THE FATHERS
OF THE CHURCH

A NEW TRANSLATION

VOLUME 95

THE FATHERS OF THE CHURCH

A NEW TRANSLATION

EDITORIAL BOARD

Thomas P. Halton
The Catholic University of America
Editorial Director

Elizabeth Clark
Duke Univeristy

†Robert B. Eno, S.S.
The Catholic University of America

Frank A. C. Mantello
The Catholic University of America

Kathleen McVey
Princeton Theological Seminary

Robert D. Sider
Dickinson College

Michael Slusser
Duquesne University

Cynthia White
The University of Arizona

Robin Darling Young
The Catholic University of America

David J. McGonagle
Director
The Catholic University of America Press

FORMER EDITORIAL DIRECTORS

Ludwig Schopp, Roy J. Deferrari, Bernard M. Peebles,
Hermigild Dressler, O.F.M.

Laszlo G. Szijarto
Staff Editor

FULGENTIUS
SELECTED WORKS

Translated by
ROBERT B. ENO, S.S.
The Catholic University of America
Washington, D.C.

THE CATHOLIC UNIVERSITY OF AMERICA PRESS
Washington, D.C.

Copyright © 1997
The Catholic University of America Press
All rights reserved
Printed in the United States of America

The paper used in this publication meets the minimum requirements of the American National Standards for Information Science—Permanence of Paper for Printed Library Materials, ANSI Z39.48-1984.

LIBRARY OF CONGRESS CATALOGING-IN-PUBLICATION DATA
Fulgentius, Saint, Bishop of Ruspe, 468–533.
   [Selections. 1996]
      Fulgentius of Ruspe : selected works / translated by Robert B. Eno.
      p. cm. — (Fathers of the church ; v. 95)
      Includes bibliographical references and index.
        1. Theology. 2. Catholic Church—Doctrines. I. Eno, Robert B.
   II. Title. III. Series.
BR65.F852E5 1996
270.2—dc20
96-19713
ISBN 0-8132-0095-4 (alk. paper)
ISBN 978-0-8132-2629-3 (pbk.)

CONTENTS

Acknowledgments	vii
Abbreviations	ix
Select Bibliography	xi
Introduction	xv

SELECTED WORKS

The Life of the Blessed Bishop Fulgentius	1
To Peter on the Faith	57
On the Forgiveness of Sins	109
To Monimus	185
The Letters of Fulgentius	277

Indices

General Index	569
Index of Holy Scripture	576

ACKNOWLEDGMENTS

Fulgentius, as an author of the sixth century, makes use of earlier authors. The translator wishes to acknowledge the use of the following translations of authors cited by Fulgentius and to thank the publishers for their permission to use them. To Liturgical Press, for permission to use the translation of Augustine's "Sermon 272" (by Professor Daniel Sheerin, as found in *The Eucharist*, vol. 7, of the Message of the Fathers series, edited by Professor Thomas Halton). To Paulist Press, for permission to use excerpts from Cyprian's *De Unitate Ecclesiae*, as translated by Maurice Bevenot in the Ancient Christian Writers series, vol. 25, and works of Prosper of Aquitaine, Ancient Christian Writers, vol. 32, translated by P. DeLetter. And, finally, in translating certain citations of Ambrose and Augustine by Fulgentius, I have made use of the translations found in the first and second series of the Nicene and Post-Nicene Fathers, currently published by Eerdmans. In the case of these last-named translations, I have sometimes modified or modernized the wording.

EDITOR'S NOTE: *Robert Eno, S.S., died on February 12, 1997, during the editing of this translation. The editorial director of the Fathers of the Church Series, Thomas P. Halton, recalls with gratitude Father Eno's willingness to undertake, as a member of the Editorial Board, whatever tasks were asked of him.*

ABBREVIATIONS

ACW   Ancient Christian Writers. New York, N.Y./Mahwah, N.J.: Newman Press, 1946–.

CCL   Corpus Christianorum Series Latina. Turnhout: Brepols, 1953–.

CSEL   Corpus Scriptorum Ecclesiasticorum Latinorum. Austrian Academy of Sciences: Vienna, 1865–.

DHGE   *Dictionnaire d'histoire et de géographie ecclésiastique.* Paris, 1912–.

DSp   *Dictionnaire de spiritualité, ascétique et mystique, doctrine et histoire.* Ed. M. Viller, F. Cavallera, and J. de Guibert, S.J. Paris, 1937–.

EEC   Encyclopedia of the Early Church. 2 vols. Ed. A. Di Berardino. New York: Oxford University Press, 1992.

FOTC   The Fathers of the Church. New York: Cima Publishing Co., 1947–1949; New York: FOTC, Inc., 1949–60; Washington, D.C.: The Catholic University of America Press, 1960–.

NPNF   A Select Library of the Nicene and Post-Nicene Fathers of the Christian Church. Series 1. Ed. P. Schaff and H. Wace. Buffalo and New York, 1888. Reprints 1956 (Grand Rapids, Mich.: Eerdmans) and 1994 (Peabody, Mass.: Hendrickson).

OECT   Oxford Early ChrisGtian Texts. Oxford: Clarendon Press, 1970–.

PL   Patrologiae Cursus Completus: Series Latina. Ed. J.-P. Migne. Paris, 1844–65.

PCBE   *Prosopographie chrétienne du Bas Empire.* Vol. 1. *Afrique.* Ed. A. Mandouze. Paris: Éditions du Centre national de la recherche scientifique, 1982.

PLRE   *Prosopography of the Later Roman Empire.* Vol. 2. Ed. J. R. Martindale. Cambridge University Press, 1980.

Tanner   Decrees of the Ecumenical Councils. Ed. N. P. Tanner. 2 vols. Washington, D.C.: Georgetown University Press, 1990.

SELECT BIBLIOGRAPHY

Critical Texts

Fraipont, J., ed. Sancti Fulgentii Episcopi Ruspensis Opera. CCL 91–91A (1968).
Lapeyre, G. G. Vie de Saint Fulgence de Ruspe de Ferrand, Diacre de Carthage. Paris: Lethielleux, 1929.

Translations
Vita Fulgentii:
French: Lapeyre, G. G. *Vie de Saint Fulgence de Ruspe de Ferrand, Diacre de Carthage.* Paris: Lethielleux, 1929.
German: Kozelka, Leo. *Das Leben von heiligen Fulgentius.* Bibliothek der Kirchenväter. München: Kösel und Pustet, 1934.
Italian: Isola, Antonino. *Vita di San Fulgenzio.* Testi Patristici 65. Roma: Città nuova, 1987.

De Fide ad Petrum:
German: Kozelka, Leo. *Das Leben von heiligen Fulgentius.* Bibliothek der Kirchenväter. München: Kösel und Pustet, 1934.
Italian: Bianco, Maria Grazia. *La Fede.* Testi Patristici 57. Roma: Città nuova, 1986.
Polish: There is also a Polish translation by W. Szoldrski in 1967.

De Remissione Peccatorum:
Italian: Bianco, Maria Grazia. *Le condizioni della Penitenza.* Testi Patristici 57. Roma: Città nuova, 1986.

Other Patristic Texts and Translations
Ambrose
De Fide. CSEL 78, ed. O. Faller. NPNF 10.
De Spiritu Sancto. CSEL 79, ed. O. Faller. FOTC 44.
Expositio Evangelii Secundum Lucam. CCL 14, ed. M. Adriaen.
Hymni. Ed. J. Fontaine. Paris: Éditions du Cerf, 1992.

Augustine
Confessiones. CCL 27, ed. L. Verheijen. FOTC 21.
Contra Faustum. CSEL 25, ed. J. Zycha. NPNF 4.

De Baptismo. CSEL 51, ed. M. Petschenig. NPNF 4.
De Civitate Dei. CCL 48, ed. B. Dombart and A. Kalb. FOTC 14.
De Peccatorum Meritis et Remissione. CSEL 60, ed. C. F. Urba and J. Zycha. NPNF 5.
De Perfectione Iustitiae Hominis. CSEL 42, ed. C. F. Urba and J. Zycha. NPNF 5.
De Praedestinatione Sanctorum. PL 44. FOTC 86.
De Trinitate. CCL 50, ed. W. Mountain. FOTC 45.
Enarrationes in Psalmos. CCL 38–40, ed. E. Dekkers and J. Fraipont. NPNF 8.
Enchiridion. CCL 46, ed. E. Evans. FOTC 2.
Epistolae. CSEL 34 and 57, ed. A. Goldbacher. FOTC 18 and 30.
Retractationes. CCL 57, ed. A. Mutzenbecher. FOTC 60.
Sermones. PL 38, trans. D. J. Sheerin. *The Eucharist.* Vol. 7. Message of the Fathers of the Church. Wilmington: M. Glazier, 1986.
Tractatus in Johannem. CCL 36, ed. R. Willems. FOTC 79.
Concilia Africae A.345–A.525. CCL 149, ed. C. Munier.

Cyprian
De Mortalitate. CCL 3A, ed. M. Simonetti. FOTC 36.
De Ecclesiae Catholicae Unitate. CCL 3, ed. M. Bevenot. OECT.

Gelasius
De Duabus Naturis in Christo. Ed. E. Schwartz. Publizisische Sammlungen zum Acacianischen Schisma. Münich, 1934.

Leo
Epistula 28. Tanner, vol. l. FOTC 34.

Optatus
Contra Parmenianum. CSEL 26, ed. K. Ziwsa. Trans. O. R. Vassall-Phillips. London: Longmans, 1917.

Prosper
Responsiones ad Capitula Obiectionum Gallorum. PL 51. ACW 32.

Victor of Vita
History of the Vandal Persecution. Translated with notes and introduction by John Moorhead. Translated Texts for Historians. Vol. 10. Liverpool: Liverpool University Press, 1992.

Secondary Literature

Lapeyre, G. G. *Saint Fulgence de Ruspe: Un évêque catholique africain sous la domination vandale.* Paris: Lethielleux, 1929. [Remains the most extensive monograph on all aspects of Fulgentius.]

Much briefer but more recent summaries:
Collins, R. J. H. "Fulgentius von Ruspe." *Theologische Realenzykopädie* 11.723–27(1983).
Jourjon, M. "Fulgence de Ruspe." *DSp* 5.1612–15(1964).
Langlois. P. "Fulgentius" *Reallexikon für Antike und Christentum* 8.632–62 (c. 1969).
PCBE 507–13(1982).

Other Studies

Cal Pardo, E. "Mariología de S. Fulgencio de Ruspe" *Miscelánea Comillas* 51(1969) 113–92.
Courtois, C. *Les Vandales et l'Afrique Paris*. RP Aalen: Scientia Verlag, 1964.
De Nicola, A. "Aspetti dell'etica matrimoniale di Fulgenzio di Ruspe." *Augustinianum* 18(1978) 361–82.
Diesner, H. J. *Fulgentius als Kirchenpolitiker und Theologe*. Stuttgart: Calwer Verlag, 1966.
Di Sciascio. *Fulgenzio di Ruspe e i massimi problemi della Grazia*. Rome: Gregorian University, 1941.
Grillmeier, A. "Fulgentius von Ruspe, *De Fide ad Petrum* und die *Summa Sententiarum*. Eine Studie zum Werden der frühscholastischen Systematik." *Scholastik* 34(1959) 526–65. "Vom Symbolum zur Summa. Zum theologiegeschichtlichen Verhältnis von Patristik und Scholastik." In *Kirche und Überlieferung*, edited by J. Betz and H. Fries. Festschrift J. R. Geiselmann. Freiburg: Herder, 1960, 119–69.
Mesnage, J. *l'Afrique chrétienne: Evêchés et ruines antiques*. Paris: Leroux, 1912.
Micaelli, C. "Osservazioni sulla cristologia di Fulgenzio di Ruspe." *Augustinianum* 28(1988) 343–60.
Moorhead, John. *Theoderic in Italy*. Oxford: Clarendon Press, 1992.
Nisters. B. *Die Christologie des hl. Fulgentius von Ruspe*. Münster: Aschendorff, 1930.
Simonetti, M. "Note sulla 'Vita Fulgentii.'" *Analecta Bollandiana* 100(1982) 277–89.
———. *La produzione letteraria latina fra Roma e Barbari (sec. V–VIII)*. Rome: Augustinianum, 1986, 48–54.
Stevens, S. "The Circle of Bishop Fulgentius." *Traditio* 38(1982) 327–41.

INTRODUCTION

Fulgentius, bishop of Ruspe (c. 467–532), considered the greatest North African theologian after the time of Augustine (died 430), did not possess an original mind, but he propagated and defended the Augustinian heritage against the adversaries of the day, notably, Arians and Pelagians (or at least semi-Pelagians). This volume gives English readers for the first time an opportunity to study a representative selection of the writings of this early sixth-century author as well as presenting the *Life* for the first time in English.

North Africa had been under the rule of the Germanic Vandals for several decades when Fulgentius was born. It may be recalled that they had crossed over from Spain c. 429 and that Hippo Regius was under siege as Augustine lay dying in August of 430. Carthage fell in 439. In 455, a Vandal fleet sacked Rome. The Vandals were Arians, and their regime in North Africa, which was to last for nearly a century, has been portrayed as extremely brutal and harsh for Catholics. The *History of the Vandal Persecution* by Bishop Victor of Vita has recently been published in English.[1] Fulgentius's family had been victimized by the Vandals earlier, and, in his own life, he too would suffer persecution and exile. He died only a short time before the Byzantine "liberation."

Life

Some things about the biography of Fulgentius are quite definite, viz., that he was in his sixty-fifth year when he died; that he had been a bishop for twenty-five years; that he died on the first of January and was buried the next day; that Feli-

---

1. *Victor of Vita: History of the Vandal Persecution*, trans. John Moorhead. Translated Texts for Historians, vol. 10 (Liverpool: Liverpool University Press, 1972.)

cianus, his successor as bishop of Ruspe, was ordained to the episcopate one year to the day after the burial of Fulgentius. The only problem is that no years are attached to these facts so that our view of the major dates of his life are not firmly tied down to anything. Since the *Life* is the first of the works to be translated in this volume, there is no point in reviewing all the details of his biography here, but it would be helpful to attempt to pin down some of these dates.

We may start with the fact that at this time the ordination of African Catholic priests to the episcopate took place on Sunday. Since the second of January fell on a Sunday in 528 and 533, the date of the death of Fulgentius must have been January 1, 527 or 532. Thus he must have been born in either 462/463 or 467/468 and ordained bishop of Ruspe in 502 or 507. There are reasons for preferring one date to the other, but the majority of scholars today come down in favor of the later dates, giving him a life span of 467 to 532. In this case, he was bishop of Ruspe from 507 to 532.

He was born in the inland city of Thelepte in the African province of Byzacena, well south of Carthage, of a prominent family. With a good education and great prospects, he became procurator or tax-collector (of his city?) at an early age. But he soon turned away from this life and chose the monastery. Most of his biography revolves around his life after this conversion.

One other certain date in his life is the year 500. It was in this year that the Ostrogothic king of Italy, Theoderic, made his only visit to Rome. According to the *Life*, Fulgentius was by chance visiting Rome himself at that moment, a side trip from Sicily where he had been staying with Bishop Eulalius of Syracuse. Having been discouraged by that bishop from pursuing his ambition of proceeding to Egypt to live with the monks there, he returned to Africa, then suffering under the harsh rule of Thrasamund (496–523). Against his will, Abbot (and Bishop) Faustus ordained Fulgentius a priest.

A few years later the Catholic bishops who remained decided that they must risk defying the king's prohibition

INTRODUCTION xvii

against the ordination of new Catholic bishops. Try as he might, Fulgentius was ultimately unable to avoid being chosen as one of these new bishops and c. 507, he was ordained bishop of Ruspe, a town on the Mediterranean coast of Byzacena. He was just in time to be exiled to Sardinia by an angry king. He remained there from c. 508/509 to 516/517. Though he was among the most junior of the bishops in the exiled group, his theological learning and literary ability brought him to a leadership position.

King Thrasamund brought him back to Carthage for approximately two years so that he, the king, could do theological battle with the Catholic champion. Ultimately convinced that Fulgentius's presence was doing the Arian cause more harm than good, he was sent back to Sardinia. There he stayed with the others until the death of the Arian king in 523. The new Vandal king, Hilderic, was much more favorable to Catholics and to Constantinople. The exiled bishops were allowed not only to return home but to resume their episcopal ministry. Fulgentius is portrayed as enjoying a triumphal march from Carthage to Ruspe where he lived out his life and died only a short time before the Roman, i.e., Byzantine, reconquest of 533, an event which would bring mixed blessings for the Catholics of North Africa.

Writings

Many writings of Fulgentius have been lost. Of those that have survived, the most significant, including those translated here, are dated to the period of his second exile and the period of his return to North Africa from Sardinia until his death, in other words, a period of about sixteen years. There are also works which obviously date to his sojourn in Carthage between the two periods of Sardinian exile, those works dedicated to answering the theological arguments of King Thrasamund. In addition, there are some thirty-nine fragments, many lengthy, of a work against Fabianus. Like the works against Thrasamund, this work also was concerned with Trinitarian questions, as was the *On the Trinity* against Felix. There are also eight undisputed sermons as well as a treatise "On the Truth of Predestination."

There was another North African author of the same name whom some scholars identify with the bishop. This is Fulgentius the 'mythographer'. The majority of scholars today, however, reject the identification on the grounds that the literary genres of the two authors are too different to be reconciled. Those who have paid more attention to the style of the two corpora of writings seem less sure, however. That the same author could produce such totally diverse types of writings may seem, a priori, extremely unlikely to us, but there is also the danger that such a judgment may be anachronistic. That the *Life of Fulgentius* says nothing about such 'secular' literary activities is not decisive. The works of the 'Mythographer' were dedicated to a priest of Carthage named Catus. On the other hand, if it is maintained that Fulgentius wrote such works in "his younger days," that too would seem unlikely, given the fairly early age at which he abandoned worldly interests. Thus the most prudent position would seem to be not to identify the two Fulgentii.

THE LIFE OF THE BLESSED BISHOP FULGENTIUS

Introduction

The question of the authorship of *The Life of the Blessed Bishop Fulgentius* remains a matter of dispute. No manuscript of the work indicates the Carthaginian deacon Ferrandus as the author. Yet this was the hypothesis of the seventeenth-century Jesuit scholar and editor of Fulgentius, Pierre-François Chifflet,[1] who brought the name of Ferrandus forward in this connection. His suggestion has been taken for granted by the great majority of scholars since then. However, Antonino Isola,[2] a recent translator of the *Life* into Italian, takes a more hesitant view to the extent that he lists the author as Pseudo-Ferrandus. Isola grants that Ferrandus in Carthage was a correspondent of Fulgentius but does not see that there was that much close association between the two men. In the prologue to the *Life*, the author indicates that he was a monk in Fulgentius's monastery in Sardinia during the second period of exile. Is this true of Ferrandus?

Evidence in favor of Ferrandus's authorship includes the statement made by Ferrandus himself at the end of a letter to Abbot Eugippius in Italy, apparently not long after the death of Fulgentius, of his desire to spread the knowledge of Fulgentius's exemplary life and work. One can only conclude that while Ferrandus's authorship continues to be widely accepted, the question has not yet been definitively resolved.

The *Life* itself is episodic, giving a series of vignettes. The emphasis appears to be more of Fulgentius the monk than of Fulgentius the bishop or theologian. His devotion to asceticism is stressed though, like other western monks, he is not in competition with the Egyptians or Syrians in this field. The lesson of the episode with the Arian priest Felix near Sicca is that Fulgentius participated in the suffering of the martyrs. (chap. 6–7). The comments on his ability to combine the life of the monk with that of the bishop (chap.15) recall similar points made about Martin of Tours. But, unlike that life and those of most other holy men, the miraculous has almost no role to play here. Hence the comments in chapter 23 on his 'moral miracles'. Chapter 25 is devoted to listing some of his writings.

---

1. On Chifflet, see Bernard de Vregille, "Pierre-François Chifflet, S.J., découvreur et éditeur des Péres (1592–1682)," in *Les Péres de l'Église au XVIIe siècle*, E. Bury and B. Meunier (Paris: Cerf, 1993) 237–51.

2. Antonio Isola, trans., *Pseudo Ferrando di Cartagine: Vita di San Fulgenzio*, Collana di Testi Patristici 65 (Roma: Città Nuova, 1987), 5–8.

Perhaps the aspect of the *Life* which most strikes the contemporary reader is the apparent restlessness of soul that Fulgentius exhibits. After having rejected the world for the ascetic life, he moves from one monastery to another, founds his own monastery, attempts to travel to Egypt to find even greater ascetic challenges. Even after being made a bishop and spending a great deal of his time in exile, he attempts at the end to go off to a monastery again. Yet, despite this restlessness, his writings manifest an orderly and rather prosaic mind.

If Ferrandus did not write this *Life*, the author may well have been one of those who lived in the monastery with him in Africa as well as in Sardinia. It has been said that one of the purposes of the work was to remind the new bishop of Ruspe, Felicianus, to whom the *Life* is dedicated, of the privileges of the local monks.

This is the first translation of the *Life* into English. The critical edition of Lapeyre[3] (1929) has been used, but, as more recent authors have pointed out, much still needs to be done for a more complete critical edition.

Prologue

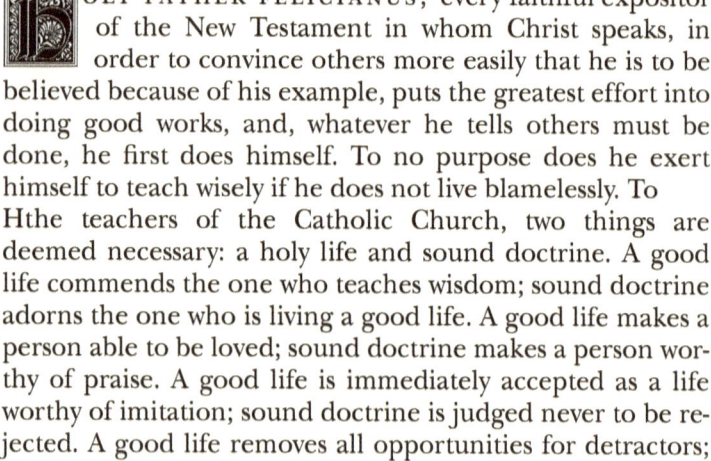OLY FATHER FELICIANUS,[4] every faithful expositor of the New Testament in whom Christ speaks, in order to convince others more easily that he is to be believed because of his example, puts the greatest effort into doing good works, and, whatever he tells others must be done, he first does himself. To no purpose does he exert himself to teach wisely if he does not live blamelessly. To Hthe teachers of the Catholic Church, two things are deemed necessary: a holy life and sound doctrine. A good life commends the one who teaches wisdom; sound doctrine adorns the one who is living a good life. A good life makes a person able to be loved; sound doctrine makes a person worthy of praise. A good life is immediately accepted as a life worthy of imitation; sound doctrine is judged never to be rejected. A good life removes all opportunities for detractors;

---

3. G. G. Lapeyre, *Vie de Saint Fulgence de Ruspe de Ferrand, diacre de Carthage* (Paris: Lethielleux, 1929).

4. Felicianus, to whom this life is addressed, was a companion of Fulgentius in Sardinian exile. He became his successor as bishop of Ruspe, ordained on January 2, 533, one year and a day after his predecessor's death. See "Felicianus 11," PCBE, 404–5.

sound doctrine resists those who contradict it. For a long time, while I pondered the renown and the sanctity of the blessed bishop Fulgentius, your predecessor, by whom we were both nurtured, many times the outstanding teacher came before the eyes of my heart. Then I lamented that the consolation of so great a man was now lacking to the peoples of Africa. And, although he has gone to better things, now enjoying the delights of heaven, still I, so conscious of his wisdom, groaned that there was no teacher like him with us now.

Some relief was granted to my sad recollections whenever I either read, or heard others reading, his wonderful books or the letters or the sermons he gave to the people. While, in silence, I considered that in these noted works, the genius and the wisdom of the man could become known, while I did not doubt that most people were aware of his justice, honesty, and mercy, and how laudable a life he led, as you well know, with his friends, following his own teachings; nevertheless, I felt that these things were unknown to an even larger proportion. Looking to the future, I feared more strongly each passing day that forgetfulness would soon overtake so good a life. After thinking for a long time, I said, "See how the sound teaching of the blessed Fulgentius shines forth since his books are read by all. When a book bearing his name is read, it is as if he were speaking. What is to be done in order that his holy life may also be known to all? As long as those who knew him are still alive, or they can hear something about his virtues from reliable witnesses, the present generation can bear true testimony to him. But what will the generation to come do? What will the great number of faithful far away, across the sea, do? When they come to read his works, in which the blessed bishop, though absent, still speaks, and, though dead, still lives, they will soon come to admire his wisdom; but how will they know of his blameless life? Just as his teaching is famous, may his life become even more renowned.

Let us speak out and tell our brethren how so great a pontiff lived. Nor should there be any fear that I, because of my poor ability, do an injustice to a bishop who has won so great a renown throughout all the world's churches. Whatever value my words may have, they cannot either increase or reduce the merits of one so great. But I shall proceed to bear witness to the love because of which, ever desiring to stay close to him, I, by his salutary exhortations, was converted and was persuaded to take up the monastic vocation at that small monastery which he had built in Sardinia, where he had been exiled for the name of Christ."

You were already living there as a priest. Days and nights, I lived with him where the rivers of his heavenly eloquence, sweeter than honey from the comb, daily refreshed me, and, had it not been for the sterility of my withered spirit, my earth would have brought forth fruit a hundredfold. But, unworthy as I am, I was scarcely able to draw even a little from that fullness. Trusting to the prayers of your Paternity, I have decided to take up the work of this present booklet. I shall put down here whatever I can remember about what he said to us, and, even more, what we saw with our own eyes. Knowing his doctrine, then, we shall not be ignorant of what he did. I shall briefly explain—in no way fearing to incur the charge of falsification—because all these things are not hidden from your aged Paternity. Nor are things being said as if to one who did not know, but only those things will be said which can be confirmed by your testimony.

Chapter 1

The truly blessed Fulgentius, born of a noble line in the eyes of the world, had among his ancestors some of senatorial rank in Carthage. When King Gaiseric[5] entered Carthage as a conqueror, he compelled very many, indeed, all the senators, to sail to Italy after he confiscated their possessions. His grandfather, Gordianus[6] by name, was among those who

---

5. Gaiseric was the leader of the Vandals who crossed from Spain to North Africa and conquered the Romans there. He was their king until his death in 477. See EEC I.342.

6. Fulgentius's grandfather. See PCBE, 542.

willingly undertook the journey imposed on them, wishing at least, having lost his fortune, not to lose his freedom.

After his death, two of his sons came back to the province of Africa in the hope of reclaiming their heritage, but they were not able to stay in Carthage, for their house had been given to Arian priests. But, with the partial restoration of their property by royal authority, they went to Byzacena,[7] and there in the city of Thelepte, one of them, Claudius[8] by name, whose wife was named Mariana,[9] a Christian and a good woman, happily begot that one to whom so great a glory was due, and his mother, as if knowing what he would become in the future, named him Fulgentius.[10] Since his father died not long after, his religious mother first made him study Greek literature, and soon he had committed all of Homer to memory; he knew a great deal of Menander as well, but she did not permit him to be taught Latin literature. She wanted him, still in his tender years, to learn a foreign language by which he might more easily be able, having to live among the Africans, to speak the Greek tongue with expert pronunciation, as if he had been brought up there.

His mother was not mistaken in making such a careful arrangement. Ever after, whenever he wished to speak Greek, even after a long period of disuse either in speaking or reading it, he still pronounced it so well that one would think that he had spent all his time living among Greeks. After having been taught a knowledge of Greek letters, he began the study of Latin letters at home, even though schoolmasters usually teach Latin, but he later went to a grammar school. The greatness of his mind and memory enabled him to retain all he had been taught. But then the necessity of household affairs forcing him, he was quickly taken

---

7. Byzacena was the Roman province of North Africa which corresponded roughly to the central and southern sections of modern Tunisia. The city of T(h)elepte is well inland in west central Byzacena near the border with the province of Numidia. See J. Mesnage, *l'Afrique chretienne*, 110–13.

8. Claudius was Fulgentius's father. See "Claudius 3," PCBE, 211.

9. Fulgentius's mother. See PCBE, 700.

10. A play on Fulgentius's name, meaning "Bright" or "Famous."

away and accepted, even as a young man, the responsibility of managing family business. Even though submissive to his mother's wishes, here too, he stood out as an imitator of Christ, of whom the holy Gospels bear witness: "And he was subject to them,"[11] i.e., his parents. His venerable mother was made happy, and the outstanding nature of her wise son consoled her in her sadness over the loss of her husband. He came to be, in that family, one who, benevolent, rendered honor to his friends, reasonably put off his enemies, both kindly and severely, ruled and corrected the slaves, diligently administered his patrimony, and became valued by the powers that be. By virtue of this, with his reputation growing every day, of a sudden he was named procurator.[12] This was the beginning of his being able to command, advise, and govern very many.

Chapter 2

Having accepted this power, while he used it in a mild manner, acting from his innate goodness, he wished to harm no one, and, when ordered to be merciless in requiring payments, the burden of this world's business began to weigh heavily on him and its vain happiness to be displeasing. Little by little, with a laudable patience taking over, love for the spiritual life began to rise in him, and, furthermore, a desire for reading and a tireless search for prayer. Henceforward, frequently visiting the most agreeable flocks of the monasteries, he learned the customs and the purpose of the servants of God. Among these ascetics, he knew that there are not the joys of the world, but neither is there boredom.

Living in the greatest self-denial, he saw no one afraid of slander, but loving each other. He noted that a great many young men, dedicated to perpetual continence, were able to keep themselves from all sexual intercourse. He was tossed

---

11. Lk 2.51.
12. This vague reference indicates that Fulgentius was named a civil tax collector, but it is not clear of what jurisdiction.

about by such thoughts within him when he cried out with these words: "Why, I ask," he said, "do we labor in the world without hope of future goods? What will the world be able to offer us? If we wish to be happy, although it is better to weep in a good cause than to rejoice in a bad one, how much better do they rejoice whose conscience is at peace with God, whom the violence of the unjust tax collectors frightens not at all, who fear nothing except sins, who do nothing except those things with which they can fulfill God's commandments. They are not weary from the journeys involved in public service; they are not compelled either to weep in misery or disgracefully fear the loss of their patrimony. They work with their hands; they do no harm to the interests of others; they live in peace among themselves, lives that are sober, meek, humble, and harmonious. They have no concern for lust; rather, there is a great concern for and vigilance over perpetual chastity. Let us imitate such praiseworthy men. Let us waste no time seizing upon this constancy in living a good life. Let what we have merited to know as better, thanks to God's gracious revelation of it to us, be of use to us. Let us renounce our former way of life and change our work. Formerly we strove to appear more noble among our noble friends; let us now strive to become poorer among the poor servants of God. If we were forced to coerce debtors, let us now try to convert sinners. Christ our Lord was able to make teachers of the Church out of public officials. Matthew was called from the tax collector's booth to become an apostle. Not that we believe such an honor befits our person; but, if he, putting aside the office of tax collector, accepted the ministry of preaching, will it not be permitted to us, after putting aside the procuratorship, to assume the lamentations of a penitent? God is our refuge. Let no excuse be found in the weakness of our age; he who is powerful enough to grant continence to so many young persons whom we saw living in a monastery, can give me, a sinner, a similar grace."

After lengthy meditation on these words in his heart, with the inspiration of the Holy Spirit, he decided to renounce worldly joy altogether and to associate himself with that way of life which he had been praising. At first, wary that too abrupt a change, disturbing both mind and body, amid the first stirrings of conversion, might generate a very great burden for himself or a scandal for others, secretly he began to practice fasting; from there, progressing little by little, he began to abandon the company of his old friends. Frequently separated from society, on his own lands, though all, both family and business associates, were unaware, he remained apart, as if melancholy because of his affairs. There he used to pray, read, fast; he cut down on the excessive amount of his meals, ceased to visit the baths, and, although still a layman, lived increasingly the full life of a monk. All who knew him were amazed at the marvelous moderation of such a refined person and attributed the cause of this change to a narrow meanness. But, within him, with each passing day, the love of the holy profession and a more ardent love of mortification grew. At a certain point, then, having experienced everything which seemed hard to him, he knew that, with the help of the Holy Spirit, his will would be able to put up with them. Assured by what St. Augustine wrote in his *Enarratio* on the thirty-sixth psalm,[13] he resolved to make public his intentions. Eagerly he changed his manner of dress, lest he feel obliged to receive as friends those who came to him with whom he had formerly lived in a worldly way. Wise man that he was, he realized that the conversion of his heart would be of use only to him if he were able to keep it secret, but, if made public, it would offer a good example to many others for giving up their old, sinful ways. What middle class or poor person would be ashamed to become a monk, when he saw Fulgentius, with the arrogance of his inborn pride decreasing, walking with unhurried steps the hard path of self-denial?

---

13. According to Antonio Isola, Simonetti believes that the third sermon of Augustine on Ps.36 is the place referred to. See Isola, *Vita di San Fulgenzio*, 46, n. 16.

Chapter 3

There was at that time a certain bishop worthy of all praise by the name of Faustus,[14] who, for the Catholic faith, had been ordered into exile, though not far from his see. The sly malice of the persecuting tyrant Hunneric had ordered this in the case of many bishops, so that they, undergoing the rigors of exile so close to their homes, might the more easily be brought to deny God. In that same place where he had been exiled, he built a monastery for himself in which he lived as a man of the spirit and was held in honor by all Christians. It was to this holy man that Fulgentius, who was already well known to him, eagerly came and made known to him with confidence the intentions of his heart. He, knowing that he had lived in a completely worldly life-style, hesitated to believe the one who promised such things. So he said to him, "Why, my son, are you telling lies and taking delight in deceiving the servants of God? Will you be a monk, or will you thus so quickly change your habits of pleasure so that this renunciation, with its food of poverty ill-prepared and second-hand clothing, will not break your spirit? What you should do, to start, is to live the life of an ascetic layman, and, then perhaps, I shall deem it credible that you want to, or are able to, renounce the world." At this, the young man, even more eager, as a supplicant, kissed the hand of the one who was trying to push him away, and begged him, with his eyes cast down on the earth, "Father, he who gave the desire to the one who did not want it, is able to give the ability to the one who does want it now. Allow me to follow in your footsteps; open to me the door of the monastery; give me the help of your holy example; make me one of your disciples; and God knows how to free men from my sinful ways." When he heard this, the blessed old man judged it a serious mistake to put off the supplicant any

---

14. Faustus, bishop of Praesidium Diolele in Byzacena. The location of his see is uncertain, but it may have been a few miles to the southwest of Thelepte. Forced out by the decrees of Hunneric, king of the Vandals after Gaiseric until 484, he founded a monastery. See "Faustus 6," PCBE, 398.

further and was inclined to give permission. "Remain with us, my son," he said, "as you wish; after a few days, let us see whether your deeds correspond to your words. I hope that my concerns are groundless and your profession is found to be solid." After the holy bishop Faustus had given his permission to the supplicant, the news quickly spread among his relatives and friends that Fulgentius had become a monk. The good were happy; the wicked confounded. His life, lived in comfort up until then, gave little hope to some. But certain others who knew the outstanding depth of his singular genius were rapidly convinced to hope for great things from him in the future. Some of his friends to whom he had been a dear and faithful companion since his childhood, desiring to imitate him, now scorned the world and, giving up their own will, went to join the monasteries.

Chapter 4

With many coming to tell her, his mother heard that Fulgentius had fled to the monastery, that he had completely given up his task of running the household and managing his patrimony, and that it was completely impossible that he be turned aside from this resolve. Upset and fearful, with the emotion of excessive love stirring her as if Fulgentius were already dead (although it would be a good death for anyone so dying), she battered heaven with superabundant tears and cries, and, as mothers usually do at the funerals of their sons, she was unable to stop her weeping. In a rage, she was swept along with great speed to the monastery; with no hesitations, she berated the holy Faustus with insults and reproofs, saying, "Give a mother back her son. Give the servants back their master. Bishops have always done many good deeds for widows; why is the house of a widow now going to perish because of you?" To which the bishop responded patiently, "If you had taken my son, woman, I would have to condemn you to the degree my sorrow required; but, as it is, you justly berate me because I have taken your son. When you are displeased that he is to serve Christ, you do well to berate Faustus." Tolerating words such as these with equanimity and gently teasing her, he absolutely refused to allow her even to see her son. She, knowing how much she was loved by her son, called out with loud cries before the gate of the monastery; and frequently calling out the name of Fulgentius, she made known to all her piteous and desolate state.

That was the first of the temptations to beat upon Fulgentius with great strength. For, he heard with his own ears his sainted mother, whom he had always loved and whom he had served with the greatest devotion, weeping. But, raising his heart to heaven, he heard and did not hear; he did not think it worthy to be swayed by her prayers because he overcame his accustomed filial piety by a religious cruelty. Here he was already beginning to furnish an outstanding example to many of the patience he would show in the future and, almost as if inebriated with the grace of the Spirit, he in some way no longer knew her as his mother. Now, for the first time, the blessed bishop Faustus believed that he was wholeheartedly converted and with joy said to the other brothers, "This young man will easily be able to tolerate whatever labor we impose on him, since he is able to resist his mother's sorrow." That mother, when she realized that her son was not coming to her, even though she lamented even more, did not believe that he was still in the same place, because she, not yet realizing his strength, thought that, if he had been there, he would not have been able to resist his mother's wailing. Frequently coming and going, she caused the bishop much trouble and laid many traps for her son, until, finally overcome, she went back to her own home.

Chapter 5

The blessed Fulgentius tortured himself to an incredible degree with feats of abstinence, eating and drinking so poorly and so little, without wine and oil, that his terrible fasts caused the dried out skin of his body to break open with many abscesses, and, with the onset of the skin disease called impetigo, the beauty of his well-formed body was disfigured. Many were of the view that at that point the blessed Fulgentius could on the occasion of this illness either back away from his previous decision to seek sanctity or, at least, would, from then on, settle for mediocrity to the point that he would no longer observe the fasts required by the common rule. But he, contrary to everyone's expectations, governed by the aid of God's prevenient mercy, took greater strength of soul from the weakness of his body, and, the weaker he got, the more he fasted, thinking only of his eternal salvation; he entrusted the health of his body to the Lord's will, saying this to many, "We all know that life is usually preserved by eating but that health cannot be thus conferred. For, in order that infirmity be cured, if it sufficed for the desires of the palate to be satisfied, then why do even they who daily are sated by sumptuous banquets get sick?" Therefore, he tolerated sickness with patience and practiced self-denial with sufficient humility. Considering everything that he did to be small, day after day, he acted so as to become better. Sustaining the resolve of his heart with the aid of his heavenly assistance, the merciful and kind God swiftly restored the health of his body. Then the soul of the wise man, moved by a higher piety, with his whole mind crucified the world to himself, and he, crucified to the world, walked the path of righteousness from his youth, as it is written. He gave over as a gift to his mother alone, even though he had a younger brother named Claudius,[15] the property that belonged to him, in order that, later, it might be given to this brother by his mother if he served her well. Thus, by a wise plan, desiring to subjugate the pride of his younger brother so that he who was unwilling to be humble from pious motives might learn to be humble for the sake of his heritage; and his holy mother, who could not bask in his affection after the departure of her beloved son, still deserved to be consoled by his good deed. Then what praises and thanks all now gave to the Lord! When they saw the blessed Fulgentius, having tram-

---

15. The younger brother of Fulgentius. See "Claudius 4," PCBE, 212.

pled upon the greed of this world, renounce completely the goods which he was unable to give and distribute to the poor, lest he offend his good mother, to deserve to have Christ as his teacher.

Now all those things which had seemed to afflict him in the first stages of his conversion had been disposed of. But, because this life can never pass without its temptations, again such a persecution of the faith sprang up which forced the blessed bishop Faustus of holy memory to seek refuge in a succession of hiding places and did not allow him to remain in peace at the monastery. Then blessed Fulgentius, fearful either that he would be the only one left in that place or that he would have to move frequently from one place to another, after first talking it over with Bishop Faustus, went to a neighboring monastery, where an abbot named Felix[16] presided over a few brothers of little sophistication. He was a friend from adolescence with whom he had always been on familiar terms even when he was still a layman. Then Felix the abbot, receiving him with joy, knowing himself to be inferior to him in virtue, gave over to him both the title and the power of abbot. But he, in his desire for humility, refused the privilege of power and, after many pious struggles, having undergone the 'violence' of charity, with the agreement of the entire body of monks, he barely agreed to share the task with his good colleague. Thus two very holy men, equally loving God and neighbor, both similar in morals, both aspiring to still better things, equal in their manner of life, one superior to the other in knowledge, accepted the gentle yoke of ruling the brethren.

O how fortunate the group of God's servants over which Fulgentius began to be the head! O how brightly shone that monastery which had kept Felix as its administrator! Each one, in giving the other his name, gave the other the prospect of undiminished praise. Fulgentius, running along the path of the Lord, was called happy [*felix*], and, with the increasing fame of Fulgentius, Felix benefited from the

16. See "Felix 89," PCBE, 440.

fruits of his high achievements. One of them, namely the blessed Fulgentius, had as his special assignment, the teaching of the brethren. The other labored conscientiously to look after daily needs. When brethren arrived, one in particular preached the word of God while the other carefully saw to the hospitality and was happy to offer it. Nothing was done by one without the consent of the other, but both gave orders in such a way that the monks thought they were under one superior. So, since Felix was afraid to offend Fulgentius and Fulgentius Felix, with their wills in subjection each one lived, and they were praiseworthy for the well-being of the brethren which they consulted, and great by the mutual subjection which they showed to each other. Who had words to explain the power of this affection? Those whom quiet peace had brought together, cruel war could not separate. But, when suddenly the province was disturbed by the incursion of a horde of barbarians,[17] they, seeing temporal safety assured only by flight, accepted the dangers brought about by a journey, and, having considered the consequences, they went far away where there seemed to be no danger of a new war and offered the complete possibility for constructing a new monastery. These great leaders of a heavenly army moved their spiritual camp, and, accompanied by the crowd of their monks, they passed through unknown regions of Africa; everywhere they brought joy to the good and jealousy to the wicked.

Chapter 6

They intended to settle finally in the area of Sicca,[18] attracted by the region's rich soil, welcomed by the faithful. But there was a certain priest of the Arian sect, preaching heresy on the estate of Gabardilla. His name among men

17. This monastery in the southwest mountainous corner of Byzacena was subject to raids from the nomads, the Mauri or Moors.
18. Sicca Veneria (Le Kef) was a small city in the northern province of Africa proconsularis, about 135 kilometers north of Thelepte.

was Felix,[19] but his will was always malevolent toward God, by race a barbarian, cruel in his morals, powerful by his resources, a fierce persecutor of the Catholics. Aware that the name of the blessed Fulgentius was well known in these regions, he foresaw that Fulgentius would secretly reconcile many of those whom he had subverted. He did not believe that such a man, worthy of the priesthood, was even now still just a monk but thought that in his monk's habit he was carrying out the ministry of a priest. And, in truth, even then, he did fulfill in a praiseworthy fashion the office of a priest, not by reconciling people, but, with salutary words, leading all whom he could reach to reconciliation. His words were challenging but not harsh, and he softened even hardened hearts so that not without reason was this priest afraid for his false religion. Driven by the spurs of a mad frenzy, the priest undertook to persecute cruelly the servants of God and, with lookouts stationed on all the roads, he set upon those who walked those roads all unsuspecting. It was necessary for those brave athletes, prepared for anything through their voluntary labors of self-denial, to be handed over for a little while into the hands of the persecutors, so that, being made sharers in the sufferings of the martyrs, they learn to put up with all the tortures used against them; they would test how much progress they had made to the extent that they did not deviate even in the slightest way from the true faith despite the tearing of all their limbs by the lash. Unaware of the intentions of the wicked serpent, having confidence in their conscience, fearing nothing, the two walked on together, talking. And, behold, suddenly as by the violence of a terrible storm, the unsuspecting were assailed; the serpent divided those who were joined, tied together those who were divided, and, crushed by the cruel chains which bound them, they were brought to the priest. Suddenly, without being guilty of anything, they found themselves accused, prisoners without a war. The Moors had not been able to harm them during their flight, but now the Arians inflict

19. See "Felix 90," PCBE, 441.

punishment on them. Then, before they were seized, Abbot Felix threw away a few gold coins which were meant to meet the needs of the brethren, in all innocence, out of fear, and thus committed to God himself the keeping of God's servants. O singular power of a divine miracle! No one could have known where these coins were thrown; no one was allowed to take away from the poor their sustenance. But they alone, who were to be tested, were held, tied up, and led to the priest. With menacing words, the violent priest addressed them, "Why have you come secretly from your own area to overthrow Christian kings?" Well did that wretch call Christians kings out of whom sadly he had driven Christ Jesus, King of Kings, by breathing on them and whom he, like an Antichrist, had taught to deny that Christ was equal to the Father. While they were preparing a true reply to his words, he first ordered them to be beaten.

Then, Abbot Felix was moved by an overwhelming charity. "Spare," he said, "Brother Fulgentius, who cannot stand torture. Don't beat him, for he may die at your hands. Let your cruelty be turned on me; I know what to confess; I am to blame for everything." Then, overcome by admiration for such love, he ordered the blessed Fulgentius to be taken away for a little while and commanded Felix to be beaten even more by the cruel servants. Then Abbot Felix with joyful heart submitted to the stripes. He sustained the suffering with joy, because he believed that the blessed Fulgentius would not suffer.

See how the blessed Fulgentius was revered by his friends that he merited to be loved until death. That charity of the blessed Felix bears outstanding witness to the holiness of that life. For he would not have despised his own safety in favor of his unless he had early on felt the usefulness and the pleasing nature of that life for himself and for many others. Let those who wish to please God imitate both. Let the blessed Fulgentius teach others to live among the brethren in such a way that they be loved, cherished, and deemed worthy of assistance in their greatest need, even if this aid is not devoid of danger. May others learn from the heroic deed of Abbot Felix to give their all with good heart to the brothers who are better and more advanced in the fear of God. When there is such charity among brothers, such as there was between these two very holy men, the power of every temptation is easily overcome, and the stubbornness of enemies is immediately broken. Yet this cruellest of priests was not in the least satiated by the sufferings of Abbot Felix and had no thought of sparing the blessed Fulgentius.

Chapter 7

But the blessed Fulgentius, a man of very delicate constitution, being born of an upper-class family, had difficulties, as he himself later told us, in standing the violent blows of the cudgels with the ever-increasing sharpness and sudden pain. He thought that he might be able either to calm the rage of the furious priest if possible, or, at least for a short time, to divert his attention before his wrath should be rekindled, so that, with this respite, he might more easily have a breathing space lest the non-stop punishment become completely unbearable. While being beaten, he cried out, "I have something to say—if I am allowed to speak." Then the priest, thinking that he wanted to convert, commanded the torturers to rest, and so, commanded him, still under the threat of the lash, to say what he wanted. At which the blessed Fulgentius began to tell the story of his travels with the attractive words of his habitual eloquence, and the priest was struck with astonishment and for a long time was softened by the charm of his words, making him almost forget his cruelty completely. The priest marveled at the eloquence of the blessed Fulgentius, approved his wisdom, and, perceiving in him some great man, began to be ashamed of his violence, but, fearful of letting his men think that his malice had been mastered, said, "Beat him again harder, and batter the talkative one with multiple lashes; I know he thinks that he can distract me. I do not know what he is trying to accomplish with the long, drawn-out account of his foolish story." The wrathful hands of the torturers began again, and the blessed Fulgentius was furrowed by innumerable lashes. At length the priest, brought to confusion by this torture for which he was responsible, recognized the merits of praiseworthy men and did not dare to hold them any longer, but, having shamefully shaved their heads and deprived them of all their clothes, threw them out of his house, naked and without a penny. But this shaving brought no shame on these holiest of men, nor did nakedness cause confusion, because the injuries sustained out of hatred for their religion had for the first time adorned them with the glory of confessing the faith, sustained by grace from on high. Therefore, they went away from the priest's house as from the site of a glorious contest, crowned by the laurels of an outstanding victory. Retracing their steps through the field where they had been captured, they found there the gold pieces, which, as we said, Abbot Felix had thrown away, all of them without exception, and they accepted them with joy as if restored by God's hand. Giving ineffable thanks to God, who consoles the lowly in their trials, they rejoined the brethren who had remained in the neighborhood. The detestable story of this cruel act saddened the entire region and was spoken of even in Carthage. The news also reached the so-called bishops of the Arians that the blessed Fulgentius had been seriously beaten, and, because a bishop knew Fulgentius's family and had loved the blessed Fulgentius himself while he was still a layman, he was motivated to take action against the priest of his own religion and diocese who instigated the beating, proposing to revenge the blessed Fulgentius if the latter were willing to swear out a complaint against the above-mentioned priest. But the blessed Fulgentius, even though many urged him to do this, said, "It is not permitted for a Christian to seek revenge. God knows how to deal with the injuries to his servants. If that priest, because of me, is punished by men for his serious crime, we would lose the reward from God for our suffering. In addition, it might scandalize many little ones, if I, a Catholic and a monk, albeit a sinner, were to seek justice from an Arian bishop." Unwilling to render evil for evil and knowing that

LIFE OF FULGENTIUS

his life was of use to good people, lest perchance, they again suffer violence at the hands of the heretics, they again left that province and swiftly returned to regions closer to their own province, choosing rather to have the Moors for neighbors than to suffer further indignities from the Arians.

Chapter 8

They set about founding a monastery near the city called Medidi,[20] where very quickly they, as servants of the Lord, gave themselves up to works of charity. But, all of a sudden, the blessed Fulgentius, reading the admirable lives of the Egyptian monks, as well as being inspired by meditating on the *Institutes* and *Conferences*,[21] decided to set out by ship for these lands; for two reasons, in particular, viz., firstly, that, giving up the title of abbot, he could live more humbly, subject to the rule, and, secondly, that he might submit himself to a stricter regime of self-denial. And, because his intention might be hindered if it became public knowledge, he immediately sought an opportunity to go to Carthage. Coming to the walls of the city with only one brother, whose name was Redemptus,[22] the companion he had chosen for his voyage, he boarded a ship headed for Alexandria. Bringing no money with him as was usual for such a voyage but firmly placing all his hope in God who is rich, he sang sweetly with David, "The Lord is my shepherd; there is nothing I shall want."[23]

With a fair breeze and favorable winds, they quickly arrived at the port of Siracusa.[24] Guided by the Providence of God most high, he came to the city where the blessed Pope

20. Medidi, a town in Byzacena, about 55 kilometers southeast of Sicca.
21. These are works of the monastic writer, John Cassian (c. 360–435), who came from the East but settled in southern Gaul and wrote in Latin. It is curious that he is read by Fulgentius, since Cassian was a favorite target of disciples of Augustine such as Prosper who saw in him a "semi-Pelagian." See EEC I.149.
22. Redemptus. See "Redemptus 1," PCBE, 956.
23. Ps 22(23).1 LXX; Ps 23.1.
24. Syracuse in Sicily. See EEC II.806–807.

Eulalius[25] then led the Catholic Church, a man of outstanding holiness, of admirable hospitality, of perfect charity, in whose heart was hidden a treasure of spiritual wisdom; he enriched many by using the talents he had received from the Lord. Adorned above all with the virtue of discernment, he had a special love for the monastic calling. He even had his own monastery where he spent time as often as he was not taken up by Church business. It was to him therefore that the blessed Fulgentius came, welcomed willingly with other travelers, to the bishop's hospitality, nor was he able to conceal himself for long. For, soon enough, as was customary at the bishop's table, talk turned toward matters theological; immediately his speech revealed a man of unusual knowledge. From the distinction of his speech and the reserve of his answers, the bishop realized that, under that monastic habit, there lay a notable theologian; but he put off asking during the meal, in the presence of the other guests, either who he was or why he had come there. But, after the dinner, during the afternoon hours, as the bishop was walking through his house, looking out the window, he saw the blessed Fulgentius, along with the other guests, looking up at him. Right away he called him aside, "You had begun to speak of the *Institutes* and the *Conferences* during our dinner; I would like you to bring me these books, if you have them with you." Without delay, obedient to his wishes, he brought the books and, when urged, explained the contents in his own words. The holy Eulalius was struck by the young man's learning and, delighted with such a guest, earnestly inquired why he had come from Africa. But he, afraid of being thought presumptuous, if his intentions were revealed, said, "I am looking for my parents who, I heard, were living as strangers in this area." In truth, he was seeking his parents, those whose holy lives he sought to imitate. The bishop, realizing that this answer was concealing something, sought the reason for the whole voyage from his companion, who was

---

25. Eulalius, bishop of Syracuse at the beginning of the sixth century. See DHGE, v. 15., cols. 1385–86.

simple and guileless. Then the blessed Fulgentius, happily betrayed, confessed the truth openly; he said that he was going to the furthest desert region of the Thebaid, where, as the text urged, he would live, dead to the world, where the larger number of ascetics would pose no obstacle to his progress, but, rather, would offer examples.

"You are doing well," the bishop answered, "in seeking to follow the better things, but you know that 'it is impossible to please God without faith'.[26] A wicked schism[27] has severed those lands to which you want to go from the communion of blessed Peter; all those monks, whose marvelous acts of self-denial are made widely known, will not share with you the Sacrament of the altar. What good will it do therefore to afflict your body with fasts when your soul, which is so much better than your body, will lack spiritual consolation? Go back home, my son, lest, by the desire for a higher life, you put your orthodox faith in danger. Once, when I was a young man, before the grace of the honor of being a bishop came to me, however unworthy, I thought a long time about seeking to follow this very holy calling in the monasteries of that province, but this same reason kept me from carrying out my intention."

The blessed Fulgentius, heeding the salutary counsel of the bishop and laying aside the fervor of his original intention, let himself be persuaded to stay in Siracusa for a few months, with the holy Eulalius supplying fitting lodging and meals. But, because strong characters cannot remain idle, always carrying on the works of charity, even in the very modest quarters he had accepted, he began to offer hospitality to many who came; still a stranger himself, needing the assistance of others, he took in strangers. The holy Eulalius marveled at the freedom which blossomed in his soul, and, expanding with happiness as he saw Fulgentius, to whom, as

---

26. Heb 11.6.
27. The Acacian schism. See EEC I.5. Behind the schism lay the Monophysite controversy stemming from the refusal of some eastern Christians, especially in Egypt, to accept the Tome of Leo and the decisions of the Council of Chalcedon (451).

one who had nothing, he supplied food for each day, himself giving something to eat to those in need. And, if it may be said, the great are accustomed to grow by comparison with the lesser, although the holy Eulalius was altogether perfect in dealing with the poor, still, watching the activities of the blessed Fulgentius, he became still more merciful and generous.

Chapter 9

When the winter of the present year was over, a strong desire drove the blessed Fulgentius to visit without further delay a certain bishop by the name of Rufinianus,[28] who, fleeing the violence of persecution, leaving behind the bishops of Byzacena, sailed away and there, near the province of Sicily, was staying on a very small island and living in a praiseworthy way the life of a monk. Fulgentius wanted to go so that, assured by a second opinion, he would know what he ought to do. He wanted this, not because he lacked confidence in Bishop Eulalius but because he realized that, in doubtful matters, the advice of several was always most useful. After many labors of a journey on foot, he came to that place in Sicily which was closest to the island on which the holy bishop Rufinianus was living. Carried across in a small boat, he quickly presented himself to the venerable bishop. He also advised him not to continue on his journey to Egypt. He then decided to return to his own monastery but not to pass up the opportunity to visit the tombs of the Apostles.

When the occasion presented itself, taking ship, he came to Rome and quickly entered that city always praised with one voice by worldly writers and truthfully called the head of the world. It was a time of great celebration in the city; the presence of King Theoderic[29] brought great rejoicing to the

28. Rufinianus. See "Rufinianus 6," PCBE, 1005.
29. Theoderic was Ostrogothic king of Italy from 493 to 526. Though an Arian, he was generally tolerant of and even friendly toward Roman Catholics. His lived in Ravenna, and his one visit to Rome was made in the year 500. See EEC II.828 and J. Moorhead, *Theoderic in Italy* (Oxford: 1992), especially for the

Roman Senate and people. So it happened that the blessed Fulgentius, for whom long since the world had been crucified, after piously touring the sacred burial places of the martyrs and humbly paying visits to all the servants of God, whose acquaintance he could make in such a short period, by chance was in that place called the "Golden Palm"[30] while the aforementioned king Theoderic was delivering an address. He saw the noble appearance of the Roman Senate and the varied ranks of the aristocracy, each with its own distinctive insignia. Hearing with his inexperienced ears the acclamations of a free people, he recognized the nature of the glories of this world. But he was not willing to recognize anything worthwhile in this spectacle, nor was he attracted by the useless enjoyment of such worldly vanities; rather, he burned all the more to enjoy the happiness of the heavenly Jerusalem. He wisely said to the brethren who were with him, "How lovely the heavenly Jerusalem must be if the earthly Rome shines so brightly! And, if, in this world, the dignity of such great honor is paid to those who love vanity, how great the honor and glory to be given to the saints who contemplate the truth!"

Chapter 10

On the same day, the blessed Fulgentius said many similar things to the profit of the others, and, now, longing with his whole heart to see his monastery again, he quickly sailed back to Africa via Sardinia. With their joy the monks had a hard time believing that the blessed Fulgentius had really come back. The holy community was uncertain what it should do first: whether to complain about the long absence of their father or to rejoice in his presence. None dared to reproach him for his departure; rather, all hastened to thank God for his return. The laity joined in the rejoicing of the

---

complications of the Laurentian schism in Rome involving prominent people whom Fulgentius may have met during his visit to Rome.

30. For the "Golden Palm," see "Ad Palmam" in L. Richardson, Jr., *A New Topographical Dictionary of Ancient Rome* (Baltimore: 1992), 283.

servants of God; all the good and upright were happy that the blessed Fulgentius, destined to be the teacher of the Church in Africa, did not remain in the regions across the sea for a longer time. As in a form of rivalry, each one now hastened to offer greater consolations of piety by which the heart of the one who had returned might be comforted. A man named Silvestrius,[31] a good Christian and a leading man in the province of Byzacena, offered a piece of land well suited for building a monastery. Its soil was rich and fertile, perfect for planting gardens that would yield much fruit, and, something even more desirable, situated far from the furies of war, it promised full security and peaceful tranquility. Furthermore, in that vicinity lived very many good people, people whose frequent assistance bid fair to facilitate the lives of the monks so that no care about their material needs would distract them in their pursuit of the Kingdom of God.

Chapter 11

Willingly taking up the pious offer of the religious man, blessed Fulgentius without delay founded a monastery in the location given to him, and, with pious exhortation, inviting many to be converted, he greatly increased the number of monks and became the father of a large community. Although he kept wanting to meditate on spiritual things, he was compelled by his greater range of cares to be frequently distracted; seeking from love of the truth a space of time for holy withdrawal and rest, the needs of brotherly love and responsibility forced him to be busy about many other things. At times nourished by the contemplation of higher things and desiring to give himself up to reading and prayer, he long tried to think of how he might divest himself of the burden he now bore and how, under the authority of others, he himself might live under a rule rather than impose on others a rule of life. According to the precept of the Lord, he judged it more profitable to obey the commands of others

---

31. Silvestrius. See PCBE, 1084.

than to give commands for others to obey. Thinking these things over for a long while, suddenly he came to a decision.

Chapter 12

By the shoreline near Junca,[32] where the sea is fairly shallow, by Benefensa for the greater part, the narrowness of the cliff does not permit the planting of gardens. Not even the minimum resource of wood and drinking water is possible, but each day these basic necessities are brought by small boats. In this monastery, the old discipline of the strict observance is maintained, with many living holy lives there from their childhood to extreme old age and carrying out in an exemplary manner lives befitting their holy vocation. There two exceptional priests, marvelous in their merits and venerable by the honor of an old age without reproach, fulfill the office of abbot. They never leave the cloister but train many men worthy of a calling in the Church. To this monastery the blessed Fulgentius went secretly and, there in the very large community, he laid aside the title of abbot and, joining himself to a large number of monks, still stood out above the others with his marvelous knowledge and spiritual eloquence but was still subject to all by a praiseworthy humility and outstanding obedience, recalling indeed that phrase from the Gospel where Our Lord said, "I have not come to do my will but the will of him who sent me."[33] He mortified all his desires, giving himself up to fasting, especially to prayers, vigils, and self-denial, crucifying himself and everything with his worldly vices and lusts. He was happy to work with his own hands; in a praiseworthy way, he practiced the art of the copyist; often he wove palm leaves into fans. He had done this as well in his own monastery even when he was abbot. Frequently he would read in his cell in the presence of the brethren, loved, honored by all, and a joy to

---

32. Junca, about 110 kilometers down the Mediterranean coast of Byzacena, southwest of Ruspe. Bennefa is the next town south of Junca.
33. Jn 6.38.

them. But, as great as was the rejoicing in that monastery, just as great a sadness arose in his former monastery. Those who had received him rejoiced, but those who had lost him were saddened. Thus arose a battle of love between the two communities. One community tenaciously held on to its new member, while the other asked and begged that their former father be given back to them. The former asserted that his presence was a feather in their cap, but the other lamented the loss brought about by his departure.

Chapter 13

The blessed Fulgentius, greatly desiring to learn rather than to teach, preferred to stay as a subject there where he was and feared to return to that place where he would be superior over all. Then the unhappiness of Abbot Felix and all the brethren whom he had left behind, taking counsel of necessity, assailed the monks on the island with the backing of the holy bishop Faustus. Right off, by his episcopal authority, he claimed that Fulgentius was a monk belonging to his jurisdiction and commanded him to be sent back and that he ought to live where he ordered him to. He threatened those who resisted with excommunication. He asserted that even Fulgentius himself would be subject to a judgment analogous to those who were disobedient if he did not yield. What more need be said? The blessed Fulgentius again returned to his own monastery; he was ordered to take up the office of abbot again. And, lest he again be tempted to stray because of his spiritual aspirations, without warning the bishop ordained him a priest. Now, adorned with the offices of abbot and priest, he could neither leave the monastery nor be ordained in another church. Now, conquered and bound by the fetters of honor, the blessed Fulgentius began to rule his monastery with good heart. His fame and praises grew; he was becoming known through all the provinces of Africa; even in the territory of the Nunti,[34] he was honored as their own bishop, and, whenever there was an episcopal vacancy,

---

34. Unknown.

all were ready to seek with minds and voices the blessed Fulgentius as their high priest, nor was any other except the blessed Fulgentius allowed to be consecrated. God saw the desire of the peoples, and the blessed Fulgentius himself was not unaware of it. But, because at that time the royal authority forbade the ordination of bishops and would not allow widowed sees to be provided with pastors, he lived through this period in safety, judging the solution of flight pointless as a way of avoiding an honor which it was unlawful either to offer or to accept.

Later, the whole group of bishops who still remained, having conferred together, decided, despite the royal prohibition,[35] to proceed with the ordination of bishops in all places. They reasoned this way: either the king's anger, if it eventuates, will abate, and they will be able to live among their people more easily, or, if the violence of persecution breaks out, those recently found worthy of ordination will now be crowned as confessors of the faith and will fulfill their ministry more easily, offering consolations to their people amid the tribulations. All of a sudden, there was a general rush to elect, bless, and consecrate priests, deacons, and anyone the popular choice could find, with all the towns hurrying as if in a competition, lest in such a race any appear to be too slow or to have let others get ahead of them. Then the blessed Fulgentius, by fleeing, kept ahead of those who chose him; he hid in a place unknown, and they could not find him when they searched. The people of the place where the monastery was located first thought of putting off their election until they found the blessed Fulgentius. But, afraid lest the search for the blessed Fulgentius take too long and concerned that the report reach Carthage and set off another royal prohibition, with the necessity for speed urging them on, they decided to elect one of their own clergy. So, in many locations where the blessed Fulgentius was either the first choice or the only choice, after he could not be located, they gave the highest honor to someone else.

Now the province of Byzacena was filled with new bishops,

---

35. A decree of Thrasamund, king of the Vandals 496–523.

and only a few sees remained unfilled. But the cruelty of the king was again stirred up, and he decreed exile for them all, with the sentence given first of all against the ordainer himself, the primate by the name of Victor,[36] who, taken prisoner by the king's men, was brought to Carthage. Then came a greater sadness with the happiness that had accompanied the ordinations being turned into public mourning. While the news was circulating that the time for ordinations had passed, the blessed Fulgentius, thinking that the sees nearest him now had their own bishops, returned to rule the community of his monastery, neither hesitating nor fearful but rejoicing totally that he had escaped the burden of the episcopal dignity. Nevertheless, our God, bringing to fulfillment what he had predestined by his higher counsel, now wanted to give to him, to whom he had given the ability to teach well the doctrine of salvation, the authority to do so, lest there be lacking a faithful preacher of the Catholic faith against the Arians. In a time of tribulation, he was no longer willing to leave hidden the vessel of election through whom he had provided the fulfilling of the office of preaching.

Chapter 14

There was Ruspe,[37] a noble town, quite famous for its illustrious citizens. But it had no bishop because a certain deacon, Felix[38] by name, had sought the honor of the office of bishop. Having been himself refused by that place, he was not going to allow another in his stead. His brother, a friend of the procurator, fed the fires of his ambition through his use of secular power. A strong feeling of resentment stirred

36. Victor, primate of Byzacena. As with the province of Numidia, the provincial primacy was not attached to one see but depended on seniority in the episcopate. Victor is a very common name, and this Victor may be one of three, viz., Victor of Gaguari ("Victor 71"), Victor of Nara ("Victor 77"), or Victor of Vita ("Victor 85")—not the historian. See PCBE, 1178–80.

37. Ruspe, on the Mediterranean coast of Tunisia, about 40 kilometers east of Thysdrus (El Djem) and down the coast about 80 kilometers southeast of the Byzacenan capital of Hadrumentum (Sousse).

38. See "Felix 91," PCBE, 441.

the hearts of the good citizens. Why did they alone remain without a spiritual father, they who seemed to be superior to others in worldly honors? Then suddenly there came to these unhappy people the accurate report that the blessed Fulgentius who in many places had been deemed worthy of the first place in the priesthood, having been unable to be found at the time of the ordinations, had remained a priest. He appeared clothed with even greater glory because he had so trampled on the lust for higher honors. As the proud and ambitious deacon displeased them, so the one who had tried to escape appeared praiseworthy and desirable.

All agreed that Fulgentius had been saved for them since he had not been ordained even though the people of so many towns had sought him. Though Fulgentius remained in ignorance of this, the citizens of Ruspe besought the primate Victor while traveling through the town, and permission was granted for Fulgentius to be ordained by neighboring bishops. So the crowd gathered and went to the monastery. Suddenly the blessed Fulgentius, suffering from an eye ailment, was found in his own little cell; they entered, seized him, led him away, and he was forceably made a bishop without ever being asked first. Thence he was brought to the bishop who had been told to ordain him; he became the father of a people he did not know, so that in him the prophetic word seemed to be fulfilled: "A people I did not know served me."[39]

The very pleasing appearance of the wise man increased the good favor of the people who had elected him, though he then seemed unknown to them. And to anyone to whom he was still unknown, the poverty of his dress charmed them, and the modesty of his manner made him venerated. When, according to the time and circumstances, he wished to address them, the entire crowd hung on his every word. His familiar speech enabled one to know the nature of the future teaching of this spiritual master. And so, in whatever areas he traveled, the people came out to honor him, pro-

39. Ps 17(18).44.

claiming that, though the Church at Ruspe had to wait a longer time, so much the better was the bishop it received.

The deacon, seeing that the attempts prompted by his ambition had failed, did the only thing left to one who had been deluded; he finally burst forth in anger. Gathering a great crowd, he, as the sacred psalm says, ". . . placed a stumbling block in the path"[40] for the son of peace who was coming. The hostile and ambitious cleric placed himself across the path which the chosen servant of God was traveling. But, whenever Christ comes to the assistance of simple souls, the election of a bishop cannot be stopped by human intervention, an election in which ambition played no part. I do not know by what urging of the Holy Spirit the crowd of people that went before Fulgentius took another road and, even while his enemy sat waiting on the other road, placed the blessed Fulgentius on the bishop's chair. The divine sacraments were celebrated that very day, and, after receiving communion from the hands of the blessed Fulgentius, the happy crowd dispersed. When he heard what had happened, the deacon, albeit tardily, bowed to the divine will. When this man returned, the blessed Fulgentius received him with kindness, mercy, and love, so much so that he afterwards ordained him a priest. But divine justice quickly exercised divine vengeance, and the deacon become priest was dead within a year, and the procurator who had supported him was reduced to poverty. They both received their just deserts in this life for their audacity, but, in the life to come, the all-powerful God will prepare for them the grace of heavenly pardon. We have thought this incident worth recalling that we might show that henceforward greater authority accrued to the blessed Fulgentius among the people because of it, since they acknowledged in such incidents that the divine justice was always on the alert.

---

40. Ps 139(140).5.

Chapter 15

So the blessed Fulgentius took up the office of bishop without ambition but with the greatest devotion, while those who contradicted him received divine retribution. But, in becoming a bishop, he did not cease to be a monk; having received the episcopal dignity, he continued to observe the commitments of his first profession in their entirety. Indeed, in so doing, he further added to the dignity of a bishop. Never did he seek expensive clothing or forego his daily fasts, nor even in the company of guests did he eat dainty dishes, nor even when lying down to rest did he seek to relax his strict regime in the slightest. But, summer or winter, he continued to wear his simple tunic. Unlike other bishops, he never wore the *orarium*,[41] but, like a monk, used a leather belt. In his zeal for humility, he so avoided wealthy vesture that, refusing to make use even of clerical shoes, he simply used common, ordinary shoes in winter or, in summer, sandals. While in the monastery, he sometimes wore sandals; frequently he walked around barefoot. He permitted neither himself nor his monks to have an expensive hooded mantle nor one of bright colors. Beneath this cloak, he went about covered with a black or white pallium. During periods of mild weather, he went about in the monastery with this pallium only. We never saw him with bare shoulders, nor did he take off his belt to go to bed. With God as his witness, observing faithfully his continence, he offered the holy sacrifice in the very tunic in which he slept and used to say at the time of the sacrifice that hearts were to be changed rather than clothes.

Chapter 16

No one was able to force this blessed bishop to eat meat of any kind, but he ate only vegetables, barley, and eggs, and,

---

41. The *orarium* was probably the pallium, the symbol of episcopal rank in Africa.

while he was still young, without oil. Later, as he got older, he ate these things with a sprinkling of oil. He was persuaded to do at least this, to accept the oil, lest his eyesight deteriorate and prevent him from fulfilling his duty of reading. While he was in good health, he always abstained from wine. But, when the necessity of failing health compelled him and he had to drink a little wine, pouring a small amount of wine into a glass filled with water, he experienced no pleasure in either the taste or odor of wine. Before evening prayers were announced by the brethren, he, always at watch in body and heart, was either praying or reading or dictating or giving himself up to mental prayer, because he knew well that throughout the daylight hours he would be taken up with the needs of the Church's children.

Sometimes he went down to celebrate the evening office with God's servants, but he used, much more praiseworthily, to have his own prayer by himself in the duties I have mentioned. Never did he live except with other monks. And so, when ordained their bishop, he asked of the people of Ruspe this first favor—that they would donate a place suitable for building a monastery. Then, from among the many citizens who hastened to be of service, one, Posthumianus[42] by name, a Christian and among the noblest citizens of the town, faithfully offered the great bishop a small piece of land which belonged to him, not far from the church. There a hill rose upward, covered with pines, offering the prospect of a lovely small forest. The blessed Fulgentius willingly accepted the offer of the spot which he saw also possessed the wood necessary for the construction. He quickly persuaded the blessed abbot Felix to come as well, together with the larger part of his community, though a small number were left behind in the other monastery, and one of their number, Vitalis[43] by name, was made the prior. He ordered both monasteries to live under such a rule of charity as to be joined together by such great unanimity that they would not

---

42. Posthumianus. See PCBE, 897.
43. Vitalis. See "Vitalis 12," PCBE, 1224.

be seen to be divided by distance. If Christ should receive new monks in either the new or the old monastery, they would reckon their seniority from the time of their entry into either of the two monasteries. And, whenever they came to visit, the superiors giving their permission, they were to be received not as guests but as members, as it were, of the same community. Governed as one by the regulations of the blessed bishop Fulgentius, they venerated and loved him as their spiritual father. The blessed Fulgentius had so arranged things that he would not lose the consolation of the monks while taking on the burden of governing the clergy.

Chapter 17

Then suddenly the ministers of the royal wrath were sent abroad so that the noble confessors of Christ, having been taken prisoner, would, together with others, be forced into exile in Sardinia. Carried off quickly, he lamented that his church would be widowed right from the start before he had been able to instruct it with his eloquent words. Yet, with a greater joy, he wisely overcame this sadness because he was now beginning to share the glories of martyrdom. Accompanied by both monks and clergy, this outstanding teacher of both orders went forth, amid the tears of the laity, from his honorable chair to the place of the blessed combat. With mind unencumbered, with full voice, he was now ready to profess the Catholic faith before kings and potentates. Carthage welcomed him when he came and, in the persons of a very few, enjoyed the fruits of his knowledge. They brought him many gifts, which the blessed Fulgentius ordered to be reserved for that monastery which he had ordered to be built.

He boarded the ship with crucified heart and naked body. But he had the vast riches of his unique knowledge, which he shared unceasingly with all with whom he came in contact. Among all the bishops with whom he was to share a common exile, he was the most junior in rank by date of ordination, but was not inferior to them by virtue of his patience and charity. When uncertain questions arose and the views of all were sought, when the blessed confessors discussed the common good among themselves, Fulgentius sat in the last place; yet, the primate, and all those behind him, wanted to hear Fulgentius's views and wanted to follow him. He, however, attributing nothing to himself via empty vainglory, deferred all such honors to his seniors. If asked to reply to those who sought his views, nevertheless, he was always ready to obey their commands; nor did he presume to wrest anything from those who did not want to agree. After long periods of deliberation, whatever decisions the group made, it was left to the eloquence of the blessed Fulgentius to persuade others.

Chapter 18

All imposed on him the task of responding, in the name of all, in letters for those across the sea, whenever the bishops were asked about faith or a variety of other questions.[44] Just as once Aurelius,[45] bishop of the church of Carthage, of blessed memory, had among his many privileges, that of drafting the letters for the councils of Africa, so Fulgentius was given the privilege of himself writing the letters for this council. There were at that time sixty and more bishops bound by the chains of exile, whose tongue and mind the blessed bishop Fulgentius was. Hence, whenever replies were sent to those seeking advice, the names of all the bishops were mentioned in the letter, but in fact the blessed Fulgentius alone was the author.

In addition to these letters which treated public issues, if any of these bishops wished to correct or admonish his distant flock, he went to ask the blessed Fulgentius and, by means of the latter's talents, fulfilled the duties of his office.

---

44. Fulgentius's ordination to the episcopate took place c. 508. Very soon afterward he joined other African bishops in exile in Sardinia. His own exile lasted about eight years until 516 or 517. Letters 15 and 17 of his collection are letters written by Fulgentius in the name of the exiled bishops.

45. Aurelius, bishop of Carthage 388–430. See "Aurelius 1," PCBE, 105–27.

O marvelous man, born not for yourself alone but for all! The Church of Ruspe alone deserved him as its teacher, but most of the province of Byzacena lived by his words. A certain cleric in the diocese of one of the exiled bishops sought to stir up trouble or to ignore the command of his bishop. But, through the letter dictated by the blessed Fulgentius, he, though absent, was corrected in such a way that, seeking to make up for his sins and crossing the sea, he immediately came into the presence of him by whose eloquence he had found himself excommunicated, and, salutarily brought low, he also besought mercy through the blessed Fulgentius himself. For, the blessed Fulgentius was himself both avenger and mediator, avenger for a colleague and intercessor for the cleric. From him came forth the sword by which the stiff necks of the proud were bent, and through him as well the medicine of kindness was proffered so that the spiritual maladies of brothers who sought him out were cured.

Chapter 19

At the very beginning of his glorious exile, he was not able to found a monastery, since he had few monks with him. But, not being able to live without some kind of community, he persuaded his fellow bishops, viz., Illustris and Januarius,[46] to live with him. Moved solely by love, he served them and in his wisdom brought about the likeness of a great monastery in which clerics and monks were mixed together. They had a common table and living quarters; they prayed and studied together. No one insolently raised himself above another, nor did any pay greater or more specific attention to his own brothers. But those monks who followed the blessed Fulgentius kept a rule of stricter austerity, possessing nothing of their own, and, although they lived among the clergy, they did not live like them. Such was the learning of the blessed Fulgentius, that he by his spiritual ad-

---

46. Illustris and Januarius. See "Illustris," PCBE, 599 and "Januarius 38 or 39," PCBE, 596.

monitions could turn away from earthly pleasures to spiritual and heavenly delights the hearts of his followers, so that, persevering in their good resolutions, they were not seduced into wanting to imitate the examples of the weaker brothers, which examples were present daily before their eyes. Who can worthily sing the praises of this establishment? That house was a house of prayer for the city of Cagliari.[47] There the afflicted came to receive the remedy of consolation; there were concluded among those separated by strife agreements establishing peace and concord. For those who wanted to have a more careful understanding of the divine Scriptures, there the Lord provided a deeper explanation. It was a delight for the leading men of the region, when possible, to go to hear the blessed Fulgentius in discussion. It pleased those in need of help to have to seek material assistance there where they also received spiritual nourishment. For, frequently the blessed Fulgentius was able by his wise admonitions to bring those whom he had freed from material hunger by his alms to renounce the world. Although they had nothing, he persuaded them to renounce even the desire to have something. He was so desirous of always gaining more adherents for the monastery that, although he knew that he was all things to all people, he desired and willed to associate all men with the profession of the monastic life. This renown, growing from one day to the next, evoked great joy in the people of the church of Carthage. The testimony of certain ones from that province who journeyed to see the blessed Fulgentius carried back the reports to those who could not go.

Chapter 20

Meanwhile, the implacable hatred and fearsome wrath of King Thrasamund[48] against the Catholic religion went on.

---

47. Cagliari, principal city of Sardinia, on its southern end.

48. Fulgentius was recalled from exile for a period of about two years 516/517–518/519. These exchanges gave rise to two works: *Obiectiones Regis Trasamundi et Responsiones Fulgentii* (CCL 91.67–94) and the *Ad Trasa-mundum* in three books (CCL 91.95–185).

Between harsh persecutions there were deceptive measures trying, sometimes by terror, at other times by promises, to force Catholics to deny that Christ was equal to God the Father. With the intention of deceiving, he began to simulate the desire to find out more about the Catholic religion, thinking that no one could be found whose arguments could convict him of error. He proposed the trap of foolish questions to many. If any were found willing to respond, he neither disdained nor refused them. He listened as if patiently but boasted that none satisfied him. And, indeed, who was able to shine the light of truth on one so hardened in heart? The daring steadfastness of their faith enabled a number of religious men on these occasions, prepared by the Lord, to refute the blasphemies of this king who was interested in learning. The king continued to seek someone who could most fully prove the truth of Catholic teaching by proofs accepted on both sides. They told him that among the bishops in exile there was the blessed Fulgentius who lacked nothing in knowledge, who abounded in grace, and who by his wisdom and eloquence could satisfy the king.

Immediately, the king, wanting to test this bishop to whom the whole Church of our religion bore favorable witness, quickly sent an eager servant, by whom Fulgentius was taken and without delay brought back to Carthage, which he entered joyfully. Here, as a faithful dispenser, finding the opportunity for using the talents entrusted to him, in the little room where he was staying, he diligently began to instruct orthodox Catholics who came to him; explaining how the Father, the Son, and the Holy Spirit, while the distinction of the three persons was maintained, were still preached as one God by the faithful. So pleasant was the eloquence of the blessed Fulgentius, such joy radiated from his countenance, that, almost as in a contest, holy charity drew all the faithful either to question the learned man or to hear how he answered the questions. But he, proclaiming the word of God, without any of that envy that irritates all questions, disdaining no one, judging no one insolent, prepared himself, if God through the Holy Spirit should reveal something to the other person, to listen and to learn to accept, to follow, to give approval. Even as a teacher, he, kind and mild, showed the humility of a disciple. So it came about that he became even better and more learned, even as he sought new gains for Christ. Those who had already been rebaptized he taught to lament their mistake, and he reconciled them. Others he warned lest they destroy their souls in exchange for worldly gains. Those whom he perceived to be close to perdition, he calmed by soothing words, so that, because of his kindness, they were ashamed to go through with the planned evil and, turning back, they quickly began to do penance. Others, strengthened by his words and renewed in their faith by the salt of his teaching, confuted the Arian heretics with all confidence. Thus, by a marvelous grace, it came about that through one bishop, whose wisdom the king wished to put to the test, the number of wise men in Carthage grew and, through the ministry of the persecutor, the strength of the Catholic faith, rather than being diminished, actually increased.

Chapter 21

All these things the king learned through his secret informers. He put the genius of this outstanding bishop to the test, his wisdom, learning, faith, piety, mildness, purity, and he acknowledged that the man deserved his reputation and was indeed such as he had been depicted. He sent him a book to be read right away, one full of the poison of infidelity, and demanded a rapid response. The most learned pontiff accepted the challenge, dividing up the collected fallacies of this very long statement into chapters, and adding his responses, which were brief, probative, of ineluctable logic, weighty with the authority of the witnesses invoked and bright with the logic of reason. Having discussed his answers in detail and at length with a number of wise men and having brought his work to the attention of the faithful, he then sent it to the king, who had been waiting impatiently for some time. The barbarous king read them over carefully, but, because he was never predestined for salvation, though he praised the wisdom, marveled at the eloquence, extolled the humility, still he did not deserve to recognize the truth. The people of Carthage, however, sensing a spiritual triumph, spread the word joyously but quietly that the king's views had been refuted, and they gloried that the Catholic faith was still victorious, all this joined to the praises of the blessed Fulgentius.

But the king desired to put the most learned man to the test once again and asked him questions about still other matters. He ordered that his questions be read to the blessed Fulgentius only once, allowing him no time to think about them or to write them down. For he was afraid that Fulgentius would put the king's words into his own responses as his arguments were refuted and that, in the eyes of the entire city, he would be ridiculed again as having been bested. The blessed Fulgentius, having difficulty recalling what had been read to him but once, put off his response. But the king became ever more insistent, asserting that the delay and the caution of the holy man indicated fear on his part. Because of this, the same pontiff, relying on the virtue of discretion, lest perchance lies be spread about through the populace to the effect that the blessed Fulgentius was not able or was not willing to counter the king's questions, wrote three marvelous little books. In these booklets, he addressed the above-mentioned king in all simplicity. He discussed all sides of the questions he had barely heard posed in passing. He taught that in the Incarnation, Christ the Lord had not been without a rational soul. Thereafter, the king, filled with great admiration, no longer dared to ask him anything. But one of his bishops, Pinta by name, attempted a response, more because he was unwilling to remain silent than because he had anything to say. Against him, the blessed Fulgentius then wrote another work in which he upheld the truth, a work entitled, *Against Pinta*,[49] and he showed that the adversaries who had been conquered in his first defense were foolhardy in trying to return to the fray.

---

49. This work is lost. On Pinta, see PCBE, 876.

To a priest named Abragil,[50] who asked a question about the Holy Spirit, he wrote a short *Admonition*, in which he brought forward much evidence, teaching that, together with the Father and the Son, the Spirit is to be confessed as one God. This *Admonition* he ordained should be written down between the other two works of this period; all faithful Catholics read these works and marveled. The Arians, on the other hand, were put to shame and murmured against him in their chagrin. They found occasion for an evil suggestion which they brought to the king. The latter wanted to keep him in Carthage for a longer time, but these wicked men objected, "Your work is in vain, O King; your efforts have accomplished nothing. Bishop Fulgentius's teaching has been so successful that he has received some of your own priests. Unless you do something quickly to support our religion, it will go down to defeat, and whoever has been baptized by us will be reconciled and will again confess the *homoousion*.[51] And, if you try to stir up a persecution again, the royal wrath will no longer be feared. The very presence of Fulgentius strengthens many and reinforces all their bishops in their faith."

The king, as if compelled by a greater necessity, agreed with those who put forward such arguments and had the blessed Fulgentius sent back to exile in Sardinia. In the dead of night (for, so the king had ordered), the blessed Fulgentius, unbeknownst to the people, was taken to the ship. But the winds were blowing the wrong way, and they had to wait by the shore so that for many days almost the entire city came out, and, in bidding them farewell, he gave them communion with his own hand. Then, filled with prophetic grace by the Holy Spirit, he said to Juliatheus,[52] a religious man grievously afflicted who gravely lamented the departure of the great pontiff, "Do not weep a long time. We shall soon

---

50. Abragil. See PCBE, 29.

51. *Homoousion*, the key word of the Council of Nicea (325) against the Arians, teaching that the Son is of the same substance (i.e., divine nature) as the Father.

52. Juliatheus. See PCBE, 617.

return to you; you will see us when freedom is restored to the Catholic Church. But, I ask, keep this to yourself—this thing which my great love has forced me to tell you."

Chapter 22

The blessed Fulgentius always carefully avoided boastfulness and never sought human glory from the gifts of the Spirit, content with the witness of his own conscience and trusting only in the mercy of God. Similarly, he never delighted in working miracles and in no way sought that such graces be given him. But, whenever he was asked to pray to God on behalf of the sick, the suffering, and those being tried by temporal misfortunes, he poured forth his prayers in this fashion: "You know, O Lord, what is fitting for the salvation of our souls. May your mercy grant to us who ask that which necessity counsels, so that our spiritual needs will not be injured. May the prayer of our lowliness be heard then, if it is for our good, so that your will above all may be done." And, very often indeed, almighty God granted many things to the prayers of his bishop. But he never attributed anything to his own merits, but, rather, everything was assigned to the faith of those for whom his prayers had been heard. He maintained that it had been granted to them and not to him.

Rather than spend much time on such things, let us mention one of his views on the working of miracles. Miracles, he said, do not confer righteousness on anyone, but notoriety on human beings. A person, well-known in the world, unless he is righteous, will end up condemned to eternal punishment. But the one who, having been justified by the work of heavenly mercy, will have lived as a righteous person in the sight of God alone, even if he be little known in the world, will be crowned and receive the joys of the saints.

Chapter 23

This man of miracles[53] feared receiving praise for miracles even though each day he performed greater miracles. By his most holy exhortation, he brought many believers to faith, and many heretics were reconciled; he made many who were sunk in the worst forms of immorality accept the laws of continence. By his most salutary admonitions, drunkards learned sobriety, adulterers followed chastity, misers and the greedy were taught to distribute everything to the poor. With their lives turned around, humility became sweet to the proud, peace to the quarrelsome, obedience to the disorderly. To miracles of this kind, the blessed Fulgentius always devoted his pious efforts. They accompanied him everywhere and made him glorious always and in every place.

With a favorable and mild wind, his ship brought him back to Sardinia. His return cheered the hearts of his fellow bishops in exile. The province itself, adorned with the presence of so many bishops, was rendered more brilliant by the light of his return. From all sides, Christians came running joyfully to see the strong athlete of Christ, who, in singular combat had broken the attack of the cruel king, now returning to the divine camp, adorned with the laurels of victory, and rejoining his former fellow soldiers. He demonstrated so much greater humility to each of them in proportion as he knew his courage shone forth, recalling, I do not doubt, the words of Scripture which warn, "My son, the greater you are, the more you must humble yourself; so you will find favor in the sight of the Lord."[54]

Chapter 24

The blessed Fulgentius was no longer willing to continue to live in his former house since there were now so many

---

53. Unlike many lives of bishops in early times, this life is devoid of miracles. (The other exception is the life of Augustine by Possidius of Calama.) Perhaps these considerations are apologetic in nature.

54. Sir 3.19.

monks there. He found an available spot not far from the noise of the city near the basilica of the holy martyr Saturninus.[55] Having first asked Primasius, the venerable bishop of the city of Cagliari, at his own expense he had a new monastery built in which, together with forty or more brothers, he kept without exception the rule of monastic discipline. He gave to none permission to depart from the rule of the monastic profession. Above all, he required his monks to observe this, that none of them would claim anything as his own but that all things would be held in common. For, he often said, "He must not and can not be considered a real monk who wishes to continue to have his own property." That a monk might perchance have need of special food sometimes required because of bodily infirmities; but that he wish to claim the right to have his own property over even the smallest things was evidence of a proud will and avarice. He himself gave the necessities of life to the servants of God with the greatest discretion, taking into consideration the strength or weakness of each person. But, to those who received more, he urged that they be more attentive to humility, telling them, "Whoever receives more from the common property becomes a debtor to all, since what he has comes from their property. Humility alone is fitting for a debtor."

He said this lest anyone be scandalized when, because of that person's weakness, he was seen giving him something extra. He was greatly concerned to anticipate the needs of all his monks, to give whatever was necessary or what was a reasonable request before it was actually sought. However, if anyone presumed to request something before it was offered, he refused the request immediately even if the monk deserved to receive it, saying, "Monks must be satisfied with what they receive." But, for the rest, for those who ask as if they had a right to something, they are still slaves to carnal desires; they are not at all thinking about the things of heaven so long as they seek to provide for themselves what is nec-

---

55. According to Isola, there is probably a textual problem here. The Sardinian martyr is Saturnus; Saturninus would refer to the third century bishop of Toulouse (Vita, 98, note 81).

essary for them by asking first, since they cannot buy it for themselves. He said that those were real monks who, with their passions mortified, were prepared to wish for nothing or to refuse nothing, but to observe only the counsels or commands of the abbot. Thus he did not permit even the brother who exercised the office of prior to do anything without consulting him. Those brothers, who worked untiringly at manual labor but had little affection for study, he esteemed less and did not consider them worthy of consideration for higher tasks. But, for the one who loved to study the things of God, even if he were weak in bodily strength and never able to work with his hands, such a person was more pleasing and loved.

When discussing matters in the presence of the community, he was pleased when someone proposed very difficult questions for him; he worked at answering them with great keenness of intellect. Usually he permitted all the brothers, even those of simple nature and little intellectual endowment, to ask whatever they wanted; nor would he cease his explanations because of boredom and fatigue, until they declared themselves satisfied with his explanation. He had the great and marvelous grace of rebuking turbulent souls with a peaceful heart. Even at the moment when others thought him to be very angry, in fact, the greatest serenity prevailed within him. Though unperturbed himself, he appeared to be upset and, with a salutary burst of anger, he shook up many a malefactor. Hating vice but loving human beings, he appeared to be severe just as long as the cause of spiritual discipline required it. At other times, with most people, he was kind, simple, and approachable, never calling any of the brothers simply by name. He gave no commands, even to the least among them, in the style of worldly authority.

Chapter 25[56]

During the same period, he wrote to the Carthaginians a letter noteworthy for its sublime exhortations in which, with

---

56. This chapter recounts Fulgentius's writings during his second exile. I

great sadness, he enumerated almost all the tricks and misleading allurements by which unfortunate souls are lured to their death. In addition, he swiftly replied in two booklets concerning the forgiveness of sins to the religious man, Euthymius, who had sought his counsel. He usefully discussed the proofs for predestination and instructed one who wanted to know about the varieties of grace. He wrote numerous friendly letters in which much spiritual edification is contained to people living near him in Sardinia, to those living in Africa, to people in Rome, especially senators, and to widows and virgins whose good reputations were well known. He wrote two brief books concerning fasting and prayer to the virgin of Christ, Proba. Fulgentius thus became better known to all people. Thus it was that two books were sent to the blessed Fulgentius to be critically evaluated by several monks in Constantinople who had been upset by them. Faustus, a bishop in Gaul, had written them with misleading guile—against grace, secretly favoring the Pelagians, though he wanted to appear Catholic. Lest the harmful material spread unnoticed, Fulgentius replied in seven books, working more to expound than to refute, since just to expose his deceitful speech was to refute the arguments of a deluded person. The great labor involved in writing this work found its due reward almost immediately. For, very soon, just as he was completing its dictation, the chains of his long captivity were broken. King Thrasamund died, and there was the marvelous goodness of Hilderic,[57] who began his reign. He restored freedom to the Catholic Church throughout Africa; he gave the people of Carthage their own bishop and by his

---

shall note those not translated in this volume. The letter to the Carthaginians is unknown; the treatise against Faustus of Riez, which concerned questions of grace, is lost.

57. Hilderic, king of the Vandals 523–30. His mother was a daughter of the western emperor Valentinian III. This partially accounts for his favorable attitude toward the Romans and "Catholic emancipation," which led to the return of Fulgentius and the other bishops exiled in Sardinia. This in turn led to his overthrow by Gelimer in 530. Finally this led to the Byzantine reconquest under Belisarius in 533, probably only a few months after the death of Fulgentius.

most clement authority ordered that ordinations of bishops be held everywhere.

Chapter 26

Therefore, the blessed Fulgentius, after having battered the Pelagians in his wisdom, deserved to see Catholics rejoicing. Then, just as the Holy Spirit had foretold through him, he returned to Carthage with all his fellow bishops whence he had departed alone. Those whom he had left in sadness he now found joyous. Those whom he had left suffering the violence of persecution, he now found delirious with happiness. Those whom he had left lamenting the sorrows of their mother the Church, he now found with a spiritual father. Those whom he had left in mourning, he now found awaiting his return with joy.

So great was the longing of the citizens of Carthage, desirous of seeing the blessed Fulgentius once more, so ardent the expectation of the whole people for the one whom they had seen engaged in serious combat in their midst, that, as the other bishops left the ship before him, the multitude stood on the shore in silence, straining with eyes and minds to pick out among all the bishops Fulgentius, whom they knew so well, looking for him through all the ships. When his face appeared, a great shout went up there; they disputed among themselves as to who would be the first to greet him, who the first to be recognized, who would bow his head for a blessing, who would deserve to touch him, at least with the tips of his fingers as he passed by, who would with his eyes see him standing there at least from a distance. The praise of God resounded from the lips of all. With some of the people going on before and some following the blessed confessors, they formed a noble triumphal parade up to the basilica of St. Agileus. A great crowd, gathering quickly, pressed in on the blessed Fulgentius, whom it honored more than the rest. With happy inspiration, certain Christians formed a circle around him, sweating as he was, so that a path was cleared for him to pass through the midst of the crowd.

The Lord, still seeking to test the love of the faithful, miraculously poured down a cloudburst as they were walking about. But who is able to tell of the deeds of piety without seeming to discount the truth? The downpour frightened no one, nor did it prevent any from paying homage to the glorious bishops. On the contrary, it was as if heavenly blessings were raining down; so much did the faith of noblemen increase that, joyously spreading out their cloaks over the blessed Fulgentius, they kept the rain-showers from him and, with their improvisational charity, invented a new kind of baldaquin. They became imitators of those who in earlier times spread out their cloaks on the ground, as the Gospel says, for the Savior who was seated on the foal of an ass and was coming to Jerusalem. Such things were done by others who, as one person, with their own clothing covered the bare head of the blessed Fulgentius. Evening was coming on when they came to bishop Boniface[58] of happy memory. All together and in common they blessed and praised God. Then the blessed Fulgentius, going through all the streets of Carthage, wheresoever he passed, was singled out by all hands and eyes; he was extolled with praises beyond number.

Chapter 27

Later, moving rapidly, he visited and blessed the homes of all his friends and deigned to rejoice with those who rejoiced; he who had previously wept with the sorrowing, satisfied the wishes of all. Bidding farewell to his brothers, he left Carthage. All along the long route of his journey, he was greeted with great joy, people coming out to meet him with candles, lamps, and tree branches, giving thanks to the ineffable God who had marvelously made the blessed Fulgentius so blessed in the eyes of all. In every church he was greeted as if he were their own bishop, and the whole province of Byzacena rejoiced as one people over his return. What man, I ask you, would not have such glorification go to his head?

58. Boniface, bishop of Carthage and Primate of Africa ca. 523–36. See "Bonifatius 26," PCBE, 159–61.

But in the blessed Fulgentius it brought about a more profound effort at humility. Arriving, covered by popular acclaim, and adding to the dignity of the episcopate the privilege of special veneration, after he had reclaimed his episcopal chair, still he desired to live with the monks. But lest, because of his return the authority of Abbot Felix seem to be diminished, he voluntarily surrendered all rights to command the monks, wishing to do not his own will, but the will of another. He who up until then as a monk had undertaken the direction of his brothers, now as a bishop was no longer willing to rule in his own monastery. So solicitous was he, fearing to upset Abbot Felix, that, when he was to entertain guests and it was necessary to buy more bread or to get more supplies, he would first consult Abbot Felix. In any council held in the province of Byzacena, he was the first to be consulted on all matters of importance; but, in his own monastery, even in the smallest matters, he humbly consulted Abbot Felix. It was not enough for the blessed Fulgentius to observe and demonstrate this humility by words and deeds; he would also confirm in writing that he claimed nothing for himself in this monastery and that he lived with the monks, not for the sake of some power he had over them but for reasons of charity. Looking to the future, this man took steps lest the simple servants of God be made subject to some loss later on. By this document, he avoided any future disagreement between the monks and his successors, because he put nothing ahead of the welfare of the monks, the servants of God. Near the Church he bought land and put a great deal of care into building a home on it so that a future successor of his would not lack a place to live in. When vacancies occurred in the ranks of the clergy, he filled them by transferring many proven brothers from among the monks to the Church's militia; here too he was taking charity into consideration. Practically all the clerics he ordained were from that monastery, the fact that they already knew each other would insure that there would be no disagreements at some future time to divide monks and clerics. He showed the greatest concern lest any cleric be clothed in expensive vesture or be taken up with worldly business and thus drift away from his churchly concerns for a long time. He commanded that all should live not far from the church, should cultivate their gardens with their own hands, and exercise great care in singing the psalms well and in reading. Each week, he set the fast on Wednesday and Friday for all clergy and widows, as well as for whoever of the laity was able. All were commanded to be present at the vigils each day as well as at morning and evening prayers. Some turbulent souls he lashed with words, but others whose fault was public he had beaten with blows. Thus he attacked the vices of all with salutary words, so that, while not mentioning names, he would cause all to be afraid and because of that salutary fear to abandon their hidden sins. For, how could he have a lesser concern for his own clergy, who had eliminated the long-standing contentions and angry battles of neighboring peoples? With salutary admonitions he pacified the anger of the people of Maximiana,[59] who were unwilling to accept the bishop ordained for them. Bringing a necessary end to this serious scandal, he modestly and wisely put everything in order and brought back peace among them.

By the judgment of all the bishops who met in the council of Junca,[60] Fulgentius was to be placed ahead of and above a certain bishop named Quodvultdeus,[61] who laid claim to seniority over him. That day Fulgentius kept silence, unwilling to diminish the authority of the council by declining. But, when the council was over and he saw that the other bishop had been hurt, he was not willing to have his honor become an occasion of sin for his brother, judging it better to take a lower place out of charity than a higher place at the expense of charity. In attendance a little later at the glorious council of Sufes,[62] in the presence of all, he asked that now bishop Quodvultdeus be placed before him as he wished that his

59. Exact location uncertain; perhaps in the vicinity of Hadrumetum.
60. On this council, see "Liberatus 7," PCBE, 638–39 (CCL 149.276 ff.).
61. Quodvultdeus. See "Quodvultdeus 23," PCBE, 955.
62. Sufes is Sbiba in central Tunisia.

own name be called after that of Quodvultdeus so that he might live happily, his soul reconciled to that of his fellow bishop. The bishops marveled at the humility of the one who asked this, nor did they want to disappoint the one offering this sacrifice of humility to God for the preservation of the communion of the spirit in the bond of charity. Where are they now, those who were dominated by the desire to lord it over others, who set themselves above their superiors and demanded privileges not due to them? Look to the blessed Fulgentius, not willing to defend the primacy which he deserved because he did not wish to be placed ahead of anyone at the expense of charity.

Unique master and teacher of the Catholic Church, to whom, because he had so many tasks to do here in Africa, so little time was available, still he dictated many ecclesiastical sermons which would be preached to the people. Whenever he preached, he entranced the souls of all, not to induce vain and empty applause but to generate within them compunction of heart. Boniface, of holy memory, bishop of the church of Carthage, present to dedicate a church in Furnos,[63] invited him to preach two days afterwards in his presence. He was so moved to hear the word of God from his mouth that, until he finished the sermon, Boniface watered the ground with his tears, thanking God whose grace continued to raise up great and outstanding teachers in the Catholic Church.

After his return from exile, Fulgentius wrote many new works: ten books refuting the false doctrines of the liar Fabianus,[64] three small works on the truth of predestination and grace, as well as many others which he wrote. If you wish to find out about them, you will find authentic copies in his monastery. But, now it is time for us to speak of how, after all his good works, he rested, taken up to the heavenly kingdom.

---

63. Furnos Maius in Africa Proconsularis, today Ain Fourna.
64. Fabianus, an Arian refuted by Fulgentius. Some thirty-nine fragments remain of this work (CCL 91A.761–866). See PCBE, 380.

Chapter 28

About a year before he was taken from this world, moved by a profound compunction of heart, he suddenly gave up his church duties. And, secretly departing from his monastery, accompanied by a few brothers, he sailed to the island of Cercina. There, on a rocky promontory named Chilmi,[65] he ordered a monastery to be built. Giving himself up to reading, prayer, and fasting, as if he knew that his final days were approaching, he did penance with his whole heart. And, although his entire life, from the moment of his conversion, when he took up the life of a monk with all his heart, had been a time of penance, now, on this island, all the more amply and seriously like a beginner, he mortified his body and wept in the sight of God alone. But many complained about the absence of their bishop, and so, constrained by the requirements of charity, he went back to his monastery. Ministering to religious people the customary consolations, he patiently put up with the most trying labors for the welfare of others.

But not many days had passed, and behold the good Lord called his faithful servant home. Suddenly the sharp pains of bodily illness hit him, and the malady burdened him for about seventy days. With frequency he kept repeating, "Lord, give me patience now, and forgiveness hereafter." He did not stop uttering these words either when the pains afflicted him or when he was afire with fever or worn out with fatigue. The physicians tried to persuade him to use the baths. "Can baths keep a mortal man from dying when the time for living has come to an end? But if death is close and the warm waters of the baths cannot hold it back, why, I ask you, are you trying to have me give up at the end the regime I have long observed as a monk?" Thus, trustingly putting his salvation in God's hands, as he felt the approach of death with certainty, calling all his clergy together, with the monks

---

65. The Kerkenah islands are about 20 kilometers off the Tunisian coast at Sfax. Chilmi is one of the smaller islands.

present as well, he spoke to them, saying, "Brothers, out of concern for the salvation of your souls, perhaps I have been hard and tough on you. And so, if anyone has suffered anything, I ask you to forgive me. And, if perhaps my severity has gone beyond what it should have, pray that the Lord will not impute this to me as a sin." When he had said this, the blessed Fulgentius burst into sobs and all fell together on their knees, proclaiming that he, good and kind, had always watched over them for the salvation of all, as was fitting. "May the Lord provide for you," he said, "a pastor worthy of him!" Then, ordering silence, he rested a while. A little later, continuing his care for the poor, when a sum of money was brought from which, as a most faithful steward, he gave to the needy each day, he ordered all of it to be given away. He recalled the names of each widow, orphan, stranger, and all the others in need, and with careful reflection determined what should be given to each one; having no heirs in this world he left to the poor the heritage of his charitable solicitude. Nor did he deprive his clergy of their due blessing; mercifully taking into account their poverty, in secret he carefully took care of everything in advance. He continued in prayer, giving a blessing to all who came in to see him. He remained lucid until his final hour. The last day of the kalends of January, after evening prayer, he happily gave up his blessed spirit into the hands of the Lord, completing the twenty-fifth year of his episcopate and the sixty-fifth year of his life as a whole, as he had indicated to many of the brothers shortly before his death. His holy body was not to be buried on that same day but was brought to the monastery church where he invited the monks as well as the clergy to watch the whole night with psalms, hymns, and spiritual canticles. The following morning a great crowd of people from neighboring areas came to the funeral; he was conveyed by the hands of priests to a church in the city which is called *Secunda*, in which he had placed relics of the Apostles; there he was given an honorable resting place. He was the first bishop to deserve to be buried in that basilica where no dead person, priest or laity, had ancient custom permitted to be buried. But the great power of love removed the obstacles posed by tradition. With all the people gathered round, with the greatest devotion they demanded that where the holy man, the one beloved of God, had been ordained a bishop was the place where he should be joined in perpetuity to the prayers of each one. For, they had experienced how much good the prayers of the blessed Fulgentius had done for them and how much evil he had turned away, as was shown by clear indications shortly thereafter. Not many days after Fulgentius's departure, the hostile nation of the Moors suddenly fell upon the territory of Ruspe, devastating the area with rapine, murder, and arson, even slaughtering those they found within the walls of a church. Who did not marvel at the grace of the blessed Fulgentius? As long as he lived, the city entrusted to him did not experience the horrors of war. And, even when the entire province underwent a terrible captivity, Ruspe remained exempt, because of its venerable bishop whose very life was a wall protecting the city.

Chapter 29

I have decided not to let this be passed over in silence, that, while a worthy successor was being sought, with considerable disagreement among clergy and laity, the prolonged wrangling consumed nearly an entire year. But your holiness sat in his chair on the very anniversary day of his death. The first solemn anniversary of his burial deserved to be adorned with this additional honor—that it was made even more venerable by the celebration of your ordination. Do you want to know how these things came about not by chance but how they can be shown to have been granted because of his prayers?

Let me remind you of the very precise vision of the blessed Pontianus,[66] bishop of Thenae, which he himself recounted, "As I was traveling to help elect a bishop for the

---

66. Pontianus or Ponticanus, bishop of Thenae in Byzacena. See "Ponticanus 2," PCBE, 883–84.

church of Ruspe, in accordance with the commands of Datianus,[67] the primate, the very blessed Fulgentius himself appeared while I was resting, greeting me as usual in friendly fashion and with his cheerful face, 'Where is your holiness now going in such haste?' To which I answered, 'To elect a bishop for the church of Ruspe.' He laughed. 'He's already ordained,' he said." Isn't it obvious that what he had come to announce had already been accomplished because of his prayers? He, who had known of the confirmation of one not yet chosen or ordained, by his prayers had merited to know the day on which the one ordained was to sit in the chair. By continual prayers and faithful devotion, we pray always that, having become a participant in his glory for eternity, you live happily, not unworthy of so great a predecessor. May you give thanks to the Lord with us for the completion of this work, and may you, with us, ask pardon of all learned readers for those parts which are not as well expressed as they should be.

67. Datianus, Primate of Byzacena, successor to Liberatus ca. 533. See "Datianus 4," PCBE, 266–67.

TO PETER ON THE FAITH

Introduction

This is probably the most popular of the works of Fulgentius, a relative term, to be sure. In the Middle Ages, it was widely attributed to St. Augustine. In the twentieth century, it has been translated into French, German, Italian, and Polish. Peter, probably a layman, intended to make a pilgrimage to Jerusalem. But he found the same problem which had kept Fulgentius himself from journeying to Egypt to visit the monks there, namely, the growing reality of the divisions in the eastern Church brought about by the widespread rejection of the decisions of the Council of Chalcedon in 451. Peter asked Fulgentius for a basic doctrinal guidebook. It dates probably to the time of his return from the second period of exile in Sardinia.

In answer to Peter's request, Fulgentius discusses the teachings of the Church on the Trinity, the Incarnation, Creation, the Fall, Redemption, the sacraments of Baptism and Penance, and Marriage and Virginity. While most believe that Fulgentius is the author of the entire work, there have been some who have posited a second author for the second half which constitutes a recapitulation of the first half with each section beginning: "Hold most firmly and never doubt. . . ." This is the first English translation of this work.

Y SON PETER,[1] I have received a letter from your charity, in which you indicated your desire to travel to Jerusalem, and you requested instruction by a letter from me concerning the rule of the true faith you would have to hold in those parts so that no one could catch you unawares with some heretical falsity. I am glad indeed that you have such a concern for keeping the true faith with no shade of unbelief, a faith without which conversion not only would be of no use but would not really be conversion at all.

---

1. Peter. The identity of the one who requested this doctrinal guide from Fulgentius is uncertain. The majority of scholars views this Peter as a layman who intended to travel to Jerusalem and asked for instruction in view of the doctrinal dissidence there, especially that stemming from the rejection of the Council of Chalcedon after 451.

Indeed, apostolic authority tells us that, "without faith, it is impossible to please God."[2] For, faith is the foundation of all things. Faith is the beginning of human salvation. Without it, no one can belong to the number of the children of God, because, without it, neither will anyone gain the grace of justification in this world nor possess eternal life in the world to come. If anyone here will not walk by faith, he will not attain the vision. Without faith, all human effort is empty. A person, trying to please God through contempt for the world but without the true faith, is like someone striving toward the homeland where he knows he will live in blessedness but who leaves the path of righteousness and foolishly embarks on the path of error; such a person will never arrive at the blessed city but will fall into the abyss, that place where joy is not the lot of the one who arrives but death is inflicted on the one fallen.

2. Nevertheless, there is not a sufficient amount of time for an adequate treatment of the faith to be produced, since you want to have my answer quickly. So great is the work of this treatise that it can scarcely be fulfilled even by the great. You did not say that you had to be instructed concerning the faith in such a way that you designated one particular heresy against which our work should be especially vigilant. Rather, you seek a clarification of the faith without any further specification, and you ask for this to be done in such a short time that surely you see how impossible it is for us to encompass such a great matter in so brief a time and space. In any case, we ourselves are not adequate for such a task, even if there were a sufficient amount of time and our own mental capacity were greater so that we were able to write the many volumes on this subject you seek from us. But, because "the Lord is near to all who call on him in truth,"[3] who "has executed sentence decisively and quickly on the earth,"[4] I hope that, as he gave you a holy concern for this faith, so also, he will grant me sufficient ability that I may respond to your good and praiseworthy desire. I hope that, although I shall

2. Heb 11.6. 3. Ps 144(145).18.
4. Rm 9.28.

not be able to say everything by which every heretical error can be recognized and unmasked, overcome, or avoided, still, in the name of, and with the help of, the Holy Trinity, which is the one, true, and good God, I may say those things in which, at least for the most part, the Catholic faith may stand forth without any of the fog of error. If you keep these things with you, you will be able to recognize and flee those things which, even if they do not seem to be explicitly refuted in this work, still, from those things which are here in a more general and complete way, that which people without faith wish to whisper in the ears of the faithful, things not handed down by the rule of divine truth but invented by the wickedness of human error, may be exposed.

3. Therefore, in whatever place you may be, because you know that you have been baptized in the one name of the Father and the Son and the Holy Spirit, according to the rule promulgated by the command of our Savior, retain with your whole heart, from the start and without hesitation, that the Father is God and the Son is God and the Holy Spirit is God; i.e., the holy and ineffable Trinity is by nature one God, concerning whom it is said in Deuteronomy, "Hear, O Israel, the Lord your God is one God," and, "You shall adore the Lord your God and him alone shall you serve."[5] Indeed, since we have said that this one God who alone is true God by nature, is not the Father only, nor the Son only, nor the Holy Spirit only but is at one and the same time, Father, Son, and Holy Spirit, we must be wary that, while we say in truth that, as the Father, Son, and Holy Spirit are one God, in so far as this is a unity of nature, we dare not say or believe something altogether blasphemous, that he who is the person of the Father is the same as either the Son or the Holy Spirit; or that he who is the person of the Son is the Father or the Holy Spirit; or that we dare to say or to believe that the person who is properly called the Holy Spirit in the confession of this Trinity is either the Father or the Son, something that is altogether wicked.

4. The faith which the holy patriarchs and prophets re-

5. Dt 6.4 and 6.13.

ceived from God before the Incarnation of the Son of God, the faith which the holy Apostles too heard from the Lord himself, living in the flesh, and, instructed by the teaching of the Holy Spirit, not only preached orally but also left behind instilled in their writings for the salutary instruction of posterity—this faith proclaims one God, the Trinity, i.e., Father, Son, and Holy Spirit. But it would not be a real Trinity if one and the same person were called Father and Son and Holy Spirit. For, if, just as there is one substance of the Father and the Son and the Holy Spirit, so there would be one person, then there would be no way at all in which it could truly be called a Trinity. Again, it would be a real Trinity, but that Trinity would not be one God if, just as Father, Son, and Holy Spirit are distinct from one another by what is proper to their persons, so likewise they would be different by a diversity of natures. But, since in that one true God, the Trinity, not only because God is one but also because he is a Trinity, it is naturally true therefore that the true God is in himself a Trinity of persons but in nature is one. Through this unity of nature, the whole of the Father is in the Son and the Holy Spirit, and the whole of the Son in the Father and the Holy Spirit, and, as well, the whole of the Holy Spirit in the Father and the Son. No one of these is outside of any of the others, because none either precedes the others in eternity, or exceeds them in greatness, or overcomes them in power; because the Father is neither prior to nor greater than the Son or the Holy Spirit, in so far as it pertains to the unity of the divine nature. Neither is the eternity nor the immensity of the Son either prior to or greater than; nor does it by nature either precede or exceed the eternity or the immensity of the Holy Spirit. Just as the Son is neither later nor less than the Father, so neither is the Holy Spirit later or less than the Son. And the Son is eternal and without beginning, because the Son, born from the nature of the Father, has always existed. And the Holy Spirit is eternal and without beginning, because the Holy Spirit[6] proceeds from the nature

---

6. Obviously here and in many other places in his writings, Fulgentius teaches the procession of the Holy Spirit from the Father and the Son.

of the Father and the Son. So, therefore, rightly do we believe and say that the three are one God, because there is a single eternity, a single immensity, a single divinity by nature of three persons.

5. Therefore, let us hold that the Father and the Son and the Holy Spirit are by nature one God; neither is the Father the one who is the Son, nor the Son the one who is the Father, nor the Holy Spirit the one who is the Father or the Son. For, the essence, that which the Greeks call the *ousia*, of the Father and the Son and the Holy Spirit, is one, in which essence the Father is not one thing and the Son a second thing and the Holy Spirit still a third thing, although in person the Father is different, the Son is different, and the Holy Spirit is different. All of this is demonstrated for us in the strongest fashion at the very beginning of the Holy Scriptures, when God says, "Let us make human beings in our image and likeness."[7] When, using the singular number, he says "image," he shows that the nature is one, in whose image the human being was made. But, when he says "our" in the plural, he shows that the very same God in whose image the human being was made is not one in person. For, if in that one essence of Father, Son, and Holy Spirit, there were one person, "to *our* image" would not have been spoken but "in *my* image." Nor would he have said, "Let *us* make," but, "I shall make." If, in reality, in those three persons three substances were to be understood or believed, "to *our* image" would not have been said; rather, "to our *images*"; for there could not be one image of three unequal natures. But, while the human being is said to be made according to the one image of the one God, the divinity of the Holy Trinity in one essence is announced. Then and shortly thereafter, in place of what he had said above, "Let us make human beings in our image and likeness," Scripture thus told of the making of the human being by saying, "And God created humankind in his image; in the image of God he created them."[8]

7. Gn 1.26.
8. Gn 1.27.

6. The prophet Isaiah did not keep silent about this Trinity of persons and unity of nature revealed to him, when he says he saw the Seraphim crying out, "Holy, holy, holy, Lord God of Sabbaoth."[9] Therefore, where the triple "Holy" is repeated, there is the Trinity of persons; where "Lord, God of Sabbath" is said but once, we recognize the unity of the divine nature. Therefore, in that Holy Trinity—and I keep on saying it so that it may be fixed in your heart the more firmly—the Father is one, who alone by his nature has generated the one Son from himself; and the Son is one, who alone has been born from the nature of the one Father, and the Holy Spirit is one, who alone proceeds from the essence of the Father and the Son. All of this is not possible for one person, i.e., both to generate oneself and to be born of oneself and to proceed from oneself. Therefore, because generating is different from being born and proceeding is something different again from generating and being born, it is obvious that the Father is different, the Son is different, and the Holy Spirit is different. The Trinity, therefore, refers to the persons of the Father and the Son and the Holy Spirit; unity, to the nature.

(II) 7. Just as, according to that divinity by which the Father and the Son and the Holy Spirit are one, we do not believe that either the Father or the Holy Spirit were born, but only the Son, so also the Catholic faith both believes and preaches that only the Son was born according to the flesh. And in that Trinity it was not the property of the Father alone that he was not born, but he begat the one Son (nor was it the property of the Son alone, that he did not beget, but he was born from the essence of the Father; nor was it the property of the Holy Spirit that he was neither born nor begot, but alone proceeds from the Father and the Son in unchanging eternity), if, according to the divine nature, God the Father would be born of no God, but, according to the flesh, he would be born of a virgin. If, however, the Father were to be born of a virgin, the Father and the Son

---

9. Is 6.3.

would be one person. But this one person, from the fact that it was born not of God but only of a virgin, would truly be called not the Son of God but only a human son. For, the very Son of God himself says that "God so loved the world that he gave his only-begotten." And again, "God did not send his Son into the world to judge the world but that the world might be save through him."[10] Nor would the blessed John have said, "He who loves the Father loves the one who was born of him."[11] Nor would the Son himself have said, "My Father is at work until now, so I am at work."[12] For the one who is called the Son, if he were the same as the Father, would not truly be called the Son of God, because he would be born not of God but only of the virgin. Finally, the Father himself would not have born witness from heaven and with a bodily voice pointed out his Son, saying, "This is my beloved Son in whom I am well pleased."[13] Nor would the Apostle Paul have said of God the Father, "He who did not spare his own Son but gave him over for all of us."[14]

8. But, since all these things have been revealed by God for our instruction and what has been revealed by God is invariably true, what the Catholic faith teaches is true, viz., that, according to the divinity, the only Son has been born from the Father, eternal with the Father, immortal, impassible, and unchangeable God, and, according to the flesh, not the Father but his only-begotten Son, one born in time, with no effect on his eternity, one who suffered without affecting his impassibility, one who died without affecting his immortality, one who was truly raised without affecting his changelessness, by which he is true God and eternal life. One who has everything in common with his Father, which from all eternity he had by nature without beginning and has nothing in common with the Father of those things which he, the eternal and exalted one, humbly accepted in his person in time.

10. Jn 3.16–17.
11. Jn 5.1.
12. Jn 5.17.
13. Mt 3.17.
14. Rm 8.32.

9. Again, if not he who is properly the only-begotten Son of God the Father but the Holy Spirit had been born of the virgin, the Holy Church would not believe with its heart for its justification and confess with its mouth for its salvation the very Son who was made of the woman, made under the Law, accepted in the Creed as "born of the Holy Spirit from the virgin Mary." But, if the Holy Spirit itself, who is the Spirit of the Father and the Son, had accepted the form of a servant, it would not have been the Spirit itself who came from heaven[15] under the form of a dove upon the one who became a human being.

10. Therefore, God the Father, begotten by no God, once from his own nature, without a beginning, begot God the Son, equal to himself and co-eternal in divinity by that same nature by which he himself is eternal. But the very same God the Son since he is God eternal and true and with the Father by nature one God in his divinity, in accordance with which he says, "The Father and I are one";[16] the same was made human for our sake, true and complete. True in his case because that God has a true human nature; full in his case because he assumed human flesh and a rational soul. The same, the sole-begotten God, was born twice, once from the Father, once from the mother; for, God the Word was born from the Father and the Word made flesh was born from the mother.

11. Therefore, the one and the same God, the Son of God, born before the ages and born in time—and each birth is that of the one Son of God—divine, according to which the Creator, in the form of God, co-eternal with the Father, is God; human, according to which, emptying himself and taking the form of a servant, he not only formed himself in the conception of the maternal womb where he became human, with the same taking up of the form of a servant, but also, the same God made human came forth from the same womb of the mother, and the same God

---

15. There is a misprint in the CCL text (p. 718, line 200): "adverniret" should be "adveniret."

16. Jn 10.30.

made human hung on the cross, and the same God made human lay in the tomb, and the same God made human rose from the dead on the third day; but in the tomb the same God lay according to the flesh alone and descended into Hell according to the soul alone. Returning from among the dead according to the flesh on the third day, the same God, according to the flesh with which he lay in the tomb, rose from the tomb; and, on the fortieth day after the resurrection, the same God incarnate, ascending into heaven, sat at the right hand of God, and thence he will come at the end of the world to judge the living and the dead.

12. The Word incarnate is the one Son of God, the Lord Jesus Christ, the mediator between God and human beings—mediator because he is true God and truly human, having one nature of divinity with the Father and one substance of humanity with his mother, having from us up until his death, the penalty of our iniquity; having unchangeable justice from God the Father; dead in time because of our iniquity, because of his justice, he both lives forever and will grant immortality to us mortals. He who preserved the perfection of his humanity in the very perfection of his divinity; through the taking on of death, he caused the truth of his mortality to be absorbed by the truth and unchangeableness of his immortality.

13. This is what the blessed Peter testifies to: that "Christ swallowed death, in order that we might be made heirs of eternal life."[17] The blessed Paul as well teaches that Christ swallowed up death and illuminated life and incorruption. Christ therefore tasted death because he is truly human; and he likewise swallowed up death because he is truly God. The same one, indeed, as the Apostle says, ". . . was crucified out of weakness, but he lives by the power of God";[18] one and the same, who according to the prophecy of blessed David "was made man" in Zion and "the Most High himself has established it."[19]

17. Not in the New Testament; cf. 2 Cor 5.4 and Ti 3.7.
18. 2 Cor 13.4.
19. Ps 86.5 LXX; Ps 87.5.

14. Therefore, the divinity of Christ is not foreign to the nature of the Father, according to this: "In the beginning was the Word and the Word was with God and the Word was God. It was in the beginning with God. All things came to be through him and without him nothing came to be."[20] Nor is his humanity foreign to the nature of his mother, according to this: "The Word became flesh and dwelt among us."[21] For that nature which, having been generated from all eternity by the Father, remains; he took upon himself our nature without sin that he might be born of a virgin. In no way could eternal and divine nature have been conceived in time and born in time from human nature unless the ineffable divinity had taken upon itself according to the taking up of human reality a true conception and birth in time. Thus was the eternal and true God truly conceived by and born of a virgin in time. For, "when the fullness of time came, God sent his Son, born of a woman, born under the Law, that he might redeem those who were under the Law in order that we might receive the adoption of sons,"[22] viz., with that God having been made a human son by nature who is by nature the one only-begotten Son of God the Father. This John the Evangelist confirms when he later said, "And the Word was made flesh and dwelt among us," and added subsequently, "And we saw his glory, a glory as of an only-begotten of the Father, full of grace and of truth."[23] Thus he, Creator and Lord of all spirits and of all bodies, i.e., of all natures, who would be created from the virgin, created the virgin. He who is her maker made his mother for himself, when he who would be conceived and begotten from her flesh, the infinite and eternal God, received the true material of the flesh in order that, according to the truth of the form of a servant, God, in his mercy, would become human, and, according to the form of God, remaining human, the same God would not lack the truth of his nature.

15. Therefore, believe that Christ, the Son of God, i.e.,

20. Jn 1.1–3.
21. Jn 1.14.
22. Gal 4.4–5.
23. Jn 1.14.

one of the persons of the Trinity, is true God, so that you do not doubt that his divinity has been born of the nature of the Father. And so, also, believe that he is truly human, so that you do not think that his flesh is of a celestial, or heavenly, or some other kind of, nature, but that his is the flesh of every human being, i.e., that which God himself fashioned for the first human being from the earth and fashions for other human beings, whom he creates through human reproduction. But, although the flesh of Christ is of one and the same nature as that of all human beings, still, that which God the Word deigned to unite to himself from the virgin Mary, conceived without sin, was born without sin, just as the eternal and just God was in his mercy conceived and born, and the Lord of Glory was crucified.

16. By these words will be explained the singular excellence of that flesh whose divine person comes from that very same conception, whose birth is the unusual origin by which the Word has become flesh in such a way that the only-begotten and eternal God, conceived in the very conception of his flesh, might be one person with his flesh. It is certain that that flesh of all other human beings is born through human sexual intercourse with the male inseminating and the female conceiving and giving birth. And, because man and woman are joined to each other to bear children, the sexual intercourse of the parents is not without concupiscence, because of which the conception of children born from their own flesh cannot come about without sin where the lust, not the propagation as such, transmits the sin to the children; it is not the fecundity of human nature that causes human beings to be born with sin, but the filth of lust which human beings have from the most just condemnation of that very first sin. Thus, the blessed David, although himself born of a legitimate and just marriage in which indeed neither the guilt of infidelity nor the stain of fornication could be found, because of Original Sin, by which children are bound by nature to be children of wrath and not just the children of unholy people but even all those who are born of the sanctified flesh of the just, he exclaims and says, "Be-

hold in iniquity was I conceived and in sin my mother bore me."[24] Even the holy Job says that not one person is clean from stain, not even if one's life is but a single day on this earth.[25]

17. Therefore, the only-begotten Son of God who is in the bosom of the Father, in order to purify the human flesh and soul by taking up the flesh and rational soul, was incarnated; and he who is true God became a true human being, not that another God became another human being but the very same God, the very same human being. In order that he might take away that sin which the act of human generation contracts in the sexual intercourse of mortal flesh, he was conceived in a new way, God incarnate in a virgin mother, without copulation with a male, without the lust of the virgin conceiving, so that through the God-man whom the inviolate womb of the virgin put forth, conceived without lust, the sin which all human beings contract when they are born might be wiped away. In them, in the body of this death, such is the condition of being born, that their mothers cannot fulfill the task of fruitfullness without first losing the virginity of the flesh. Alone, therefore, the only-begotten God took away the sin of human conception and birth who, when conceived, took the truth of his flesh from the virgin, and, when born, preserved the integrity of virginity in his mother. This was the way by which God was made the son of the virgin Mary, and Mary the virgin mother of the only-begotten of God—in order that the one whom the Father begot in eternity, the virgin, might bring forth, conceived in time, that virgin whom God, who was to be born of her, had previously visited and filled with singular grace that she might have him as the fruit of her womb, the one whom the universe has from the beginning as its Lord; and she would see subject to her by the solemnity of birth, the one whom not only the human but also the angelic creature knows and adores as the Most High in the unity of his Father's substance.

24. Ps 50.7 LXX; Ps 51.5.
25. Job 14.4.

18. Thus the sin and the punishment for the sin which through the crime of a corrupted woman entered the world, is taken away from the world through birth from an inviolate virgin. And, because in the condition of the human race [brought about] by a woman made from a male only, it came about that we were held in custody by the chains of death; in the redemption of the human race, the divine goodness accomplished that through a man who was born from a woman only, life was restored to human beings. Thence, by a most wicked deception, the Devil associated the human race with himself through the likeness of sin; here God took up human nature in the unity of person. There the woman was deceived, that she might be made a daughter of the Devil; here the virgin was filled with grace that she might become the mother of the Most High and unchangeable only-begotten of God. There the angel, cast down by pride, gained the heart of the woman who had been seduced; here God, humbling himself through compassion, filled the womb "of the uncorrupted virgin from whom he was to be born. Jesus Christ, the Son of God, who was in the form of God, (which he could not be unless he had been born of the nature of the Father); he, according to the teaching of the Apostle, "emptied himself, taking the form of a servant." God accepted into his own person the form of a servant, i.e., the nature of a servant, and so the Creator of human beings, "made in human likeness" was "found human in appearance;" he "humbled himself, becoming obedient to death, even death of a cross."[26]

19. Think this statement of the Apostle over carefully and, by means of it you will realize how you may believe that the Lord Jesus Christ is at the same time God and a human being. In him, however, you are neither to confuse nor divide the truth of each nature in the one person. Therefore, when you first hear concerning the Lord Jesus Christ that he was in the form of God, it is necessary for you to recognize and hold most firmly that, by that expression, "form" must

26. Phil 2.7–8.

be understood the fullness of nature. Therefore, the Lord Jesus Christ was in the form of God because he was always in the nature of God the Father from whom he was born. Since he is of one nature with the Father, he is equally with him immortal and unchangeable, equally invisible and inexpressible, equally good and just, equally "merciful and gracious, slow to anger and abounding in steadfast love and faithfulness,"[27] equally strong and gentle, equally wise and all- powerful.

20. Accordingly, all these things which we have said concerning the Son of God, holding them with most firm faith (because having all these qualities in the unity of nature with the Father, he is, without a doubt, the equal of the Father; because of this, the Apostle too added immediately and said, "Who ... did not regard equality with God something to be grasped";[28] for that equality of divinity of the Son with the Father was not "grasping" but nature); also those things which the Apostle added subsequently, saying that "He emptied himself, taking the form of a slave, made in human likeness, and found human in appearance" and that "he humbled himself, becoming obedient unto death, even the death on a cross," all of these things are said of that only-begotten God, the Son of God, of that God the Word of whom the evangelist says, "In the beginning was the Word and the Word was with God and the Word was God,"[29] concerning that strength of God and wisdom of God, concerning which it is said to God, "In wisdom you have made all things."[30] From that beginning with which the Father himself is one beginning and in which, co-eternal with himself, he made heaven and earth, i.e., every nature, corporeal and spiritual; as I said, take all these things as coming in person from the only-begotten God who is in the bosom of the Father, saving, however, his eternity, immensity, immortality, immutability, the invisibility of his divinity. By nature, God the Son has all these things in common and equally with

27. Ps 85.15 LXX; Ps 86.15.
28. Phil 2.6.
29. Jn 1.1.
30. Ps 103.24 LXX; Ps 104.24.

God the Father so that, although he was truly made a human being for us, still he remained equal to the Father, from whom he was born true God and the truth. Therefore, "he emptied himself," but "from his fullness we have all received," which fullness, if having emptied himself, he lost, he would not give us from that which he did not have. Likewise, if he had nothing, without a doubt we could receive nothing. But "from his fullness, we have all received." From the fact that he has given us of his fullness, he shows that, even when he emptied himself, he did not lose the fullness he had, because, if he lost his fullness, he could never give us of it. Therefore, he accepted the form of a servant; nor was the self-emptying of the Most-High God anything other than the taking on of the form of a servant, i.e., human nature.

21. Each form is in Christ, therefore, because each substance is in Christ truly and fully. Therefore, the holy evangelist proclaims that he is full of grace and truth; that he is complete in his divine nature, in which God is Truth; and he is complete in his human nature in which he has become truly human by grace. In that fullness, he is God, in the form of God, equal to God; in that other fullness, a servant in the form of a servant, because, "coming in human likeness, [he was] found human in appearance."[31] Emptying himself, he took the form of a servant that he might become a servant; but he did not lose the fullness of the form of God in which he is always the eternal and unchangeable Lord, made truly human according to the form of a servant, of that same nature of which his handmaid his mother is, and, remaining in the form of God, true God, of that same nature of which the Lord is the Father. In the form of God with the Father and the Holy Spirit, the one and only creator of all things, God; according to the form of a servant, formed by his own working and that of the Father and the Holy Spirit; because he is creator, having a common nature with the Father and the Holy Spirit; because, however, he was created, alone in having a person in himself. And his coming birth according to

---

31. Phil 2.7.

the flesh and his death and resurrection and ascension into heaven, the Law and the Prophets never ceased to proclaim, just as he commanded, obedient in words and deeds.

22. For, in the sacrifices of carnal victims which the Holy Trinity itself, who is the one God of the New and the Old Testament, commanded be offered by our ancestors, was signified the most gracious gift of that sacrifice by which God the only Son according to the flesh would mercifully offer himself up for us. For, he, according to the teaching of the Apostle, "handed himself over for us as a sacrificial offering to God for a fragrant aroma."[32] He, true God and true priest, who for us entered once in the Holy Place, not with the blood of bulls and goats, but with his own blood. He signified that other priest who each year used to enter the Holy of Holies with blood. Therefore, this is the one who in himself alone provided everything he knew to be necessary for the effecting of our redemption, for he was both priest and sacrifice, both God and temple; the priest, through whom we are reconciled; the sacrifice, by means of which we are reconciled; the temple, in which we are reconciled; God to whom we are reconciled. By himself he is the priest, sacrifice, and temple, because God according to the form of a servant is all these things; not, however, God alone, because he together with the Father and the Holy Spirit is God according to the form of God.

23. Therefore, we have been reconciled through the Son alone according to the flesh but not to the Son alone according to the divinity. For, the Trinity has reconciled us to itself through this, that the Trinity itself made only the Word flesh. In him, the truth of the human and divine nature remains unchangeable in such a way that, just as his divinity is always true, which he has unchangeable from the Father, so his humanity is always true and unchangeable, which the highest divinity bears united to itself.

24. I have inserted these few things concerning the faith of the Holy Trinity, which alone is true God by nature, in so

---

32. Eph 5.2.

far as brevity, time, and speech permit. Now I shall familiarize you with the things about creation you must believe without a doubt.

(III) 25. First of all, believe that every nature which is not God the Trinity (which alone is the true and eternal God) has been created out of nothing by the Holy Trinity itself. And so everything in the heavens and on earth, visible and invisible, whether thrones or dominions, principalities or powers, are the work and creation of the Holy Trinity, which is the one God, Creator and Lord of all things, eternal, omnipotent, and good, existing by nature so that it always is and can never be changed. This God who always exists, without beginning, because he exists to the highest degree, has given to beings created by him that they may exist; not, however, without beginning, because no creature is of the same nature as is the Trinity, the one, true, and good God, by whom all things have been created. And because he is good to the highest degree, he has given to all natures which he made that they are good; not, however, so good as the Creator of all good things who not only is good to the greatest degree but is also the greatest and unchangeable good, because he is the eternal good; having no defect, because he is not made from nothing; having no history, because he has no beginning. Thus, of course, the natures made by God can have a history because they began; therefore, they can fall away as well because they have been made from nothing. The condition of their origin brings them to fall away; but the work of the Creator brings them forward. In this, therefore, first of all, is the natural eternity without beginning of the Trinity, which is true God, recognized because he made them in such a way that, though they have begun to exist, still they cannot at some time cease to exist. In this is his omnipotence understood, that he made from nothing every creature visible and invisible, i.e., corporeal and spiritual. These things, in their very diversity, commend the goodness and the omnipotence of the Creator even more. For, unless he were omnipotent, he would not have made the greatest and the least of things with one and the same ease; and, unless he were the greatest good, he would not have given himself to the governing of even the smallest things.

26. Therefore, the goodness and omnipotence of the Creator is just as great in the making of small things as in great things. For, the highest and true Wisdom has made all things wisely; for him, wisdom is of his nature and to do things is to do them wisely. Therefore, the simplicity of the multiple wisdom of God manifests the greatness of his exaltedness, not only in the greatness of sublime creatures but also in the smallness of the least; while all the good things which he has created not only are greatly below and dissimilar to their Creator, in so far as they are not taken out of him but are made from nothing; but also they do not all exist in the same manner among themselves but each being exists as it has been given by God to exist, one in one way, another in a different way. Nor has it been given to corporeal things to exist in the same way as spiritual things, since even corporeal things do not exist to the same degree and, whether in the heavens themselves or on earth, there is considerable diversity; whether heavenly or earthly, they differ not only by being of varying dimensions, but they also shine forth with varying degrees of brightness. For, as the Apostle says, the brightness of heavenly bodies is one thing, that of earthly bodies another. Among the heavenly bodies themselves, "the brightness of the sun is one kind, the brightness of the moon another, and the brightness of the stars a third. For, star differs from star in brightness."[33] Therefore, the diversity of corporeal natures demonstrates that each one of them is not what it is because of what it could always have had of itself but because of what it has received from the plan and working of the omnipotent, unchangeable, and all-wise Creator.

27. If any corporeal creature whatsoever were of one and the same nature as the Holy Trinity, which is the one God, it would not exist in a place locally, nor would it ever undergo change because of the passage of time, nor would it move

---

33. 1 Cor 15.41.

from one place to another, nor would it be circumscribed by the fact of its mass. All of this goes to show that he is the Creator of natures of this type for whom no space is big or small, because he exists totally no less in small spaces than in large. Nor is he changed by the passage of time; he alone who is able marvelously to put into order the revolutions of the days and hours, not by the unfolding of time but by the unchanging peace of eternity. For, he does not think in terms of time as the times pass by the coming into existence and departure of things; nor is he bounded by any quantity of mass, because he cannot be enclosed; nor is he spread out in his parts throughout the parts of the universe, so that he fills the larger parts of the world with his larger parts; and, by filling the lesser with his smaller parts, the whole of him does not fill any place. For, he is the God who says, "I fill the heavens and the earth."[34] Therefore, all the things that he has made, i.e., the spirits and the bodies, the highest and the lowest, the heavenly and the earthly, the living and those things to which he has not given the capability of living, ineffably and everywhere the whole Lord God both fills and contains; nor is he divided in those things which are divided, nor does he vary with any change in those things which are changed. For, unless he were unchangeable by nature, never in these changeable things would the good order of his foresight and providence have remained unchangeable.

28. Therefore, God, the unmeasured Creator of things corporeal and incorporeal, by this first of all shows that he himself is not a body, because he has not bestowed life on certain corporeal things, though he himself created all bodily things. He himself is life by nature, because, if he were not life, he did not make living corporeal things. Nor does he make something not living unless he himself is a living thing. Therefore, corporeal things are not of one nature with God, because the former cannot exist of themselves. And so, neither are those corporeal beings of one nature with God, in each of whom he has placed individual brute

34. Jer 23.24.

and irrational spirits by which the same corporeal beings are given life and senses. But neither are those brute spirits of one nature with God, which, although it is recognized that he implanted in these bodies what is necessary for life and gave them the capability of sensing, still, he granted these same souls no light of understanding by which they could either know or love their Creator.

29. Even of those spirits of which there is no doubt that they are rational and intelligent, who, with blaspheming spirit and blind heart, would dare to think or say that they are of the same nature as God, since God is by nature altogether unchangeable and unmeasurable? He who, since he is unable to have any diversity within himself, shows forth the diversity of his works in those same spirits whom he has made rational and intellectual. In certain ones (i.e., those which have been placed in earthly and mortal bodies, although there is no spatial movement, because, when they are in bodies, they are not there part by part, distributed throughout the parts of the bodily space, but are whole as in the whole body, so they are whole in the parts of the same bodies), still, the variety of thoughts demonstrates diversity in those who have movement and change over time; at times, they do not know something, at others, they do know; sometimes they will, at others, they do not will; sometimes they are wise, at other times, foolish; sometimes, from being just, they become wicked, at other times, having been wicked, they become just; sometimes they are bright with the light of piety, at other times, they are vicious with the error of dark impiety.

30. Even those whom no muddy matter of earthly bodies weighs down, i.e., angelic spirits, who does not see that they are not of one nature with God but are made out of nothing? Their mutability by nature is seen in this, that a portion of the same creatures has been changed for the worse. Then, because those who were not wicked (albeit by the gift of the one by whom they were made when they did not exist and, in so far as it has freely been given to the angelic creature by the tireless and perfect love, they ceaselessly partake of the

abundance of the sweetness of the Lord by their contemplation and exultation, nor do they fall away from it by their natural condition), although in those who cling to God there is no temporal variation, because, by the gift bestowed on them of eternal incorruption and unchangeability, they feel within them no change, still, there is in each of them a natural boundary by which they are distinguished one from another—because none of them is in another; and, when some task is enjoined on one of them, another, by the decision of divine power, is assigned to fulfill some other work. All of these things show that the holy angels are also a creation of the Holy Trinity, who, through individual things which indeed it made as it wished, appears marvelous both in the wisdom of its planning and strong in its execution.

31. God so created certain spirits that they might exist forever; others, however, that they might cease to be spirits at some time. Of those who would cease to exist, the Almighty produced some from water, others, as he willed, from the earth. But the higher spirits he made to have no natural admixture of bodily elements, those whom he also created eternal, and he implanted in them the ability and the intellect to contemplate, know, and love the divinity. And he so created them that they might love him before themselves, by whose work they knew that they had been created the way they were with no preceding merits of their own, by which they might become the way they were. In order that this love might have a just and fitting praise, he also granted them freedom of will, so that it would be possible for them either to raise the attention of their holy love to him who is above them or to lower themselves to themselves, or to those things which are beneath them because of the weight of wicked concupiscence.

32. It is not nature, therefore, which can subsist for eternity, either in misery or living in bliss, except that it can think about God by the gift of God himself. This intellectual nature exists in the souls of human beings and in the spirits of angels. For, God has instilled the ability to know and to love him only in angels and human beings. To them, on ac-

count of the freedom of the will which had most notably to be conferred on an intellectual creature by the kindness of the Creator, he has given them the ability and the will to know and love him in such a way that each one is able both to have it and to lose it. But, if anyone of his own will were to lose it, from then on, he would not be able to regain it on his own initiative. In order that he might again be willing to infuse the beginnings of holy thought, by the gratuitous gift of free goodness, into those who must be renewed, he, that is, whose it was, at the very beginning of creation, without pre-existing merits, marvelously to order spirits and bodies into just the right places and relationships, as he, the wise one, wished. Therefore, angels and human beings, because of the fact that they have been created as rational, have received from God in the very creation of a spiritual nature, the gift of eternity and happiness. This was done in such a way that, if they adhered uninterruptedly to the love of the Creator, at the same time, they would remain eternally blessed; if, on the other hand, by a decision of their own free will, they would endeavor to do their own will against the command of the Most High Creator, blessedness would immediately depart from the recalcitrant, and there would be left for them as a punishment eternal misery, henceforward subjected to error and grief. Concerning the angels, God has decided this and carried it out, that, if any of them loses the goodness of will, he will never restore it by divine gift.

33. Therefore, that portion of the angels which, by its own voluntary turning away, went away from God its Creator, by whose goodness alone it was blessed, by the judgment of the highest justice, found the beginning of its condemnation in the very turning away of the will. For it, the beginning of punishment would be nothing other than the deprivation of the love of that blessed and good being. God ordered all of that portion to remain in eternal punishment for which he prepared eternal fire, where all those wicked angels could never lack either their evil will or punishment; but, as the evil of their unjust aversion remains in them, so also does their just retribution of eternal condemnation. The Devil,

the originator of these evils, because out of envy he led the first human beings to involvement in sin, infected not only them but their entire progeny with the sentence of death, together with the vice of sin. But God, merciful and just, even as he confirmed the other angels in the eternity of his love, after the Devil and his angels fell by their own will, so also he did not permit the whole mass of the human race to perish forever. His free goodness predestined to be brought back to the light those whom he willed, after the darkness in which every human being lives, because of the condemnation of Original Sin, had been removed—showing in this especially that, by the undeserved grace of the liberator, he freed them from the chains of Original Sin, while eternal condemnation would hold on to others with unbreakable board, especially little children who had neither good nor evil merits of their own will.

34. That the beginning of a good will and mind is not born from a human being himself but is prepared and bestowed by God, God clearly shows in this, that neither the Devil nor any of his angels, cast down into the lower darkness because of their deserved ruination, could or will be able to regain a good will. If it were possible that human nature, which, after turning away from God, lost the goodness of the will, could of itself regain it, how much more possible would this be for the angelic nature, which, to the degree that it is less weighed down by the burden of an earthly body, how much more would it have been endowed with this ability? But God shows from what source a good will is given to human beings. The angels, when they had it, lost it in such a way that henceforward they cannot have what they lost.

35. Therefore, since, through the grace of God, the same good will is deserving of the reward of eternal bliss, and angelic and human iniquity must not remain unpunished, wherefore, according to the rule of the Catholic faith, we await with faith the future coming of the Son of God to punish all sinful angels and to judge human beings living and dead. The blessed Peter bears witness that "God did not

spare the angels when they sinned, but, casting them into the prisons of smoky hell, he handed them over to be kept for punishment in the judgment."[35] Concerning the coming judgment of human beings, living and dead, the blessed Paul says this: "I bear witness in the presence of God and of Christ Jesus, who will judge the living and the dead, and by his appearing and his kingly power."[36] At his coming, from that body of the first man which God fashioned from the earth, up until the bodies of all human beings which began to live when they were infused with a soul, all will be raised by him by whose action they were created. In the resurrection, individual bodies will be restored to their individual souls, which they began to have in the wombs of their mothers, in order that they might begin to live—in order that, in that examination of the just judge, souls might receive in their very same individual bodies their reward, of the kingdom or of punishment, in those bodies in which they had led a good or an evil life in this world.

36. The quality of an evil life begins with lack of faith, which takes its beginning from the guilt of Original Sin. In it, each one begins to live in such a way that, before he ends his life, which is ended when freed from its bonds, if that soul has lived in the body for the space of one day or one hour, it is necessary that it suffer with that same body the endless punishments of Hell, where the Devil with his angels will burn forever, he who committed the first sin and led the first human beings to sin. With him there also are "fornicators, those who serve idols, adulterers, male prostitutes, sodomites, thieves, the greedy, drunkards, revilers, robbers" and all who "do the work of the flesh"[37] (concerning whom the blessed Apostle says that "they will not inherit the kingdom of God"[38]); if, before the end of this life, they will not have been converted from their evil ways, they will be burned in eternal fire. For, every person who in this world persists until the end in his love of wickedness and hardness

---

35. 2 Pt 2.4.
37. 1 Cor 6.9–10.
36. 2 Tm 4.1.
38. Gal 5.19–20.

of heart, just as his harmful love of his sins held him here, so eternal torture will hold him without end.

37. There will be a resurrection of the wicked but without change, which God will give only to the faithful and those living justly by faith. For, this is what the blessed Paul says, "For, we shall all indeed rise, but we shall not all be changed."[39] Showing that the just must be changed by divine gift, he says, "And we shall be changed."[40] For, the wicked will have a resurrection of the flesh in common with the just, but they will not have the grace of transformation which will be given to the just. Since corruption will not be taken away from the bodies of the wicked, ignobility and infirmity will be sown in them; for this reason, these will not be extinguished by death, so that that endless torment may be as a punishment of eternal death for body and soul. But just souls, which God the Redeemer has here freely justified by faith and has given to the justified perseverance in good living until the end, in the very bodies in which here they received from God the grace of justification, and in which, justified by faith, they lived in the love of God and neighbor, they will receive the eternal bliss of the heavenly kingdom; and, when their bodies have been glorified, with the nature of the flesh which God created truly persisting, without a doubt, they will then have spiritual bodies, not animal ones, as they do here. In the saints, "a natural body is sown; a spiritual body rises."[41] In them, there will be fulfilled, through that change which will be given only to the just, what the Apostle says must be: "That which is corruptible must clothe itself with incorruptibility, and that which is mortal must clothe itself with immortality."[42] The masculine and feminine sexes will remain, just as the same bodies were created; and their glory will vary according to the diversity of their good works. For, all bodies, whether of men or of women, all that will exist in that kingdom, will be glorious. For, that judge knows how much glory he is to give to each one who, in this

---

39. 1 Cor 15.51.
41. 1 Cor 15.44.
40. 1 Cor 15.52.
42. 1 Cor 15.53.

life, he first freely justified by his mercy, and whom he rewards with glory in the next life through justice.

38. God has given human beings the opportunity to win eternal life only in this life, where he also desired a fruitful penance. Penance is fruitful here because here, a human being, when malice has been put aside, can live well and, when his will is changed, can change his merits and his works at the same time and in the fear of God do those things which please God. For, the person who has not done it in this life will indeed have penance to do in the next world for his sins but will not find forgiveness in the sight of God; for, although there will be motivation for regret there, there will be no correction of the will there. His wickedness will be blamed in such a way that justice can never either be loved or desired by them. For, their will will be such that it always has in itself punishment for their wickedness yet can never accept the love of goodness. Because, just as they who will reign with Christ will have in themselves no vestiges of an evil will, so they who, relegated to the punishment of eternal fire with the Devil and his angels, just as they will never again have rest, will in no way be able to have a good will. And, just as the perfection of grace for eternal glory will be given to the co-heirs of Christ, so their very malignity will pile up punishment for the Devil's confederates; they will be enlightened by no interior light of truth.

39. Accordingly, penance can be of use to everyone in this life, which, at whatever time one does it, however evil, however aged, if he, with his whole heart, will have renounced his past sins, and poured out tears for them, not only of the body but also of the heart, in the sight of God, and taken care to wash away the stains of all evil works with good works, he will soon have the forgiveness of all his sins. For, with prophetic words, the Lord promises this to us, saying, "If you are converted and weep, you will be saved."[43] And in another place, it is said, "Have you sinned, my child? Do so no more, but ask forgiveness for your past sins that they may be forgiv-

---

43. Is 30.15.

en you."[44] Prayer for sins would never have been proclaimed to the sinner, if forgiveness would not have to be granted to the one praying. But penance is fruitful for the sinner, if he does it in the Catholic Church; to which God in the person of blessed Peter granted the power of binding and loosing, when he says, "What you will bind on earth will also be bound in heaven; and what you loose on earth will also be loosed in heaven."[45] Therefore, at whatever age a person will do true penance for his sins and change his life for the better under the illumination of God, he will not be deprived of the gift of forgiveness, because God, as he says through the prophet,[46] does not wish the death of one dying but that he be turned from his evil path and his soul live.

40. Indeed, no one should delay a longer time in his sins out of hope for the mercy of God, since no one wishes to be ill for a longer time in the body because of the hope for future health. Those who decline to give up their sins and vices and promise themselves forgiveness from God, not infrequently are thus visited beforehand by the sudden fury of God, so that they find neither time for conversion nor the blessing of forgiveness. Therefore, Holy Scripture mercifully forewarns each one of us when it says, "Do not delay to turn back to the Lord and do not postpone it from day to day; for suddenly the wrath of the Lord will come upon you and at the time of punishment you will perish."[47] Blessed David also says, "Today, if you hear his voice, harden not your hearts."[48] The blessed Paul agrees with this in these words: "Take care, brothers, that none of you may have an evil and unfaithful heart, so as to forsake the living God. Encourage yourselves daily while it is still 'today' so that none of you may grow hardened by the deceit of sins."[49]

Therefore, he lives "with a hardened heart" who either is not converted, despairing of the forgiveness of his sins, or who so hopes for the mercy of God that, up until the very

---

44. Sir 21.1.
46. Cf. Ez 33.11.
48. Ps 94.7–8.
45. Mt 16.19.
47. Sir 5.7.
49. Heb 3.12–13.

end of this present life, he remains in the perversity of his crimes.

41. Accordingly, loving the mercy of God and fearing his justice, let us neither despair of the forgiveness of our sins nor remain in our sins, knowing that that justice of the most just judge will exact what is due from all people, all that the mercy of the most clement Redeemer has not forgiven. For, just as mercy takes up and frees the converted, so justice will repel and punish the recalcitrant. These are the ones who, sinning against the Holy Spirit, will receive forgiveness for their own sins neither in this world nor in the world to come. Therefore, the intellectual soul of a human being is a spirit, in order that it may seek, recognize, and discern both the time of his works, for which he is going in the judgment what divine judgment has ordained, and the time of the retribution for these works, when it will not be permitted either to change the works or to ask for the forgiveness of his sins from the divine mercy with any hope of success. The other spirits of all the animals, in whom there is no understanding, because certain of them take their origin from the earth and others from the waters (from the waters come reptiles and birds; but, from the earth, some which crawl and others which walk, have arisen); their "souls" live only so long as they are in their bodies. For, their soul, which has not been made capable of reason by God, both begins and ceases to live with its flesh. Because, when it does not give life to the body and does not live itself, and thus in a wonderful way the soul is the cause of living in all flesh, still the irrational spirit lives only so long as it can remain in the flesh, and, when it is separated from its flesh, it is extinguished. And so it is that, since it is the life of its flesh, it cannot live when it ceases to provide life for the flesh; and, if there is no flesh to which it can give life, it also will not have life henceforward. Therefore, eternity has not been given to irrational spirits, nor is any judgment being prepared for them in which bliss will be awarded to them for good works or damnation for evil works. Therefore, no such distinction of works will be sought from them because they have received from God no

ability to understand. So their bodies are not going to rise because there was neither justice nor wickedness in their souls for which eternal bliss or punishment must be dealt out to them.

42. Therefore, these animals accomplish their life and purpose in this world according to the incomprehensible will of the Creator, to render no account for their deeds because they are not rational. "Is God concerned about oxen?"[50] Human beings, however, because they have been made rational, will render an account to God for themselves and for all the things which they have received for use in this present life and, according to the nature of their works, will receive either punishment or glory. "For, we must all appear before the judgment seat of Christ, so that each one may receive recompense, according to what he did in the body, whether good or evil."[51] Then, indeed, according to the words of our Creator and Redeemer himself, when "all who are in the tombs will hear his voice and will come out, those who have done good deeds to the resurrection of life, but those who have done wicked deeds to the resurrection of judgment."[52] In order that, to be more precise, those who have done evil may go into the eternal fire to burn forever with the Devil, the prince of all evildoers, but, on the other hand, those who have done good things will go into eternal life, there to reign without end with Christ, the King of all the ages. Those will reign with Christ whom God by his free goodness has predestined for the Kingdom. Because, by predestining them, he has seen to it that they are worthy of the kingdom; he has seen to it that according to his decree those who are to be called are obedient; he has seen to it that those who are to be justified, having received the grace, believe rightly and live well; he has seen to it as well that those who are to be glorified, having been made co-heirs with Christ, will possess the kingdom of heaven without end.

43. Throughout history, by the mysteries Christ has insti-

50. 1 Cor 9.9.
51. 2 Cor 5.10.
52. Jn 5.28–29.

tuted through the faith of his Incarnation, they have arrived at that kingdom, those whom God has freely saved with no merits of good will or good works preceding. Just as from that time onward when our Savior said, "If anyone is not reborn from water and the Spirit, he cannot enter the Kingdom of God,"[53] without the Sacrament of Baptism, apart from those who poured out their blood for Christ in the Catholic Church but without Baptism, no one can receive either the kingdom of heaven or eternal life. And so, anyone who receives the Sacrament of Holy Baptism in the name of the Father and of the Son and of the Holy Spirit, whether in the Catholic Church or in any heresy or schism, receives the complete Sacrament; but he will not have salvation which is the effect of the Sacrament if he receives the Sacrament outside the Catholic Church. Therefore, that person must return to the Church, not to receive the Sacrament of Baptism again, which no one must repeat in the case of any person already baptized, but in order that he receive eternal life in the Catholic community. Anyone who has received the Sacrament of Baptism but remained away from the Catholic Church is never prepared to obtain eternal life. Such a person, even if he is very generous with almsgiving and even pours out his blood for the name of Christ, because of the fact that in this life he has not held tightly to the unity of the Catholic Church, he will not have eternal salvation. Wherever Baptism can be of use to anyone, it is there that almsgiving can be of avail. Baptism indeed can exist outside the Church, but it can be of no avail except within the Church.

44. Therefore, only within the Catholic Church can the reception of Baptism and the works of mercy and the glorious confession of the name of Christ be of use to anyone—provided, however, one lives well in the Catholic Church. For, just as outside the community of the Catholic Church, Baptism will be of no avail to anyone nor the works of mercy, except perhaps that one may be tormented a bit less,[54] still he will not be numbered among the children of God. So,

---

53. Jn 3.5.
54. "... tormented a bit less"? See Augustine *Enchiridion*, 112.

within the Catholic Church, eternal life is not gained solely by Baptism, if, after Baptism, we lead an evil life. For, even those who lead a good life must ceaselessly give themselves up to the works of mercy, knowing that daily they contract some sins, albeit light ones, for which even the holy and just ones must always say to God while in this life, "Forgive us our trespasses as we forgive those who trespass against us."[55] And these sins frequently steal in upon people even in licit matters and things granted by God. The more the body is filled with stronger foods and the human heart entangled with carnal deeds and desires, so the more frequently is guilt contracted in this mortal life.

45. Wherefore, humble servants of Christ, who wish to serve their Lord without impediment and apart from any harmful preoccupation of mind, do not seek marriage and abstain from meat and wine, in so far as their body's health permits.[56] Not that it is a sin either to have a spouse or to drink wine and eat meat. For, the blessed Apostle says, "For, everything created by God is good, and nothing is to be rejected when received with thanksgiving, for it is made holy by the invocation of God in prayer."[57]

For, God instituted and blessed marriage among the first human beings. So the Apostle says, "Let marriage be honored among all and the marriage bed be kept undefiled. . . ."[58] Therefore, the servants of God, when they abstain from meat and wine, do not spurn them as impure things, but they are following the rules of a purer life; and, when they do not marry, they do not think that the good of marriage is a sin, but they do not doubt that perpetual continence is better than a good marriage—above all in this age of ours when it is said of continence, "Let the one who can take it, take it."[59] Of marriage, however, it is said, "Anyone who cannot control himself, let him marry."[60] In one case, virtue is stimulated by exhortation; in the other, weakness is

---

55. Mt 6.12.
56. The "humble servants of Christ" are presumably monks.
57. 1 Tm 4.4–5.   58. Heb 13.4.
59. Mt 19.12.   60. 1 Cor 7.9.

allayed by a remedy. So, since weakness must always be taken into account, if it happens that anyone is deprived of his first marriage, if he wishes to enter into a second or even a third wedding, this will not be a sin, if he holds to them chastely, i.e., if the one man and woman, legitimately joined together, keep fidelity so that he is joined to no woman other than his wife and she to no man other than her husband. In such instances, even if there be any conjugal excess, which still does not violate the legitimate marriage bed, there is only a venial sin.

46. But such things belong to those who have not vowed continence to God. Otherwise, anyone who will have made himself a eunuch for the kingdom of heaven and in his heart vowed continence to God, not only if he be stained with the mortal sin of fornication, but also if he, as a man, wishes to take a wife, or, as a woman, to marry, according to the statement of the Apostle, he or she will be damned because he or she has made void his or her first pledge of fidelity. Therefore, just as, according to the declaration of the Apostle, it is worthy that "a man fulfill his duty to his wife and likewise the wife toward her husband,"[61] because, if anyone take a wife, he does not sin, and, if a virgin marry, she does not sin, so according to the statement of the same Apostle, "The one who stands firm in his resolve . . . , who is born not under compulsion, but has power over his own will. . . . ,"[62] and who vows continence to God must, with the fullest attention of his mind, keep it until the end, lest he incur damnation, if he render his first pledge of fidelity void. Likewise, married men or married women, if by mutual consent they vow perpetual continence to God, know that they are held accountable for their vow and that they no longer owe to each other that sexual intercourse which earlier was permitted to them, but now they owe to God the continence which they have vowed. Then each one will possess the kingdom of heaven which is promised to the saints, if, forgetting those things which are behind and stretching themselves to-

---

61. 1 Cor 7.3.
62. 1 Cor 7.37.

ward those things which lie ahead, according to what is said in the psalm, "Make vows to the Lord your God and perform them,"[63] he both willingly vows and swiftly fulfills that which he knows is licit and knows pertains to making progress toward a better life. Because he fulfills what he has vowed, he will make even greater progress with each new effort. To everyone who makes a vow to God and fulfills the vow, God himself will give the reward of the heavenly kingdom which he has promised.

(IV) 47. Hold most firmly and never doubt that the Father and the Son and the Holy Spirit are by nature one God, in whose name you have been baptized. Even though Father is one name, the Son another, and the Holy Spirit a third, this is just the one name of the nature of these three, which is called God, who says in Deuteronomy, "See now that I, even I, am he; there is no God beside me,"[64] and concerning whom it said, "Hear, O Israel, the Lord is our God, the Lord alone," and, "the Lord your God you will adore and him alone will you serve."[65]

48. Hold most firmly and never doubt that the Father and the Son and the Holy Spirit, i.e., the Holy Trinity alone, is true God by nature. For, since it is not lawful for us to worship three gods but only the one, true God, still, just as the Father is called true God with the testimony of the Apostle who says, "Having turned from idols to serve the living and true God and to await his Son from heaven whom he raised from the dead, Jesus,"[66] the Apostle John thus also shows that the Son is true God, when he says, "We know that the Son of God has come and has given us discernment to know the one who is true. And we are in . . . this true Son, Jesus Christ. He is the true God and eternal life."[67] Since he is true God, he is also the Truth, just as he himself teaches us when he says, "I am the Way, the Truth, and the Life."[68] Concerning the Holy Spirit as well, John the Apostle says, "The

---

63. Ps 75.12 LXX; Ps 76.11.
64. Dt 32.39.
65. Dt 6.4, 13.
66. 1 Th 1.9–10.
67. 1 Jn 5.20.
68. Jn 14.6.

Spirit is Truth."[69] And, indeed, he could not be true God naturally, who is the Truth. And Paul the Apostle confesses this God saying, "Do you not know that your body is a temple of the Holy Spirit within you, whom you have from God and that you are not your own? For, you have been purchased at a price. Therefore, glorify God in your body...."[70]

49. Hold most firmly and never doubt that the Father and the Son and the Holy Spirit, i.e., the Holy Trinity, the one true God, is eternal, without beginning. Wherefore it is written, "In the beginning was the Word and the Word was with God and the Word was God. It was in the beginning with God."[71] Again this eternity is expressed in the psalm where it is said, "Yet God my king is of old,"[72] and, in another place, "Eternal also his power and divinity."[73]

50. Hold most firmly and never doubt that the Holy Trinity, the only true God, just as it is eternal, is likewise the only one by nature unchangeable. He indicates this when he says to his servant Moses, "I am which I am."[74] Hence, it is said in the psalms, "In the beginning you laid the foundation of the earth, and the heavens are the work of your hands. They will perish, but you endure. They will wear out like a garment. You change them like clothing and they pass away, but you are the same."[75]

51. Hold most firmly and never doubt that the Holy Trinity, the only true God, is the Creator of all things, visible and invisible—concerning which it is said in the psalms, "Happy are those whose help is the God of Jacob, whose hope is in the Lord their God who made heaven and earth, the sea and all that is in them."[76] Concerning this the Apostle too says, "For, from him and through him and in him are all things. To him be glory forever."[77]

52. Hold most firmly and never doubt that of the Father and the Son and the Holy Spirit, there is one nature but

---

69. 1 Jn 5.6.
70. 1 Cor 6.19–20.
71. Jn 1.1–2.
72. Ps 73.12 LXX; Ps 74.12.
73. Rm 1.20.
74. Ex 3.14.
75. Ps 101.26–28 LXX; Ps 102.25–27.
76. Ps 145.5–6 LXX; Ps 146.5–6.
77. Rm 11.36.

three persons; and it is the Father alone who said, "This is my beloved Son in whom I am well pleased,"[78] and the Son alone over whom that voice of the Father alone sounded when the only-begotten God who alone had taken on flesh was baptized in the Jordan according to the flesh. Only the Holy Spirit is of the Father and the Son who in the form of a dove descended on Christ, baptized and ascending from the water, and, on the fiftieth day after the Resurrection, coming in an appearance of fiery tongues, filled the faithful of Christ gathered in one place. That voice, by which God the Father alone spoke and that flesh by which only the only-begotten God became human; and that dove, in whose form the Holy Spirit descended upon Christ; and those fiery tongues in the appearance of which he filled the faithful gathered in one place, were the works of the entire Holy Trinity, i.e., of the one God who made all things in the heavens and on earth, visible and invisible.

(X) 53. Hold most firmly and never doubt that only God the Son, i.e., one person of the Trinity, is the Son of the only God the Father; that the Holy Spirit, itself also one person of the Trinity, is the Spirit, not only of the Father, but simultaneously of the Father and the Son. God the Son, showing that he alone is begotten of the Father, says, "God so loved the world that he gave his only-begotten Son."[79] And right after that, ". . . Whoever does not believe has already been condemned, because he has not believed in the name of the only-begotten Son of God."[80] That the Holy Spirit is the Spirit of the Father and the Son, the Apostle teaches who says, "But you are not in the flesh; on the contrary, you are in the Spirit, if only the Spirit of God dwells in you." And immediately he adds, "Whoever does not have the Spirit of Christ does not belong to him."[81]

(XI) 54. Hold most firmly and never doubt that the same Holy Spirit, who is the one Spirit of the Father and the Son, proceeds from the Father and the Son. For, the Son says,

78. Mt 3.17.
80. Jn 3.18.
79. Jn 3.16.
81. Rm 8.9.

"When the Spirit of Truth comes, who has proceeded from the Father,"[82] where he taught that the Spirit is his, because he is the Truth. That the Holy Spirit also proceeds from the Son, the prophetic and apostolic teaching shows us. So Isaiah says concerning the Son, "He shall strike the earth with the rod of his mouth, and with the breath of his lips he shall kill the wicked."[83] Concerning him the Apostle also says, "Whom the Lord Jesus will kill with the breath of his mouth."[84] The one Son of God himself, showing who the Spirit of his mouth is, after his resurrection, breathing on his disciples, says, "Receive the Holy Spirit."[85] "From the mouth," indeed, of the Lord Jesus himself, says John in the Apocalypse, "a sharp, two-edged word came forth."[86] The very Spirit of his mouth is the sword itself which comes forth from his mouth.

(XII) 55. Hold most firmly and never doubt that God the Trinity is unbounded in power, not in mass; and that every creature, spiritual and bodily, is bound by his power and his presence. For, God the Father says, "I fill the heavens and the earth."[87] For, it is said of the Wisdom of God, which his Son is, that, "it reaches mightily from one end of the earth to the other and orders all things well."[88] Concerning the Holy Spirit we read that "The Spirit of the Lord has filled the whole world."[89] And David the prophet says, "Where can I go from your Spirit? Or where can I flee from your presence? If I ascend to heaven, you are there; if I make my bed in Sheol, you are there."[90]

(XIII) 56. Hold most firmly and never doubt that one person of the Trinity, i.e., God the Son, who alone was born of the nature of God the Father and is of one and the same nature with the Father, that he in the fullness of time according to the taking up of the form of a servant was voluntarily conceived in a virgin and born from a virgin, the Word

---

82. Jn 15.26.
83. Is 11.4.
84. 2 Th 2.8.
85. Jn 20.22.
86. Rev 1.16.
87. Jer 23.24.
88. Wis 8.1.
89. Wis 1.7.
90. Ps 138.7–8 LXX; Ps 139.7–8.

made flesh; and that he is essentially born from the Father and essentially conceived by and born of the virgin; that he is one, born of one nature with the Father and of one nature with the virgin, who says of God the Father, "Ages ago I was set up; before the hills, he begot me."[91] Concerning him also the Apostle said, "When the fullness of the time had come, God sent his Son, born of a woman, born under the Law."[92]

(XIV) 57. Hold most firmly and never doubt that Christ, the Son of God, just as he is from God the Father, complete and perfect God, so from the virgin Mary is he begotten the complete and perfect God-Man, i.e., God the Word, having the true flesh of our race and a rational soul without sin. God the Son clearly points this out himself when he says of his flesh, "Touch me and see, because a ghost does not have flesh and bones, as you can see I have."[93] He also shows that he has a soul by these words when he says, "This is why the Father loves me, because I lay down my life in order to take it up again."[94] Further, he shows that he has the intellect of the soul when he says this: "Learn from me, for I am meek and humble of heart."[95] And, concerning him, God says through the prophet, "See, my servant shall prosper; he shall be exalted and lifted up, and he shall be very high."[96] And the blessed Peter, following the prophecy of holy David, confesses that there are flesh and soul in Christ. For, speaking of the blessed David, he says, "But, since he was a prophet and knew that God had sworn an oath to him that he would set one of his descendants upon his throne, he foresaw and spoke of the resurrection of the Messiah, that neither was he abandoned to the nether world nor did his flesh see corruption."[97]

(XV) 58. Hold most firmly and never doubt that one is God the Word who himself with God the Father and God the Holy Spirit created all the ages and on Mount Sinai gave the Law to Moses through the ministry of angels, and God

---

91. Prov 8.23, 25.
92. Gal 4.4.
93. Lk 24.39.
94. Jn 10. 17.
95. Mt 11.29.
96. Is 52.13.
97. Acts 2.30–31.

the Word himself made flesh who, when the fullness of time came, was sent by the Father and the Holy Spirit; he alone was made from the woman whom he made, alone was made under the Law which he gave.

(XVI) 59. Hold most firmly and never doubt that the two natures of God the Word who became flesh remain in unconfused and inseparable union; the one truly divine which he possesses in common with the Father, as he himself says, "I and the Father are one,"[98] and, "He who sees me, sees the Father also,"[99] and, "I am in the Father and the Father is in me";[100] for this reason, the Apostle says that he is the "refulgence of his glory" and the "very imprint of his being";[101] the other nature is truly human, and for this reason God incarnate himself says, "The Father is greater than I."[102]

(XVII) 60. Hold most firmly and never doubt that God the Word, having become flesh, has one person of his divinity and his flesh. For, God the Word deigned in truth to unite to himself a complete human nature and, with his divinity remaining, the Word became flesh in such a way that, although by nature this Word is not what the flesh is, because the truth of the two natures remains in Christ, still, according to a single person, the same Word became flesh from the very beginning of his conception in his mother. God the Word did not receive the person of a human being but the nature; and into the eternal person of the divinity, he received the temporal substance of the flesh. Therefore, Christ the Word made flesh is one, who comes from the fathers "according to the flesh" and "God, who is over all, blessed forever,"[103] one Jesus to whom the Father says, "From the womb before the dawn I begot you,"[104] where an eternal birth before all time, without a beginning, is meant; concerning whom the evangelist also says that "he was named Jesus, the name spoken by the angel before he was conceived in the womb."[105]

(XVIII) 61. Hold most firmly and never doubt that it was

---

98. Jn 10.30.
99. Jn 14.9.
100. Jn 14.10.
101. Heb 1.3.
102. Jn 14.28.
103. Rm 9.5.
104. Ps 109.3 LXX; Ps 110.3.
105. Lk 2.21.

not the flesh of Christ without the divinity that was conceived in the womb of the virgin before he was taken up by the Word; but God the Word himself was conceived by the taking up of his flesh and the very flesh was conceived at the Incarnation of God the Word.

(XIX) 62. Hold most firmly and never doubt that the only-begotten God the Word himself become flesh offered himself for us as a sacrifice and victim to God with a pleasing fragrance. In the time of the Old Testament, animals were sacrificed by the Patriarchs and Prophets and Priests to him, together with the Father and the Holy Spirit. In the time of the New Testament, the sacrifice of bread and wine, in faith and holy charity, the Holy Catholic Church throughout the whole world does not cease to offer to him with the Father and the Holy Spirit, with whom there is one divinity with him. In those fleshly victims was signified the flesh of Christ, which he himself, without sin, would offer for our sins, and the blood which he would pour out for the forgiveness of our sins. In this sacrifice, there are thanksgiving and a memorial of the flesh of Christ which he offered for us and of the blood which the same God poured out for us. Concerning this the blessed Paul says in the Acts of the Apostles, "Keep watch over yourselves and over the whole flock of which the Holy Spirit has appointed you overseers, in which you tend the Church of God that he acquired with his own blood."[106] In those sacrifices, therefore, was signified in a figure what was to be given to us; but in this sacrifice is clearly shown forth what has already been given to us. In those sacrifices, it was foretold that the Son of God would be killed for sinners; in this, however, it is proclaimed that he has been killed for sinners, as the Apostle bears witness that "Christ, while we were still helpless, yet dies at the appointed time for the ungodly," and that, "while we were enemies, we were reconciled to God through the death of his Son."[107]

(XX) 63. Hold most firmly and never doubt that the Word made flesh always has the same truly human flesh with

---

106. Acts 20.28.
107. Rm 5.6, 10.

which God the Word was born of the virgin, with which he was crucified and died, with which he rose and ascended to heaven and sits at the right hand of God, with which he will come again to judge the living and the dead. For this reason, the Apostles heard from the angels, "He ... will return in the same way as you have seen him going into heaven,"[108] and the blessed John says, "Behold, he will come amid the clouds, and every eye will see him, even those who pierced him; and all the tribes of the earth will see him."[109]

(XXI) 64. Hold most firmly and never doubt that God the Trinity, i.e., the Father and the Son and the Holy Spirit, is by nature the highest and unchanging good; and that, by it, all natures have been created good, indeed, because they have been created by the highest good; but changeable because they have been created from nothing; that no nature is evil because every nature, in so far as it is nature, is good. But, since in it good can both be decreased and increased, it is said to be evil to the degree that the good in it is decreased. For, evil is nothing other than the privation of good. From this it is clear that evil in the rational creature is two-fold, i.e., (first) because of its own will, it has fallen away from the highest good, its Creator; (second) because, against its will, it will be punished by the penalty of eternal fire; this it will suffer justly because it has unjustly incurred this; and, since it has not kept the order of the divine teaching in what concerns itself, neither will it escape the order of divine vengeance.

(XXII) 65. Hold most firmly and never doubt that neither the angels nor any other creature is of the same nature as is the Most High Trinity according to its natural divinity, which is one by nature, God the Father and the Son and the Holy Spirit. Nor were they, He who made them and those whom he made, able to be of one nature.

(XXIII) 66. Hold most firmly and never doubt that every creature made by the unchangeable God is changeable by

---

108. Acts 1.11.
109. Rev 1.7.

nature; nor can any of the holy angels be changed for the worse now, since they have received eternal bliss in which they enjoy God enduringly, so that they cannot lose him. But this state—that they can in no way be changed for the worse from that state of blessedness in which they are—this was not implanted in them by their nature, but, after they were created, was conferred on them by the generosity of divine grace. For, if the angels had been made unchangeable by nature, the Devil and his angels would never have fallen away from their company.

(XXIV) 67. Hold most firmly and never doubt that in every creature which the Most High Trinity has made, spiritual and corporeal, only human and angelic spirits have received from God the ability to understand, while the other spirits of brute animals have not received rational intelligence and are altogether incapable of possessing it. So it is said to human beings, "Do not be like the horse and the mule, who have no understanding";[110] and so the souls of human beings and the souls of beasts are not of one nature; nor can the souls of human beings pass into beasts.

(XXV) 68. Hold most firmly and never doubt that the first human beings, i.e., Adam and his woman, were good, righteous, and created without sin, with free will by which they could have, if they were willing, always served and obeyed God with a humble and good will; but with that power of discretion they could also, if they so willed, sin by their own will; and they did sin, not out of any necessity, but by their own will; and, by that sin, human nature was so changed for the worse that, through that sin, death obtained the rule not only in the first human beings themselves but also that the dominion of sin and death would pass on to all human beings.

(XXVI) 69. Hold most firmly and never doubt that every human being who is conceived by the sexual intercourse of man and woman is born with Original Sin, exposed to impiety and subject to death, and for this reason is born by na-

---

110. Ps 31.9 LXX; Ps 32.9.

ture a child of wrath. Concerning this the Apostle says, "And we were by nature children of wrath, like the rest."[111] From this wrath no one is freed except through faith in the mediator between God and human beings, the man Jesus Christ, who, conceived without sin, born without sin, dying without sin, was made sin for us, i.e., he became a sacrifice for our sins. In the Old Testament, sacrifices which were offered for sins were called sins,[112] in all of which Christ was signified, because he is "the lamb of God who takes away the sins of the world."[113]

(XXVII) 70. Hold most firmly and never doubt that, not only adults with the use of reason but also children who either begin to live in the womb of their mothers and who die there or, already born from their mothers, pass from this world without the Sacrament of Holy Baptism, which is given in the name of the Father and of the Son and of the Holy Spirit, must be punished with the endless penalty of eternal fire. Even if they have no sin from their own actions, still, by their carnal conception and birth, they have contracted the damnation of Original Sin.

(XXVIII) 71. Hold most firmly and never doubt that Christ, the Son of God, will come to judge the living and the dead. To the human beings whom he justifies through faith here by the free gift of his grace, to these same ones who have been justified he gives the gift of perseverance in the faith and charity of Holy Mother Church until the end. At his coming he will raise, glorify, and make them the equals of the holy angels according to his promise. He will lead them to that state in which they, in so far as God gives to each one, are perfectly good, and cannot, from that point on, be turned aside from that perfection where the glory of the saints will vary, but eternal life will be the same for all. But the Devil and his angels will be sent by Christ into the eternal flames, where the punishment which the divine justice has prepared for them will never end. With that Devil

---

111. Eph 2.3.
112. Cf. Lv 4.21 [LXX].
113. Jn 1.29.

will be those impious and evil human beings, about whom Scripture says, "They imitate him who belong to him"[114] in this, that they imitated him in evil deeds and did not do appropriate penance before the end of this present life. When their bodies have been taken up again, they will burn with the punishment of eternal fire.

(XXIX) 72. Hold most firmly and never doubt that there will be a resurrection of the flesh at the coming of the Lord, common to all people, good and bad. There will be retribution from the justice of God, differing for the good and the wicked. So says the Apostle: "We shall all rise, but we shall not all be changed." The just who will go into eternal life will be changed. The Apostle points this out when he says, "And the dead will be raised incorrupt, and we shall be changed;" and, showing what this change will be, he added, "For, that which is corruptible must clothe itself with incorruptibility, and that which is mortal must clothe itself with immortality."[115] In their bodies there will be what the Apostle himself says, "It is sown corruptible; it is raised incorruptible. It is sown dishonorable; it is raised glorious. It is sown weak; it is raised powerful. It is sown a natural body; it is raised a spiritual body."[116] What he called "spiritual" is not so because the body itself will be a spirit, but because, with the Spirit giving life, it will remain immortal and incorruptible. Then it will be called a spiritual body, although it is not a spirit but remains as body; just as now it is called "natural," although still it is not a soul but a body.

(XXX) 73. Hold most firmly and never doubt that, with the exception of those who are baptized in their own blood for the name of Christ, no one will receive eternal life who has not been converted from his sins through penance and faith, and freed through the sacrament of faith and penance, i.e., through Baptism. For adults it is necessary both to do penance for their sins and to hold the Catholic faith according to the rule of truth and to receive the Sacra-

---

114. Wis 2.24.
116. 1 Cor 15.42–44.
115. 1 Cor 15.51, 52, 53.

ment of Baptism. For children, on the other hand, who are able neither to believe by their own will nor to do penance for the sin which they contract at the beginning of life, the sacrament of faith and penance, which is Holy Baptism, suffices for salvation, since their age is not yet capable of reason.

(XXXI) 74. Hold most firmly and never doubt that no one here below can do penance unless God will have enlightened him and converted him by his generous compassion. As the Apostle says, "It may be that God will grant them repentance that leads to knowledge of the truth and that they may return to their senses out of the Devil's snare. . . ."[117]

(XXXII) 75. Hold most firmly and never doubt that a man whom neither illiteracy nor some weakness or adversity keeps back, can either read the words of the holy Law and the Gospel, or hear them from the mouth of some preacher. But no one can obey the divine commands unless God first come to him with his grace in order that what he hears with his body he may also accept in his heart and, having accepted the good will and the power from God, he both wills and can perform the commands of God. For, "neither is he who plants anything nor the one who waters, but God gives the growth,"[118] who also is at work in us both to will and to carry through for the good will.

(XXXIII) 76. Hold most firmly and never doubt that, to the unchanging God, not only the past and present but also all future things are completely known in an unchangeable way. To him it is said, "O God, you know what is secret and are aware of all things before they come to be."[119]

(XXXIV) 77. Hold most firmly and never doubt that the Trinity, the unchangeable God, most certain knower of all things, both his own works and those of human beings, knows before all ages to whom he will grant grace through faith. Without it no one could, from the beginning of the world until its end, be freed from the guilt of sin, original

117. 2 Tm 2.25–26.
118. 1 Cor 3.7.
119. Dn 13.42.

or actual. "Those" God "foreknew, he also predestined to be conformed to the image of his Son."[120]

(XXXV) 78. Hold most firmly and never doubt that all whom God by his gracious goodness makes vessels of mercy were predestined by God, "before the foundation of the world, for adoption as children"[121] of God. Further, not one of those whom God predestined can perish, neither can anyone of those whom God has not predestined for life be saved by any means. Predestination is that preparation by a free gift by which the Apostle says that we are predestined "for adoption as children through Jesus Christ, in accord with the favor of his will."[122]

(XXXVI) 79. Hold most firmly and never doubt that the Sacrament of Baptism can exist not only within the Catholic Church but also among heretics who baptize in the name of the Father and of the Son and of the Holy Spirit. But, outside the Catholic Church, it can be of no use. Indeed, just as within the Church salvation is conferred through the Sacrament of Baptism on those who believe rightly, so for those baptized outside the Church destruction is increased by that same Baptism, if they do not return to the Church. So much does the communion of ecclesiastical society count for salvation that the one is not saved by Baptism[123] to whom it is not given where it ought to be given. The one baptized outside the Church has Baptism, but, for that one separated from the Church, it is for his judgment. And, because it is obvious that, wherever it is given this Baptism is to be given only once; therefore, although it will have been given by heretics in the name of the Father and the Son and the Holy Spirit, it is to be recognized with respect and for that reason not to be repeated. For the Savior says, "Whoever has bathed has no need except to have his feet washed."[124]

(XXXVII) 80. Hold most firmly and never doubt that

---

120. Rm 8.29.   121. Eph 1.4–5.
122. Eph 1.5.
123. There is a misprint on p. 757, line 1351: "Baptismo" rather than "batptismo."
124. Jn 13.10.

everyone baptized outside the Catholic Church cannot be a partaker of eternal life, if before the end of this life they will not have returned to the Catholic Church and have been incorporated into it. Because, "if I have," says the Apostle, "all faith and know all mysteries, but I do not have charity, I am nothing."[125] So, in the days of the flood, we read that no one could have been saved outside the ark.

(XXXVIII) 81. Hold most firmly and never doubt that not only all pagans but also all Jews and all heretics and schismatics who finish this present life outside the Catholic Church will go "into eternal fire which has been prepared for the Devil and his angels."[126]

(XXXIX) 82. Hold most firmly and never doubt that any heretic or schismatic whatsoever, baptized in the name of the Father and of the Son and of the Holy Spirit, if he will not have been gathered to the Catholic Church, no matter how many alms he may have given, even if he shed his blood for the name of Christ, can never be saved. In everyone who does not hold the unity of the Catholic Church, neither Baptism nor alms, however generous, nor death taken up for the name of Christ, can be of any profit for salvation, as long as in him either heretical or schismatic depravity continues which leads to death.

(XL) 83. Hold most firmly and never doubt that not all those who are baptized within the Catholic Church will receive eternal life, but those who, once Baptism has been received, live rightly, i.e., those who abstain from vices and the concupiscence of the flesh. For, just as infidels, heretics, and schismatics will not possess the kingdom of heaven, neither will sinful Catholics be able to possess it.

(XLI) 84. Hold most firmly and never doubt that here below no one can live without sin, even just and holy people except those who were baptized as small children. And it is always necessary for every person both to wash away his sins by alms up until the end of this present life and in humility and truth to ask God for forgiveness.

125. 1 Cor 13.2.
126. Mt 25.41.

(XLII) 85. Hold most firmly and never doubt that everything created by God is good and nothing which is received with thanksgiving is to be rejected. The servants of God who abstain from flesh or wine are not repudiating what has been made by God as if it were unclean, but abstain from stronger food and drink, solely for the mortification of the body. Marriage has been instituted and blessed by God, and it is better if anyone remain unmarried that he may more freely and fully meditate on the things of God, on how to please God. Still, for those who have not vowed continence, there is no sin if either a woman marry or a man take a wife. For, not only were first marriages instituted by God but also second and third, a concession to the weakness of those who cannot contain themselves. For, those who, either married or free from marriage, have vowed continence to God, it is totally damnable if they now wish to seek marriage, something they vowed they would not do, or to seek it again after having gone away from it, the one having professed continence with a free will, the others with a common will.

(XLIII) 86. Hold most firmly and never doubt that the Catholic Church is the threshing floor of God, and to the end of the age within it the straw is mixed with the grain, i.e., that the evil are mixed with the good in the communion of the sacraments; and that in every calling, whether clerics, monks, or laity, there are the good along with the bad. The good must not be deserted because of the bad, nor the bad because of the good, in so far as the meaning of faith and charity demands that the former be tolerated, i.e., provided either that they do not sow the seed of faithlessness in the Church nor that they lead the brethren to some evil work by deadly imitation. It is not possible for anyone who rightly believes in the Catholic Church and lives well to be stained by the sin of someone else provided that he show neither approval nor favor to the sinner. It is useful for the evil to be tolerated by the good in the Church, if, by living well or dying well with them, it happens that, seeing and hearing the things that are good, they look at their evil deeds, become aware that they are going to be judged by God for their evil works, and thus, with the gift of grace coming first, they are put to confusion by their iniquities and, through the mercy of God, are converted to a good life. The good must now be separated from the evil in the Catholic Church at least by the distinction of their deeds, so that, while they are in communion with them in the divine sacraments, they do not have evil works in common with those who are wicked. At the end of the world, the good must be separated from the evil even in body, when Christ will come having "his winnowing fan in his hand. He will clear his threshing floor and gather his wheat into his barn, but the chaff he will burn with unquenchable fire,"[127] when with a just judgment he will separate the just from the unjust, the good from the bad, the right from the perverse. He will set the good on his right, the evil on his left, and, when the everlasting and unchangeable verdict has come forth from the mouth of the just and eternal judgment, all the wicked "will go off to eternal fire, but the just to eternal life";[128] the wicked to burn forever with the Devil, the just, however, to reign with Christ without end.

(XLIV) 87. Faithfully believe these forty chapters which belong most firmly to the rule of the true faith, courageously hold on to them, and defend them with truth and patience. And, if you know anyone who teaches what is contrary to them, flee him like the plague and reject him as a heretic. These things which we have detailed are fitting to the Catholic faith in such a way that, if anyone should wish to contradict not only all of them but even any one of them, in so far as he stubbornly repudiates even one of them and does not hesitate to teach something contrary to them, he is a heretic and an enemy of the Catholic faith, and as such is to be cursed by all Catholics. Although the shortness of time and the haste of the messenger have compelled us to pass over in silence some of the things which should have been included for recognizing and avoiding diverse heresies, still,

127. Mt 3.12.
128. Mt 25.46.

if you are careful not to neglect reviewing all the material which is contained in this work and to be thoroughly informed about it, with these things you will be able with careful discretion also to make judgments in a spiritual way about other matters. For, the Apostle says that "the spiritual man judges all things,"[129] and, until then when each of us arrives, may he walk there where he has arrived, i.e., may he faithfully persevere in that which he has accepted as certain. And, if anyone thinks otherwise, God will also reveal this to him. Amen.[130]

129. 1 Cor 2.15.
130. Cf. Phil 3.15.

ON THE FORGIVENESS OF SINS

Introduction

At the request of Euthymius, a pious layman, Fulgentius produced this treatise during his second period of exile in Sardinia (c. 517–523). It may well rank among the most repetitive of his works. Surprisingly, it does not discuss technical questions about the system of canonical penance then prevalent, though perhaps little used, in the Church. This treatise provides a more general treatment of the question of repentance for sins. In the first book, Fulgentius discusses the issues of to whom God forgives sins and where he forgives them. The answer is that God forgives sins only to those in the Catholic Church who have the true faith and who live good lives (doing good works). In the second book, he emphasizes the question of time, that sins must be forgiven while one is still in this life. Those who die in a state of serious sin will be damned. This work has been published recently in an Italian translation.

TO EUTHYMIUS. BOOK I

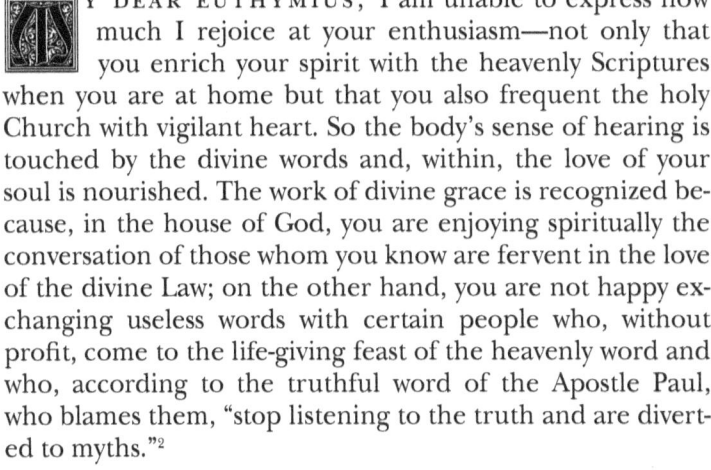

MY DEAR EUTHYMIUS,[1] I am unable to express how much I rejoice at your enthusiasm—not only that you enrich your spirit with the heavenly Scriptures when you are at home but that you also frequent the holy Church with vigilant heart. So the body's sense of hearing is touched by the divine words and, within, the love of your soul is nourished. The work of divine grace is recognized because, in the house of God, you are enjoying spiritually the conversation of those whom you know are fervent in the love of the divine Law; on the other hand, you are not happy exchanging useless words with certain people who, without profit, come to the life-giving feast of the heavenly word and who, according to the truthful word of the Apostle Paul, who blames them, "stop listening to the truth and are diverted to myths."[2]

1. Euthymius: a layman otherwise unknown. See PCBE, 377.
2. 2 Tm 4.4.

2. Of such people, I shall say, not undeservedly, that they are like those whose stomach, overcome by some deadly complaint, enjoys fasting more than food; and, for this reason, in vain do they study the abundant medicines brought to them. Since they refuse to take them, they acquire from them neither strength nor health, and, in the doctor's office, spurning the remedy of the spiritual cure offered them, they enter it only to go away more ill than before. To them God is able to grant a knowledge of and a love for his word, that they may be inflamed by the example of good people. Having been warned by these people, let them cast aside their negligent procrastinating and let them seek salvation in the salutary precepts of the Doctor himself—so that, together with those who, searching the word of the Lord, seek him, they too for their salvation may not stop seeking what can be found by those who seek.

II. 1. Therefore, the letter which you sent me, although it did not tell me anything unknown about your heart, still, it did furnish a great increase in happiness to my heart. I was aware, for example, that, with the divine grace mercifully at work in you, you often gave a great deal of thought to the forgiveness of sins. Nevertheless, I said that our happiness increased because you desire to obtain the forgiveness of sins in such a way that you inquire frequently and carefully about the way the same forgiveness works.

2. You say that the question arose among you and, although you yourself recall it, still, I preferred to insert in this small work the words which are found in your letter in the precise order you wrote them, so that you might recognize the product of your own dictation, but also so that anyone else reading it, while he may be given an idea of your request for knowledge, may also be taught to understand the answer more easily. You ask therefore, "The Lord, the Creator of all things, in this world forgives sins only for those for whom he wishes to do it, and thus someone goes forth from this world free; or, through his omnipotence, those whose sins he did not forgive in the present world, he forgives those sins when they leave the body before the day of judgment, or on that

very day in the world to come." These words I have written, you recall immediately as contained in your letter, as I have already said.

III. 1. In the solution of this question, I see you clamoring for the views of our littleness. To this end, I hope in the abundance of God, by which he is always rich, that from it our poverty can also be enriched, and from which he gives to others as much as he wills, so that he himself abides in its fullness—that he will deign to pour such things into our heart which it will be profitable for us and for you to hear. These words which in the grace of God we minister to you, thus are also of profit to us if what we say externally, verbally, and with pen for your salvation, we too hear within, meekly and humbly. Not in vain then did the very holy David say, "Let me hear what the Lord God speaks in me."[3] This kind of hearing properly belongs to the humble.

2. For which reason in another text the same prophet says, "Let me hear joy and gladness; let the bones that you have crushed rejoice,"[4] and, in another place, the majesty itself speaks thus, "But this is the one to whom I will look, to the humble and contrite in spirit, who trembles at my word."[5] Nor indeed does this Spirit of God rest on the humble and peaceful so that it is not he who makes him peaceful and humble, but he is going to rest on the one he finds humble and peaceful. That is, he deigns to rest on the humble and peaceful, because he makes peaceful and humble the one on whom he rests. The Holy Spirit does this that he may expel from the man on whom he rests the vice of pride and dissatisfaction; and thus, with the work of the Holy Spirit preceding and mercifully changing the will of the person, the forgiveness of sins freely given looses every chain of past human wickedness.

IV. 1. Thus we are not speaking of some small matter, nor are we seeking something worthy of scorn, when, insofar as the divine generosity helps us, we discuss the forgiveness of

---

3. Ps 84.9 LXX; Ps 85.8.   4. Ps 50.10 LXX; Ps 51.8.
5. Is 66.2.

sins. By it, those whom God will assign to the kingdom of his beloved Son are snatched away from the power of darkness. By it, they are freed from eternal punishment that they may attain eternal bliss. Through it is left behind that burden, either that which a birth in sin has contracted or what the wickedness of an evil life has added. Through it Christ refreshes those who labor and are heavy burdened, who come to him, and on them he imposes the mild yoke and the light burden of his love. Through it the sinner is freely justified that his faith may be accounted justice. Through it he leaves behind the evil life in which he was ensnared and freely receives a good one, of which he was unworthy. Through it come about that, from now on, enlightened by the gift of prevenient mercy, he may walk in the path of goodness, and, led along on it, may persevere with further gifts of mercy; so that, by an undeserved grace, the gift of good living will start in a person, and the forgiveness of sins having been given, this will be brought to perfection when the power of perseverance has been granted.

2. By the forgiveness of sins, people are freely separated from those who will be tortured for eternity with the Devil, and they will be added to those who will reign with Christ without end. Finally, such is the forgiveness of sins that, for it, the Only-Begotten of God became a human being; for it, even his blood was poured out. The first of these the voice of the angel disclosed at his visitation; the other the Lord himself disclosed. For, "when his mother Mary was betrothed to Joseph," and, as the evangelist bears witness, "But before they lived together, she was found with child through the Holy Spirit,"[6] the cause of this conception was announced by an angel to Joseph who did not know it, in these words: "Joseph, son of David, do not be afraid to take Mary your wife into your home. For, it is through the Holy Spirit that this child has been conceived in her. She will bear a son, and you are to name him Jesus, because he will save his people from their sins."[7]

6. Mt 1.18.
7. Mt 1.20–21.

3. What is "saving from sins" except "forgiving sins"? For our Savior himself, who came to save what had been lost, testifies that he came for this reason, to call sinners to penance.

V. The principal benefit of this call to penance is the free forgiveness of sins. For which our Redeemer, when the feast of the paschal meal had been completed, proclaims that his blood must be poured forth. "Drink from it," he says, "all of you, for this is my blood of the [New] Covenant, which will be shed on behalf of many for the forgiveness of sins."[8] This forgiveness, therefore, I think, either all or almost everyone who in any way is called by the name of Christian, wishes to find; what is significant is where or when or how someone seeks it. For no one will be able to attain the forgiveness of sins if he either does not hold the true faith or neglects the duty of good works or, blinded by deadly vice, scorns the time granted by God for living a good life inspired by right belief. For these three things, i.e., faith, works, and time are, taken together, so necessary for people in this life that, if one of the three is lacking to anyone in this present life, he will not be able to share in eternal life; and neither in this way will he attain the forgiveness of sins through which one arrives at the reward of eternal life. That this is necessary, with the help of the Lord, let us demonstrate with the corroboration of the divine testimonies.

VI. 1. Therefore, before all else, it must be held with firm faith by us that our Lord God is merciful and just. From this point, it can easily be seen by those who seek to know to whom God forgives sins, where he forgives, when he forgives. When these things are known, let no one continue to hold an unworthy idea of God, nor put off his conversion, nor depart from the Catholic Church. If anyone has left, let him quickly return. Concerning the matter of time, no one should desire to delude himself with foolish thoughts, if, unwilling to be converted to God in this life and remaining a servant of evil until death, anyone believes that he is going to receive the forgiveness of sins after this life when, already

---

8. Mt 26.27–28.

judged at the time of divine tribulation, converted, sin cannot be avoided. Rather, he remains condemned to an eternity of torture. With many and manifold tricks, the Devil struggles to close and to conceal the path of the journey to heaven; this is his unending work that he may draw on the seduced crowd or force the unwilling crowd of the wretched to share his suffering, as many as he is able.

2. Some he brings to consider only the mercy of God, putting aside all consideration of divine justice; in order that they may put off their conversion, thinking that they, even though they will have led an evil life up until the end, will receive the blessing of forgiveness. Others he either forces or seduces. Having abandoned the bosom of the Catholic Church, corrupted by blindness of heart, they move to heresies or schisms. These souls he ensnares through the deception of a false promise so that either they think they are being strengthened by a false teaching or they hope that in the future the blessing of forgiveness will be theirs by reason alone of the faith in their heart. Even if they have acted with a bad conscience because of some temporary advantage or fear, they are held tied to the death-dealing communion of heretics until death. They are not paying much attention to that declaration of our Savior who says, "Everyone who acknowledges me before others, I will acknowledge before my heavenly Father; but, whoever denies me before others, I will deny before my heavenly Father."[9] And in another text: "Whoever is ashamed of me and of my works, the Son of Man will be ashamed of when he comes in his glory and in the glory of the Father and of the holy angels."[10]

3. In many others, the enemy of the human race strives to insist upon the recollection of their sins, that he may instill even in the stubborn a despair about forgiveness and exclude them from the remedy of conversion. All of these things he does, always concealed under the cover of fraudulent deception, for no other reason than that he may remove the opportunity available in this time by which forgive-

9. Mt 10.32–33.
10. Lk 9.26.

ness may be given to the converted; and thus, insofar as it depends on his malevolence, if it can be done, no one attains salvation. He knows that God is merciful and just, and he is not unaware that only true conversion of heart can draw the forgiveness of sins from God. He knows as well that not elsewhere than in the bosom of the Catholic mother alone can sins be forgiven to the converted. Nor is it hidden from him that only in this present world can the forgiveness of all sins be granted to the converted; where the human race, through the divinely constituted order of the departure of the dying and the arrival of those who are born, is not unjustly constrained by the bond of carnal birth and is graciously loosed by a spiritual birth. Where as well conversion either liberates every guilty person or renders him impossible to free either because fed by the neglect engendered by a foolish hope or with despair strengthened and carried forward till the end because of the wickedness of a hardened heart.

VII. 1. But now the urgency of the work I have taken up compels me to instruct you about all the matters I have indicated above, with due discussion and proofs from the Sacred Scriptures. For the true unfolding of the Testaments is not silent about those things which are relevant to the advance of human salvation that there is no excusing factor from the coming condemnation of the scorner. At the start then, all of the divinely-inspired Scripture proclaims that the one true and only God, i.e., the Trinity, Father, Son and Holy Spirit, is merciful as well as just. In the person of the Church, it is said to them: "I will sing of mercy and justice to you, O Lord."[11] Concerning God, it is also sung: "The Lord is merciful and just and our God takes pity."[12] And in another text: "For the Lord ... loves righteous deeds; the upright shall see his face."[13] And again it is said: "All the paths of the Lord are mercy and truth."[14]

2. And again: "Because the Lord loves mercy and truth."[15]

11. Ps 100.1 LXX; Ps 101.1.
12. Ps 114.5 LXX; Ps 116.5.
13. Ps 10.7 LXX; Ps 11.7.
14. Ps 24.10 LXX; Ps 25.10.
15. Ps 83.12 LXX; Ps 84. 12.

In the very first commandment of the decalogue, the same God indicates that he is just and merciful in the following way: "For I the Lord your God am a jealous God, punishing children for the iniquity of parents, to the third and fourth generation of those who reject me, but showing steadfast love to the thousandth generation of those who love me and keep my commandments."[16] Wherefore Moses says, "The Lord, a God merciful and gracious, slow to anger, and abounding in steadfast love and faithfulness, keeping steadfast love for the thousandth generation, forgiving iniquity and transgression and sin, yet by no means clearing the guilty but visiting the iniquity of the parents upon the children and the children's children to the third and fourth generation."[17] Through Isaiah also, the Lord recalls his mercy and justice, saying, "I am God and there is no other besides me; just and saving, there is no other besides me. Turn to me and you will be saved."[18]

VIII. 1. With these and innumerable other texts of the same kind, in which the Lord our God is proclaimed as merciful and just, is shown how much his mercy must be loved and how much his justice must be feared. "You, O Lord, are merciful and gracious, slow to anger and abounding in steadfast love and faithfulness."[19] Just as he knows how to remove the punishment from the one who is converted, so in the one who refuses to be converted, never does he allow the sin to remain unpunished. Therefore, if there are those whom the pious goodness of God does not free from the domination of sin in this present world, his just severity condemns them in the future. From this it comes about that the evil ones are tirelessly admonished for their salvation by the divine words lest they remain in the servitude of sin, but they are exhorted rather to seek the mercy of a just God while they are in this life.

2. The good are also enjoined, that serving the Lord in fear and exulting with him with trembling, they may acquire

16. Ex 20.5–6.
17. Ex 34.6–7.
18. Is 45.21–22.
19. Ps 85.15 LXX; Ps 86.15.

discipline lest at some future time the Lord grow angry and they perish from the way of justice. Therefore, God himself who is merciful and just so admonishes that he be feared and loved by the wicked because of his justice and mercy, that, when converted, they may avoid the punishment which justice threatens and receive the forgiveness which mercy promises; he thus admonishes that he be loved and feared by the good on account of his justice and mercy, by which they who are good because of his prevenient mercy and remain in good works by love of his mercy and fear of his justice are able carefully to keep themselves from sins; and instructed by the consideration of their own weakness, they never trust in their own strength but continually and humbly ask for the help of divine strength.

IX. 1. Therefore, his mercy must be loved and his justice feared by both the good and the wicked, lest either the good, loving the mercy of God, do not fear his justice and fall into the traps of the Devil who seduces, or the wicked, considering only the severity of his justice, do not seek the blessing of his mercy when they can find it in their life, and so hardened, not only reject the forgiveness of sins but also do not cease to multiply sins. The Devil frequently captures in this twofold trap those who are not careful so that, either dulled by the vain hope of a future forgiveness, they are unwilling to be converted by the fear of justice, or, in all ways despairing of forgiveness, they neglect their way of living and loosing the reins to wickedness, while they despair of forgiveness, they plunge headlong into Hell. And so that fervid enemy of the human race hurls some down because of reckless despair, but others he trips up with the deception of a false hope. Wherefore blessed Paul in whom Christ spoke, writing to those who lived good lives, commends their obedience, so that he orders them to act cautiously, with fear and trembling, in their salutary acts.

2. For he says to the Philippians, "So then, my beloved, obedient as you have always been not only when I am present, but all the more now when I am absent, work out your salvation in fear and trembling. For God is the one who, for

his good purpose, works in you both to desire and to work."[20] With these words, the blessed Paul conveys the idea that God is indeed just when he commands that fear and trembling must accompany the good works of the faithful. He also proclaims him merciful whom he says is at work in them both to desire and to bring to perfection according to a good will. Nor would he be justly feared by those who do good works, if he were not just; nor would he bring to perfection in them every good work and will, if he were not merciful.

3. Once again he strongly instills in the just this fear of the divine justice when with a fearful proclamation he says, "Whoever thinks he is standing secure, should take care not to fall."[21] And again: "Brothers, even if a person is caught in some transgression, you who are spiritual should correct that one in a gentle spirit, looking to yourself, so that you also may not be tempted."[22] When their own weakness is denounced to the Apostles themselves by the heavenly teaching, it is shown that the caution of a due fear is to be kept in humility of heart, as the Lord says, "Watch and pray that you may not undergo the test. The Spirit is willing but the flesh is weak."[23]

X. 1. Thus, everything which is contained in the divine oracles has been put there for the safe-keeping or restoration of human salvation; the divine Word has taken care that, while the fear of divine justice is instilled in the just, on the contrary, deadly despair not be engendered in sinners, if the hope for forgiveness were not manifested. It recalls to the path of truth those who have strayed while it promises to the converted that whatever evil he has done prior to conversion will be forgiven by the divine mercy. So, the Apostle in the letter which he wrote to the Romans, just as he warns the faithful and the good with his teaching about the divine severity, so he invites those without faith and the wicked to conversion with the most certain hope of heavenly good-

---

20. Phil 2.12–13.
21. 1 Cor 10.12.
22. Gal 6.1.
23. Mt 26.41.

ness, so that as the good learn not to be arrogant but to fear, so the wicked may be able to acquire the remedy of eternal salvation without any impediment of doubt.

2. Therefore, the most blessed Paul says, "See, then, the kindness and severity of God; severity toward those who feel but God's kindness to you, provided you remain in his kindness; otherwise, you too will be cut off; and they also, if they do not remain in unbelief, will be grafted in, for God is able to graft them in again."[24] Therefore, when the Apostle says that the one who has not remained in goodness must be cut off and that the one who has not remained in unbelief must be grafted in, what just man does not, trembling, fear the justice of God, or what evil person, having been encouraged, will not run to the mercy of God? Who would not be compelled to be solicitously fearful for any good person or who would dare despair of the salvation of any wicked person, if he is converted with his whole heart, since the heavenly medicine with its salutary precepts looks after both the healthy and the sick equally, pointing out to them fear of his justice as the safeguard for salvation already received, assuring them of the blessing of mercy, so that, lifted up by the remedy of hope, they may receive back the salvation they had lost.

3. Fear of justice is required of the healed person to whom it is said: "Look, you are well; do not sin any more, so that nothing more may happen to you."[25] The hope of mercy is shown to the sick when it is said: "Those who are healthy do not need a physician, but the sick do. I have not come to call the righteous to repentance but sinners."[26] The words of the prophets never cease to show the mercy and justice of God, as when God says through the prophet Ezechiel, "But if the wicked turn away from all their sins they have committed and keep all my statutes and do what is lawful and right, they shall surely live; they shall not die. None of the transgressions that they have committed shall be remembered against

---

24. Rm 11.22–23. 25. Jn 5.14.
26. Lk 5.31–32.

them; for the righteousness that they have done shall live. Have I any pleasure in the death of the wicked, says the Lord God, and not rather that they should turn from their ways and live?"[27] When the blessing of the divine patience and kindness has been made clear to convert the wicked, then the word of the prophet is directed to frightening off the just as well: "But when the righteous turn away from their righteousness and commit iniquity and do the same abominable things that the wicked do, shall they live? None of the righteous deeds that they have done shall be remembered; for the treachery of which they are guilty and the sin they have committed, they shall die."[28]

XI. 1. Innumerable are the testimonies of the Scriptures in which a merciful and just God is proclaimed, nor does every text of the divine word do anything other than admonish the wicked to put an end rapidly to their evil deeds out of fear of God's justice and [admonish] the good to abide humbly and carefully in their good deeds. [Every text of the divine word admonishes] both that every evil person, fearing the justice of God, runs to the mercy of the just goodness and that every just person, rejoicing in God's mercy, not neglect the judgment of the most benign justice. For where mercy and justice are perfect, neither can the just one grant favor to sins nor can the merciful one deny forgiveness to the converted.

2. From this, therefore, the fact that he who forgives sins is proclaimed to be just and merciful, we know with the greatest of ease that the forgiveness of sins is granted only to the converted, and the punishment of eternal damnation is inflicted only on those who remain in sin. For this reason the psalmist sings, "If one does not repent, God will whet his sword; he has prepared his deadly weapons, making his arrows fiery shafts (and in him has prepared vessels of death)."[29] In Isaiah also is found a similar declaration from the divine word against the recalcitrant who scorn the divine

27. Ez 18.21–23.   28. Ez 18.24.
29. Ps 7.13–14 LXX; Ps 7.12–13.

clemency. In this declaration it is made known that one obeys the divine commands not without reason and that one does not remain in evil without punishment. He says, "Wash yourselves clean; make yourselves clean; remove the evil of your doings from before my eyes; cease to do evil, learn to do good; seek justice, rescue the oppressed, defend the orphan, plead for the widow. Come now, let us argue it out, says the Lord; Though your sins are like scarlet, they shall be like snow; though they are red like crimson, they shall become like wool. If you are willing and obedient, you shall eat the good of the land; but if you refuse and rebel, you shall be devoured by the sword; for the mouth of the Lord has spoken."[30]

3. Who, I ask, is so hard and altogether inert that, in these words of the highest admonition, if he is not called to conversion out of the pleasure of what is promised, he is not at least compelled by the fear of punishment? Salvation will not accept the one who scorns the divine words but the sword will devour him. Hence it is that in another text in the book of the same prophet, it is shown that other than through conversion, no one will attain salvation. Thus it is said: "If you are converted and groan, you will be saved."[31] In this conditional statement, God uses both the precept and the promise. Saying, "If you are converted and groan, you will be saved," he shows that on the condition of conversion depends completely the promise of salvation.

4. Therefore, this is the condition between God and human beings, i.e., between the Lord who gives the command and the servant who asks, between the judge who grants in advance mercy without justice and the sinner who awaits mercy from the one who judges justly. Therefore, this Lord, merciful and just, severe and pious, says: If you will do this, you will have this; if you keep what I say, I will give you what you seek; I command conversion for you, you seek salvation from me; if you obey the command, you will receive

30. Is 1.16–20.
31. Is 30.15.

the benefit; If I see what has been commanded being done, I will grant what has been asked: "If you are converted and groan, you will be saved."[32]

XII. 1. When it is said to the sinner who seeks to receive the blessing of salvation that if he is converted and groans, he will be saved, fittingly it is understood that, even if he groan but still is not converted, he will not be saved. It is not to no purpose that the divine word has brought together both these things, except so that we may know that these two elements, i.e., conversion and groaning, are necessary to gain salvation. Some, indeed, terrified by the thought of their crimes, groan in prayer because of their misdeeds, yet they do not abandon their evil works. They confess that they have done evil, but they are unwilling to put an end to their evil deeds. Humbly in the sight of God, they accuse themselves of the sins by which they are held in servitude and the very same sins of which they accuse themselves of in humble speech, they stubbornly pile up with a perverse heart. The forgiveness which they seek with tearful cries, they themselves push away with their evil works. They ask for a remedy from the physician and, to their own destruction, they provide assistance to the disease. Thus to no avail do they seek to placate the just judge with words when with their evil deeds, they stir him up to rage.

2. Such people never cleanse their sins by their groans because they do not give up sinning after the groaning. For they groan for their crimes, and, after the groaning, they return to their crimes. Of such people, the divine Scriptures in the book of Ecclesiasticus say, "If one washes after touching a corpse and touches it again, what has been gained by washing? So if one fasts for his sins and goes again and does the same things, who will listen to his prayer?"[33] Most rightly, therefore, does God say to human beings, "If you are converted and you groan, you will be saved."[34] With the severe and good God, the prayer of the one who groans is heard,

32. Is 30.15.
33. Sir 34.30–31.
34. Is 30.15.

then the tears of the one who seeks are attended to, then salvation is granted to the one who weeps, if he will have been converted to God in the humility of a contrite heart. It is necessary that God, taking pity, forgive the sinner, if the sinner, having been converted, acknowledges his iniquity.

3. Finally, holy David successfully gained divine mercy because, having been converted by the humility of a contrite heart, he condemned the evil he had done by acknowledging it and did not put off punishment by doing penance for the lust of the evil deed he had fallen into; because, if he had not punished the cause of the guilt in which he was held, without a doubt he would have been punished. Having been converted to penance, he acknowledged his crime, fearing lest he would have to acknowledge the penalty by being condemned. By doing penance, he punished himself by acknowledging what he wanted to be overlooked by the Lord in himself. Finally, since he said, "Have mercy on me, O God, according to your steadfast love; according to your abundant mercy blot out my transgressions. Wash me thoroughly from my iniquity and cleanse me from my sin."[35] Immediately following this he added, "For I know my transgressions and my sin is ever before me."[36] He acknowledged his sin, not that by sinning, he might increase it the more, but that, by repenting, he might wash it away; and so the domination of sin which blameworthy enjoyment had brought in, true conversion removed. And because David, converted with all his heart, groaned, he was immediately saved and thus in him was fulfilled what is commanded through the prophet: "If you are converted and groan, you will be saved."[37]

XIII. 1. Conversion from both impiety and iniquity is commanded. For both provoke the wrath of God against one, because God detests and condemns both, as Paul says, "The wrath of God is indeed being revealed from heaven against every impiety and human wickedness."[38] And Solo-

---

35. Ps 50.3–4 LXX; Ps 51.1–2.
37. Is 30.15.
36. Ps 50.5 LXX; Ps 51.3.
38. Rm 1.18.

mon says, as the blessed Peter had also inserted among his own words, "And if the righteous one is barely saved, when will the godless and the sinner appear?"[39] Whence not undeservedly, the vessel of election who had been filled with divine charity, just as he was shaken with great sadness and sorrow of heart because of those faithful who sinned, so he testified that he was in mourning over those who, while living impurely and scandalously in the Church, did not do penance. Concerning Jews whom the impiety of an unbelieving heart possessed, he speaks thus: "If I speak the truth in Christ, I do not lie; my conscience joins with the Holy Spirit in bearing me witness that I have great sorrow and constant anguish in my heart. For I could wish that I myself were accursed and separated from Christ for the sake of my brothers, my kin according to the flesh. They are Israelites."[40]

2. Concerning those who, though within the Church persisted in their evil deeds, he spoke thus to the Corinthians with these words of comfort: "I fear that when I come again, my God may humiliate me before you, and I may have to mourn over many of those who sinned earlier and have not repented of the impurity, immorality, and licentiousness they practiced."[41] The Apostle would not be saddened or humiliated in mourning over them, if he believed that the forgiveness of sins would be granted to sinners and the wicked who continue to exasperate the divine justice, without conversion of heart. The forgiveness of sins has no effect except in the conversion of the heart. They, we mean, who, using their own freedom of choice, are converted by the offer of divine aid and, their lives changed for the better, do not cease to hasten to ask for the forgiveness of sins, they whom either ignorance pushes unknowing to the carrying out of these things or, worse, stubbornness of will has lured knowingly. For this reason the prophet prays to God in this way: "Do not remember the sins of my youth or my transgressions."[42]

---

39. 1 Pt 4.18; Prov 11.31.
40. Rm 9.1–4a.
41. 2 Cor 12.21.
42. Ps 24.7 LXX; Ps 25.7.

3. And our Savior says, "That servant who knew his master's will but did not make preparations nor act in accord with his will shall be beaten severely, and the servant who was ignorant of his master's will but acted in a way deserving of a severe beating shall be beaten only lightly."[43] And so the Apostle confesses with these words that he himself had sinned in ignorance: "I am grateful to him who has strengthened me, Christ Jesus our Lord, because he considered me trustworthy in appointing me to the ministry. I was once a blasphemer and a persecutor and an arrogant man, but I have been mercifully treated because I acted out of ignorance in my unbelief."[44] Lest anyone delude himself because of ignorance, the words of the Apostle must be carefully scrutinized. He declares that he acted out of ignorance, but he does not thereby deny that he sinned; indeed, he says that he was the greatest of all sinners, not the greatest, of course, in the passage of time but in seriousness of evil.

4. Therefore, he won mercy for this reason, that the sins which he had committed in ignorance, when enlightened, he acknowledged and, having been converted, he immediately renounced. This happened so that, as the Apostle James teaches us, every good gift and every perfect gift, we know comes from above, from the Father of lights. He, when he finds in a sinner that for which he ought to be justly damned, he freely gives that sinner the gift of conversion through which the well-deserved, just damnation can be taken away.

XIV. Therefore, in every sinner who makes use of his own free will, the blessing of the divine gift begins to work through conversion of heart. For the rest, we know that small children are saved, not by their own will, but by the orthodox faith of those who make confession on their behalf. It is fitting that young children be absolved by the judgment of truth, by the ministry of the confession of faith of others. It is plain that they are bound by the chains of someone

---

43. Lk 12.47–48.
44. 1 Tm 1.12–13.

else's sin, so that, with others confessing spiritually, they may receive the blessing of justification who, since others generated them carnally, bear original sin. As the sexual intercourse of their parents was harmful to their first birth, even though they were not yet born and had done nothing, so the spiritual love of the faithful who make a confession of faith on their behalf is of value for their second birth, even if they are unaware of it. But as for how this affects those who are now capable of rendering an account for their own actions, no one will become blessed except the one who, renouncing his evil actions, will be converted to God in all humility of heart. For, "Happy are those whose transgression is forgiven, whose sin is covered."[45] Therefore, whoever of his own free will and action carries on his evil way of life, cannot receive any blessedness unless he is converted to the giver of blessedness himself.

XV. 1. For the heart is blinded by sins but illumined by forgiveness. Since to be blind is nothing other than to be deprived of light, the eye is cured to the extent that it can possess the vision of light. To that extent it lacks the defect of blindness. For the eye will never be able to see light unless light will have poured itself into it. Therefore, the eye can perceive the vision of light through the infusion of light. Thus when the forgiveness of sins is given to human beings, without a doubt blindness of heart is driven out so that the light of justice is discerned by the interior eye. For the rest, how can it happen that the obscurity of darkness is removed if the infusion of light is not given? God therefore pours the light of true conversion into those whose sin he forgives. Just as any blind person, as long as he is blind, cannot see the light, so any evil or sinful person does not receive the forgiveness of sins unless, having been given beforehand the free gift of justification, he is converted to God with his whole heart; for the effect of the forgiveness itself consists in conversion of heart.

2. To the one who is not granted the grace of conversion,

---

45. Ps 31.1 LXX; Ps 32.1.

the forgiveness of sins is not granted. For what is it to gain the forgiveness of sins other than to be freed from the domination of sin? "Everyone," as the Truth says, "who commits sin is a slave to sin."[46] How is it believed that someone who does not lack the most vile servitude of sin, acquires the luminous gift of freedom? Wherefore for those who say, "Let us do evil that good may come of it,"[47] there is a just condemnation, we know, with the teacher of the nations teaching, as he proclaims, we likewise hear [that] "neither fornicators nor idolaters, nor adulterers, nor boy prostitutes, nor practicing homosexuals, nor thieves, nor the greedy, nor drunkards, nor slanderers, nor robbers will inherit the kingdom of God."[48] The same great teacher also warns the Galatians in this way: "Now the works of the flesh are obvious: immorality, impurity, licentiousness, idolatry, sorcery, hatreds, rivalry, jealousy, outbursts of fury, acts of selfishness, dissensions, factions, occasions of envy, drinking bouts, orgies, and the like. I warn you, as I warned you before, that those who do such things will not inherit the Kingdom of God."[49]

3. Because God is just, as long as these people do such things, they will not gain the Kingdom of God. Since, however, the same God is merciful, the evil, if they cease doing the things that exasperate God and, humbled and corrected, are converted to God; they will surely gain the Kingdom of God. For, as the work of justice is not overcome, so neither is the work of mercy removed. And so God has arranged the possession of his kingdom in such a way that, because he is just, he does not give it to sinners and the evil; but because he is merciful, neither does he deny it to any person who is truly converted.

XVI. 1. Conversion is shown to be genuine in a person if impiety and wickedness are expelled from the heart. Nevertheless, this distinction is usually made between impiety and wickedness, that impiety has either a false faith in God or none at all; whereas wickedness soils life with evil morals.

46. Jn 8.34.
48. 1 Cor 6.9–10.
47. Rm 3.8.
49. Gal 5.19–21.

Impiety blasphemes God; wickedness harms the neighbor. Impiety, from the lowliness of the flesh, measures the most High, striving to present the mystery of unsurpassed mercy by slandering the divine nature; or it denies that the Son of God was conceived and born as God in human flesh and assigns to the true God, not the reality of the flesh, but only the manifestation of a false appearance; or it speaks of the flesh of Christ from the flesh of the virgin in such a way that it denies that it was conceived in the assuming of the flesh; or, with impious confusion, it states that the Father is the same as the Son and the Holy Spirit; or, with perverse separation, it leads to the idea of diverse natures of the Father, the Son, and the Holy Spirit; or it does not believe that the flesh of the Son of God was assumed from the flesh of the virgin Mary, but it does not hesitate to assert that it was brought down from heaven; or it seeks to remove some element of human nature from Christ, so that, having received human flesh, it denies that the only-begotten God received a rational soul, i.e., the complete soul of the human being.

2. It is the crime of impiety if anyone says that not every spiritual and corporeal nature was created good by God but, on the contrary, wishes to assign to evil its own substance. Although every evil exists not from an origin or state of its own nature but arises from a defect of thoughtful willing, not because a good nature receives an evil nature, since there is no such thing as an evil nature, but because, with the order of love abandoned, the rational creature, which was made for the love of the Creator, when the Creator has been scorned, either adheres to created things or false thoughts, becomes worse, and places temporal things ahead of the eternal, the lowest ahead of the highest, the changeable ahead of the unchangeable. Likewise, there are those who say that the just and the unjust ought to be judged, not by the diversity of their deeds but from the communion of the sacraments, wishing it to be of no avail to anyone if he lives justly in the Catholic Church among the unjust. It is as if eternal reward, whether it be punishment or the Kingdom, is to be awarded a person not for the quality of his deeds but for the communion of the sacrament.

3. All these things which have been indicated above by us and many other things which are put forward by heretics and schismatics against the Catholic and apostolic faith are assigned to the vice of impiety. The very separation designates the impious, this separation which makes such people not sharers but adversaries in the body of the Church. They are not separated in a bodily or in a spatial sense from the meeting of the unity of the Church unless, with corrupted heart, they previously have departed from the faith of the Church. They are not severed from legitimate union with the Word of God with open impiety, unless by the adulterous insemination of the Devil's defilement, they conceive faithless and perverse thoughts. If they nurture these thoughts with internal assent, they bring them forth later with evil words so that like vipers, bursting apart, they die of their own offspring. For vipers, giving birth is the same as dying.

4. Their offspring, so it is said, after the organs in which they have been conceived have burst apart, come forth into the light in such a way that they bring death to their mothers. So when any impious vice is either conceived by agreement or, in addition, given birth to by avowal, it kills the soul with an eternal death. Consenting to the corruption, it is puffed up by conceiving this unfaithfulness to God so that, split apart by this birth, it later dies. The authority of the Apostle points up such cases with these words: "Just as Jannes and Mambres opposed Moses, so they also oppose the truth—people of depraved mind, unqualified in the faith."[50] Therefore, if anyone, discussing contrary things and cutting himself off from the good, perversely opposes the faith of the Church, he without a doubt is to be called impious. But if someone staying on in the body of Catholic unity and still united in the communion of the sacraments is given over to vices and crimes, he is normally called wicked but not impious. Where such terminology comes from is not up to us to discuss here. Still we say this: that not every wicked person is impious although every impious person is wicked.

XVII. 1. Therefore that conversion is pleasing in the sight

---

50. 2 Tm 3.8.

of God and accepted by him in which, at one and the same time, both the rightness of faith is preserved and the rule of a good life is maintained, i.e., in order that first of all, the right view be held concerning God, then the divinely commanded charity be shown to the neighbor. For then does a person love himself in the right way when, devout and humble, he prefers the love of God to himself. Then he loves his neighbor if, insofar as he is able, he is mindful of his neighbor, that the neighbor with orthodox faith and a virtuous way of life, may attain to God. For the love of neighbor is to be maintained in a two-fold way, viz., nothing is to be done to the other that one would not wish done to oneself; nor, insofar as it is possible, would one deny to the needy the assistance of a good work, because one would not want it denied to oneself, if one were seriously in need. Hence we recognize that we are trained by these words of our Savior when he says, "Do to others whatever you would have them do to you. This is the Law and the Prophets."[51]

2. Christ did not say: What people will have done to you, you do the same things to them; lest we believe that evil should be done for evil to him who did something evil to us or that we should think that some benefit should be denied to someone by whom, we know, nothing beneficial has been done for us; since a Christian must either offer or render benevolent aid to every person; so that he both renders good for good and forestalls evil with goodness. For it is said to us by the Lord: "Love your enemies and pray for those who persecute you that you may be children of your heavenly Father, for he makes his sun rise on the bad and the good and causes rain to fall on the just and the unjust."[52] However, the good-living faithful not only suffer persecution from those who on the outside struggle against the teachings of the Catholic Church with their faithless and perverse screaming but also from those who indeed seem to be within the Church but who, living evil lives, repudiate the tradition

---

51. Mt 7.12.
52. Mt 5.44–45.

of the Church not in word but by their deeds. When the good see such people, they groan loudly and, moved by holy feelings, the good spirit is tormented when it does not refuse to understand the reason for the others' bad state, although it cannot agree with it.

XVIII. 1. In the present age, the wicked are held to be mixed with the just within the Catholic Church, i.e., in the communion of the sacraments but not of morals, i.e., by a common belief but not by a like manner of living. Not, therefore, in the heart but in the body; by words, not by deeds. Now, therefore, but for the present time, according to the statement of the blessed Paul: "In a large household there are vessels not only of gold and silver but also of wood and clay, some for lofty and others for humble use;"[53] for, within the Church, there are the wicked and the just, but outside the Church, no one is just.

2. And within the field of the Lord, while the feared-coming of the winnower and the selection process by the winnower is put off to the end, the chaff is mixed with the wheat in the Church in each place. Whatever place is outside the Lord's field, even though the word "farmer" is used there, in that place there can be only the chaff which is driven by the wind. To be sure, so great is the omnipotence of our "farmer" that none can overcome his will; anyone who, converted in this present life runs to the real location of the Lord's field, if he perseveringly holds on to his intention in right faith and lives a good life, he will not be chaff but wheat; he will not be handed over to be bound in the fires, but he will be gathered into the barn, enriched with fruits pleasing to the Lord.

XIX. 1. Therefore, only in the Catholic Church is the forgiveness of sins given and received. This Church the bridegroom himself calls his one dove, his chosen one, which he founded upon a rock, to which he gave the keys of the kingdom of heaven, to which he also granted the power of binding and loosing, just as the Truth itself truthfully promised

---

53. 2 Tm 2.20.

blessed Peter, saying, "You are Peter and upon this rock, I will build my Church and the gates of the netherworld shall not prevail against it. I will give you the keys to the kingdom of heaven. Whatever you bind on earth shall be bound in heaven, and whatever you loose on earth shall be loosed in heaven."[54]

2. Whoever is outside this Church which has received the keys of the kingdom of heaven is not teaching the path to heaven but to hell; nor is he heading to the house of eternal life, but he is hurrying toward the punishment of eternal death; not only if he remains a pagan without baptism but also, even if he perseveres as a heretic, if he is baptized in the name of the Father and the Son and the Holy Spirit. Nor does one gain the true life because of the merit of baptism, if one is baptized in the name of the Father and of the Son and of the Holy Spirit whether within the Church or outside the Church, if one does not end this life still within the Catholic Church. Nor will one live because of the sacrament of the Church's baptism, who has not held to the communion of the Church's faith and charity. That one is saved by the sacrament of baptism whom the unity of charity will have held within the Catholic Church until the end of this present life.

XX. 1. For the rest, if any baptized person leaves the Church or was baptized in the name of the Father and of the Son and of the Holy Spirit outside the Church, if, before the end of this present life, he will not have been restored to the Catholic Church, he will not lack death but rest. Just as at the time of the flood, if anyone did not enter the ark of Noah, he was not saved from the flood but was killed; he did not find salvation in the water but death. That water, in which was prefigured the sacrament of baptism, whomever it found in the ark, it raised up to the heavens after they had been raised up from the earth; the remainder, however, which it found outside, it killed after they were crushed. And as Jericho was being destroyed, any whom the house of

---

54. Mt 16.18–19.

Rahab the prostitute held, Jesus (Joshua) ordered kept unharmed; but the rest, whom that house did not contain, the destruction of a single death consumed.

2. Therefore, in that ark and in that house, one and the same Church was prefigured; but in those who perished outside the ark in the flood and in those who died by the sword outside that house, a mystery of two-fold significance can be considered. For I think, insofar as it seems to me now for the current time, that not unfittingly, in the significance of the flood, the baptism of the Christian confession can be believed to have preceded; that we may recognize that heretics, if they remain outside the Church, by their baptism, merit punishment, not life, and that those, who, denying Christ, leave the Catholic Church, will perish in eternal punishment. For blessed Peter expounds the mystery of the ark in these words: ". . . while God patiently waited in the days of Noah during the building of the ark in which a few persons, eight in all, were saved through water: this prefigured baptism, which saves you now; it is not a removal of dust from the body but an appeal to God for a clean conscience."[55] And where is there a good conscience except where there is a sincere faith? For the Apostle Paul teaches: "The aim of this instruction is love from a pure heart, a good conscience, and a sincere faith."[56]

3. Therefore, because the water of the flood did not save those outside the ark but killed them, without a doubt, it prefigured that every heretic who, although he has the sacrament of baptism, must be plunged down to hell, not by any other waters but by those very waters by which the ark was lifted up to heaven. Nor for any other reason is death begotten by the water for them except that the bosom of the ark did not hold them, in which alone anyone who does not wish to perish in the life-giving waters can live.

XXI. 1. Cyprian, the most blessed martyr, writing about the unity of the Church, expounds the mystery of the ark

---

55. 1 Pt 3.20–21.
56. 1 Tm 1.5.

with these words: "The spouse of Christ cannot be defiled; she is inviolate and chaste; she knows one home alone; in all modesty she keeps faithfully to one only couch. It is she who rescues us for God, she who seals for the kingdom the sons whom she has borne. Whoever breaks with the Church and enters on an adulterous union, cuts himself off from the promises made to the Church; and he who has turned his back on the Church of Christ shall not come to the rewards of Christ; he is an alien, a worldling, an enemy. You cannot have God for your Father if you have not the Church for your mother. If there was escape for anyone who was outside the ark of Noah, there is escape too for one who is found to be outside the Church."[57]

2. Therefore, it is certain as much by the preaching of the blessed Apostle Peter as by the exposition of the holy martyr Cyprian that in the ark of Noah is found the figure of the Church and in the waters of the flood, the figure of baptism. Also in that house of Rahab[58] the prostitute, which house as Jericho perished at Joshua's command was alone kept unharmed along with all whom it held within, in the mystery of the Christian confession, so it seems to me, was signified the Catholic Church from the gentiles. And having rejected the filth of earlier fornication, she secretly took in the two spies of Joshua; that is, either the chaste knowledge of each testament or love of God and neighbor; since both in these two testaments, love of God and neighbor is indicated and, in these two commandments, the whole Law and the Prophets is opened to be recognized.

3. This woman, who earlier as a sinful whore had prostituted herself to idols, receiving Joshua's spies, became faithful and chaste; protecting them from the enemies pursuing them, she did not bury them in the basement but secretly hid them high upon the roof terrace of her house. It is called a solarium for the simple reason that it is suffused by the light of the sun. But who is the sun of the human heart,

---

57. Cyprian, *De unitate* 6. CCL 3.253. Bévenot translation. ACW 25.48–49.
58. Cf. Jos 2.

except he of whom it has been said through the prophet. "But for you who revere my name the sun of righteousness shall rise, with healing in its wings."[59] Concerning the sun as it rises, Zachariah prophesies in the Gospel that "the daybreak from on high will visit us to shine on those who sit in darkness and death's shadow."[60]

4. And the prophet Habakkuk proclaims the ascension of Christ and the strength of the ecclesiastical order under the titles of the sun and the moon: "The sun raised high its hands; the moon stood still in its exalted place."[61] So the heart of each of the faithful is not improperly called a spiritual sun-terrace, because it is illumined for its salvation by the rays of that sun above. Therefore, Rahab the harlot hid those spies of Joshua on the terrace of her house, that is, she kept them in the upper parts because of the deep love of a heart illumined by spiritual knowledge so that she might sing this prophetic word by the truth of her deed: "I treasure your word in my heart, so that I may not sin against you."[62]

5. Therefore, the true faith, which is announced by divine words, is not betrayed to persecutors at one time, at other times is guarded inviolate and unharmed in the hearts of the faithful, if the spirit holds on affixed, not to earthly and perishable and fleshly promises but to heavenly and spiritual ones, and contemplates not the things which are seen but those which are not seen. "For what is seen is transitory," as the Apostle says, "but what is unseen is eternal."[63] For the rest, whoever holds the Christian faith so that he acquires earthly and transitory goods, such a one places Joshua's spies, not in the upper parts of his house, but in the lower; when they have been placed there, they can more easily be found by enemies and perish. For every persecutor and enemy of the Church kills them spiritually and inflicts eternal death on those whose hearts he finds tied down by earthly and perishable things.

59. Mal 4.2.
60. Lk 1.78–79.
61. Hab 3.11.
62. Ps 118.11 LXX; Ps 119.11.
63. 2 Cor 4.18.

6. For those who either fear to lose or lust to acquire earthly riches do not hide the precepts of Christ, i.e., Joshua's spies, in the sun terrace of the heart but hands them over to the pursuing enemy, either because they are terrified by fear or they are on fire with wicked lust. They who confess the faith but deny its mysteries do not hold the crimson cord in which sign that house was saved, hanging from the window of her house. For the crimson cord showed forth beforehand the mystery of the blood of Christ; which [cord] he holds suspended from the windows of his house, he who, under God's protection, strengthened in faith against the pagans or against any heretics and guarding his faith carefully, confesses that he has been redeemed by the blood of Christ.

7. So the Savior himself says, "Everyone who acknowledges me before others, I will acknowledge before my heavenly Father. But whoever denies me before others, I will deny before my heavenly Father."[64] Therefore, although the persecuting enemy attempts to kill the spies of Joshua in the lower quarters, i.e., he strives to weaken the strength of the Christian faith with earthly promises or terrors, if anyone has placed in the higher quarters the faith of the Trinity by which he believes that the Father and the Son and the Holy Spirit are one in substance, he will not fear all the black errors of the persecutor and all the snares of the seducer.

XXII. 1. Accordingly, not only those whom the guilt of a repeated baptism holds entangled must speedily rush to the Church and beg God with tears and alms for such a great crime, but also if any, perhaps without the repetition of baptism but because of the enjoyment of gifts or fear of punishments, denying the mystery of the Catholic faith, have fallen into the deadly companionship of heretics, let them take up again the faith which they have denied and swiftly return to the Church. In this way, with Jesus coming, they can be found within that house, outside of which no one can be freed from death, because just as in Jericho anyone who was

---

64. Mt 10.32–33.

outside that house could gain no assistance for his life, so outside the Catholic Church, no one will receive the forgiveness of sins; and just as within the Catholic Church, "One believes with the heart and so is justified, and one confesses with the mouth and so is saved,"[65] so outside the same Church, unorthodox faith does not procure justification but punishment, and a wicked confession does not acquire salvation for the one who confesses but brings death. Outside this Church, neither does the Christian name help anyone, nor does baptism save, nor is a pure sacrifice offered to God, nor is the forgiveness of sins received, nor is the happiness of eternal life found.

2. For the Church of Christ is one, one dove, one beloved, one spouse; in it the Trinity is believed to be one God, of one nature and substance; in it no slander is inflicted on the Son or the Holy Spirit, to the effect that they are lesser; in it one and the same worship and one honor is offered to the one Trinity, which is the true God. This is the one true Church which so believes and preaches the one essence of the Trinity that no one dares to place any one person of the three before another. Thus it does not manifest any diversity of worship in the substance of the divinity, so that, confessing the Father and the Son and the Holy Spirit, i.e., the Trinity itself as one, true and only God, it does not in the unity of the name incur the error of Sabellian confusion and in the word Trinity is careful to avoid the deadly ruination of Arian diversity. Retaining as its norm the preaching of the Apostles, as it knows the Trinity in the persons of the Father and the Son and the Holy Spirit; so it proclaims the orthodox faith of one God, because it proclaims the unity of nature in the Father and the Son and the Holy Spirit.

XXIII. 1. If there are any who, in a variety of errors, are outside, away from this Church, then they will receive forgiveness of sins, if, while they are still in this world, they go to this same Church with orthodox faith and are converted with the humility of a contrite heart. Therefore, while there

---

65. Rm 10.10.

is still time, let them run to their legitimate mother who, just as she carefully holds and nourishes these children born from her womb, so those born from a maidservant, she not only does not repudiate when they return but also in the bowels of her mercy, seeks them out as they wander and, out of love, ceaselessly calls to them whom she leads back into the communion of the Father's inheritance. Nor does she devote attention to them on the condition of coming from the womb of the maidservant but recognizes in them the reality of the paternal seed.

2. What is the reality of the father's seed, except baptism received in the name of the Trinity? Whomever she finds like this, as the legitimate mother, she recognizes as belonging to her. For, like Rachel, she knows not only that she begets children from her own womb, but also, as the legitimate mother, she claims those begotten by the maidservant in her name. It is necessary then that such people not neglect to seek out again the company of their brothers and sisters, if they do not want to miss out on the gift of the father's inheritance. Therefore, leaving heresy behind, let them quickly return to the Catholic Church; and let them not doubt about the possession of the inheritance nor despair of the forgiveness of sins. For he who does not believe that within the Catholic Church all sins can be loosed, that person denies himself the forgiveness of sins, if, persisting in that same hardness of an impenitent heart, he goes forth from this life, separated from the communion of the Church.

XXIV. 1. Such a person speaks the word against the Holy Spirit which must not be forgiven either in this world or in the world to come. For "the love of God," which "covers a multitude of sins,"[66] "has been poured out," as the Apostle says, "into our hearts through the Holy Spirit who has been given to us."[67] This love, because it maintains unbroken the communion of brotherly unity, therefore covers a multitude

66. 1 Pt 4.8.
67. Rm 5.5.

of sins and does not allow to perish those who persevere with most certain hope in the unity of faith. Therefore, if anyone, holding the faith "that works through charity"[68] does penance for any earlier error whatsoever in such a way that no false communion later holds him, and no chain of death-dealing despair fetters him, he will be free from that word which is spoken against the Holy Spirit which is not forgiven the one who says it, either in this world or in the world to come.

2. With this word, Our Lord and Savior did not convey the idea that in the world to come sins will be forgiven which have not been forgiven in this world; but to those who understand such things well, he shows that not other sins but only those are to be forgiven in the world to come which will have already been forgiven in this world in the one and true Catholic Church. For the Lord gave the power of binding and loosing only to it, when he says, "I will give you the keys of the Kingdom of Heaven. Whatever you bind on earth shall be bound in heaven; and whatever you loose on earth, shall be loosed in heaven."[69] Therefore, what holy Church will not have so loosed in this world remains unloosable so that even in the world to come, it can never be loosed. Everyone whom the Church has not loosed, has been bound; nor will he gain any benefit of loosing who, not being converted to penance in the Church, will hope that the forgiveness of sins will be given to him. Therefore, he speaks the unforgivable word against the Holy Spirit who, scorning the "riches of the goodness of God"[70] "and his patience and forebearance," "by [his] stubbornness and impenitent heart" is storing up "wrath for [himself] for the day of wrath and revelation of the just judgment of God who will repay everyone according to his works."[71]

XXV. 1. Whether it be "charity," and that "from a pure heart," or the communion of brotherly unity, or the Father's gift of a heavenly inheritance, all are in the gift of the Holy

---

68. Gal 5.6.
70. Rm 2.4.
69. Mt 16.19.
71. Rm 2.4–6.

Spirit. Concerning charity, the teacher of the nations says, "The love of God has been poured into our hearts through the Holy Spirit that has been given to us."[72]

The Spirit also commends unity with the same charity, saying, "I, a prisoner for the Lord, urge you to live in a manner worthy of the call you have received, with all humility and gentleness, with patience, bearing with one another through love, striving to preserve the unity of the Spirit through the bond of peace."[73] He also confirms that this is the communion of the Holy Spirit, saying, "The grace of the Lord Jesus Christ, and the love of God and the fellowship of the Holy Spirit be with you all."[74] Concerning our inheritance, he speaks as follows: "You were sealed with the promised Holy Spirit which is the first installment of our inheritance...."[75]

2. The blessed Apostle also assigns to the Holy Spirit that hope which drives out the vice of despair, saying, "May the God of hope fill you with all joy and peace in believing, so that you may abound in hope by the power of the Holy Spirit."[76]

Therefore, he receives an eternal share of the heavenly inheritance, who, preserving the unity of fraternal charity within the Catholic Church before he ends this present life, puts away the fatal hardness of an impenitent heart and does not despair that in the one and truly Catholic Church, the forgiveness of all sins is given through the Holy Spirit to those who are converted. Our Savior himself shows this. For, after he rose, breathing on his disciples and giving them the gift of his Holy Spirit, he gave them the power to forgive sins, saying, "Receive the Holy Spirit. Whose sins you forgive are forgiven them and whose sins you retain are retained."[77]

XXVI. 1. Therefore, let not those who, separated from the Catholic Church by the error of whatever heresy or schism they are held fast, close the gate of forgiveness against themselves because of death-dealing despair. Let them put aside hardness of heart, if they do not wish to be tortured by un-

72. Rm 5.5.
74. 2 Cor 13.13.
76. Rm 15.13.
73. Eph 4.1–3.
75. Eph 1.13–14.
77. Jn 20.22–23.

ending evils. For it has been written that: "A stubborn mind will fare badly at the end, and whoever loves danger will perish in it."[78] What is more dangerous than not to be obedient to the divine words and to spurn the will of God who calls? In the book of the holy Job, just as a glorious eternity is promised to those who are converted, so the gifts of salvation are denied to sinners because they do not obey. For so it has been written: "[Those who return from iniquity] if they listen and serve him, they complete their days in prosperity and their years in pleasantness. But the impious he does not save because they were unwilling to know God and when they were warned, they were disobedient."[79] Therefore, let them not spurn the time allowed for obedience but let them return to the Catholic Church; in which alone, through the gift of the Holy Spirit, "charity covers a multitude of sins."[80]

2. If there are any who are even in the Catholic Church and live evil lives, before they finish this life, let them hasten to give up the evil life, and let them not think that the Catholic name is enough for salvation, if they do not do the will of God. For our Savior says, ". . . not everyone who says to me, 'Lord, Lord' will enter the Kingdom of Heaven, but only the one who does the will of my Father in heaven."[81] In the book of Psalms as well, it is written that: "The Lord is near to all who call on him, to all who call on him in truth. He fulfills the desire of all who fear him; he also hears their cry and saves them."[82] Wherefore also in Proverbs each one of us is commanded both to fear the Lord and to depart from evil. There it is said: ". . . fear the Lord and turn away from evil. It will be a healing for your flesh and a refreshment for your body."[83]

3. And in the book of Ecclesiasticus, each of the faithful is thus warned against doing evil: "Do no evil and evil will never overtake you. Stay away from wrong and it will turn away from you. Do not sow in the furrows of injustice and

78. Sir 3.26.
79. Job 36.10–12.
80. 1 Pt 4.8.
81. Mt 7.21.
82. Ps 144.18–19 LXX; Ps 145.18–19.
83. Prv 3.7–8.

you will not reap a sevenfold crop."[84] Again in the same book, lest anyone, adding sins to sins, wish to comfort himself vainly with the mercy of God, the salutary teaching comes to our attention in words such as these: "Do not be so confident of forgiveness that you add sin to sin. Do not say, 'His mercy is great' for both mercy and wrath are with him and his anger will rest on sinners."[85] And again the holy Job says, "Does not calamity befall the unrighteous and disaster, the worker of iniquity?"[86] In Proverbs it is written: "The iniquities of the wicked ensnare them, and they are caught in the toils of their sin. They die for lack of discipline and because of their great folly, they are lost."[87]

XXVII. 1. And lest anyone think that some human sins can be hidden from God, let us be instructed by the words of holy Job when he says, "You have numbered my thoughts and none of my sins is hidden from you. You have sealed my iniquities in a bag, you have taken note if I erred unwittingly in anything."[88] Lest anyone indeed think that he will go unpunished if he is not willing to be converted, let him listen carefully to the words of the same holy man who speaks. Let no one since he is wicked trust that he will go unpunished, as many as provoke God to wrath, as if there would be no judgment for them. In Ecclesiasticus, there is a clear salutary admonition to the effect that we may lack neither conversion by which sins are avoided nor entreaty by which past sins can be forgiven. So it is said: "You have sinned, my child! Do so no more but ask forgiveness for your past sins. Flee from sin as from a snake, for if you approach sin, it will bite you; its teeth are lion's teeth and can destroy human lives."[89]

2. But let there not be silence about this: that the impious and sinners, who are not willing to do penance for their

---

84. Sir 7.1–3.
85. Sir 5.5–6.
86. Job 31.3.
87. Prov 5.22–23.
88. Job 14.16–17 LXX. The current translation (New RSV) reads: "For then you would not number my steps, you would not keep watch over my sin; my transgression would be sealed up in a bag and you would cover over my iniquity."
89. Sir 21.1–2.

impiety or iniquity, in the end are to be sentenced to eternal torments, but to those who do penance, my Lord grants mercy. It is just this way in the book of Ecclesiasticus: "For the most High also takes pity on the penitent and will inflict punishment on the impious and sinners."[90] Again, in the same volume, it is said: "Remember that wrath does not delay. Humble yourself to the utmost, for the punishment of the ungodly is fire and worms."[91] Isaiah also says that "Their fire shall not be quenched and their worm shall not die."[92] Again it is set down in Ecclesiasticus: "An assembly of the wicked is like a bundle of tow and their end is a blazing fire. The way of sinners is full of offenses but at its end is the pit of Hades [and darkness and pains.]"[93]

XXVIII. 1. This is the death which those living according to the flesh will receive, as the holy statement of the blessed Paul bears witness when he writes thus: "Consequently, brothers, we are not debtors to the flesh, to live according to the flesh. For if you live according to the flesh, you will die, but if by the spirit, you put to death the deeds of the body, you will live."[94] He follows the deeds of the flesh who either yields to desires of worldly things or, in impiety, prefers to remain captive to them; since the spiritual teaching teaches us nothing other than that when impiety has been rejected, we also put away worldly desires. This is what the teacher of the nations conveys with these words: "For the grace of God has appeared, saving all and training us to reject godless ways and worldly desires and to live temperately, justly and devoutly in this age, as we await the blessed hope, the appearance of the glory of the great God and of our Savior Jesus Christ."[95]

2. Therefore the blessed hope, the certain expectation, the future happiness, belong to those who, rejecting impiety and worldly desires, live soberly and justly and piously in this world. Therefore sobriety and justice and piety must be most

90. Sir 12.7.
91. Sir 7.16–17.
92. Is 66.24.
93. Sir 21.9–10.
94. Rm 8.12–13.
95. Ti 2.11–13.

scrupulously kept by Christians. He keeps sobriety who reconciles his morality and his life. And he lives justly who does no evil to his neighbor and, insofar as he can, offers assistance with good works. He lives piously who neither believes nor says anything wicked about God. Therefore, whoever wants to attain the Kingdom of Heaven, let him live soberly in his own life, be just toward his neighbor, and persevere in piety with regard to God.

XXIX. 1. These things then will be of avail in the future life, if they are a reality in the life of this present world. The blessed Apostle knew and taught this when he ordered that "we live soberly, justly and piously in this life,"[96] teaching that they will receive mercy in the judgment who, before the judgment, have led a just life in this world. The divine Scripture warns us in the book of Ecclesiasticus, when it says, "Before judgment comes, examine yourself; and at the time of scrutiny, you will find forgiveness."[97] Therefore, anyone who desires to find compassion in the sight of God must prepare justice for himself here. That which a person will not have stored away for himself in this present world, he will not have in the time of future retribution. Since this can be shown as much as is necessary by the witness of the divine Scriptures, let us end the first book that, subsequently, we may be able to give a fitting end to what remains of the question.

TO EUTHYMIUS. BOOK II

AM NOT unaware that at the beginning of the earlier book we undertook to treat of the question of the forgiveness of sins in the name of God and with his help, in such a way as to initiate a three-fold division of the discussion. And since we said that with our Lord, who is the true God, there is lacking neither mercy nor justice (which we took care to demonstrate with the manifest witness of the divine Scriptures), hence we said that the truth could more

---

96. Ti 2.12.   97. Sir 18.20.

easily be apparent to those who seek it, to whom God forgives sins, where and when he forgives them. Though I have already acquitted myself of two of the parts of this three-fold division, I am not unaware that I still owe the third. To whom God forgives sins and where he forgives them, how much assistance God has given us from his piety, I think has been sufficiently shown in the former book.

2. It is certain then that forgiveness of sins is not given except to those who are the converted within the Catholic Church. There conversion can be true where true faith is adorned with an accompanying holy way of life and a zeal for good living is polluted with no stain of depraved belief. For a good life is not truthfully so named which is depraved by the vice of perverse belief, nor does the faith of an orthodox believer suffice, if his way of life is befouled by obscene morals and deeds. So, just as the blessed James calls faith without works dead, so Paul in his teaching confirms that everything which is not from faith is sin.

II. 1. Now insofar as the assistance of illumination is given to us by the true light "which illuminates every man coming into this world,"[1] we are going to show when the forgiveness of sins is granted to penitents. A sterile penance will be deprived of the fruit of forgiveness, if the opportunity of the time offered by God is missed. So the blessed Peter says, "The Lord does not delay in his promise, as some regard 'delay,' but he is patient with you, not wishing that any should perish but that all should come to repentance."[2] I beg you, then, dear Euthymius, that it not irk you to consider carefully how much that is weighty there is in the power of the Apostle's words. Nor should it be passed over as unimportant that the blessed Peter for this reason states that God bears patiently because he does not want anyone to perish but that all be converted to penance.

2. For here penance can profit the sinner when God does not hasten to punish the sinner, so that he may grant the forgiveness of sins to the person converted to penance. For if there could be any kind of fruitful penance for the wicked

1. Jn 1.9.   2. 2 Pt 3.9.

after this life, the blessed Peter would not say that God bears patiently because he does not want anyone to perish, namely of those whom "he foreknew and predestined to be conformed to the image of his Son."[3] No one of these perishes. "For who opposes his will?"[4] These are visited freely by the mercy of God before the end of this present life; they are moved for their salvation with a contrite and humbled heart and all by divine gift are converted to penance to which they are divinely predestined by free grace, so that, converted, they may not perish but have life eternal. Without a doubt, these are all whom, according to the proclamation of the blessed Paul, "God wills . . . to be saved and to come to the knowledge of the truth."[5] Because he who has done all the things he wanted wants this, what he wants he always does invincibly. And so that is fulfilled in them which the unchangeable and invincible will of almighty God has, whose will, just as it cannot be changed in its plans, so neither is his power stopped or hindered in its execution; because neither is anyone able justly to censure his justice, nor can anyone stand opposed to his mercy.

3. Whence our Savior reproves the malevolence of the unbelieving city with these words: "Jerusalem, Jerusalem, you who kill the prophets and stone those sent to you, how many times I yearned to gather your children together, as a hen gathers her young under her wings, but you were unwilling."[6] Christ said this to show its evil will by which it tried in vain to resist the invincible divine will, when God's good will neither could be conquered by those whom it deserts nor could not be able to accomplish anything which it wanted. That Jerusalem, insofar as it attained to its will, did not wish its children to be gathered to the Savior, but still he gathered all whom he willed. In this it wanted to resist the omnipotent but was unable to because God who, as it is written, "Whatever the Lord pleases, he does,"[7] converts to himself whomever he wills by a free justification, coming beforehand

3. Rm 8.29.
5. 1 Tm 2.4.
7. Ps 134.6 LXX; Ps 135.6.
4. Rm 9.19.
6. Mt 23.37.

with his gift of superabounding grace on those whom he could justly damn if he wished. Therefore, when the Apostle Peter says that God "is patient, not wishing that any should perish, but that all should come to repentance,"[8] let us not so understand the word 'all' as stated above, as if there is no one who will not do a fitting penance, but we must understand 'all' here as those to whom God gives penance in such a way that he may also give them the gift of perseverance, i.e., those who are converted by the prevenient divine mercy in such a way that by the same subsequent mercy, they will never go back to the serious sins which they have renounced. These are the ones to whom, as Paul says, "God grants ... repentance that leads to knowledge of the truth and that they may return to their senses out of the Devil's snare, where they are entrapped by him, for his will."[9] Anyone who is careful to practice this penance in this life will be able to find the fruit of his penance with God.

III. 1. Further, we read in the book of Wisdom that on the day of judgment, certain ones will receive penance, indeed, but not forgiveness from God. This is the way it is expressed: "Then the righteous will stand with great confidence in the presence of those who have oppressed them and those who make light of their labors. When the unrighteous see them, they will be shaken with dreadful fear and they will be amazed at the unexpected salvation of the righteous. They will speak to one another in repentance and in anguish of spirit they will groan and say, 'These are persons whom we once held in derision and made a byword of reproach—fools that we were! We thought that their lives were madness and that their end was without honor. Why have they been numbered among the children of God? And why is their lot among the saints?'"[10] No one, however, when he reads the statement that the wicked will be amazed at the sudden, unexpected salvation will think that at some time an unexpected salvation is going to be conferred by divine gift on those

8. 2 Pt 3.9.   9. 2 Tm 2.25–26.
10. Wis 5.1–5.

who end the present life in serious sins. He spoke of the unexpected salvation of the just, which, although its giving was despaired of by the wicked, it still remained a hope for the just.

2. Whence blessed David in the text of a psalm sang of the hope of the just and their salvation as one thing, saying, "The salvation of the righteous is from the Lord; he is their refuge in the time of tribulation. The Lord will help them and will rescue them; he will snatch them from the wicked and will save them, because they take refuge in him."[11] Hence it is that the wicked, destined for eternal torments, will say of the just, "These are persons whom we once held in derision and made a byword of reproach—fools that we were! We thought that their lives were madness and that their end was without honor."[12] This is the unhoped for salvation, since they thought that the life of the just was madness; and although they themselves were mad, they believed that they were sane and did not hope for the retribution of divine justice and thus did not make an effort to reform their lives. They delighted to live licentiously here below for a few short days and did not believe that after a little while they would be tortured with eternal punishments.

3. So, when they will see the just in that glory of the children of God concerning which the blessed Paul says, "... [that glory] in which we stand and we boast in the hope of the glory of God,"[13] thus the wicked will be amazed at the glory of the just, i.e., of the children of God, because the just are the children of God. So the wicked, having a repentance that is fruitless because it comes after the end of time and groaning because of anguish of spirit: "Why have they been numbered among the children of God? And why is their lot among the saints?"[14] An unexpected salvation, therefore, i.e., what was not hoped for by the wicked, will immediately be given to the just, not the wicked. For it will not be given to

11. Ps 36.39–40 LXX; Ps 37.39–40.
12. Wis 5.4.
13. Rm 5.2.
14. Wis 5.5.

those who, despairing of it, lead evil lives but to those who, hoping for it well and abstaining from fleshly desires, keep the salutary commands of blessed Peter, who says, "Beloved, I urge you as aliens and sojourners to keep away from worldly desires that wage war against the soul. Maintain good conduct among the Gentiles...."[15] By that same good conduct, the just make of their bodies a living sacrifice, holy, pleasing to God because through their good conduct, they are the very Temple of God. That the faithful are, the Apostle testifies, saying, "Do you not know that you are the Temple of God and that the Spirit of God dwells in you?"[16] Lest this Temple be polluted by evil deeds, not only does he assiduously forewarn but also strongly frightens our spirits saying, "If anyone destroys God's Temple, God will destroy that person, for the Temple of God which you are, is holy. Let no one deceive you."[17]

4. Who, I ask, living an evil life, when he hears from the Apostle that "If anyone destroys God's Temple, God will destroy him," and the foolish human being deceives himself with the very wicked thought, saying, Even if I destroy the Temple of God and live an evil life to the end, I shall be saved. Is not the Apostle speaking about such people because he says, "Let us do evil that good may come of it? Their penalty is what they deserve."[18] Are not these the ones whom Holy Scripture calls unhappy and proclaims that their hope is altogether useless, saying, "Those who despise wisdom and instruction are miserable. Their hope is in vain, their labors are unprofitable, and their works are useless"?[19]

IV. 1. That salvation, therefore, will not be given to the wicked but to the just; at least to those who have been corrected and converted before the end of this life. That salvation will be given to the good, those who have hastened to God's friendship through conversion, not to the wicked who, remaining friends of the world, rightly deserve to be

15. 1 Pt 2.11–12.
17. 1 Cor 3.17–18a.
19. Wis 3.11.

16. 1 Cor 3.16.
18. Rm 3.8.

called, according to the apostolic warning, enemies of God. The blessed James reproves such people in this way: "Adulterers! Do you not know that to be a lover of the world means enmity with God? Therefore whoever wants to be a lover of the world makes himself an enemy of God."[20] Whoever, therefore, drawing away from evil and doing good, does penance for his evil deeds in this life and, converted to God with his whole heart, renounces wicked deeds, that person's hope will not be in vain.

2. On the other hand, he deceives himself in vain, whoever thinks that he will attain life by the broad and wide road; when the Lord commands us to walk on the narrow road and shows us the entrance through the narrow gate by which one arrives at the Kingdom. "Enter through the narrow gate; for the gate is wide and the road broad that leads to destruction and those who enter through it are many. How narrow the gate and constricted the road that leads to life. And those who find it are few."[21] Our road is the present life, in which, if anyone does not obey the word of God, he will not receive the forgiveness of sins; but in wailing and the gnashing of teeth, he will lament his punishment without end; not undeservedly, he will never merit an end to his torment, who for as long a time as he lived here, was unwilling to renounce sin.

V.1. So the Savior forewarns each one of us, saying, "Settle with your opponent quickly while on the way to court with him. Otherwise your opponent will hand you over to the judge, and the judge will hand you over to the guard, and you will be thrown into prison. Amen, I say to you, you will not be released until you have paid the last penny."[22] A person makes the Word of God his enemy, as long as he does those things which the divine Word forbids. To him it is said in the psalm: "For you hate discipline and you cast my words behind you."[23] If anyone on the road, i.e., if anyone in this life, does not quickly consent to this word of God, he will

20. Jas 4.4.
22. Mt 5.25–26.
21. Mt 7.13–14.
23. Ps 49.17 LXX; Ps 50.17.

never have rest again, having been sent into a prison of eternal fire. This adversary is a good one, who continually presses with salutary adversity so that he may expel from us the adversity of death-dealing wickedness. Hence this which divine Scripture in another place exhorts us to, viz., to be converted quickly lest deadly procrastination beget destruction for the procrastinator, not salvation. Therefore, it says, "Do not delay to turn back to the Lord, and do not postpone it from day to day; for suddenly the wrath of the Lord will come upon you and at the time of punishment, you will perish."[24]

2. And so the word of God shows that when the time of vengeance comes, conversion will not then help the evil person evade punishment but avenging wrath will destroy him with the due damnation. For that will be a time, not of remission but of retribution, not of forgiveness but of revenge. This is put off by the divine patience so that the number of the saints can be filled up. The blessed John in the Apocalypse recalls that it is the saints who asked for this vengeance in these words: "How long will it be, holy and true master, before you sit in judgment and avenge our blood on the inhabitants of the earth?"[25]

3. And to teach those who are joined to his company that the time for vengeance is being put off by the highest ordinance, he adds right away, "Each of them was given a white robe and they were told to be patient a little while longer until the number was filled of their fellow servants and brothers...."[26] For the blessed Paul also knew the distance between the present world and the world to come. He knew that only in the present world could the blessing of salvation be acquired but that only in the world to come could a just reward be given to individuals according to the quality of their works, good or wicked. So, when he had repeated the prophetic testimony which God speaks: "In an acceptable time, I heard you, and on the day of salvation, I helped

---

24. Sir 5.7. 25. Rev 6.10.
26. Rev 6.11.

you,"[27] he immediately followed it up by adding, "Behold now is a very acceptable time, now is the day of salvation."[28] But concerning the future, he says, "For we must all appear before the judgment seat of Christ, so that each one may receive recompense according to what he did in the body, whether good or evil."[29]

VI. 1. Therefore, eternal life will be given in the future only to the one to whom forgiveness of sins has been given in this world. Only he will receive the forgiveness of sins here who renounces his sins and hastens to the highest and true God with true conversion of heart. For that will not be a time of forgiveness but of retribution. There mercy will not justify the sinner but justice will distinguish the just and the sinner. This is written in the psalm: "The Lord tests the righteous and the wicked."[30] And, so that he might show that in iniquity lies the destruction, not the salvation, of the soul, he goes on to say, "He who loves iniquity, hates his own soul."[31] Lest they who perdure in iniquity to the end of the present life promise themselves mercy, it is said subsequently concerning God: "On the wicked he will rain coals of fire and sulphur; a scorching wind shall be the portion of their cup. For the Lord is righteous; he loves righteous deeds; the upright shall behold his face."[32]

2. Therefore, whoever, hearing these things, is unwilling to seek the mercy of God through conversion in the present time, will never be able to find it in the future life. The just judge commanded that this be denounced to us by the blessed Apostle James, with the same saying, "For the judgment is merciless to one who has not shown mercy."[33] The order of mercy holds that the mercy which a person is commanded to show to another, he first bestows on himself, as Scripture says, "Have mercy on your soul, pleasing God.[34]

---

27. 2 Cor 6.2; Cf. Is 49.8.   28. 2 Cor 6.2b.
29. 2 Cor 5.10.   30. Ps 10.5 LXX; Ps 11.5.
31. Ibid. The Latin says, "He who loves iniquity hates his own soul." The New RSV text reads, "... his soul hates the lover of violence."
32. Ps 10.6–7 LXX; Ps 11.6–7.
33. Jas 2.13.
34. Sir 30.24.

Hence if anyone does not wish to please God, he refuses mercy to his own soul; and he who is unwilling to have mercy on his own soul in the present world, never will he be able to find mercy with God.

3. "For the judgment is merciless to one who has not shown mercy." And for this reason, he goes on to say, "Mercy triumphs over judgment;"[35] this will happen in that one who now has mercy on his own soul by pleasing God. For the Lord himself says, "Blessed are the merciful for they will be shown mercy."[36] For when the blessed Apostle warns that "everything must be done properly and in order,"[37] so it is also said in the Canticle of Canticles, "Order charity in me."[38] How will he be said to hold the order either of charity or of mercy, he, I do not speak of any other person, but he who refreshes his own body with food, lest he collapse; clothes it, lest it be cold; while it is healthy, he fears, lest it become ill; while it is ill, he is busy about getting cured; with great concern he ceaselessly does what is necessary for his flesh: food, clothing, medicine, and by living an evil life, he seeks destruction for his soul. He feeds his flesh with the necessary foods and destroys his soul with evil deeds. He refuses harmful foods for his flesh and supplies his soul with evil works like deadly poisons. He desires to prolong the life of his flesh which is ended in a few days and procures death for his soul of whose punishment there will be no end.

4. And because of this, he who is convicted of hating his own soul is a cruel enemy of his flesh as well; because, as good acts bring it about that the flesh enjoys heavenly beatitude along with the soul, so evil deeds bring it about that the soul is tortured in eternal flames along with the flesh. He, therefore, is his own most deadly enemy who, living an evil life, does not change his life before it is over.

VII. 1. On the end of this life depends the beginning of that life in which the retribution does not end. So it is aptly said by the Apostle John: "Everyone who hates his brother is a murderer, and you know that no murderer has eternal life

---

35. Jas 2.13.
36. Mt 5.7.
37. 1 Cor 15.40.
38. Sg (Song) 2.4.

remaining in him,"[39] and when holy David says, "He who loves iniquity hates his own soul."[40] If a murderer is one who hates his brother, what is he who, loving iniquity, hates his own soul? And if the one who hates his brother does not have eternal life remaining in him, how will he who ends this life in the love of iniquity and hatred of his own soul be able to attain the forgiveness of sins through which one attains life? Since our God himself clearly shows how each one attains life when he says, "If you wish to enter into life, keep the commandments."[41]

2. He therefore will attain life who keeps the commandments. But who keeps the divine commandments except the one who, converted to God before the end of this present life, has departed from his earlier sins? So the blessed Peter warns us, "Let everyone who calls upon the name of the Lord avoid evil."[42] He said this, knowing that penance is done fruitfully in this world in which forgiveness is given to penitents. Otherwise there will be the penitence of the wicked in the future world, but it will bear no fruit because there will be no conversion of the wicked. They will be sent into the exterior darkness where there will be wailing and the gnashing of teeth.

3. There they will be tortured endlessly, not only with the hellish punishment of soul together with body but also by the very darkness of the will set in evil. Here for such people there will be the evil will itself for a heaping up of punishment, because of which there remains for them torment without end. They now scorn the opportunity offered by the acceptable time and on the day of salvation, they do not seek to be helped by God. God has conveyed this time to us in the words of the prophet, saying, "In an acceptable time, I heard you and on the day of salvation, I helped you."[43] When the blessed Apostle inserted this testimony in his letter, he im-

---

39. 1 Jn 3.15.
40. Ps 10.5 LXX; Ps 11.5. (Same comment as in n.30.)
41. Mt 19.17.
42. 2 Tm 2.19.
43. Is 49.8; Cf. 2 Cor 6.2.

mediately added, "Behold, very acceptable time; behold now is the day of salvation."[44]

4. In another passage, the same Apostle clearly commends this time so that each person who, illumined by the divine gift, carefully reads and adequately understands, does not deceive himself and does not seek some other time for his conversion or forgiveness; knowing that whoever in this life is not willing to seek forgiveness, never will he be able to find it after this life. The blessed Paul, therefore, writing to the Galatians, says this: "Make no mistake. God is not mocked, for a person will reap only what he sows because the one who sows for his flesh will reap corruption from the flesh, but the one who sows for the spirit will reap eternal life from the spirit. Let us not grow tired of doing good, for in due time, we shall reap our harvest, if we do not give up. So then, while we have the opportunity, let us do good to all but especially to those who belong to the family of the faith."[45] What lazy person is not stirred up to the love of good works by these words of the Apostle? Who, straying from God, does not, frightened, seek the right way? Who is not happy to press on with the sowing of seed, when he knows that in the harvest he will not gather in anything other than what he sows?

VIII. 1. Therefore, it is necessary that we pay greater attention to these words of the apostolic proclamation. It is not in vain that he so weightily warns us, saying, "Make no mistake," and then adds, "God is not mocked." Afterwards, he showed that he knew in what matter some erred, saying, "A person will reap only what he sows."[46] Therefore, whoever thinks that he, in the future retribution, will reap what he is not sowing in his works in this life, errs. On the contrary, since the diversity of the sowing and the reaping was obviously to be communicated, so the expert farmer makes the distinction in the following words. Continuing, he says this: "Because the one who sows for his flesh will reap corruption

---

44. 2 Cor 6.2. 45. Gal 6.7–10.
46. Gal 6.7.

from the flesh, but the one who sows for the spirit will reap eternal life from the spirit."[47]

2. This is the error which he forbade in the exordium of this declaration; by which any may think that he is going to reap something different from what he sowed. Anyone who sows in the flesh, from which corruption is reaped, errs who thinks that he will reap eternal life which is reserved for those who sow in the spirit. Following up, the Apostle says, "Let us not grow tired of doing good, for in due time, we shall reap our harvest, if we do not give up." Here he clearly shows that the works of each person are being designated by the word 'seed'. For he said above, "For a person will reap only what he sows." Now he says, "Let us not grow tired of doing good, for in due time, we shall reap our harvest if we do not give up."[48]

3. Truly, the disciple of the Truth and, because of this, outstanding teacher of the nations who, as he taught that justice will not be absent in the retribution for deeds, so made the distinction between the time of sowing and of reaping, i.e., of working and rewarding; lest anyone with inadequate thought, confusing the time for sowing and reaping, either demand the results of the future harvest in the time of sowing or hope that the beginning of a good sowing will be granted him at the time of the harvest and so, the lazy and slothful worker, caught in the nets of his sloth or, what is worse, intent on working on a death-dealing sowing, not rejoice in the harvest but mourn when he then begins to reap the due results of his sowing, when he will no longer be able to change the nature of the evil seed.

4. We must pay closer attention to the fact that in this place three elements in the teaching of the apostolic word are shown, i.e., that we do good and that we do not weary of it and that at the proper time, we shall reap if we do not grow weary. Of these three, two concern the command to work, the third resides in the promise of reward. In two,

47. Gal 6.8.
48. Gal 6.9.

work is indicated for the workers, in the third, the spirit of the laborers is lifted up by the hope of the future harvest. It is usual for the one who hopes for an assured reward for the quality of his work to take more strength from his work. The Apostle therefore enjoins perseverance in the good work, so that whoever delights to rejoice without end in the harvest may not grow weary in the sowing. Hence, according to the saying of the blessed Apostle, it is necessary that he arrive at the joy of the future harvest who in the present time perseveres in the sowing of the good work. Otherwise, he greatly deceives himself, either the one who up until the end of this present life, sowing no seeds of good works, thinks that he will reap good things sometime; or the one who, misled, lacks perseverance in good works and yet hopes for happiness in the giving of rewards. The blessed Apostle bears witness that anyone will receive at the harvest what he has sown with perseverance.

5. Such is that very experienced winnower who will thoroughly cleanse his field so that in the separation of the wheat and the chaff, he is deceived by no secret fraud; nor does he send into the barn the chaff to be thrown in the fire nor put in the flames the grains which are to be assigned to the barn. In the time of the future harvest, good sowers, those, namely who now sow in tears with perseverance, will reap in joy and those who now weep on the way to sowing their seeds, when they come back, they will come in joy, carrying their sheaves.

6. Just as he will be deprived of the joy and the company of the harvesters who, although he sowed good things at some point, did not persevere in sowing good things; neither will he be able to rejoice in the participating in forgiveness or happiness, who, insofar as he enjoys serving and favoring the nocturnal sower, i.e., the Devil, so that up until death, he does not rest from sowing those things which, gathered up by the selection of the harvesting angels and gathered into sheaves by the judgment of the Lord, with unchanging command, are destined for the inextinguishable fire. Because all the just man's good work of the past is ren-

dered void by the defect of subsequent evil, and the reward of iniquity remains, all his work is evil. For the Apostle says that "Each will receive wages in proportion to his labor."[49] That is, the labor in which each one is engaged when he is commanded to go forth from the present world. Hence as the Apostle warns, "While we have the opportunity, let us do good to all, but especially to those who belong to the family of the faith."[50]

IX. 1. In the letter which was written to the Hebrews, not only is conversion in the present time shown to be necessary, but it is commanded as well that one must persevere until the end. For he says, "Take care, brothers, that none of you may have an evil and unfaithful heart so as to forsake the living God. Encourage yourselves daily while it is still 'today' so that none of you may grow hardened by the deceit of sin. We have become partners of Christ if only we hold the beginning of the reality firm until the end."[51] Who, however, would not be frightened by the example of the Apostle himself so that, leaving behind evil works, in penance and conversion, he runs to God and is concerned and fearful that, if the course of perseverance is abandoned, he will become a reprobate.

2. For, all the faithful should consider with what concern the blessed Paul himself ran, with what vigilance he fought, with what severity he chastised his body. Therefore, he says, "Thus I do not run aimlessly; I do not fight as if I were shadowboxing. No, I drive my body and train it, for fear that, after having preached to others, I myself should be disqualified."[52] He said these things, aware that God has spoken through Ezechiel, "When the righteous turns away from his righteousness and commits iniquity, he shall die for it; for the iniquity that he has committed he shall die."[53] Uselessly with vain thoughts does he dream of forgiveness of sins for himself, whoever does not persevere in the commandments of the Lord up until the end of the present life, or whoever

49. 1 Cor 3.8.
51. Heb 3.12–14.
53. Ez 18.26.
50. Gal 6.10.
52. 1 Cor 9.26–27.

does not depart from the most evil pathways before the end of the present life.

3. For it is necessary that every just person work out his salvation in fear and trembling and that every wicked person cease to offer his members to sin as weapons of iniquity. Rather, let him present himself, as it were, a living person from among the dead, and his members as weapons for the justice of God, and cease doing those things whose wages is death, as Paul the Apostle says, "For the wages of sin is death."[54] This death is also called the wrath of God to come which will be inflicted on the wicked and on those who persevere in evil. Whence also John the Baptist inveighs against the Pharisees and Sadduccees so that he touches as well with his reproof Christians who lead evil lives. For he says, "You brood of vipers! Who warned you to flee from the wrath to come? Produce good fruits as evidence of your repentance and do not begin to say to yourselves, 'We have Abraham as our father.' For I tell you, God is able to raise up children to Abraham from these stones. Even now the ax is laid to the roots of the trees. Therefore, every tree that does not produce good fruit will be cut down and thrown into the fire."[55] When the Lord's forerunner said these things, without a doubt he was speaking to the wicked and evil whom he called 'a generation of vipers" because of their likeness to serpentine, i.e., diabolical, works.

4. He showed them by these words what they do in this world, also what they fear in the judgment to come. Commanding that they bring forth fruits worthy of penitence, he shows that human beings can be changed here and that, by the conversion of a repentant heart, they pass from deserving punishment to the reward of the kingdom. Adding, however, that "Every tree that does not produce good fruit will be cut down and thrown into the fire,"[56] he foretold the time of the future judgment, in which to the evil, to those who lead a sinful life until the end, as to trees that bear no fruit,

54. Rm 6.23.
55. Lk 3.7–9.
56. Lk 3.17.

it is not the forgiveness of sins that will mercifully be given but eternal burning that will justly be rendered. Therefore, also he foretells that our Savior will come for the separating of the wheat from the chaff, who, having "his winnowing fan in his hand to clear his threshing floor and to gather the wheat into his barn, but the chaff he will burn with unquenchable fire."[57] So he informs every Christian with this text from the Gospel that, when the separation has been made, he considers what was given to each one with most affectionate generosity at the Savior's first coming and what may be expected for each one in the second coming when just retribution must be rendered.

X. 1. For our Savior and judge himself, who comes now to save, then, however, will come to judge. Now he comes to make the evil good by an affectionate forgiveness, then, however, he will come to separate the evil from the good by a just scrutiny. He points out the benefit of his first coming when he says, "For the Son of Man has come to seek and to save what was lost."[58] He thus indicates the justice to be feared at his second coming: "For the Son of Man will come ... and then he will repay everyone according to his conduct."[59] Once more showing the mercy of his first coming, he says, "For God so loved the world that he gave his only Son, so that everyone who believes in him might not perish but might have eternal life. For God did not send his Son into the world to condemn the world but that the world might be saved through him."[60] But speaking of the judgment of his second coming, he says, "I have much to say about you and to condemn."[61]

2. And in another place: "The word that I spoke, it will condemn him."[62] And in another place: "I judge as I hear and my judgment is just."[63] Again he indicates the benefit of his first coming, in which he, finding no one alive, freely raises the dead, whom thereby he makes just from being sin-

57. Lk 3.17.
58. Lk 19.10.
59. Mt 16.27.
60. Jn 3.16–17.
61. Jn 8.26.
62. Jn 12.48.
63. Jn 5.30.

ners with words such as these: "Amen, Amen, I say to you, the hour is coming and is now here when the dead will hear the voice of the Son of God and those who hear him will live."[64] He subsequently foretells the scrutiny of the second coming in which he is to judge the living and the dead, saying, "Amen, Amen, I say to you that the hour will come in which all who are in the tombs will hear his voice and will come out, those who have done good deeds to the resurrection of life, but those who have done wicked deeds to the resurrection of condemnation."[65]

3. Therefore, the hearing of his voice now gives life to the dead, when he gives the grace of faith to those who do not believe and those whom he finds evil he makes good; affectionately he justifies sinners; mercifully he saves sinners; kindly he makes the blind see. The hearing of his voice the second time, as it will render the crown of justice to the just, so it will assign punishment to the wicked for their iniquity. In the hearing of his first voice, the mercy of the Redeemer has encountered sinners ahead of time; in the hearing of his second voice, the retribution exacted by the judge follows upon the doers of evil. In the first case, it is said to all: "Come to me, all you who labor and are burdened and I will give you rest."[66] In the second, it will be said only to those on the right, "Come, you who are blessed by my Father. Inherit the Kingdom."[67] But to those on the left, it will be said, "Depart from me, you accursed, into the eternal fire."[68]

4. The shepherd's most certain knowledge of merits, by which the sheep will be separated from the goats, is so great that no goat will be placed on the right just as no sheep will be located on the left. Those merits with which people go forth from this life will remain ceaselessly and unchangeably with them in that other life, whether they be good merits which here divine piety has bestowed or bad ones which human wickedness has procured here below. And for this reason, there will be no removal of evil merits although

64. Jn 5.25.
66. Mt 11.28.
68. Mt 25.41.

65. Jn 5.28–29.
67. Mt 25.34.

there will be an advancement for good merits. The former will remain for punishment; the latter will be perfected in glory. Therefore, that is the time in which God, as it is written in the psalm, "... does not deal with us according to our sins, nor repay us according to our iniquities. For as the heavens are high above the earth, so great is his steadfast love toward those who fear him; as far as the east is from the west, so far he removes our transgressions from us."[69]

5. In that judgment, the just judge will give the crown of justice, as the Apostle says, to those who love his coming, but to workers of evil, as the psalm shows, he will give according to their works and according to the evil of their efforts, and he will reward them according to the works of their hands, he will exact retribution of them. For this reason, namely, that the state in which each one goes forth from this life, without a doubt is the state that will be rewarded in the future life; nor will there be any alteration in that just judgment, from corruption to incorruption for the one who remained earlier unchanged in this world, the one who did not go from wickedness to justice and from an evil life to a good life.

XI. 1. So Paul says, "We shall indeed all arise, but we shall not all be changed."[70] Since the blessed Apostle said this, lest the meaning of his words remain uncertain for some, he knew that he had to go on to show the faithful that certain ones, as he said, would be unchanged in the time of the future resurrection. For, if he had said indeed: We shall all arise but we will not be changed, it would be understood that no one would be changed. And again, if he had said: For we shall all rise and we will be changed; just as all are believed to be going to rise, all also would be believed in similar fashion to be going to be changed. Yet when he predicted the future resurrection of all and still did not assert that all would be changed, he was giving us a warning to examine carefully who was to be changed in the resurrection of the coming scrutiny.

69. Ps 102.10–12 LXX; Ps 103.10–12.
70. 1 Cor 15.51.

2. The blessed Paul, unwilling to leave the matter ambiguous, lest the wicked misbehave even more boldly if they were to hear that the gift of a future change would be common to them along with the just, took care to show the gift of this change with the following words: "In an instant, in the blink of an eye, at the last trumpet, for the trumpet will sound, and the dead will be raised incorruptible and we shall be changed."[71] When he says 'we', he shows that those will acquire the gift of change with him, those whom in this world the communion of the Church and of living rightly holds with Paul and his companions. Conveying the nature of the change itself, he says, "For that which is corruptible must clothe itself with incorruptibility and that which is mortal must clothe itself with immortality."[72] In order that the change of a just reward will later follow in these people, now the change of free generosity precedes. Showing this change, the blessed prophet David says, "I have said. Now I begin; this change at the right hand of the Most High."[73]

XII. 1. To those then who in the present life have been changed from evil to good, the reward of future change is promised. Hence it will come about that each one who, converted, has changed his life here for the better, in that reward will also be changed, acquiring the gift of being equal to the angels; something the Savior himself, who is faithful in his words and holy in all his works, promises not to the evil or sinners but only to the just and those who lead good lives. They are not just who do not live good lives and not unjustly will they be punished who, though loving God, scorn his commandments; they love him who keep his commandments as the Lord himself says, "He who loves me, keeps my commandments."[74] They truly love God who obey his precepts, God who can neither be loved unjustly nor can he be justly scorned. These are the ones who, according to

---

71. 1 Cor 15.52.
72. 1 Cor 15.53.
73. Ps 76.10 LXX; Ps 77.10. The new RSV translation is: "And I say, 'It is my grief that the right hand of the Most High has changed.'"
74. Jn 14.15.

the word of God, will be changed and will be equal to the angels of God, made incorruptible, that is, and immortal by the gift of that change. And not only their soul alone will be changed for the better so that it is no longer able to sin, but the flesh as well, which they possessed as corruptible and mortal, will be so changed in the resurrection that it will indeed be what it now is but cannot be either corruptible or mortal such as it is now.

2. And through this, the flesh of both the wicked and the just, which now dies, will be raised. The flesh of the wicked will rise to eternal misery, but that of the just will remain in eternal happiness. And just as the one flesh will rise to torture, so the other will rise to joy. It will be given life for this reason, that it may be tortured with the soul in eternal death; the other will live for this reason, that, together with the soul, it may enjoy the bliss of eternal life. The body of the just, therefore, according to the preaching of the Apostle, "is sown corruptible; it will rise incorruptible. It is sown dishonorable; it will rise glorious. It is sown weak; it will rise powerful. It is sown a material body; it is raised a spiritual body."[75]

3. This then is done in them through grace so that the change brought about by divine gift may begin in them, here, first through justification in which there is a spiritual resurrection and afterwards, in the resurrection of the body, in which the change of the justified is brought to completion, the perfected glorification, remaining for eternity, is not changed. To this end, first the grace of justification, then the grace of glorification changes them so that the glorification itself remains, unchangeable and eternal in them. For here they are changed through the first resurrection by which they are enlightened that they may be converted; by which, that is, they change from death to life, from iniquity to justice, from infidelity to faith, from evil acts to a holy way of life. Therefore, the second death has no power over them.

---

75. 1 Cor 15.42-44.

4. Concerning such people, it is said in the Apocalypse: "Blessed is the one who shares in the first resurrection. The second death has no power over them."[76] Again it is said in the same book: "The victor shall not be harmed by the second death."[77] Therefore, just as the first resurrection is found in conversion of the heart, so the second death is found in eternal punishment. Let every person who does not wish to be condemned by eternal punishment of the second death, hasten here to become a participant of the first resurrection. If any are is changed in the present life by divine fear, they change from an evil life to a good life, they move from death to life and afterwards will be changed from obscurity to glory.

XIII. 1. Just as the most holy David blames the stubbornness of the miserable and unhappy who decline to be changed from evil to good in the time of this life, so he announces the coming punishment of divine retribution, saying, "For them there is no change and they have not feared God."[78] And lest they who were not willing to be changed, vainly promise themselves the forgiveness of sins to be granted when this life has run its course, he then added, "He extended his hand in retribution."[79] The beginning of this retribution comes about when the wicked person, receiving the reward which was required for his error in itself, by a just judgment is allowed to remain in his wickedness; the completion comes when, for these same iniquities, he will be tortured by eternal fire. Nor should this retribution be considered small by which the wicked person, deprived of the light of justice, is permitted to wander in his darkness, prejudged not by blindness of the flesh but of the heart; where this also is relevant to the cumulation of retribution, if the blind person not only is unable to perceive the light but also with pleasure seeks to increase the darkness of his blindness.

2. To such people the Lord says in the psalms, "But my people did not listen to my voice; Israel did not pay atten-

76. Rev 20.6.
78. Ps 54.20 LXX; Ps 55.19.
77. Rev 2.11.
79. Ps 54.21 LXX; Ps 55.20.

tion to me. So I gave them over to their stubborn hearts to follow their own counsels."[80] Concerning such people, the teacher of the nations says, "Therefore, God handed them over to impurity through the lusts of their hearts."[81] And a little later he says, "Therefore, God handed them over to degrading passions."[82] And again: "God handed them over to their undiscerning mind to do what is improper."[83] Therefore, they are first of all handed over to their unjust desires, to be handed over later to suitable punishments. Here they are handed over to deeds that suit them, to be handed over later to fitting punishments. Nor because the evil person delights in sinning should it be thought that he is foreign to the suffering of retribution; since by the very delight in sinning, he is now gravely punished, he who is subject by his own consent to such delight, from which the degree of deserved punishment is increased.

3. By the degree to which what he unjustly enjoys is increased the more, by so much more will the unjust person receive more to be mournful over. If anyone here is unwilling to be converted to God, to be changed from an evil life to striving for a good life, he will not be changed there where, when the just have been blessedly changed, immortality and incorruption are conferred. Accordingly, the evil or sinners, i.e., either those who believe wrongly or those who live evil lives and do not before the end of this present life give up their infidelity or iniquity, in the retribution to come, will be neither immortal nor incorrupt. They will be corrupted but they will not be annihilated. They will die but they will not be extinguished. The power of the dead to feel the torments will perdure forever, where death is not granted to the dead in their pain. There death for those in misery will be the kind in which the soul is not taken from the body of the sufferer but rather stays in the suffering body unendingly for this purpose that it may afflict soul and body together with an eternity of suffering.

80. Ps 80.12–13 LXX; Ps 81.11–12.
81. Rm 1.24.   82. Rm 1.26.
83. Rm 1.28.

4. And to this purpose, the soul will always die together with the body; with which it will endlessly be forced to participate in eternal torments. There the death of soul and body does not die, because the torture of body and soul is not ended. This indeed will be the eternal death of the wicked, that they do not die in the eternal fire and can never at any time be without punishment. Nor can anything be taken away there from the burning body, although the unhappy soul is continually burning in its body; but in order that the whole body does not cease to burn, the whole continues endlessly in the fire with the soul. In that body in which the soul lived justly or wickedly, in the same body it will receive eternal punishment or happiness without end.

XIV. 1. Therefore, it behooves each person, before he finishes the present life, to be converted by the fear of punishment to come, if truly he does not wish to be tortured without end after the end of this life. Wherefore, it is a foolish belief that the unchanged wickedness of evil people in the sight of God is to be forgiven; in his sight the absence of good works will not be permitted to go unpunished. It is not said to anyone who is placed at the left side, to go into eternal fire, because he took away bread from someone who was eating it but because he did not give it to the hungry; nor did he take away the clothes from someone who was clothed but because he did not give clothes; not because he expelled anyone from his own house but because he did not receive one of Christ's least ones into his dwelling. Therefore, if he who did not give his bread to the hungry will go into eternal fire, what will he receive who has taken away someone else's bread? And if he who did not cover the naked with his clothes will be sent into the pool of fire and sulphur, what is he who cruelly steals someone else's clothes going to suffer?

2. And if the greedy possessor of his own property will not have rest, how does the insatiable plunderer of other people's property, if he is unwilling to be converted in this life, vainly promise forgiveness for himself from the just judge afterwards? Let us consider that unhappy rich man once clothed in purple linen, burning in the inextinguishable

flames for no other reason than that, endowed with a deadly evil, he was never willing to share even the crumbs of his meal with poor Lazarus, struggling with continuous hunger. He, condemned to endless torture, continued unworthy of the refreshment of the finger of the poor man rejoicing in eternal peace, as Abraham the Patriarch in his clear response, showed that after this life, the good are not able in any way to cross over to the wicked, nor can the evil at any time change from their punishments to the rest of the blessed. For so he says, "My child, remember that you received what was good during your lifetime while Lazarus likewise received what was bad; but now he is comforted here, whereas you are tormented. Moreover between us and you a great chasm is established to prevent anyone from crossing who might wish to go from our side to yours or from your side to ours."[84]

XV. 1. Accordingly, it is good for us now to do good while it is time for doing; and in order that we may be very rich at the harvest, we must remain neither slothful nor sterile. It is good for each one to apply the remedy of conversion and penance to his wounds, while the one converted can still receive the forgiveness of sins; since the penitence of the time to come will be such that it cannot merit forgiveness. Nor will there then be some who are to do penance, those whom God has predestined to life. What is according to God, sadness, according to the saying of the Apostle, belongs to them in the present time, bringing about a lasting salvation so that in the future a lasting and eternal salvation will be rendered to those who do penance and are converted in this time. But in the future, penance will not be lacking to those who will not have done penance in the present life.

2. Penance of this latter type will not come from God's generosity but will consist in the torture of punishment. In penance of this type, the mourning will be eternal because there will be no fruit for such penance there. There, the evil will not be converted by doing penance; when the wicked

---

84. Lk 16.25–26.

person in his punishment will have penance for this purpose only that he can never at any time lack either penance or punishment. And so that will which here held itself unchangeably wicked until the end, to this purpose it will have penance without end for its crimes, that from then on it can never be converted nor can it ever for eternity lack torment. It is not always penance when the sinner, touched beforehand by the grace of a pitying God, declares his sin by doing penance in such a way that through conversion, he seeks the grace of forgiveness. Otherwise, he is like someone who repents the sins he committed but does not, changed by conversion, run to God, just as someone might be gravely suffering from wounds and does not seek the help of a doctor. He announces the pain he is suffering but does not look for a remedy by which he might be healed. Wherefore, not everyone who confesses his sin, receives forgiveness, because our God does not pay attention only to the words that come from our mouth but rather what we carry about in our heart. Concerning him, the psalm says, "God who tests minds and hearts."[85] And the Savior says, "Why do you call me 'Lord, Lord' but do not do what I command?"[86] And so it is that we read in the Scriptures that certain ones consistently confess their sins in word but just as consistently do not receive the benefit of forgiveness.

3. King Saul, ordered by God to destroy Amalek, incurred sin because he barely kept the precept of God. When the prophet Samuel had come to reprove him, he, terrified, confessed his sin but still did not obtain forgiveness because his heart was not right with God. That confession of sin came from fear; it was from a horror of punishment, not of sin. He did not hate what he had done but feared what he did not want; nor did he blame his guilt in conversion but, momentarily struck with terror of the divine fury, he trembled. King David as well, overcome by the snare of carnal desire, not only committed adultery with the wife of one of his soldiers

---

85. Ps 7.10 LXX; Ps 7.9.
86. Lk 6.46.

but also killed the innocent husband who was not only guilty of no crime of his own but also unaware of his thoroughly dishonored wife.

4. When the prophet Nathan was sent to him by the Lord, he, terrified by the prophet's reproof, exclaimed, I have sinned. And the prophet replied as follows: "Now the Lord has put away your sin; you shall not die."[87] Behold, Saul said, I have sinned. And David said, I have sinned. Since, therefore, in the confession of sin there was one word for both, why was not one forgiveness granted to both? Only because in the similar confession God saw a dissimilar will. He did not pay attention to the sound of the word but made a distinction in the intention of the heart of each one. The one being converted immediately rejected the desire to sin and by doing penance himself punished his own admission; but the other brought forth a confession of his sin verbally but, held tight by the vice of a perverse heart, did not cast away from himself the love of sinning.

XVI. 1. Therefore, the confession of sins avails if the sinner having confessed what evil he had done would do it no longer and by his exertion for good works sought to overcome what he deserved because of past serious sins; so that according to the words of the Apostle: "Wherever sin abounded grace may abound the more."[88] So some, not knowing the power of penance, do not do penance to this end that hoping for the help of divine mercy they are converted; rather in doing penance they commit still worse sins since they despair of the forgiveness of sins. Such was the penance of the traitor Judas which did not win salvation for the penitent but procured destruction for the one who despaired. Finally when he killed himself who was guilty, he bound himself with an even worse chain of evil than he did when he betrayed Christ who was innocent. For the sin of betraying Christ could have been forgiven Judas, if he had been converted while still alive; but his suicide is never forgiven him when dead.

87. 2 Sam 12.13.
88. Rm 5.20.

2. After the betrayal of Christ, therefore, the betrayer had time in which, through that blood which was poured out for the forgiveness of sins, the sin of even Judas himself could be forgiven; since Christ, who dies for sinners, would not have denied to his own betrayer the benefit of forgiveness, if he, by despairing, had not removed from himself the time granted for forgiveness. Therefore, he did not do penance in the right way nor did he permit himself to be the just avenger of his own crime. Therefore, the unjust avenger increased; he did not remove the punishment merited by his crime, who, having killed himself, deprived his killer of the time for conversion. And in this way, because he killed himself, he took away from himself the time for conversion by killing himself. Most miserable Judas, who when he admitted having evilly committed the crime of betrayal, did penance worse than that crime, because he did not seek forgiveness from the bottom of his heart; and so that penance for a grave sin was deemed worse than the sin itself. That sin of betrayal of the Lord later had time in which it could be washed away; but that penance which brought about not conversion, but despair, therefore did not help the penitent but destroyed him because he took away the time for conversion from himself by killing himself and, by his despair, took away forgiveness.

XVII. 1. So greatly avails the opportunity of time granted for the forgiveness of sins! And although it is much more serious to have betrayed Christ than to have murdered any person, still the killers of Christ, any such as are converted in the present life with all their heart, have gained the forgiveness of sins by the blood of Christ himself. But, whoever, I do not say heretics or pagans, concerning whom there is no doubt that they will be punished with eternal fire, by which also a Catholic Christian will be punished if he commits a murder or commits adultery or steals what belongs to others or violates an oath by perjury or does not hesitate to bear false witness and is not converted before the end of this present life, even though he appears to have sinned much less than he who killed Christ; nevertheless, Christ's killer, if he is converted in the present life, will be saved. The Catholic, on the other hand, for the reason that he is not converted in the present life, after the end of this life, will be relegated to torments which have no end.

2. This happens, not because he sinned more than the impious person who killed Christ, but because, recognizing the omnipotence of the good doctor, he came to the healing remedy at the right moment, he will gain eternal life. The other is condemned by eternal death because, despairing of mercy, he did not seek the remedy of salvation from the doctor at the right moment, and thus, even though his sin, when compared to the killing of Christ, is deemed a lesser crime, still he, in that same lesser crime, is much worse because although he did not kill Christ, still his sin was worse than if he killed Christ for this reason, that he ignored the right moment which was granted by divine patience for the forgiveness of sins.

3. Thus it is recognized that there is no forgiveness of sins if penance is not done at this moment; nor is penance in this time of any avail if the forgiveness of sins is despaired of. But in the future time, there is to be no conversion for the wicked and the penance of such people will be endless as well as useless. Just as forgiveness will never be given to them, so their penance will never be ended. For they neglect the time in which penance is fruitfully done by sinners and in which divine pity grants the forgiveness of sins. Because of which the Lord himself in the Apocalypse of John, consoling his faithful and directing the attention of the wicked to the penalty of future punishment, speaks thus: "Let the wicked still act wickedly and the filthy still be filthy. The righteous must still do right and the holy still be holy. Behold, I am coming soon. I bring with me recompense I will give to each according to his deeds. I am the Alpha and the Omega, the first and the last, the beginning and the end. Blessed are they who wash their robes so as to have the right to the tree of life and enter the city through its gates. Outside are the dogs, the sorcerers, the unchaste, the murderers, the idol-worshipers, and all who love and practice deceit."[89]

---

89. Rev 22.11–15.

4. Who, I ask you, can be of such a stiff neck or who is of such an uncircumcised heart and ears, who is not terrified by these words, not prostrated, not converted? Who does not wail? Who does not tremble in his innermost being? Who, frightened by the fear of the judgment of that just judge, does not hasten to conversion that he may find the forgiveness of sins and the grace of everlasting salvation? Woe to the one who before the time of the last winnowing does not hasten to become wheat from chaff! Woe to the one who, before the harvesting angels come to gather the weeds to be burned from the midst of the grain, does not run to be converted from weeds to grain! Nor shall the thoughtful admonition of divine Scripture be scorned which gives us the salutary command both for a rapid conversion and reminds us of the coming wrath of divine vengeance for those who delay. For thus he says, "Do not delay to turn back to the Lord, and do not postpone it from day to day; for suddenly the wrath of the Lord will come upon you and at the time of punishment, you will perish."[90]

XVIII. 1. In order that we may more fully recognize that only the time of this present world is allotted for conversion, let us pay attention to those workers whom the Lord called to his vineyard. Although he called for them at various hours, still at the eleventh hour he ended the call, i.e., just before the end of the day. In those hours at which the call went out for workers are recognized the ages of this world, in which God has called to a good work those whom he converted to himself by a free justification. It is understood that the morning of this day means the world from its beginning until the flood; the hiring at the third hour, from the flood until Abraham; the hiring at the sixth hour, from Abraham to David; from David up until the exile of the people in Babylon, the ninth hour has been completed; then the eleventh hour came in the first coming of Christ, in which he came in humility in mortal flesh, in which he, the immortal one, deigned to be killed for the sin of the world.

2. This then is the final call for workers, something that is

90. Sir 5.7.

going on from now until the end of this present age, i.e., from his coming in humility until his coming in majesty; from his coming in which the good one came to be judged by the evil, in order that in his mercy he might make good out of evil, until his coming in which he will judge justly both the evil and the good; from the coming of pious forgiveness until the coming of just retribution; from the coming in which he freed the souls of the poor from usuries and iniquities until the coming in which he will come to demand his money with interest from those in whom he will find it used up and not doubled by any effort at good works. This is the hour which the blessed John called the last, saying, "Little children, this is the last hour."[91]

3. After the end of this hour, the Lord does not call workers to the vineyard, but he will come to render to each one the reward for his work, as he himself says, "Behold, I am coming soon; I bring with me the recompense."[92] Let each one hope that the denarius of divine reward will be given to him, who, before the "day" of the present age is finished, work in the Lord's vineyard in a praiseworthy fashion. And that work is nothing other than true conversion of the heart; that one is converted to God as is necessary in whom there is, as the Apostle says, "the faith which works through love."[93]

4. That diversity of the hours, although it is worthily understood, as we granted above, as the differentiation of the ages of the world, still we are able, not in any far-fetched way, to see in this diversity of hours also the ages of the individual person. Morning is human infancy until it is finished; then the end of childhood completes the third; the end of adolescence completes the sixth; the end of youth finishes the ninth; maturity takes care of the eleventh; and then old age moving toward the end, marks the sunset of the whole day. Thus in whatever age of the present life, any sinner or evil person will be converted to God with his whole heart, he will immediately receive forgiveness for all his past sins.

---

91. 1 Jn 2.18.   92. Rev 22.12.
93. Gal 5.6.

XIX. 1. Whoever is able to find in the Gospel or to teach that any worker is called into the vineyard[94] *after* the end of the day, that person may worthily hope, and with the greatest certainty preach, that to any wicked person who will *not* have been converted in the present world, the ability to do good works or the grace of forgiveness is to be granted in the time of the world to come. Likewise, whoever shows that to whomever the denarius has been given by the command of the Lord, though not called to work in the Lord's vineyard before the end of the day, he may hope worthily and fittingly that on such a person, though not converted before the end of the present life, the kingdom of heaven may be conferred by the Lord's generosity. If they, whom the pious labor of the day's work in the vineyard has employed, to them alone after the end of the day, he pays the wage of a denarius. As for ourselves, if we wish to receive the denarius of eternal life, let us labor in the present time in the Lord's vineyard. Let us not scorn the voice of the one who hires, if we do not wish to be excluded from the generosity of the one who pays.

2. The one who does not labor in the vineyard before the end of the day, when the day is over, he will not be able to receive the denarius; because [that time] will not be the time when anyone is mercifully called to work in the vineyard but rather when the payment is given for past work. At that time, there will not be a pious hiring but a just payment. That denarius will not be given to the non-worker nor to the one who works outside the vineyard. The non-worker is the Catholic who does not bother doing good works "because faith without works is useless and dead of itself."[95] He works outside the vineyard who, in any heresy, makes an effort at good works but by his false belief denies to himself the effect of salvation. For the blessed Apostle Paul says that "whatever is not from faith is sin."[96] "Without faith it is impossible to please God."[97]

94. Mt 20.1–16.
96. Rm 14.23c.
95. Jas 2.17 or 20.
97. Heb 11.6.

3. Therefore, both deprive themselves of the denarius, both put themselves outside the company of the workers; the one because though within the Lord's vineyard, he was not willing to concern himself with making efforts to work; the other because he worked outside—because before the end of the day, he should have been at work within the Lord's vineyard. And for this reason, the one because he did not do any of the work whereby he could be saved; the other because he did not work there where he could receive the gift of salvation. Thus when the day is ended, the latter is not allowed to enter the vineyard, and the ability to do good works is taken away from the former; because the evil-living Catholic did not have on the wedding garment at the Lord's banquet (something Paul informed the faithful was to be feared, saying, "If, indeed, when we have taken it off, we shall not be found naked"[98]); but the heretic refused to come to the same banquet at the acceptable time.

4. And so, the one will be thrown out and the ability to come in will not be given to the other. Therefore, now is the time for the chaff to be changed into wheat; now is the time for every wicked person to become wheat from weeds if he does not wish to be burned in an eternity of inextinguishable fire. If anyone, rejecting the grace of the present time in which the Lord has deigned to come, not to judge, but to save sinners, believes that he must remain in his iniquities, he will find no mercy in the judgment to come; because at the time of the winnowing, that winnower will not allow the chaff to be mixed with the wheat, just as the divine severity will not grant to the lazy, worthless servant the possession of a talent in the time of reckoning; but, just as he will burn the chaff with inextinguishable fire, so eternal wailing and gnashing of teeth will greet the wicked and lazy servant consigned to darkness. For what does ordering that servant bound hands and feet mean, except that in the hands is shown that the guilt of evil works and in the feet the love of an evil will are to be punished?

---

98. 2 Cor 5.3.

XX. 1. The holy Isaiah, inspired by God, recognized the opportunity available at this time; he never ceases to urge us to conversion with these words: "Seek the Lord while he may be found, call upon him while he is near; let the wicked forsake their way and the unrighteous their thoughts; let them return to the Lord, that he may have mercy on them, and to our God, for he will abundantly pardon."[99] The Lord must be sought *now*, therefore, when he can be found by seekers. He must be called upon *now* while he is near to the one calling. Now the path of impiety, now thoughts of iniquity must be left behind.

2. Now is the necessary conversion of the sinner by which he can shed the guilt of all sin by the blessing of divine forgiveness. Otherwise, he will not see the good things of God in the land of the living, if he, in this land of the dying, will not accept the forgiveness of sins. For our Savior and judge has himself foreordained this, that when he forgives sins, he does so in this land. So he says to the unbelieving Jews, "But that you may know that the Son of Man has authority on earth to forgive sins. . . ."[100] He did not say this because he was not able to forgive, if he wished, the sins of this time to people passing from this earth but in order that human beings might recognize that the time for forgiveness and reward has been unchangeably established by divine decree and that human foolishness would not hope pointlessly to hear what divine truth promises.

3. This is why also to the blessed Peter, i.e., to his Church, he granted the power of binding and loosing on earth that we might know that in the time of this life free mercy is granted in the forgiveness of sins, but in the future, just deserts will be handed out to all according to the nature of our deeds; let us not doubt that now all sins can be forgiven and whatever sins have not been forgiven now will be paid for then. Recognizing this by the revelation of the Holy Spirit, holy David, to whom, as he himself bears witness, God had

---

99. Is 55.6–7.
100. Mt 9.6.

shown the uncertain and hidden corners of his wisdom before he left this world, asks for the forgiveness of sins, saying, "Turn your gaze away from me, that I may smile again, before I depart and am no more."[101] The blessed prophet would not have carefully asked that the forgiveness of sins be given him *before* the end of the present life, if he knew that after this life either there would be penance for anyone or that the forgiveness of sins would then be granted to those doing penance by divine gift.

XXI. 1. Indeed, after this life, although there is a future penance for the wicked, still no forgiveness of sins will be granted them, but the penance itself will increase the punishment. It will contribute to the amassing of eternal torture; where the hardness of the perverse heart, which before the end of the present life will not have been forgotten by a salutary confession, when he will be violently burned without end by the avenging flames, he will be the more gravely punished by regret. For what is worse than to be so torn by a perpetual regret about the past so that the regretful one can never be freed from the torment of the crime committed? Nor will this be considered in a person ending the present life in his evil deeds, that, because his evil deeds seem finished, his torments should also be ended at some time; but let the perversity of his evil will be noted which the evil person loves and holds until the end of the present life, although he unwillingly loses life itself which he lives very badly.

2. The one who does not take care to change his bad will before the end of the present life shows without a doubt that he so loves his own wicked deeds that if he could live here without end, he would wish to remain in his wicked deeds without end. Wherefore no wicked person will be spared because he is unable to fulfill the desires of his evil will; rather, he will be tormented without end because so long as he was able to sin here, he did not stop sinning. And for this reason, there will be no end to the punishment for the evil person

---

101. Ps 38.14 LXX; Ps 39.13.

because before he ended the course of this life, he did not put an end to his serious sins. Although he was unable to prolong his evil life as much as he wished, whoever was unwilling here to be converted while he lived, still he was able to change for the better if he wished it, before he unwillingly ended his evil life, to remain in the evils of Hell without end.

3. That they who end the present life in evil morals and works will be tormented in eternal fire, is up to the justice of the just judge, rendering to each one according to his works. Nor is it an unjust reward by which it is brought about that they never lack punishment, whose will in this life was not willing to forego sin. Such people delight more in sinning than in living; nor do they sin for this reason that they may live forever, but rather they wish to live here forever so that they may never cease sinning while they live.

4. But no one ends the present life safely unless, before he finishes life, he abandons iniquity; lest he then wish uselessly to bemoan his crimes, when he will never be able to avoid torments. Therefore, it is not pointless that in this present world penance is enjoined on all, nor is conversion proclaimed in vain for this life. For here the penance of forgiveness finds fruit, if the sinner, while still alive here, puts aside his affection for sinning. The merciful and just Lord has designated the time of the present world only for the blessing of forgiveness; he is saving the future world for just retribution in which each one will receive reward befitting the quality of his faith and work, retribution that will never end.

XXII. 1. Henceforward, now let every wicked person within the Church repudiate his evil way of life and hasten to grasp the course of a good life so that he can attain eternal life. Now let every impious person put away his wicked view of the faith and not put off returning to the Church. Now let everyone prepare himself to deserve to be on the right side, if he does not wish to share the torments of those on the left side. Now let him trod the path of justice that he may come to the native country in which he will have eternal rest. Now let everyone who angered God with his evil deeds, pass over to a good life by which a kindly God is gained so that he may receive eternal life which God grants to the good without end.

2. Let no one despair of the mercy of God, out of consideration of the atrocious nature of any sin; nor still should anyone remain in his sins on the pretext of hoping for the mercy of God, but let the confidence of the person with hope seek the harbor of penance without faltering in such a way that the humility of the one with hope may drive away the deadly shipwreck of despair. And may he so love God's mercy that, with fear, he also take into consideration his justice. Let him hope that everything can be forgiven him when converted but let him think that nothing is forgiven to the one who is stubborn. In this time, let the wicked person change his life and he will not find punishment. Let him flee guilt and he will receive mercy. For in this time, he receives the blessing of forgiveness when also a change of reward accompanies a change of will. Now everyone who labors and is burdened, let him come to be refreshed to God who calls; now let him take upon himself the light yoke and light burden of the Savior; now let him learn from him because he is meek and humble of heart, if he desires to find rest for his soul; now, turned away, let him hasten to conversion, now let the wicked person depart from iniquity; wandering now, let him return to the way.

3. Now let him who does not wish to suffer misery without end seek the mercy of the Lord. Now let him who does not wish eternal death seek eternal life. Now let him who does not wish to be damned with eternal punishment hurry to confess before the face of God. For now is the time when doing penance bears fruit; now the forgiveness of sins is granted to the one who does penance; now possession of the Kingdom of Heaven in which one lives and rejoices without end is not denied to the converted; where neither does death take life away from the happy nor can sadness take away happiness from the living. In whatever faith and works the end of this life finds any human being, the reward which will have no end will be given to him. Because just as everyone who will not have been converted before the end of the

present life and ends in his sins, will not have peace in the beyond, so everyone who in this time, obeying the divine commandments, will have been converted from his sins, if he will persevere to the end on the right path and a good life within the Catholic Church, this person will be saved.

TO MONIMUS

Introduction

This work too is the product of Fulgentius's second exile in Sardinia c. 517–23. While it is not ranked among the letters, it is not essentially different in form from some of the later letters translated in this volume, lengthy and devoted to doctrinal questions submitted by a correspondent. Monimus is otherwise unknown.

The first and longest section defends the Augustinian view of predestination. God predestines some to eternal blessedness, but he does not predestine others to damnation, in the sense that he predestines them to evil. The latter choose evil (or at least the lesser good) themselves, and God predestines them to punishment for their sins.

The second question reverts to the more familiar Trinitarian discussion in the context of the Eucharist. The Eucharistic sacrifice is offered to the Trinity, not to the Father alone as certain Arians argue. The final and shortest book contests an Arian quibble over the Johannine verse: "The Word was with God." They claimed that what was 'with' God was not 'in' God, and, therefore, the Logos should not be held to be fully divine.

This is the first translation of "To Monimus" into a modern language.

PROLOGUE

GIVE THANKS to the Lord that you do not cease "to bring forth good things" "out of the store of goodness"[1] of your heart, "and an affable tongue, which abounds in a good man,"[2] conveys the purity of your heart. Although this abounds in those to whom God grants a flow of eloquence, still I do not believe that as much is expressed in words as I know is contained in the depths of your heart. Alight with the divine fire, you continuously suffer with us in such a way that even those tribulations which, although they happen to us, still, with the help of the Lord, have been

1. Mt 12.35.
2. Sir 6.5.

overcome, you almost always suffer them for us in such a way that, as often as you go back over these things in your heart, so often are you in some way forced to suffer them. Behold how much good charity has, behold how much praise it possesses before God and humankind, so that, while it is saddened over what happened to the one it loves, more frequently it endures even more by recollection. In addition, there is this, that what charity itself was accustomed to doing, you continuously do for us. But what else is this, except that you are always praying for us to him in whom you love us purely? For charity also intercedes on behalf of those whom it loves, while also it fears those things which are free from risk. But he feared, not with that fear which charity drives out, for "perfect love drives out fear,"[3] but with that fear which one was used to having, not for fear, but for love. Therefore, he is afraid, not with a fear-filled fear, but with a chaste fear. For he does not fear with a fear of sin but with the strength of purity and firmness of virtue. Now you require of me a debt which, with the help of the Lord, I pledge myself to repay quickly. I do not confess this debt as your Virgil recalls about someone, that "he confessed it but denied he could repay";[4] but I affirm that I owe in him, in whom I do not deny that I am able to repay. I pledge myself to do so. For he who gave me the ability to owe is the one who gives me the means to repay. For unless we received from him, not only would we be unable to repay, but not even to owe. For what is it we owe each other except love? As the blessed Paul, saying these things to the faithful, clearly shows: "Owe nothing to anyone, except to love one another."[5] For who admits a debt if he denies receiving? Just by the fact that we say we owe, we immediately show that we have received. For the blessed Apostle says, "What do you possess that you have not received? But if you have received it, why are you boasting as if you did not receive it?"[6]

And in another place, he bears witness: "Because the love

3. 1 Jn 4.18.
5. Rm 13.8.
4. Virgil *Eclogues* 3.24.
6. 1 Cor 4.7.

of God has been poured out into our hearts through the Holy Spirit that has been given to us."[7] Therefore, he who gave us what we owe by paying back will give us the ability to be able to pay back what we owe. He who is the source of the gift is the source of the debt. By his generosity he has deigned to make himself a debtor, not because, in need, he received something from someone, but because, out of his abundance, he has given generously. Having put the half-dead victim on his own mule and handing him over to the inn-keeper to be cared for, leaving the two denarii, he professes himself a debtor in such a way that he may say," If you spend more than what I have given you, I shall repay you on my way back."[8] What does it mean "If you spend more" unless more than what you received from me? For he who spent more, not because he received a commandment but because he was giving an example of charity, professed that he too had received mercy. For he says, "Now in regard to virgins, I have no commandment from the Lord, but I give my opinion as one who by the Lord's mercy is trustworthy."[9] So he won mercy, not only that he might receive what would be asked, but also that he might ask for more. See how Our Lord is—that by giving, he might owe, and the more he gives, the more it does not displease him to be a debtor. To the extent that he gives freely, to that extent is he a debtor. No one can have him as a debtor, except for the fact that he himself deigned by his free generosity to give. Therefore, keep asking him, on my behalf, that he may grant me the ability to repay the debt, he who gave that I might owe the free servitude of charity to you in him.

In order that I might truly confess all to your heart, which is my heart, since, just as from my own heart, I am unable to conceal anything from your heart, this reasoning has brought about in me a delay in repaying the debt. Since I have been forced to respond to the foolishness of some heretic who not only did not hesitate to assail my name with

7. Rm 5.5.
8. Lk 10.35.
9. 1 Cor 7.25.

the reproach of the error of Photinus[10] but also wanted to turn against me even the words of Saints Augustine and Jerome as contrary to my own profession. Now I have deferred introducing his name into the letter, but, without a doubt, you are able to remember it. For when you were there at Carthage with us, his words were brought to me and, if I remember well, also came to your attention; for with you there, I could read nothing which I could not offer for your perusal. Therefore, if the Lord wishes, I shall quickly send these same booklets to your charity. And I do not doubt that you will deign to bear patiently my tardiness in the matter of your debt. Since I know how much you enjoy or how much you yourself always urge us, so that, with the help of the Lord, it does not irk you for us to reply to heretics.

BOOK I

MY DEAR SON, Monimus, your letter shows the delightful sincerity of your spirit and the laudable ardor of your spiritual zeal as much as it seems to condemn with complaining kindness the lateness of our response. As if because of this, I appear to love you less than I ought because I did not make efforts to respond to your questions rapidly.

2. But believe me that as in the charity of Christ, I in no way hold your person as unimportant in my heart, so also my reply was delayed not by my will but by a variety of concerns. On the contrary, among the concerns which I am unwillingly compelled to put up with, I praise your zeal as much as I delight in your charity.

3. For this reason, embracing the holy proposal of your eagerness all the more because like a truly spiritual trader, seeking the profits of the inner person and desiring to increase more and more the income of the heavenly rewards,

---

10. The heretic here is unknown. On Photinus, see letter 8, n. 56.

the first debt you are pressing me for, constantly you amass with questions as interest, in order that our unavoidable tardiness may serve the increase of your profits.

4. Hence, I trust that in the mercy of our God, by which, if there is anything in the work of this investigation and discussion that is not granted to me for my own merits, it will be granted to me on behalf of your desire. Nor will God in any way permit your question to be defrauded of the effect of a solution, he who set you afire spiritually to seek, since the faithful promise will never be made void by him who says, "Ask and you will receive; seek and you will find; knock and the door will be opened to you."[11]

5. The master within, therefore, from whom we receive the help of heavenly teaching, not only opens the secrets of his words to us who seek, but, in order that we may seek, he freely inspires the desire. Because we are unable to hunger for that bread "which comes down from heaven"[12] unless the appetite be given to those who are not hungry by him who deigns to give himself to satisfy the hungry.

6. It is also given to us that, thirsting, we run to the fountain by him who gives himself that we may drink. Therefore, he must be praised in the grace of each gift whether when he awakens us from sleep to seek him or when he gives himself to be found by us who seek. He is never found unless he himself bestirs us to seek him.

II. 1. Going over your writings as my documents to learn from them for how many and for which questions I was in debt to you, I was able to discover two letters that were relevant. One, containing the words of St. Augustine, which he is known to have written among other things in the book, *On the Perfection of Justice*, concerning those who are predestined to death. The other question I seem to have found is immediately attached to it, i.e., "Concerning the sacrifice which certain ones think is offered only to the Father." In the other letter, I found the subject of esquire stated: "What is it

11. Lk 11.19.
12. Jn 6.33.

that the Apostle will be able to pay in addition to the two denarii he received?"

2. When I found only these two letters, I immediately also remembered a third which was not offered to me by the secretary. This was the one containing the question on the Holy Spirit, "Why is the Father asked to send someone to consecrate the sacrifice of the body and blood of the Lord?" These are four questions: three are from your two letters; the fourth I remembered when my memory recalled it.

3. But if perchance there are others which you have sent us for solution and you do not find them either mentioned or resolved in this work, I ask that you do not ascribe it to contempt or distaste but that you patiently attribute it to forgetfulness, especially since I was unable to pass over in silence the one on the Holy Spirit which I recalled (even in a letter not found). But because you have doubtless remembered all (if perchance there are some), let it not be troublesome for you that, if you write back, I will remember. And I hope that insofar as the Lord helps, our answer will follow, if it is sustained by the assistance of your prayer preceding.

III. 1. Seeking an understanding of the first question in the name of him concerning whom it has been written that "the Lord gives wisdom; from his mouth come knowledge and understanding,"[13] I have thought it more fitting and easier that I consider your own words as well as those of the blessed Augustine which you have in your letter, so that, when these have been reread, the purpose as well as the solution of the question may be recognized more easily.

2. While I was reading, you say, the book on the perfection of human justice, rereading the testimony of the prophet in order, after a wary hearing, slowly and carefully I thought over the text where it is said, "There is no one who does good, no, not one."[14] And without any cloud, without any hesitation, the most true interpreter himself declared that such a type of human beings that does not do good has been predestined to death.

13. Prov 2.6.
14. Ps 13.3 LXX; Ps 14.3.

3. And in order that your words be supported by the pronouncement of the aforesaid-holy man, you added the same words which were spoken by the blessed Augustine: "For," you say, "the same most glorious Augustine says, 'For we must suppose the Psalmist here to mean that 'good' which he describes in the context, saying, 'God looked down from heaven upon the children of men to see if there were any that did understand and seek God.'[15] Such good then as this, seeking after God, there was not a man found who pursued it, no, not one; but this was in that class of men which is predestined to destruction. It was upon such that God looked down in his foreknowledge and passed sentence.'"[16]

4. Ending your citation from St. Augustine here and directing the attention of your letter to me, you say that I already knew why you are again urging these views, namely, very often you had urged upon me who resisted that predestination be spoken of in the case not only of the good but also in the case of the evil, while you said that you opted for predestination in the case of the evil, while I, when teaching, had always said that another predestination could be spoken of, to punishment owed but not to doing evil. You too confirm this, as you wrote.

5. You assert that you do not know what I will answer here to maintain my view that, except for death, destruction is not being spoken of here. And you add that in the meantime you have read this and have declared that these people are predestined to destruction as well. Then you admonish me to consider the words of this text and, as a teacher of my disciples and not as a champion of my own ideas, to bring you to a knowledge of what is to follow.

IV. 1. My dear friend, insofar as the Lord grants free grace, I am able to recognize the measure of my own littleness. Placed in his school, under the one Lord and Master, I do not aspire to be called the master or teacher of my brothers. In truth, I always desire to be their fellow disciple.

15. Ps 13.2 LXX; Ps 14.2.
16. Augustine *De perfectione iustitiae hominis* XIII.311. CSEL 42.32. English translation, NPNF, ser. 1, 5.170.

2. So, I do not cease to ask this of that true Lord and Master of ours that he may deign to teach me either through the words of his Scriptures or through the conversations of my brothers and fellow students or also through the interior and sweeter teaching of his inspiration (where without the sounds of words and without written letters, the truth is spoken more sweetly as well as more secretly) teach me those things, which I shall propose and assert in such a way that in my own propositions and assertions, I shall always adhere to the truth (which does not deceive and is not deceived), and I shall always be obedient and agreeable to it.

3. In order that I may be able to obey and agree with the truth, the Truth itself illuminates me, it assists, it confirms; I ask that it, from which I have received the few things I do know, teach me many more things which I do not know. I ask that, with mercy preceding and following, it may teach me whatever I do not know but should know for my salvation. In those things which I know are true, may it preserve me; in the things which as a human being I am mistaken, may it correct me; in those true things about which I am uncertain, may it confirm me. May it snatch me away from the false and the harmful, so that in my thoughts and words it may find what it gives for salvation. May it bring forth from my mouth those things which are from the start pleasing in his sight and that, as such, they be accepted by all the faithful.

V. 1. To the extent, therefore, with Truth itself (which is the true light) "lighting up my darkness"[17] in the study of this question, the ability to understand has been to this point granted to me, I think that in these words of St. Augustine, nothing else is to be accepted, except that he confirms that certain ones are predestined to destruction but to the destruction of punishment, not of sin; not to evil, which they unjustly admit, but to suffering which they will most justly suffer; not to sin, whereby they either do not accept or lose the benefit of the first resurrection but to torment which their own wickedness evilly bears for them and divine justice

---

17. Ps 17.29 LXX; Ps 18.28.

gives as a good reward; not to the first death of the soul in which children are born or into which (as blessed James says) the sinful fall back ("lured and enticed by his own desire"[18]) but to the second death which they must suffer, with the most just judge exacting retribution or those who, before they have received the grace of baptism, pass from this world or those who, "receive the grace of God in vain"[19] after receiving baptism, prefer to be slaves of sin until the end of this present life and do not wish while it is the acceptable time and the day of salvation to be converted from their evil path that they may live. Unaware that God's kindness is leading them to penance, they, according to their hard and impenitent heart, are storing up for themselves wrath on the day of wrath and of the revelation of the just judgment of God.

2. Concerning that death which sinners with their hands and words have been inviting for themselves and thinking it friendly, have fallen away, it is said: "Do not invite death by the error of your life or bring on destruction by the works of your hands; because God did not make death and he does not delight in the death of the living."[20]

3. And in another place, it is said of this death: "Through the Devil's envy, death entered the world and those who belong to his company, experience it."[21] And that we may know that this death is foreign to the work and predestination of God, God himself speaks through the prophet: "Repent and turn away from all your transgressions; otherwise iniquity will be your ruin. Cast away from you all the transgressions that you have committed against me, and get yourselves a new heart and a new spirit! Why will you die, O house of Israel? For I have no pleasure in the death of anyone (says the Lord God). Turn, then, and live."[22] This is the death of impiety, which God did not make, which came into the world through the Devil. In this they who are of his company imitate him.

18. Jas 1.14.
20. Wis 1.12–13.
22. Ez 18.30–32.

19. 2 Cor 6.1.
21. Wis 2.24.

VI. 1. To this one death, which the sinner has invited for himself through the contempt of the divine command by unjustly lusting, God, by justly judging, has added a double death, i.e., the first death consisting in the separation of soul and body, the second, in the eternal torment of soul and body.

2. And through this the first death by which, with the departure of the soul, the flesh alone dies; but the second when the soul returning to the flesh is tortured in the same and with the same flesh in which it sinned. With the one it communicated the death of sin which the goodness of God forbade to the human race, with the same it communicated the death of punishment which divine justice prepared for the sinner.

3. Concerning this death, our Savior says, "And do not be afraid of those who kill the body but cannot kill the soul; rather, be afraid of the one who can destroy both soul and body in Gehenna."[23] Because the evil perish before Gehenna, it is not a divine but a human work. That they are to perish in Gehenna, the justice of God brings this about—God for whom no wickedness of the sinner is pleasing. "He who loves wickedness, hates his own soul."[24] And John says that: "Everyone who commits sin, commits lawlessness, for sin is lawlessness."[25] And through the prophet, God says that "the soul which sins will die."[26] Concerning the Son of God, John says, "You know that he was revealed to take away sins and in him there is no sin."[27]

4. Just as there is no sin in him, so there is no sin from him. And because it is not from him, it is not his work. And what is never in his work was never in his predestination.

VII. 1. Thus the evil are not predestined to that which they do that is evil, "lured and enticed by their own desire,"[28] but to what they justly suffer unwilling. By the name of predestination is not expressed some forced necessity of the

---

23. Mt 10.28.
24. Ps 10.6 LXX; Ps 11.5.
25. 1 Jn 3.4.
26. Ez 18.4.
27. 1 Jn 3.5.
28. Jas 1.14.

human will but the merciful and just eternal order of God's future work is proclaimed. The Church sings to God of "mercy and judgment"[29] of whom this work is in humankind so that by his hidden will, but not by unjust decision, either he gives in advance free mercy to the wretched or he renders due judgment to the unjust.

2. Indeed, either may he mercifully give to the debtor what he could demand if he willed justly or demand justly with interest what is his and render to the wicked debtor what is owed to his evil deeds. And so, may his mercy go before the unworthy one or find him worthy of wrath. For he gives grace freely to the unworthy. By it, the justified impious person is enlightened by the gift of a good will and with the ability to do good so that, with mercy going on before, he may begin to will the good and, with mercy following after, he may be able to carry out what he wills. By predestining, God has prepared each one in that unchangeable will in which he has set in order the future effect of renewing the person so that his will cannot be new in a new work.

VIII. 1. He also gives grace to the worthy in the distribution of eternal rewards so that whether, when the just one piously justifies the impious because the Apostle says of him ". . . that he might be righteous and justify the one who has faith in Jesus,"[30] or, when the pious justly glorifies the just one, "and those he justified he also glorified,"[31] it is the same working of grace which both initiates a person's good merit to justice and consummates it to glory. First, initiating the good will in a person, then helping the same will now begun so that the same will both may be good by divine gift and can overcome evil concupiscence by divine assistance and, with God perfecting it, the very same will is later such that it cannot have evil concupiscence.

2. And so in the present life, with the help of grace, it does not give in to weakness, and in the future life, by the blessing of grace, it does not have weakness. And now, let it

29. Ps 100.1 LXX; Ps 101.1. 30. Rm 3.26.
31. Rm 8.30.

be re-created by the ongoing assistance of medicine; then, let it enjoy the eternal fulness of health. God does these things just as he always had in predestination, then he does by grace just as he had predestined. Therefore, the acknowledgment of predestination itself is made known when Scripture says, "And the will is prepared by the Lord."[32]

3. It is not said to be "prepared" for any other reason except it is said beforehand that it is to be given. "It is prepared" by him through eternal goodness; it is given by the same through undeserved grace. As the Lord himself bears witness in the prophecy of Ezechiel, saying, "A new heart I will give you and a new spirit I will put within you; and I will remove from your body the heart of stone and give you a heart of flesh. I will put my spirit within you and make you follow my statutes and be careful to observe my ordinances."[33] Therefore, God gives a new heart so that we may walk in his justifications which pertain to the beginning of a good will. He also gives that we may observe and do his judgments which pertain to the doing of good works.

IX. 1. Hence we know both the will to do good and the ability to do good come from God. David agrees completely with this, showing that by the command of divine generosity the grace of a good will is granted: "Our steps are made firm by the Lord when he delights in our way."[34] We have no good works in us unless they come from God, and we bear witness that it is done in God, saying, "Show your strength, O God, as you have done for us before."[35] And in another place: "With God we shall do valiantly,"[36] i.e., the work of virtue. So here in the place of the work of virtue, he said "virtue" just as John, for the work of justice, spoke of doing justice. For he says, "The person who acts in righteousness is righteous."[37] Paul also wants us to do the will of God, saying, "May the God of peace, who brought up from the dead the great shepherd of the sheep by the blood of the eternal covenant,

---

32. Prov 8.35.
33. Ez 36.26–27.
34. Ps 36.23 LXX; Ps 37.23.
35. Ps 67.29 LXX; Ps 68.28.
36. Ps 59.14 LXX; Ps 60.12.
37. 1 Jn 3.7.

Jesus our Lord, furnish you with all that is good, that you may do his will."[38]

2. What is doing his will except to do the works which he inspires in us and which his will works in us? This is what we also find in the words of our Redeemer himself when, for the work of the Truth, he speaks of the truth being done. He says the following: "For everyone who does wicked things hates the light and does not come toward the light so that his works might not be exposed. But whoever lives the truth comes to the light, so that works may be clearly seen as done in God."[39]

But we do this in God because it is given to us to do it when God is in us doing it. This is clearly shown in the letter to the Hebrews where, when it is said of God: "May he furnish you with all that is good that you may do his will." There immediately follows: "May he carry out in you what is pleasing to him."[40] Therefore, every work which is done by us in God, God does in us. "For from him and through him and for him are all things."[41] From him come both good will and good works. The teacher of the nations affirms this with these words: "For God is the one who, for his good purpose, works in you both to desire and to work."[42]

3. So, just as Solomon says, "The will is prepared by the Lord,"[43] Paul also asserts that our good works have been prepared by the Lord, i.e., set in order in predestination. Therefore, he says, "For by his grace you have been saved through faith and this is not from you; it is the gift of God. It is not from works so that no one may boast. For we are his handiwork, created in Christ Jesus, for the good works that God has prepared in advance, that we should walk in them."[44] Just as the will by which we will the good has been prepared by God through predestination, so also God has prepared good works that we may walk in them.

38. Heb 13.20–21.
39. Jn 3.20–21.
40. Heb 13.21.
41. Rm 11.36.
42. Phil 2.13.
43. Prov 8.35.
44. Eph 2.8–10.

X. 1. Let us also pay attention to eternal life and the kingdom of heaven prepared by God for the faithful. Christ himself showed that he would say to those on his right, "Come, you who are blessed by my Father. Inherit the kingdom prepared for you from the foundation of the world."[45] But this too is the work of grace. For from grace is given not only a good life to the justified but also eternal life to the glorified. We consider this as proved by the statement of Paul when he says, "For the wages of sin is death, but the gift of God is eternal life in Christ Jesus our Lord."[46]

2. But why is death called "wages" and eternal life, on the other hand, grace, except that the first is paid and the second given? But when God pays it, he punishes the evil deeds of the human sinner, which the human being would never have done, had he not departed from God.

3. When God gives eternal life, the work which he had begun by justifying the impious, he now completes by glorifying the just person. Each of these graces, i.e., both a good life and eternal life are in Christ Jesus, our Lord. "From his fulness we have all received," indeed, "grace in place of grace,"[47] i.e., the grace of eternal glorification for the grace of unowed justification so that the grace of justification destroys all evil merit by unowed blessing and confirms the good merit by continuous assistance to which the grace of glorification is justly rendered in reward.

4. Grace itself, therefore, is not unjustly so named, because not only does God crown his gifts with his gifts but also because the grace of divine reward so abounds there that it incomparably and ineffably exceeds all merit, human will, and work, however good and given by God. Although Paul shows that not only the light for believing in Christ but also the strength to suffer for him is given to us by God when he says, "For to you has been granted for the sake of Christ, not only to believe in him but also to suffer for him,"[48] because each pertains to the grace of the present good life, still he

45. Mt 25.34.
46. Rm 6.23.
47. Jn 1.16.
48. Phil 1.29.

places that grace of the future life ahead of all the sufferings of the present time, saying, ". . . the sufferings of this present time are as nothing compared with the glory to be revealed for us."[49] And in another place: "For this momentary light affliction is producing for us an eternal weight of glory beyond all comparison."[50]

XI. 1. He says that the grace remains not only in the justification of the present life but also in the reward of the life to come, and he asserts that in the goodness of God it abounds in us, i.e., over all the good merits of any human being, saying, ". . . that in the ages to come he might show the immeasurable riches of his grace in his kindness to us in Christ Jesus."[51] Grace, therefore, is a pious remuneration by which God in the present time gives good things to evil people, to those whom he justifies who were unholy that their faith might be considered as justice. Concerning this remuneration David says, "What shall I return to the Lord for all his bounty to me?"[52]

2. Grace is also that just remuneration by which, giving better things to his good people, God is going to glorify the just. And this will be the work of grace. That they may merit this, by coming first, it begins mercifully; but coming afterwards, it guards it. In the Scriptures this grace is also called mercy. Concerning this, David says, "My God in his steadfast love will meet me."[53] And in another place: "Surely goodness and mercy will follow me all the days of my life."[54]

3. He has gone before the sinner that he may become just; he has followed after the just person lest he become impious again. He has gone before the blind man that he may give him the light he did not find; he has come after the person who can see that he may preserve the light which he brought. He has gone before the broken person that he may rise; he has come after the raised person lest he fall. He has gone before, giving the human being a good will; he has

---

49. Rm 8.18.
50. 2 Cor 4.17.
51. Eph 2.7.
52. Ps 115.12 LXX; Ps 116.12.
53. Ps 58.11 LXX; Ps 59.10.
54. Ps 22.6 LXX; Ps 23.6.

come after the person who wills the right thing, accomplishing in him the ability to do good works. This mercy of God in humankind comes after that which, in going before, it granted. And therefore not only does it recall the wanderer to the right path by justifying him but also guards the one walking correctly and gives him help in order that he may attain the gift of eternal glorification.

4. All of these things, i.e., both the beginnings of our call and the increase of justification and the rewards of glorification, God has always had in predestination; because both in the call and in the justification and in the glorification of the saints, he foreknew the future works of his grace. The Apostle attributes all of this to God, saying, "For those he foreknew, he also predestined to be conformed to the image of his Son, so that he might be the first-born among many brothers. And those he predestined he also called; and those he called, he also justified; and those he justified he also glorified."[55]

5. Nevertheless, when we hear at the same time of the justified and the glorified, let us not assign both the work of justification and glorification to the same moment in the present time. For the grace of justification is given in the present time but the grace of glorification is saved as a future grace. The one is of faith, the other of sight. Paul says that now "we walk by faith, not by sight."[56]

What the saints believe now, then they will see. For this reason it is said to the Church: "Hear, daughter, and see." Since faith comes from hearing, the just man living by faith says with trusting faith, "I believe that I shall see the good things of the Lord in the land of the living."[57] This, therefore, is the order of divine redemption and reward in humankind so that, having been justified, he believes now what, having been glorified, he will receive then. For this reason, Paul says, "It is not that I have already taken hold of it or have already attained perfect maturity...."[58]

55. Rm 8.29–30.
56. 2 Cor 5.7.
57. Ps 26.3 LXX; Ps 27.3.
58. Phil 3.12.

XII. 1. Therefore, in this justification, the saints "go out weeping, bearing the seed for sowing," but in that glorification, they "shall come home with shouts of joy, carrying their sheaves."[59] In the former, the householder's workers are at work in the vineyard; but in the latter, the workers will no doubt take possession of the denarius as their reward. God now gives the former so that the unworthy one may now freely receive the beginning of good merit; he keeps the latter set aside for the future by which the worthy one who received the beginning of good merit when he was unworthy is able to receive worthily the reward of good merit. Therefore, when Paul says that "those he justified, he also glorified,"[60] he does not assign both to the present life but by that faith he affirms that which is to be as it were already done, by which faith, the prophet says of God: "Who has made the things that are to be."[61]

2. In the immutability of his plan, ". . . in accord with his favor that he set forth in him, as a plan for the fulness of time, to sum up all things in Christ, in heaven and on earth,"[62] in him from the eternity of his plan, he has already done in predestination whatever he planned to be done at the fitting time by the carrying out of his work.

3. For just as every work of the Creator could not be without a beginning nor could come into being, so that eternal will of his is never subject to change because it does not have a beginning of existence. What has always existed in such a way that it never began to exist is doubtless this way so that what it is, it cannot not be. Therefore, true immutability is worthily called true eternity. In that eternity of his unchangeable will, the Creator is said to have already done what in a mutable creature, to the extent that he had arranged that it is to be done at the proper moment, he thus causes to be properly arranged.

4. And therefore whatever he has promised, we say is already done because we must not doubt about what must

---

59. Ps 125.6 LXX; Ps 126.6.
61. Is 45.11.
60. Rm 8.30.
62. Eph 1.9–10.

come to be. For Abraham our father (as the Apostle says) "did not doubt God's promise in unbelief; later he was empowered by faith and gave glory to God and was fully convinced that what he had promised he was also able to do."[63] Therefore, there is no falseness in God's promises because for the all-powerful there is no problem about doing things. And so the effects of the will are never lacking because the will itself is nothing other than power. Whatever he wills, he can do; he can do as much as he wishes.

5. So it is rightly said of him alone: "He does whatever he pleases."[64] And again: "For you have power to act whenever you choose."[65] So we have said that there is as much power of will there as there is will itself for the power. Since for the one to whom it is subject, when he shall will, he can, willing being nothing other than power.

XIII. 1. Because God is compelled by no necessity to promise something against his will, he is not impeded by any obstacle or adversity so that he end by doing less than he promised or doing it later. Accordingly, he was able, as he willed, to predestine certain ones to glory, certain others to punishment. But those he predestined to glory, he predestined to justice. But those he predestined to punishment, he did not predestine to guilt. A sin could be from God's predestination if it were possible for anyone to sin justly. But no one sins justly, although God justly permits him to sin. Justly is he who deserts God deserted by God. And because a person deserting God sins, God preserves justice by deserting the sinner. What is more just than that he who because of a desire to sin now sins, because desiring to sin, he does harm to himself, he is permitted to do injury to himself by his sin?

2. Therefore, in the saints, God crowns the justice which he has freely given them, freely preserved for them, and freely perfected in them. The wicked, however, he will condemn for their impiety or injustice, which he did not work in them. For in the former, he glorifies his own works; in the

63. Rm 4.20–21.
65. Wis 12.18.
64. Ps 113.11 LXX; Ps 115.3.

latter, he condemns works that are not his own. Therefore, God has predestined this, that which he himself was going to do or that which he was going to bestow. But he has never predestined what he himself was not going to do either through grace or through justice. Accordingly, it seems that what God accomplishes in those in whom he works, whom he freely justifies, must be sought most diligently; and what in the others whom he justly condemns.

3. For the outstanding teacher of the nations says, "But if our wickedness provides proof of God's righteousness, what can we say? Is God unjust, humanly speaking, to inflict his wrath? Of course not!"[66]

He, however, has substituted wrath for condemnation, just as John the Baptist says elsewhere, ". . . But whoever does not believe in the Son, will not see life, but the wrath of God remains upon him."[67] He makes this wrath known to the Pharisees and Sadduccees, with a rebuke, saying, "You brood of vipers! Who warned you to flee from the wrath to come?"[68] The Lord Christ has snatched us from this wrath as Paul has assured us with his truthful proclamation, saying to the Thessalonians, ". . . how you turned to God from idols to serve the living and true God and to await his Son from heaven, whom he raised from the dead, Jesus, who has delivered us from the coming wrath."[69] This wrath, i.e., punishment, which has been prepared for the evil, in another place he calls destruction, saying, "When people are saying 'Peace and Security,' then sudden disaster comes upon them, like labor pains upon a pregnant woman and they will not escape."[70]

XIV. 1. Let us enquire whether God must be believed to have predestined the works of the wicked for which he condemns them just as he is said to have predestined what he crowns in the saints? When we enquire about the cause of the condemnation of the wicked and of the glorification of

---

66. Rm 3.5–6.
68. Mt 3.7.
70. 1 Thes 5.3.

67. Jn 3.36.
69. 1 Thes 1.9–10.

the saints, we do not deny that the former are predestined to punishment or the latter to glory. But whether, just as the good works for which the just will be glorified are believed to be divinely predestined, must the evil works for which the unjust will be punished forever, be believed to be divinely predestined? For it is said in the book of the psalms: "The unjust will be punished and the seed of the impious will perish, but the salvation of the just is from the Lord."[71] Concerning both, our Savior also says, "And those will go off to eternal punishment but the righteous to eternal life."[72]

2. In both, therefore, i.e., in the just and the unjust, I think that there are three things which must be considered: the beginning, the will; the unfolding, the work; the end, reward or punishment. That we may attribute to the just and good God whatever we see in them as just and good; we know that those things in which we find neither goodness nor justice are unworthy of God. And having considered the quality of works, we believe those things which are found to be worthy of and befitting the divine mercy or justice are predestined by God, "the gracious, merciful and righteous Lord."[73]

3. And first we confess that the beginning of the whole of a good will is predestined and given by that eternal Trinity which is the one, sole, and true God. With a free justification, he has given this prepared to humankind, that which he had prepared to be given in eternal predestination. I have shown this preparation of the will above, by the testimony of Holy Scripture, where it is said: "The will is prepared by the Lord."

4. Therefore, the will is prepared by him who mercifully accomplishes in us both the willing and the completion. For the Apostle says, "For God is the one who, for his good purpose, works in you both to desire and to work."[74] God, speaking through the prophet, confirms that it is he who empowers the faithful to do what they do, according to that oracle

---

71. Ps 36.28 LXX; Ps 37.28.
72. Mt 25.46.
73. Ps 111.4 LXX; Ps 112.4.
74. Phil 2.13.

which has been cited by us above, where he says, "[I will] make you follow my statutes and be careful to observe my ordinances."[75] But what is "I will make you follow. . . ." except: all the good you will do is my doing. So he does that we may do. With him at work in us, every good thing we do comes about. Concerning this it is said in Hebrews: "[May he] furnish you with all that is good. . . . May he carry out in you what is pleasing to him."[76]

5. Since it has now been demonstrated that the grace of God is at work in the good will and work of a human being, who would argue that the glory of future reward as well, which will be given to the saints, is not of divine grace? Since whether believing or doing, although the faith is ours and the works are ours, just as the Lord himself says, "Let it be done to you according to your faith." And blessed John proclaims, "And the victory that conquers the world is our faith."[77] Paul also writes as follows: "I give thanks to my God through Jesus Christ for all of you, because your faith is heralded throughout the world."[78] Our Lord himself testifies that the works are ours, saying, "Just so, your light must shine before others, that they may see your good deeds and glorify your heavenly Father."[79] Still, these things when we have them, we do not have them as originating in ourselves but as given by God, as the Apostle says, "We have not received the spirit of the world but the Spirit that is from God, so that we may understand the things freely given us by God."[80] As for whatever he gives us to do, just as we cannot possess anything unless he gives it to us, so we cannot do it, unless he himself does in us what he has granted.

XV. 1. We are in no way permitted, indeed, in a salutary way, we are forbidden, as much in our faith as in our works, to claim anything for ourselves as if it were our own. For the vessel of election says, "What do you possess that you have not received? But if you have received it, why are you

75. Ez 36.27.
77. 1 Jn 5.4.
79. Mt 5.16.

76. Heb 13.21.
78. Rm 1.8.
80. 1 Cor 2.12.

boasting as if you did not receive it?"[81] And in the holy Gospel, the word of the Lord's precursor is "No one can receive anything except what has been given him from heaven."[82] James the Apostle testifies, "All good giving and every perfect gift is from above, coming down from the Father of lights. . . ."[83]

2. What is there that is a more perfect gift than the future glorification of the saints? For this is not yet the moment of the final perfection of the divine gifts (so to speak) since every perfect person is in need of perfecting. For he who said, "Let us then who are 'perfectly mature' adopt this attitude"[84] is the same one who said, "It is not that I have already taken hold of it or have already attained perfect maturity."[85] So he was perfected in the hope of future glorification but was imperfect with the weight of corruption and mortality. "For a perishable body weighs down the soul and this earthly tent burdens the thoughtful mind."[86]

3. He was perfect in the awaiting of the gift; he was imperfect in the weariness of the struggle. He was perfect in that he served the Law of God in his mind; he was imperfect because he served the law of sin in the flesh. He was perfect "longing to depart this life and be with Christ,"[87] but he was imperfect because as long as he was in the body, he was away from the Lord. He was perfect "fully convinced that what (God) promised, he was also able to do;"[88] but he was imperfect because God has not yet done in his saints certain things of all the things which he has promised. For this reason, even all the just people of old (just as the same Apostle says) "though approved because of their faith, did not receive what had been promised. God had foreseen something better for us, so that without us they should not be made perfect."[89]

4. Therefore, just as the earlier saints, though approved

---

81. 1 Cor 4.7.
82. Jn 3.27.
83. Jas 1.17.
84. Phil 3.15.
85. Phil 3.12.
86. Wis 9.15.
87. Phil 1.23.
88. Rm 4.21.
89. Heb 11.39–40.

by the testimony of their faith, were not perfected without the perfecting of those who came after, likewise the saints who came after cannot be perfected without those who went before. Therefore, the gift of perfection will be given to all when the eternal glorification will be given to the saints. Then as the Truth states: "The righteous will shine like the sun in the kingdom of their Father."[90] This gift of perfecting too comes from him from whom is the beginning of the total gift. So it would not be called a gift, if this too were not given by grace.

XVI. 1. For it is the one God who freely both calls the predestined and justifies those called and glorifies those justified. Just as "to justify" is nothing other than to make just, so "to glorify" is nothing other than to make glorious. Accordingly, because God both justifies and glorifies his own, just as it is the work of his grace when he makes people just, so it will be the work of his grace when he will make them glorious. Just as no one can have true justice unless he be justified, so no one can have true glory unless he be glorified.

2. Where true glory comes from, our Savior shows when he reproves the Jews, saying, "How can you believe, when you accept praise from one another and do not seek the glory that comes from the only God?"[91] Paul, having this mind and saying truly, "But we have the mind of Christ,"[92] as he knew true glory is from God, so he confirms that true justice is from God, saying, "That [I may] be found in him, not having any righteousness of my own based on the Law but that which comes through faith in Christ, the righteousness from God, depending on faith. . . ."[93]

3. And although many examples abound by which it is clear that not only the grace of a good will and good works but also the very glorification of the saints are both indeed begun and brought to perfection by God, still I think that those which have been cited by us are enough in any event.

XVII. 1. And so, in order that these pages not go on in-

90. Mt 13.43.
92. 1 Cor 2.16.
91. Jn 5.44.
93. Phil 3.9.

definitely, we must also consider the will, deeds, and reward of the wicked. We need to find out whether a just God has predestined the evil to do that which he is going to punish them for doing. Whether for that reason he justly predestined the wicked to punishment because he foreknew their evil works, albeit future ones, still he did not predestine that they come to be in the future, because he did not cause them to come into being. So, if an origin of sin is being sought, nothing other than pride is found. For Scripture says, "Pride is the beginning of all sin."[94]

2. This had its beginning when the angel rose up against God. Cast down by that rising and wishing through concupiscence (which is the root of all evils) to usurp what was not given him by God, he departed from God and fell. If he had stood firm in him, he would not have fallen. But because of evil concupiscence, by which he lusted to go beyond himself, he became less in himself. Although he was unable to fulfill this concupiscence in deed, still he retained it in his will.

3. Thus he became a punishment unto himself so that a bad will is always a punishment for the wicked person, just as blindness is for the blind person. And a lust for sinning became a torment for the sinner and the rebel. The runaway who flees that undisturbable rest in turn is enslaved to disorder and is justly abandoned by a good Lord whom he abandoned unjustly. Thus it came about that in a persistent disorder of his own making, he would be re-ordered toward himself and in him who lost order in himself, the plan of divine order would not perish. And this is what happened in the human being whom the Devil himself cast down by serpentine cunning. Disobeying the good Lord and consenting to the evil servant, he was unable to attain to the full effect of the evil will because the wickedness itself of the will was not from God. For he would not have had this, if he had not deserted God.

XVIII. 1. Therefore, the good God is the founder of good natures. For "God saw" (as it is written) "everything that he

---

94. Sir 10.13.

made and it was very good."[95] In all that he had made, he made the rational creature better than the rest. So he wanted the greater good to be in the more powerful creature so that no evil would be in the substance of even the least creature. And for this reason, the better-created good would be superior to the least good, over which the highest good (which is not created and by which every changeable good has been created) would justly dominate.

2. By participating in this, it would be blessed, if with humble love, it would serve the highest good. There could not be nor can there be nor will there ever be able to be any other blessedness for the rational creature unless by acknowledging not only the one by whom it was made but also the one by whom it was made rational, it shows greater love for the good Creator than for itself. Nor could there be any reason in it, unless there could be love of the Creator in it because there is nothing else which is the true wisdom or understanding of the rational creature, except the love of the Creator. In the creature, love of the Creator is inversely proportional to love of self.

3. The will of the rational creature cannot be without some kind of love; nor can it love itself in such a way that it does not wish its love to be anchored to something. The creature has been placed in a middle position between the highest good, by whom it was created, and the least good, over which it is set. Assuredly, then, it is necessary either that it lie miserably in the least good or truly and happily rest in the highest good. When swept away by a certain love, either it is lifted up by obedience and well subjected to the good Creator, or it is pressed down by pride so that it evilly dominates over the good creature. For just as it is laid low by pride, so it is raised on high by humility.

4. Our Lord and Master says, "For everyone who exalts himself will be humbled but the one who humbles himself will be exalted."[96] For this reason, it is likewise written: "God

---

95. Gen 1.31.
96. Lk 14.11.

resists the proud but gives grace to the humble."⁹⁷ God does not find the humble to whom he gives grace humble before the grace was given; but, by giving the grace, he makes them humble. God gives this through grace, so that anyone who accepts it becomes humble. Wherefore the only-begotten teacher and giver of holy humility himself says, "Learn from me, for I am meek and humble of heart and you will find rest for yourselves."⁹⁸

5. They have lost this rest who, having rejected humility, have become inflated with pride against their own life and have fallen into death through pride. Concerning such people, it has been said: "You made them fall to ruin."⁹⁹ For God resists such people because he did not bring about the pride in them, through which they justly deserve to remain in sin.

XIX. 1. Accordingly, because pride is the beginning of an evil will which is not from God, it is perfectly clear that the destruction for persons resulting from evil works is not from God, but the destruction of retribution is payment from the just judge for the evil. The evil will does not belong to the best Creator but a just condemnation of the unjust angel and human being does belong to the most just knower. Therefore, God did not predestine the man to an evil will because he was not the one who was going to give it to the human being. For how could God predestine the human being whom he had made in his image to an evil will which he did not make?

2. Therefore, the human being began to sin in the matter by which he departed from God. For it is written that "the beginning of human pride is to forsake the Lord."¹⁰⁰ And in another place: "Indeed those who are far from you will perish; you put an end to those who are false to you."¹⁰¹ Therefore, they who are far from God and are false to him indeed perish by sinning through their evil will which is not from God. God will destroy them by his just judgments as is prop-

---

97. Jas 4.6; 1 Pt 5.5.
99. Ps 72.18 LXX; Ps 73.18.
101. Ps 72.27 LXX; Ps 73.27.

98. Mt 11.19.
100. Sir 10.12.

er to God. For God would not destroy them by his judgment, unless they had perished through their iniquities. For it is written: "How they are destroyed in a moment, swept away utterly by terrors."[102]

3. Falling away from the highest good to the lowest good, this is the proper and voluntary evil of the sinner. By this evil the unjust person destroys himself. And because the depraved person, not God, is the author of this evil, it is totally fitting that eternal destruction in torments is paid to that person who destroyed himself by sin. So he who wished to perish, perishes although he does not perish in the way he wished. Seduced by the pleasure of sins, he perishes in such a way that if it were possible, he would remain forever in his sins, such a person is justly dispatched to the destruction brought about by sin because he has fallen by his own will.

4. But he must not be dispatched without punishment lest the faithful God, in whom there is no iniquity, who is just and holy, if he always left the sinner unpunished in sin, he would be thought to be pleased by the sin. Through Malachy the prophet, God rebukes the view in certain people who say, "All who do evil are good in the sight of the Lord, and he delights in them. . . . Where is the God of justice?"[103] Justly, therefore, does the severity of the judge follow where the evil of the sinner has preceded, because God is the avenger of that thing whose author he is not, i.e., of iniquity, which God can punish but cannot do. For it is written: "Everyone who commits sin commits lawlessness, for sin is lawlessness. You know that he was revealed to take away sins and in him there is no sin. No one who remains in him sins."[104] And again: "A faithful God without deceit, just and upright is he."[105] Therefore, iniquity, because it is not in God, does not come from God.

XX. 1. What is iniquity but evil concupiscence? The Apostle John shows that this does not come from God when he says, "If anyone loves the world, the love of the Father is not

---

102. Ps 72.19 LXX; Ps 73.19.　　103. Mal 2.17.
104. 1 Jn 3.4–6.　　105. Dt 32.4.

in him. For all that is in the world, sensual lust, enticement for the eyes, and a pretentious life, is not from the Father but is from the world."[106] Here, by the word "world" he means "human beings," lovers of this world, who are not therefore to be punished for their love of the world because they love some evil substance, since no substance is evil by nature but because, not holding to the order of loving, when they love the world more than justice, they love God less than they ought to love him.

2. God did not make anything that was out-of-order, nor did he predestine that anything out-of-order come into being, he who commands through the medium of the Apostle, that "everything must be done properly and in order."[107] So also in the sacred texts, it is ordered that charity follow a proper order in order that sin may be avoided. For it is written: "Put my charity in the right order."[108] The Apostle rejoices in this right order, saying, "For even if I am absent in the flesh, yet I am with you in spirit, rejoicing as I observe your good order. . . ."[109] If we take a closer look at the origin of sin, I think that it is nothing else than the inordinate love by a rational creature of the things set in order by God. By deliberately abandoning the order of love, he loses salvation as well. The rational creature was not predestined by God for this. Nor is there any other predestination of his, except the eternal preparation for his future works in which the cause of no one's evil will be able to be found because the origin of sin never proceeded from the will of God.

XXI. 1. For the "Lord is merciful and just"[110] concerning whom it is written in another place: "The Lord God loves mercy and truth."[111] Therefore, in all his works, either a just truth is kept or a pious mercy is given beforehand. Furthermore, since we cannot deny that the human being has been made good by God, if we were to say that he had been predestined by God to some evil work, we would be ascribing to the merciful and just God a work of this kind (which God

---

106. 1 Jn 2.15–16.
107. 1 Cor 14.40.
108. Sg (Song) 2.4.
109. Col 2.5.
110. Ps 114.5 LXX; Ps 115.5.
111. Ps 83.12 LXX; Ps 84.12.

forbid), one in which he is neither merciful nor just. If, since a human being was made by God, he was good in the present work of God in such a way that he would be evil in his predestination, without a doubt, he was to become evil by the work of God, by whom he had been predestined to sin.

2. So it is that this absurdity follows immediately, as it is said, that God, about whom the prophet says, "He made those things which shall come to be,"[112] had within himself the origin of iniquity (which God forbid) if he had predestined a person made by him to be a sinner; for his predestination is a preparation for his works. And just as it is proper for the good God that he be the cause of the entirety of his works, so it is unfitting that the cause of any evil work whatsoever be thought of in him. So let us take note that no reason is given by which a human being should be believed to be predestined by God to sin. For if in those of whom it is said, "Blessed be the God and Father of our Lord Jesus Christ who has blessed us in Christ with every spiritual blessing in the heavens, as he chose [them] in him; before the foundation of the world, that they might be holy and without blemish before him. In love, he predestined [them] for adoption to himself through Jesus Christ, in accord with the favor of his will."[113] If, therefore, the cause of predestination in them is sought, there is no other cause except the free mercy of God alone.

3. He is the one about whom the psalm says, "The Lord is merciful and gracious, slow to anger and abounding in steadfast love. He will not always accuse, nor will he keep his anger forever. He does not deal with us according to our sins nor repay us according to our iniquities. For as the heavens are far above the earth, so great is his steadfast love toward those who fear him. As far as the east is from the west, so far does he remove our transgressions from us. As a father has compassion for his children, so the Lord has compassion for those who fear him."[114] In all of these great, good things

112. Is 45.11.
113. Eph 1.3–5.
114. Ps 102.8–13 LXX; Ps 103.8–13.

which the Lord gives to the wicked, what else is being sung than undeserved mercy? What else other than free piety is being proclaimed? For in this, that "He does not deal with us according to our sins, nor repay us according to our iniquities,"[115] the free justification of the impious is shown forth. And in this that "as a father has compassion for his children, so the Lord has compassion for those who fear him,"[116] the free adoption of children shines through by the same justification by faith. For not as a father has compassion on his children unless becoming our father through grace, he deigned to make us his children. "To those who did accept him, he gave power to become children of God . . ."[117]

XXII. 1. This is the cause of divine predestination in the saints, viz., the preparation for unowed justification and adoption which, because the evil will of the human being did not deserve it, there is no cause for it except only the good will of God. In the case of those who are thought to be predestined not to suffer punishments but to commit sins, when the cause of the predestination itself is sought, I am unable to find what anyone who thinks he can assert such a thing can reply.

2. Is it not, as we rightly say, that the saints are predestined to this, that with God mercifully at work in them, from evil people, they become good, and from impious people, just (which, when we say it, we say it to the glory of God)? Will we not be able to say rightly as well, that the evil are predestined to this, that with God at work in them, albeit not mercifully but at least justly, from being good people, they become evil and from just people, they become impious?

3. Far be it from us and from all Christians that anyone dare to assign to the divine justice the cause of any sin; since he could not be the cause of any evil or impiety except in one who is evil and impious.

4. Therefore, the mercy of God ought to be praised for the fact that people become good from being evil and just

---

115. Ps 102.10 LXX; Ps 103.10.   116. Ps 102.13 LXX; Ps 103.13.
117. Jn 1.12.

from being impious. But that people become evil after being good or wicked after being just, if divine predestination is claimed as the cause, it will be a justice that must be declared defective (God forbid!). And furthermore, justice is not rightly so called if it is proclaimed that it did not find a person guilty and deserving of punishment but made him so. Indeed, the injustice will be greater if God inflicts punishment on the fallen, whom it is claimed he predestined to ruin when he was standing.

XXIII. 1. I seek to know why he could predestine the first man, whom (as it is written) God made right, to sin, i.e., to an evil will, which is the origin of all sin. It must be believed either that God gave an evil will to the person who was not yet a sinner or that he gave it to the sinner as retribution. If he gave this to the person who was not yet a sinner, he (God forbid) was the author of the wickedness because he gave an evil will to a good person. That person sinned and so deserved to be punished with eternal torment.

2. And where is it that "God did not make death"?[118] And that "there is no wickedness in God"?[119] And that "The Lord is righteous; he loves righteous deeds; the upright shall behold his face"?[120] If, however, he did not give the beginning of an evil will to the sinful person but God was making retribution, so that the sin is believed to have begun from the person, then the beginning of the evil will is said to have been paid back by God as by a just judge. But what sin could a person commit who did not have an evil will? No fruit of wickedness could arise unless the root of an evil will brought it forth. "For from the heart" (as the Truth says) "come evil thoughts, murder, adultery, unchastity, theft, false witness, blasphemy. These are what defile a person...."[121]

3. God himself through Jeremiah reproves the evil of the human will in such a way that he teaches that it is foreign to him. For he says, "Yet I planted you as a choice vine.... How then did you turn degenerate and become a wild vine?"[122]

---

118. Wis 1.13.
119. Dt 32.4.
120. Ps 10.8 LXX; Ps 11.7.
121. Mt 15.19–20.
122. Jer 2.21.

He says that the vine is foreign to him not because of some defect in the divine creation but by an aversion of his own will, which is justly blamed because it brought forth bitterness, something God himself did not produce in it. It had the bitterness not from God's predestination, nor from God's work, but from the evil of its will.

4. Because of that bitterness God rebukes it a second time through the prophet mentioned above: "Know and see that it is evil and bitter for you to forsake the Lord your God; the fear of me is not in you."[123] Since, therefore, it is evil and bitter for a person to have left the Lord and not to have in him a fear of God, who is contrary to the truth in such a way that he thinks it comes from a good and kind God about whom it is written: "How good is the God of Israel to the pure of heart"?[124] And that "no one is good but God alone"?[125] Concerning him, the Apostle says, "That in the ages to come he might show the immeasurable riches of his grace in his kindness to us."[126] And concerning his kindness is sung: "Taste and see how sweet is the Lord."[127]

5. And concerning his words, it is proclaimed a second time: "How sweet are your words to my taste, sweeter than honey to my mouth."[128] And again: "The ordinances of the Lord are true and righteous altogether. More to be desired are they than gold, even much fine gold; sweeter also than honey and drippings of the honeycomb."[129] Therefore, who would think that a person has been predestined by a good and kind God either to an evil will by which he abandons the good God or to a bitter recalcitrance by which he does not fear a kind God? Accordingly, it is fitting for the faithful to believe and confess that the good and just God indeed foreknew that people were going to sin because no future thing could be hidden from him (since these things would not come to be if they did not exist in his foreknowledge),

---

123. Jer 2.19.
124. Ps 72.1 LXX; Ps 73.1.
125. Mk 10.18.
126. Eph 2.7.
127. Ps 33.9 LXX; Ps 34.9.
128. Ps 118.103 LXX; Ps 119.103.
129. Ps 18.10 LXX; Ps 19.10.

still that he did not predestine any person to sin because if God did predestine a person to some sin, he would not punish the person for his sins.

6. By the predestination of God, there is prepared either a pious forgiveness of sins or a just punishment for sins. Therefore, God could never predestine a person to this because he had arranged to forbid by his commandment and wash away by his mercy and punish by his justice. Therefore, God has predestined to be punished with endless torment, the wicked who God foreknew would finish this life in sin. Just as the foreknowledge of human iniquity must not be blamed for this punishment, the predestination of the most just vengeance must be praised in such a way that it may be recognized not that a person has been predestined by him to some kind of sin but rather that he has been predestined to punishment because of the merit of his sin.

XXIV. 1. Therefore, God foreknew all human works, whether good or evil, because nothing could be hidden from him, but he predestined only the good works which he foreknew he would do in the children of grace; by his most powerful divinity he foreknew the future evil works of those whom he did not predestine to the kingdom but to destruction, and he arranged it with provident goodness; and because he foreknew not only that he was not going to do the same evil things but also that the person, insofar as he humbly clung to him would not do them either, in this he further showed us the unconquerable power of his foreknowledge because he did not allow the predestination of his justice to be made void even in the case of the evil. Therefore, God, to show that what he foreknew must be paid and what must be given, predestined to punishment those whom he foreknew would depart from him because of the vice of an evil will.

2. And he predestined to the kingdom those whom he foreknew would return to him because of the assistance of prevenient mercy and would remain in him with the help of subsequent mercy. In the case of the latter, keeping mercy, holding justice in the former; giving the latter what he pi-

ously promised, justly giving as retribution to the former as well what he predicted. Thus God did not promise all the things he predicted, although he predicted all the things which he promised. Just as he did not predestine all the things he foreknew, although he foreknew all the things that were predestined.

3. He foreknew human wills good and evil, but he predestined not the evil ones but only the good ones. And although it was not in his predestination that he gave evil to the human will, still it was in his predestination that he would give to the human willing of evil what it deserved. For this reason, as the psalmist bears witness: "The Lord is merciful and just,"[130] he predestined the just to glory, the wicked to punishment. He equally predicted and promised the predestined work of his mercy in those who were to be justified and glorified. But to the wicked, he only predicted, not promised, the predestined work of his justice.

XXV. 1. But if someone asks why God predicted all the things predestined and still did not promise all the predestined things, we answer that it cannot be called a promise unless when it is predicted that something is going to be done, what is done can be of use to the one to whom it is promised. What is promised is always something of a gift but not always something of a judgment, since the gift of what is promised always brings happiness while the severity of a judgment sometimes saddens.

2. As the prophet, fearing something of this sort, pours out his prayer to God: "Do not enter into judgment with your servant, for no one living is righteous before you."[131] For he knew that all would have to be restrained by the equal chain of punishment unless God, in those whom he willed, made mercy surpass judgment. Justification and glorification which do not exist in a human being from a human being, but from God, have been both predicted and promised because they were to be of great benefit to the saints.

130. Ps 114.5 LXX; Ps 115.5.
131. Ps 142.2 LXX; Ps 143.2.

3. But punishment, which for all eternity was to be prejudicial to the impious, was only predicted, not promised. This is more easily demonstrated by divine testimonies. Indeed, in one place in the prophet each is found expressed equally, where God through Isaiah rebukes those who do not serve him with these words: "My servants shall eat but you shall be hungry; my servants shall drink but you shall be thirsty; my servants shall rejoice but you shall be put to shame; my servants shall sing for gladness of heart, but you shall cry out for pain of heart, and shall wail for anguish of spirit."[132] In all these things, whatever has been predicted only, not promised, pertains to the persons of the wicked. Nor should that which because of the merit of wickedness, severity threatens to be inflicted be said to have been promised by the generosity of goodness. If there are things which pertain to the persons of those who serve God, these have been both predicted and promised.

4. This is also the point of the words of our Savior where he says, "And these will go off to eternal punishment but the righteous to eternal life."[133] He predicted and promised the reward which the just would enjoy, but he did not promise but predicted the torments with which the unjust would be punished. Not as he predestined the saints to receive justice, did he predestine the wicked to lose that same justice, because the "merciful and just Lord" could freely deliver from depravity whomever he wished. But he was never the doer of the depravity, because no one was ever depraved except insofar as he went away from God. Nor did God predestine anyone to go away, even though by divine knowledge he foreknew that he would go away.

XXVI. 1. Therefore, God, although he is not the author of evil thoughts, still is the arranger of evil wills, and from the evil deeds of any evil person, he himself does not cease to bring about good. Nor in the very works of the unjust will does he desert the just order of his own works, because this is part of the order itself, that he justly deserts the evil will.

132. Is 65.13–14.
133. Mt 25.46.

He deserts the one going away from him by his own evil works in such a way that the good work of God who permits it is not lacking. There, while also in the unjust will of the sinner, he himself fulfills justice, and from the evil for which he judges the sinner, he himself fulfills justice, and from the evil for which he judges the sinner, blessings in advance to those to whom he wishes.

2. Therefore, in the saints, the Lord is going to perfect what he freely gave them that they might be good. What he foreknew he was going to give, he predestined in the eternal arrangement of his goodness. For this is the predestination of God, viz., the eternal arrangement of the future work of God. He is going to punish in the evil what he did not give in order that they might be evil, nor did he predestine them to any evil since he was not going to give this to them that they might will evilly.

3. And because the perduring wickedness of an evil will must not remain unpunished, he predestined such to destruction because he prepared the torment of a just punishment for such people. This the Lord himself taught in clear words because he showed that what he had prepared was not only a kingdom where the good might rejoice but also an eternal fire where the evil will be tortured. He will say to the good, "Come, you who are blessed by my Father. Inherit the kingdom prepared for you from the foundation of the world."[134] But to the evil he will say, "Depart from me, you accursed, into the eternal fire prepared for the Devil and his angels."[135]

4. See to what the Lord has predestined the wicked and the impious, i.e., to a just torment, not to some unjust work; to punishment, not to guilt; to punishment, not to transgression; to destruction which the wrath or the just judge rendered to sinners, not to destruction by which the wickedness of sinners has provoked the wrath of God against themselves. The proclamation of the blessed Apostle shows this,

---

134. Mt 25.34.
135. Mt 25.41.

he who calls the evil one whom God is going to condemn for eternity vessels of wrath, not of guilt. For he says, "What if God, wishing to show his wrath and make known his power, has endured with much patience the vessels of wrath made for destruction? This was to make known the riches of his glory to the vessels of mercy, which he has prepared previously for glory."[136]

5. I ask you, my dear Monimus, to pay attention carefully to this text of the Apostle. For it is known that the wrath of God cannot be spoken of except in cases where human wickedness is believed to have come first. Nor could God be either ignorant or unjust who could either not recognize the guilt of a sinful human being or inflict the judgment of punishment on one who has not sinned. Also the blessed Paul himself proclaims that proof is provided for the justice of God in human wickedness so that he shows that the wrath of the almighty is not inflicted unjustly. For he says, "But if our wickedness provides proof of God's righteousness, what can we say? Is God unjust, humanly speaking, to inflict his wrath? Of course not! For how else is God to judge the world?"[137]

6. Therefore, a distinction like this made by him between those to be punished and those to be glorified is not a vain one. He calls the former vessels of wrath and the latter vessels of mercy to show that their own wickedness came first just as much in the vessels of wrath as in the vessels of mercy. For such is the true God whose mercy is free and his wrath not unjust; and for this reason he comes before those unworthy whom he justifies by his goodness and finds others worthy of punishment whom he condemns. Let it be very clear that both in the case of vessels of mercy, that they are good not from themselves but from God, and in the case of the vessels of wrath, that they are evil of themselves not because of God. For the Apostle might have been able to name those who he said were vessels of mercy, rather, vessels of justice. But if they were called vessels of justice, perhaps they

---

136. Rm 9.22–23.
137. Rm 3.5–6.

might be thought to have justice of themselves. Now, however, when he speaks of vessels of mercy, without a doubt he did not keep silent about what they were because he clearly shows what was bestowed on them by God.

7. For if they were just of themselves, the Lord would reward them for their works, he would not give them mercy in advance, just as the same Apostle says in another place, "A worker's wage is credited not as a gift but as something due."[138] Therefore, the vessels of mercy have been prepared for an undeserved glory, because they have freely gained mercy. Concerning them, even the same blessed Apostle testifies that he himself is one, saying, "I was once a blasphemer and a persecutor and an arrogant man, but I have been mercifully treated because I acted out of ignorance in my unbelief."[139]

8. This is the work of God in the vessels of mercy, that the deserved destruction not be rendered to blasphemers and persecutors and the arrogant but that the free gift of mercy be given. For God would never reward the vessels of wrath with destruction if a person were not found to have a voluntary sin, because God would not justly inflict his wrath on a sinful person if the person contracted guilt from the predestination of God. But because the person had the cause of his wickedness in his own will, so the blessed Paul asserts that "God with much patience" has put up with "the vessels of wrath, fitted for destruction." Therefore, this wrath has brought about destruction for such vessels because he found in them the desserts for their voluntary wickedness. When would the just Lord have inflicted his wrath on a sinful servant, if the servant has sinned because of the predestination of the Lord?

9. Therefore, God fitted those vessels for that to which he predestined them, i.e., to destruction, indeed to that destruction which Paul announced would come suddenly on the evil, saying, "When people are saying, 'Peace and Securi-

138. Rm 4.4.
139. 1 Tm 1.13.

ty,' then suddenly disaster comes upon them."[140] But if God had predestined such people to sin, the Apostle would have preferred to call them not vessels of wrath but vessels of guilt, and such vessels would be said to be fitted not for destruction but for sin. Now, however, they are called vessels of wrath that it may be shown that in such persons the evil committed by them is not from the predestination of God but that such people are given what they deserve.

XXVII. 1. God does well by rewarding the evil with destruction, although destruction is an evil for them who now are justly deserted and afterwards will be justly tortured. In these people, God begins his judgment with desertion and ends with torture. For in this present time as well in which God deserts the evil ones who go away from him, he does not work in them what displeases him but works through them what pleases him. Afterwards, he is going to give them what they deserve from his justice. They will receive it not because God has made good use of their evil works but because they have badly used the good work of God.

2. Such people God has fitted for destruction as punishment which the just judge by his just predestination has decreed for the sinner. Not to a sin which a person, not from divine predestination but from his own will, has begun by his evil lusting and completed by his evil action. Concupiscence, conceiving, has given birth to sin but the mature sin has begotten death.

3. The wicked, therefore, have not been predestined to the first death of the soul but have been predestined to the second, i.e., to the pool of fire and sulphur. Concerning this the blessed John says, "The Devil who had led them astray was thrown into the pool of fire and sulphur."[141] And in another place: "The Death and Hades were thrown into the pool of fire.... [This pool of fire is the second death.] Anyone whose name was not found written in the book of life was thrown into the pool of fire."[142] Again he says, "But as for

---

140. 1 Thes 5.3. 141. Rev 20.10.
142. Rev 20. 14–15.

cowards, the unfaithful, the depraved, murderers, the unchaste, sorcerers, idol-worshipers and deceivers of every sort, their lot is in the burning pool of fire and sulphur, which is the second death."[143]

4. He calls the second death that which follows from the sentence of the just judge, not that which went before in the evil concupiscence of the sinner. By this death, the Savior indicated certain dead ones, saying, "Let the dead bury their dead."[144] And the Apostle says of the widow: "The one who is self-indulgent is dead while she lives."[145] To the Ephesians he also says, "You were dead in your transgressions and sins in which you once lived following the age of this world, following the ruler of the power of the air, the spirit that is now at work in the disobedient. All of us once lived among them in the desires of our flesh, following the wishes of the flesh and the impulses and we were by nature children of wrath, like the rest. But God who is rich in mercy, because of the great love he had for us, even when we were dead in our transgressions, brought us to life with Christ...."[146] Concerning this death in which a human being had died in his sins, God says, "For I have no pleasure in the death of anyone.... Turn then and live."[147]

5. So how is God believed to have predestined a human being to the death of sin, something which he testifies that he does not want? That death of the one who dies is his own evil way; which, because it is evil, is unknown to God. For it is written: "Do not swerve to the right or to the left; turn your foot away from evil."[148] Therefore, he knows the ways which God made; those which he did not make, he destroys because he does not know them. So it is written: "For the Lord watches over the way of the righteous, but the way of the wicked will perish,"[149] he who knows all things before they come to be, and whose eyes observe the good and the evil in every place, and whose "face is against evildoers, to cut off

143. Rev 21.8.
144. Mt 8.22.
145. 1 Tm 5.6.
146. Eph 2.1–5.
147. Ez 18.32.
148. Prov 4.27.
149. Ps 1.6.

the remembrance of them from the earth."[150] Therefore, he does not know the evil way, not because something in the works of human beings escapes his knowledge, but because he did not bring about the death of the one who dies. He justly rendered death to the dead person.

6. Therefore, the first death of the soul which a person inflicted on himself, is the cause of the second death. And the second death which God has rendered to the person is the punishment for the first death. And because the unjust person has unjustly inflicted the latter on himself, he has justly received the former from the just judge, so that, because in the latter, the short-sighted sinner willingly sows the seed of wickedness, in the former, unwillingly, he reaps the fruit of punishment. "The one who sows for his flesh will reap corruption from the flesh, but the one who sows for the spirit will reap eternal life from the spirit." But "the one who sows for the spirit will reap eternal life from the spirit"[151] has as a gift from God both the harvest and the seed. With Paul as a witness we know this. For he speaks as follows: "The one who supplies seed to the sower and bread for food will supply and multiply your seed and increase the harvest of your righteousness."[152] But the one who sows in the flesh will also reap corruption from the flesh; therefore, he will not rejoice at the harvest because he has as the supplier of the seed, not God, but himself.

7. God has foreknown in the sinners all the future sins of human beings; and, because he did not predestine them to be done, he has justly predestined them to be punished at the judgment. If you think about the very words of St. Augustine which you included in your letter, you will know right away, for afterwards he said, "The good which consists in seeking God, there was no one to do it, there was not even one, but in a race of human beings devoted in advance to destruction."[153] Continuing on, he immediately added: "For

---

150. Ps 33.17 LXX; Ps 34.16.   151. Gal 6.8.
152. 2 Cor 9.10.
153. Augustine *De perfectione iustitiae hominis* XIII.31.

the foreknowledge of God looked down on them and pronounced sentence."[154] To be sure, with these words, he shows sufficiently and clearly that God by his foreknowledge saw human sins, to which he prescribed a sentence by predestination.

8. What else are we to understand by this pronouncement of God's sentence except the torment prepared for the sinner? Justly is he who by divine knowledge is foreknown as a sinner predestined to punishment by divine justice, as is natural, for one who was going to do evil by his own will, evil to which he was not predestined by God. As by his foreknowledge, God saw in him the future unjust work, through the sentence of predestination, he would prepare a just torment for him.

XXVIII. 1. Although you yourself and others like you in their zeal for reading or swiftness of understanding, from this citation from the works of St. Augustine which you have noted in your letter, you very easily know what a Catholic understanding holds concerning those we hear have been predestined to destruction, still lest some are slower and think that this citation alone is not sufficient for them in this question, I have included some things from other books of St. Augustine in which he taught that the sole cause of human wickedness is pride and that human beings are not predestined by God to sin but to damnation. The cause of their not being helped by God is in themselves, not in God.

2. Therefore, in the second book concerning the baptism of children, written to Marcellinus, he says among other things, "Ignorance, therefore, and infirmity are faults which impede the will from moving either for doing a good work or for refraining from an evil one. But that what was hidden may come to light and what was unpleasant may be made agreeable is of the grace of God which helps human wills; and that they are not helped by it has its cause likewise in themselves, not in God, whether they be predestined to condemnation on account of the iniquity of their pride or

---

154. Ibid.

whether they are to be judged and disciplined contrary to this very pride, if they are children of mercy."[155]

3. Here immediately St. Augustine has added the testimony of a prophet, saying, "Accordingly, Jeremiah, after saying, 'I know, O Lord, that the way of human beings is not in their control, but mortals as they walk cannot direct their steps,' immediately adds: 'Correct me, O Lord, but in just measure, not in your anger.'"[156] As if he were to say: I know that it is for my correction that I am too little assisted by you, for my footsteps to be perfectly directed; but you do not in this so deal with me as you do in your anger when you determine to condemn the wicked; but as you do in your judgment whereby you teach your children not to be proud.

4. Accordingly, he says in another place, "And let your ordinances help me."[157] The holy Augustine instructing the above mentioned Marcellinus with this teaching, follows up by saying, "You cannot therefore attribute to God the cause of any human being's guilt, for pride is the cause of all human vices."[158] Pay attention to these words of St. Augustine, I ask, my friend. First, that people are not helped by God, the cause is said to be in themselves, not in God. Then, because of the wickedness of pride they are said to be predestined to be damned, something that pertains to judgment, not predestined to be depraved, something that pertains to sin.

5. Thirdly, also consider that he warns that the reason for human guilt is not to be referred to God. If any wickedness of a sinner is believed to be predestined by God, the cause of the wickedness itself is to be placed in the divine predestination. That such a thought is impious and contrary to the Christian faith, I trust that no Christian can escape. And in another place of the same book, the aforementioned St. Au-

---

155. Augustine *De peccatorum meritis et remissione et de baptismo parvulorum* II.xvii. CSEL 60.99. English translation, NPNF, ser. 1, 5.55.

156. Jer 10.23–24.

157. Ps 118.175 LXX; Ps 119.175 and Augustine *De peccatorum meritis* II.xvii.

158. Ibid.

gustine speaks as follows: "To be lifted up, indeed, to pride, is the result of the human being's own will, not of the work of God; for to such a thing God neither urges us nor helps us."[159]

XXIX. 1. And in order that our statements may be strengthened by even clearer evidence from his words, something else must be set down by us from the book which he wrote, *On the Predestination of the Saints*. Here he showed more clearly that there can be foreknowledge on God's part without predestination but that, on the other hand, there could not be predestination without foreknowledge; and that God foreknew even what he himself did not do, i.e., sins. Therefore in the above-mentioned book, this is the view of the same blessed Augustine: "Predestination cannot exist without foreknowledge, though there can be foreknowledge without predestination. By predestination God indeed foreknew that which he himself was going to do, whence it is said: 'He has made that which shall be.'"[160]

2. Furthermore, he can foreknow even those things which he himself does not do, such as whatever sins there may be. For even though there are certain things that are sins and at the same time punishment for sins, so that it is written: "God delivered them up to a reprobate mind, to do those things which are not fitting,"[161] this is not the sin of God but the judgment of God."[162] I think that in these words of the blessed Augustine, it is clearly shown that God foreknew and predestined his good works, i.e., whether those which pertain to mercy or those which pertain to justice; but the evil works, i.e., sins, he only foreknew but did not predestine, because this is not said to be the work of God but judgment.

3. Therefore, the work of God is not in sin, because it has not been predestined by him that there be a sin. Therefore,

159. Augustine *De peccatorum meritis* II.xix. CSEL 60.103–104. NPNF, ser. 1, 5.57.
160. Is 45.11.
161. Rm 1.28.
162. Augustine *De praedestinatione sanctorum* X.19. PL 44.975. English translation, FOTC 86.241.

it is judgment because what the evil person does without God's acting is not left unpunished.

XXX. 1. You are not unaware that in time past objections were made by certain Gauls to that most excellent work of St. Augustine, which he wrote, *On the Predestination of the Saints* [they objected] that the blessed Augustine in the assertion of divine predestination said that sinners were predestined, not only to judgment, but also to sin. Because Augustine died shortly thereafter, Prosper, a learned and holy man, defended his words with orthodox faith and abundant speech.

2. From among the chapters of the Gauls, we do not cite many lest they seem to make even longer this book which the necessity of the argument forces us to make long, we have brought citations of two responses to be included. The fourteenth objection of the Gauls goes as follows: "Objection: If some do not believe in the message of the Gospel, they do so owing to God's predestination. His decree is such that those who do not accept the faith do so owing to his disposition." Therefore, to this bit of impropriety which is an objection constructed using the words of the blessed Augustine, not from the truth but from malice, Prosper replies with these words: "The unbelief of those who do not believe in the message of the Gospel is in no way produced by God's predestination.

3. God is the author of good, not of evil. And so the object of his predestination always is what is good, whether he renders justice or bestows grace. For 'all the ways of the Lord are mercy and truth.'"[163] Accordingly, the unbelief of unbelievers should not be referred to God's disposition but to his prescience. The infallibility of this prescience, which could not err about their future unbelief, does not entail that they refused to believe of necessity."[164] The fifteenth objection was put in these words: "Prescience and predestination are one and the same thing."

163. Ps 24.10 LXX; Ps 25.10.
164. Prosper *Responsiones ad capitula obiectionum Gallorum* XIV. PL 51.169. English translation, ACW 32.155.

4. To which Prosper responds in this way: "If you make no distinction whatever between God's prescience and his predestination, then you endeavor to attribute to God with regard to evil what must be ascribed to him with regard to what is good. But since what is good must be ascribed to God as to its author and helper and what is evil to the willful wickedness of the rational creature, it is beyond doubt that God both foreknew and predestined at one and the same moment the good that would be done and of which he would be the author or the just punishment which he would render to evil merits; but he only foreknew and did not predestine those actions of which he would not be the author in any way."[165]

5. My friend, we have preferred to include in this book these few things for the present from the books of St. Augustine and from the responses of Prosper for this reason—that all may know what they ought to think about the predestination of the saints and of the impious. And, at the same time, that it be clear that the course of our views fits right in with the words of the same blessed Augustine. Accordingly, since (I believe) we have shown sufficiently that the wicked are predestined, not to sin, but to torment, we must bring this volume to a conclusion, so that the distinctive flavor of the books may renew the interest of the reader for considering the discussion of other questions more attentively.

BOOK II

HE TEXT ABOVE (insofar as the Lord has deigned to aid our littleness) contains, I think, dear Monimus, enough of the question concerning the diversity of predestination of the just, that is, and the wicked—i.e., about those whom the free mercy of God, going before and justifying, has converted and is going to glorify those

---

165. Prosper *Responsiones ad capitula* XV. PL 51.170. ACW 32.156.

converted, and about those whom the just severity of God abandons in their sins to be punished by damnation—the text above has treated it at length and resolved it. In such a way that many, although they are accustomed to be swayed not lightly in this matter, can easily be instructed by both the testimonies of the divine books and informed by the books of St.Augustine and the responses of Prosper, a most learned man, in which they recognize that the predestination of God is nothing other than the preparation of his works which he foreknew he would do in his eternal arrangement either mercifully or justly. In sins neither is mercy found nor justice, and, therefore, every evil will of the wicked, by which they sin, though foreknown by God, still has not been predestined by God, since they were not going to have the evil will itself in any other way except because they were going to depart from God.

2. Nor did God predestine this departure of a human being from himself, since the sole voluntary cause of the departure itself was the aversion of the sinner. Since this future departure was not hidden from God in his eternal foreknowledge, [the sinner] found prepared for him the punishment of a just retribution.

II. 1. Now therefore, let the thrust of our discussion be directed to the investigation of remaining questions, with the Lord leading us. You state that several people have asked you questions concerning the sacrifice of the body and blood of Christ, which some think is offered to the Father only. This is, you assert, the prize question, as it were, of heretics. But there is nothing new in this, that heretics, deprived of the light of truth, think that they are going to overcome the truth with their propositions, by which they are most easily overcome. "Their glory is in their shame, their minds are occupied with earthly things."[1]

2. Seeking this, heretics seem to propose these things as if, in their own eyes, they were master-strokes and unanswered, so that they do not see the confusion which hangs

---

1. Phil 3.19.

over them. But when they are overcome by the truth, this is fulfilled in them, so that they are confounded by the very thing in which they glory. Therefore, it is no marvel, if they, whom, blinded by their own malice (as it is written), the truth itself (which is the true light) has deserted and the darkness of vile error has surrounded the clouded gaze of their perverse heart, impiously strive to break up the inseparable Trinity which they do not hesitate to proclaim diverse with differences of substance, consequently with unequal duty of honor.

3. And since they are convicted of sinning in wisdom itself, the word of that very wisdom is fulfilled in them, so that while they are sinning in it, they admit the sin of impiety into their souls; for thus says wisdom itself: "Those who miss me injure themselves; all who hate me love death."[2] For how do they not hate the Son of God whom by their words they are not able to deny is the only-begotten but with thoughtless perversity distinguish him from the nature of the Father? Or how do they not act impiously against their own souls who neither are in agreement that the only begotten Son of God, indeed true God, is glorified with the Father nor permit him to be equally honored in one and the same sacrifice?

4. Responding briefly to them, with the help of God, (to the extent the sequence of this work allows) by way of preface, we ask this question: Tell us whether God gave this faith to his Church by which our father Abraham, by believing, pleased God and in which he received all the nations of the earth to be blessed in his seed? Or do they profess that some other norm of religion has been divinely handed down to them so that they think that the faith of the patriarchs and prophets must be repudiated? And although they are regarded as in every way foreign to this faith (as the truth will demonstrate) still they claim that it has been given to the Church and they contend that it remains inviolate with them.

---

2. Prov 8.36.

III. 1. Therefore, while the question of sacrifice is controverted between ourselves and them, we must have recourse to those fathers whom God has glorified like lights in the world to be guides for our instruction in the true faith. He has deigned to show that their faith has been inspired by him so that he most clearly calls himself their God, saying, "I am the God of Abraham and the God of Isaac and the God of Jacob. This is my name forever; and this my title for all generations."[3]

2. While we say that the sacrifice is offered not to the Father alone, but at the same time the one sacrifice is offered to the Father and the Son, they think the immolation is made to that Father alone. Let us seek the evidence of the true immolation that is pleasing to God in the sacrifice of the patriarchs. With it our series of types must begin [with them] because in their seed is the promised future blessing of all nations, as Paul says, "Now the promises were made to Abraham and to his descendant." It does not say, 'and to his descendants' as referring to many but as referring to one. "And to your descendant, who is Christ."[4] And again: "that the blessing of Abraham might be extended to the Gentiles through Christ Jesus, so that we might receive the promise of the Spirit through faith."[5]

3. Therefore, let it be altogether verified that they are sharers in the divine blessing and participants in the spiritual grace who, it is apparent, are followers of the faith of Abraham in sacrifice. In the book of Genesis we read: "Then the Lord appeared to Abraham and said, 'To your offspring I will give this land.' So he built there an altar to the Lord who had appeared to him. From there he moved on to the hill country on the east of Bethel and pitched his tent with Bethel on the west ... and there he built an altar to the Lord God and invoked the name of the Lord God."[6] Now let the heretics choose what they want, that either they confess that the Father was seen by Abraham or certainly agree that

---

3. Ex 3.15.
4. Gal 3.16.
5. Gal 3.14.
6. Gen 12.7–8.

the altar was built by Abraham to the Son. The reading of the Old Testament frequently indicates that the altar was built for no other reason than that sacrifice must be offered to God.

4. Moses speaks concerning Noah, the just man in this way: "And Noah built an altar to God," and, as if he were being questioned as to why the just man built that altar, he added, "And he took of every clean animal and of every clean bird and offered burnt offerings on the altar."[7] It is clear, therefore, that the holy Abraham, the faithful friend of God and father of the gentile faithful, built an altar to God who was seen by him for this reason, that he might be able to offer to him the sacrifice of a fitting immolation.

5. But lest, while he is said to have invoked in the name of the Lord God, anyone think that another God was being invoked in the name of another God, since there was nothing else in the invocation in the name of the Lord God than an invoking of the name of the Lord God, subsequently, this also the divine Scriptures took care to show with a clear proof. For a bit later, it is said: "Now Abram was very rich in livestock, in silver and gold. He journeyed on by stages from the Negeb as far as Bethel, to the place where his tent had been at the beginning, between Bethel and Ai, to the place where he had made an altar at the first; and there Abram called on the name of the Lord."[8]

6. Therefore, we recognize that to invoke in the name of the Lord God is the same as to invoke the name of the Lord God. So let the heretics say whether they think that Abraham built his altar to the Father or to the Son? Because he invoked the name of the one for whom he built the altar. He built an altar to none except to the God who was seen by him, whom the heretics are accustomed to call the Son. Striving to teach that the substance of the Father and the Son are different, they think that all the visible forms of corporeal things (to which the omnipotent Godhead, the Lord

---

7. Gen 8.20.
8. Gen 13.2–4.

of every creature, adapted himself to let himself become known to human beings, just as he wished and knew was fitting to times, places, and persons) are to be assigned to the Son only. From this they assert that the Son is unequal to and different from the Father, that his nature could have been capable of changing forms.

7. And just as if the more his divinity by nature was visible, the more he did not spurn to show himself in visible things in order to form human minds. But it is not for us here in this work to discuss this matter since the point of the present question requires only this, that because the holy Abraham is known to have sacrificed to that God, whom divine Scripture testifies was seen by him, either let them say that the Father was seen by Abraham, or let them agree that Abraham sacrificed to the Son. Let the assertion of a nefarious diversity be struck down by either one as by a sharp two-edged sword; because, if they say that God the Father was seen by Abraham, so that they may claim that the sacrifice was offered to him alone, because it is asserted that he was seen, the as-it-were invisible Father will not have to be given priority over the visible Son; if, however, the Son was seen, and the holy patriarch offered the sacrifice to him, the Son is not to be placed below the Father in anything. For Abraham would not have offered a sacrifice to him if he believed that any other was more powerful than he.

8. And so those people who think that our faith is going to be shaken by the blow from this question, in both cases it is necessary that they recognize the falsity of their own belief. And would that they, having recognized this, would walk away from it, and now, having been humbled and made peaceable in a salutary way, would return to the true faith (which they stupidly attack in rebellion)! For Abraham who built an altar not to another God, but to him who had been seen by him, so that heretics might be confounded according to that knowledge, either saw the Father or sacrificed to the Son.

IV. 1. This God, who was seen by Abraham and to whom Abraham, not to another, built an altar to offer sacrifice,

Isaac also saw and, holding on to the faith of his father, constructed an altar to him. For it is written concerning Isaac (the book of Genesis contains this): "From there he went up to Beersheba. And that very night the Lord appeared to him and said, 'I am the God of your father Abraham; do not be afraid, for I am with you and will bless you and make your offspring numerous for my servant Abraham's sake.' So he built an altar there and called on the name of the Lord."[9]

2. Without a doubt of his Lord the one who was seen by him promised the assistance of his presence and the gift of blessing and growth by multiplying his seed. Jacob too is known to have built an altar, not to another God, but to the one who was seen by him. And what is more, he did not receive it of his own accord, but, obeying divine commandments, he fulfilled it. Holy Scripture bears witness to this in these words: "God said to Jacob. 'Arise, go up to Bethel and settle there. Make an altar there to the God who appeared to you when you fled from your brother Esau.'"[10] And following this, it is said: "Jacob came to Luz (that is, Bethel) which is in the land of Chanaan, he and all the people who were with him and there he built an altar and called the place El-Bethel, because it was there that God had revealed himself to him when he fled from his brother."[11]

3. Behold in the mouth of two or three witnesses, the word of our faith stands; behold, the oblation of the Catholic Church is in complete agreement with the sacrifice of the friends of God, the Church which thus sacrifices to the Father in such a way that at the same time it sacrifices to the whole Trinity; since the holy patriarchs too knew that the sacrifice which they were ordered to offer to the Son, they were providing at the same time to the Father and the Son with due respect. Therefore, the divine command was given to them to build an altar to the Son, not because they were not to sacrifice to the Father, but so that what was immolated by the saints would be offered at one and the same

---

9. Gen 26.23–25. 10. Gen 35.1.
11. Gen 35.6–7.

time to the Son and the Father, and not in order that the Son be preferred to the Father, but lest the one begotten be thought to have been considered inferior to the Begetter in anything.

4. Accordingly, there should be no doubt in anyone's mind that the rightness of our faith is strengthened by the testimony of the sacrifice of the patriarchs. As long as anyone with hardened heart thinks he must offer resistance to this, he wanders as an alien, far from the faith and communion of the saints. On this matter we will be able to join together the testimonies on not unequal firmness and strength from the prophets, unless recalling the whole debt that must be repaid, we prefer to hurry on as quickly as possible to solve the remaining questions.

V. 1. Nevertheless, lest under the cover of abundance anyone think that we are concealing a lack of defense, we shall bring forward one testimony from the prophets by which it can clearly be shown that the holy prophets, divinely inspired, predicted with a certain and most faithful prophecy, that in the time of the New Testament, spiritual sacrifices were to be offered not to the Father only but also to the Son by the faithful. For Zephaniah says, "Therefore, wait for me, says the Lord, from the day when I arise as a witness. For my decision is to gather nations, to assemble kingdoms, to pour out upon them my indignation, all the heat of my anger; for in the fire of my passion, all the earth shall be consumed. At the time I will change the speech of the peoples to a pure speech, that all of them may call on the name of the Lord and serve him with one accord. From beyond the rivers of Ethiopia, my suppliants, my scattered ones, shall bring my offering."[12]

2. What, I ask, is clearer than that prophecy? Or how can heretical infidelity find a hiding place for their subborn darkness, where it can flee the light of such a great demonstration? "Its rising is from the end of the heavens, and its circuit to the end of them; and nothing is hid from its

12. Zeph 3.8–10.

heat."[13] Since if there is anyone who hides himself, numbed by the glacial cold of infidelity, the assistance of mercy can rescue him from it, but he cannot conceal himself from the punishment. See that the one who commands that he is to be awaited on the day of his resurrection shows that victims are to be offered to him by all nations, in order that that sacrifice be recognized as acceptable to God, the suppliant and pure devotion of the faithful offers it in common to the Father and the Son.

3. Would that the heretics, having been warned by this and similar testimonies, would not listen with deaf ears but may they acknowledge the truth of the faith by the illumination conceded to them by God, so that, receiving the saving light from now on, they may cease to wander in the darkness of death-bringing infidelity. Those who do not offer sacrifice with the Son and with wretched stubbornness defect from the faith of the patriarchs and prophets, impiously delinquent, show that they have been condemned by themselves. The apostolic sentence is known to have condemned every heretic by such a declaration to the effect that a heretic must be avoided in every way after a first (and second) correction, because not only will one be subverted by the same, but also because [the heretic] has been condemned by his own judgment.

4. If there are Catholic faithful who seemed to be unaware of this mystery up to now, from now on they ought to know that every act of this kind of honorific or saving sacrifice is offered by the Catholic Church equally to the Father and the Son and the Holy Spirit, i.e., to the Holy Trinity. And it is obvious that in its single name, holy baptism is also celebrated. There is no disrespect shown to the Son and the Holy Spirit when a prayer is directed by the offerer to the person of the Father.

5. The completion of this prayer, when the name of the Son and the Holy Spirit is attached, shows that there are no divisions in the Trinity. When words of honor are directed to

---

13. Ps 18.6 LXX; Ps 19.6.

the person of the Father only, the Trinity is honored by the integral faith of the orthodox believer, and when the intention of the offerer is directed to the Father, the tribute of the sacrifice is offered to the whole Trinity by one and the same act of the offerer. Therefore, when we offer a sacrifice to the Trinity, which is the one and true God, we are not moved by the vain objections of the heretics, for we are both instructed by the divinely-promulgated oracles and strengthened by the examples of the saints who have gone before to follow this and to hold on to it most strongly.

VI. 1. Now that question has come around to us concerning the mission of the Holy Spirit: If a sacrifice is offered to the Holy Trinity, why is the sending of the Holy Spirit only asked for, for the sanctifying of the gift of our oblation, as if (so to speak) God the Father himself, from whom the Holy Spirit proceeds, could not sanctify the sacrifice offered to him; or the Son himself was unable to sanctify the sacrifice of his body which we offer, since he sanctified his body which he offered to redeem us; or that the Holy Spirit was to be sent to consecrate the sacrifice of the Church, as if the Father or the Son was missing from the sacrifices.

2. First, therefore, it behooves us to recall that in speaking about this mission, the Holy Spirit must not be understood as inferior or lesser; because if lesser, then inferior, and if inferior, then lesser. We bring this up in advance, knowing how strongly this objection to our faith is frequently made by heretics, that the Holy Spirit must be believed to be less than the Father and the Son because he has been sent by the Father and the Son. Moreover, if the one who sends must be believed to be more powerful than the one sent, let them recognize that in this they are convicted of faithlessness, because as the Holy Spirit is recorded as being sent by the Father and the Son, so the Son too is sent by the Father and the Holy Spirit.

3. The Son himself said it through the prophet, long before he was sent, and confirmed it by his own testimony, after he was sent. For, coming to Nazareth and entering the synagogue, when the book of the prophet Isaiah had been

passed to him to read, he unrolled it to that place where it is written: "The Spirit of the Lord is upon me, because he has anointed me to bring glad tidings to the poor."[14] When the scroll had been handed back, he bore witness that the truth of this prophecy was fulfilled by his acts that day, saying, "Today this Scripture passage is fulfilled in your hearing."[15]

4. And in another place in the same prophet, he showed that he had been sent by the Lord and by his Spirit with these words: "And now the Lord God has sent me and his spirit."[16] In this way before his passion, he announces that the Holy Spirit is being sent by him to his disciples: "When the Advocate comes whom I will send you from the Father, the Spirit of Truth that proceeds from the Father, he will testify to me."[17] Above, he had taught that the same Spirit was also sent by the Father: "The Advocate, the Holy Spirit that the Father will send in my name—he will teach you everything...."[18] The Son has been sent by the Father and by the Spirit, and the Spirit has been sent by the Father and the Son. Nevertheless, no Christian ought to understand that the mission of the Son or of the Holy Spirit has been carried out in the sense of place or space, but by that word "mission" let us understand the work of a revelation freely granted.

5. So the Son has not been sent in some spatial sense; neither has the Holy Spirit, just as there is no spatial coming of the Father himself anywhere. When the Son promises to those who love him not only his own coming but that of the Father too, he says, "Whoever loves me will keep my word and my Father will love him and we will come to him and make our dwelling with him."[19] Therefore, just as the Father and the Son are nowhere absent and still they come to whom they wish (for they come by grace, they who are nowhere absent through power), so also in the mission or coming of the Holy Spirit, no spatial movement on his part is to be understood, but the effect of our sanctification is to be believed in.

14. Lk 4.18.
15. Lk 4.21.
16. Is 48.16.
17. Jn 15.26.
18. Jn 14.26.
19. Jn 14.23.

6. For if the Son is sent according to his divinity in a spatial sense, or the Holy Spirit is thought to be sent in a spatial sense, therefore, God the Father too should be believed to exist in some place (which God forbid). And when God himself indicates his unmeasurability to us in such a way, saying, "I fill the heavens and the earth,"[20] the prophet's words also underline for us the unmeasurability of the Son. Concerning him, the holy Jeremiah says, "It is great and has no bounds."[21] And because he is the power and the wisdom of God, concerning him it is also said: "She reaches mightily from one end of the earth to the other and she orders all things well."[22] Because of the Apostle's declaration, we hold it as certain that "in him were created all things in heaven and on earth, the visible and the invisible whether thrones or dominions or principalities or powers; all things were created through him and for him. He is before all things and in him all things hold together."[23]

7. Therefore, what is there that his presence cannot fill, in whom the Apostle declares all things in the heavens and on earth, visible and invisible hold together? Scripture speaks thus of the unmeasurability of the Holy Spirit also: "The Spirit of the Lord has filled the world."[24] So David also, not only believing in his heart to justification but also confessing with his mouth for salvation the unmeasurability of the Holy Trinity, one in substance, says thus: "Where can I go from your Spirit? Or where can I flee from your presence? If I ascend to heaven, you are there; If I make my bed in Sheol, you are there. If I take the wings of the morning and settle at the farthest limits of the seas, even there your hand should lead me and your right hand shall hold me fast."[25]

VII. 1. Since, as we have said, the whole Trinity remains by

---

20. Jn 23.24.
21. Bar 3.25.
22. Wis 8.1. Wisdom became a traditional term for Christ. Because it is a feminine noun, the new RSV uses "she" here.
23. Col 1.16–17.
24. Wis 1.7.
25. Ps 138.7–10 LXX; Ps 139.7–10.

nature with the unmeasured and infinite unity of its divinity and thus in a spatial sense is nowhere so that it is nowhere absent, it is totally everywhere so that neither can it be divided up into parts of a whole creature bit by bit nor can it be limited by the totality of a whole creature. Whenever the Holy Spirit is sought by the Father for consecrating a sacrifice, a basic consideration of the faith, a first caution to be retained for salvation by all Christians is that the coming of the Holy Spirit is never to be thought of or conceived of in some spatial sense.

2. The Apostle says to the faithful, "Do you not know that you are the Temple of God and that the Spirit of God dwells in you?"[26] And in another place: "With all prayer and supplication, pray at every opportunity in the Spirit."[27] And the Savior himself says to his disciples, "If you love me, you will keep my commandments. And I will ask the Father and he will give you another Advocate to be with you always, the Spirit of Truth which the world cannot accept because it neither sees nor knows it. But you know it, because it remains with you and will be in you."[28]

3. Paul too thus proclaims that we have received the same Spirit of adoption: "For you did not receive a spirit of slavery to fall back into fear, but you received a spirit of adoption through which we cry, 'Abba, Father'."[29] To the faithful, therefore, who are the Temple of God and in whom the Spirit of God lives, indeed, who are the Temple of the Holy Spirit, the Apostle says, "Do you not know that your body is a Temple of the Holy Spirit within you, whom you have from God?"[30] How is the Holy Spirit believed to be sent as if absent before by those whom the same Apostle orders to pray in him and to be vigilant in him since no one can pray worthily and vigilantly unless the Holy Spirit will have poured itself into him?

4. So, as the Apostle says, "describing spiritual realities in spiritual terms,"[31] and in the Spirit, who is God by nature,

26. 1 Cor 3.16.
27. Eph 6.18.
28. Jn 14.15–17.
29. Rm 8.15.
30. 1 Cor 6.19.
31. 1 Cor 2.13.

thinking nothing corporeal, nothing spatial, nothing temporal, nothing mutable, we must consider that sometimes under the name of the Holy Spirit, the gifts of the Holy Spirit are designated. For we read in the book of Kings that when Elijah was about to be carried off by divine gift and before he was carried off, he gave to his disciple the confidence to ask for what he wanted, he asked that a double portion of the Spirit which Elijah had received be given to him. Here is a place where we understand by the name of the Spirit, a gift of spiritual grace is being designated. For the substance of the Holy Spirit can neither be increased nor diminished who, just as he is eternal, without beginning and without end, so is he perfect without increase or decrease.

VIII. 1. These gifts, according to his inscrutable and irreproachable will, just as we believe they can be increased in human beings, so we do not deny that they can be decreased in them. For when the gifts are of the Holy Spirit, "love, joy, peace, patience, kindness, generosity, faithfulness, gentleness, self-control"[32] and when "to one is given through the Spirit, the expression of wisdom; to another, the expression of knowledge according to the same Spirit; to another faith by the same Spirit"[33] in human beings all of these can both be increased and decreased.

2. From where does that increase of faith come which the Apostles themselves ask that they be given by the Lord, saying, "Lord, increase our faith"?[34] That we increase also in charity, the blessed Apostle himself shows who says, "Living the truth in love, we should grow in every way into him who is the head."[35] But how do we grow in love, unless we receive an increase of love with the gift of spiritual grace? "The love of God has been poured out into our hearts through the Holy Spirit that has been given to us."[36]

3. This is also known concerning the other spiritual gifts which, according to the capacity of each person, are said either to increase or decrease in us. Increases and decreases of

32. 2 Kgs 2.9–10.
34. Lk 17.5.
36. Rm 5.5.

33. 1 Cor 12.8–9.
35. Eph 4.15.

such charismata are spoken of in this sense, that they exist in certain people to a greater or a lesser degree, not that they can, in themselves, be increased or decreased. For the sun, too, so great as it is when seen by healthy eyes or however it may seem when viewed by injured eyes, it is not made less when perceived as smaller by disturbed eyes nor increased when pouring more amply into healthy eyes.

4. Because, that difference of vision did not originate in differences in the sun but consists in diversity of health and illness. And although it illumines one less and the other more, still it has one and the same light in itself, of which one sees less and the other more. So it is with the Holy Spirit, in itself remaining immutably without growth or loss, Elisha asked for a double portion of the Spirit because he asked for an increase of spiritual grace.

IX. 1. Therefore, when the coming of the Holy Spirit is sought for the sanctifying of the sacrifice of the whole Church, nothing else is being sought for, it seems to me, than that through the spiritual grace in the Body of Christ (which is the Church) the unity of charity may be preserved endlessly unbroken. For this is the principal gift of the Holy Spirit without which any "speaking in human and angelic tongues . . . like a resounding gong or a clashing cymbal"[37] can give faith a sound but cannot have life. "Although" he has "the gift of prophecy" and knows "all mysteries and all knowledge, even if" he have "all faith so as" to move "mountains, but" does not have "love, he is nothing." "Even if" he give away "everything he owns as food for the poor," and he hands over "his body to be burned but has not love, it does him no good."[38] The Apostle says that the Law "was promulgated by angels at the hand of a mediator;"[39] they spoke with the tongues of angels, who, with their mouth, taught what is of the Law and, by depraved actions, fought against the Law. Concerning them, the Savior himself says, "Therefore do and observe all things whatsoever they tell you, but do not

37. 1 Cor 13.1.
38. 1 Cor 13.2–3.
39. Gal 3.19.

follow their example. For they preach but they do not practice."⁴⁰

3. Saul also had prophecy and Simon Magus believed and received the sacrament of baptism; for the demons too, while they believe and tremble, seem to have faith, but it is of no profit to them because they do not have charity. Many, giving away their goods to the poor, because they did not make an effort to acquire charity, have given away their goods, but it profited them nothing, because they lost themselves by not acquiring charity which they should have acquired. By these indications, it is shown that the Holy Spirit is there where the "end of the Law" is, i.e., "love from a pure heart, and a good conscience and a sincere faith."⁴¹

3. For where there is no love along with the faith, whatever gifts of the Holy Spirit there can be, the Holy Spirit itself cannot be there; and for this reason the granting of those gifts accomplishes nothing where some gift of the Spirit is present in such a way that the Spirit itself is not present. Accordingly, such people, although they seem to be participants in certain gifts of the Father, still they are not sharers in the inheritance of the Father, since "the Holy Spirit is the pledge of our inheritance."⁴² "The God and Father of our Lord Jesus Christ [who] has blessed us in and with every spiritual blessing in the heavens, as he chose us in him, before the foundations of the world, to be holy and without blemish before him. In love. . . ."⁴³

X. 1. When the Church asks that the Holy Spirit be sent from heaven upon itself, it is asking that the gift of charity and concord be conferred on it by God. But when does the holy Church (which is the Body of Christ) more fittingly ask for the coming of the Holy Spirit than for consecrating the sacrifice of the Body of Christ? It knows that its own head according to the flesh was born of the Holy Spirit. So by the word of an angel, Mary is informed: "The Holy Spirit will come upon you and the power of the most High will over-

---

40. Mt 23.3.
42. Eph 1.14.
41. 1 Tm 1.5.
43. Eph 1.3–4.

shadow you. Therefore the child to be born will be called holy, the Son of God."[44]

2. The evangelist Matthew, as well, filled with the same Holy Spirit, affirms that "When his mother Mary was betrothed to Joseph but before they lived together, she was found with child through the Holy Spirit."[45] And he thus recalls that the angel said to Joseph in dreams: "Joseph, son of David, do not be afraid to take Mary your wife into your home. For it is through the Holy Spirit that this child has been conceived in her."[46] What was accomplished by the mystery of this Incarnation of the Lord except that things divided are united and discordant things are subdued? For Paul is the witness concerning Christ that: "For he is our peace, he who made both one and broke down the dividing wall of enmity, through his flesh, abolishing the Law with its commandments and legal claims, that he might create in himself one new person in place of the two, thus establishing peace, and might reconcile both with God, in one body, through the cross, putting that enmity to death by it. He came and preached peace to you who were far off and peace to those who were near, for through him we both have access in one Spirit to the Father."[47]

3. This was done by divine love so that from the Spirit itself, the body of that head might be reborn, from which the head itself is born. And for this reason, it is necessary for us that, just as Christ was born from the Holy Spirit, united to his man "came out like a bridegroom from his wedding chamber,"[48] so the Church by the gift of the Holy Spirit, adheres to Christ, as a woman to her husband and as a body to its head. For the Apostle says, "For . . . Christ is the head of the Church, he himself the savior of the body."[49] And again: "Because we are members of his body [from his flesh and his bones]. For this reason a man shall leave his father and his mother and be joined to his wife and the two shall become

44. Lk 1.35.
46. Mt 1.20.
48. Ps 18.6 LXX; Ps 19.6.
45. Mt 1.18.
47. Eph 2.14–18.
49. Eph 5.23.

one flesh."[50] Explaining this, he added: "This is a great mystery, but I speak in reference to Christ and the Church."[51]

4. Immediately following he added this testimony from the Old Testament when the Lord exposed the temptations of the Pharisees: "So they are no longer two, but one flesh. Therefore what God has joined together, no human being must separate."[52] As in that holy matrimony: what was done in the marriage chamber of the virgin's womb, that there were not two now but one flesh, this was done by the grace of the Spirit. The grace of the Spirit is at work for this too—that it may remain unbroken forever; that this unity of the body may adhere to its head and that, knowing that "those who are from you will perish; you put an end to those who are false to you,"[53] grace can say chastely and sweetly: "But as for me, it is good to be near God." And again: "My soul clings to you."[54] These things the love of God does: "which has been poured out into our hearts by the Holy Spirit that has been given to us."[55]

So great is this unity of Christ and the Church through this Holy Spirit that when the vessel of election says, "That Christ is the head of the body, the Church,"[56] the very body of Christ does not doubt that it truly calls on Christ.

5. Finally, he speaks as follows, writing to the Corinthians: "As a body is one, though it has many parts and all the parts of the body, though many, are one body, so also Christ."[57] And that he may show that this body which is that of Christ, that it may be Christ, that although it has many members, it remains and holds together as one only by the grace of the Holy Spirit, he follows up immediately as he says, "For in one Spirit we were all baptized into one body, whether Jew or Greek, slaves or free persons, and we were all given to drink of one Spirit."[58] This spiritual grace never ceases for a single day to build up the body of Christ through the unity of

50. Eph 5.30–31.
51. Eph 5.32.
52. Mt 19.6.
53. Ps 72.27 LXX; Ps 73.27.
54. Ps 62.9 LXX; Ps 63.8.
55. Rm 5.5.
56. Col 1.18.
57. 1 Cor 12.12.
58. 1 Cor 12.13.

peace and love, which grace fashioned in the womb of Mary the virgin the gift of wisdom which is the head of this body.

6. Hence the blessed Apostle with these words shows that we also are built up in him: "So then you are no longer strangers and sojourners, but you are fellow citizens with the holy ones and members of the household of God built upon the foundation of the Apostles and prophets, with Christ Jesus himself as the capstone. Through him the whole structure is held together and grows into a temple sacred in the Lord; in him you are also being built together into a dwelling place of God in the Spirit."[59]

The Apostle bears witness that this building by which we are built up in the Spirit, in another place is made for nothing other than the perfection of the saints for the work of ministry, for the building up of the Body of Christ.

7. Where he indicates the unity of the same spiritual building, which consists in love, he says, "until we all attain to the unity of faith and knowledge of the Son of God, to mature manhood, to the extent of the full stature of Christ, so that we may no longer be infants, tossed by waves and swept along by every wind of teaching arising from human trickery, from their cunning in the interests of deceitful scheming. Rather, living the truth in love, we should grow in every way into him who is the head, Christ, from whom the whole body, joined and held together by every supporting ligament, with the proper functioning of each part, brings about the body's growth and builds itself up in love."[60]

XI. 1. Therefore, this spiritual upbuilding of the Body of Christ which happens in love (since according to the words of the blessed Peter, "... like living stones, let yourselves be built into a spiritual house to be a holy priesthood to offer spiritual sacrifices acceptable to God through Jesus Christ."[61]) this spiritual upbuilding, I say, is never more opportunely sought than when the very Body and Blood of Christ are offered by the body of Christ itself (which is the

---

59. Eph 2.19–22.   60. Eph 4.13–16.
61. 1 Pt 2.5.

Church) in the sacrament of the bread and chalice: "The cup of blessing that we bless, is it not a participation in the blood of Christ? The bread that we break, is it not a participation in the body of Christ? Because the loaf of bread is one, we, though many, are one body, for we all partake of the one loaf."[62]

2. And, therefore, we ask that by that very grace by which it comes about that the Church becomes the Body of Christ, by the same grace it may happen that all the members of charity, with the binding framework remaining, persevere in the unity of the Body. This we seek worthily to happen in us by the gift of that Spirit who is the one Spirit of both the Father and the Son; because the Holy Trinity, by nature unity and equality and love, which is the one, only, and true God, in total accord sanctifies those whom it adopts.

3. In that one substance of the Trinity, unity is in the origin, equality in the offspring, in the love, the communion of unity and equality. There is no division of that unity, no difference in that equality, no pride in that love. There nothing is out of harmony, because the equality, dear and one, and the unity, equal and dear, and the love, equal and one, persevere by nature and immutably. Because from the very (if it must be said) communion of the Holy Spirit, the one love of the Father and the Son is shown. The blessed Apostle points out this communion with these words: "The grace of the Lord Jesus Christ and the love of God and the fellowship of the Holy Spirit be with all of you;"[63] and in another place: "If there is . . . any solace in love, any participation in the Spirit,"[64] because of which it is said: ". . . because the love of God has been poured out in our hearts through the Holy Spirit that has been given to us."[65]

4. The Holy Spirit who is the one Spirit of the Father and the Son accomplishes this in those to whom it has given the grace of divine adoption, something it has done also in those who, in the book of the Acts of the Apostles, received

---

62. 1 Cor 10.16–17.
64. Phil 2.1.
63. 1 Cor 13.13.
65. Rm 5.5.

the same Spirit. Concerning them it is said: "The community of believers was of one heart and mind."[66] The one who is the one Spirit of the Father and the Son and who is the one God with the Father and the Son made the heart and soul of the multitude that believed in God, one. So the Apostle too states with concern that this spiritual unity in the bond of peace must be preserved, warning the Ephesians in this way: "I, then, a prisoner for the Lord, urge you to live in manner worthy of the call you have received, with all humility and gentleness, with patience, bearing with one another through love, striving to preserve the unity of the Spirit through the bond of peace, one Body and one Spirit...."[67]

5. By departing, they lose this Spirit, if they, either depraved by lack of faith or puffed up by pride, are separated from the unity of the body of the Church. The Apostle Jude shows that these people are clearly without the Spirit of whom he says, "These are the ones who cause divisions; they live on the natural plane, devoid of the Spirit."[68] These, because they are natural, do not have the Spirit. Because of this Paul the Apostle says, "Now the natural person does not accept what pertains to the Spirit of God."[69] Such people, therefore, are quick to promote division because they do not have the Spirit in whom alone the members of Christ spiritually preserve precious unity.

6. Whence it is clear that among all heretics the grace of the Holy Spirit does not exist, nor can their sacrifices, so long as they are heretics, please God, nor is the sanctification of spiritual grace granted to the sacrifices of those who make their offerings while separated from the unity of the ecclesiastical body. God delights only in the sacrifices of the Church which spiritual unity makes a sacrifice to God, there where the truth of faith believes in no separation in the Trinity and the tenacity of peace preserves fraternal concord in love.

XII. 1. Lest anyone think that we, when the Church prays

66. Acts 4.32.
67. Eph 4.1–3.
68. Jude 19.
69. 1 Cor 2.14.

for the coming of the Holy Spirit in the prayer of sacrifice, unfittingly understand by the words "Holy Spirit" love which has been poured forth in our hearts through the Holy Spirit that has been given to us, we have thought it suitable to strengthen our belief with statements from the fathers. St. Augustine in his books on baptism, when he considered the question of the reception of heretics without the repetition of baptism, in the third book of this same work, among other things, says the following: "But when it is said that 'The Holy Spirit is given by the imposition of hands in the Catholic Church only,' I suppose that our ancestors meant that we should understand thereby what the Apostle says: 'Because the love of God is poured out in our hearts by the Holy Spirit that has been given to us.' For this is that very love which is wanting in all who are cut off from the communion of the Catholic Church."[70]

Note, I ask you, how the most blessed Augustine, divinely learned in the Holy Scriptures, has miraculously opened up in one place the meaning not only of the holy Apostle Paul but also that of the holy Apostle Jude, in the name of the Holy Spirit.

2. He says above, "The Holy Spirit is given by the imposition of hands in the Catholic Church only, I suppose that our ancestors meant that we should understand thereby what the Apostle says: 'The Holy Spirit has been poured out in our hearts by the Holy Spirit that has been given to us.'"[71] Subsequently also what the Apostle Jude set down in his letter, with the uncertainty of doubt removed, St. Augustine explained. For the Apostle Jude said, "These are the ones who cause divisions; they live on the natural plane, devoid of the Spirit."[72]

3. And the blessed Augustine concerning the love of God, which has been poured out in our hearts by the Holy Spirit that has been given to us, says, "For this is the very love

---

70. Augustine *De baptismo* III.16.21. CSEL 51.212. English translation, NPNF, ser. 1, 4.442.
71. Ibid.
72. Jude 19.

which is wanting in all who are cut off from the communion of the Catholic Church."[73] And who is going to say that the Holy Spirit given by the imposition of hands to heretics who return is different from the one divinely given to the spiritual sacrifice? Anyone who thinks or says this assuredly does not yet understand in what way they show themselves a living, holy victim, pleasing to God, if any schismatics and heretics, abandoning deadly error, return to the unity of Catholic truth, where, offering to God the sacrifice of a contrite heart, they themselves are a living victim, holy, pleasing to God. Because through the contrition of a humbled heart, they return to the unity of the members of that priest who loved us, as the Apostle says, "... and handed himself over for us as a sacrificial offering to God for a fragrant aroma."[74]

4. The love of God which has been poured out in our hearts through the Holy Spirit that has been given to us brings it about that they may return and become a spiritual sacrifice. God willingly accepts the sacrifice only from Catholic truth and communion; because, while he guards his love poured out in it by the Holy Spirit, he makes the Church itself a sacrifice pleasing to him. The Church can always receive the grace of spiritual love through which it can continuously show itself a living and holy victim, pleasing to God.

XIII. 1. You write concerning that place in the Apostle where he says, "Now in regard to virgins, I have no commandment from the Lord, but I give my opinion."[75] In the letter which I wrote to you recently,[76] I recalled that that opinion was relevant to the instance where, when the two denarii had been received from the Lord, the faithful innkeeper did more than was required. Although you assert that the meaning of this text[77] is not so interpreted by St. Au-

---

73. Augustine *De baptismo* III.16.21. CSEL 51.212. English translation, NPNF, ser. 1, 4.442.
74. Eph 5.2.
75. 1 Cor 7.25.
76. A letter of Fulgentius to Monimus no longer extant.
77. The work of Augustine referred to here is uncertain.

gustine, you confirm that it is so interpreted by other illustrious men.

2. It is true that St. Augustine said that here the Apostle did more than was required, that, though according to the commandment, he was able, if he wished, to live from the Gospel, still he preferred, not only for himself but also for those who were with him, to work with his own hands, as he said truly to the Ephesians: "You know well that these very hands have served my needs and my companions. In every way I have shown you that by hard work of that sort we must help the weak."[78]

And writing to the Thessalonians: "You recall" he says, "brothers, our toil and drudgery, working night and day in order not to burden any of you."[79] And to the Corinthians, he calls this his reward, that preaching the Gospel, he offers the Gospel free of charge so that he does not abuse his power in the Gospel.

3. Although St. Augustine has treated this suitably and fittingly, still it must not seem unsuitable or unfitting that St. Ambrose has located the supererogation of the blessed Paul either in his sermons and his letters or in the too great labor of mind and body.[80] St. Optatus of Milevis, in the sixth book against Parmenian, bears witness that Paul has done more than is necessary with his advice on virgins in these words: "For virginity is a matter of choice, not of necessity. So Paul the Apostle, that famous innkeeper, to whose care was entrusted a people wounded with the wounds of their sins, had received two pennies to lay out—that is the two Testaments. These he, as it were, expended by his teaching and taught how Christian husbands and wives ought to live; but, when he was asked what command he would give concerning virgins, he answered that nothing about virginity had been commanded. He acknowledged that he had laid out the two Testaments, that is the two pennies. In a certain way, the commission was exhausted, but, inasmuch as Christ, who

78. Acts 20.34–35.
79. 1 Thes 2.9.
80. Ambrose *Expositio evangelii secundum Lucam* VII.82. CCL 14.240.

had entrusted the wounded man to his keeping, had promised that he would repay whatsoever over and above might be expended upon his care, Paul, after having laid out the two pennies, gives not commandments, but counsel with regard to virginity. He does not stand in the way of those who desire it, but neither does he drive or force those who do not desire it."[81]

XIV. 1. Therefore, since this text of the blessed Apostle has been explained in three ways by three holy men whom we have named, whoever would choose one of these three does not depart from the truth, nor is it necessary that what is understood in several ways be included in multiple ways in every writing. For the saints themselves, by whose ministry God has deigned to open the secrets of his Scriptures, have said that most things are not unfittingly understood, not in one way only, but in multiple ways, without offense at any rate to the true faith. So the blessed Augustine himself is known to have done against Faustus in the case of the mystery of Noah's ark. For, with the Manichaean asserting that in the books of the Old Testament nothing is prophesied concerning the future coming of Christ in true flesh, the same most blessed Augustine showing that our old Scripture is full of prophetic meanings about Christ and because of this, divinely inspired, so, among other things, he explains that God commands that the above-mentioned ark be constructed with two and three stories, in such a way that in the fifteenth book of the *City of God*, he might give no less sweetly than miraculously the mystical explanation of the same text in two other ways, "not with words taught by human wisdom but" truly (as the Apostle says) "with words taught by the Spirit."[82]

2. In order that this may be recognized more easily, I shall cite the words of each work, just as they have been written by him. So, against Faustus, he said this: "That the lower spaces of the ark are divided into two and three chambers, as the

---

81. Optatus *Contra Parmenianum* VI.4. CSEL 26.149–50. English translation, Vassall-Phillips, 257–58.
82. 1 Cor 2.13.

multitude of all nations in the Church is divided into two, as circumcised and uncircumcised; or into three, as descended from the three sons of Noah."[83]

3. But in the fifteenth book of the *City of God*, undertaking to expound the mystery of the above-mentioned ark according to the opening offered by the text, after some other matters, where it is said that Noah must build his ark with two and three stories, he inserted mention of that explanation which is contained in the books against Faustus the Manichaean, adding this subsequently: "Biblical interpretations, of course, can vary in value—and I do not claim that mine is the best—but any interpretation which is to catch the mind of the writer who described the flood must realize the connections of this story with the City of God which, in this wicked world, is ever tossed like the ark in the waters of a deluge. Anyone is free to reject the interpretations I gave in the work against Faustus. I said, for example, that the words 'with lower, middle chambers, and third-storied shall they make it,' can be applied to the Church. The Church is gathered from all nations, and is two-storied because it has room for two kinds of men, the circumcised and the uncircumcised, or the Jews and the Greeks, as the Apostle calls them. But the Church is also three-storied because after the flood the whole world was repeopled with descendants from the three sons of Noah. Now, anyone is entitled to say something else, so long as what he says is in harmony with the rule of faith. Thus, God wanted the ark to have rooms not only in the lower story but also in the middle story—the 'middle chambers'—and even in the top story—the 'third stories'—so that there should be living space from the bottom to the top. These stories may well be taken to imply the three virtues praised by the Apostle: faith, hope, and charity. However, better application would be to the three harvest increases mentioned in the Gospel, the thirty-fold, sixty-fold, and hundred-fold, the meaning being that on the lowest level in the Church we have chaste marriage, on the next

---

83. Augustine *Contra Faustum* XII.16. CSEL 25.346. English translation, NPNF, ser. 1, 4.189.

level chaste widowhood, and on the highest level virginal purity. Still better interpretations can be expressed, so long as they square with the faith of the City of God. This is true of any other text which I may have occasion to interpret. All explanations need not be the same, but none may be proposed which is incompatible with the Catholic faith."[84]

6. Again, the same blessed Augustine asserts in the first book on the Trinity that it "is useful if many men, differing in style but not in faith, write many books even on the same topics, in order that the subject itself may reach as many people as possible, to some in one way, to others in a different way."[85] If, therefore, those things which the blessed Augustine said in one place in two ways about the ark of Noah are interpreted differently by two men in separate places, will not each one rightly be acknowledged to be a holder of the truth? Still if each seems to affirm one of the meanings found in his words in such a way that what the other says in his words equally fits the truth, let him be pacified and approve it rather than attack it contentiously.

XV. 1. So, my friend, although that meaning which was put forward by me perhaps is not found in the words of St. Augustine, still most openly, it is found in the books of St. Optatus (as you yourself are aware along with me). Nor is it hidden from your prudence that of those things which are said by the holy fathers, who in various ways defended the correct rule of the Catholic faith in the teaching of the Holy Spirit, either in their exegetical or apologetic works, whatever be said by us, we are affirming a meaning befitting the truth of that text in such a way that we do not refuse assent to other opinions of the fathers, equally befitting the truth.

2. Nor do we depart from the truth, if in the question of the Apostle's supererogation, either what St. Ambrose or what St. Augustine or what St. Optatus believed, is also believed by us, saving the truth of the faith. Since it is believed

---

84. Augustine *De civitate Dei* XV.26. CCL 48.494. English translation, FOTC 14.478–79.
85. Augustine *De Trinitate* I.5. CCL 50.33. English translation, FOTC 45.8–9.

rightly that, with the two denarii accepted, Paul has done something more than he had to do, in that, preaching the Gospel while expending himself, he did not demand the payment owed him by the faithful; rightly also is it believed that something else is being done beyond what is required in that he did not have a commandment of the Lord concerning virgins, but he gave advice. Without a doubt, he had both because He gave it without whose gift Paul would not have been able to do more than was required.

BOOK III

As OFTEN, my beloved Monimus, as the virtue of charity is considered and examined by the servants of Christ, it is found no less marvelous than sweet. For who does not marvel at it or who does not completely delight in something whose burden when borne, does not weaken the spirit with fatigue but strengthens it with enthusiasm? For when it burdens, it lifts up and, in a marvelous manner, the one whom it burdens, it does not allow to be oppressed; when it lifts up, it does not permit one to be exalted. This, while allowing my past debt to you to be resolved with the Lord's help, again makes me a debtor. For on the four questions which you sent to me for discussion, with the help of him who gives wisdom to children, I wrote two books wishing to repay you what I owed.

2. Then suddenly the statement of a certain Arian assertion grated on my ears, which, just as much as it is generated by a pointless aberration, to that degree is it "discovered" by every intellect, foreign not only to the divine Scriptures but also to humanity itself. For I find that, from the beginning of the Gospel according to John, they plant a certain now unaccustomed question.[1] They think that what has been said: "In

1. Fulgentius feels obliged to answer a question not raised by Monimus. It seems to be a particularly superficial one raised by an Arian. Basing his response on the beginning of John's Gospel ("The Word was with God"), he rais-

the beginning was the Word, and the Word was with God and the Word was God,"[2] should be understood and explained in such a way that the Word should be accepted as being with the Father, not that he is in the Father but outside the Father. One of them (to the extent that I have discovered by hearsay) when once there arose a conflict among them concerning these two prepositions, i.e., in and with, when someone had received a cloak and was holding it in his hands, asked whether that cloak which he held in his hands, was in him when it was with him.

3. And from there, as if to confirm his view, he is said to have closed his discourse with this definition: "When something is said to be in us, it is to be understood as being inside us; when it is said to be with us, it is to be accepted as outside us." And because that cloak which he held was "with him" so that it was not in him, so for that reason, that it was with him, and not in him, therefore, it was outside him, not inside him, in the same way the Word of God also (which is God) must be believed to be with the Father, not in the Father, and for this reason, is not of one substance with the Father; since something that is with someone so that it is not in him, assuredly, is with him in the sense that it cannot be of one substance with him. This is their reasoning, contrary to reason. This dispute about the law is intolerably inimical to the law of God.

II. 1. Hence, under the impulsion of Christ, my spirit was stirred to write something lest the hearing of little ones be disturbed by poisonous words; for it is part of the duty of our servanthood to prepare salutary remedies of divine words against the nascent pestilence of any deadly view. Therefore, when the holy Apostle forewarns the faithful with concern, saying, "See to it that no one captivate you with an empty, seductive philosophy according to human tradition, according to the elemental power of the world and not according to

---

es the objection that that which is "with" something is not "in" that thing and, therefore, is of a different nature from that which it is "with." Fulgentius seeks to refute this verbal quibble from Scripture.

2. Jn 1.1.

Christ. For in him dwells the whole fullness of the deity bodily."[3] They, on the contrary, pursuing the error of worldly philosophy of time past, not only thought that there must be disputation about God according to the elemental power of the world, but also they now forget religion so completely that when they discuss God, they do not pay attention even to the elements of this corporeal world.

2. And so, while they stubbornly shut the eyes of their intelligence even against those things which are seen, they never detect with their intellect the invisible things of God through those things which have been made. For what could be more absurdly said than that in order that anyone discuss God, one should employ in the discussion nothing but examples from the heavier bodies? For, that person seemed to himself to find something significant when, receiving a cloak and holding it in his hands, he asked whether, just as it was with him, was it in him.

3. Thereupon, wishing to teach that the Son was with the Father just as a cloak was with a person, that because a cloak could be with a person, it could not be in a person, so the Son was with the Father, but was not in the Father. I ask if he took delight in employing something from these tangible bodies as an example in the discussion, although to that person who argues against the truth, the elements which have been made by the truth, can never be relied upon, still, in order that he may seem to say something acceptable so that I may keep silence about other things, why does he show the cloak which he held in his hands and not pay attention to at least the breath which he drew through his nostrils?

4. Because if that cloak could be said to be with him, and not in him, that breath, which we draw from the air, when we perceive it by breathing, is both with us and in us and whatever we send back by exhaling, when we give it back, we have it neither in us nor with us. Or perhaps he is going to say the element of that air, when we take it in by breathing is only in us but is not also with us? Does he say, therefore,

---

3. Col 2.8–9.

when it can be with us or when we exhale it, we do not also have it in us?

5. But I think this, that he will not dare to speak about that cloak, if he has given it back to the one from whom he had received it. He sees that then he had it with him when he received it; but after he gave it back, he now ceased to have it with him. Just as by receiving, what he did not have before, he now had with him; so, by giving it back, what he had with him, he no longer had. Accordingly, if he said the cloak was not in him but with him, still, it seems to me, that he will not say of this breath which by turns we draw in and breathe out from the air around us, that it is not with a person, when it is in a person, because then, a person has it with him and in him, when he receives it by breathing. Then when he gives it up by exhaling, he does not have it with him anymcre than he has it in him.

III. 1. In vain, therefore, in that discussion concerning these words: "The Word was with God," did he wish to assert that what is in something is always internal, that what is with someone is always external, since the breath received into the body, is in a person in such a way that it is with a person. And again, expelled from the body, it is not with a person anymore than it is in a person. For he did not pay enough attention to this, that because of what he struggled to assert by an absurd example, now subsequently a weightier absurdity held him tightly bound. For it is said: "In the beginning was the Word and the Word was with God and the Word was God."[4]

2. If everything that was with God is external, and everything that is in God is internal, what remains to that most expert debater except to contend that we are more powerful than the Son of God? For the Apostle says about God: "That in him, we live and move and have our being."[5] And in another place: "One God the Father, from whom all things are and for whom we exist."[6] So now, let anyone who, under the name of Christian, did not fear to dispute so foolishly

4. Jn 1.1. 5. Acts 17.28.
6. 1 Cor 8.6.

against Christ, when he hears that the Word is with God and that we are in God, if he dares, let him say that the Word is external and we are internal. If anyone thinks that that must be said, let him pass judgment from his own words. In such a statement, is any other judge to be sought for when the very one who said this must without question condemn himself?

3. What will he again answer to that statement of the same blessed Paul in which he says of God: "For from him and through him and for him are all things. To him be glory forever. Amen."[7] Behold, Paul testifies that all things are from God and through God and in God; by the preaching of John the Evangelist it is recognized that the Word is with god; if, however, according to the meaning of the Arians, everything which is in God is interior and everything that is with God is exterior, since the Word which is with God is believed by the Arians not to be in God but external.

4. What is left is that that which is with God is proclaimed as inferior to everything that is in God. When this is accepted—because it has been written concerning the Word: "All things were made through him"[8]—this will be the orthodox faith according to the Arians, that what is made must be preferred to the Maker. Who does not perceive into what abyss thoughtless people fall who, resisting the true faith, try to defend a false faith? For what is being done with such words except that the creature, by the defense of this view, forgetful of his condition and redemption, dares not only to make itself equal to the Son of God but to put itself ahead of him?

5. I am amazed how they who assert this do not consider how the inferior fruit of wicked blasphemy is born from it. For they say, "What is in God must be believed to be internal, but what is with God must be thought to be external. Wherefore if something is with God and is external, it must not be believed to be of one nature with God. It follows that what is in God and is internal, is believed to be of one substance with God." That reasoning leads to this conclusion, that as the Word, because it is with God, is separated from

7. Rm 1.36.
8. Jn 1.3.

his nature, so the creature, because it is in God, is believed to be of one nature with God. From this, they are convicted of believing these things by which they dare to put us ahead of even the Son and try to make us equal to the Father. So do those who dissent from the truth confuse everything. See with what views faithless error is asserted. See with what foolishness the truth of the faith is attacked.

IV. 1. But no matter with what blows heretics struggle to shake the holy Church, we are certain from the Lord our God that they will not be able to undermine the city built on a mountain. In fact, they undermine and destroy themselves, who outrage the only Son of God, true God, with slanderous assertions. Nor do they restrain themselves even from injuring the Father while they return ingratitude for the grace of the Savior. So it seems fitting that the understanding of this word be sought from other texts of the Scriptures, so that it may be clear whether or not, whenever something is said to be with someone, we are obliged, according to their view, to think of it always as external.

2. In the book of Wisdom, we read that it is said by certain people: "For they reasoned unsoundly, saying to themselves;"[9] we require an explanation of this text from the Arians, whether he who thinks to himself, thinks inside himself or outside himself? Since the act of thinking of a person is not only not outside the person's body, neither is it the action of the body. For that which is called thinking is not only not found outside a person, neither is it found in the very body of a person. Who does not see that thought belongs only to the soul, to which thinking has been given by God through the power of reason? In a human being, the spirit rules by thinking; by working, the body shows its subordination. For there, thinking has been given to a human being where the power of distinguishing good and evil has been instilled.

3. Therefore, the inner person carries on the work of thinking who, created in the image of God, has received the

---

9. Wis 2.1.

power of understanding. When, therefore, the human being thinks "with" himself, he is thinking within himself, not outside himself; he would not think outside himself even if thinking belonged to the external person. How much more does he think within himself, inasmuch as it not the external but the internal person that thinks. According to the testimony of Scripture, one is said to think with himself because thinking is the function, not of the external, but of the internal person. For Scripture says, just as has already been cited above, "For they reasoned unsoundly, saying to themselves."[10]

What is it "to say to oneself" except to say it in one's heart? Wherefore it is said in another place: "When you are disturbed, do not sin; ponder it on your beds and be silent."[11]

4. Therefore, to speak with oneself is to speak within oneself. So that Pharisee who had invited the Lord to eat, when the sinful woman, having entered, watered the feet of the Savior with her tears and dried them with her hair, because he thought within himself, said within himself what he said by thinking. For the evangelist says, "When the Pharisee who had invited him saw this, he said to himself."[12]

What is "said to himself" except: thought within himself? Nevertheless, with Scripture teaching, we know that the one who thinks within himself, thinks with himself. Therefore, it is said: "For they reasoned unsoundly, saying to themselves."[13]

5. Still, lest the Arians wish to link this which has been said "to themselves," not to the preceding words but to what follows, so that it is not said: "They said to themselves" but "They said" and afterwards is continued, "thinking within themselves;" so let them hear the testimonies of the divine Scriptures and let them know that the function of human thought belongs not to the external, but to the internal human being. The evangelist says that when the paralytic was brought before the Lord, "When Jesus saw their faith,"

10. Ibid.
12. Lk 7.29.
11. Ps 4.5 LXX; Ps 4.4.
13. Wis 2.1.

i.e., of those who had let him down through the tiles, he "said, 'Courage, child, your sins are forgiven.' At that some of the Scribes said to themselves, 'This man is blaspheming.' Jesus knew what they were thinking and said, 'Why do you harbor evil thoughts in your hearts?'"[14]

6. They who the evangelist said, "said within themselves," the Lord says of these very ones that they had evil thoughts in their hearts. What is thinking evil thoughts in their hearts except: "to reason unsoundly, saying to themselves"? In whatever way the Arians pull apart the meaning of this text, there it is necessary that they find the confounding of their depravity. And would that they who are thus confounded about their error might be converted to the truth. For if they said that this verse of Scripture must be divided in this way, what has been written, "For they reasoned unsoundly, saying to themselves" so that, joining "to themselves" to the preceding words, they divide it up this way: "They said to themselves" so that later they bring in "reasoned unsoundly." Immediately they are convicted by the words of David that "to say to oneself" is nothing other than "to say in the heart." For he says, "What you say in your hearts."[15]

7. If they wish to distinguish them differently, so that they join "to themselves," not to the preceding words but to those that come after, as those who spoke before said, with a silent pause in between, afterwards they bring forward what has been said: "For they reasoned unsoundly," even from this they hear the reproach of the Savior and recognize that these are the thoughts of the heart; for he says, "Why do you think evil in your hearts?"[16] And in another place as well the same Lord teaches: "For from the heart come forth evil thoughts."[17] And a second time he says, "A good person brings forth good out of a store of goodness but an evil person brings forth evil out of a store of evil."[18]

---

14. Mt 9.2–3.
15. Ps 4.5 LXX; Ps 4.5. "When you are disturbed, do not sin; ponder it on your beds and be silent."
16. Lk 5.22.   17. Mt 15.19.
18. Mt 12.35.

Now do they who strive to assert that the Word is with God, not internally, but externally, recognize in what depth of error they are carrying on?

V. 1. Again, we read written about Wisdom in the same book: "... For in the memory of virtue is immortality, because it is known both by God and by mortals."[19] For how is it known by mortals if it is not within mortals but is outside mortals? Since, unless it entered the human soul, it could not be known to a human being. Concerning this, it is said: "... while remaining in herself, she renews all things; in every generation she passes into holy souls."[20] And in order that it be recognized that passing into souls is nothing other than entering into souls, again from that text of Holy Scripture, he thus recalls, "A holy people and blameless race, wisdom delivered from a nation of oppressors. She entered the soul of a servant of the Lord, and withstood dread kings with wonders and signs."[21] This "entering into" of his, by which he enters souls, he also indicates in the Apocalypse of John when he says, "Behold, I stand at the door and knock. If anyone hears my voice and opens the door, then I will enter his house and dine with him and he with me."[22]

2. By this entering, the Father and the Son come to their lover and make their home with him, just as the Son himself says, "Whoever loves me and keeps my word and my Father will love him and we will come to him and make our dwelling with him."[23] But if the Father and the Son, coming to him, make their dwelling with him, not internally but are external, are we told where they come to him and make their dwelling with him? All the while, that Christ lives in his faithful interiorly, we know from the preaching of Paul who says, "That Christ may dwell in your hearts through faith."[24]

3. Or perchance they are going to say that Christ lives through faith in our interior man in one way and, in another way, he comes with the Father to make his dwelling with his lover so that Christ all the while can live alone in our in-

19. Wis 4.1.
21. Wis 10.15–16.
23. Jn 14.23.
20. Wis 7.27.
22. Rev 3.20.
24. Eph 3.17.

terior man, the Father remaining on the outside of the one with whom he makes his dwelling. Not only is he unable to remain in the interior but also impedes the Son by the communion of his coming since he is unable to live in the interior person.

4. The Son of God promised the Holy Spirit as well to his faithful so that he remain with them and in them. For he says, "If you love me, you will keep my commandments. And I will ask the Father and he will give you another Advocate to be with you always, the Spirit of Truth, which the world cannot accept because it neither sees nor knows it. But you know it, because it remains with you and will be in you."[25] See that the Holy Spirit is in those with whom the Son remains.

5. What can the difference be here which is spoken of so that he remains with them and is in them? Each preposition is found in one text and the possibility of each position is ascribed to the Holy Spirit, so that he is in those with whom he remains. Since the Holy Spirit remains with the faithful in such a way that he can exist in the same faithful, is God the Word with God in such a way that he cannot exist in God? What shall I say to those who desire to argue about the Scriptures in such a way that they never seek the way of spiritual understanding and, averting their eyes from the true light, delight to wander in the darkness forever?

6. That to be with God is the same thing as to be in God, the Holy Scripture shows in other places. For Moses says: "A faithful God without deceit, just and upright he is."[26]

David also sings, "Just is the Lord our God and there is no iniquity in him."[27] Paul the Apostle says that there is no iniquity with God. For he speaks thus: "Is there injustice on the part of God? Of course not!"[28] Let them choose in this text what the Arians want and, to show their wisdom in an obvious way, let them pass judgment on what is said by the Law and the Prophets and the Apostle, Moses says, "A faithful

---

25. Jn 14.15–17.
26. Dt 32.4.
27. Ps 9.16 LXX; Ps 10.16.
28. Rm 9.14.

God in whom there is no iniquity."[29] David also says, "Just is the Lord our God, and there is no iniquity in him."[30] And Paul says, "Is there injustice on the part of God? Of course not!"[31] Therefore, either let them confess that the Apostle's meaning fits with the meaning in the Law and the Prophets, or let them say that Paul differs from the understanding in the Law and the Prophets.

7. Paul the Apostle says that he has the same spirit of faith which the blessed David had, which the holy Moses received, just as he himself testifies, saying, "Since then we have the same spirit of faith, according to what is written: 'I believed, therefore, I spoke.' We too believe and therefore speak."[32] How did they have the one spirit of faith, if they believed differently concerning the faithful God? For the difference in belief is great if what Paul says, "There is no injustice with God,"[33] differs from what Moses and David say, "There is no iniquity in God."[34] And if, as Paul says, he has the same spirit of faith which the prophets also had, and yet his belief is different from their faith, let the Apostle be declared a liar (God forbid), he who testifies that Christ speaks in him.

8. "You are looking for proof of Christ speaking in me?" But since Christ has truly spoken in Paul, Paul is not a liar. And when he says that he has the same spirit of faith, he does not lie; the belief of each is in agreement so that what Moses and David have said—that there is no iniquity in God, this is also what Paul says, "There is no iniquity with God."[35] But if it perhaps seems to them that they are saying something quite different, this is left to them, that they contradict either the prophets or the Apostle.

VI. 1. And although the views of the heretics, confuted by so many and such great testimonies, is recognized as supported by no truth, still let them answer what they think about that text of the Apostle James when he says, "All good

29. Dt 32.4.
30. Ps 9.16 LXX; Ps 10.16.
31. Rm 9.14.
32. 2 Cor 4.13.
33. Rm 9.14.
34. Dt 32.4; Ps 9.16 LXX; Ps 10.16.
35. Rm 9.14.

giving and every perfect gift is from above, coming down from the Father of lights, with whom there is no alteration of shadow caused by change."[36] With the one with whom there is no alteration assuredly there is no mutability; and with the one with whom there is no mutability is immutability.

2. This immutability which is with God, let them say, whether it is exterior or interior; for if it is interior, behold this is to be in God, because it is to be with God. Therefore, let them stop believing wrong things and hasten to agree with Catholic orthodoxy. But if this immutability which is with God is not believed to be internal, but external, assuredly it is not believed to be in God. And if the immutability is not believed to be in God, as a consequence, God himself is proclaimed to be mutable. And lest they wish to attribute this to the Son, let them hear "The Father of lights" named in the same text.

3. Accordingly, when we hear that there is no alteration with God, let us believe this according to the truth of the Catholic faith, that there is no alteration in God. And when it is said: "The Word was with God,"[37] let us believe nothing other than that: The Word was in God. And when Wisdom says in Proverbs: "I was beside him, like a master worker,"[38] let us not believe anything other than: I was in him like a master worker. And when it is said to God: "With you is the fountain of life,"[39] let us not understand anything other then: in you is the fountain of life.

4. And when John says, "We proclaim to you the eternal life that was with the Father and was made visible to us,"[40] we do not understand anything else than: the eternal life which was in the Father. For truly with God is God the Word because God the Word was in God. And truly with the God the wise is Wisdom because Wisdom is in the wise God. And truly with the living God is life because God the life is in the

---

36. Jas 1.17.
37. Jn 1.1.
38. Prov 8.30.
39. Ps 35.10 LXX; Ps 36.9. Misprint at the foot of CCL XC.60.
40. 1 Jn 1.2.

living God. And truly with the true God is God the Truth, because God the Truth is in the true God. And truly with God the powerful is God the Power because God the Power is in the powerful God.

5. But what is wonderful, if to be with the Father is for the Son what it is for him to be in the Father, because by nature born from the Father, he remains forever in the Father; when we read about human beings (insofar as it attains to the substance by which they are human by nature) that it is no different, when something is said to be with them than to be in them? To this, we shall bring forward very clear testimonies: in the book of Isaiah, there is the prayer of king Hezekiah which he poured out to God after fifteen years had been added to his life, where, among other things, he says, "My spirit has been made with me, as a weaver coming near to remove the cloth."[41] How else is this to be understood? "My spirit with me," except: My spirit in me?

6. Or will it be said that the person's spirit is with a person but is not in a person? Since the Apostle clearly says, "Among human beings, who knows what pertains to a person except the spirit of the person that is within?"[42] As for the text that we cited above: "Reasoning unsoundly, they said with themselves,"[43] what is this but: They said within themselves? Again it is written in the book of Wisdom: "When I considered these things inwardly and pondered in my heart that in kinship with wisdom there is immortality."[44]

7. What he considers inwardly, he ponders in his heart, what he speaks of in each case, i.e., the considering and the pondering, he showed are within him, not externally but internally. It is also said in Proverbs: "My child . . . [let not evil thoughts seize you] who forsakes the partner of her youth and forgets her sacred covenant; for her way leads down to death and her paths to the shades."[45] Therefore, if evil thoughts, which placed their dwelling with death, are outside of death, not in death, assuredly he lives.

41. Is 3.12.
43. Wis 2.1.
45. Prov 2.17–18.
42. 1 Cor 2.11.
44. Wis 8.17.

8. And if "with the shades" does not mean placed in hell, what is left is that that which is neither in death nor in hell is said to have life in heaven. Therefore, it is said to God: "For you have delivered my soul from death,"[46] because he has given life to the soul by faith, saying, "My just one lives by faith."[47] And again it is said to him: "You have delivered my soul from the depths of Sheol,"[48] because by the grace of God souls are delivered from hell that they may live in the heavens. Whence the Apostle says, "Our citizenship is in heaven."[49]

9. But the soul, which through evil thoughts was with death, how has it been freed from death, if it was not in death? And how was it snatched from hell, if, while with the shades, it was not in hell? Since, if it was not in death, it would not have been dead. Through an evil will, i.e., through sin, who does not know that the soul is dead? Since God says, "The person who sins shall die."[50] Therefore, it is certain that the soul that thinks evil thoughts when it is with death, is in death, and when it is with the shades, is in hell. What is it that the Savior says? "What is impossible with human beings, is possible with God."[51] Therefore, shall we say that all things are possible to God, that even this is possible, viz., that we say that it is with God in such a way that we say that it is not in God? For what power does God have with him, if he does not have the power itself in him?

VII. 1. With testimonies of this sort, let it be clear that when it is said: "The Word was with God," nothing else must be understood than: the Word was in God. For the Son himself who is God the Word bears witness not only that the Father is in him but also that he is in the Father, saying, "Do you not believe that I am in the Father and the Father is in me?"[52]

This being of the Son with the Father and being in the Father does not seem to be comparable to that of any human

---

46. Ps 114.8 LXX; Ps 116.8.   47. Hab 2.4.
48. Ps 85.13 LXX; Ps 86.13.   49. Phil 3.20.
50. Ez 18.20.   51. Mt 19.26.
52. Jn 14.10.

person being with another person, whether it be a question of the rule of hospitality or affection of love. For the Apostle Paul says that he remained fifteen days with the Apostle Peter by rule of hospitality and purity of love. Although by reason of unity of faith and love, they were of one soul and one heart, still Paul did not stay with Peter in the way the Word remains with God, because it is not possible for one human being with another to be as God the Word is with God the Father. For a human being is with another human being in such a way that not only can he not be with him, but also, when he is with him, he cannot be in him by way of substance.

2. Truly, one who is with another is outside him, because even when he is with him by a sincere love, he is separated by place, no matter by how great an affection each is joined to the other. But the Word is with God in this way, just as the word in the mind, just as counsel is in the heart; when the mind has a word with it, it has it by thinking, because to say that it is with it, is nothing other than to say that it is thinking with it. When, therefore, the mind thinks and by thinking generates a word within itself, it generates a word from its own substance and generates that word from itself in such a way that it has with it what has been begotten.

3. Nor does the word have something less because it is born from the mind than is the mind from which it is born because as great as the mind is which generates the word, just as great is the word itself. For just as the word is born from the whole mind, so what is born remains within the whole. And because, with the mind thinking, there is not some part of it where the word is not, therefore, so great as the word is, just as great is the mind itself from which it is, and when it is with it, it is in it, and what the mind itself is, this the word is, which is from it and in it; and as great as it is, just as great is the word because it is from the whole and in the whole.

4. Just as great as the word itself is, so great at the same time is also the mind itself with the word; the word is not born from it in such a way that it may be detached from it in

a spatial sense. That birth, which shows what it is and from what it is, itself shows that it cannot exist outside of that from which it was born, nor is it less in something but is of it in such a way that it is with it and in it, and as great as it is from it is just as great in it, and as great as it is in it, it is just as great with it.

VIII. 1. Indeed, Scripture says that we too in some way are both in God and with God but not in the way God the Word, who is the only-begotten Son, is with God and is in God. For it is said also to us that: "in God, we live and move and have our being."[53] And it is said to God himself: "For even if we sin, we are yours."[54] Nevertheless, when this is said about us, it is not a unity with God by our nature that is being demonstrated, but either the power of the Creator is understood or the piety of the Redeemer. Thus we have believed that we are in God and with God, just as, born from God, we are children of God.

2. For it is written: "Beloved, we are God's children now."[55] And again: "He willed to give us birth by the word of truth."[56] Therefore, God begot us by the word of truth, but he begot the truth, the Word. He gave us the power to become children of God, but the Son of God was not made by power; the Son of God was born from God by nature. God begot us by his will because the will preceded generation; in the generation of the only-begotten, however, no will of the begetter went first where the eternal birth by nature remains without a beginning.

3. Just as we have been begotten but not like the only-begotten God, and we are children of God but not like the only and true Son, and we are gods but not the Word who is true God, so we are in God and with God but not as God the Word is with God and is in God, who was born from God by nature. Although he is called the Son and we are called children and he, God, and we, gods, and he is begotten and we are begotten, still there is in reality a great distance between

---

53. Acts 17.28.
55. 1 Jn 3.2.
54. Wis 15.2.
56. Jas 1.18.

the realities which one name seems to express, since he is by nature what God is, what the Son is, what the only-begotten is, because he was born of the nature of the Father. But we are what gods are, what children are, what the begotten are, not by nature, but by grace, because, though we do not have it in our nature that we can be these things, it has been freely given to us that we could become these things.

4. If heretics, with God's merciful gift, grasp this distinction, they will see the true light and they will refrain from their slanders against the only-begotten Son; they disparage him not only in this, that he is "with" God, but also they strive to deny that there is a human soul in him. The Son of God himself with one verse of a psalm pointed them out saying, "May that be the reward of my accusers from the Lord, of those who speak evil against my life."[57]

5. For who disparages Christ worse with God than the one who, hearing that God the Word is with God, says that the same Word is not in God? Or who speaks greater evil against the soul of Christ than he who denies that there is a human soul in Christ? When that Word, which is God, is with God, of whom it is so in such a way that it is in God through unity of nature and through that same unity of nature, is one God with it, and that soul at the same time, was taken up with the flesh by the only-begotten God so that at the same time in Christ, both our soul and our flesh should be saved. From him without a doubt, he will receive eternal salvation, who in him knows the full truth of the divine and human nature.

57. Ps 108.20 LXX; Ps 109.20.

THE LETTERS OF FULGENTIUS

Introduction

The first seven letters of Fulgentius deal with questions of spirituality. It is probable that the letters given here are the sole remaining examples of other letters written to the same correspondents. Letters 8 to 14, on the other hand, are primarily concerned with doctrinal issues, especially, of course, of the doctrines at issue with the Arian Vandals. Two of this group, letters 11 and 13, are letters of the Carthaginian deacon, Ferrandus. They are probably kept separate because Ferrandus is an author and theologian of note in his own right. (They are letters 1 and 2 within the Ferrandan corpus.) These two letters draw out lengthy responses from Fulgentius in letters 12 and 14.

In contrast, queries from otherwise unknown correspondents are incorporated under the number of Fulgentius's letters of reply. So, in letter 9, Victor asks Fulgentius to refute the sermon of the Arian Fastidiosus and includes the Arian's text for good measure. Letter 10 includes the inquiry of one Scarila as well as Fulgentius's lengthy answer to three questions.

Of the remaining letters not translated here, two were authored by Fulgentius in the name of the African bishops exiled with him in Sardinia (letters 15 and 17). Letter 16 from Peter the Deacon, which elicits letter 17 in response, is also included in the Fulgentius corpus. Letter 18 is a relatively brief reply to Count Reginus on the subject of the incorruptibility of the body of Christ.

LETTER 1. TO OPTATUS

The closest most commentators come to giving a date to this letter is to assign it to the period of the second exile in Sardinia, 515–23. It is not even certain that the name 'Optatus' is to be trusted. Most manuscripts do not give the name, and the subject matter of the letter would argue for a high degree of confidentiality.

The problem behind the letter is brought about by the harsh conditions imposed on baptized Christians who had undertaken the non-repeatable canonical penance of the time. One of the many consequences of this penance was that the penitent was no longer to have conjugal relations with a spouse. Not surprisingly, because of this and other strident demands, Christians increasingly put off doing this penance until they were dying.

In this case, a young wife who was believed to be dying undertook this penance, but in fact she recovered. Now her husband expressed serious concern about the future of their marriage. In his reply, Fulgentius reviewed the question of Christian marriage. Marriage bound each spouse closely and intimately to the other. Neither was allowed to make a vow of continence without the informed consent of the other. The theologian then applied this basic consideration to the matter at hand. If the husband had made such a vow, he and his wife, the penitent, were bound to carry it out. If not, the continence resulting from the penance should not bind the other partner who had not so bound himself. Pope Leo the Great could be cited as supporting this more moderate view. See his letter 167.

ULGENTIUS, servant of the servants of Christ, sends greetings in the Lord to the deservedly venerable son.

1. Some months ago I received your letter, a sign of your holy concern. While I wanted to reply without delay, I was seized by a sudden illness in such a way that a violent excess of fever might have carried me off from the hustle and bustle of the present life unless the true physician of souls and bodies who cures all our illnesses and redeems our life from destruction had deigned to grant the assistance of his medicine to remove the scourge of so great an infirmity. When deliverance had been received, the will to write was not lacking but the harshness of winter stood in the way of sending it. Now, because the Creator and ruler of the seasons has granted a moderation of the winds, I have not delayed returning as an answer to your question what I have received from the mercy and inspiration of the highest giver.

2. You say that our daughter, your wife, recently was ill almost to the point of the ultimate danger and, as often happens, having received the imposition of hands, entered upon the penitential process according to the custom of the Christian religion. But afterwards, by gift of the divine goodness, she received a full restoration of bodily health. Now, adducing the weakness of the flesh, you confess the incontinence of a youthful age in addition; and in this uncertainty of mind, in which you take the flesh into consideration, you fear the majesty of God, just as a sailor, not knowing where

he is and tossed about by the waves and winds, since you are taking precautions because of the uncertainty of the dangers, you demand that a harbor where you can avoid a shipwreck of the soul be shown to you by our response.

3. The thrust of your question forces me to weigh energetically two matters which should be considered, viz., not only what the nature of conjugal sexuality is but also what the promise of one making a vow demands in each matter.

4. Therefore, if any of the faithful in the light of reason consider sexual intercourse in itself, culpable usage will not be found in conjugal intercourse but in the excesses of the sexual partners. Conjugal sex induces guilt not from the sexual intercourse of husband and wife but from immoderate lust. In spouses, therefore, excess is censured by the law, but nuptial dignity is not deprived of the gift of honor conferred on it by God. So the authority of the apostolic proclamation cries out, "Let marriage be honored among all and let the marriage bed be kept undefiled."[1] Paul was informing the Corinthians about the purity of marriage that had to be preserved, when he prefaced his remarks with, "It is good for a man not to touch a woman."[2] Seeing their weakness and brimming with apostolic charity, the outstanding teacher, with Christ speaking in him, did not neglect to put an underpinning of consolation "as on a leaning wall, a tottering fence."[3] Finally, he adds, "Because of cases of immorality every man should have his own wife, and every woman, her own husband. The husband should fulfill his duty toward his wife and likewise the wife toward her husband."[4]

5. The thrust of the reading from the Apostle shows that the wife should have intercourse with her husband and the husband with the wife by reason of a certain mutuality of what is owed. Without a doubt, the Apostle would not have called this a debt unless he knew that it had legitimately to be paid; nor would he command that it be paid by the duty of mutual consent, if it were an evil demand on the part of

---

1. Heb 13.4.
2. 1 Cor 7.1.
3. Ps 61.4 LXX; Ps 62.3.
4. 1 Cor 7.2–3.

the one asking. Indeed the teacher of the nations has no hesitation in including marriage among the divine works so that he confirms that there is a power with equal right, of the woman over the body of her husband and of the husband over the body of his wife, saying, "A wife does not have authority over her own body but rather her husband, and similarly, a husband does not have authority over his own body, but rather his wife."[5] And in another text, the same one says that "there is no authority except from God."[6]

6. The use of this power assigned by God to the work of begetting is without blame if lustful excess is not permitted to go beyond the bounds of righteousness. And the righteous use of marriage is this, that the spouses have sexual intercourse at the proper time not to fulfill lust but for begetting children. So, among those good things which God has made is found the chaste joining of wife and husband. In these works of God, lust cannot be found. Sometimes that is not befitting to righteousness which has not come to human beings from the gift of creation but to sinners from the fault of the first sin. But without it, human progeny is not sown in the body of this death, chaste marriages do not strive for it but tolerate it, and the goodness of marriage imposes on it a means without which it cannot fulfill the duty of the fecundity of nature in the sinful flesh.

7. Fruit must be sought from marriage in such a way that the excess of lascivious pleasure is contained. So, if conjugal practice is moderated so that the spirit is not enslaved to the heat of lust but concentrates on the producing of children to be born, and, when they are born, does not neglect to see that they are swiftly cleansed in a spiritual begetting, then the sexual intercourse conceded is not allowed to the faithful spouses for the sin of the flesh because the conjugal obligation preserves chastity and modest restraint guards temperateness. Conjugal fecundity provides children to be dedicated to God so that by the help of God the Redeemer, the human being already born, may be reformed by the

5. 1 Cor 7.4.
6. Rom 13.1.

sacrament of baptism. By God's work, he is first formed in the womb and human nature has him as a father by the blessing of a second birth, the same one whom in the first birth he recognizes as the author of his creation.

8. Therefore, if a married man fornicates, he sins mortally. But if he does not desert the faith of his bed but intemperately exceeds a little bit with his wife, in the natural usage only, not only seeking to beget but sometimes obeying the lust of the flesh, he does not do this without fault; such a fault, however, is quickly forgiven to the one who does good and prays because marital love preserves the fidelity for the spouse when marital weakness is unable to guard moderation. And if nuptial modesty is not held in the case of the wife, still there is no departure from nuptial fidelity because of any lack of moderation.

9. As long as the faith of the bed is kept, it cleanses the stain which the weakness of the flesh contracts, if he does not have relations with other women. This is the case with the one who has relations with his wife not for begetting alone but also because of the weakness of the flesh. Because even if he goes beyond the determined method of having intercourse, still he has not exceeded the conjugal limits. And although carnal weakness contracts guilt, still nuptial integrity asks for forgiveness. As such he receives forgiveness, not because he demands the conjugal debt from her more than he should, but because, content with what he has received legitimately from one woman, he does not seek from another woman. Still, the works of mercy, which alone are worthwhile in the Christian religion must not be lacking so that not only those who use spouses or those who are continent, but also virgins cannot attain to the prize of virginity, if they neglect the works of mercy and charity. If someone, on the other hand, intent on good works, has so kept moderation in regard to his wife that he has relations with his wife only for the sake of procreating children, such a person is without a doubt worthy of much praise, if there is anyone in our times who can fulfill this description.

10. Fornication can never be without serious sin in which,

although we do not doubt that the man without a wife sins mortally, I think that for the husband to fornicate is an even more serious sin. Holy Scripture says that each must be condemned and is alien to the kingdom of God. For in the letter to the Hebrews, it is written that: "God will judge the immoral and adulterers."[7] And the Apostle in the letter he wrote to the Corinthians, says, "Do not be deceived; neither fornicators nor idolaters, nor adulterers, nor boy prostitutes, nor practicing homosexuals, nor thieves, nor the greedy, nor drunkards, nor slanderers, nor robbers will inherit the Kingdom of God."[8] Again, among the works of the flesh, the same blessed Apostle enumerates: fornication, impurity, and licentiousness in the conclusion of which, he says, "Those who do such things will not inherit the kingdom of God."[9] He also warns lest he "have to mourn over many of those who sinned earlier and have not repented of the impurity, immorality, or licentiousness they practiced."[10]

11. Therefore, because we have been speaking of the nature of marriage as the Lord has given it, consequently, this must be examined with the greatest care, viz., what devotion has prescribed beforehand in your will (if there could have been anything). Because the use of things conceded by God is not forbidden to human beings, one should not conclude that therefore one need not render to God what he has vowed. It is written: "I will pay you my vows, those that my lips uttered."[11] And lest anyone seek to use tribulation as an excusing cause for himself, in order to gain the freedom to evade a promise or to think of himself as free from what he has vowed, by saying that he was forced to vow something not by his own will but because of tribulation, the blessed David teaches that everything which was legitimately promised, even in tribulation, must be given back to God, when he says to God, "I will pay you my vows, those that my lips uttered." And he added immediately, "... and my mouth promised when I was in trouble."[12] But in Deuterono-

7. Heb 13.4.
8. 1 Cor 6.9–10.
9. Gal 5.21.
10. 2 Cor 12.21.
11. Ps 65.13–14 LXX; Ps 66.13–14.
12. Ps 65.14.

my, it is also written: "If you make a vow to the Lord your God, do not postpone fulfilling it; for the Lord your God will surely require it of you and you would incur guilt. But if you refrain from vowing, you will not incur guilt. Whatever your lips utter, you must diligently perform, just as you have freely vowed to the Lord your God with your own mouth."[13] And Solomon says, "When you make a vow to God, do not delay fulfilling it; . . . Fulfill what you vow. It is better that you should not vow than that you should vow and not fulfill it."[14]

12. Accordingly, the use of licit things is done licitly with moderation, as long as the renunciation of the licit thing is not vowed and as long as the perpetual promise of continence is not held from the consent of both, i.e., of the husband and wife, conjugal sexual relations are not illicit. For it is written: "If you marry, however, you do not sin, nor does an unmarried woman sin if she marries."[15] Nevertheless, although the virgin who marries does not sin, there is a type of virgin who sins if she marries; the virgin who marries does not sin, if, before she marries, she has not vowed her virginity to God in her heart. Otherwise, "If," as the Apostle said, "the one who stands firm in his resolve, however, who is not under compulsion but has power over his own will and has made up his mind to keep his virgin"[16] sins gravely later, if, after vowing her virginity to God, she wish to be enslaved in a human marriage. For the blessed Paul pronounced certain widows bound by the chain of condemnation because, after professing continence, they did not give up the habitual will to marry. He instructs Timothy to avoid such people as follows: "But exclude younger widows for when their sensuality estranges them from Christ, they want to marry and will incur condemnation for breaking their first pledge."[17] Therefore, the promise of continence removes the freedom for sexual intercourse, nor is fornication alone forbidden to such people, but conjugal sexuality is also forbidden and the guilty embrace holds the sinful will, even if in practice no ef-

13. Dt 23.21–23.
14. Eccl 5.4–5.
15. 1 Cor 7.28.
16. 1 Cor 7.37.
17. 1 Tm 5.11–12.

fect follows. For it has not been written in vain that "desire, when it conceives, brings forth sin."[18]

13. So, not only integrity promised to God by virgins but also continence promised to God by widows and wives must be preserved with fear and trembling. Because before anyone is guilty because of a vow, he is not condemned whether it be a virgin who marries licitly or a husband and wife rendering the conjugal debt to each other. But after anyone, seeking better things, has bound himself by a profession of continence or integrity, he sins most seriously, if he thinks that from then on something that was possible for him before is still an option for him. In such matters, that which the will, making a vow to God, removes from itself, from then on no necessity allows him to make use of it with impunity; nor will the violator of a vow find a justifying excuse for his transgression, he whom no one forced to make a vow.

14. Doubtless, a distinction must be made between the vow of a virgin or widow and the vow of those who are held by the conjugal vow. For the freedom or liberty to make a vow is not as great for the man or woman who does not have the power over his or her own body as it is for any widow or virgin. The full ability to vow bodily continence is not available to the married man or woman, whose body is not in his or her own power but in that of the spouse, according to that statement of the Apostle, which we have cited above: "A wife does not have authority over her own body but rather her husband, and similarly, a husband does not have authority over his own body, but rather his wife."[19] Therefore, one whose body is not within his or her own power is not allowed to assume continence apart from the will of the spouse. A person promises with right and firm vow only that which he knows is within his right. When someone wishes to make profession of the continence of his body which is under the power of his spouse, it is like someone trying to give alms or offer a sacrifice from what belongs to someone else; for our

18. Jas 1.15.
19. 1 Cor 7.4.

1. TO OPTATUS

God (as he himself bears witness) loves justice and hates robbery in a holocaust.

15. Therefore, that promise of continence between spouses is certain which has been confirmed by the consent of both. When husband and wife, giving consent with a common will, have offered it up on the altar of faith to the true and highest God in the temple of their heart, as a sacrifice for a sweet aroma, neither can the wife have any further legitimate power over the body of the husband to demand the conjugal debt nor the husband over the body of the woman. For just as before they made a vow to God together, the sacrifice made by only one was reprehensible, because the assent of the legitimate partner was lacking, so when each has offered with equal consent what is inseparably common to both, he will not go unpunished if anyone believes that the gift offered to God by a vow made voluntarily is to be violated by an illicit deed.

16. But if perchance anyone will be alleged to have made a vow but not with his whole heart, it will be the more to be condemned, because he did not go to God in an innocent but in a false way. For it is written that: "a holy and disciplined spirit will flee from deceit and will leave foolish thoughts behind."[20] In another text, Holy Scripture thus rebukes the false: "Woe to timid hearts and slack hands and to the sinner who walks a double path."[21]

17. How evil it is and how earnestly to be avoided it is if someone should attempt by death-dealing transgression to retain or to get back that which he vowed to God. Ananias and Sapphira are an example whom, unfaithfully holding back some part of the price obtained for their field, not only the apostolic voice rebuked as usurpers of divine right but also the severity of heavenly justice killed. The blessed Peter not only said that the above-mentioned Ananias was guilty because of the sin of fraud but also declared that his heart had been filled by Satan, saying, "Ananias, why has Satan

20. Wis 1.5.
21. Sir 2.12.

filled your heart so that you lied to the Holy Spirit and retained part of the price of the land? While it remained unsold, did it not remain yours? And when it was sold, was it still not under your control? Why did you contrive this deed? You have lied, not to human beings, but to God."[22] Therefore, if anyone, overcome by carnal enticement believes that something already vowed to the Lord can again be sought, he is not a legitimate possessor of his property but is declared to be one who usurps what belongs to God. Not undeservedly does the impure violator of vowed continence now hear what the swindler greedy for money heard.

18. Accordingly, with your conscience bearing witness to you, think over carefully all the things which have been discussed above. And if you, with equal assent, have vowed continence, preserve the quality of your love together with the fear of God, and, if any time, the weakness of the flesh troubles your mind, let your spirit hasten to the assistance of the divine pity and not give in to lust but as a believer pray to God with all humility and not give in to the carnal desire fighting against the soul but rather repel it. If, on the other hand, one of you has made a vow of continence without the agreement of the other, he knows that he has made the vow rashly and, with a chaste sincerity, let him render the debt to his spouse.

19. Nevertheless, in order that all of your actions may be done rightly in rendering the conjugal debt, let the conjugal practice set aside the weakness of the flesh in such a way that the flesh is not enslaved to lust but let the power of the Spirit helped by God hold in the reins of carnal lust. The business of begetting children ought to be done in such a way by the spouses, that with the help of the sense of shame, when the faithful spirit brings itself to the work of fecundity, with God's help, it keeps the modesty of natural decency. Especially, Christian spouses must be careful to flee those works which the divine severity both forbids to be done and condemns when they are done. These things the apostolic

22. Acts 5.3–4.

1. TO OPTATUS

teaching has not ceased to make known to the faithful so that it might prudently instruct and salutarily frighten them into keeping the rule of a good life.

20. Not to touch a woman is a great good which every faithful man ought to observe from the start. Still, because of fornications, anyone, whether married or free from a spouse, if he has not vowed continence to God and sees that he himself is incapable of fulfilling the continence (although when the will to be continent is full and true humility of heart has not ceased from prayer and good works, he who said, "Ask and it will be given to you; seek and you will find; knock and the door will be opened to you,"[23] because he is the truth and cannot lie, and he gives to the one who asks well and for the one seeking, prepares the one seeking for his discoveries, and to the one who knocks, [the door] opens so that [the one] may enter the inner places of a better life), still if anyone up to this point is more worried about his own weakness than secure in the power of the Lord, if he has not known the continence of the flesh, let him keep himself from iniquity and use his wife as is fitting. Let him flee evil and greed and he will not be condemned if he pays the debt to his spouse. Let him not be drunk, nor envious, nor contentious, nor a hypocrite, nor evil, nor a quarreller, nor proud, nor rapacious, nor greedy. Insofar as he is able, let him seek peace with all; let him not hold fast to destruction; let him detract from no one; let him keep faith with friends; let him never be treacherous to enemies or a perjurer; let him not steal what belongs to others; let him not prefer money to justice; let him be just in business, devout in works; meek in tolerating injuries, slow in avenging them; stable in faith, a lover of chastity and peace. Let him hearken to the saying of the Savior in which he both commands us as to what to do and shows us what we are to accept; for he says: "Forgive and you will be forgiven; Give and gifts will be given to you."[24] If, therefore, insofar as he is

23. Mt 7.7.
24. Lk 6.37–38.

able, he is generous and cheerful in giving alms, and easy and mild in forgiving sinners, and yet not think that forgiveness should be given to sinners in such a way that he believes that the discipline of his house ought to be neglected, but, retaining moderation in both force and mercy, let him maintain moderateness in correction and severity in forgiveness. Let him criticize, warn, frighten, reprove, console, delight; let him not do as much to sinners who are subject to him, as the onset of rage urges, but as much as the method of putting the question requires; and if a slave is to be flogged for a sin, let not the lust for vengeance win out, but let Christian justice counsel mercy for him whom he is flogging; and thus also when justice pursues guilt, let mercy not be lacking, which knows how to attenuate punishment by moderation.

21. Let children be nourished according to the commandment of the Apostle, "with the training and instruction of the Lord,"[25] and let them not be allowed to live impiously or in depravity, since Christian offspring ought to serve chastity and temperance. And in that fearful scrutiny the negligence of parents concerning the evil deeds of their children will have to be judged since in this world Eli the priest was reproved by the Lord and rejected, not because he supported his sons in their wickedness, but because, albeit with soft words, he admonished the sinners but he did not forbid them with adequate severity. Parents who truly love their children look after them by doing good deeds more than by accumulating wealth, lest while money is steadily piled up for the children, the opportunity for good works is passed over.

22. Above all, let faithful spouses always remember that they must stand firm in prayers and almsgiving; let them not always wish to wallow in the weakness of the flesh, but let them hasten to rise to the level of a more controlled life. And in order that the spirit may attain the virtue of continence, let the excesses of carnal lust be more and more sup-

---

25. Eph 6.4.

pressed so that while, with God's help, they will have gone beyond that level in which conjugal weakness asks for forgiveness, they can praiseworthily reach a higher level, in which the virtue of continence awaits the palm of a better life.

LETTER 2. TO THE WIDOW GALLA

This letter, which begins as a letter of consolation on the death of a young husband, quickly (by section 8) turns into a letter seeking to persuade the recipient to take up the life of a dedicated Christian widow and ends as a general exhortation to the spiritual life. Galla, a member of an illustrious Roman family, was the daughter of Quintus Aurelius Memmius Symmachus, counsul in 485 under Odoacer. Her sister, Rusticiana, was married to Boethius, consul in 510 and author of *The Consolation of Philosophy*. According to Gregory the Great, Galla became a holy woman who was favored with visions. See *Dialogues* IV.14. See "Galla 5," PLRE II.491.

ULGENTIUS, servant of the servants of Christ, sends greetings in the Lord to the illustrious lady and, in the fear of God, venerable daughter, Galla.

1. Several months ago, I found out from a reliable report of my deacon returning from the city,[1] not only of the death of your spouse but also of the holy path of your resolution in which you are already walking, with him leading who is the "way, the truth and the life."[2] He knows how, after a passing sorrow, to give to his faithful the gift of eternal happiness, and he wishes for their salvation that they may pass from the earthly to the heavens by the arrangement of his fatherly kindness.

2. The Lord, whose incomprehensible judgments and ineffable ways the Apostle Paul proclaims, did not swiftly transfer to no purpose your husband, faithful with pure religion, humble of heart, meek in sanctity, merciful in works, in his inmost depths innocent of life, young in years from the pil-

1. Rome.
2. Jn 14.6.

grimage of this life to the eternal dwelling of the heavenly homeland, except that, he gave to him eternal joys and to you the possibility of a higher life. He has given to him that, freed from the body, he will live with Christ forever; to you he has given that you may think of the things of the Lord and, according to the words of the Apostle Paul, be "holy in body and spirit."[3] Accordingly, believe without hesitation what is said by God and with love hope for what is promised that you may be able to do well what is commanded.

3. First, concerning the death of your husband, know from the Apostle Paul what you must faithfully hold. For he says, "We do not want you to be unaware, brothers, about those who have fallen asleep, so that you may not grieve like the rest who have no hope. For if we believe that Jesus died and rose, so too will God, through Jesus, bring with him those who have fallen asleep."[4]

So, if we hold on to the true faith, if we harbor no doubts about the words of God, if we, with most certain hope, progress toward the future life, if we love God and neighbor worthily, if we do not await a vain glory from human beings but the true glory of the Christian name from God, we must not like the unbelievers have any sadness concerning the faithful departed and, to speak more precisely, our people who have fallen asleep. There must remain in our heart a distinction between a salutary and a harmful sadness by which it comes about that a spirit, given over to eternal things, does not collapse because of the loss of temporal solace and assumes a salutary sadness concerning these things in which it considers that it did either something less or differently than it should have. So Paul teaches that each type of sadness is different no less in deed than in word. Finally, he shows that in one there is progress toward salvation but in the other, an ending in death, saying, "For godly sorrow produces a salutary repentance without regret but worldly sorrow produces death."[5]

---

3. 1 Cor 7.34.   4. 1 Thes 4.13–14.
5. 2 Cor 7.10.

4. Therefore, do not have an undifferentiated sadness over the death of your husband beyond the way of the Christian faith. You should not think of him as lost but as sent on ahead of you. You should not think of his youth as prematurely cut off but rather see him confirmed in an endless eternity. To the faithful souls it is said: "Your youth shall be renewed like the eagle's."[6]

5. Far be it from us, agreeing with the errors of the unbelievers to think or to say that "A black day has carried off and plunged in bitter death"[7] that young Christian man. For black day carries off those who, according to the saying of the Apostle John, "are in darkness and walk in darkness and do not know where they are going because the darkness has blinded their eyes."[8] Black day has carried off those whom the true light itself vehemently rebukes: "This is the verdict," he says, "that the light came into the world but people preferred darkness to light because their works were evil."[9] Such are they who live in such a way that when they hear the voice of the Son of God, they are called forth, not to life, but to judgment, as the Lord says, "... The hour is coming in which all who are in the tombs will hear his voice and will come out, those who have done good deeds to the resurrection of life, but those who have done wicked deeds, to the resurrection of condemnation."[10] And since neither a short nor a long life can avail these people, consequently in the book of Wisdom, it is said of such people: "Even if they live long, they will be held of no account and, finally, their old age will be without honor. If they die young, they will have no hope and no consolation on the day of judgment."[11]

6. But what is the "great day" except the day on which the Lord will come not to be judged but to judge? For when he came in order that there might be judgment given on our behalf, it was not the great day but a day of humiliation in which he was made a little less than the angels; but there will

---

6. Ps 102.5 LXX; Ps 103.5.
8. 1 Jn 2.11.
10. Jn 5.28–29.
7. Virgil *Aeneid* VI.429.
9. Jn 3.19.
11. Wis 3.17–18.

be the great day when, according to the testimony of the blessed John, all the wicked will want to be hidden in the caves in the mountains, crying to the mountains and the rocks: "Fall on us and hide us from the face of the one who sits on the throne and from the wrath of the Lamb because the great day of their wrath has come and who can withstand it?"[12] On this great day, the wicked will not have consolation but rebuke, for they will not hear: "Come, you who are blessed by my Father, inherit the kingdom prepared for you from the foundation of the world."[13] But it will be said to them: "Depart from me, you accursed, into the eternal fire prepared for the Devil and his angels."[14] Such people, however aged they may be when they die, are engulfed in a bitter death and although their age in the body may seem ripe, the deadly love of the world holds the bitterness of an immature mind in the heart.

7. But the Christian who has lived in the fear of God, at whatever age of the body he will have died, is not plunged in a bitter death but, relying on God, he is transferred at a fitting maturity. For in the same book of Wisdom we read that "Old age is not honored for length of time or measured by number of years but understanding is gray hair for anyone and a blameless life is ripe old age. There were some who pleased God and were loved by him...."[15]

Then, in what follows, he says that one who lives a good life and one that is pleasing to God is swiftly snatched away for this reason, viz., that he might endure no change brought about by the wickedness of the world nor his soul be deceived by some guile.[16] So it is said: "They were caught up so that evil might not change their understanding nor guile deceive their souls. For the fascination of wickedness obscures what is good and roving desire perverts the innocent mind. Being perfected in a short time, they fulfilled long years; for their souls were pleasing to God. Therefore

---

12. Rev 6.16–17.   13. Mt 25.34.
14. Mt 25.41.   15. Wis 4.8–10.
16. The textual reading here, CCL XCI, p. 200, l. 99, I take to be "foret" rather than "fovisset."

he took them quickly from the midst of wickedness."[17] With these words, Holy Scripture teaches us that in this world a long life does not profit faithful Christians, but a good life; and to know, insofar as it is possible, the merit of any deceased person, one must see not how long he lived but how each one lived. Just as an evil life, the longer it is prolonged in time, so much the more does it increase the punishment of those who go astray; so a good life, although ended here after a brief time, acquires great and eternal glory for those who lead good lives. But an evil life buries immature and bitter elderly people in hell, but a good life brings the dead, young and old, to the kingdom.

8. So, do not be sad that he has preceded you by a few days, but be careful and proceed on the road of this mortal life in such a way that you may be able to attain to eternal life. Accordingly, it is necessary that you recall without ceasing the word of the Apostle where he says, "An unmarried woman or a virgin is anxious about the things of the Lord, so that she may be holy in both body and spirit."[18] Here he calls a widow unmarried, not because she was never married but because she has been freed from the marriage bond to a dead husband. Concerning this he says in another text, ". . . if her husband dies, she is released from the law in respect to her husband."[19] He counsels this woman to be holy both in body and in spirit. What is it to be holy in body and in spirit except to preserve what is holy both in deed and in thought? Still she who is held bound by a bodily marriage is permitted to think of the things that are of the world, as the same Apostle says, "A married woman, on the other hand, is anxious about the things of the world, how she may please her husband."[20] Thus where mortal flesh is carnally wedded to one who is going to die, one must undergo the necessity of thinking about things of this world. And because the very requirements of the flesh hold them bound by harder chains, for this reason, the Apostle says about them: ". . . Such peo-

17. Wis 4.11–14.
19. Rm 7.2.
18. 1 Cor 7.34.
20. 1 Cor 7.34.

ple will experience affliction in their earthly life."[21] Therefore, the unmarried woman, i.e., the widow, to whom the command is given to be holy both in body and in spirit, just as she ceases to serve her husband in the body, so she must not think of carnal things in her heart.

9. The marriages of Christians are holy because in them chastity is kept in the body and purity of faith is preserved in the heart. For apostolic authority also says, "Let marriage be honored among all and let the marriage bed be kept undefiled...."[22] For marriage does not come from the pollution of sin but from the institution of God; and because the spouses pay to each other the debt of the flesh, insofar as they do it in modesty, they keep the commandments of Christ because they depart in no way from conjugal charity and chastity. But conjugal chastity abhors adulterous sexual relations and tenaciously clinging to morality and modesty, one man seeks it from one woman and one woman from one man because each knows that he or she owes it legitimately to only one. There the debt of the flesh is paid to the husband; but conjugal chastity is owed more to Christ than to the husband, because the body too is then truly chaste because it is not polluted by fleshly fornication when spiritual integrity is preserved by the fear and love of Christ.

10. Nevertheless, the unmarried woman and the virgin are distinguished from the married woman by not a small degree of dignity. Inasmuch as the married woman is held bound by worldly thoughts but the unmarried woman and the virgin are not subject to carnal trials, because they are not held by the bonds of carnal matrimony. There the freedom of bodily and spiritual continence is more certain because there is no necessity arising from conjugal servitude. Therefore, each is a gift of God, both conjugal modesty and a widow's continence. "Each has a particular gift from God,"[23] and that, in itself, is praiseworthy because good; but the latter is more praiseworthy because better. For the vile-

---

21. 1 Cor 7.28.   22. Heb 13.4.
23. 1 Cor 7.7.

2. TO THE WIDOW GALLA

ness of fornication is overcome by conjugal servitude; but the dignity of chastity increases with a widow's freedom. In the former case, faith counsels weakness lest it fall into vice; in the latter case, the faithful spirit is stretched for the increase of virtue. Concerning spouses, it is said: ". . . because of cases of immorality, every man should have his own wife and every woman her own husband."[24] But concerning the widow, it is said: "She is more blessed if she remains as she is."[25] Therefore, blessed is she who, out of horror of vice, does not seek illicit sexual relations; but more blessed she who, out of a greater love of purity, scorns licit sexual relations. Blessed she who lives bound to a husband in such a way that she pays the debt of her flesh to her husband only; but more blessed she who, now freed, remains unmarried lest she owe the debt.

11. Accordingly, because having been a wife, you have become a widow, think rather that God's gift to you has been increased, not taken away. For he who showed you the way to be followed for a better life has not deserted you. The Lord wanted you to climb to better things by degrees, so that at first you might live faithfully married to one husband, that afterwards you might remain apart from a husband without difficulty. To this end, divine grace has nourished your spirit with conjugal chastity so that you who had learned, while your husband was living, not to seek another, would learn to remain a widow apart from any man. Therefore, do not neglect the grace which is in you, and you know how much better it is to refrain always from sexual intercourse than to have relations even out of conjugal requirements. The husband that had been given to you for a time has departed in time; for he had been given to you, not for the bliss of the homeland, but for consolation on the journey.

12. There are other gifts of God, which God gives to his faithful in the present time in such a way that the use of them is considered necessary only in this life. By means of

---

24. 1 Cor 7.2.
25. 1 Cor 7.40.

them merit is acquired for the future life. Such are belief, holding the right faith, and works preserving justice and mercy in order that correct faith be not deserted by the assistance of charity which is recognized in works. Thus the Apostle gives his approval to that faith "which works through love."[26]

13. Right faith and works of mercy will cease after this life, when we shall see face to face that which when not seen is believed. Among the blessed, there will not be anyone miserable to whom mercy is given in advance. But these two things, i.e., faith and works, are not necessary after the end of this life in such a way that before the end they may not in any way be abandoned. Whoever before the end of this present life will have departed from the right faith or good works, even if he has worked at these vigorously and vigilantly before, because of the fact that he has departed from the right way, he loses the merit of the entire journey which he has run.

14. Likewise there are other things which are given to human beings in this time by divine piety in such a way that not only in this life must they remain uninterruptedly with human beings but they also grow in divine reward; such are the cleansing of sins, the knowledge of the truth, the love of God and neighbor. If anyone in this time will have perseveringly kept these in himself and, making progress by divine gift, will take care to increase the things begun, in the future he will have them remain with him with eternal perfection. Then perfect cleansing will receive perfect knowledge of the truth and perfect knowledge will allow nothing of perfect charity to be lacking in us.

15. But there are other things which are given by God in time in such a way that they are taken away in time, such as the mating of spouses, procreation of children, abundance of riches, health of bodies, and whatever things like these which in themselves are able to make people neither miserable nor happy. Therefore, these things are given by the

---

26. Gal 5.6.

Lord both to the good and to the evil and sometimes are taken away by God from both the good and the evil.

16. Job was blessed when he lived justly in riches but more blessed when he was more just in poverty. He was blessed when he was surrounded by ten children but more blessed when, struck by a loss of all of them at the same time, he remained unmoved in the love of God. He was also blessed in health of body but he became more blessed in his wounds. He was more blessed on a heap of filth than in a marble palace.

17. Also take note of the two men, one miserable in his wealth and health, the other very blessed in his want and disease. That wealthy man, who "dressed in purple garments and fine linen and dined sumptuously each day,"[27] how empty he was in those banquets, how poor in the greatness of his riches, how naked in the beauty of his clothing, how sick in the health of his body, how famished in the satiety of his belly, how miserable in rejoicings, how forsaken amid the conversations of his friends, how abject amid the subservience of his slaves! Also observe Lazarus, rich in his poverty, blessed in misery, cheerful in misfortune, healthy amid sores, without home but not without the Lord; without clothing but not without faith; with good health of body but not without the strength of charity; without food but not without Christ; exposed to the dogs but companion of angels, he received nothing of the crumbs that fell from the rich man's table, but he ate the heavenly bread interiorly.

18. Therefore, these are things which are sometimes possessed for good, sometimes for ill; sometimes they are scorned for good, sometimes for ill. They are possessed for good when, in their use, the fear of God is preserved, but they are scorned for the good when, in contempt of them, glory is sought not from human beings but from the highest God.

19. Such also is marriage which can be both taken up for good and scorned for the good. How well did Susanna pre-

---

27. Lk 16.19.

serve the work of marriage in conjugal chastity! How much better did Judith and Anna scorn it in a widow's continence! How best of all did Mary know nothing of this in virginal integrity!

20. Therefore, marriage is not to be thought of as among the outstanding gifts of God although it is not to be denied that it is a divine gift; it must not be said that the gift of blessedness, which can be held with good intent, can also be scorned with a better intention. For if it is necessary that this be reckoned among the outstanding gifts of God, they "who have castrated themselves for the kingdom of heaven"[28] would not be praised by the mouth of our Savior, nor would the Savior himself have commanded that father, mother, brothers, sisters, wife, children, fields, be left for his sake together with the one hundred-fold promise of reward and eternal life, saying, "And everyone who has given up houses or brothers or sisters or father or mother or children or lands for the sake of my name will receive a hundred times more and will inherit eternal life."[29] But saying this, Christ commanded that there be no divorce but with a precise distinction showed that even among the gifts of God, temporal things are to give way to eternal, those that pass to those that remain, the small to the great, among his faithful. He does not condemn good things but praises the better more; he does not hate the former but loves the latter more. The gain or the loss of the former is not a reward for faith but a testing of it.

21. But our faith must be fixed not on temporal things but on eternal. So, the vessel of election, exhorting us to the toleration of present trials, commands us to turn away the gaze of our inward heart from the contemplation of temporal things, saying, "For this momentary light affliction is producing for us an eternal weight of glory beyond all comparison; as we look not to what is seen but to what is unseen, for what is seen is transitory, but what is unseen is eternal."[30]

28. Mt 19.12.
29. Mt 19.29.
30. 2 Cor 4.17–18.

22. Therefore, walk, as it is written, "from strength to strength"[31] and may your spirit pass from attention to temporal things to contemplation of eternal things. Passing from the virtue of conjugal modesty to the more powerful virtue of the continence of a widow, you must be endowed with no less continence of heart than of body, and after the death of your temporal husband, all the remnants of worldly thought in your heart must be extinguished.

23. Why would a Christian widow have a spirit bound by the chain of any worldly thought, who, with her husband dead, ought to think of the world as dead with him? Thus since the reason for the worldly thought has ceased, worldly thought itself should cease; and just as formerly you were adorned bodily for your husband who delighted in the appearance of the body, so now you must be spiritually adorned for Christ, who seeks in you only the beauty of the mind.

24. Listen to what the blessed Peter commands even married women to whom he forbids the adornment of outer clothing, saying this: "Likewise your wives should be subordinate to your husbands so that, even if some disobey the word, they may be won over without a word by their wives' conduct when they observe your reverent and chaste behavior. Your adornment should not be an external one, braiding the hair, wearing gold jewelry, or dressing in fine clothes but rather the hidden character of the heart, expressed in the imperishable beauty of a gentle and calm disposition which is precious in the sight of God.[32] The blessed Apostle strengthened this commandment by the example of holy women, saying, "For this is also how the holy women who hoped in God once used to adorn themselves and were subordinate to their husbands."[33]

25. Therefore, if holy women, even married ones, are not to be provided with rings but with morals, and, for that reason, they ought to be adorned more with humility than with

---

31. Cf. Ps 83.8 LXX; Ps 84.7.   32. 1 Pt 3.1–4.
33. 1 Pt 3.5.

clothes, what ought the clothing and the manner of a widow be who seeks to please not a human husband but Christ? Ought she, released from the obligation of a bodily marriage, to seek only spiritual adornments? Therefore, let your clothing be such that it does not stir to lust but invites to continence, which does not entice to lust but constrains to fear, which does not inflame the concupiscence of the flesh but extinguishes it, which does not seduce to sexual intercourse but stirs up to progress, from which compunction of heart, not lust of the flesh, is born, by means of which you may please the Son of God, by means of which you may show yourself as truly chaste to the gaze of the heavenly spouse. For that spouse wishes to see your flesh worn down, not radiant; he makes use of the marriage of the soul, not of the flesh, but delights in the beauty of the soul. So, acquire beauty of heart by chastising the body; let the flesh be draped with cheap coverings and the soul endowed with precious clothing. Do not seek to please the eyes of human beings but seek not to offend the eyes of Christ. Let him see in you what he loves; let him find what he gave; let him recognize that by which he is delighted. "The king will desire your beauty" but, "all the glory of the king's daughter is within."[34]

26. The time for embracing is passing away; now is the time to be far from embraces. Let those who are held bound by the marriage bond cling to their husbands; to you it must be said with the prophet: "But for me it is good to be near God; I have made the Lord God my refuge."[35] So the Apostle also says, "The real widow, who is all alone, has set her hope in God and continues in supplication and prayers night and day."[36] In your case, let prayer be frequent in petition, in holy meditation and good works, unending. For in this way you will be able to fulfill what the Apostle commands, that we pray without ceasing. For in the sight of God every good

---

34. Ps 44.12 LXX; Ps 45.11–13. "All the glory of the king's daughter is within" is in the contemporary version: "The princess is decked in her chamber with gold-woven robes; in many-colored robes, she is led to the king."
35. Ps 72.28 LXX; Ps 73.28.
36. 1 Tm 5.5.

work is a prayer by which God, though needing nothing, is delighted. And that we may recognize that good works share the place of prayer in God's sight, Holy Scripture thus admonishes us: "Store up almsgiving in your treasury and it will rescue you from every disaster."[37]

27. Beware lest you be concerned for the flesh and its desires, lest you always give in to gluttony as it demands. Let not pleasure be satisfied when you eat but let weakness be supported. You should share meals with people who are not accustomed to praise the delights of the flesh but of the heart; who avidly seek the bread of angels for the interior person; who run after your spouse in the fragrance of his ointments; who taste inwardly the sweetness of God; who with pure love hunger and thirst for justice; who work for food, not that which perishes but that which remains for eternal life. Let your conversations and meals be held with people like these so that while you feed them with bodily foods, you may gain the merit of holy deeds and when you are fed with their spiritual words, progress in a holy life may accrue to you. Now you will not want to fill your table with such delights as you once filled it when you were the slave of carnal marriage. Hear the teacher of the nations who says of the widow: "The one who is self-indulgent," he says, "is dead while she lives."[38]

28. For in both the Old and New Testaments you have examples of holy widows by which you may be edified. In the Old Testament, Judith. Let Anna be considered in the New, of whom, if, with the help of the Lord, you are an imitator and trample on both the delights of the flesh and worldly boasting with true humility of heart, so that the love of that spouse who is always alive, always lives in you; just as, when he rises, he is confirmed by the witness of the angel's voice, when it is said to the women: "Why do you seek the living among the dead?"[39] Concerning him the apostolic authority also speaks as follows: "The Word of God is living and effective."[40] Therefore, he who is the Word of the Father is alive

37. Sir 29.12.
38. 1 Tm 5.6.
39. Lk 24.5.
40. Heb 4.12.

and so he is the life of the faithful. Holy widows have sought him with contrition of heart and chastising of the body. Most devoutly they have served him with complete continence of heart and body.

29. Concerning Judith it has been written: "Judith remained a widow for three years and four months at home where she set up a tent for herself on the roof of her house. She put sackcloth around her waist and dressed in widow's clothing. She fasted all the days of her widowhood. . . ."[41] And, lest anyone think that that holy widow fasted, not from devotion of heart but from the necessity of poverty, hear what is said of her in what follows: "She was beautiful in appearance and was very lovely to behold. Her husband Manasseh had left her gold and silver, men and women slaves, livestock and fields."[42]

Behold a widow, famous in family, wealthy in goods, young in age, marvelous in appearance, who despised riches, repudiated delights, trampled on the attractions of the flesh, and, putting on virtue from on high, she did not seek to be entangled in a second marriage. So, by the witness of so brilliant a deed, it is apparent how beloved of God is a widow's continence. Then when Holofernes besieged Bethulia in force and with an army and all the power of the Israelites shaken, grew weak, chastity went forth to assault lasciviousness and holy humility proceeded to the destruction of pride. He fought with armies; she with fasts; he with drunkenness, she with prayer. Therefore, what the entire people of the Israelites was unable to do, the holy widow accomplished by the virtue of chastity. For one woman cut off the head of the leader of so great an army and restored to the people of God an unhoped for freedom.

30. Let us see also in the New Testament how the way of life of St. Anna is revealed to us. Concerning her, St. Luke speaks as follows: "There was also a prophetess, Anna, the daughter of Phanuel of the tribe of Asher. She was advanced in years, having lived seven years with her husband after her

---

41. Jdt 8.4–5.   42. Jdt 8.7–8.

2. TO THE WIDOW GALLA

marriage and then as a widow until she was eighty-four. She never left the Temple but worshipped night and day with fasting and prayer."[43] These two widows, although they lived in different periods, still both served the mystery of the one faith; because Christ, whom Anna knew as born in the flesh, Judith had known as one who was going to be born. How God showed in each widow that continence pleases him greatly! For Judith, girded with spiritual weapons, cut off the head of the lustful brigand. But Anna, filled with the Holy Spirit, knew the very head of the Church. The death of Holofernes was given to Judith; to Anna was revealed the coming of the Savior. To the former, God gave it to drive away a plague from the people; to the latter, he gave it to recognize the remedy of the human race. And because the continence of the widow follows after virginal holiness as a lower degree, therefore, after the Son of God was born of a virgin, he deigned to be proclaimed by the office of a widow's tongue. Still it was not a widow given over to pleasure who spoke about him, one who "is dead while she lives"[44] but one who "never left the Temple but worshipped night and day with fasting and prayer."[45]

31. This is not the time or the place for a lengthier discussion of these fastings and prayers. For we are planning (if the Lord wills and if we live) to write something on prayer and fasting to your sister, the holy virgin of Christ, Proba, whom the Lord especially at this time in the city of Rome has deigned to give as an example of virginity and humility, just as in the letter which I have recently given to her, my promise is contained and her holy way of life ought to be imitated by you in all things. She, though she was born of a grandfather and ancestors who were consuls and she was nurtured with royal delights, so great was the humility infused in her by the gift of heavenly grace that by her love of subjection and experience of serving, she no longer knows that she had once been a lady, since by her delight in holy

---

43. Lk 3.36–37.
45. Lk 2.37.

44. 1 Tm 5.6.

servitude, she aspires to have all women as her mistresses. For she knows that the humility of the form of a servant was accepted for our liberation by the Lord to whom she vowed virginity of both heart and body. For this reason, she delights to please her spouse in the humility of this servitude, so that, associated with the company of the five wise virgins, she can reign with her spouse in eternal splendor. With what great strength she has scorned the delights of the body and how she makes her hunger be of service for feeding the poor, nor is she covered with vile clothing for any other reason than to fulfill the purpose of humility and accomplish the unending care of holy devotion in clothing the poor, you yourself know even more fully by seeing than you would wish to hear from me what I am less able to explain by words.

32. Set her as a mirror for yourself and from considering her, know what is already in you and what is still lacking in holy zeal and works. Although she surpasses you in the outstanding gift of virginity, she ought to have you as a companion in the other virtues. Therefore, learn to attribute to yourself nothing because of nobility of lineage. And although, along with your grandfather, father, father-in-law and husband who were consuls, you were an illustrious person in the world, know now that you are becoming illustrious in him, insofar as the virtue of humility grows in you. Learn from the Lord that he is meek and humble of heart and in him you will find rest for your soul. Cast away nobility of the flesh which is the kindling wood of pride and pursue nobility of spirit by perfect humility of the heart. Work on prayer, give yourself to fasts and whatever you take away from yourself, confer on the needy. Let your voluntary fast relieve the hunger of those who fast so that the fruitfulness of your fasts may be seen in the fruit of mercy. May the cheapness of your clothing be of use to you and may the nakedness of the poor be clothed by you; for then to some purpose will you flee the harmful splendor of expensive clothing if you clothe the naked; so that not by the emptiness of words nor by deceptive show, but by the witness of good works you may show that you are truly a sharer with the poor of Christ.

33. Do not believe that you are superior to those whom you feed or clothe, or, because you give and they receive, esteem your merits above the poor of Christ, as if you were greater because you scorned more things. In vain do you scorn your property, if you hold on to the harmful riches of boasting in your heart. For not only do they sin who, because of the riches which they possess, carry about some boasting in the heart; they sin even more seriously who wish to have boasting in their heart because of riches scorned, or who wish to place themselves ahead of the poor, because they seem to give many things to the poor. For the order is not the same with God who does not pay attention to the quantity of property scorned, but the quality of the will. Zacchaeus is said to have expended great riches for the poor on behalf of Christ, for whom Peter the Apostle abandoned the most humble tools of the fisherman's trade. Still Zacchaeus the rich man is not preferred by Christ to Peter the poor man, but the poor man Peter is preferred to the rich man Zacchaeus, so that among the rich people belonging to Christ no boasting about riches should arise.

34. God forbid that you enrich yourself with anything on earth, where you are not to leave children of the flesh, since also they who have children of the flesh do not without sin delight to enrich themselves in the world. Our Savior deigns to warn all the faithful with one statement, saying, "Do not store up for yourselves treasures on earth where moth and decay destroy and thieves break in and steal. But store up treasures in heaven where neither moth nor decay destroys nor thieves break in and steal."[46] Greatly to be feared is that rebuke of the Lord which the foolish rich man heard at the moment he was about to die: "You fool, this night your life will be demanded of you; and the things you have prepared, to whom will they belong?"[47] Therefore, send all your riches ahead to Christ; set up for yourself treasure in heaven which you cannot lose and you will be able to possess for eternity.

---

46. Mt 6.19–20.
47. Lk 12.20.

35. In all good works, be careful lest you be stirred by desire for human praise. You ought to be praised in your good works, but insofar as you do them, you ought not to expect human praises. The human tongue may praise you but desire praise from God alone. And thus it may come about that while you do not seek human praise, God may be praised in your deeds. Recall how much the Lord forbids us to do our righteous works to garner human praise, saying, "Take care not to perform righteous deeds in order that people may see them; otherwise, you will have no recompense from your heavenly Father."[48] Therefore, when he says that we should look out lest we do our righteous deeds before human beings, that we may be seen by them and again he commands that our light shine before human beings,[49] is he not commanding contrary things? Certainly not, but he commands that good deeds be done in such a way that we wish, not that we ourselves, but that God be praised in our works. For the Apostle too avoided human glory in his works but sought God's glory. So he says, writing to the Thessalonians, "Nor, indeed, did we ever appear with flattering speech, as you know, or with a pretext for greed—God is witness—nor did we seek praise from human beings either from you or from others."[50] And yet the same one, in the reports about his way of life, thus recalls with exultation God glorified by the churches: "And I was unknown personally to the churches of Judea that are in Christ. They only kept hearing that 'the one who once was persecuting us is now preaching the faith he once tried to destroy.' So they glorified God because of me."[51] Accordingly, let your hand not slacken from doing good works, nor your spirit work in such a way that the reward of good works be rendered useless by attention to human praise. For the Apostle, as he bears witness, wants us to be "pure and blameless for the day of Christ, filled with the fruit of righteousness that comes through Jesus Christ for the glory and praise of God."[52]

48. Mt 6.1.
49. Mt 5.16.
50. 1 Thes 2.5–6.
51. Gal 1.22–24.
52. Phil 1.10–11.

36. In your zeal for good works and your contempt of human praise, be careful lest you wish to assign the good that you do, not to the grace of God, but to your own strength. Hold firmly that there can be no ability in you for good will or good works unless you received it by the free gift of divine mercy. Know, therefore, that it is God working in you both to will and to do, for a good will. Accordingly, work out your salvation in fear and trembling. Humble yourself in the sight of God that he may exalt you. Ask from him the beginning of a good will. Ask from him the effects of good works. Seek from him the gift of perseverance. Do not think at any time that you can either will or do anything good, once his assistance has ceased. Ask him to turn away your eyes lest they see vanity; ask him to show you the way in which you should walk; petition him to direct your steps according to his word and let no wickedness rule over you. Pray to him that he direct the works of your hands for you. "Be strong and let your heart take courage; wait for the Lord."[53]

37. You should not lack confidence concerning the divine power and devotion in anything because I said that you must assign nothing to your own strength. For the "Lord is faithful in all his words and gracious in all his deeds."[54] Neither will he deny you help in this age nor will he withhold a reward in the age to come. He has shown you the right way and he is your guide to the homeland. "Trust in the Lord and do good."[55] Do not think that you can fail if he will deign to guard you. For it is written: "Has anyone trusted in the Lord and been disappointed? Or has anyone persevered in the fear of the Lord and been forsaken? Or has anyone called upon him and been neglected?"[56] Do not, therefore, lose your confidence which has a great reward. Be stable and unmoved, knowing that your work will not be useless in the Lord. Always seek greater things and stretch your spirit toward an increase of virtue. Never cease from the divine

---

53. Ps 26.14 LXX; Ps 27.14; Ps 54.23 LXX; Ps 55.22.
54. Ps 144.13 LXX; Ps 145.13.   55. Ps 36.3 LXX; Ps 37.3.
56. Sir 2.10.

310   FULGENTIUS

words and indulge all the pleasures of your heart in the Holy Scriptures. Do not be held fast by the ties of worldly love and you will be successful in triumphing over the Devil.

38. And in order that the present letter to you end with the testimony and admonition of Holy Scripture, I shall add this too to all the other things which have been said above: "Perform your tasks with humility; then you will be loved by those whom God accepts. The greater you are, the more you must humble yourself; so you will find favor in the sight of the Lord."[57] May the Lord direct you in the way of his righteousness and bring you to the promises of the heavenly kingdom, my Lady, illustrious daughter.

LETTER 3. TO PROBA

Similar in tone to letter 2, letter 3 is another offering of spiritual advice to an aristocratic Roman lady. Galla is a widow; Proba, a consecrated virgin. In the previous letter, Fulgentius referred to Proba as Galla's sister, a title which scholars have been unable to agree is a familial or spiritual one. Proba, in any event, like Galla, comes from a prominent family with ancient roots and several of her male relatives have held the post of consul. See "Proba 1," PLRE II. 907.

This is Fulgentius's treatise on "virginity and humility." As such treatises go, it may be classified as a moderate one, reminiscent of Augustine's own treatment of the question. Marriage is good but virginity is better. But humility is a basic prerequisite for the Christian virgin. Humility is the "interior virginity of virginity" (36). In several places in this discussion, Augustine's teachings of grace also clearly play an important role.

Letter 4, Fulgentius's briefer reply to her answer to letter 3, continues the emphasis on the Augustinian doctrine of grace but stresses prayer and penance as well.

ECAUSE of your spiritual desire and your way of life, Proba, holy servant of God, I would like to express suitably in words how much I congratulate you and rejoice with you, if my speech were able to match my thoughts with equal capacity. Nor should it be thought evi-

57. Sir 3.17–18.

dence of a slight resolution that although it is clear that, with him from whom is "all good giving and every perfect gift"¹ working in you, you are endowed with spiritual strengths, you think that you are lacking as it were and must be advised about the virtues. Therefore, I praisegreatly in God, in whom your soul must be praised this zeal, with our holy brother, a trusted servant of God, insisting with frequent writings you strongly urge me to present you with instruction containing something on virginity and humility. But as much as I ought to praise, I am unable to praise; and as much as I perceive that I am unequal to this desire by giving worthy praise, so much the more am I afraid of offending God in you either by a callous refusal or by a lengthy delay. Indeed Christ is offended whenever due service is denied to his members, since he wished to free from the slavery of sin those once free for evil for no other reason than to teach us how to serve each other with a free charity. Those whom he found oppressed by the yoke of the worst, servile liberty, he uplifted by the gift of the best free servitude. Finally, in place of that harmful freedom, in which it is more pleasing to serve sin than God, we have happiness announced to us by the apostolic word; for he says, "For when you were slaves to sin, you were free from righteousness."² And he adds, "But what profit did you get from the things of which you are now ashamed? For the end of those things is death."³ That servitude, which when liberated we accepted in order freely to serve God our liberator, we find in the words of his teaching which follow when he says, "But now that you have been freed from sin and have become slaves of God, the benefit that you have leads to sanctification and its end is eternal life."⁴ Behold where this holy servitude leads and goes, in which is the gift of true freedom; namely, to eternal life, in which one lives and reigns forever, in which no human being will live except the one who is mortified in this world; in which no one will reign, except the one who perseveres, humble in the Lord. For that life is promised to

1. Jas 1.17.
2. Rm 6.20.
3. Rm 6.21.
4. Rm 6.22.

this mortification and that height is reserved for this humility by humility itself which you seek efficaciously and eagerly and in which you keep holy virginity, with God as guardian. You compel me as well to serve it devotedly and willingly.

2. And I, holy daughter, insofar as "the love of God," which "has been poured out into our hearts through the Holy Spirit that has been given to us,"[5] urges me to serve the members of Christ with delight as well as freely, I wish to fulfill suitably what you imposed on me; knowing that he serves Christ who serves the members of Christ through that charity, through which Christ himself first served, in order that he might become a member of the same Christ. So the Apostle, that we might attain to eternal freedom, commands the members of Christ that they must freely provide service for one another, saying, "For you were called for freedom, brothers; but do not use this freedom as an opportunity for the flesh, rather, serve one another through love."[6]

3. Therefore, the more that I am compelled to pay what you demand by the command of this servitude, the more I am discouraged by the consideration of my abilities. There is such a union of each virtue concerning which I should have something to say insofar as God will give it to me, so that in the present life it is the perfecting of all and the peak of the virtues because neither in the body is there anything better than integrity nor in the soul is there anything loftier than faithful humility. Still I have confidence in the divine assistance, because I am aided by your prayers. Because of this, God inspires his sons and daughters with the fervor of holy desire so that when they press for a spiritual debt from their fellow servants, they do not also rest from praying to the Lord for them and demand the debt which is owed to them by the duty of mutual charity in such a way that what they demand, they pay to the debtors.

4. There is no one of the faithful who demands that charity be rendered to him in such a way that he must not render it to his own debtor. This charity which, albeit in different

---

5. Rm 5.5.
6. Gal 5.13.

gifts according to the grace which has been given to us, seems to be paid with different effect to different people, still in the assistance of mutual prayer makes all sharers of the one debt, in which it makes individuals debtors to all. See how he who professes himself a debtor to the wise and the foolish, both pays the debt of prayer to all and demands it from all. To the Romans he says, repaying this debt, "God is my witness, whom I serve with my spirit in proclaiming the gospel of his Son, that I remember you constantly, always asking in my prayers. . . ."[7] But see how the conscientious repayer of this debt is also its avid demander. He says again to the same people, "I urge you, brothers, by our Lord Jesus Christ and by the love of the Spirit, to join me in the struggle by your prayers to God on my behalf."[8]

5. In this debt which you demand from us and you repay do not doubt that I am assisted, so that God, who works in us both to will and to bring to completion the work of the good will, himself gives that I may worthily think and worthily speak. For in good thoughts, "Not that of ourselves, we are qualified to take credit for anything as coming from us; rather our qualification comes from God."[9] And for this reason we do not fail for want because by a free gift, our sufficiency is from him in whom there is no want. Just as he does not need our goods, so he always abounds in giving, nor does he become needy by giving who gives that by which he is always filled; nor is there any pleasing gift of thought, word, or deed offered by us to him which he himself has not given with free kindness. Wherefore the holy giving of God is always free because no demand based on human merits has ever preceded, because even if a human being has any good merit, it comes from him from whom comes "every good and perfect gift."[10] A human being cannot have it, unless it be given by him, nor does he have it steadfastly, unless it be preserved with him as its guardian. Therefore, I ask from him the ability to pay this debt, the very one from whom I received the will to pay. Nor would I even will to pay

7. Rm 1.9–10.
9. 2 Cor 3.5.
8. Rm 15.30.
10. Jas 1.17.

anything unless he mercifully gave that I might will. Therefore, if in this work, I say anything that is pleasing and sufficient or, if it is not sufficient, at least pleases your holy desire, it does not come from my poverty but from God's sufficiency. If perchance I should say something so as to be able neither to be sufficient for your holy desire, nor to please, it does not come from God's sufficiency but from my poverty. Accordingly, let Christian charity in both cases show the parts of its work, so that it may both humbly recognize God's sufficiency and patiently make allowances for its servile lack.

6. By a free gift, he has made you a sacred virgin for himself, he who "does whatever he pleases"[11] by whom grace is given with no merits preceding, so that a pure act of thanksgiving may always be given to him in humility of heart. He is the only begotten Son of God, also the only-begotten son of the virgin, the one spouse of all sacred virgins, the fruit of holy virginity, its adornment and gift; whom holy virginity bore corporeally; to whom holy virginity is wedded spiritually; by whom holy virginity is made fruitful so that it remains intact; by whom it is decorated that it remain beautiful; by whom it is crowned that it reign gloriously for eternity.

7. Wherefore, "guard what has been entrusted to you,"[12] and the merit of so great a good which God gave that you might have it and he brought it about that you might vow it to God. Reflect on it from the significance of its very name; for God willed that the good of virginity be so great that it was not worthy to be named from anything other than the word 'virtue'. Therefore, if anyone is willing diligently to consider the word 'virgin', he will find it derived from the word 'virtue'; for a virgin (*virgo*) is named as if 'virago'. Holy Scripture says that a virgin is called this for no other reason than that she was taken from the male (*vir*). For this the translation done by St. Jerome specifically from the Hebrew text of the book of Genesis teaches it this way: "So the Lord God sent a deep sleep to fall on Adam and when he slept, he took one of his ribs and filled up flesh for it. And the rib that

11. Ps 113.11 LXX; Ps 115.3.
12. 1 Tm 6.20.

the Lord had taken from Adam, he made into a woman and brought her to Adam. Then Adam said, 'This at last is bone of my bone and flesh of my flesh; this one shall be called woman (*virago*) for out of man (*vir*) this one was taken."[13]

8. Therefore, since the word *virago* came from the word *vir*, who will doubt that *vir* has been called after 'virtue'? And because as Paul teaches, "those things happened as examples for us,"[14] undoubtedly in that virgin, who a rib from a man became, the Church to come was prefigured. She truly was taken from a male, and she was joined to the one from whom she was taken. Hence, she has in truth virtue from which she has the true name of *virago*. So, the *virago*, i.e., virgin who has been taken from a male, Paul does not hesitate to call by the name, not only of 'virgin' but also of 'male', for he says to the faithful, "Since I betrothed you to one husband to present you as a chaste virgin to Christ."[15] Christ indeed is the male from whom this virgin has been taken. The same Apostle says again to the faithful, "Until we all attain to the unity of faith and knowledge of the Son of God, to mature manhood, to the extent of the full stature of Christ."[16] Through the holy David also, in common for men as well as for women, this spiritual exhortation is put forward: "Be strong (*viriliter*) and let your heart take courage, all who wait for the Lord."[17]

9. Through typology, therefore, the word 'virgo' is taken from 'vir' because the name 'Christian' is taken from Christ. For Christ is the power of God and the wisdom of God, from whom is the Church which, remaining a virgin in faith and charity, possesses both wisdom and power (*virtus*); therefore, neither is it misled by seduction nor overcome by violence because it is supported by the integrity of virginity within. To this virgin, Isaiah says, "For the Lord delights in you, and your Lord shall be married. For as a young man marries a young woman, so shall your builder marry you."[18] And in order that he show that the young man is none other than

13. Gen 2.21–23.
15. 2 Cor 11.2.
17. Ps 30.25 LXX; Ps 31.24.
14. 1 Cor 10.6.
16. Eph 4.13.
18. Is 62.4–5.

her spouse and that the virgin is none other than the spouse and that the spouses are Christ and the Church, he added immediately after, "... as the bridegroom rejoices over the bride, so shall your God rejoice over you."[19] The virgin mother is the one to whom it is said: "Your sons shall live in you,"[20] and this mother is the virgin about whom it is said: "A young man shall live with a virgin."[21] This is the virgin spouse concerning whom it is said: "And the husband will rejoice over his wife."[22] Therefore, this Church is the one and true Catholic spouse because it clings to Christ; it is a mother because it is inseminated by Christ; it is a virgin because uncorrupted, it perseveres in Christ. Neither is the virginity of this spouse corrupted by fecundity; nor fecundity impeded by virginity. For such is the marriage of this man and virgin that this virgin is made fruitful by this man, because in this marriage there can never be any corruption and so great is the integrity of the virginity that remains in this mother that unless she always was a virgin, she could not be a mother. Isaiah thus announces before the fact the new name of this mother and virgin: "And you shall be called by a new name that the mouth of the Lord will give."[23] Therefore, because Christ is power (*virtus*), just as the Church has taken the word virgin from virtue, so it has received the name Christian from Christ.

10. She, though she has in her diverse members different gifts, according to the grace which has been given to her, still she has received the greater grace of a gift in those members, in whom she is spiritually called a virgin so that she also gains the integrity of bodily virginity. For in other faithful members, who believe in God correctly according to the rule of the Catholic faith and observe conjugal and widow's chastity, who are not splattered by any stain of any act of fornication and remain exempt from any illicit sexual act of infidelity, the Church gains a spiritual virginity only; but in these members in whom he guards the correct faith

19. Is 62.5.
20. Is 62.4.
21. Ibid.
22. Is 62.5.
23. Is 62.2.

in such a way that they keep the flesh untouched by any sexual intercourse, the more the Church has a fuller virginity, the more fully and perfectly it possesses the name of the same virginity. In the former it has nothing less of its life; in the latter, however, it acquires something more for glory, because just as Paul says, "The brightness of the sun is one kind, the brightness of the moon another, and the brightness of the stars still another. For star differs from star in brightness. So also is the resurrection of the dead."[24] Finally, under the name of eunuchs (whom also in the gospel the Lord affirms have castrated themselves for the sake of the kingdom of heaven) the Lord through Isaiah again promises virgins a better place in his house and within his walls. For so it is written: "For thus says the Lord, 'To the eunuchs who keep my sabbaths, who choose the things that please me and hold fast my covenant, I will give in my house and within my walls, a monument and a name better than sons and daughters; I will give them an everlasting name that shall not be cut off.'"[25] Also in the Apocalypse of blessed John, they are the ones who "follow the Lord wherever he goes"[26] who have remained virgins.

11. Therefore, it is clear that among the other gifts of the Church, that is the principal gift of a spiritual charism, where the very virtue of integrity deserves to be called by the perfect name of virtue. Although there is ". . . prophecy, in proportion to the faith; if ministry, in ministering; if one is a teacher, in teaching; if one exhorts, in exhortation; if one contributes, in generosity; if one is over others, with diligence; if one does acts of mercy, with cheerfulness."[27] These different gifts are called by their own names. But the integrity of the flesh faithfully consecrated to God and in virginity of heart, preserved with God's help and protection, this is properly called virginity so that there the perfection of true virtue is shown to be present within.

12. Therefore, unstained virginal holiness is better than the other gifts, which by the grace of a divine gift seems to

24. 1Cor 15.41–42.
26. Rev 14.4.
25. Is 56.4–5.
27. Rm 12.6–8.

take the origin of its name from virtue, so that from the name itself it may always be aware that it is being warned that it must preserve those things which are from virtue. Whence not undeservedly does the vessel of election distinguish with such a definition the celibate and conjugal life so that he cautions that the former is concerned about the things of God to please God in the sanctification of body and spirit; the latter is given over to worldly thoughts, being eager to please a human being. "An unmarried man," he says, "is anxious about the things of the Lord, how he may please the Lord. But a married man is anxious about the things of the world, how he may please his wife, and he is divided. An unmarried woman or a virgin is anxious about the things of the Lord so that she may be holy in both body and spirit. A married woman, on the other hand, is anxious about the things of the world, how she may please her husband."[28]

13. Nevertheless, the Apostle, saying this, did not ascribe sanctity of body and spirit to virgins in such a way as either to take it away from the married or deny it to widows; especially one who in an earlier text of the same letter, calls the bodies of the faithful, members of Christ and a temple of the Holy Spirit, for he says, "Do you not know that your bodies are members of Christ?"[29] And a little later: "Do you not know that your body is a temple of the Holy Spirit within you, whom you have from God and that you are not your own? For you have been purchased at a price. Therefore glorify God in your body."[30] And in order that he might show that he is also writing to married people, he immediately added, "Now in regard to the matter about which you wrote: 'It is a good thing for a man not to touch a woman,' but because of cases of immorality, every man should have his own wife and every woman her own husband."[31] In the letter to the Ephesians, he also spoke to spouses to whom he said, "Husbands, love your wives even as Christ loved the Church. . . ."[32]

28. 1 Cor 7.32–34.
29. 1 Cor 6.15.
30. 1Cor 6.19–20.
31. 1 Cor 7.1–2.
32. Eph 5.25.

And a little later: "He who loves his wife, loves himself. For no one hates his own flesh but rather nourishes and cherishes it even as Christ does the Church, because we are members of his body."[33] Also Peter the Apostle does not hesitate to call faithful spouses holy, saying, "For this is also how the holy women who hoped in God once used to adorn themselves and were subordinate to their husbands, thus Sarah obeyed Abraham, calling him 'Lord'"[34] Therefore, the Apostle Paul does not separate the married faithful from the sanctification of the body and the spirit, but he says that they think of this, where he knows their thoughts are more fully held. For who does not know that the thoughts of holy virgins run more to spiritual things and the thoughts of holy spouses serve more conjugal requirements?

14. Therefore, we know that marriages are not a sin but the work and gift of God; the Lord himself has linked them with the bond of faith, has graced them with the gift of blessing, has multiplied them by the increase of propagation. We know that "marriage is honored among all and the marriage bed kept undefiled."[35] We know that, not marriages, but fornications and adulteries will be judged by God. "God will judge the immoral and adulterers."[36] We say that the faith of marriages, the charity of spouses, the fecundity of nature are from God; but because "each has a particular gift from God, one of one kind and one of another,"[37] we also so distinguish the importance of the gift of each person so that we do not deny that each gift is given by God to the faithful. Therefore, we are not reducing a lesser gift of God to a matter of blame when we bring forward the grace of a greater gift; nor when we prefer the gift of chastity as first, do we condemn the second or third gift; nor because we acknowledge virginal integrity as the peak are we asserting that conjugal chastity is a sin; nor do we set virginity among the grain in such a way that we may assign marriage to the chaff. Marriage is not the fruit of the one who sows at night because an envious sower

33. Eph 5.28–30.
34. 1 Pt 3.5–6.
35. Heb 13.4.
36. Ibid.
37. 1 Cor 7.7.

has not sown this afterwards in the Lord's field, but the good Lord has established it.

15. Nevertheless, pondering the importance of each thing with fitting distinctions, we say only that holy virginity because of its more potent merit is as far above holy matrimony where they who are unable to restrain themselves marry, as better things are far above good things, the exalted from the low, the heavenly from the earthly, the more blessed from the blessed, the holier from the holy, the more pure from the pure, immortal marriage from mortal marriage, the spirit from the flesh, strength from weakness, the fruit of the offspring that will remain from the state of infancy that will pass, safety from tribulation, tranquillity from disturbance, the better which is eternal with happiness from the good which is temporary with trials.

16. Nor do we have any qualms about saying that the sexual intercourse of Christian spouses (albeit conceded by God) of this weak and mortal flesh is as far from holy virginity of flesh and spirit as the likeness of livestock is distinguished from the imitation of the angels. In the one, the spirit is brought down to earth by the earthly pleasure of the flesh; in the other, the earthly flesh is raised up to the heavenly by the heavenly enjoyment of the spirit. To please carnal marriage, often worldly cares preoccupy the mind; but to please spiritual marriage, the mind, intent on the sweetness of heavenly thoughts, castigates its body, growing rich with spiritual delight.

17. In the work of bodily marriage, virginity of the flesh is lost so that fecundity of the flesh may be attained. Still when at times human pleasure is defrauded of the fruit of uncertain hope in such a way that she who has ceased to be a virgin, is unable to become a mother, and forced by the obstacle of sterility neither is able to undo what she lost in the body nor is able to have what she wants from the body. Often (which is more serious) offspring of the flesh which she carried with great pain are lost with even greater pain; and carrying the pregnancy to this point, she puts up with danger and groans, so that losing the one she had borne with

groans, she moans all the more. But in the union of spiritual matrimony, the soul is joined with Christ the spouse in such a way that the flesh is also preserved intact. The more that virginal integrity thrives, the stronger is immortal fecundity. There there is not mortal fruit from the body so that immortal offspring are not lacking from the heart; there marital intercourse does not corrupt the body because the spiritual embrace of Christ preserves both soul and body. In such a marriage, no efficacy is permitted to the heat of lust, because the fervor of holy charity is fed by spiritual refreshment. O more than human strength in human beings for imitating the angels! O the ineffable ornament of a supernal and eternal gift! They who accept it, reflect on this in mortal flesh, viz., that they are to be taken up in immortality. They choose the good part which will not be taken away from them but will be brought to completion in them. For what is now preserved inviolate by them in deed, this, gathered together, will be paid them as a gift with the glory of immortality.

18. Wherefore, she who is not a virgin of the world but of Christ, just as she ought not to be adorned with jewels, ought to be adorned with virtues. The adornment of a virgin is to preserve the good of virginity, not less in the mind than in the flesh, so that she may always present herself as worthy of so great a gift, and so hold to the way of the truth, that she turns neither to the right nor to the left. The mob of carnal vices besieges the left, the proud boasting about spiritual virtues holds the right. The former strives to beguile the flesh with manifest delights, the latter does not cease to whisper in its own mind the praises of its own virtues. The former soothingly tries to persuade the virgin that so long as the integrity of the flesh is preserved, let the virgin love, seek, and hold whatever pertains to the delights of food, the splendor of clothes, the warmth of the baths, the softness of rugs, the soothing of ointments, the hilarity of jokes, under the guise of avoiding illness or guarding bodily health; and as on an easy slope he points out the sloping descent of the wide road to the one who is going along, by which she does

not mount to heaven, but by which she falls down to hell; he conveys to them that the hard work of the narrow way must be avoided lest one arrive at rest.

19. But the other prepares a fall for the virgin more obscurely as well as more dangerously all the while it cleverly praises the upward path. Even if abstinence is observed in the matter of food, your clothing is not bright but despicable, fasts generate a boxwood paleness in your body, when the ruddiness has been lost, contempt for washing beclouds the whiteness of the flesh, sleep is given to the weary body on harder bedding, the softness of the skin is made rougher when ointments are rejected, a sadder face always resists laughter and jokes, she does not refer all these things to the divine help but attributes them to the strength of human ability.

20. Accordingly, the virgin must always be on the alert with concerned caution to preserve her virginity without and within. Let the sacred virgin altogether flee the delights of the flesh and the pleasures of the body which not so much necessity as pleasure demands for itself. The spiritual spouse of virgins does not seek in the virgin the flesh carefully prepared by delights but chastened by fasts. The teacher of the nations when he says that he does this, is conveying that this should be done by us as well: "I drive," he says, "my body and I train it."[38] And again: "Through many sleepless nights, through hunger and thirst, through frequent fastings."[39] Concerning a widow, he says, "The one who is self-indulgent is dead while she lives."[40] Therefore, let not the virgin of Christ seek the delights of the flesh which she sees are not granted to the widow. Living in the satiety of food, Sodom deserved to become food for the fire; and the people of Nineveh warded off the divine wrath which hung over the necks of all by fasting and tears. Therefore, if visible covetousness is overcome in the body, the invisible enemy power does not rule in the heart. We happily conquer it if we

38. 1 Cor 9.27. 39. 2 Cor 11.27.
40. 1 Tm 5.6.

contend bravely with it and triumph over it comes when it is trampled upon.

21. Nevertheless, moderation must be used in the matter of fasts in such a way that neither satiety stirs up our body nor immoderate lack of food weakens it. Let a meal of such a kind follow a virgin's fast that it neither entices the body with its pleasantness nor inflames it with satiety. Alms for the poor are diminished by pleasantness; the body is made bellicose by satiety. Then what is owed to brothers is devoured; here assistance is furnished to the enemy. For us who wish to seduce the lust of gluttony with a variety of flavors, pleasure consumes what the poor man ought to receive. Accordingly, let neither weakness usurp nor satiety do away with fasting. Each one is at the service of our adversaries because one removes the usefulness of the fast that precedes, the other obstructs the possibility of the subsequent fast. Satiety brings it about that we fast to no purpose; weakness brings it about that we are unable to fast.

22. Let the clothing of the sacred virgin be such that it bears witness to an inner chastity. Let no glitter be sought in the clothing of the external person lest the clothing of the interior person be soiled. The virgin who affects splendor in her bodily dress, strips her soul of the splendor of the virtues; nor does she have true chastity who prepares allurement for those who look at her; nor does she keep faith with Christ who seeks to please men more than her spouse. Logically, it is necessary that she who sows lust in the eyes of men reap wrath in the eyes of God. "The one who sows for his flesh will reap corruption from the flesh, but the one who sows for the spirit will reap eternal life from the spirit."[41]

23. But concerning these things and those like them which pertain to the care of the flesh and, under the name of virginity, make the soul negligent in matters of concupiscence, they rather ought to be warned, virgins who are desirous of pleasure, vagabonds who are given over to joking. But now we are speaking to the spiritual virgin concerning

---

41. Gal 6.8.

those snares to be avoided, something must be called to mind which the adversary holds out (so to speak) not in earthly things but in heavenly things; nor does he seduce from the path with obvious error but (as the prophet says, "On the path where I walk, they have hidden a trap for me.")[42] where he sights people walking in good works, there more vehemently and more dangerously, under the pretext of a feigned peace, he fights with hidden snares; and, unable to destroy the virginity of the flesh, he tries to carry off the virginity of the spirit.

24. Wherefore, the virgins of Christ must not more negligently consider how much virginity of heart surpasses virginity of the flesh. For if in this life, this will be kept by faithful spouses and widows in the faith "which works through love,"[43] even if without bodily virginity, in the future she will not be deprived of virginity of the flesh and she will enjoy the bliss of the heavenly kingdom; for bodily virginity, even dedicated to God, if it has not preserved virginity of the heart, will be kept in the body to no avail if spiritual chastity is corrupt in the mind.

25. The Devil attacks each one; he pursues each one with insidious counsels. But he strives to ravish virginity of the flesh in advance through a human being; he tries to carry off virginity of the heart personally. For often he does not attack the virginity of the flesh which is inferior, for this purpose, so that he may undermine the foundations of that which is superior. As with different siege engines, he makes use of innumerable arguments; and when he openly withdraws from the contest, he shows that he has been conquered to this purpose, viz., that he may conquer; he simulates flight for this purpose, that he may kill his pursuer with arrows shot from behind his back. He provokes with obvious vices, while he attacks the virginity of the body in those into whom, if he is openly overcome, he most perniciously hurls pride; and the author of vices, because he cannot conquer

42. Ps 141.4 LXX; Ps 142.3.
43. Cf. Gal 5.6.

with his vices, rises to be conquered by the virtues of others, by arms by which he is crushed and casts down by the virtue by which he is cast down. He praises virtue by which he sees himself being overcome so that when conquered, he can capture the conqueror; he places boastfulness within the heart so that he can cast down from a height with a more serious lapse, if he sees some among the humble fighting with a firmer step. To take an example, when he puts forward the delights of gluttony, if it is taken up, he adds the stimulant of lust; if it is rejected, he sows boasting about abstinence. He introduces the love of money; if he gets assent, he stabs the careless soul with the sword of avarice; but if he is repulsed, the traps which he was unable to set out though tenacity, the most wicked one sets out through liberty; and in a work of mercy, he causes pride of heart to sprout so that because of what he gave to the needy person, he seems to have greater merits for himself. He does these things in many cases, and he especially has been accustomed to attack men and women who are the spiritual servants of God; so that if anyone is not conquered by harmful and death-dealing things, he is killed by life-giving remedies. He makes bad things from good, harmful from healthful, unjust from just, and produces unfavorable things from favorable. This he first accomplished in himself, he who did not have the origin of his sin from his creation but from pride in virtue; he wanted to hold on to the truth in injustice and, fallen through injustice, he did not stand firm in the truth. For how could he stand firm, who, because of his pride, resisted him who never falls? "For the beginning of pride is sin. Wherefore God resists the proud but gives grace to the humble."[44]

26. Thus this pride is said to be the beginning of all sin, so that every sin is shown to sprout from it as from a root. Bringing death to the wretched in many ways, it casts down the carnal in a public contest; but the spiritual, if he finds any, it brings down in a more obscure combat. For who does not know that careless fornicators, idolaters, adulterers, boy

---

44. Sir 10.13.

prostitutes, homosexuals, thieves, the greedy, drunkards, slanderers, robbers raise their proud necks against God and fight more for the Devil with their very evil works? There are others whom, in the sight of human beings, pride shows as his enemies and within he possesses them as his most wicked soldiers. By these, wickedness is cleverly carried on so that to human sight, righteousness is deceptively shown forth. Our Lord thus rebukes them, "You justify yourselves in the sight of others, but God knows your hearts."[45] That he might clearly show them to be proud, he immediately added, "For what is of human esteem is an abomination in the sight of God."[46]

27. To those who live under the Christian profession and, by sinning openly, scorn the commandments of Christ, Christ himself speaks as follows: "Why do you call me, 'Lord, Lord' but do not do what I command?"[47] The teacher of the nations rebukes such people with these words: "They claim to know God but by their deeds they deny him; they are vile and disobedient and unqualified for any good deed."[48] And the blessed James also says, "What good is it, my brothers, if someone says he has faith but does not have works? Can that faith save him?"[49] Humility, which Christ taught, saying, "Learn from me for I am meek and humble of heart,"[50] does not consist in faith alone, but simultaneously in faith and works. For it is written that "Even the demons believe and tremble,"[51] who, however, are not humble. Whence the Apostle Paul asserts, "For the concern of the flesh is hostility toward God; it does not submit to the Law of God, nor can it."[52] Such wisdom, according to the statement of James, ". . . does not come down from above but is earthly, unspiritual, demonic."[53]

28. Open pride is detected when there is open sin. But when wickedness is covered with a disguise, that pestilence of pride creeps in more venomously; it crawls in more dan-

45. Lk 16.15.
46. Ibid.
47. Lk 6.46.
48. Ti 1.16.
49. Jas 2.14.
50. Mt 11.29.
51. Jas 2.19.
52. Rm 8.7.
53. Jas 3.15.

gerously when either the life of others is despised as unworthy or in good works something is attributed to human strength by those who exercise a zeal for righteousness. Finally, that pride by which others are despised as sinners by those who seem to themselves to be righteous, is condemned in the Pharisee just as the holy evangelist bears witness, saying, "He then addressed this parable to those who were convinced of their own righteousness and despised everyone else. Two people went up to the temple area to pray; one was a Pharisee and the other a tax-collector. The Pharisee took up his position and spoke this prayer to himself, 'O God, I thank you that I am not like the rest of humanity—greedy, dishonest, adulterous—or even like this tax collector. I fast twice a week and I pay tithes on my whole income.' But the tax collector stood off at a distance and would not even raise his eyes to heaven but beat his breast and prayed, 'O God, be merciful to me a sinner.' I tell you, the latter went home justified, not the former; for everyone who exalts himself will be humbled and the one who humbles himself will be exalted."[54] In the sight of the merciful and just judge, proud boasting about good works is not accepted but rather a humble confession of sins. Those who proudly strive to attribute the virtue of a good will or of good works to their own strength are spoken of by the Apostle in the following way: "... in their unawareness of the righteousness that comes from God and their attempt to establish their own righteousness, they do not submit to the righteousness of God."[55] Therefore, assuredly, he fails in his unrighteousness who does not bow his proud neck to the righteousness of God.

29. There are these four types of pride on which the Devil travels as on a chariot drawn by four horses and with a death-dealing fall is carried off to the hell of the wretched in whom he dwells. With two kinds he oppresses souls whom he sees wallowing in the flesh; with the two others, he casts

---

54. Lk 18.9–14.
55. Rm 10.3.

down souls which he knows fly from the flesh. The former he captures with the delights of the vices; the latter he tricks with the pride of the virtues. He snatches away the virginity of the former in such a way that they are in no doubt that they are fornicating; the latter he violates and defiles in such a way that they do not realize that they are being defiled.

30. Accordingly, in order that virginity dedicated to God remain whole, just as the wholeness of the body is guarded, much more must humility of heart be guarded. If any woman is really a virgin of Christ, she cannot be joined to Christ except by humility of heart. The nuptial bed of the Son of God does not receive the proud, and the humble spouse expels the proud from his marriage. Therefore, let your zeal be to pursue righteousness, as befits a sacred virgin, devotion, faith, charity, patience, mildness; not, however, that in your thoughts you look down on certain Christian women even those placed in a lower state or, on the presumption of your own virtue, extol yourself by good works. Whatever spiritual gifts you may have more of than others, it is not a small loss of virtue if you do not excel others in the very principal virtue which is humility, when you know that it is written: "The greater you are, the more you must humble yourself; so you will find favor in the sight of the Lord."[56] Therefore, be attentive to the love of your spouse in you; consider the devotion of the Lord. The Lord who has made you his handmaid is faithful; the handsome spouse who has sanctified you as his spouse. Still, the same one, because he is the true Lord and the true spouse, accomplishes the parts of each power. He requires humble service from his handmaid; in a spouse he seeks complete chastity. Serve the Lord with fear and exult with the spouse with trembling. For, because he is the Lord, he frightens, and because he is a spouse, he is jealous. Therefore, in fear guard the domain of the Lord who terrifies and, trembling, love the affection of the jealous spouse. In the handmaid of the Lord, let the brigand find nothing of his own; in the spouse of Christ, let

---

56. Sir 3.18.

the adulterer find nothing of his own. Just as lust does not rule in the body of a virgin, so let not pride rule in the heart of a virgin. Work out your salvation in fear and trembling. For it is God who works in you both to will and to carry out in view of a good will.

31. As often as you think of the perfection of the virtues, do not consider what others have less than you have but what you have less than you ought to have. You should not think that you are perfect in virtue if you see some other women given over to sins; nor consequently should you credit yourself with any greater speed if you see some women either backsliding or walking feebly. Nor, therefore, must one with watery eyes be proclaimed to have healthy eyes because a blind man seems thoroughly closed off from the light, nor must someone be declared healthy who lies half-dead with a serious wound, if another is found dead because of a more serious wound. Nor must anyone lay claim to glory as a victor who, although not killed by the enemy, still is being held captive by the enemy.

32. Therefore, do not compare yourself to others but to yourself. Hear the Apostle doing this and salutarily warning us to do the same. For, writing to the Corinthians, he says, "Not that we dare to class or compare ourselves with some of those who recommend themselves. But when they measure themselves by one another and compare themselves with one another, they are without understanding."[57] Therefore, let the virgin of Christ compare herself to herself, and, in order that she attain perfect health, she must not be lulled by the graver danger of others than herself, but let her take care to be saddened by her own infirmity; concerning which he was unendingly saddened who used to say, "All day long I go around mourning. For my loins are filled with burning and there is no soundness in my flesh."[58] And in order to show that humility must be joined to this sadness, he immediately added, "I am utterly spent and crushed.[59] And to

---

57. 2 Cor 10.12.
58. Ps 37.7–8 LXX; Ps 38.6–7.
59. Ps 37.9 LXX; Ps 38.8.

teach that this must be done by himself out of a desire for health, he added, "I groan because of the tumult of my heart,"[60] and "O Lord, all my longing is known to you; my sighing is not hidden from you."[61] But he who said this confesses that sometimes he was proud of health as of virtue and for this reason experienced the danger of very grave illness; for he says in another psalm, "As for me, I said in my prosperity, I shall never be moved."[62] And because, saying this, he was deserted by the assistance of divine grace and disturbed by his weakness, he had succumbed, he spoke as follows: "By your favor, Lord, you have established me as a strong mountain; you hid your face, I was dismayed."[63] And that he might show that the help of divine grace, even if it is now possessed, must be humbly asked for without ceasing, he also adds this, "To you, O Lord, I cried, and to the Lord I made supplication."[64] No one prays and asks who does not know that he has less of something or, that what he has, he can preserve only by his own power.

33. Therefore, whoever both asks for a blessing and clamors for assistance, it is necessary that he acknowledge both the evidence of his own weakness and need. So our need asks that it be given what it does not have, and our weakness asks that what it has received be guarded for itself. Need hears, "What do you possess that you have not received?"[65] And "No one can receive anything except what has been given him from heaven."[66] Weakness hears, "Commit your way to the Lord; trust in him and he will act."[67] He also hears from strength itself, "Without me, you can do nothing."[68] He hears from the prophet, "Unless the Lord guard the city, the guard keeps watch in vain."[69] Therefore, let need say to him who "for your sake, became poor although he was rich, so that by his poverty, you might become rich;"[70] let him say,

60. Ibid.
61. Ps 37.10 LXX; Ps 38.9.
62. Ps 29.7 LXX; Ps 30.6.
63. Ps 29.8 LXX; Ps 30.7.
64. Ps 29.9 LXX; Ps 30.8.
65. 1 Cor 4.7.
66. Jn 3.27.
67. Ps 36.5 LXX; Ps 37.5.
68. Jn 15.5.
69. Ps 126.1 LXX; Ps 127.1.
70. 2 Cor 8.9.

"Give me understanding that I may learn your commandments."[71] Let weakness also say to him who for us "was crucified out of weakness but he lives by the power of God,"[72] and who was made so infirm because of our sins that he is always himself the power of God and the wisdom of God, therefore, let human weakness say to him, "Keep me, O Lord, as the apple of your eye; hide me in the shadow of your wings, from the wicked who despoil me. . . ."[73]

34. The souls of all, even those now justified and living by faith are gravely afflicted here, but indeed only those souls understand in what affliction they have been placed, into which the true light is being poured, that light which enlightens every human being who comes into this world. For they see that although they are freed from the contagion of evil works by the gift of grace, still they are held captive by the trickery of thoughts. "Who can say 'I have made my heart clean; I am pure from my sins'?"[74] Let us see what and how great a just person is who says, "We all fall short in many respects,"[75] and who said, "If we say, 'We are without sin,' we deceive ourselves and the truth is not in us."[76] He who delighted in the law of God according to his interior self saw another law in his members, fighting against the law of his mind and taking him captive in the law of sin which was in his members, until the grace of God through Jesus Christ our Lord freed him, conscious of his unhappiness, from the body of this death.

35. From this law of sin which is in our members, not the strength of any strong person, not the diligence of the wise person, but only the grace of the Savior frees us, which grace is given freely to none save the humble: "God resists the proud, but gives grace to the humble."[77] Nevertheless, this grace, just as it is not given except to the humble, so a person cannot be humble unless it is given. For it is given that they may begin to be humble and it is given that they do not

71. Ps 118.73 LXX; Ps 119.73.
72. 2 Cor 3.4.
73. Ps 16.8–9 LXX; Ps 17.8–9.
74. Prov 20.9.
75. Jas 3.2.
76. 1 Jn 1.8.
77. Jas 4.6.

stop being humble. Therefore, the grace of God brings it about both that we may be humble and that we are able to stay humble. For he who was able to give what we did not have is able to guard what we have received.

36. Accordingly, in order that you may have true humility, which is the interior virginity of virginity, may you not be unaware of how much poverty of spirit must be in the sacred virgin so that she may merit to receive the kingdom of heaven; how much mildness, that she may possess that land of the living in which David with complete faith trusts that he will see the good things of the Lord. With how great a care must the distressing happiness of the present age be fled by the virgin, who in this life, always awaiting the coming of her heavenly spouse, must mourn more from spiritual desire that she may obtain interior and certain consolation. How much must the virgin of Christ experience hunger and thirst for justice that she may merit to rejoice with a satiety, full of eternal sweetness; with what depths of mercy must she also be endowed that in the sight of God, she may be able to find mercy; how much zeal for the cleansing of the heart must the sacred virgin have that she, with blessed eyes, may merit to see that spouse, handsome beyond human sons, to whom virginity of the flesh cannot attain unless it is supported by a humble heart, the virtue of interior virginity. How much of a virtue of peaceful calm must the virgin of Christ possess in order that she may subdue the wars of carnal desires, having taken up spiritual weapons. Your spouse wishes you to use and enjoy such jewels, who has espoused you to himself with faith, confirmed it by hope, joined it with charity.

37. Nor would you, with the truth of faith and integrity of the flesh, have spiritually wedded such a spouse, if you had not loved him, having scorned the vanity of the world. You would not be going to love him in any way, unless you had first been visited by the free love of the spouse. I said that you had been preceded not only by the love, with which he loved you, but also by the love which he infused into you freely that he might be loved by you. Everything and anything of the holy love you have in you toward your spouse,

you indeed have in you, but you do not have it of yourself. The very rich spouse has accepted you, a poor person. Whatever good you have in you, you have not from yourself but you have it from him, and whatever you do not yet have, then you will have it if the spouse will give it, who, with free generosity has already given all the good things you have. Therefore, humbly give thanks to him for what you have received, ask him humbly to receive more. You have such a rich spouse that he does not miss the things he has given and is eager to give much better things than he has already given. With humble sorrow always meditate on these things and preserve the virginity which you have vowed to God not only by the integrity of the flesh but also with humility of heart. Always ask from him the guardianship of your virginity and humility, him the guardian of Israel, who will neither slumber nor sleep.

38. Behold, holy daughter, insofar as the Lord has given, I have written to you a short booklet on virginity and humility; choosing rather to transmit a few things to you who desire them than to refuse the duty of due service to the spouse of the Lord.

LETTER 4. TO PROBA

ULGENTIUS, servant of the servants of Christ, sends greetings in the Lord to the very venerable Lady in Christ and Servant of God, to be named with all honor, his daughter Proba.

1. I have taken up the letter of your holiness with all joy of heart, a letter which displays with certain evidence not only your zeal for good works but also the humility of your heart. So, holy daughter, it is well that you are lifted up for the praise of God, not by the wind of pride, over good works, but you testify that you are infirm and weak in the matter of fulfilling the commandments of the Lord. Thus should anyone feel who desires to be "Not a hearer who forgets but a

doer who acts,"[1] one who does not expect to receive her reward from human beings here but from God on the day of retribution; who is not carried away by the vanity of empty glory in the present time but who ascends by the holy fire of divine love. This Christ has come to cast on the earth that it may burn up every sprout of pride and may implant the fervor of holy compunction in the humbler heart. Thus it comes about that we truthfully accuse ourselves in our sins and in our good works we praise God with true humility of heart; let us attribute to him what his devotion gives to us; let us impute to ourselves those matters in which our weakness angers him.

2. And since he is frequently offended by us, it is necessary that he be appeased by frequent prayer and uninterrupted compunction of heart. Compunction of the heart stirs up love for prayer, humble prayer wins divine assistance; compunction of the heart looks to its wounds, prayer asks for the cure of health. And who is fitted for this? Who can pray as is needed unless the physician himself instills the beginning of spiritual desire? Or who is able to persevere in prayer unless God increases in us that which he began, nourishes what he sowed and that which, with mercy preceding, he freely gave to the unworthy, with mercy following up, he brings to final completion? For thus the merit of our good works will be able not to perish if God, author and helper, is always glorified in the works.[2]

3. Let us not think that the author of good works must be viewed as if only at the very beginning of creation God gave to human nature the ability to do good works in such a way that, after his assistance ceased, human nature by itself was able of itself to will or to do anything good. Not even the very first human being was able to fulfill this by his own effort when human nature was not yet wounded by sin. Therefore, how will infirm human nature be able to restore its own

---

1. Jas 1.25.
2. There is an error in the Latin text of CCL XCI, lines 31–32. There is one 'a' too many.

health without the assistance of a physician, since when it was whole, it was unable to preserve its own health?

4. Therefore, let not earth and ashes glory because in its life it has abandoned its inmost thoughts; wounded, let it not exult as if healthy concerning that which it thinks healthy in itself. But with the humility of an afflicted heart, let it meditate on the rottenness of its wounds in order that, crying out with the prophet, "My wounds grow foul and fester because of my foolishness,"[3] it can receive healing from the divine piety, not of its own merits, but by a free gift. For what does a person have that he has not received? But if he has received, why is he glorying as if he had not received? Therefore, God alone can give to all to whom he wishes the means by which true salvation can be acquired.[4] He alone is able to safeguard what he has given in the one receiving: "Unless the Lord guards the city, the guard keeps watch in vain."[5] Therefore, he will not permit the stealthy entry of the most wicked brigand in that person to whom the assistance of the vigilant Lord will not be lacking. For he "will neither slumber nor sleep, he who guards Israel."[6]

5. Just as one who returns to his homeland always has more of the trail ahead of him until he arrives, so we also, as long as we are in this mortal body, are away from the Lord. For us the present life is a road in which we always have room for being able to make progress, until, with God leading us, we are able to reach that eternal homeland of blessed immortality. Therefore, it is a great blessing in the present age to love in such a way that each member of the faithful applies himself to spiritual progress but not, however, at any time proudly attributing this to his own power. Rather, with humble heart he asks God for a ceaseless guarding of the gift received, from whom emanates not just the beginning but also the perfecting of every good will.

3. Ps 37.6 LXX;Ps 38.5.
4. There is an error in line 52 of the Latin text. It should be 'acquiri' instead of 'acquirit'.
5. Ps 126.2 LXX; Ps 127.1.
6. Ps 120.4 LXX; Ps 121.4.

6. The preaching of the Apostle James cannot be shaken by any argumentation. He says, "All good giving and every perfect gift is from above, coming down from the Father of lights."[7] Nor can any human being be fit either for thinking or for doing anything good unless he is first helped by the free gift of divine assistance. "For God is the one who, for his own good purpose, works 'in them' both to desire and to work,"[8] as the vessel of election affirms; also by his teaching, we know that "we of ourselves are not qualified to take credit for anything as coming from us; rather our qualification comes from God."[9] Therefore, he supplies us with all the sufficiency of good and his fullness is not lessened when he gives who kindly shares every good with us that we may have them. In himself he remains full without any diminution which neither angelic nor human nature—thus, although spiritual, no created substance—can provide. Everything which is created, just as before it was created it did not exist, so before it receives, was unable to possess; and just as it cannot subsist without the working of him who made it, so it is unable to will or to do good unless God continuously deigns to help. For from him is the beginning of a good will, from him the ability to do good works, from him perseverance in a good way of life, from him in the present age is given true humility of heart and in the future, the happiness of eternal reward, that they may without end be happy who now without falsity are humble. They do not deceive themselves by their pride, but they view the dangers of the present life with fear and trembling. In this life there can be no total safety for the good because hostility creeps in the more easily at the moment prosperity deceptively puts in an appearance.

7. There is no period in this life in which the enemy does not set a trap for people; no one can escape his snares with his own strength except that one whom God has deigned to free by his grace through Jesus Christ our Lord. Therefore, the vessel of election when he knew that he was enslaved by the law of sin, cried out, saying, "Miserable one that I am!

---

7. Jas 1.17.   8. Phil 2.13.
9. 2 Cor 3.5.

4. TO PROBA

Who will deliver me from this mortal body? The grace of God through Jesus Christ our Lord."[10] So the prophet too proclaims that his feet will be freed from the snare, not by his own power but by the divine gift, saying, "My eyes are ever toward the Lord for he will pluck my feet out of the net."[11] And in another text, in the person of the saints, liberated from the snare of this age, whom the Lord has deigned to transfer to safety and happiness for eternity, it is said: "Our soul has escaped like a bird from the snare of the fowlers; the snare has been broken and we have escaped."[12]

8. Nevertheless, so that each one of us will know that his soul lives among the adversities and snares of the enemy and that in this world it may never grow slothful with a false sense of security, the same prophet says, "All day long, I go around mourning. For my soul has been filled with illusions and there is no soundness in my flesh."[13] What is "to go around mourning all the day long" except to be saddened by the memory of sins in the time of this life? How is the soul filled with illusions except that it is buffeted by frequent temptations of carnal concupiscence? Although he does not give in with consent at the time, he grows weary. Although the Lord repeatedly grants assistance to his own in the struggle lest they fall, still, burdened mortality is allowed to grow weary by the weight of its own infirmity so that when it finds in itself no firmness of strength, it may hasten quickly to ask for the help of divine piety.

9. Here we overcome the adversary if we fight with tears and prayers and continuing humility of heart. It is written that "The prayer of the humble pierces the clouds . . . and it will not desist until the Most High responds."[14] Therefore, the weeping of the humble contributes greatly to the destruction of carnal concupiscence. The tears which come from compunction of heart both conquer the enemy and gain for us the gift of triumphal happiness. For those "who go out weeping, bearing the seed for sowing, shall come

---

10. Rm 7.24–25.   11. Ps 24.15 LXX; Ps 25.15.
12. Ps 123.7 LXX; Ps 124.7.   13. Ps 37.7–8 LXX; Ps 38.6–7.
14. Sir 35.21.

home with shouts of joy, carrying their sheaves."[15] How well does the holy prophet teach that the seeds of good works must be watered by a river of tears! No seeds germinate unless they are watered; nor does fruit come forth from the seed if deprived of the aid of water. Accordingly, we too, if we wish to keep the fruits of our seeds, let us not stop watering our seeds with tears which must be poured out more from the heart than from the body. Therefore it is said to us through the prophet that we rend "our hearts and not our clothing;"[16] something we can do when we recall that we ourselves, even if not in deed, frequently sin at least in thought. Because the "earthly tent burdens the thoughtful mind"[17] and our land does not cease to produce thorns and thistles for us. We are unable to get to eating our bread, unless we will have been worn out by weariness and the sweat of our brow.

10. We are wearied by sweats when we fight against our own lusts. In conquering them, the difficulty of the struggle is greater because the adversary, carnal concupiscence, is generated, not extrinsically from someone else, but interiorly, from within the struggling person himself. This instills weariness in human weakness when it is born, although it is conquered by the assistance of divine power. "For the flesh has desires against the spirit and the spirit against the flesh; these are opposed to each other, so that you may not do what you want."[18] Hence it is that we are not yet altogether subject to God because there is born from us something that resists the divine command. For although by the grace of God, there is in us a good will which makes us humble before God, still there is not lacking in us a source of depraved desires which makes us recalcitrant.

11. Therefore, by the grace of God, we are now in part subject to God; through our own fault, we are up until now in part not submissive. So it is said to the Hebrews that all things have not yet been subjected to Christ; for he says, "In subjecting all things [to him], he left nothing not "subject to

---

15. Ps 125.6 LXX; Ps 126.6.   16. Jl 2.13.
17. Wis 9.15.   18. Gal 5.17.

him." Yet at present we do not see all things subject to him."[19] We are subjected to God in this way, that, with him at work in us, we take pleasure in "the law of God, in my inner self."[20] But we are not yet subjected in this, that we see "another law in [our] members, at war with the law of [our] mind and taking [us] captive to the law of sin, that dwells in [our] members."[21] We are subjected to God because we are snatched away from temptation because of his mercy; for we sing to him, "He is a shield for all who take refuge in him,"[22] but we are not yet altogether subjected because "Do not human beings have a hard service on earth?"[23] We are subjected to God, in whom he keeps "our steps steady according to [his] promise and never lets iniquity have dominion over us."[24] But we are not altogether subjected because "we all offend in many things."[25] We are subjected insofar as by his gift, "walking in the flesh, we do not battle according to the flesh,"[26] but we are not yet altogether subjected because although, by the gift of God, we have it that with our mind, we serve the Law of God, still from the vestiges of sin, we have it that we serve the law of sin with the flesh. So the Apostle says, "Therefore, I myself, with my mind, serve the law of God, with my flesh, the law of sin."[27]

12. Everyone who now lives justly serves the law of sin with the flesh, while he knows that carnal concupiscence is born in him; but with his mind, he serves the law of God because he does not consent to the same carnal concupiscence. We serve the law of sin with the flesh when the children of Babylon as they are born disturb our soul; but with our mind we serve the law of God when the same children of Babylon are smashed against the stone. For Babylon is interpreted as confusion whose daughter is all the carnal lust which confusion of heart begets. As long as we are in the body, away from the Lord, this confusion implants its offspring in us. From that confusion every depraved thought is

19. Heb 2.8.
20. Rm 7.22.
21. Rm 7.23.
22. Ps 17.30 LXX; Ps 18.30.
23. Jb 7.1.
24. Ps 118.133 LXX; Ps 119.133.
25. Jas 3.2.
26. 2 Cor 10.3.
27. Rm 7.25.

born. This is the girl child which is then smashed against the stone, when, overcome by a swift calling to mind and the assistance of Christ, it is trampled underfoot.

13. Therefore, although we have reason to have to thank God, because by his free mercy, he has subjected us to himself so that we are humble, still we have reason to have to besiege the divine ears with continuous prayers; because as long as we are in this mortal body, just as we cannot be without sin, so we are not yet able to show forth perfect humility to the divine commands. So, thanks must be given to God inasmuch as he gives us that we may do well, lest we be ungrateful for his gifts; and we must exert ourselves that we may make progress toward better things, lest we fall into deadly pride if we think that our way of life is perfect in every way.

14. Accordingly, let us sigh and weep before the Lord who made us, that he may free us from "sensual lust and from enticement for the eyes" and "a pretentious life [which is] not from the Father but from the world,"[28] and may he lead us to that subjection in which nothing of the vice of mortality fights against us but from the gift of immortality, everything which is within us be submitted to God. Then there will truly be in us the perfect and elevated humility when, both in the flesh and in our mind, no depraved lust will remain in us; nor will the spirit be wearied by thoughts nor the body tormented by labors; there will be no worry about the struggle but there will be perfect, peaceful security; there will be no lack of righteousness for us but full satiety with enjoyment. There we will be blessed with perfect grandeur because we shall be subjected to God with perfect humility of flesh and spirit. There our love will not be less than our praise, nor our praise inferior to our love. Our praise will be full because then there will be in us perfect love of God and neighbor. Then we shall praise and we shall possess; then we shall possess and we shall love; then we will be sated with delight and we shall be filled with delight to the point of satiety.

28. 1 Jn 2.16.

LETTER 5. TO THE ABBOT EUGIPPIUS

One of Fulgentius's correspondents was Eugippius, abbot of Lucullanum near Naples where a number of monks driven from Noricum by barbarian incursions, had settled around the relics of St. Severinus, the apostle of Noricum. Eugippius, the author of the *Life* of St. Severinus, was in correspondence with many of the important figures of the day in the Church. Charity is the main subject of the letter.

ULGENTIUS, servant of the servants of Christ, sends greetings in the Lord to the most blessed and many times venerable holy brother and fellow presbyter, Eugippius,[1] desired with all the affection of charity.

1. Would, holy brother, sufficiently great ability be given to my speech so that I might find words capable of explaining the spiritual sweetness which I received from reading your letter. While I wish it, I am not up to it. Yet I know that something wonderful has happened to me, seeing the joy that I received from your words, something that cannot be explained by my words. Namely, what you wrote to me, after it was devised and formulated in thought, you so organized with a letter that either you wrote it with your own hand or dictated it as the author. How has it come about that my mouth by composing is unable to produce the enjoyment which my heart has conceived from the words of your mouth? What is this destitute opulence or opulent destitution that more affection urges me on; and what I say because I am delighted, I put into words insufficient to express the degree of my delight? What is it, I ask, that I wish to express by speech and am unable to do? Without a doubt, it is something which is expressed by physical eloquence and pen in such a way that it is possessed not physically but spiritually.

---

1. Unlike some of Fulgentius's other correspondents, Eugippius is not only known but is himself an author. Born c. 460, he became the abbot of Lucullanum near Naples after fleeing Noricum. His best known work is his life of St. Severinus. A translation of this work as well as further information on the author can be found in FOTC 55 (1965.) See also *The Encyclopedia of the Early Church*, I.296. Recently a new edition of the *Life* has appeared as vol. 374 of *Sources chretiennes* (1991).

2. Among the gifts of the Spirit, the first fruit is charity. Hence the vessel of election was not improper when he put it this way: "The fruit of the Spirit is love, joy, peace,"[2] and the rest. In another text, he wished to show the principal among the heaven-sent charisms when he said, "Because love of God has been poured out in our hearts through the Holy Spirit that has been given to us."[3] This love which we received by the gift of the Holy Spirit, though we were unworthy, is so good, so holy, so infinite that even he who has it in his heart is never able to explain it in words. O how excellent a love, greatly to be wondered at, greatly to be praised and greatly to be loved.

3. Nevertheless, not all those who admire and praise charity immediately love charity; and therefore, unless someone love it, the fact that he admires and praises it, is of no avail to him. The admiration and praise of charity is fruitful, then, if love is not lacking in the one who admires and praises. But just as those who do not have it can admire and praise it, can they love it who do not yet have it? Certainly not. For charity itself is love. How does he who has not yet begun to have love now love love? For we see many things with our bodily vision, where this is not sight itself but is that which we see, because the sense by which we see is one thing, the sensible thing we see, another. When that which is seen is removed from before our eyes, if the eyes are healthy so that what was seen is removed from before the senses of the one who sees, so that the sense itself is in no way taken away from the one who sees, it happens in such a way that the sense of sight remains in a human being although the sight itself departs from that which was seen. When charity is loved, because it is not loved except by love, a person is not able to turn away the aim of the love like the eyes of the body from some seeable thing so that it is able both not to love charity and to have love. For charity, i.e., love, is never loved unless love is possessed by which love itself is loved. Therefore, love itself is loved because it is loved when it is

2. Gal 5.22.
3. Rm 5.5.

5. TO THE ABBOT EUGIPPIUS 343

possessed, and it is not loved unless it is possessed. In truth, it can be loved by us, also, when we ask that it be increased in us, but he does not love its increase who does not have the beginning.

4. Therefore, charity is not loved in the way a coin or something like that is loved. A person may possess not even one coin and still love and desire a pile of coins. Therefore, this person loves a pile of coins although he possesses not even one; he does not have one coin with him and he seeks innumerable coins outside. We find this also in other matters of the body, that something of them can be loved in such a way that the very thing which is loved is in no way possessed. Such is the case also with many spiritual gifts; just as if someone loves (for example) to have the gift of prophecy which no one denies is numbered among the spiritual gifts in the apostolic letter: "To one is given through the Spirit the expression of wisdom; to another the expression of knowledge according to the same Spirit; to another, faith by the same Spirit; to another, gifts of healing by the same Spirit; . . . to another prophecy; to another discernment of spirits; to another varieties of tongues; to another interpretation of tongues. But one and the same Spirit produces all of these, distributing them individually to each person as he wishes."[4]

5. Since, therefore, in order that we may keep silent about the other spiritual gifts, prophecy can be loved and not possessed, but charity is not possessed if not loved and is not loved if not possessed. Therefore, the other gifts of the Holy Spirit, i.e., tongues, prophecy, the knowledge of mysteries, faith, the distribution of goods to the poor, even the giving of one's body to be burned, these can be possessed without a good will to this point, namely, that they may be a burden, not an honor, to the one who has them; charity cannot be possessed without a good will because it does not allow the will in which charity exists to be a bad will; for "Love is not jealous, does not think evil," and "it does not rejoice over

---

4. 1 Cor 12.8–11.

wrong-doing,"[5] it is necessary that in that in which it is, it brings about a good will.

6. The malevolent spirit does not exercise charity toward another because it does not have any in itself; but when it starts to have the beginning, if I may so speak, of charity, it cannot be malevolent or sterile. And because while he remains in charity, he remains in God and God remains in him, he will always have it, if he always expends it but when he ceases to expend it, he will not have it. For it is the property of charity, that as the course of the present life is concerned, it increases in the one who expends it, but it departs without delay from the one who wanted to have it only for himself. Therefore, that person will have it the more, who will have expended it freely; because, just as the malevolent person can neither expend it nor have it, so someone who is reluctant neither has it nor expends it. The benevolent person is the dwelling place of charity. This word, i.e., benevolent, is made up of two Latin words *bene* and *velle* (wish well); therefore, if someone wishes another ill, insofar as he is an ill-wisher, he is not benevolent and because of this is malevolent. "Wisdom will not enter a deceitful soul."[6] But not every person who wishes for or seeks for something contrary either for himself or for another is properly called malevolent, but the person who carries out the will to do harm whether what he wants can be either good or evil.

7. But that a will is either good or harmful not from the doing of a thing, but from its purpose, is something that should be weighed by anyone; because it is not from what he does but from that on account of which he does it that a person shows the nature of his will. For Paul also wished for something contrary to himself when he asked that the sting be taken away from him which, for his salvation, he had accepted against the sin of pride; nor did he have a malevolent mind, although he exercised a will contrary to his own utility. In order that he ask that the sting by which he was ill-treated be removed from him, he wished for the health of

5. 1 Cor 13.4–6.
6. Wis 1.4.

his body to be of use, more for his preaching than for himself, not seeking what would be useful to himself but what would be useful to the many that they might be saved. For he wished that his health be of use to them; for he knew that his life was also useful for them. Finally, when he had the desire to be dissolved and to be with Christ, which would have been much better, he knew that it was necessary for him to remain in the flesh for the sake of those for whom he fulfilled the ministry of Apostle. Therefore, the charity of Christ urged him on, whether when he asked that the sting be taken away from him or when he wished to remain in the flesh, although desiring something else; for he was forced by the depth of charity that he both desire to be with Christ and wish to fulfill the duty of devout necessity; therefore, in both instances, he loved charity which he always breathed in a good will.

8. Therefore, whoever loves his brother according to charity, which God is, loves charity itself in him as much as possible. When our savior deigned to renew his Apostles with a new commandment, he said, "A new commandment I give you, that you love one another,"[7] ordering that fraternity be loved in itself, through the Apostle Paul, he commands also that charity itself of the fraternity be loved. When Christ speaks in himself, the teacher of the nations wishes us to have love without pretense: "Hate what is evil, hold on to what is good; love one another with mutual affection."[8]

9. Hence it is that in the eleventh book of the *Confessions*, that outstanding doctor, the blessed Augustine, when he confesses his love for God, which he had accepted from him in order that he love him, he says, "I have already said it, and I shall say it again; in the love of thy love am I doing this."[9] Also, expounding the 118th psalm, when he was explaining the understanding of that text, where it is said, "I live in an alien land; do not hide your commandments from me,"[10]

7. Jn 13.34.
8. Rm 12.9–10.
9. Augustine *Confessiones* XI.1. CCL 27.194. FOTC 21.327.
10. Ps 118.19 LXX; Ps 119.19.

after which he says, "What is loved by loving if not love itself? Whence consequently that alien on the earth, when he prayed that God's commandments not be hidden from him, in which commandments, love is commanded, either alone or the most, and he declares that he wants to have the love of love itself, saying, 'My soul is consumed with longing for your ordinances at all times.'"[11] Does not the statement of the blessed Augustine with prophetic and apostolic words deal[12] openly with loving love?

10. So, the love of God and neighbor, which is the fullness of the law and the purpose of the commandment, in God, loves the charity which God is and, in the neighbor, loves charity which is from God; thus God and neighbor are rightly loved, if love itself is loved both in God and in the neighbor. Thus it comes about that without a doubt we love both God himself in God and God in the neighbor. Nor is it in vain that after the love of God, no other love has been commanded us except only the love of neighbor, viz., that we recognize that we must love that creature where we can find charity itself. For every irrational animal, just as it does not have reason, so it does not have charity; nor does there appear to me to be a special reason other than that fitting and ordered love which is owed by a human being only to God and neighbor.

11. You see, holy brother, how prolix is the speech of your fellow servant with you about charity. I love charity itself in you too much, which you yourself also love in us. You are so filled with that gift of God that you wish all those whom you love to be filled with it in a similar way. Because you love us purely, you deign to pray for us urgently so that God who first loved us and gave us the charity by which it is loved by us, just as he grants it to those who do not have it by his prevenient grace, so he may destroy in us all the remnants of worldly desires and perfect us, fervent in the Spirit, in charity and make in that bliss in which just as there is no de-

---

11. Augustine *Enarrationes in Psalmos* CXVIII, s.8.3. CCL 40.1687.

12. Page 239, line 151 of the Latin text should read 'tractat' rather than 'tracta'.

praved enjoyment, so death is not feared as a punishment where no one experiences anything from the weakness of the flesh, but all the saints reign in the always perfect charity of God and neighbor.

12. May the divine mercy keep your holiness, praying for us, as I wish, holy sir and most blessed brother. Januarius[13] greets your holiness with all the affection of purity and veneration; with great joy, I have received the blessing sent by you. As you commanded, I have sent the book written to Monimus in fascicles in which, if anything please you, would that I know that it is of truth and not only of love! These are the offering of my littleness which the purity of your heart will cause to be accepted by you. When the suggestion of a brother we have in common has been accepted, I ask that diligence be present to assist your charity. I ask that the books which we have need of, your servants make copies of from your codices.

LETTER 6. TO THEODORE THE SENATOR

Fulgentius sends words of spiritual encouragement to a prominent Roman senator, Theodore, who, together with his wife, has decided to lead a life of greater asceticism. Theodore had been consul in 505 and in 526 was selected by the Gothic king Theodoric to accompany Pope John I on a mission to Constantinople. As was the case with the letters to the two aristocratic women, Fulgentius warns against the attractions of worldly prestige. See PLRE II. "Theodorus 62," 1097–98.

ULGENTIUS, servant of the servants of Christ, sends greetings in the Lord to the illustrious and deservedly outstanding Lord and most excellent son, Theodore.

1. That one unknown in body take the trouble to bring my acquaintance to you in the words of a letter, I ask that you not impute to impudence nor that you assign a work of

---

13. Januarius may be one of the African bishops living in exile in Sardinia with Fulgentius. See "Januarius 38 or 39," PCBE, 596.

charity to lack of consideration. First, there was the lovely letter of the holy brother Romulus,[1] then the letter of the brothers coming from there who were kindly received by you in the Lord. The more suggestion compelled me to write, the more gladly the knowledge of your spiritual resolve invited me to do so. For they reported that, compelled by the love of Christ, you kindly made mention of our name in a conversation, saying that you were delighted by our letter. Therefore, I willingly did what I know you willingly wanted, preferring to appear uncultivated in speech rather than be cold in charity, O illustrious and deservedly outstanding Lord and most excellent son.

2. I rejoice greatly that you are not held by the ties of worldly love, and, scorning the world, you tread underfoot that by which you were being trampled when you loved it. Now you are being carried forward by the consulship, now with happy triumph you are most certainly raised up not as one whom the Roman people applaud but as one because of whom the angelic choir rejoices, "Blessed are you.... For flesh and blood has not revealed this to you but my heavenly Father,"[2] among which heavens, you also have become a heaven. Into how much mourning do you think the Devil has been plunged because he sees that the world has been scorned by you and he knows that you have been converted to Christ, because he sees that you are deserting the things in which you seem to be and are moving in your heart from the love of temporal and earthly things to those heavenly and eternal things? Although Christ died equally for all the faithful and expended the equal benefit of redemption for all, as the Apostle says, "For all of you who were baptized into Christ have clothed yourselves with Christ. There is neither Jew nor Greek, there is neither slave nor free person, there is not male and female; for you are all one in Christ Jesus,"[3] still the conversion of the powerful of the world is of great service to the acquisitions of Christ.

---

1. Romulus is otherwise unknown.   2. Mt 16.17.
3. Gal 3.27–28.

3. For just as many brothers and friends, clients and subjects, equally known and unknown, are stirred to an ardor for earthly love by the influence of such people, so they are enkindled with the fire of worldly lust the more they see that the lofty are willingly held captive by the worldly love of the age. So just as often does he "look on the earth and it trembles, who touches the mountains and they smoke,"[4] while he regards hearts taken up with earthly matters, mercifully and by the consideration of his judgment, he compels them to tremble and he touches the proud hearts of the lofty like the tops of the mountains, so that they smoke with the confession of sins. By the shaking of such people, many begin to fear, and in the conversion of such people, many flee to the support of the divine pity. And so it happens that those who find themselves in the highest positions in this world either destroy many along with themselves or they take many with them on the road to salvation. Either a great punishment awaits such people if they provide the snare of bad example for many or great glory if they show many the example of a conversion to holiness. For who does not despise a small cell, when a senator despises a home of marble? Who, scorning earthly things, would not tell himself to seek the things of heaven, when a consul of Rome, with the scorning of earthly things, hastens to heaven?

4. Truly we see fulfilled in deed in your case what the prophet sang of: "The right hand of the most High has changed."[5] For who could have accomplished this in you, except the one who knows how to rule the order of mutable things according to the immutable and to dispense counsel? Because in order that individual things may be changed either for the worse or for the better according to the opportuneness of the times or for a variety of reasons, it comes about by the immutable counsel of him who is changed neither by things better or worse. Nor does he have the possibility either of progressing for the better or falling into some-

---

4. Ps 103.32 LXX; Ps 104.32.
5. Ps 76.11 LXX; Ps 77.10.

thing worse. He is what he always is and just as he is, that is the way he is; he does not have it in himself not to be able to be what he is because he does not have it in himself to be able to be what he is not. And what he is was not preceded by a beginning nor concluded by an end point; it does not extend through time nor is it contained by places nor changed by ages. Nothing is missing there because everything is in him; nothing is left over there because there is nothing beyond him.

5. Therefore, if they who, having contemned the love of temporal and mutable things, change to the love of him, they will be filled in him in whom nothing is lacking; safe in him in whom there is nothing to be feared; truly and always glorious in him whose true and eternal glory is neither taken away nor diminished nor increased. Who would not despise the present life by desire for that other life? Who would regard with horror the riches of a time that is collapsing because of the delights of his abundance? Who would not disdain all earthly kingdoms for love of that kingdom?

6. Therefore, we shall then receive that life if we see ourselves as dead to this life; and then we shall possess those riches, if we live as poor in spirit here. Then we shall arrive at the peak of that kingdom if with a true heart we hold on to humility here which God the teacher taught. The blessed Apostle says to those that are dead as follows: "For you have died and your life is hidden with Christ in God. When Christ your life appears, then you too will appear with him in glory."[6] Concerning the poor of this sort, the Lord himself speaks, saying, "Blessed are the poor in spirit, for theirs is the kingdom of heaven."[7] And concerning the humble of this sort, he says, "Whoever humbles himself will be exalted;"[8] and in another place, "Learn from me for I am meek and humble of heart and you will find rest for yourselves."[9]

7. They who love the world or they who attribute it to their own strength when they scorn the things that are in the world do not have this humility. These two types of pride

6. Col 3.3–4.
7. Mt 5.3.
8. Mt 23.12.
9. Mt 11.29.

the Holy Spirit has pointed out with one verse in a psalm when David says, "Those who trust in their wealth and boast of the abundance of their riches."[10] Those boast of the abundance of their riches who love their riches in such a way that they place their ultimate happiness in them. They trust in their own strength who scorn riches in such a way that they attribute this contempt to their own strength. For this reason, both types are proud; the former, because they trust in their wealth, not in God; the latter, because they wish to attribute the fact that they spurn riches to themselves, not to God; the former, because they love badly that which cannot be loved well; the latter because they do not spurn well that which can be spurned well; and for this reason, the former do evil badly, the latter do good badly.

8. Accordingly, since, with the Lord working mercifully in you, you have now learned not to boast of the abundance of your riches, it remains that you do not trust in your strength, i.e., that you do not assign to your own strength the fact that you scorn the goods and riches of the age, that you consider the honor of the world as nothing, that you are on fire with desire for the heavenly kingdom, that you delight to run in the path of God's commandments. You would never have all these things unless you had received them by a free gift from God; not nature, but grace, gives this to a human being; this is not possessed from the nature of the human condition but is acquired from the kindness of divine enlightenment.

9. The human being has been made by God in such a way as to be able to possess these things, but he cannot possess them unless he receives them by the gift of a merciful God, for the eye too was made in such a way so that it can see the light but it is unable to see the light unless light penetrates it. Therefore, that the eye sees is a benefit of the light but if it is lacking, it will remain blind in the darkness. Not everything which something can be is now that which it can be unless by nature it has the possibility of being what it always is. This is the one God, the Trinity itself, i.e., The Father and

---

10. Ps 48.7 LXX; Ps 49.6.

the Son and the Holy Spirit, who alone is the Creator of all things, because he alone has been created by no one. All things, since they have been created by him, not from him, by nature are subject to growth and loss. Therefore, in order that some things not fall into worse things, his grace governs them; and in order that some things may rise to better things, his grace raises them; and in order that they may abide forever, his grace gives life and preserves it.

10. The assistance of this grace must always be sought from God by us, but we must not attribute the very thing we seek to our own powers; nor can the very love of prayer at least be possessed unless it is given us by God. That we desire the assistance of grace is itself also the work of grace. For it begins to be poured in, in order that it can begin to be asked for; it is poured in more fully when it is given to those who ask. For who can ask for grace unless he wanted it? But unless God worked the very will in him, he could never want to. Wherefore the blessed Apostle bears witness that not only does God work the good works of human beings but also the good will, saying, "For God is the one who, for his good purpose, works in you both to desire and to work."[11] That is, because recommending to the faithful concern and humility, he first said, "Work out your salvation with fear and trembling,"[12] and then he added, "For God is the one who for his good purpose works in you both to desire and to work."[13] We run that we may come to God; and therefore we run because we want to run. But lest we attribute either the will to run or the running itself to our strength, the same Apostle informs us, saying, "So it depends not upon a person's will or exertion but upon God who shows mercy."[14]

11. So that you may abide and advance in these good things which you have received from God; that you may neither remain on the road nor turn back, nor turn to the right or to the left, whatever you have of good will or of good works, attribute to God who gave it and humbly ask him

---

11. Phil 2.13.
13. Phil 2.13.
12. Phil 2.12.
14. Rm 9.16.

both to preserve and increase what he has given. Do not attribute anything good to yourself as if it were yours, lest you not receive what you were able to receive and you lose what you did receive. The pride of the human heart is detestable by which a human being does what God condemns in human beings; but that is even more detestable by which a human being attributes to himself what God gives to human beings. That one is held to be guilty of the worse pride, the more ungrateful he is for the better gifts. The one who uses badly the substance of the world is damnable but even more damnable is the one who is made proud by the spiritual gifts.

12. Therefore, may humility of spirit grow in you. This is the true and whole greatness of the Christian. And the more the grace of God increases in you, all the more may you seem to have humility of heart abound in you. Work out your salvation in fear and trembling that you may always have it and that you may keep advancing. Do not let reading be absent from your good works nor good works be absent from your zeal for reading. Provide good things before God and human beings. Expend the zeal of your heart on the Holy Scriptures; and in them know who you were, who you are, and who you ought to be. If you approach them humbly and meekly, there assuredly you will find both prevenient grace by which the crushed person can rise and accompanying grace by which one can run along the way of the right route and subsequent grace by which one can arrive at the blessedness of the heavenly kingdom.

13. I ask you to greet your holy mother, venerable in Christ, who is at one with your spiritual zeal in both the Christian faith and truly maternal charity and also the one who now is your venerable sister in Christ, your wife. May the inseparable Trinity keep you, as I wish, with the protection of its strength, illustrious son.

LETTER 7. TO VENANTIA

Through Junillius, perhaps one of those living in Sardinia with him, Fulgentius contacted Venantia, otherwise unknown. We do not have her letter but it had obviously asked about the question of the forgiveness of sins, the sole topic of the letter. See "Venantia," PLRE II.1152.

ULGENTIUS, servant of the servants of Christ, sends greetings in the Lord to the illustrious and deservedly venerable Lady, his daughter Venantia.

1. Just as the true light is never obscured, so eternal truth never lies. God is truth and light. Concerning him it is written: "The true light which enlightens everyone was coming into the world."[1] The light and the truth itself says, "I am the light of the world."[2] And again he says of himself, "I am the way, the truth, and the life."[3] We are warned by his teaching that "every good tree bears good fruit,"[4] and that "a tree is known by its fruit."[5] In him, illustrious lady and deservedly venerable daughter, although you are unknown, I already know you; in him, I rejoice with you, although you are so far away.

2. Through the letter of my outstanding son, Junilius, I have come to know your way of life and at the same time the ardor of your Christianity. Insofar as he took care to mention to me the grace which God has given you, in his letter he gave me an indication of your greetings. Without a doubt you would not have done this unless you loved Christ in his servants with complete purity of mind nor would you have greeted in the Lord an unknown servant so kindly unless you put on the Lord with a devout heart. Thanks be to him who multiplies our joy from the charity of the faithful. For it is charity which leads believers to God because God is love itself. So John the Apostle says, "God is love and whoever remains in love, remains in God and God in him."[6]

3. Where this begins to dwell; it does not permit sin to

1. Jn 1.9.
2. Jn 8.12.
3. Jn 14.6.
4. Mt 7.17.
5. Mt 12.33.
6. 1 Jn 4.16.

dominate but "covers a multitude of sins";[7] nor does it cause only present sins to be avoided but also it causes all past sins to be loosed. The proud and recalcitrant who despair of the forgiveness of sins repudiate it, and not only do they with pitiable blindness reject the care for their own salvation but also do not rest from upsetting faithful souls with deadly words if they are unable to pervert them. Often, either the frightfulness of their sins or the length of a wicked life takes away from them the hope of salvation and drives them to perpetrate even worse things in such a way that in such people that statement of Holy Scripture is fulfilled: "When wickedness comes, contempt comes also."[8] And truly the depth of evils kills, if the despair of forgiveness does them injury by a detestable hardening of the heart.

4. Who does not see how impious and how sacrilegious it is if a person, who has been converted to good things through penance for his past evils, believes that there can be no forgiveness for any sin? What else is being done with these words than that the hand of the all-powerful physician is being pushed away by the vice of despair, from effecting human salvation? For the physician himself says, "Those who are healthy do not need a physician, but the sick do."[9] If our physician is expert, he can cure all maladies. If God is merciful, he can forgive all sins. A goodness which does not conquer every evil is not a perfect goodness nor is a medicine perfect for which any disease is incurable. It is written in the sacred writings: ". . . Against wisdom, evil does not prevail;"[10] and the omnipotence of our physician is made known by such words in the psalm: "Bless the Lord, O my soul, and all that is within me, bless his holy name. Bless the Lord, O my soul, and do not forget all his benefits—who forgives all your iniquity, who heals all your diseases, who redeems your life from the pit, who crowns you with steadfast love and mercy, who satisfies you with good as long as you live so that your youth is renewed like the eagle's."[11] What, I ask, do we think

---

7. 1 Pt 4.8.
9. Lk 5.31.
11. Ps. 102.1–5 LXX; Ps 103.1–5.
8. Prov 18.3.
10. Wis 7.30.

cannot be forgiven us when the Lord forgives all our iniquities? Or what do we think cannot be healed in us, when the Lord heals all our diseases? Or how is there anything still lacking to the healed and justified person whose desire is satisfied with good things? Or how is he not believed to gain the benefit of complete forgiveness to whom a crown is given together with love and mercy? Therefore, let no one despairing of the physician remain in his infirmity; let no one, downplaying the mercy of God, waste away in iniquities. The Apostle calls out that "Christ died for the ungodly."[12]

5. But perhaps it is said that those sinners can be saved who after their sins, deserve to be cleansed by the washing of baptism; but from that point on, the sins which the baptized person seems to commit, remain unforgivable. Was the Apostle John speaking to the unbaptized, to whom he said, "My children, I am writing this to you so that you may not commit sin. But if anyone does sin, we have an Advocate with the Father, Jesus Christ the righteous one. He is expiation for our sins"?[13]

6. Whatever kind of sin it may be, it can be forgiven by God to the converted person, but that person does not allow it to be forgiven for himself who by despairing closes the door of forgiveness against himself. Otherwise, the truth does not lie which said, "Ask and it will be given to you; seek and you will find; knock and the door will be opened to you."[14] Hence also the most holy prophet Isaiah exhorts sinners and the wicked to the effect that the forgiveness of sins is never to be despaired of, saying, "Seek the Lord while he may be found, call upon him while he is near; let the wicked forsake their way and the unrighteous their thoughts; let them return to the Lord that he may have mercy on them and to our God for he will abundantly pardon."[15] Let the wicked forsake his way, in which he sins; let the unrighteous abandon his thoughts with which he despairs of the forgiveness of sins and according to the prophet's statement, "re-

---

12. Rm 5.6.
14. Mt 7.7–8.

13. 1 Jn 2.1–2.
15. Is 55.1–7.

turn to the Lord for he will abundantly pardon."[16] In this 'abundantly', nothing is lacking. Here mercy is omnipotent and omnipotence is merciful. For so great is the kindness of omnipotence and the omnipotence of kindness in God that there is nothing which he is unwilling or unable to loose for the converted person.

7. A salutary conversion consists of two aspects: If neither penance deserts the one who hopes nor hope deserts the one who does penance, and through this, if with his whole heart, someone renounces his sin and with his whole heart places his hope of forgiveness in God. But sometimes, either the Devil takes the hope away from a person doing penance, or he removes the penance from the one who hopes; when he burdens one, he crushes him; when he lifts up the other, he casts him down. Judas who betrayed Christ did penance for his sins but lost salvation because he did not hope for forgiveness. The evangelist speaks about him in this way: "Then Judas his betrayer, seeing that Jesus had been condemned, deeply regretted what he had done. He returned the thirty pieces of silver to the chief priests and elders, saying, 'I have sinned in betraying innocent blood.' They said, 'What is that to us? Look to it yourself.' Flinging the money into the Temple, he departed and went off and hanged himself."[17] He repented worthily because he sinned, betraying innocent blood, but he denied himself the fruit of his penance, because he did not hope that the sin of his betrayal was to be washed away by the very blood which he had betrayed.

8. The Devil holds many in their sins by a vain hope for forgiveness and forces them not to fear the justice of God, and he persuades them foolishly to rejoice in God's goodness. Such people say, according to the rebuke of the Apostle, "Let us do evil that good may come of it. Their penalty is what they deserve."[18]

9. With these indications, we recognize clearly that a person does penance in vain if, while penance is being done,

16. Is 55.7.   17. Mt 27.3–5.
18. Rm 3.8.

forgiveness is despaired of and forgiveness is hoped for in vain without penance for sins; and through this, neither must anyone sin in security under the hope of forgiveness nor, considering the multitude of his sins, remain bound by the chain of despair. For Holy Scripture exhorts us to stop sinning now and not to give up hope that what we have done will be forgiven us; indeed he says, "Have you sinned, my child? Do so no more but ask forgiveness for your past sins."[19] Holy Scripture has forewarned each and shown that neither ought we to remain in sin nor to doubt the forgiveness of any sin. Why is it ordered that we are not to add sins to sins, if we are to remain in sin? Or why is it ordered that we pray concerning past sins that they be forgiven us if there are some which can never be forgiven to those who pray? Or perhaps the length of time can foreclose someone's case so that just as, after a space of thirty years no one is permitted to try to get possession of things appropriated under human laws, so, under divine laws, after a long period of sinning, it is not permitted to ask for forgiveness? Far be it that this be the case with our God as the human condition has it in lawsuits. For our God is just as merciful and good as he is infinite and unconquered. Accordingly, the goodness of the unconquered is not conquered and the mercy of the infinite knows no bounds.

10. Finally, he demonstrates that the whole time of the present life is most apt for conversions, saying, "But if the wicked turn away from all their sins that they have committed and keep all my statutes and do what is lawful and right, they shall surely live. They shall not die. None of the transgressions that they have committed shall be remembered against them; for the righteousness that they have done, they shall live. Have I any pleasure in the death of the wicked, says the Lord God, and not rather that they should turn away from their ways and live? But when the righteous turn away from their righteousness and commit iniquity and do the same abominable things that the wicked do, shall

---

19. Sir 21.1.

they live? None of the righteous deeds that they have done shall be remembered; for the treachery of which they are guilty and the sin they have committed, they shall die."[20] And further on he says, "When the righteous turn away from their righteousness and commit iniquity, they shall die for it; for the iniquity that they have committed, they shall die. Again, when the wicked turn away from the wickedness they have committed and do what is lawful and right, they shall save their life. Because they considered and turned away from all the transgressions that they had committed, they shall surely live. They shall not die."[21] Each statement is true because each is divine, whether it be that the just person when he will have turned away from his righteousness, all his righteous deeds will be consigned to oblivion, or whether it be that the wicked person when he will have been converted from wickedness to righteousness, will be saved, and all his wicked deeds will not be remembered.

11. Indeed, it is wicked if we think that the just person can be condemned at whatever time he is turned away; and let us think it wicked that he cannot be saved at whatever time he is converted. God is just and merciful. Therefore, just as he can through justice condemn the one who had turned away, so he is always able through mercy to save the one who has been converted. No length of time closes off either the divine justice or mercy. Penance is never late with God in whose sight things past as well as future things are always taken as present. If a long period of sinning were to overcome the mercy of God, Christ would not have come in the last age of the world to take away the sins of a perishing world, concerning which John says, "Behold the Lamb of God, who takes away the sin of the world,"[22] and the Savior says of himself, "The Son of Man has come to seek and to save what was lost."[23]

12. Our Samaritan would never have mercifully brought the wounded man to the inn on his mule, if he had made

---

20. Ez 18.21–24.
22. Jn 1.29.
21. Ez 18.26–28.
23. Lk 19.10.

the judgment that there was some incurable wound in him. He would never have promised that he would pay the innkeeper whatever he asked, beyond the two denarii given, if he did not know beforehand that that generous offer would not be useful for full restoration to health. For why would the innkeeper ask for something more, if the injured man had a wound which could not be healed? Just as there is no illness that is incurable for our physician, so the heavenly medicine cannot be powerless in any wound or for any length of time. Therefore, the physician himself testifies that he is always able to restore health to the one converted, saying, " In returning and rest, you shall be saved."[24] Wherefore God through Jeremiah does not cease to reprove the hardheartedness of certain ones in this way: "When people fall, do they not get up again? If they go astray, do they not turn back? Why then has this people turned away in perpetual backsliding? They have held fast to deceit; they have refused to return."[25] God does not punish the sins in the sinner, if the neck of the sinner is not stiffened.

13. Therefore, it is good for us if we flee to the mercy of him whose justice we are incapable of escaping. The justice of God is such that it condemns those who turn away, saves those who turn to him. So he says, "Be converted to me and I will save you."[26] He is always delighted by our conversion nor has he set a time for a human being, so long as he is in this life, at which time he cannot be merciful to the one who turns to him; on the contrary, the whole time of the present life is known to have been destined for our conversion. For the blessed Peter says, "The Lord does not delay his promise as some regard 'delay', but he is patient with you, not wishing that any should perish but that all should come to repentance."[27]

14. If the Lord were to judge any age unfitting for the remedy of conversion he would not have called the workers to his vineyard at different times. Not unfittingly the difference of ages is seen in the difference of hours. In this way,

24. Is 30.15.
26. Is 54.22.
25. Jer 8.4–5.
27. 2 Pt 3.9.

the age of childhood is seen as the morning, adolescence in the third hour, young adulthood in the sixth, the gravity of declining age in the ninth and in the eleventh, the very last age, old age. Therefore, in whatever age one is called, if he does not scorn the kindness of the Lord who calls, it is necessary that he receive the denarius of eternal life. He is always delighted by our conversion, concerning which the prophet Joel cries out to us, "Yet even now, says the Lord, return to me with all your heart, with fasting, with weeping, and with mourning; rend your hearts, not your clothing. Return to the Lord, your God, for he is gracious and merciful, slow to anger and abounding in steadfast love and relents from punishing."[28]

15. So the Apostle Paul rebukes hardness of heart in those who neglect to do penance for their sins; for he says, "Therefore, you are without excuse, everyone of you who passes judgment. For by the standard by which you judge another, you condemn yourself, since you, the judge, do the very same things. We know that the judgment of God on those who do such things is true. Do you suppose, then, you who judge those who engage in such things and yet do them yourself, that you will escape the judgment of God? Or do you hold his priceless kindness, forbearance, and patience in low esteem, unaware that the kingdom of God would lead you to repentance? By your stubbornness and impenitent heart, you are storing up wrath for yourself for the day of wrath and revelation of the just judgment of God who will repay everyone according to his works."[29] Also in another text, he does not lament so much those who seemed to sin gravely as those who were unwilling to do penance for their sins. Then he says to the Corinthians, "I fear that when I come again my God may humiliate me before you and I may have to mourn over many of those who sinned earlier and have not repented of the impurity, immorality and licentiousness they practiced."[30] Not undeservedly does the Apostle mourn over those who do not do penance for he knows

28. Jl 2.12–13. 29. Rm 2.1–6.
30. 2 Cor 12.21.

that "there will be more joy in heaven over one sinner who repents than over the ninety-nine righteous people who have no need of repentance."[31] Fittingly, therefore, does the blessed Apostle mourn over them for their impenitence of heart, those over whom the angelic choir does not rejoice.

16. The kindness of God leads us to penance; he afflicts us with trials, he corrects us with infirmities, teaches us with cares, so that we who have sinned in the health of the body may learn to abstain from sins in infirmity. We who scorned the mercy of God in frivolity, corrected by the lash of sadness should fear his justice. Thus it comes about that we who, by abusing health, have begotten infirmity for ourselves, through that infirmity, may again procure the benefits of health, and we, who through frivolity have fallen into trials, through these trials, may regain happiness. Holy Scripture bears witness that God's love for us is shown more by the lash and correction; for it says, "My child, do not despise the Lord's discipline or be weary of his reproofs for the Lord reproves the one he loves, as a father the son in whom he delights."[32] And the Savior himself says that he loves those he reproves, saying, "Those whom I love, I reprove and chastise."[33] And the teaching of the Apostles does not cease to proclaim that "It is necessary for us to undergo many hardships to enter the kingdom of God."[34] The Lord himself also says that the road which leads to life is constricted and the gate narrow.

17. That we may know that those who are beguiled by temporal joys and scorn the divine commands must be burned in eternal flames but that those who with the fear of God patiently put up with temporal evils will gain eternal rest, let us have a look at the rich man garbed in purple and Lazarus, the poor man, the former delivered over to eternal flames after his banqueting; the latter, after his afflictions, is safe in the eternal peace of Abraham's bosom. When the rich man, burning up, asked that a drop of water bedew his tongue by the finger of the blessed poor man, this answer

31. Lk 15.7.
33. Rev 3.19.
32. Prov 2.11–12.
34. Acts 24.22.

was given to him forthwith by the blessed Abraham: "My child, remember that you received what was good during your lifetime while Lazarus likewise received what was bad; but now he is comforted here, whereas you are tormented."[35] There was no other reason why the rich man suffers punishments and the poor man gains joy and rest, except that the former received good things in this life and the latter, bad.

18. But not all who have the good things of the present life receive the good things of the present life, nor do all who suffer the evils of this life, receive bad things in this life; but they receive good things in their life who exult in the joy and delights of the present Life and believe for that reason that they are blessed because they perceive that they are struck by no adversity, but those receive bad things in their Life who tolerate the pressures and trials of the present life with the fear of God and with contrite and humbled heart, they sigh for, not temporal joys, but eternal ones. They desire, not the good things that pass, but those that abide.

19. Thus to those who wish to have happiness in the goods of present things, the psalm says, "How long, you people, shall my honor suffer shame? How long will you love vain words and seek after lies?"[36] And in another text, "Put no confidence in extortion and set no vain hopes on robbery; if riches increase, do not set your heart on them."[37] The blessed James does not cease to reprove such people, saying, "Come now, you rich, weep and wail over your impending miseries. Your wealth has rotted away, your clothes have become moth-eaten, your gold and silver have corroded, and that corrosion will be a testimony against you; it will devour your flesh like a fire. You have stored up treasure for the last days. Behold the wages you withheld from the workers who harvested your fields are crying aloud, and the cries of the harvesters have reached the ears of the Lord of Hosts. You have lived on earth in luxury and pleasure; you have fattened your hearts for the day of slaughter."[38] He commanded that the laughter and the joy of such people be turned to

---

35. Lk 16.25.
37. Ps 61.11 LXX; Ps 62.10.
36. Ps 4.3 LXX; Ps 4.2.
38. Jas 5.1–5.

mourning and dejection, saying, "Cleanse your hands, you sinners, and purify your hearts, you of two minds. Begin to lament, to mourn, to weep. Let your laughter be turned into mourning and your joy into dejection. Humble yourselves before the Lord and he will exalt you."[39]

20. We should not think that the sadness of the humble and the happiness of the proud, the mourning of the devout and the joy of the impious can be deprived of future reward and retribution. A fitting payment remains to be paid by the divine judgment for both. This the judge himself is known to have decreed by this declaration, "Woe to you who are filled now, for you will be hungry. Woe to you who laugh now, for you will grieve and weep...."[40] Blessed are you who are now hungry, for you will be satisfied. Blessed are you who are now weeping, for you will laugh."[41] "Blessed are they who mourn for they will be comforted."[42] David also speaks of people who sow in tears but does not keep silent that they will reap the harvest in joy and exultation; for he says, "May those who sow in tears reap with shouts of joy. Those who go out weeping bearing the seed for sowing shall come home with shouts of joy, carrying their sheaves."[43] Also he asserts that the Lord is now near to these people, saying, "The Lord is near to the brokenhearted and saves the crushed in spirit."[44] So useful are trials for Christians that through them, our spirit becomes a sacrifice to God. For it is written in the psalm: "The sacrifice acceptable to God is a broken spirit; a broken and contrite heart, O God, you will not despise."[45]

21. Enlightened by this and innumerable other texts of this type, let us hasten as rapidly as possible to be converted to God absolutely. For Scripture says, "Do not delay to turn back to the Lord and do not postpone it from day to day; for suddenly the wrath of the Lord will come upon you and at the time of punishment, you will perish."[46] Converted, let us never despair of the forgiveness of sins, holding on to the

39. Jas 4.8–10.
40. Lk 6.25.
41. Lk 6.21.
42. Mt 5.4.
43. Ps 125.5–6 LXX; Ps 126.5–6.
44. Ps 33.19 LXX; Ps 34.18.
45. Ps 50.19 LXX; Ps 51.17.
46. Sir 5.7.

faithful promise of the Lord who says, "In returning and rest, you will be saved."[47] Let us put up with the pressures and trials of the present time with patient courage and let us never depart from the fear of the Lord. For the Apostle commands us to "endure in affliction."[48] He bears witness that the correction of the present time is of great avail to us for avoiding the punishment of the future judgment, saying, "But since we are being judged by the Lord, we are being disciplined so that we may not be condemned along with the world."[49]

22. But in the very trials, let us give thanks to the Lord and that which the holy Azariah said in the furnace, let us say in our trials: "Blessed are you, O Lord, God of our ancestors and worthy of praise; and glorious is your name forever! For you are just in all you have done; all your works are true and your ways right, and all your judgments are true. You have executed true judgments in all you have brought upon us and upon Jerusalem, the holy city of our ancestors; by a true judgment you have brought all this upon us because of our sins. For we have sinned and broken your law in turning away from you; in all matters we have sinned grievously. We have not obeyed your commandments; we have not kept them or done what you have commanded us for our own good. So that all you have brought upon us and all that you have done to us, you have done by a true judgment."[50] A bit later he says, "And now with all our heart we follow you; we fear you and seek your presence. Do not put us to shame."[51]

---

47. Is 30.15.
48. Rm 12.12.
49. 1 Cor 11.32.
50. Prayer of Azariah 3–8 (Dn 3.26–31).
51. Prayer of Azariah 18–19 (Dn 3.41–42).

LETTER 8. TO DONATUS

Donatus, a faithful Catholic of some learning though not versed in Theology, asked Fulgentius to refute the Arians who had been asking him questions he was unable to answer. Fulgentius obliged at length and from section 20 on, quickly passed in review the heretics whose ideas had helped to provoke the development of the classic Trinitarian and Christological syntheses of the patristic period.

ULGENTIUS, servant of the servants of God, sends greetings in the Lord to the outstanding Lord and, in the charity of Christ, very much desired son, Donatus.

(I) 1. I bless the Lord greatly, my dearest son, because by his grace you, although younger in age, do not crave for fleshly things but for the things that are of the spirit. On fire with fervor for the faith, you now praiseworthily begin to meditate, not on those things by which pleasure damnably nourishes the flesh, but on those things by which the truth, recognized spiritually, feeds the soul. I do not doubt that this came about by his inspiration so that although you are accustomed to spend your time on the study of secular literature, now you expend your devotion on the divine words. You wish to grasp more earnestly, not that from which swollen eloquence is learned but that by which eternal life is prepared. For whosoever holds the true faith, possesses life. "The just man lives by faith."[1] And whoever wishes to be instructed in the mystery of the same faith, desires to gain the knowledge of life. One grows in it the more one learns what is true and salutary. The one who will hold without a doubt the beginning of this knowledge will arrive at perfection, and he who will not scorn to accept humbly the milk of the Apostle's words will deserve to rejoice in the reception of solid food. Whether one is nourished by milk or fed by food within the Catholic Church, only if he does not go away from the lap of mother Church, will he remain a participant in life, because, holding on to the righteousness of faith, he

1. Rm 1.17.

8. TO DONATUS

will possess life as well. He who remains in unbelief will not possess this life nor will he who perseveres in serious sin. Each of them is convicted of being among those who, according to the true statement of the blessed Paul, "live . . . in the futility of their minds, darkened in understanding, alienated from the life of God because of their ignorance, because of their hardness of heart";[2] for that blindness of heart is unaware of what it believes and of what it does.

(II.) 2. You say that a question was proposed to you by certain Arians concerning the Father and the Son. They asserted that the Father was greater and the Son less. But you, because of your ignorance of divine letters in which you have been given less instruction, did not come up with anything with which you might answer them in defense of the true faith. In the name of the Lord, therefore, I first praise this in you, that if you did not have much ability to answer, nevertheless there remained in your heart a firm faith in the truth. For not all who are sharers in Christ have the ability to defend what they believe by giving a response. But this is also assuredly a part of victory that as long as one is unable to defend the truth in word, still, with a faithful heart, he avoids error. It is profitable that we follow the very salutary words of Peter the Apostle commanding that we be "always ready to give an explanation to anyone who asks for a reason for the faith and hope which are in" us.[3] Wishing to be better prepared to answer, you ask that, instructed by our words, armed with the divine words, you know how you may be able to counter the heretics who wish to attack our faith.

3. Accordingly, I advise that first of all you hold on to this: that the Holy Trinity, i.e., the Father and the Son and the Holy Spirit, are by nature God most high, true and good, of one nature, of one essence, of one omnipotence, of one goodness, of one eternity, of one infinity. So, when you hear of one God, Father, Son, and Holy Spirit, understand one nature of that most high Trinity. And when you hear of the Trinity, Father, Son, and Holy Spirit, recognize the three

2. Eph 4.17–18.
3. 1 Pt 3.15.

persons of that one most high divinity. For there are three persons, the Father and the Son and the Holy Spirit; thus, it is called the Trinity but there is one substance of the Father and the Son and the Holy Spirit. Therefore, the Trinity itself is truly proclaimed as one God by the faithful.

(III.) 4. The words of Truth itself show that the three persons are the Father and the Son and the Holy Spirit. Hence, our Savior says, ". . . I am not alone but it is I and the Father who sent me."[4] Concerning the Holy Spirit, he also says, "And I will ask the Father and he will give you another advocate . . . the Spirit of Truth."[5] He also commanded that the nations be baptized "in the name of the Father and of the Son and of the Holy Spirit."[6] With these and other testimonies of this sort, it is shown that the Father and the Son and the Holy Spirit are three persons but that they are not three natures. Hence that Holy Trinity is worthily believed in the persons, but unity of nature does not permit them to be called three gods, the Father and the Son and the Holy Spirit. And because in the one nature of the Trinity, there can be no diversity, therefore, the property remains unconfused in the three persons and equality of substance reigns unchangeably in the unity of nature. So it is said of the Son: "Who, though he was in the form of God, did not regard equality with God something to be grasped." And "because he not only broke the sabbath, but he also called God his own Father, making himself equal to God."[7] To this equality of nature and power, that also belongs of which the Son himself says, "What he does, his Son will also do," and "For just as the Father raises the dead and gives life, so also does the Son give life to whomever he wishes."[8] Therefore, in that nature of the Trinity, it is all so much one that nothing there can be either separated or divided; it is all so equal that nothing there can be greater or less. Truthful authority shows this one God of the New and Old Testament to us. Concerning this one God, the blessed Moses says, "Hear, O

4. Jn 8.16.
6. Mt 28.19.
8. Jn 5.19,21.

5. Jn 14.16–17.
7. Jn 5.18.

8. TO DONATUS

Israel, the Lord is our God, the Lord alone . . . ," and "the Lord your God you shall fear; him you shall serve."[9] And the Lord himself says concerning himself, "See now that I, even I, am he; there is no god besides me."[10] Concerning this, the blessed David also says, "For who is God except the Lord? And who is a rock besides our God?"[11] Also the holy James the apostle, proclaiming this one God, says, "You believe that God is one. You do well . . . ; even the demons believe and tremble."[12]

5. Nevertheless, we are not unaware that these testimonies or if there are any similar ones found in the divine words by which God is asserted to be one and sole are assigned by heretics, not to the Holy Trinity itself, but only to one person, i.e., to God the Father alone. Accordingly, insofar as we are able, with the Lord God himself giving, let us seek understanding of those texts which we put forward, i.e., of the one where it is said: "Hear, O Israel, the Lord your God is one God,"[13] and of the other one, where it is said: "The Lord your God you shall adore and him alone you shall serve."[14] We recall that the first text which we cited was the one where it is said: "Hear, O Israel, the Lord your God is one God."[15] Therefore, we say this most firmly to each one in such a way that no one think that he can depart in any way from this text.

6. Accordingly, since the rule of this commandment in no way permits that two gods be worshipped by the faithful, either let them believe that the Father and the Son are by nature one God, if they wish without transgressing this command, to worship one God in such a way that they neither worship the Father without the Son nor the Son without the Father. Or, because a greater God and a lesser God cannot be one, it is necessary that either they say that the Father alone is their Lord God and deny that the Son is in any way their Lord God. Or, let them assert that only the Son is their

---

9. Dt 6.4,13.
10. Dt 32.39.
11. Ps 17.3 LXX; Ps 18.31.
12. Jas 2.19.
13. Dt 6.4.
14. Dt 6.13.
15. Dt 6.4.

Lord God and let them depart from the worship of God the Father. But they are unable to deny God the Father, the Lord their God. While they confess that he is the Lord God of all, they also strive to subordinate the divinity of the Son, as of a lesser god, to him by the right of subjection. But, as for the Son, if they wish to deny that he is the Lord their God, they are immediately convicted by the voice of the Father himself. For through the mouth of the prophet, in the person of God the Father, it is said: "But I will have pity on the house of Judah and I will save them by the Lord their God."[16] The authority of the Gospel truth also points out that the Lord himself is our God when the confession of the blessed Thomas the Apostle assuredly contradicts heretical depravity as he exclaims and says, "My Lord and my God."[17]

7. Therefore, when they confess without a doubt that the Father is the Lord God and are forced by prophetic and Gospel truth to say that the Son is the Lord God, either let them say that the Father and the Son, the properties of the persons being preserved, are by nature one Lord God or, confessing that the Father alone is the one Lord God, consequently let them say that the Son is neither their Lord nor their God. When they say this, they will never dare assert that they are Christians, since indeed the Christian has received his name from Christ. He can never be a Christian who says that Christ is not his Lord God.

8. Therefore, let them say that the Father and the Son are not two Lord Gods but their one Lord God, if they wish to hold to the truth of the faith and they are unwilling to be found in rebellion against the commandments of the Law and the Gospel. For thus they will be able to preserve equally the understanding and the obligatory force of that text where it is said: "The Lord your God you shall adore and him alone shall you serve."[18] Nor is it right for anyone to adore the Father as God in such a way that he does not adore the Son as God, for indeed it has been written about the Son himself in Deuteronomy: "Praise O heavens, his

16. Hos 1.7.   17. Jn 20.28.
18. Dt 6.13.

people, worship him, all you gods."[19] Concerning him as well, the blessed David says in the psalms, "May all kings fall down before him, all nations give him service."[20]

(IV.) 9. But if the Son were not, according to his divinity, one God with the Father, he would not be of one nature with him; and if he were of another nature, he would undoubtedly be a creature. If, however, he were a creature, the authority of the Holy Scriptures would not order that he must be served but rather would forbid it. In the first commandment of the Decalogue, just as the worship and service of the one Lord God is most clearly commanded, so for adoration and service to be shown by the faithful to any creature is most vehemently forbidden. For it is said there: "I am the Lord your God, who brought you out of the land of Egypt, out of the house of slavery; you shall have no other gods before me."[21] If this is taken as spoken simultaneously by the Father and the Son, the Father and the Son are believed to be one Lord God; but if either the Father is believed to have said this without the Son or the Son without the Father, it is necessary that the Father or the Son be denied to be the Lord God. Concerning this he said, "I am the Lord your God who brought you out of the land of Egypt, out of the house of slavery; you shall have no other gods before me." Concerning him, the holy Moses said, "Hear, O Israel, the Lord your God is one God."[22] And because God himself, commanding that only he be served and ordering that he be adored by the faithful, in fact forbade that anyone adore a creature and serve a creature. So, at the end of that first commandment, he speaks as follows concerning everything which he created: "You shall not bow down to them or worship them; for I am the Lord your God."[23]

10. Knowing this, the blessed Apostle asserts that "the

---

19. Dt 32.43. LXX. This verse is not found in the Hebrew Bible. The English text given is from the New Revised Standard Version. The Latin is translated: "Rejoice, O heavens, together with him and let all the angels of God adore him." The LXX speaks of "Sons of God" which gives rise to the divergent translation of 'angels' or 'gods'.

20. Ps 71.11 LXX; Ps 72.11.　　21. Ex 20.2–3.
22. Dt 6.4.　　23. Dt 20.5.

wrath of God is being revealed ... against every impiety and wickedness of those who suppress the truth by their wickedness ..., and they revered and worshipped the creature rather than the Creator who is blessed forever."[24] To hold the truth of God is to worship one God; to convert the truth of God into a lie is to serve the creature. For true religion consists in the service of the one true God. For the one God is Truth itself and just as when one truth has been set aside, there is not 'another' truth, so, apart from the one true God, there is not another true God. For the one truth is that by nature there is one true divinity. And so there cannot truly be said to be two true gods, just as the one truth itself cannot by nature be divided.

(V.) 11. Holy Scripture which truthfully and salutarily points out to us that there is one Lord God, just as it makes known to all the faithful that the Father is true God, so also it makes known that the Son is true God. Concerning the Father, the blessed Apostle says, writing to the Thessalonians, "... You turned to God from idols to serve the living and true God and to await his Son from heaven, whom he raised from the dead, Jesus who delivers us from the coming wrath."[25] Here Jesus Christ is not the Son of God the Father in the way that we are; he is in the proper sense, we are redeemed; he is born, we are made; he is true, we are adopted. He, who is the true Son, is also the true God, not generated by adoption, but born from the Father by nature. In this true God and true Son is the true divinity because the birth from the Father is natural to him. So, the blessed John in his letter declares that he is the true Son of the Father, true God, saying, "We also know that the Son of God has come and has given us discernment to know the one who is true. And we are in the one who is true, in his Son Jesus Christ. He is the true God and eternal life."[26] Therefore, to worship the true God and to serve the true God is not to change the truth of God into a lie. That one, however, changes the truth

24. Rm 1.18,25.   25. 1 Thes 1.9–10.
26. 1 Jn 5.20.

of God into a lie who thinks that the not-true God is to be served; that one worships the not-true God and serves the not-true God who serves a creature and worships a creature; because where the not-true God is worshipped and the not-true God is served, there the truth of God is changed into a lie.

12. Therefore, since by the witness of words from heaven, we know both that God the Father is true God and God the Son is true God; either let them assert with the Catholics that the Father and the Son are by nature the one true God; or let them not be afraid to profess that they are worshipers of a creature, so that they may know by the very clarity of things that they have changed the truth of God into a lie. The one truth of the one true God, indeed, one Truth, one true God, does not permit the serving and worship of the true God to be joined to that of a creature. The true religion allows that the duty of worship and service be shown by the faithful to no god, except to the one true God.

(VI.) However, every nature which is less than the nature of God the Father is without a doubt a created nature. But what is a created nature except a creature? But every creature, since it is a work of the truth, is a true creature; still it is not the truth. That alone is by nature the truth which by nature is the true divinity. Therefore, they do not change the truth of God into a lie but hold the saving mystery of the true faith who believe in their heart unto righteousness and confess with their mouth to salvation that not the Father alone, nor the Son alone, but the Father and the Son together are their one Lord God. Because not only God the Father but also God the Son by nature is truthful God, true God, God the Truth, remaining by nature with the Father, one Truthful, one True, and one Truth because the one truth which alone is the true divinity, altogether forbids that two gods be believed in or spoken of.

13. Thus, God the Son according to his divine nature is not less than the Father but equal to the Father because the Son is called true God in such a way that the Father is not called a truer God. For the very recognition of the Truth al-

lows that nothing in God be considered less. Therefore, the one equality of true divinity remains in the Father and the Son by nature and one immutable and eternal majesty. For we truly say that the Son is equal to the Father in such a way that we do not deny truly that he is less. For we know that God the Son was born from the nature of God the Father, born also from the nature of the virgin mother and through this, true God from the truth of the nature of the Father, truly human from the truth of the substance of the mother. The eternity of the divinity shows that he was born without a beginning and the taking of the flesh in time teaches without a doubt that he is lessened. Therefore, the Son is equal to the Father and the Son is less than the Father, equal in true divinity, less in true humanity. Equal because "in the beginning was the Word and the Word was with God and the Word was God";[27] less, however, because "The Word became flesh and dwelt among us."[28] Equal because, "though he was in the form of God, he did not regard equality with God something to be grasped";[29] but less because "he emptied himself, taking the form of a servant."[30] The Son is equal to the Father because as the Lord he was born from the Lord; but the Son is less than the Father because he was made a servant, born from the handmaid. Hence it is that he says, "Since my mother bore me, you have been my God."[31] And again: "O Lord, I am your servant, the child of your serving girl."[32] The Son is equal to the Father because "All things came to be through him and without him nothing came to be."[33] The Son is less than the Father because "He was born of a woman, born under the Law."[34] And so, just as the Son of God is truly recognized as coeternal with God the Father, so truly he is later than his mother.

14. The eternity of the Father in no way came before the first birth of the Son but the birth in time of his mother preceded his second birth. In that nature of God the Father

---

27. Jn 1.1.
28. Jn 1.14.
29. Phil 2.6.
30. Phil 2.7.
31. Ps 21.11 LXX; Ps 22.10.
32. Ps 115.7 LXX; Ps 116.16.
33. Jn 1.3.
34. Gal 4.4.

which had no beginning, the coeternal Son was inexpressibly born from the eternal Father; in the nature of the virgin which had a beginning in time, the same Son was mercifully begotten in time by a temporal mother. Therefore, in one nature, the Son of God is equal to the Father, the nature in which before all things he is coeternal with the Father; and in the other nature, the Son is less than the Father, in which nature he is also later than his mother. In one nature, the Son is equal to the Father, in which nature he is the Creator of the angels, and in the other nature, the same Son is less than the Father, in that nature he is the redeemer of the human race. In the one nature, the Son is equal to the Father; in that nature from the beginning of creation, he is adored and praised by the angels. In the other nature, the Son is less than the Father; in that nature he is a little less than the angels.

(VII.) 15. Apostolic authority did not cease to give an account of the mystery of this lessening, saying, "We do not see Jesus 'crowned with glory and honor' because he suffered death, he who 'for a little while' was made 'lower than the angels'."[35] To which nature this lessening must be attributed has been clearly shown above when that text of the prophet was put forward, in which it is said: "What are human beings that you are mindful of them, mortals that you care for them? Yet you have made them a little lower than the angels."[36] Before the taking up of the flesh, the Son of God, "though he was in the form of God, did not regard equality with God something to be grasped,"[37] because in that form of God, the Son is equal to the Father; but if he were less, he would not be in that same form of God; but apostolic authority bears witness that the Son is in the form of God. Therefore, for him, to be equal to God was not grasping but nature; because, unless he were true God, he would not be in the form of the true God and the very unity of the form of God is the equality of nature of the one deity. Where the unity of form was in nature, equality was not a grasping. It

---

35. Heb 2.9. 36. Ps 8.5–6 LXX; Ps 8.4–5.
37. Phil 2.6.

was impossible to take away from the true God the equality in nature of the divinity which was in the form of God.

16. Hence it is that, keeping the truth of the divinity and accepting the truth of the flesh, the one and the same is Son of God and Son of Man and has been made less than the Father and remained equal to the Father. Therefore, the truth itself has said of both that "The Father is greater than I,"[38] and "The Father and I are one."[39] Truly, therefore, Christ is less than God the Father because by nature he is from his father's according to the flesh; and truly the same Christ is equal to God the Father because by nature he is God, above all, blessed forever. Concerning the one Christ, the Son of God, the blessed Apostle says, "Theirs the Patriarchs, and from them, according to the flesh, is the Messiah. God who is over all be blessed forever."[40] Accordingly, the true faith, which believes in one and the same Christ, the Son of God both made less according to the truth of the flesh and according to the truth of the divinity believes and confesses him equal to God the Father. So, in truth, the true faith adores one God the Son with the Father and this faith knows that the one God must be served by all creatures just as it knows that the honor of divine service is not owed to any creature.

(VIII.) 17. Hence it is that the true faith asserts that the Holy Spirit as well is the Creator, not created. How is it to be denied as Creator, by which the power of the heavens has been strengthened, as David says, "By the word of the Lord the heavens were made and all their host by the breath of his mouth."[41] And in another text: "When you send forth your spirit, they are created."[42] Indeed it is the Creator of all things who is the maker of human beings. Concerning it, the blessed Job says, "The Spirit of God has made me."[43] The Holy Spirit, then, as it has created all things, so, as infinite, it fills all things. And the one who fills all things is by nature true God. It is written that: ". . . the Spirit of the Lord has

---

38. Jn 14.28.
39. Jn 10.30.
40. Rm 9.5.
41. Ps 32.6 LXX; Ps 33.6.
42. Ps 103.30 LXX; Ps 104.30.
43. Jb 33.4.

filled the whole world."⁴⁴ The blessed David as well bears witness that the Spirit of God is everywhere, saying to God himself, "Where can I go from your Spirit? or where can I flee from your presence?"⁴⁵ How do the Arians deny that the Holy Spirit is God since we are the Temple of the Holy Spirit, just as we are the Temple of the Father and the Son? For the Apostle says, "Do you not know that you are the Temple of God and that the Spirit of God dwells in you? If anyone destroys God's Temple, God will destroy that person; for the Temple of God which you are is holy."⁴⁶ The Apostle asserts that we are the Temple of God in such a way that in the same letter he also says that we are the Temple of the Holy Spirit. For he says, "Do you not know that your body is a Temple of the Holy Spirit within you, whom you have from God?"⁴⁷ And in order that he may show that the Holy Spirit is God, he immediately added, "Therefore glorify God in your body."⁴⁸

18. Therefore, the Holy Spirit is equal to the Father and the Son because it is the Creator of all things just as the Father and the Son. The Holy Spirit is equal to the Father and the Son because, infinite, it fill all things, just as the Father and the Son. The Holy Spirit is equal to the Father and the Son because he holds the members of all the faithful as one Temple, just as the Father and the Son. Who would dare to deny that the divinity of the Father and the Son and the Holy Spirit is one, when the bodies of the faithful which are the members of Christ, are themselves the Temple of the Holy Spirit?

(IX.) 19. Therefore, the Trinity is God, the one, sole Creator of all things, the Trinity is one and alone infinite, God by nature. The human being is recognized as having been made according to the image of this Trinity; baptized in its name, he is renewed a second time. Our Savior taught that the nations are baptized "in the name of the Father and of the Son and of the Holy Spirit,"⁴⁹ so that just as we have received the beginning of creation by the work of the Trinity,

---

44. Wis 1.7.
46. 1 Cor 3.16–17.
48. 1 Cor 6.20.

45. Ps 138.7 LXX; Ps 139.7.
47. 1 Cor 6.19.
49. Mt 28.19.

so in the name of the Trinity, we assume the grace of divine adoption. One, therefore, is the true God, Father and Son and Holy Spirit, who by his most omnipotent goodness, creates human beings and by his free mercy, justifies sinners. Other than this one true God, there is no God because when he says, "See now that I, even I, am he; there is no God besides me,"[50] he teaches and warns us that it is a serious sin if anyone believes that there is another God besides the one God. Without a doubt, anyone believes this who thinks that there is a difference in nature among the Father and the Son and the Holy Spirit; since that God who alone has true divinity in no way grants the possibility of worshipping another God; nor in the mystery of human redemption ought anyone to be named in any way who is alien to the nature of the one true God. The mystery of human redemption is in no way complete if, in baptism, the name of the Son or of the Holy Spirit is left out.

(X.) 19 bis. Accordingly, since the form of a letter does not allow the words of our discussion to be extended and the beginnings of your enjoyment must not be wearied by the length of the reading but rather, stirred by its brevity so that while you may read a short work with pleasure, you may be more ardently inflamed for a long reading. The few things which I am about to say, read with attention, understand with caution, and hold to without doubts that by means of them you may be able to distinguish the true from the false in statements of faith and may be able to retain the Christian faith with the assistance of our enlightener himself.

(XI.) 20. The Holy Trinity is one God, the Father and the Son and the Holy Spirit. There is one nature of the Father and the Son and the Holy Spirit but not one person. Accordingly, that, with the truth being retained, you may be able to refute or certainly repudiate falsity, if you see anyone confessing the one nature of the Father and the Son and the Holy Spirit in such a way that he wants to proclaim one per-

---

50. Dt 32.39.

son, do not think him a Catholic Christian but recognize him as a Sabellian heretic.[51]

(XII.) 21. If you hear anyone speaking of the three persons of the Father and the Son and the Holy Spirit in such a way that they want to assert three natures of these three persons, understand without a doubt that he is an Arian heretic.[52] It is true that the Sabellians believe in the one nature of the Father and the Son and the Holy Spirit; but it is false because they do not believe in the three persons. It is also true that Arians say that there are three persons of the Father and the Son and the Holy Spirit; but it is false because they strive to persuade us that there are three natures of these three persons. Therefore, perversely do the Arians divide the nature of the Trinity and Sabellians confuse the persons; since the nature of the Father and the Son and the Holy Spirit is one in such a way that there is one person of the Father, another of the Son, and a third of the Holy Spirit.

(XIII.) 22. If you see anyone confessing the one nature of the Father and the Son but proclaiming that the substance of the Holy Spirit is other, so that he says the Son is equal to the Father and asserts that only the Holy Spirit is less, that one does not hold the truth of the Catholic faith but follows the error of faithlessness born from Macedonius.[53] Accordingly, because he is not a Catholic Christian

---

51. In the early Church, some were concerned that the worship of Christ rendered Christian monotheism suspect. They stressed the oneness of God and sought to support this by arguing that the persons of the Father and the Son were not real but only a human attempt to understand the various facets of God's activity. Hence Sabellianism, Modalism, and Patripassianism. See EEC II.748–49.

52. Arianism was a form of subordinationism which taught the inferiority of the Son to the Father. The Logos was not coeternal with the Father but had been created by him before the creation of the material universe. As such, he was superior to all other creatures but a creature nonetheless. The council of Nicea (325) taught the ontological equality of the Father and the Son *(Homoousia)*. See EEC I.76–78.

53. Macedonius was an early bishop of Constantinople. His name is associated with the denial of the divinity or the consubstantiality of the Holy Spirit. See EEC I.516.

but a Macedonian heretic, he must be repudiated by all the faithful.

(XIV.) 23. Now turn to a few matters concerning the mystery of the Lord's Incarnation. Christ, the Son of God, who truly proclaims himself the Truth, just as he is true God, so he is truly a human being, in whom just as there is the fullness of divine nature is also the fullness of human substance. For there is in him the natural truth of divinity, the natural truth of a rational soul, and the natural truth of the flesh; and through this, the natural divinity is common to him with the Father; the natural humanity is common to him with the virgin.

(XV.) 24. Therefore, if anyone proclaims that true divinity is in Christ in such a way that he strives to deny his true flesh, he is not a Catholic Christian but a Manichaean heretic,[54] since Christ himself said to his doubting disciples, "Touch me and see because a ghost does not have flesh and bones as you can see that I have."[55]

(XVI.) 25. Again, if anyone proclaims the truth of the soul and flesh in Christ in such a way that he is not willing to accept the truth of the deity in him, i.e., anyone who speaks of Christ as a human being in such a way that he denies the God, he is not a Catholic but a Photinian heretic.[56] For Christ, in the manner in which according to true divinity, is God the Creator of human beings, so according to his true flesh, he is the mediator between God and human beings. But he would in no way be mediator if either he did not have a nature of divinity with the Father or he did not have a common substance of flesh and blood with human beings. In this, the true mediator for human beings is Christ Jesus the human being in that both by nature he has the form of God from the Father (through which he saves us) and he re-

---

54. Manichaeism was a dualistic, quasi-gnostic movement which stressed the equality and the eternal conflict of a good and an evil principle. See EEC I.519–20.

55. Lk 24.39.

56. Photinus was bishop of Sirmium in Pannonia. His name is usually associated with those who denied the divinity of Christ, but his theology, related to that of Marcellus of Ancyra, is somewhat more complex than that. See EEC II.685–86.

ceived from the virgin the form of a servant (which he saved in us). For a human being would never receive the grace of salvation from God if the communion of divine and human nature did not remain in the one person in Christ.

(XVII.) 26. Therefore, the truth about Christ is that, just as he has a true nature of divinity from the Father, so he has the true nature of humanity from the virgin. For the only begotten God deigned to become in the womb of the virgin, a taker-on of human flesh and soul so that he might be the savior of human flesh and soul. He is one in whom there is a double inseparable and unmixable nature and one person of both natures; in whom again two other heretics believing contrary to each other are known to have initiated different errors, namely Nestorius and Eutyches.[57] Nestorius, because he knew that there were two natures in Christ, tried to proclaim two persons in him. Thus having a heart blinded by the darkness of falsity he did not hesitate to join the lie of his faithlessness to the Christian faith. For the true faith, just as it preaches that there are two natures in Christ, so it denies that there are two persons in him. But Eutyches, believing correctly that there is one person in Christ perversely strove to proclaim that there is one nature in him, when the true faith knows that at the same time in Christ there is the property of each nature and understands that there is one person of the divinity and the humanity.

(XVIII.) 27. Indeed Christ is one who "in the beginning was the Word and the Word was with God and the Word was God."[58] And also: "The Word was made flesh and dwelt among us."[59] Hence the Sabellian is conquered because, insofar as "the Word was with God," it is shown that there is

---

57. In the Christological controversies of the fifth century which culminated in the councils of Ephesus, 431, and Chalcedon, 451, the names of Nestorius, bishop of Constantinople, and Eutyches, a monk of Constantinople, are linked as representatives of two extremes. Nestorius, a theologian of the tradition of Antioch, was accused by Cyril of Alexandria of dividing the incarnate Christ into two persons. Eutyches, on the other hand, a follower of Cyril, was accused of blending the divine and the human in Christ into one nature. Such views were later labeled Monophysitism. See EEC, Nestorius II.594; Eutyches I.304–305; Monophysites I.569–70.

58. Jn 1.1. 59. Jn 1.16.

one person of the Father and another of the Son. Hence also the Arian is overcome because, insofar as "the Word was God," it is shown that there is one nature of the Father and the Son. To show the property of the person, it suffices that only the Son is called the Word; to show as well that there is a communion of the one nature, it is relevant that just as God is called Father, so also is God called the Son. Hence, also both Mani and Photinus are confounded insofar as it is said: "And the Word became flesh."[60] In the name of the Word, true divinity is recognized, and in the name of the flesh, true humanity is found; so that Christ, the Son of God, both true God and truly human, may be known in the natural truth of each name; and so, neither let Mani dare to proclaim a false flesh in him nor let Photinus be able to take the natural deity away from him.

(XIX.) 28. Likewise, Nestorius and Eutyches are convicted by the words of the Apostle; the former, that he may acknowledge that the one person of Christ cannot be doubled; the latter, that he may know that the two-fold nature of Christ cannot be confused. For Christ himself is one, concerning whom that which has already been cited above, the Apostle says, "Theirs the Patriarchs, and from them, according to the flesh, is the Messiah. God who is over all be blessed forever."[61] Here, filled with the Holy Spirit, he has shown both the one person of Christ and his double nature. Saying indeed, "From them, according to the flesh, is the Messiah. God who is over all be blessed forever," just as by the name of God and the flesh, he undoubtedly shows us the truth of each nature, so in the one name of Christ, he has taught the one person of the divinity and the humanity. For Christ who is "from the Patriarchs according to the flesh" is "God over all, blessed forever." The nature which the Son of God has from the Father is not confused with that nature which the same God assumed from the virgin. But neither did Christ have at some time two persons because the same only-begotten God both according to the divinity was born

---

60. There is a misprint in the Latin text, vol. XCI.272, line 465. "Et verbum caro factum est."

61. Rm 9.5.

9. THE LETTER OF VICTOR 383

from the Father and according to the flesh came from the virgin. And because God the Word was born of God, the same Word became flesh "like a bridegroom coming out of his wedding canopy."[62] He is one who, the property of each nature being preserved, both "was crucified out of weakness" and "lives by the power of God."[63]

(XX.) 29. Most dear son, I am sending these things to you for your holy desire and enjoyment, by means of which may a taste for instruction be offered to you. From that taste may the affection for a longer reading grow in you so that as much as you will be able to make progress with God's help, so much the more diligently may you begin to seek the words of the holy fathers and when found, may you study them more frequently and attentively. So, from them, with God's help, may the grace of a fuller knowledge come to you, by which you may be able not only to hold on to the true faith but also to confute the deadly falsity of heretics, believing and firmly holding onto one nature and three persons in God the Trinity and one person and two natures in the only-begotten Son of God, our Lord Jesus Christ.

LETTER 9. THE LETTER OF VICTOR, THE SERMON OF FASTIDIOSUS THE ARIAN, AND THE BOOK OF FULGENTIUS TO VICTOR

The lengthy letter 9, entitled a 'book', was written in response to the plea of Victor who was concerned about the sermon of an apostate Catholic priest and monk, Fastidiosus. Since the latter's text is included, we have a rare example of an Arian sermon. Langlois places the letter in the final period of Fulgentius's life after the return from his second exile in Sardinia.

Fulgentius's explanations are more technical than in the previous letter. If the three persons of the Trinity are inseparable and the workings of the Trinity are of all three persons together, then why was not the entire Trinity incarnated? Fulgentius argues, "... The entire Trini-

---

62. Ps 18.6 LXX; Ps 19.5.
63. 2 Cor 13.4.

ty made the humanity of the Son of God but . . . only the Son, not the entire Trinity, received it into his person." (XIX.3) Once again, Fulgentius's debt to Augustine's theology, here the *De Trinitate*, is clear.

ICTOR[1] SENDS GREETINGS to the most blessed, the holy Father, bishop Fulgentius, equal in merits to the Apostles.

1. The time, divinely-appointed, for the desired matter has arrived, the moment in which our petition obtains its effect. For it was wicked that I who had frequently asked your blessedness to answer a clever attack, should put you off though you were willing; something that among those with the best morals often is considered a lie, when something promised is put off. But because of this, as your blessedness well recognizes is the case with us, it was not done by our will, but preoccupation with various matters posed an obstacle by which we were led this way and that to no purpose, matters in which nothing is accomplished for salvation and eternal life. Rather by various concerns, the mind is turned away from seeking the usefulness of the future life, so that, when it is time, at the prompting of diabolical envy, who of us is allowed to do in the least something which would be of profit for eternal salvation?

2. We are led astray by various lusts and desires of this world which vanish suddenly like smoke. Insatiably because of worldly allurements, our attention has melted away to the extent that we live in this world as if we were here forever. Concerning eternity to come, we think hardly at all about the danger of life or death which exists on both sides. But we are preoccupied by this alone, viz., what we know in the present is coming because of our desires. However much that is useful accrues to our will, we think it little, according to the statement of the blessed Cyprian: "What else is carried on daily in the world but the fight against the Devil?" And a little later there follows: "If greed is cast down, lust arises; if lust is repressed, ambition comes next; if ambition is scorned, anger irritates, pride inflates, drunkenness beck-

---

1. For Victor, see PCBE, p.1183, "Victor 90."

ons, envy breaks harmony, jealousy destroys friendship," etc.[2] The venerable man sees the soul daily being wounded by so many spears of the enemy, a situation from which, not our own virtue, but the divine mercy alone can rescue us.

3. So in tears, we beg you, together with all those whom you have acquired for the Lord and torn away from the filth of this world, you have caused to be converted to the life of the Spirit, to deign to obtain by prayer from his piety that the light of his mercy shine on us, that he not inflict punishment for our sins, that we not die in our sins, that we may be extricated from the snares and traps of the enemy, that he not rejoice that he has gained a soul which the Lord redeemed with his blood. We beg this most earnestly, that you join our supplication to your just prayers and our groans to your holy tears, that, by your intercession, we may merit to bring back assistance for the life to come so that we who are dead because of sin may rise again by your holy prayers. The prophet Elisha could not raise a dead body in any other way than, drawing in the contours of his members, he shaped himself to the outline of that body.[3] A large bulk lessened itself a little so that when the dead person was kissed, he breathed in a soul and life to the child. One lay down and two rose up. Suddenly, he who lived again by the spirit of another is restored unharmed to his mother. And so I trust that by your intercession, I am restored living to Mother Church, I who, with my sins weighing me down, seem held down by the sting of death. I know that in my youth many years ago, you sought the salvation of my soul and for this reason very often begged the Lord to snatch me from the temptations of this life. And because up until now, bent over by the mass of my own sins, I was not able to merit it, I ask that you, with assiduous supplications, deign to pray to the Lord for us, so that in some order or at some time, we may gain the forgiveness of our sins.

4. And lest our plaintive and long-lasting prayer generate

---

2. Cyprian *De mortalitate* 4. CCL IIIA.18–19. FOTC 36.202.
3. The Elisha incident, see 2 Kgs 4.34.

aversion *(fastidium)* in the senses of your Paternity, once again we must ask that a prompt response follow from your promises and to this evil work of one who disdainfully *(fastidiose)* scorns the spiritual, and in the eyes of the world, as it were, most vile, life of venerable monks, who, escaping, boasted that he had gotten as far as the cedars of Lebanon. Unless I am mistaken, I clearly seem to have written his name in the order of words in a line above. I have sent a copy of the treatise of one who, with words borrowed from here and there, seems to bark against the right faith and Catholic truth and, as if wounding with the spear of his objections the homoousians[4] (as he called us) and the Donatists, afterward he laid claim to the *Catholica* for himself, as your Paternity will note from your careful reading. Thus we ask from the honeyed spring of your Paternity that the vanity not only of this person but also of its author, the serpent, on whose evil grasses this one has fed, who seems to have sent forth a certain, as if new, error, be refuted. Yet there was an excellent response, and all wickedness devised against God should be crushed, lest those who read him think that he said something right against the faith of true teaching. Let the cunning of the ancient serpent be confounded who with various allurements has gathered to himself such preachers of seductions and pleasures. Destroy with your holy answers his viper's poisonous forked tongue. With your response may the false scheme which he who for a time fulfilled the office, not of teacher, but of flatterer, left behind to the wicked, vanish from the minds of those who wish to fight against the mystery of God. Wherefore, we ask that in this part, with the help of the Lord, you may extend to all your intelligence both famous and deserving its good reputation. And since the present heat seeks some new things, I, possessed by a love of an old familiarity, have boldly expressed the desire of my mind. And, just as you outshine other bish-

---

4. Since the key word of the council of Nicea (325) in the condemnation of Arianism was '*homoousios*', that the Son was equal or consubstantial with the Father, the Arians used the term in a derogatory fashion as a sectarian label attached to the supporters of Nicea.

9. THE SERMON OF FASTIDIOSUS

ops in the eyes and minds of observers; so we frequently want you to appear even more brilliant *(fulgentiorem)* with your flowering works both to us and to all people.[5]

5. Confident because of this devout love, I, ignorant of things, have written and, thirsting with too great ardor, I have enthusiastically run to the font of knowledge and doctrine with my rustic speech. From it we wish to have our thirst and ignorance satisfied so that I may merit to gain not only the reward of the future life, just as at the beginning of the letter I sought the aid of your prayers, but also that we may rejoice that by this work we have been satisfied in all things; so that not only we but also every religious sentiment of our fellow servants, your children, who depend on you with devout affection and together with us, await this from you, I may give thanks with them for the divine grace. And we seek that you overlook our rusticity since you yourself have commanded that I dare this. And although it has imbued us with little or no knowledge of a teacher, it has also happened that if we, entangled by other preoccupations, retain anything conceived in the heart, we have almost lost the use of Latin speech, according to that saying, "Your breasts not admitting two cares." But pray that the Lord grant and do what we want. Therefore, direct and equip the servant whom you have nursed and put forth the teaching which you have taught so frequently. May the eternal Divinity keep your blessedness praying for us, as we wish, sir.

THE SERMON OF FASTIDIOSUS[1] THE ARIAN

OST WISE BROTHERS, we speak what the Divinity itself deigns to grant our littleness. The God of justice and the author of life is himself our justice and our life. He did not make the human being for sin or for

---

5. Victor plays with the names of Fastidiosus ('scornful') and Fulgentius ('fulgeo': glisten or shine).

1. On Fastidiosus, see "Fastidiosus 2," PCBE.382.

death, as Scripture says, "God did not make death and he does not delight in the death of the living."² Because death did not happen to humankind which God had made, it is not of God the Creator, but of the Devil, the deceiver. Afterwards, the human race was deceived by the Devil, though he did evil willingly, unwillingly he incurred death. He transgressed unjustly and was punished justly. God, when he saw these two things in humankind, guilt and death, the one which he did badly, the other which he bore justly, since humankind was held bound by these two most insidious chains, he commanded that the Lord Christ take on flesh, not because he became a debtor to sin but so that without the debt of sin, on behalf of debtors, he might endure death without incurring debt. Not in order that the Son of God might be bound by the chain of evil but in order that sinful humankind might be freed from the chain of evil. This is what the Apostle says, "Undeniably great is the mystery of devotion, Who was manifested in the flesh, vindicated in the spirit, seen by angels, proclaimed to the Gentiles, believed in throughout the world, taken up in glory."³

2. And, indeed, most learned Christians, what greater devotion could there have been than that the Son of God, obeying his Father's command, would take up human flesh on behalf of carnal human beings, and life would endure death for mortals? That he who was born before the ages, created by the Father, in the last days would be born of a virgin? That he who gives life to the world would lie dead in the tomb? With how many tears must we now weep or with what affliction of heart must we now mourn because most from then on were not willing to abandon the persistence of their most hard obstinacy while, without reflection, they wish to devote themselves to the harmful assumption. They who acquiesce with remedies that are not at all salutary and reject the will to be corrected, holding up their hands against the life-giving words, like surgical instruments, by

2. Wis 1.13.
3. 1 Tm 3.16.

means of which they wound themselves by the very means by which they should have been cured and turn against themselves the strength of spiritual remedies, so that they increase the rottenness of their words, by means of the source from which they could have gained health. For a long time now, a twofold error has penetrated. Until the present, binding the souls of the lost, it does not permit them to breathe to seek the truth, with the homoousians asserting that the Trinity is inseparable and undivided and that the Son was not less than the Father or that the unbegotten Father is the maker of his Son; with the Donatists[4] preaching that the good are polluted by communion with the evil while they cast off the gift of Holy Scripture as a remedy of salvation.

3. Among them, holy Mother the Catholic Church knows how to sing with Davidic sound, just as we have sung in the present psalm, "Lead me, O Lord, in your righteousness, because of my enemies."[5] For in your righteousness I am led when I believe that you, the almighty God, unbegotten and uncreated, are the maker of your Son, the Lord Christ; as John the Baptist bears witness, "The one who is coming after me ranks ahead of me because he existed before me,"[6] and with Peter the Apostle preaching and saying, "Therefore let the whole house of Israel know for certain that God has made him both Lord and Messiah, this Jesus whom you crucified"[7]; also with Solomon prophesying in the person of Christ, "The Lord created me at the beginning of his work," and a little later declaring, "Ages ago I was set up."[8] Behold

---

4. Donatism was a North African schism that had begun during the great persecution under Diocetian at the beginning of the fourth century. It had prospered under its first two leaders, Donatus and Parmenianus. With the coming of Augustine and Aurelius of Carthage, the fortunes of the Catholics began to change for the better. The great Conference of Carthage of June, 411 seemed to put an end to them but the remarks of the preacher show that they still exist. However, note the remarks of Fulgentius to the effect that Fastidiosus had stolen the material about the Donatists from Fulgentius's own letter to Stephania, a letter now lost. (X.l)

5. Ps 5.9 LXX; Ps 5.8.   6. Jn 1.15.
7. Acts 2.36.
8. Prov 8.22–23. A key proof-text for the Arians.

Scripture bears witness that he has been made and created, something which the sacrilegious refuse to believe. Likewise, as was said above, they assert that the Trinity is inseparable and undivided. And if the Son of God, concerning whom the Evangelist says, "The Word was made flesh and dwelt among us,"[9] the power of his Divinity hidden for a little while, alone entered the bridal chamber of the virginal womb, without a doubt he was separated from the Father and the Holy Spirit. But the Trinity, which it is clear is in no way divided, could never be separated from one, according to this absurdity of theirs.

4. Did the entire Trinity take on flesh; did the entire Trinity feel the sufferings of the injuries; did the entire Trinity lie in the tomb; did the entire Trinity descend to Hell; did the entire Trinity rise from the dead on the third day; did the entire Trinity ascend to Heaven on the fortieth day? And at whose right hand does the entire Trinity sit? And what Spirit did the entire Trinity send on the Apostles on the day of Pentecost? Or to what God in heaven was the entire Trinity able to say, "My God, my God, why have you forsaken me?"[10] or to what Father did the entire Trinity say, "Father, into your hands I commend my spirit"?[11] If they can, let them speak up. And if they are unable to do that, let them kill themselves with their own spears, they who claim that the Trinity is inseparable. The Donatist vanity does not pay attention to the fact that, because of this blessing of baptism bestowed on humankind, they who from the origin are weighed down with the burdens of others, once relieved by the help of healing grace, henceforward bear only their own burden. Communion in the sacrament does not condemn anyone for sins, but consent does. Since, just as the Lord says that he will repay the sins of the fathers to the third and fourth generations to those who hate his name—because the earthly and carnal birth is shown to be subject to the original fault—so, in another text, he testifies that, just as the soul of the father, the soul of the son is his own so that

9. Jn 1.14.
10. Ps 21.2 LXX; Ps 22.1.
11. Lk 23.46.

the second and heavenly birth is recognized as completely free from the sins of others.

5. Immediately he concludes, "It is only the person who sins that shall die."[12] With this view, the warning of Solomon is in accord, and he shows that one is not burdened by the sins of another, saying, "Son, if you are wise, you are wise for yourself; if you scoff, you alone will bear it."[13] Therefore, the Catholic faith, fleeing the difficulties of each error, and with the Lord leading, entering upon the path of the heavenly way, with sober faith, singing, says, "Lead me O Lord, in your righteousness because of my enemies."[14] And from there, clamoring to the Holy Spirit from the Father through the Son, with rightness of path, by whose free gift, it has acquired the ability to make progress, just as it confesses that those not yet baptized are subjected not only to their own sins but also to the sins of others, who it knows were conceived in iniquity, so it asserts that those washed in life-giving waters are freed from the iniquity of others, if assent of the will is not given in a sin.

6. John the Evangelist says, "But to those who did accept him, he gave the power to become children of God, to those who believe in his name, who were born not by natural generation nor by human choice, nor by a man's decision, but of God."[15] Therefore, just as those who spring from the will of the flesh and from the will of a man bear the sins of others, although they do not yet have any of their own, so those born from God, if they have no guilt of their own will in them, are splattered with no injury from the iniquity of another. Since, just as the first birth, by bringing forth, has fixed something that the one being born did not do, so the second birth, when original sin[16] has been washed away, imputes only the sin done by the will. Therefore, on this count, we must be separated from the evil in which we "who have the first fruits of the spirit, buried with Christ in baptism,"[17]

---

12. Ez 18.4.
13. Prov 9.12.
14. Ps 5.9. LXX; Ps 5.8.
15. Jn 1.12–13.
16. It is interesting to note the Arian's acceptance of original sin. Is it due to Augustine's influence or the African tradition?
17. Rm 8.23; Col 2.12.

have arisen. In him, with the grace of God going before and accompanying, we lay aside the old person who is being corrupted according to the desires of error, so that we may put on the new person who has been created according to God in righteousness and in the sanctity of charity.

THE BOOK OF SAINT FULGENTIUS THE BISHOP TO VICTOR AGAINST THE SERMON OF FASTIDIOSUS THE ARIAN.

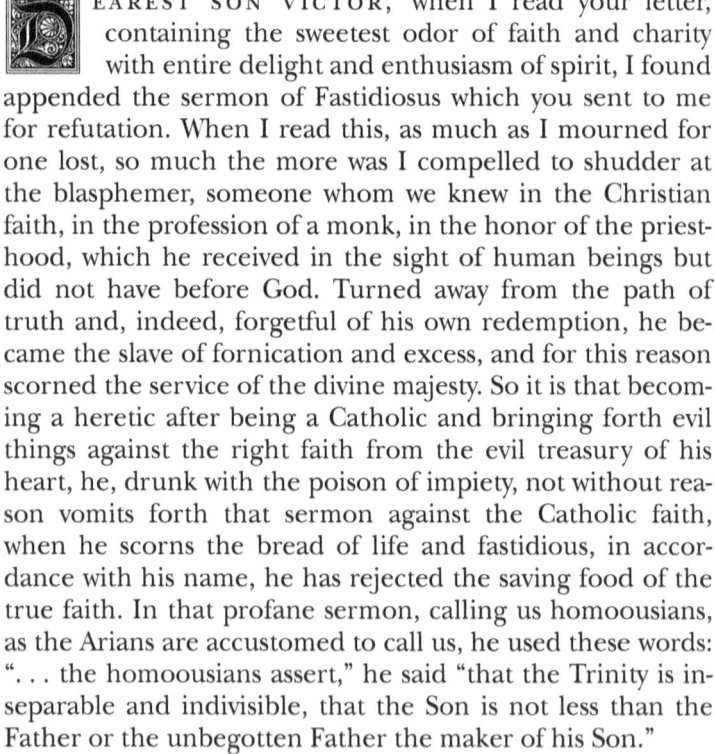EAREST SON VICTOR, when I read your letter, containing the sweetest odor of faith and charity with entire delight and enthusiasm of spirit, I found appended the sermon of Fastidiosus which you sent to me for refutation. When I read this, as much as I mourned for one lost, so much the more was I compelled to shudder at the blasphemer, someone whom we knew in the Christian faith, in the profession of a monk, in the honor of the priesthood, which he received in the sight of human beings but did not have before God. Turned away from the path of truth and, indeed, forgetful of his own redemption, he became the slave of fornication and excess, and for this reason scorned the service of the divine majesty. So it is that becoming a heretic after being a Catholic and bringing forth evil things against the right faith from the evil treasury of his heart, he, drunk with the poison of impiety, not without reason vomits forth that sermon against the Catholic faith, when he scorns the bread of life and fastidious, in accordance with his name, he has rejected the saving food of the true faith. In that profane sermon, calling us homoousians, as the Arians are accustomed to call us, he used these words: "... the homoousians assert," he said "that the Trinity is inseparable and indivisible, that the Son is not less than the Father or the unbegotten Father the maker of his Son."

2. Pay attention, I ask you, in these words of Fastidiosus, to something so badly put that they can never be asserted in

an acceptable fashion; but something so impiously spoken by him that they could be, if piety were present, equally both spoken and listened to. For that by which he thought we would be confuted, that we say that the Trinity is inseparable and undivided, he expressed so badly and impiously in such a way that no one could express this well. For who does not see with what great impiety a separable Trinity is asserted by the Arians? When the blessed Apostle says of us, "What will separate us from the love of Christ? Will anguish or distress or persecution or famine or nakedness or peril or the sword?"[1] And a little later: "For I am convinced that neither death, nor life, nor angels, nor principalities, nor present things, nor future things, nor powers, nor height, nor depth, nor any other creature will be able to separate us from the love of God in Christ Jesus our Lord."[2]

II. 1. Since the blessed Apostle trusts that through the grace of God we cannot be separated from his love, how do they not think that they are caught in a deadly trap of impiety, they who do not hesitate to proclaim that the Holy Trinity is separable, whose works they are unable to prove are separable in anyone? For in what the evangelist says of the Son of God, "All things came to be through him; and without him, nothing came to be,"[3] and in what the blessed David says, "O Lord, how manifold are your works! In wisdom you have made them all,"[4] the blessed Apostle professes that Christ is the power of God and the wisdom of God. Concerning him he says, "For in him were created all things in heaven and on earth, the visible and the invisible, whether thrones or dominions or principalities or powers; all things were created through him and for him."[5] It is obvious that all the works of the Father are the same as the works of the Son, the same also are the works of the Holy Spirit.

2. The Holy Trinity works inseparably; there is no work which the Father has done and the Son has not done; or which the Son has done and the Holy Spirit has not done.

1. Rm 8.35.
2. Rm 8.38–39.
3. Jn 1.3.
4. Ps 103.24 LXX; Ps 104.24.
5. Col 1.16.

For it is written: "By the word of the Lord, the heavens were made and all their host by the breath of his mouth."[6] Of wisdom also which we say was created in the angels, we read written in the book of Ecclesiasticus: "Wisdom was created before all other things and prudent understanding from eternity."[7] Where it would show that also the angels were made by the Word of God, by which all things were made, Holy Scripture immediately added, "The font of Wisdom is the Word of God on high and his entry eternal commands."[8] And a bit later, in order that angelic wisdom may be shown to pertain to the works of the Holy Spirit, the following is said: "There is but one who is wise, greatly to be feared, seated upon his throne—the Lord. It is he who created her."[9]

3. Therefore, what will be denied to have been made by the Holy Spirit by which the power of the heavens is described as having been made firm and by whose work wisdom is declared to have been created? For also concerning the divine gifts which God gave to his Church, when the blessed Apostle spoke and said, "There are different kinds of spiritual gifts but the same Spirit; there are different forms of service . . . but the Son of God who produces all of them in everyone,"[10] after the enumeration of the diversity of heavenly gifts, he added, "But one and the same Spirit produces all of these, distributing them individually to each person as he wishes."[11] But what in all creatures among which wisdom "reaches mightily from one end of the earth to the other, and she orders all things well"[12] can be found apart from the work of the Holy Spirit, since Christ, who is the power of God and the wisdom of God, declares that he casts out devils in the Spirit of God? For he himself has said, "But if it is by the Spirit of God that I drive out demons, then the Kingdom of God has come upon you."[13]

4. How then does Fastidiosus deny that the Trinity is inseparable when no Christian dare deny that the works of the

6. Ps 32.6 LXX; Ps 33.6.
7. Sir 1.4.
8. Sir 1.5 LXX; not in the text.
9. Sir 1.8–9.
10. 1 Cor 12.4–6.
11. 1 Cor 12.11.
12. Wis 8.1.
13. Mt 12.28.

Trinity are the same and inseparable in all creatures? The one God, i.e., the Father and the Son and the Holy Spirit, works inseparably. The only-begotten God himself declares that his works are the same as those of the Father when he says, ". . . a son cannot do anything on his own but only what he sees his Father doing; for what he does, his son will do also."[14] And yet what the Son does, he does in the Holy Spirit, in whom he casts out demons.

III. 1. But lest, because of what we said that the Son does whatever he does in the Holy Spirit, the Arians wish to assert some question of diversity, thinking that he in whom something is done must be considered as less than the one who does them, let them listen to our Savior completely rejecting this perversity when he says, "But whoever lives the truth, comes to the light, so that his works may be clearly seen as done in God."[15] Here let the Arians choose whom they wish to accept as the God named by the Son of God, whether the Father or the Son or the Holy Spirit. If they think that here the Father in whom good works are done by human beings must be accepted, they will destroy what they propose, blaspheming the person of the Holy Spirit. Nor will they dare to say that the Father is less to whom, according to his divinity, they are unwilling to proclaim the Son equal. And for this reason, since a human being does good works in the Father and Christ casts out devils in the Holy Spirit, let them acknowledge the equality of the Father and the Holy Spirit.

2. If they say that here the Son must be understood because good works are done in the Son and in the Holy Spirit, not only will they be found to confess that the Son and the Holy Spirit are equal, but also they will confess that the works of the Father and the Son and the Holy Spirit are the same and inseparable: "But one and the same Spirit produces all of these,"[16] as the blessed Apostle bears witness. But if the Arians think that in this text the Holy Spirit must be understood, it is necessary that from this text they are compelled to confess that the Holy Spirit is God.

14. Jn 5.19. 15. Jn 3.21.
16. 1 Cor 12.11.

3. For the Spirit of the Lord did not say, He who does the truth, that his works be clearly seen as done in the Holy Spirit, but "as done in God"[17] which we say are done not in the Father alone, nor in the Son alone, nor in the Holy Spirit alone. But we confess that the truth is done by a human being in the Holy Trinity itself, which is one God, in whom the blessed David indicates is the power of what is done by the faithful, saying, "With God we shall do valiantly; it is he who will tread down our foes."[18] For he is the one God concerning whom the blessed Apostle says, "For from him and through him and for him are all things. To him be glory forever."[19]

IV. 1. Therefore, how is the Holy Trinity said by the impious to be separable since it works inseparably? Insofar as it is possible to understand, they do not think that, as the truth of the matter demands, there is any separation in the Spirit, as it is said. From our God, i.e., from the Holy Trinity itself, nothing can be separated in a spatial sense, because the same most high God, true and good, as he made all things, as infinite, contains and fills all things. He is not corporeal nor spatial and, therefore, corporeal things themselves cannot be separated from God spatially because every body is in some place and there is no place without God. For God is so contained in no place that he contains every place; in whom there is no mass and whose power is infinite. Therefore, since bodies which cannot exist without a place, cannot be spatially separated from God, without a doubt neither are the spirits which God created spatially separated from God.

2. For every spirit which God created exists in some place and God is there. Although he who is not in evil spirits through grace by means of which he grants to whom he wishes a holy life and blessedness, still he is always in all his creatures through his natural power. Thus there is no creature that can be found in whom God is not present through his power. Therefore, that nature can be separated from

17. Jn 3.21.
19. Rm 11.36.
18. Ps 59.14 LXX; Ps 60.12.

9. FULGENTIUS TO VICTOR

God which was or is able to be subject to sin. There is no other thing which can go away from God except that substance which is able or has been able to sin with its own will. For Isaiah says, "See, the Lord's hand is not too short to save, nor his ear too dull to hear. Rather your iniquities have been barriers between you and your God."[20]

3. Also in the book of Wisdom, it is shown that human beings are separated from God, not by places, but by wicked thoughts and evil acts. For it is said there: "For perverse thoughts separate people from God and when his power is tested, it exposes the foolish; because wisdom will not enter a deceitful soul or dwell in a body enslaved to sin; for a holy and disciplined spirit will flee from deceit and will leave foolish thoughts behind."[21] Who does not see here the Trinity announced by the properties of the persons? For it is said that "perverse thoughts separate from God" by which name the person of God the Father is recognized. Then it is added that "wisdom will not enter a deceitful soul" by which name Christ is shown, whom Paul calls the power of God and the wisdom of God.

4. Then it is said that: "The Holy Spirit will flee from deceit and will leave foolish thoughts behind." Lest anyone think that certain evil or impious people can be spatially separated from that Holy Trinity, which is the one, true, and good God, a little later Scripture speaks thus: "For wisdom is a kindly spirit but will not free blasphemers from the guilt of their words; because God is witness of their inmost feelings and a true observer of their hearts and a hearer of their tongues. Because the spirit of the Lord has filled the world. . . ."[22] The divine words do not cease to proclaim the infinity of the Holy Trinity. The blessed David most certainly knew it and so said to God, "Where can I go from your Spirit? Or where can I flee from your presence? If I ascend to heaven you are there; if I make my bed in Sheol, you are there."[23] Concerning wisdom also, i.e., the Son of God, Scripture says

20. Is 59.1–2.
21. Wis 1.3–5.
22. Wis 1.6–7.
23. Ps 138.7–8 LXX: Ps 139.7–8.

that "She reaches mightily from one end of the earth to the other."[24]

5. Therefore, nothing can be spatially separated from the Holy Trinity which is everywhere in its totality; only evils and perverse thoughts separate from God, as we have just taught. Whoever seeks to assert that the Trinity is separable must of necessity be saying that either the Father or the Son or the Holy Spirit can by nature be subject to wicked thoughts and evils. Who catches himself in the trap of such impiety that he thinks that there is some separation in that Trinity where unity is natural, since, through grace received, just as it has been shown by us above, the faithful Paul trusts that he can never be separated from the love of God which is in Christ Jesus our Lord? The blessed John the Apostle confirms both that love is from God and that God is love, with these words: "Beloved, let us love one another because love is of God; everyone who loves is begotten by God and knows God. Whoever is without love, does not know God, for God is love."[25] This love, which is from God and God is, cannot be separated from himself, because it is inseparable.

6. For since it, itself unseparated, not only possesses human beings who can be separated from one another but from many hearts and souls makes one heart and one soul, what madness is it to say that love which is accustomed to join separated minds in an inseparable love, is itself separable? Hence it is that Paul said, "For even if I am absent in the flesh, yet I am with you in spirit, rejoicing as I observe your good order."[26] And in the Acts of the Apostles, it is written that the "community of believers was of one heart and mind ... ,"[27] something that was not brought about except by the Spirit of faith and love. For "the love of God has been poured out into our hearts through the Holy Spirit that has been given to us."[28] Through the Holy Spirit itself it comes about that all believers, as the Apostle says, are "one body and one spirit."[29] Whence he says in another text, "For in one Spirit,

24. Wis 8.1.
25. 1 Jn 4.7–8.
26. Col 2.5.
27. Acts 4.32.
28. Rm 5.5.
29. Eph 4.4.

we were all baptized into one body, whether Jew or Greek, slaves or free persons, and we were all given to drink of one Spirit."[30] For the only-begotten Son of God with his own mouth commanded that all nations be baptized in the name of the Father and of the Son and of the Holy Spirit.

V. 1. Therefore, since baptism is given in the name of the Trinity, it comes about that all the faithful are baptized into one body and, for this reason, it makes all one body, as the blessed Apostle says that "we are one body in Christ, and individually parts of one another."[31] Since of the multitude of believers there was one heart and one soul through the love of God which has been poured out into our hearts through the Holy Spirit that has been given to us, assuredly it is clear with how great impiety the Trinity itself is said to be separable since any creature is separated from God neither by place nor by time but only by evils. Hence it is that God says about certain ones: "This people honors me with their lips, but their hearts are far from me."[32] And when he says, "Am I a God nearby, says the Lord, and not a God far off. Who can hide in secret places so that I cannot see them? says the Lord. Do I not fill heaven and earth?"[33] The blessed David says to him, "Indeed, those who are far from you will perish." And in order to show what it is to be far from God, he added, "You put an end to those who are false to you."[34]

2. Therefore, one approaches God with the heart and with the heart, one departs. For it is clear that God is totally everywhere but is in no way spatially contained. For God is a spirit, indeed the Creator, not created, the maker of all bodies and all spirits, immutable, eternal, infinite, just, and good. Through the infinity of his nature, he never departs from all the things which he has made. Nor can it be that God himself can be absent by his power from anything which has its existence from God. And still through his mercy and judgment, because of which the Church never ceases to sing to him, it is not unfittingly said both that he is

30. 1 Cor 12.13.
32. Mt 15.8.
34. Ps 72.27 LXX; Ps 73.27.

31. Rm 12.5.
33. Jer 23.23–24.

present to the faithful and far away from non-believers. For what concerns nature, the whole, whatever has been created, whether corporal or spiritual, the Holy Trinity alone, i.e., one God who is Father and Son and Holy Spirit, with one will, one operation, one power, one benevolence, and one omnipotence, has made it. Just as the Father fills the whole creature with power, not with mass, so the Son fills the whole, so the Holy Spirit fills the whole.

3. Nor does the Trinity so fill the whole creature that the Father fills part, the Son fills a part, and the Holy Spirit fills a part nor yet that the whole is filled by the Father alone nor by the Son alone nor by the Holy Spirit alone. Whoever would dare to think of the Trinity, i.e., of the one God, in this way, I do not call stupid but altogether sacrilegious; since the power of God and his Divinity are necessarily infinite by nature, just as he is by nature eternal. But human beings given over to carnal feelings are unable to think of God himself except carnally. And they think that the Father and the Son and the Holy Spirit can thus be separated from one another, just as human beings are separated from one another, who, just as they are different because of the capacity and quantity of each body, it is necessary that they also be distinguished by spatial location.

4. Such people, while they wrap their souls in the mud of the flesh, blinded by their appearances and weighed down by the weight of vanity, the more they are caught up with the thought of those things which with bodily eyes they take in bodily mass, so much the less are they able to rise to understanding the Godhead. Nor do they hear the command being given by the Lord God through holy Isaiah that we do not wish to think about him in such a way as about creatures which we know were made by him, because he does not think as we human beings think. So Isaiah says, "For my thoughts are not your thoughts, nor are your ways my ways, says the Lord. For as the heavens are higher than the earth, so are my ways higher than your ways and my thoughts than your thoughts."[35]

35. Is 55.8–9.

VI. 1. Therefore, God the Father and his Word and his Spirit, i.e., the Holy Trinity, the only one, true, and good God, just as there is not thought in him which varies with the passing of time (nor, like human beings, did he think one way before he made the world, nor does he think another way after he made the world, nor will he think still another way after the appearance of this world has passed away; for the "counsel of the Lord stands forever"[36]), so he is inseparable just as he is unchangeable. For the Trinity, one God, is neither a body nor a created spirit; because a body is enclosed in a space and every spirit which is created is circumscribed by the limitation of its nature. But the Trinity, one God, just as it is eternal and no times are coeternal with it, so it is infinite which no creature can enclose; and because infinite, everywhere in its totality; because not contained in a place, it is neither spread out nor compressed in space. Therefore, God is wisdom, God is truth, God is love. This the Father is, this the Son, this the Holy Spirit, this the Trinity itself which is the one, true, and good God.

2. Therefore, if anyone is able to teach that there is any division, whether in wisdom or in truth or in love, let him dare, without hesitation, assert that the Trinity is divisible. But from the fact that neither wisdom nor truth nor love is divided in any way, let the indivisible and inseparable Trinity be recognized. Therefore, the impiety of Fastidiosus appears to have been great by which he thought that we were altogether to be blamed for this, that we confess an inseparable and undivided Trinity; since, as the preceding discussion has taught, (which not only reason but also a sufficient group of divine witnesses has strengthened) neither can the infinite nature of the Trinity be contained in a place nor can any person in the Trinity be subject to sin, because the Trinity itself is by nature eternal, perfect, and unchangeable in justice. Heretical depravity strains badly to assert that the Son is less, which, when devotion has been saved, Catholic truth well confesses that he is equal.

3. Heretics, not thinking of the incorporeal divinity ex-

36. Ps 32.11 LXX; Ps 33.11.

cept in a corporeal way when they, under the appearance of the Christian name which they mistakenly lay claim to, say that according to the divine nature the Son is less, they are enveloping themselves in the unspeakable crime of idolatry. For what is speaking of a greater god and a lesser god in individual persons, except to set up idols of different nature and different power, not on the walls, but, what is worse, in hearts? Hence the Arians clearly show that they worship two gods when they deny that the Son is equal to the Father; and they assert that he is less, not because of the assumption of the flesh (which the truth of faith teaches) but because of the nature of infinite divinity, although it is said concerning him who is the wisdom of God that "he is a reflection of eternal light."[37] Concerning him also in the letter to the Hebrews it is said: "who is the refulgence of his glory, the very imprint of his being."[38] Let them pay attention to the "reflection of eternal light" and let them recognize that, just as that eternal light is also infinite, it so has its reflection as well and is not in any way either inferior or lesser by nature; but eternity has infinity, infinity has eternity equally.

VII. Therefore, the Christian faith which knows the only-begotten God both alone born from the nature of the Father and created from the virgin Mary, knowing that each substance remains true of him, so confesses him truly and piously equal to God the Father so that without the sin of lying and impiety, it proclaims him also as less. For because there is one divinity natural to him with the Father and one natural humanity with the mother, in the one, he is Son, equal to the Father, in which he is true God from the Father, and in the other, the Father is greater than the Son in whom the only-begotten God himself is truly human. This is the true faith, this holy piety, this Christian belief in one and the same Son of God; to believe in the nature of the Father's divinity and not to deny the substance of the mother's humanity; nor to believe that the divinity of the Son is different

37. Wis 7.20.
38. Heb 1.3.

from the divinity of God the Father, nor to separate the humanity of the Son from the humanity of the virgin mother, but to believe that the whole and true humanity of our race is in the same true God, to believe that the true and full deity of the Father's nature is in the same true and complete human being. Whoever denies the unity of the divinity in the Father and the Son is polluted by Arian impiety; he who denies the truth of the flesh in the only-begotten God is profaned by the crime of the Manichaean plague; he who denies that there is a human, i.e., rational, soul in the same Son of God is immediately befouled with the sacrilege of the Apollinarians.[39]

VIII. 1. Wherefore, because of the truth of the Father's and the mother's nature in the only-begotten God, believed to the fullest, and with the natural property of the double substance being preserved in the one person of Christ, piously and truly the Son is said to be equal to and less than the Father, devoutly and truly declared to be co-eternal and later, devoutly and truly asserted both to be born from eternity and born in time and forever immutable and changed in time. Therefore, the Son is equal to the Father because he always has this from the Father. He is also less than the Father, because he received this in time from the virgin.

2. Wherefore, just as the Son is piously said to be equal to the Father when the humanity in him by which he is less than the Father is not recognized; so impiously the same Son is said to be less when the unity and equality of divinity with the Father in him by nature is denied. Therefore, we say that the Son is equal by nature and less. We say that he is born equal according to the form of God, but, according to the form of a servant, lessened by his manner of being. We say that he is equal to the Father, in whom we know that he was born without a beginning from the Father; we say also

---

39. In order to solve the problem of the true unity of the divinity and humanity in Christ, Apollinarianism suggested that the Logos united with a human body and soul but not a human mind. The last named was supplied for by the Logos. This was rejected and the aphorism was coined: "What is not assumed, is not healed." See EEC I, 58–59.

less, because "When the fullness of time had come, God sent his Son, born of a woman, born under the Law."[40] Accordingly, just as without hesitation, we proclaim that he was born, so likewise we also proclaim that he was made. We say also that he was born from the heart of the Father without a beginning; we say that he was made in time by the work of the Trinity. The Father begot his own Son, both from his nature and made him from the nature of the virgin.

3. But whatever he made, he made with the Son and the Holy Spirit working with him. The Father alone begot his Son but he did not make him alone. In the only begotten Son is the eternal generation of the Father only and in the same created Son, one work of the whole Trinity. The Creator of humanity, the only-begotten God, was created a human being from a woman. Whence it appears that the testimonies which Fastidiosus impiously brought forward from the Gospel and from the Acts of the Apostles and Solomon do not take away the unity of the Father's nature from the Son but show forth the mystery of the divine Incarnation. Knowing most certainly of this, John the Baptist said, "This was he of whom I said, 'The one who is coming after me, ranks ahead of me, because he existed before me.'"[41] Proclaiming the truth of this mystery, the Apostle Peter says, "Therefore let the whole house of Israel know for certain that God has made him both Lord and Messiah, this Jesus whom you crucified."[42]

4. Well does he say "made" of the one whom he proclaims as crucified, the only-begotten God, incomprehensible and immortal, made by no one and eternal maker of all things, deigned to become Christ by his own work, that he could be crucified by the work of the Jews. The cross would never have carried the betrayed redeemer of the world if the work of the virgin had not given birth to the conceived maker of the world. Through Solomon, pointing out the truth of his generation and creation, he said, "The Lord created me at

---

40. Gal 4.4.
41. Jn 1.15.
42. Acts 2.36.

the beginning of his work." But before he said this, he first gave clear evidence of the future incarnation, saying, "If I shall announce to you what happens each day, I shall recall what is from the ages."[43] Then, summing up, he added, "The Lord created me at the beginning of his work."[44]

5. This creation is from the ages, not before the ages. For afterwards he says, "Ages ago I was set up," and a little later, "Before all the hills, he brought me forth."[45] Here because he says "Before the ages" and "before the hills," he wished the eternity of his divine birth to be understood. For both before the ages and after the age is eternity. And so the eternity of the Son of God does not have a beginning before the age, just as his eternity does not have an ending after the age. So, taking time past for time future, Wisdom said, "The Lord created me" for this: He is going to create me and so he spoke of as having been made that which was to be made; just as he said through blessed David: "My hands and my feet have shriveled; I can count all my bones. They stare and gloat over me. They divide my clothes among themselves, and for my clothing they cast lots."[46]

6. Therefore, when he says, "The Lord created me," he showed how he would be made. Saying "My hands and my feet are shriveled," he shows how he will be crucified. Just as this was to come, which as already done, the Son of God through David says of his passion, so he who is the Wisdom of God prophesied through Solomon what was to happen concerning his Incarnation as if it were already done. For Solomon himself says a little later, "Wisdom has built her house; she has hewn her seven pillars,"[47] which pertains to the mystery of the Lord's Incarnation. Isaiah also speaks thus of Christ's passion so that he speaks of what he prophesies as future as if it were past. For he says about Christ: "Like a lamb that is led to the slaughter and like a sheep that be-

43. Prov 8.21a LXX not in the text.
44. Prov 8.22.
45. Prov 8.25.
46. Ps 21.17–19 LXX; Ps 22.16–18.
47. Prov 9.1.

fore its shearers is silent, so he did not open his mouth."[48] For he predicts the very birth of the only-begotten God according to the flesh from the virgin, not only at times as future but at other times, he also speaks of it as past. In a certain place, he says, "Behold, a virgin shall be with child and will bear a son...."[49] Still, in another text, pointing to it as something over and done, he says, "For a child has been born for us; a son given to us."[50]

7. Therefore, who does not see that all of that which was said concerning the human birth and passion of the only-lbegotten God through the prophets, at that time was in the future in truth, just as now it is in truth past. To show the immutability of the divine counsel, it came about that prophetic Scripture would in word speak of as past what in fact was awaited as future. For God, concerning whom the prophet says, "He who made the things that will be,"[51] therefore, the things that were to be done, he willed them to be spoken of as if done, because these things which come about changeably in time, he has made firm with the unchangeable eternity of his plan. Therefore, in those things as well, in which the effect of the work has not yet come to be, the plan of the Creator remains firm from eternity. So, therefore, the Son of God, when he was to be created by his own work, said that he had been created, just as he did not hesitate to say that he had been crucified when he was going to be crucified.

IX. Still raving with perverse heart and sacrilegious mouth, Fastidiosus for this reason wished to assert that the Son was separated from the Father and the Holy Spirit because it is clear that he alone entered the wedding chamber of the virgin's womb. Concerning him in the book of the Psalms, it is said: "[He] comes out like a bridegroom from his wedding chamber."[52] Wishing to support the statement of his perversity, he did not hesitate to assert even that blasphemy, saying that if the Trinity:

48. Is 53.7.　　　　　　　49. Is 7.14.
50. Is 9.6.　　　　　　　　51. Is 45.11.
52. Ps 18.6 LXX; Ps 19.5.

could in no way be separated, it is clear that it can in no way be divided. Therefore, did the entire Trinity take on flesh, the entire Trinity suffer the injuries of the passion, the entire Trinity lie in the tomb, the entire Trinity descend to Hell, the entire Trinity rise from the dead on the third day, the entire Trinity ascend to heaven on the fortieth day? And at whose right hand does the entire Trinity sit? Or what Spirit on the day of Pentecost did the entire Trinity send on the Apostles? Or to what God, could the entire Trinity say in heaven, "My God, my God, why have you forsaken me?" Or to what Father did the entire Trinity say, "Father, into your hands, I commend my spirit."? If they are able, let them state it publicly. If they are unable to speak, they destroy themselves with their own weapons, they who argue that the Trinity is inseparable.

X. 1. These, then, are the words of Fastidiosus in that profane statement against the Catholic faith. With the exception of those which are a blasphemous affront to the Holy Trinity, almost all his words, whether those that come before or those that come after, he, most wicked as he is, has stolen from the words of others. Finally, all the things which he said against the Donatists, he stole from those two letters which all of us exiled in Sardinia wrote to the religious daughter of the Church, Stephania,[53] against the Pelagians and Donatists. Indeed, the same very wicked person has fraudulently placed them there under his own name with the very order of the words. That you may not lack knowledge of this affair I have had appended to this little work the two letters which the above-mentioned Stephania sent to us, and those which we wrote back to her. You will recognize in that sermon only those things which are from Fastidiosus, the words in which, rushing to the attack against the Holy Trinity itself, with blind heart, he attempted to assault Catholic truth.

XI. Now, therefore, with God's help I reply to his blasphemies. For the entire Trinity did not take on flesh nor did the entire Trinity feel the injuries of the passion, nor did the entire Trinity lie in the tomb, nor did the entire Trinity descend into Hell, nor did the entire Trinity rise from the dead on the third day, and if there are any other things which are

---

53. Stephania. See PCBE, 1093.

found in the mystery of his Incarnation, they belong to the person of the Son alone. Those things with which Fastidiosus objected to the Catholic faith are full of falsity and perversity and cannot be put forward truthfully as objections except by the Sabellians, i.e., the Patripassians in which, indeed, painted into a corner and proved wrong, they collapse, they who strive to claim that there is one person of the Holy Trinity just as there is one nature. Their perversity as a consequence forces them to this absurdity, that they in no way believe in the divine birth; and so they assign to the Father the birth according to the flesh, likewise, the suffering and death, also the resurrection from the dead and ascension into heaven, and all those things which in the mystery of the Incarnation belong to the person of the one Son. But the Catholic Church, divinely-inspired, holding the truth of the faith, just as it knows how to assert the one nature of the Holy Trinity, so most carefully it attributes to each person its own. Therefore, the Son of God, mercifully to redeem us, for this reason is alone rightly believed to have assumed, because he did not take up human nature in such a way that there would be in him one nature of divinity and flesh. In Christ, the deity will not be able to be that which the flesh is because, with each nature retaining its property, it could not come about that either of them either cease to exist or change into the other with total destruction. If this were to happen, rightly would the flesh be said to have been taken up by the entire Trinity when the Son would change his flesh into that divinity which we profess remains common to him with the Father and the Holy Spirit.

XII. But now, because we say that in Christ there is a divine and a human nature, so we believe and confess that the human nature, i.e., the flesh and the rational soul were taken up, not by the entire Trinity, but by the Son alone. The only-begotten God took up the flesh and the soul into a unity of person, not into a unity of nature; and thus the person of the Son is not the same as that of the Father or of the Holy Spirit. The unity of person, with the property of each substance remaining, just as in Christ, he did not make a two-fold person, so he did not make the taking up of human nature common to the Holy Trinity. For not, as there is one common nature for the Son of God with the Father and the Holy Spirit, is there one common person.

XIII. 1. Therefore, it is proper to the Son alone mercifully to have received the form of a servant. That taking up of the form of a servant pertained to the person of God the Word, which did not with resulting confusion pass into the divine nature. Therefore, that taking up of the form of a servant, according to which the Son of God who is the Lord of all things and in whom dwells all the fullness of divinity, became a true and complete human being, took away from him nothing of his divine fullness. It took away nothing of the power, because in that one person remained without confusion a divine nature and a human nature. Hence it is that in one and the same Christ both the truth of the human nature shone forth and the eternal immutability of the divine nature remained.

2. Neither was anything diminished in him at all or changed which he had by nature from eternity, through that which he received from time. In his exterior aspect, he became a servant, but he did not cease to be by nature the Lord of all things. According to the flesh, he became poor; nonetheless, according to his divinity, he remained rich. Hence it is that the blessed Apostle asserts that Christians have been enriched by his poverty, saying, "For you know the gracious act of our Lord Jesus Christ, that for your sake he became poor although he was rich, so that by his poverty you might become rich."[54] He would in no way have made us rich by his poverty if, having become poor, he did not have in himself the riches of his divine nature. He became poor according to the form of a servant; he remained rich according to the form of God. Therefore, the poverty of the form of a servant is not common to him with the Father and the Holy Spirit because with the poverty of the human nature having been taken up into unity, the divine substance in him remained rich.

54. 2 Cor 8.9.

3. What was the poverty of the rich Son of God except our weakness and our mortality? Whatever in the weakness and death according to the flesh the only-begotten God bore, the divinity did not experience. For "God sent his own Son in the likeness of sinful flesh,"[55] in which was true flesh but there was no pollution of sin. Therefore, that likeness of sinful flesh was in the flesh of Christ, though that was not the flesh of sin because it was weak, because it was passible and mortal, because it was susceptible to wounds and subject to pain.

4. Nevertheless, all these things were common to the divinity and the humanity of Christ, not in the substance, but in the person. For the person of Christ is altogether distinguished from the person of the Father and the person of the Holy Spirit. This one person of the divinity and the humanity in Christ so remains that it does not permit one nature to be separated from the other, nor both to be confused. Therefore, Christ who is the way, the truth, and the true life is the way for us who in the truth of the flesh possessed true weakness; and he is the true life for us because the true strength remained in his true divinity. And the Apostle saw this when he said, "For indeed, he was crucified out of weakness, but he lives by the power of God."[56]

XIV. 1. Therefore, in one and the same Christ, just as the weakness of the human flesh could not either give or give back life to himself because that power of laying down or taking up again did not come from human weakness but from divine power; thus, the eternity of the divine power, to whom it is proper by nature to live immutably and without tiring, could experience nothing of infirmity or death on the cross. Therefore, the only-begotten Son of God in him both born true God from the Father and made a true human being from his mother is recognized both because he showed evidence of the weakness in the truth of the flesh and showed instances of his power in the truth of the divinity; showing in the unity of the person that there were some

55. Rm 8.3.
56. 2 Cor 13.4.

things common by nature with the Father and the Holy Spirit.

2. For Christ, communion of soul and flesh with us is natural; with the Father and the Holy Spirit, communion of deity is natural for him. Therefore, how could the Son of God have those things which are of the flesh as common with the Father and the Holy Spirit, he who in no way confused his flesh with his divinity? This does no harm to the Catholic faith that we believe that our nature was taken up in the unity of person by the only-begotten Savior, when we confess that there remains one divine substance of the Holy Trinity. The entire Trinity made that humanity of the Son, but, though it made it as a whole, the entire Trinity did not take it up because that person which is not common to the Son with the Father and the Holy Spirit is the one in Christ for both the divinity and the flesh. Where there is any distinction either of persons or of substances, whatever there is in the commonality of work is not always referred to the communion of taking up. Because this seems obscure when it is put forward by words alone, it is better that facility of understanding be provided by an apt example insofar as the subject matter permits.

XV. 1. There is a likeness to knowledge readily available to the faithful which God has placed in his image. This image is the human mind. For one reads that the Lord said, "Let us make humankind in our image, according to our likeness."[57] In these words, the heretical Arians find much to sadden them, they who read the Holy Scriptures but do not understand them; and put to confusion by their blindness of heart, they do not recognize the unity of nature in the Holy Trinity in which they distinguish the persons of the Father and of the Son and of the Holy Spirit in their preaching. Since in that testimony which we cited above, the Trinity itself, which is the one God, true and good, both teaches the unity of its divinity and clearly points out the evidence for the three persons.

57. Gen 1.26.

2. For he said, "Let us make humankind to our image, according to our likeness," lest unity of substance be denied in the three persons. He did not say, "Let me make humankind to my image and likeness," lest in that divine nature there be believed to be only one person, but he salutarily mixed the plural with the singular number, and when we read that God says, "Let us make humankind to our image, according to our likeness", that which is in the singular we say is in the nature as we said that the plural is in the persons. Therefore, this image, i.e., the interior person, is found to have by nature three things within itself, i.e., memory, understanding, and will.

3. The memory is the power of the soul by which we remember. The understanding is that by which what we conceived in memory, we ponder in thought. The will is that by which we either seek something or avoid it, i.e., by which we either love something or hate it. Therefore, these three, although they do not have their own persons in a human being, still are distinguished one from another; and so in these three, there is one person of a human being and one substance of the human mind so that still in the very nature of the rational soul in which it is clear there is the image of God, we find that the memory is one thing, the understanding another and likewise the will, a third.

4. For though we are unable either to think of anything or to love or hate that which we do not have in the memory because what forgetfulness has taken away from the heart, neither thought nor will can in any way find there; still to recognize the distinction of memory, thought, and will, we remember much which we neither ponder in thought nor seek by the will; likewise, we think of some things which we do not love. Therefore, our thought, which is born from and formed by memory, is well called an interior word. For what is thought except a speaking within?

5. So it is written: "When you are disturbed, do not sin; ponder it on your beds and be silent."[58] Also in the Gospel,

---

58. Ps 4.5 LXX; Ps 4.4.

when the Lord Jesus said to that paralytic whom he healed, "As for you, your sins are forgiven."[59] Luke the evangelist added, saying, "Then the Scribes and Pharisees began to ask themselves, 'Who is this who speaks blasphemies? Who but God alone can forgive sins?' Jesus knew their thoughts and said to them in reply, 'What are you thinking in your hearts?'" Where Luke said, "The Scribes and Pharisees began to ask themselves", Matthew said this, "At that, some of the Scribes said to themselves, 'This man is blaspheming.' Jesus knew what they were thinking and said: 'Why do you harbor evil thoughts?'"[60] Also in the book of Wisdom, it is said concerning certain people: "For they reasoned unsoundly, saying to themselves."[61] Obviously therefore, this is what thinking is, i.e., to speak within oneself. Thus, the word will be spoken invisibly where it is thought invisibly. Therefore, without any sound of a bodily voice, anyone speaks what he thinks which does not come to the hearing of another except by a physical speaking.

XVI. 1. Therefore, that word which was born from the memory, according to nature alone, by which it is born from memory, cannot be brought to the ears of any person without a bodily voice. Accordingly, in order that it be able to be brought to others, it is clothed with a bodily voice. To this word a bodily voice from the mouth is joined. And thus it comes about that that word which was wholly spiritually in the mind comes to others through a bodily voice but does not go away from the spirit from which and in which it remains spiritual. It is necessary that it remain totally in the mind, even when the totality is brought forth in the voice. We are still not able to say that that bringing forth of the word alone does not happen from the memory or from the will. For everyone who speaks both remembers and thinks what he speaks; and therefore he speaks because the will equally together with the memory and thinking brings about that speaking.

59. Lk 5.20.
61. Wis 2.1.
60. Mt 9.3–4.

2. For insofar as whatever a person speaks knowingly, he does not speak unless willing so that even whatever a person is forced to say unwilling, he does not say as long as the will is in no way disposed to speak. Hence, it is that not only those who, blinded by their lust for temporal things, have denied God, but also whoever, oppressed by the fear of worldly trials or tortures or by sadness, abandoning the truth of the Catholic faith, have gone over to impiety and infidelity, they will be able to find no excuse so that they may say that they denied the true faith unwillingly, when it appears that they did this with their own will. Even if their spirit was led to deny the faith because of trials or torture, still they did not deny it unwillingly. To deny the faith, first he thought and willed and so brought forth that denial; that this came about, thought, together with the will, decreed.

XVII. 1. To return to that with which I was dealing; in the very image of God, i.e., in the very mind of a human being, the thinking which is born and formed from the memory and is rightly called a word, receives a corporal voice only in order to be heard by corporal ears. So, therefore, in that holy and divine Trinity, only the Word of the Father, which is a mirror without stain and the image of the goodness of God, the refulgence of his glory and the very imprint of his being, "who though he was in the form of God, did not regard equality with God something to be grasped. Rather, he emptied himself, taking the form of a servant."[62] Therefore, only the Son of God took on flesh so that he could be seen by bodily eyes and touched by bodily hands; alone he thus received a human nature so that he might make it his own and through it might mercifully instill in human beings the knowledge of his divinity as well. Revealing himself, he also revealed the Father also in himself.

2. Giving knowledge of his divinity, he gave knowledge of the Father as well at the same time. The divinity which is one for the Father and the Son, also brings it about that the Son is not known without the Father and the Father is not known

---

62. Phil 2.6–7.

without the Son. Hence it is that he says, "Have I been with you for so long a time and you still do not know me, Philip? Whoever has seen me has seen the Father."[63] Thus the Son, who alone took up flesh, showed in himself the Father by right of the one divine nature; just as our speech, when we speak the truth which we recall, that which it points out by bringing it forth, it shows that this was found within the mind. That bodily voice with which the spiritual word is clothed in order that it be brought to the attention of hearers comes about simultaneously both from the memory and from thought and from the will; but from thought alone, i.e., it is taken up by the interior word in order that knowledge of the interior thought may proceed to the bodily ears of those who are in the vicinity. But that word, just as the whole went forth to hearers, having received the external aspect of a bodily voice, so, in the heart, the whole exists spiritually with the memory and the will.

3. Accordingly, whoever sees this image in the human mind, will more quickly laugh at the foolishness of the heretics who, thinking carnally about spiritual things, are unwilling to believe that in that Holy Trinity anything done by the three persons, that by divine arrangement, has been taken up by only one person; although that human nature was made by the working of the entire Trinity, it was taken up into the unity of the person only by the Son. Just as it is certain that "in the beginning was the Word, and the Word was with God and the Word was God,"[64] so it is certain that "the Word became flesh and dwelt among us."[65] What have we received except that the Word is God, and who is the God, with whom the Word was, except the Father and the Son?

XVIII. 1. By the name of the Word is shown the different person of the Father and the Son; but because the Word was God, one substance of the Father and the Son is taught. Therefore, not of the Father nor of the Holy Spirit, that flesh is of the Word alone; because with God the Word there

63. Jn 14.9.   64. Jn 1.1.
65. Jn 1.14.

is not a communion of one person with the Father and the Holy Spirit. According to the working of the eternal divinity in which there is a trinity of persons, just as the Father made the humanity of the Son, so the Son made it, so also the Holy Spirit made it, but not as the Son received it, did the Father or the Holy Spirit receive it. It was fitting for that Son, who according to divinity by nature alone was born from the Father alone, that he according to the flesh by nature be born from the virgin. But in that Trinity, just as there are not two Fathers, nor two Holy Spirits, so there would not be also two Sons. For that Trinity has in itself one Father, one Son, one Holy Spirit. But one Father and one Holy Spirit according to the divine nature but one Son according to divine and human substance.

2. In the persons, the Trinity is divided, although in the nature the one divinity of the Trinity is not divided or separated. In the person of the Son alone, humanity is assumed. Because of the nature, there is always one working of the Holy Trinity; but on account of the persons, the taking up of humanity belongs to the Son only. Nevertheless, while we discuss these matters for the instruction of the faithful, we must think also of the carnal and sensual heretics who for this reason are incapable of spiritual matters. Concerning them the Apostle says, "Now the natural person does not accept what pertains to the Spirit of God, for to him it is foolishness and he cannot understand it, because it is judged spiritually."[66]

3. The apostolic authority testifies that heretics are carnal or, above all, sensual. The blessed Paul also places heresies among the works of the flesh. Also the Blessed Jude the Apostle calls 'natural' those who separate themselves from the Church, saying, "These are the ones who cause divisions; they live on the natural plane, devoid of the Spirit."[67] This is indeed what we have shown, and the blessed Paul said, "Now the natural person does not accept what pertains to the Spirit of God."[68] Therefore, let it not be a wonder that those who

66. 1 Cor 2.14.
67. Jude 19.
68. 1 Cor 2.14.

do not have the Spirit of God are not able to understand the things of God. For it is written in the book of Wisdom: "Who will learn your counsel unless you have given wisdom and sent your Holy Spirit from on high?"[69] Hence it is that also the holy Apostle asserts that the things of God are not revealed except by the Holy Spirit, saying, "This God has revealed to us through the Spirit."[70] And a little later he says, "We have received not the spirit of the world but the Spirit that is from God, so that we may understand the things freely given us by God."[71] Nevertheless, it is good that we too, insofar as we are aided by God, imitating the blessed Apostle, are zealous to become all things to all people, that we may gain all.

XIX. 1. Since the Arians do not grasp what we have said, that in that one divine nature something has been made by the entire Trinity which was not taken up by the entire Trinity. And it is not believed possible that the entire Trinity made that flesh which one person of the Trinity took up. Therefore, let us become, as the Apostle says, like little children in their midst, and let us propose this example to them to foster broadening of their spiritual understanding, something that does not weary or trouble the narrowness of their heretical heart. We know that that alone is the divine, inseparable and indivisible Trinity where neither can the one nature be divided by the Trinity of persons nor can the three persons be confused by the unity of the indivisible nature.

2. But if this is sought in any creature, it is nowhere found. For even the very mind of the human being which we said is the image of God, received it in such a way that while it has in itself some trace of the Holy Trinity, it does not have in itself a distinction of three persons. The divine Trinity has saved this for itself alone. Whence, although there is in the human mind, memory, understanding, and will, there are these three but still they cannot be three persons because in each human being in whose mind or whose mind is the divine image, there is by nature one person, not

69. Wis 9.17. 70. 1 Cor 2.10.
71. 1 Cor 2.12.

only of the mind itself but of the soul and the flesh together.

3. In the creature, insofar as the importance of so great a thing about which we are speaking permits us to seek an example, perhaps we find in natures some such thing, which we cannot find in the persons. For we said that the entire Trinity made the humanity of the Son of God but that only the Son, not the entire Trinity, received it into his person. That flesh was made by the entire Trinity, i.e., by the Father and the Son and the Holy Spirit; but only the Word became flesh. Since, as we said above, insofar as it pertains to the creature, we are unable to find three persons in one mind or in one flesh, we do not have to labor to be able to find at least two natures in one person.

4. The person of each living human being consists of a rational soul and body. Yet many things are done by it in such a way that although they are done together by the soul and the body, they sometimes pertain only to the soul or only to the body. For who is unaware that only the body is restored and nourished by bodily food, though eating is a work common to the flesh and the soul? For the soul does it through the body, indeed with the body, when the body eats; and still, only the body receives it, which, in order that it be received, the soul works together with the body. Therefore, in that eating, there is one work of the soul and the flesh, but the receiving is of the flesh alone. Insofar as the flesh alone is fed by bodily food, so that it alone, if it receives it, becomes fat, it alone, if it does not receive it, grows weak.

5. The feeding and fatness of the soul, however, consist not in bodily bread but in spiritual bread. "One does not live by bread alone, but by every word that comes forth from the mouth of God."[72] In the receiving of this word in order that the soul be fed with its food, the flesh is associated with it in the work. This is done when either the soul moves the ears of the body with words to hear or moves the eyes of the body to read the Scriptures. See that here there is a working together of the flesh and of the soul, where there is a receiving by the soul alone. Let the Arians see this in creatures and let

---

72. Mt 4.4.

them not doubt that there is one divine nature of the Holy Trinity and that what could have been done, indeed was done, that that flesh was made by the one and inseparable working of the entire Trinity, which in the mystery of the Incarnation, would pertain only to the person of the only-begotten God.

XX. 1. Therefore, the entire Trinity did not assume flesh, nor did the entire Trinity suffer the injuries of the passion, nor did the entire Trinity rise from the dead on the third day, nor did the entire Trinity ascend into heaven on the fortieth day but, just as we have shown above, only the Son assumed flesh. One in him, because as the property of each nature remains unconfused, he is one and the same who also remained according to his true divinity altogether incapable of suffering. By nature, that divinity suffers nothing, just as by nature, it is not changed. To be subject to sufferings belongs to a changeable nature. Therefore, no suffering could happen to that nature, in which change could not be present by nature. Only the Son lay in the tomb, but that nature of the only-begotten God which could die could be buried. According to the nature of the flesh, therefore, the only-begotten God lay buried in the rock, according to which affixed by nails, he hung on the cross. How could his divinity, which can be contained by neither the earth nor the heavens, be confined in the tomb?

2. The unity in the person in Christ made that suffering and that burial to be one of the divinity and of the flesh, but the property of each substance in Christ made only the flesh of Christ subject to suffering and death by nature, with the impassibility and immortality of the divine and immutable substance remaining. Therefore, Christ, who is not the Trinity, but one person of the Trinity, according to the truth of the flesh, truly hung on the cross and lay dead in the tomb, as the Apostle says that "Christ died for our sins in accordance with the Scriptures; that he was buried; that he was raised on the third day in accordance with the Scriptures."[73] All of this the whole Christ has done according to the unity

---

73. 1 Cor 15.3.

of person; according to the property of the nature, they pertain only to the truth of the flesh. Thus, according to the soul alone, he descended to Hell.

3. So at one and the same time, in the interval between the death of Christ and his resurrection, one and the same Christ, both according to the truth of the flesh, truly lay in the tomb and according to the truth of the rational soul, truly descended to Hell. And for this reason, according to the truth of human nature, from the time Christ hung on the cross, having lowered his head, gave up the spirit, up to the time, having received the spirit back, he rose from the dead, wherever he was according to the flesh, there he was not according to the soul. According to the flesh, dead, he lay in the tomb; but according to the rational soul, he descended to Hell; according to his divinity, by which he is one God with the Father and the Holy Spirit, infinite, he filled the whole of creation.

4. Therefore, according to the flesh, he was in the tomb only, so that according to the soul, he would have been only in Hell, but according to the divinity, by which he is confined in no place but is found everywhere complete ineffably, so that he did not abandon his flesh in the tomb nor did he desert his soul in Hell, as he could not be absent from earth or heaven at any time. Also the same Son of God who, according to the flesh only lay in the tomb, and according to the soul alone, descended to Hell, since he himself had said of his soul, "I have the power to lay it down and power to take it up again,"[74] afterwards he lay down his soul and took it up again, according to his entire humanity, he ascended into heaven and sits at the right of the seat of God, as Mark the evangelist bears witness, saying, "So then the Lord Jesus, after he spoke to them, was taken up into heaven, and took his seat at the right hand of God."[75]

5. All of these things, which happened in time in the only-begotten God, partly according to the soul alone, partly according to the flesh alone, partly according to soul and flesh together, just as they are worthily referred to the one person

74. Jn 10.18.
75. Mk 16.19.

of the divinity and humanity which is in the Son of God, so in no way can they be referred to his divine substance. And for this reason, none of these things can be assigned to the person of the Father or of the Holy Spirit, because there is not one person of the Father and the Son and the Holy Spirit.

6. Nor can anyone ascribe the assumption of the suffering of the flesh to the Father or the Holy Spirit, because it is wicked to proclaim the nature of the Word mutable in anything or passible; according to which Christ also remained without a beginning, always born from the Father when he took a beginning of his conception and birth from his mother, and incomprehensible when he permitted himself to be comprehended; and impassible when he underwent the injuries of his passion and immortal when he submitted to death; and undivided when according to the flesh, he lay in the tomb and according to the soul, he descended into the lower parts of the earth; and infinite, when he ascended to the heights of heaven from the lowliness of this earth.

XXI. 1. If the wretched Fastidiosus did not deny this faith, without a doubt, he would not perish. But since he has denied it both in deeds and in words, it is no surprise that he has become worst in deeds and now, perverse in speech and walking in darkness, he has become an enemy of the light. Bodily fornication, which first took possession of his mind and flesh, consequently dragged him to the disaster of spiritual fornication. For he took the members of Christ and made them members of a prostitute. And, therefore, he did not hesitate to destroy the chastity of faith because he did not mourn losing chastity of the body. Behold how great an evil is the sexual pleasure of the flesh which was able to lead that wretch all the way to the denial of the truth! This was the storm that snatched that chaff from the Lord's threshing floor and planted it among the thorn-bushes of heretical impiety. This made him speak against his conscience and indeed, with false words, to be involved in a slanderous attack against the Trinity itself.

2. He did not believe that what he said was true, but now with double heart he preferred to speak differently from

what he believed. Because possessed by despair and depriving himself of the hope of forgiveness, he wished more boldly to fulfill the delights of lust. Therefore, from his own mouth by which he ought to have been justified, he received an increase of condemnation when his tongue, which ought to have brought forth words of repentance, brought forth words of blasphemy. To that place, therefore, the wretched Fastidiosus preferred to move where he might bark against God with sacrilegious impudence and in his fornications, he who did not have fear of God would not fear human beings as well. Woe to that wretch who wished to be deprived of the Church's communion to this point, that he can never lack punishment; and he wished to sin without any fear to this point, that he deserves to burn without end.

XXII. 1. Where now are those two, as it were, delightful years which Fastidiosus had, because he used them up as he wished, full of lust in fornicating? How quickly they passed! And even if they had been, not just twenty, but even two thousand, they would have passed rapidly. What will the wretch do when he comes to the judgment seat of him whom he denied? What will he receive for such deeds and words? What will he receive, that one, lustful in body, blind in heart, and blasphemous in mouth who first violated the Temple of God in himself by fornication; then, separated from the Church, left it in body? What will he receive from that holy Trinity, he who preferred to be the slave of lust and infidelity? What but eternal fire which it is clear has been prepared for such works? And in this time, the fornication of Fastidiosus has rapidly come to an end, but for him in that fire the eternal burning will not be ended. Therefore, let Christians flee both kinds of fornication, which the wretched Fastidiosus has incurred; and guarding their souls, let them preserve chastity of both heart and body.

2. Within the Church, let them hold the Catholic faith. Let them believe in and confess the inseparable and undivided Trinity, which in its divine nature has nothing made, nothing begun in any way. By its one and inseparable working all things have been made in the heavens and on earth, visible and invisible. Likewise let them believe in and confess

the only-begotten God, alone according to his true divinity, born from the Father, alone according to his true humanity, created from the virgin. Let them further believe that the flesh and soul of the only begotten God were made by the work of the Trinity and that the same flesh and rational soul in the unity of the person were taken up by the only-begotten God alone for the salvation of the world. Holding on to this most firmly, let them move forward and continue in good works. For "in Christ Jesus," the only thing that counts is "the faith that works through love,"[76] and if anyone depart from it, he will be guilty of his own soul. But everyone who will persevere in it to the end will be saved.

LETTER 10. THE LETTER OF SCARILA TO FULGENTIUS AND THE BOOK OF FULGENTIUS TO SCARILA

An unknown correspondent, Scarila, asked Fulgentius to enlighten him about questions which had arisen at a dinner party. Once again, as in letter 9, the relation of the Trinity to the Incarnation is a prominent issue in the discussion as well as a lesser question that comes under the general heading of the problem of evil. In the case of the latter question, concerning the origin of flies and other vermin, Fulgentius sees the danger of Manichaeism lurking behind the hypothesis that such nuisances for the human race were not created by God. The reply is very lengthy and is called not unfittingly a 'book'. Its date is unknown.

THE LETTER OF SCARILA TO FULGENTIUS

OUR SERVANT SCARILA[1] sends greetings to the holy, most blessed Father, Fulgentius the bishop, equal in merits to the Apostles.

1. The desires of the unlearned greatly desire the learning of your paternity because it has been written: "Ask your father and he will inform you; your elders and they will tell

76. Gal 5.6.
1. Scarila. See PCBE, 1044.

you,"[2] and because that which we are unable to understand, we desire to know from the learning of your holiness.

2. While at the table of your Christian son of the Catholic Church, Eventus,[3] a discussion arose about the Incarnation of God, one of us asserting this about the Incarnation itself, viz., that not God the Father but God the Son took on flesh. And another said that God himself who is one in three deigned to assume flesh in order that he might lead to freedom our servitude by which we were being held bound because of the transgression of our father Adam.

3. And we wish to know if God the Father himself descended and took on flesh or, with himself remaining, he commanded the Word who assumed flesh, since we know that the Word became flesh that he might dwell among us? But between the Word who is God and the Father who is God, one majesty of both descended to take on flesh because we read, "This is our God; no other can be compared to him . . . afterward he appeared on earth and lived with humankind."[4] And when we brought this testimony to the forefront, he, to the contrary, said this, "He said this about the Son, not about God the Father." At that moment, I said to him, "Because we are equally ignorant, let us have recourse to the holy father, Bishop Fulgentius, to whom God has deigned to give knowledge of such power. Through the disclosure of the divine Scriptures, he will show the way for our ignorance with plain words." Then, commending myself to your holy prayers, I ask through him who gifted your sanctity with such great grace, that you, as a good father, may wish us to be instructed in what we do not know and that you inundate us from that fountain from which all who thirst are filled.

4. When that discussion was over, another of our number said that flies, fleas, and scorpions and that kind of filthy animals which are called bed-bugs,[5] God did not make but, after

---

2. Dt 32.7.   3. Eventus. See PCBE, 360.
4. Bar 3.35, 37.
5. Bizarre as the subject may seem at first sight, Fulgentius is not the only one to discuss it. See, for example, Augustine, *Tractatus in Johannem* I.14, CCL 36.8.

the fall of that angel, the unworthy Devil, all these things were made by the Devil himself; and while we were saying that God made all things, and these were very good, he said that we ought to consult your holiness about this also, so that you might wish to be satisfied concerning this also, whether before the transgression, when God made all things, then these things were made or after the transgression of Adam. Pray for us, holy Lord and most blessed father.

THE BOOK OF ST. FULGENTIUS THE BISHOP TO SCARILA CONCERNING THE INCARNATION OF THE SON OF GOD AND THE AUTHOR OF VILE ANIMALS.

WHEN THE LETTER which you sent had been read, my very dear son Scarila, I rejoiced in the Lord and my heart exulted in God my Savior, because he has endued you with a zeal for salvation and mercifully infused your heart with a desire for righteousness by which you wish to know the true faith. Through faith, abundance of life comes to human beings, as God himself bears witness through the prophet, saying, "My just man lives by faith."[1] That faith must be called true which is true, not feigned, which the Apostle commends, saying, "The aim of this instruction is love from a pure heart, a good conscience, and a sincere faith."[2] Since the same blessed Apostle says that we have been saved through faith by grace, which he asserts is not from ourselves but is a gift of God, then indeed there will be no true salvation where there is not the true faith, since it is infused by God, without a doubt it is given by free gift; and where through true faith, there is a profession of true Christianity, the truth is accompanied by salvation. Whoever will have deviated from the true faith will not have the grace of true salvation. Accordingly, the faithful soul

---

1. Hab 2.4.
2. 1 Tm 1.5.

must not be slow to ask questions if he perceives in his own mind something uncertain in the mystery of faith, and, above all in the mystery of the Lord's Incarnation, through which righteousness is given to the impious, life to the dead, health to the sick, and the grace of true freedom to prisoners.

2. Therefore, you have written to us your words that, while at the table of my Christian son of the Catholic Church, Eventus, a discussion arose about the Incarnation of God, one of you asserted this about the Incarnation itself, that not God the Father but God the Son took on flesh. And another said, "God himself who is one in three deigned to assume flesh in order that he might lead to freedom our servitude by which we were being held bound because of the transgression of our father Adam." Then you say that you wish to know whether God the Father himself descended and took on flesh or, with himself remaining, he commanded the Word who assumed flesh. You say that you also know that the Word became flesh that he might dwell among us. At that point you add these words, saying, "But between the Word who is God and the Father who is God, one majesty of both descended to take on flesh, because we read," you say, "'This is our God; no other can be compared to him . . . afterward he appeared on earth and lived with humankind.'[3]" Then you add and say that "When we brought this testimony to the forefront, he, to the contrary, said this, 'He said this concerning the Son, not God the Father.'" And you, at that moment, said to him that because you are equally ignorant, you will have recourse to us. With the gift and help of God, an answer must be given now by us to this question which is found in the first part of your letter; when that is finished, it will not bother us to reply to the other question insofar as God gives it to us to do so.

3. To start with, every Catholic Christian must know that there is one God, the Holy Trinity, i.e., the Father, the Son, and the Holy Spirit; that the Trinity itself which is one God,

---

3. Bar 3.35, 37.

is indeed one in nature, not, however, one in person. The fact that it is said that the one God is the Trinity is a truth and that he is not called the Father who is called the Son or who is called the Holy Spirit is, nonetheless, true. The one God is the Trinity because the Father does not have one nature and the Son another and the Holy Spirit a third, but the Trinity itself is one nature, God. Nor are the Father and the Son and the Holy Spirit one person, but the person of the Father is of the Father only, and the person of the Son is of the Son only, and the person of the Holy Spirit is of the Holy Spirit only. In person, therefore, the one who is the Father is not the Son and the one who is the Son is not the Holy Spirit. What the Father is by nature, this the Son is, this the Holy Spirit is, because in nature the Trinity is one God; where neither greater nor lesser is spoken of because none is prior to another, nor found to be later. There the eternity and immensity belong just as much to each person as they do to the three persons in nature. It is the Father alone who begot the Son; only the Son who is born of the Father; it is only the Holy Spirit who is neither born of the Father nor begot the Son but proceeds from the Father and the Son. Therefore, the Father is Father only of the Son and the Son is the Son only of the Father, but the Holy Spirit is not of the Father only nor of the Son only, but the Holy Spirit is at the same time one and common to the Father and the Son.

4. Therefore, in this Trinity, there are certain things proper to the individual persons. By these properties, the persons are shown but are not separated. The nature of these properties is this that, though they are inseparable, they cannot be confused, but the individual properties remain in each of the persons for this purpose, that they show forth both the unity of nature of the true Trinity and the Trinity of persons of true unity. It is the property of the Father alone that he was not born but begat; it is the property of the Son that he did not beget but was born; it is the property of the Holy Spirit that he neither begat nor was born but proceeded from the begetter and the begotten. Just as the eternal generating of the Father is without beginning, and the eternal

birth of the Son without beginning, so naturally the eternal procession of the Holy Spirit is without beginning. Like the eternity of God the Father which remains without a beginning, such is the birth of the Son and the procession of the Holy Spirit, so that both that birth and that procession are co-eternal with the origin, where a beginning can never be found. Since, therefore, that truth of the Trinity in nature has this in itself, that being born is proper to the Son alone, the one who alone has in himself the true birth from the divinity of the Father, is alone found to have the true birth in humanity from the virgin. To him it was according to the true flesh to have a mother by nature, who according to his divinity has a true Father by nature. Accordingly, the one who is begotten without beginning from the eternal Father, the Son is born in time from a time-bound mother; therefore, not only in his divinity but also in the flesh is he truly called the only-begotten Son of God, because he alone is begotten both according to the divinity and according to the flesh.

5. The property of the sole, only-begotten of God is each birth, one from the truth of divine nature, the other from the grace of humanity assumed. So the blessed evangelist John asserts that the only-begotten of the Father is full of grace and of truth. Accordingly, that death-dealing and in all ways diabolical blasphemy must be feared by which it is believed or said that the Trinity itself at the same time took on flesh. This the Catholic faith does not accept but the wickedness of the Sabellian error invented. For Sabellius knew that it was preached, with the Scriptures bearing witness, that the Father and the Son and the Holy Spirit are not three gods but one true God. He heard what was true so that he might beget from himself what was false. Finally, because he knew that there was one nature of the Father and the Son and the Holy Spirit, he did not scruple to preach one person of the same nature. He was cast down by the madness of his error to this point, that he asserted that the Father himself was born of the virgin. Of necessity, it followed that as he attributed to the one the truth of human birth, to the same he

assigned the truth of the passion and death. The Catholic Church has named the followers of the same Sabellius, not only Sabellians, but also Patripassians, and has condemned them along with their author with the bond of anathema.

6. Let this perversity be far from the faithful, nor may God permit anyone redeemed by the blood of his only-begotten Son to be thus profaned by the death-dealing sense of faithlessness. It is a matter of great impiety if anyone either wishes to proclaim one person because of one nature in the Father and the Son and the Holy Spirit or, because of the three persons, asserts three natures as well. Inasmuch as he who asserts that there is one person of the Father and the Son and the Holy Spirit is caught in the snare of the Sabellian error; on the other hand, the one who confirms that there are three natures of the Father and the Son and the Holy Spirit is entangled in the cords of Arian faithlessness. And although the assertion of each form of infidelity seems different, the condemnation for each type of impiety is one. Because of the unity of nature, what is proper to the persons is impiously confused; no less impiously is unity of nature broken up because of the properties of the persons. The Father has one true Son by nature and born of him without a beginning and of the virgin in time. He sent him into the world that the world might be saved through him. The Son himself shows this when he says, "For God so loved the world that he gave his only Son, so that everyone who believes in him might not perish but might have eternal life. For God did not send his Son into the world to condemn the world, but that the world might be saved through him. Whoever believes in him will not be condemned but whoever does not believe has already been condemned because he has not believed in the name of the only Son of God."[4]

7. See how in this text our Savior himself says three times that he is the Son and twice named the only-begotten. He asserted that he had been sent by the Father to save the world; since, if the Trinity itself had come in the flesh as the same

---

4. Jn 3.16–18.

time, the Son would not have said that he had been sent by the Father. Because Christ could not lie, without a doubt one person did the sending and the other was sent. The true Father sent the Truth which he begot; he sent Wisdom in which he made all things; he sent the Word which he wrote in the heart. Accordingly, in that sending, the coming must not be thought of as spatial, as if the Son of God had been sent to earth from heaven, so that he was not on earth before he received flesh or deserted heaven when he took on flesh for our salvation. Since he is the wisdom of God concerning which it has been said: "It reaches mightily from one end of the earth to the other and orders all things well,"[5] that divinity which by nature is one of the Father and of the Son and of the Holy Spirit, thus is not spatial, just as it is not temporal; it is not confined in a space, just as it does not change with time. That divinity by nature is infinite and eternal; it did not begin at some initial point nor is it confined in a space. Therefore, the one God, the Father and the Son and the Holy Spirit,[6] fills up the whole, contains the whole; as the whole is in each thing, so the whole is in everything; as the whole is in small things, so the whole is in the largest creatures. This is true of nature but not of grace. When it creates human beings, it does not by the same act save them. While it makes them, it does not by the same act remake them. While it makes that sun to rise over the good and the evil, it does not do the same when the sun of justice rises on those on whom the light, not of the flesh but of the heart, is poured by the gift of prevenient mercy. As it belongs to all to be born through nature, it does not in the same way belong to all to be reborn through grace. Since the Father and the Son and the Holy Spirit by nature are one God, eternal and infinite, there is nothing in heaven, nothing on earth, nothing above the heavens, nothing in any nature which he made that has not been made, where the same one God, Father, Son, and Holy Spirit, could be missing. In God, just as

---

5. Wis 8.1.
6. There is a printing error in CCL XCI.317, line 160, 'Spiritus'.

10. FULGENTIUS TO SCARILA

there is no mutability of times, so there is no spatial capacity. As Solomon truly said at the dedication of the Temple in these words, "Even heaven and the highest heavens cannot contain you, much less this house that I have built."[7]

8. Therefore, the ineffable God, and altogether marvelous ineffably and marvelously, by the infinity of his nature, both is wholly in individual things and not confined by all things. Thus the Father alone, thus the Son alone, thus the Holy Spirit alone, thus the Trinity all at once is one God, Father, Son, and Holy Spirit, because neither is there the Father alone without the Son or the Holy Spirit, nor the Son alone without the Father or the Holy Spirit, nor the Holy Spirit alone without the Father or the Son. Accordingly, it must be very carefully thought out, how the Son could be sent into the world, he who could not be lacking to the world; or how he came into the world whence he never departed, since the one to whom it is natural to fill up the whole can neither withdraw for a while nor enter in. That nature of infinite divinity neither is stretched to fill up what was empty before nor is it contracted to empty what it had filled. Such is the power of the Creator and such the condition of every creature that while, unless he created it, no substance could exist, so, unless he sustained it, no substance could continue to exist. Accordingly, because according to his divinity, God does not move from one place to another, the truth of the Christian faith holds this, that as the Son of God is believed to have come into the world, so it is known that he accepted the form of a servant. For the Son of God thus came into the world, when, preserving his equality of nature with the Father, he deigned to become a sharer in the substance of his mother; when he became human, preserving his divinity; he came into time, preserving his eternity; he came into a certain place, preserving his infinity; he became changeable, preserving his immutability; he became mortal, preserving his immortality.

9. But the coming of the Son of God is not always to be

---

7. 1 Kgs 8.27.

understood in one and the same way. For he comes in one way with the Father sending him; in another way, he deigns to come with the Father. Since he deigns to come as an equal with the Father, when sent by the Father, he came, diminished, a little less than the angels; he is known to have come once, sent by the Father; with the Father, he deigns to come innumerable times. For he set neither the way nor the number of his comings when he said, "Whoever loves me will keep my word and my Father will love him and we will come to him and make our dwelling with him."[8] Accordingly, that coming by which the Son alone comes into the world once sent by the Father was manifested not only to the good, but also to the evil; to some that they might believe, to others, that they might crucify him; to some, that they could be freed from sin, to others, that they could not have any excuse to offer for their sins. The Apostle shows that believers have been freed from sin, saying, "But now that you have been freed from sin and have become slaves of God, the benefit that you have leads to sanctification and its end is eternal life."[9] The Savior himself has shown that unbelievers can have no excuse for their sin when he says, "If I had not come and spoken to them, they would have no sin; but as it is, they have no excuse for their sins."[10] Nor would the Jews have the sin of unbelief, if the presence of the Savior had not been made known to them. Therefore, that coming by which the Son was sent into the world once by the Father was for the fall and rise of many. He, when he comes with the Father, is concerned only with the rise of many because the love which covers a multitude of sins merits him. At that coming by which the Son was sent by the Father, he came once in the fullness of time. But in the one when he is accustomed to come with the Father, from the beginning to the end of the world, he has not ceased nor does he cease now to come to those to whom it was and still is fitting. Hence it

8. Jn 14.23. This is the key text for the doctrine of the divine indwelling. On this see, DSp 7/2, cc.1735–67, 'Inhabitation'.
9. Rm 6.22.
10. Jn 15.22.

10. FULGENTIUS TO SCARILA

is that before he came in the flesh, the prophets asked for his coming, saying, "Stir up your might and come to save us."[11] They would never seek the future coming of the Son of God, if they did not have within them the grace of the same one who comes and abides.

10. They who do not believe in the equality of the Father and the Son altogether reject for themselves that coming of the Son and the Father. When they come, they construct one dwelling within the one who loves them. But there cannot be one simple dwelling for them, if the love is diverse. But if they are unequal, it is necessary that they be loved unequally. In a simple heart, one single dwelling cannot be prepared for the unequal. Scripture warns us when it says, "Think of the Lord in goodness and seek him with sincerity of heart."[12] How is God sought in simplicity of heart when a difference of love is accepted in God the Father and God the Son? Or how is there a simple love of a human being for God if there is thought to be a diversity in the divinity itself? That divinity which is believed to be simple in nature is loved with a simple heart. But when a diverse divinity is worshipped, not simplicity, then duplicity of heart is shown forth. Therefore, that faith is not true but false. "For a holy and a disciplined spirit will flee from deceit and will leave foolish thoughts behind."[13] A duplicitous heart is convicted when someone thinks that not a single divinity must be worshipped by the faithful or when he thinks that the nature of the Son is not the same as that of the Father. So, if someone, feigning goodness for his neighbor in words and doing evil in his heart, is said to be a duplicitous heart, how is the one, who under the guise of truth either believes or says false things about God, not held by the sin of a duplicitous heart? In that highest divinity, to divide what is by nature one and to fashion a greater and a lesser God, it is most certain that this belongs to the wickedness of a duplicitous heart. Holy Scripture says, "Woe to the duplicitous of heart and to

11. Ps 79.3 LXX; Ps 80.2.   12. Wis 1.1.
13. Wis 1.5.

wicked lips, and hands that do evil, and to the sinner who walks the earth on double ways."[14] And because to think of a difference in divinity for the Father and the Son is not to believe in God (because he worships one God who does not worship another one altogether, and he believes in one God who does not believe there is another God), therefore, the same text of Scripture follows up by saying, "Woe to those who do not believe in God because they are not protected by him."[15] Hence it is that our Savior as well, pointing out one divinity and sovereignty, says, "No one can serve two masters."[16] We read that "The Lord, he is God."[17] Whence it is certain that with true faith and sincere love, no one can serve either lords or gods. One is the God of gods and Lord of lords; wherefore, he alone must be worshipped because he alone is by nature the true Lord, who is the Trinity, Father, Son, and Holy Spirit.

11. Therefore, that we may seek God in simplicity of heart, let us not believe in our heart in any difference in divinity in the Father and the Son. But in order that true simplicity of heart can remain in us, let that faith remain in us by which the oneness of the Holy Trinity is believed and divinity without difference is preached. Thus will the Father and the Son and the Holy Spirit deign to remain with us when they come. For one is the coming of the Holy Trinity to its lover because God comes invisibly and constructs his dwelling invisibly. Remaining with his lover, he increases the love because of which he makes his abode in the person. He comes because he is loved and when he comes, he brings it about that he is loved more.

12. I have said these things that you may know of the nature of the coming of the Son when he was sent by the Father and the nature of the coming of the Son when he deigns to come with the Father. Because just as in the former coming, he was made a human being, he is acknowledged as less than the Father; so in the latter coming, he re-

14. Sir 2.14.
16. Mt 6.24.
15. Sir 2.15.
17. Ps 99.3 LXX; Ps 100.3.

mains God, equal to the Father. The Holy Spirit is also said to come since it too is one God with the Father and the Son, by nature, eternal and infinite, without whom neither can the Father come nor the Son. He who has charity in his heart can love the Father and the Son. "The love of God has been poured out into our hearts through the Holy Spirit that has been given to us."[18] Therefore, the Father and the Son never come to their lover without the Holy Spirit; because, in order that they come, they are given the charity by which they are loved by the gift of the Holy Spirit. The coming in common of the Father and the Son and the Holy Spirit is always invisible; they do not move from one place to another but because the Trinity itself, one God, deigns either to give the grace of charity which it may increase or to increase what it gives. The Son came in another way when the only-begotten God became a human being for us. He who did not receive the person of a human being into his own person of his divinity but the nature of a human being. We also know that the Holy Spirit has come visibly in the form of a dove; but in a very different way, i.e., not in that way in which the Father and the Son come to their lover, not without the Holy Spirit, nor in that way in which the Son alone came into the world, according to which he marvelously and in a singular way took up our nature into the person of his divinity. For the Holy Spirit did not take the form of a dove in the way the Son took the form of a servant; nor was the Holy Spirit made in the likeness of doves as the Son was made in the likeness of human beings. Therefore, the Holy Spirit came in the appearance of a dove, not, however, taking up a dove into a unity of person. Nor did the nature of doves have to be redeemed thus through the Holy Spirit, as the nature of human beings was redeemed through the Son. For the Son took up this nature, which he was without a doubt going to redeem, into the unity of his person. And since his humanity is never separated from the Son of God, consequently he rules over all angels and all human beings

---

18. Rm 5.5.

in heaven or on earth. According to his human nature, the Son of God "humbled himself, being obedient to death, even death of a cross,"[19] according to which nature, God "exalted him and bestowed on him the name that is above every name, that at the name of Jesus, every knee should bend, of those in heave and on earth and under the earth; and every tongue confess that Jesus Christ is Lord, to the glory of God the Father."[20]

Therefore, when the fullness of time had come, "God sent his Son, born of a woman, born under the Law."[21] Why this was done, the Apostle subsequently shows, saying, "To ransom those under the Law, so that we might receive the adoption of sons."[22] Therefore, human nature was taken up by the Son of God. The only-begotten God became a human being so that divine adoption might be given to us through him, in order that because that human being is true God by the natural truth of his divinity, we too, because we are his brothers, might become children of God, not because of any merits of ours, but because of his grace.

13. The Holy Spirit, coming in the form of a dove, did not become a dove, as the Son became a human being; but, through the form of a dove, he showed that love is to be given to us by his gift. For "the love of God has been poured out into our hearts through the Holy Spirit that has been given to us."[23] Later he also appeared in tongues of flame but this too he did as a sign of that very charity which he granted us. For because "the aim of this instruction is love from a pure heart, a good conscience and sincere faith,"[24] and "For in Christ Jesus, neither circumcision nor uncircumcision counts for anything, but only faith working through love,"[25] this is that simplicity of heart which is signified in the dove, by which that which we believe in the heart for justification, we must in trust confess with the mouth for salvation. Therefore, the dove shows simplicity of faith and charity that we

19. Phil 2.8.
20. Phil 2.9–11.
21. Gal 4.4.
22. Gal 4.5.
23. Rm 5.5.
24. 1 Tm 1.5.
25. Gal 5.6.

may rightly believe in God and love God and neighbor purely. The fiery tongue signifies the confession of the true faith and an admonition to holy charity. Therefore, that dove in whose form the Holy Spirit came above the baptized Christ was made to signify something and was immediately dissolved. Therefore, only the Son took up human flesh and a soul. To him alone belonged the divine birth by nature. And who alone was born of the Father, alone could be born of the virgin as well. Unless he was a human being coming from a human being, he was not a sharer in our nature. Therefore, it came about that he received true flesh from the flesh of the virgin, so that a true communion of nature remained for us with him. For how could he take up either the ancient fathers or human beings from any time into a communion of his divinity, if he did not have a natural communion of the flesh with them?

14. Therefore, the Son of God not only deigned to become a human being but also to come from human beings. Hence what the Apostle says, speaking of Christ, "Surely, he did not help angels but rather the descendants of Abraham; therefore, he had to become like his brothers in every way, that he might be a merciful and faithful high priest before God to expiate the sins of the people. Because he himself was tested through what he suffered, he is able to help those who are being tested. Therefore, holy brother, sharing in a heavenly calling, reflect on Jesus, the apostle and high priest of our confession who was faithful to the one who appointed him."[26] Hence there is that which he says again in another text of the same letter: "Every high priest is taken from among men and made their representative before God, to offer gifts and sacrifices for sins."[27] Such was that high priest in order that he offer himself up for us as an offering and victim to God as a pleasant odor for the reconciliation of the human race. Hence it is that "while we were enemies, we were reconciled to God through the death of his Son."[28] In

26. Heb 2.16–18, 3.1–2.   27. Heb 5.1.
28. Rm 5.10.

order that the blessed Apostle show that Christ, the Son of God, took the origin of his flesh from that one man, from whom the unity of nature has propagated all human beings, he says in another place, "He who consecrates and those who are being consecrated, all have one origin. Therefore, he is not ashamed to call them 'brothers' saying I will proclaim your name to my brothers."[29] But he says this about us, he who according to the flesh was both born and suffered for us. He, who became a sharer in our nature so that he might come into being from that one from whom we all have come into being, took his origin in the flesh from that one from whom we all take our origin. But if the Trinity had taken up flesh for us, since through a communion of the flesh we have become brothers of him who became incarnate, now we would be not only sons of God the Father but also brothers of the entire Trinity; and the one whom we have as a Father in heaven, a human birth would have made a brother for us as well.

15. It is a great absurdity to imagine him as begotten in time, to whom it is proper not to be born in eternity, but to have begotten. Therefore, it befits the true faith to confess not the Father, nor the Holy Spirit but the Son, just as he alone was born of God the Father, so he alone is born of the virgin Mary. Since, therefore, only the Son of God took on flesh, he made us sons of God and, freed from the slavery to sin, he gave us back to true freedom. And because only the Son of God was born of the virgin, therefore, he alone was handed over for us, as the Apostle bears witness that "God did not spare his own Son but handed him over for us all."[30] For concerning the Son himself, he says, "Insofar as I now live in the flesh, I live by faith in the Son of God who has loved me and given himself up for me."[31] And in another text, he also says, "Grace to you and peace from God our Father and the Lord Jesus Christ, who gave himself for our sins that he might rescue us from the present evil age in accord

---

29. Heb 2.11–12.
30. Rm 8.32.
31. Gal 2.20.

with the will of our God and Father, to whom be glory for ever and ever."[32] Therefore, just as the Father handed over the son, so the Son handed himself over, and just as the Son gave himself, so also the Father gave him, as the Son says, "For God so loved the world that he gave his only Son, so that everyone who believes in him might not perish but might have eternal life."[33]

16. Therefore, since all these things are known, things by which it is clearly shown that the Son alone took on flesh for our salvation and he alone was handed over for our sins and bore the punishment of the passion and death, God forbid that any of the faithful say that God the Father either was born of the virgin or was handed over for us. These things belong to the Son alone who, just as he deigned to be born in time for us, so deigned to die for us. If anyone attributes to God the Father the taking up of flesh, let him pay attention to that place in the Gospel especially, because God who took on flesh most frequently calls himself not only the Son of man but also the Son of God. He said to the man born blind whom he had illuminated, "'Do you believe in the Son of God?' He answered and said, 'Who is he, sir, that I may believe in him?' Jesus said to him, 'You have seen him and the one speaking with you is he.' He said, 'I do believe, Lord' and he worshipped him."[34] Also to the Jews, he speaks as follows: "Is it not written in your Law, 'I said, you are gods.' If it calls them gods to whom the Word of God came and Scripture cannot be set aside, can you say that the one whom the Father has consecrated and sent into the world blasphemes because I said, 'I am the Son of God'?"[35] Also in another text, he called himself at the same time both the Son of Man and the Son of God, saying, "And just as Moses lifted up the serpent in the desert, so must the Son of Man be lifted up so that everyone who believes in him may have eternal life."[36] When immediately that which has already

32. Gal 1.3–5.
33. Jn 3.16.
34. Jn 9. 35–38.
35. Jn 10.34–36.
36. Jn 3.14–15.

been cited by us in this work, the Savior himself added concerning himself, in which he called himself the Son of God, saying, "For God so loved the world that he gave his only Son, so that everyone who believes in him might not perish but might have eternal life. For God did not send his Son into the world to condemn the world but that the world might be saved through him. Whoever believes in him will not be condemned, but whoever does not believe has already been condemned, because he has not believed in the name of the only Son of God."[37] And when he named himself the Son of Man, saying to his disciples, "Who do people say that the Son of Man is?"[38] And having heard the diversity of human opinions, of those namely who, concerning truth itself, fashioned for themselves of their own free will a death-dealing lie, he said, "But who do you say that I am?"[39] In answer Peter said, "You are the Messiah, the Son of the living God,"[40] for which he deserved to be called blessed, so, with the Lord responding, "Blessed are you, Simon, Son of Jonah, for flesh and blood have not revealed this to you but my heavenly Father."[41]

17. Hence it is that he also bears witness that after the resurrection he is going to ascend to his Father in these words: "I ascend to my Father and your Father, to my God and your God."[42] If, therefore, the God who took on flesh is himself claimed to be God the Father, it is necessary that another be claimed to be the Father of the Father himself and hence God the Father also had a Father, to whom he said, "Father ... give glory to your Son, so that your Son may glorify you."[43] And from this sacrilegious interpretation full of blasphemies, one also falls back into this, that now there is thought to be not one, but two Fathers, i.e., one the Father of the Son, whom truth knows, and the other, the Father of the Father, whom foolishness concocted. Here the Apostle confesses that there is one God the Father: "For us there is

37. Jn 3.16–18. 38. Mt 16.13.
39. Mt 16.15. 40. Mt 16.16.
41. Mt 16.17. 42. Jn 20.17.
43. Jn 17.1.

one God, the Father, from whom all things are and for whom we exist."[44] And in another place: "One God and Father of all, who is over all and through all and in all."[45] Although the Son is by nature one God with him, still according to the persons, one is the Father, the other is the Son. The blessed John clearly shows these persons when he says, "Everyone who loves the Father loves the one begotten by him."[46] Likewise, he says, "In the beginning was the Word and the Word was with God and the Word was God."[47] And a bit later, to show that flesh was taken up by the Word alone, he says, "And the Word became flesh and made his dwelling among us."[48]

18. God the Word became flesh, not God with whom the Word was; because the only-begotten who is in the breast of the Father, as he is flesh, is full of grace, and as he is the Word, he is full of truth. This one is the Word become flesh that dwelt among us. Concerning him the prophet also says, "This is our God; no other can be compared to him. He found the whole way to knowledge and gave her to his servant Jacob and to Israel whom he loved. Afterward she appeared on earth and lived with humankind."[49] True faith accepts this testimony as spoken only of the Son. For he was seen on earth according to the flesh, and lived among human beings. Whence the holy evangelist Matthew with words altogether befitting prophecy says that Jesus lived with his disciples. He says this: "As they were gathering in Galilee, Jesus said to them, 'The Son of Man is to be handed over to men, and they will kill him and he will be raised on the third day.'"[50] Therefore, he had come to be killed for us. How would he be killed, if he were not handed over? Or how would he be handed over, if he were not held? And how would he be held, if he did not live with human beings, or how would he live with human beings, if he is not seen on earth? How would he be seen, if he were not born? But how

44. 1 Cor 8.6.
45. Eph 4.6.
46. 1 Jn 5.1.
47. Jn 1.1–2.
48. Jn 1.14.
49. Bar 3.36–38.
50. Mt 17.21–22.

would he be born, if he were not conceived, flesh from flesh? If all these things did not come to pass, the plan of the Lord, which remains unto eternity, would never be carried out. With that plan useless, no grace of salvation would be conferred on us sinners. And how would that be a true name in him, by which he is called Jesus? For this is interpreted as Savior. Wherefore the angel, telling Joseph that Mary was to give birth to a son, also added this: "You are to name him Jesus, because he will save his people from their sins."[51] To Mary herself, the angel spoke as follows: "Behold, you will conceive in your womb and bear a son and you shall name him Jesus. He will be great and will be called Son of the Most High."[52] Therefore, God the Father is not born of the virgin seeing that he whom the virgin bears will be called Son of the Most High. Since the Father is one and the Son is another and the Holy Spirit a third, so he who by nature is Son of the Most High, from the eternal divinity of the Father, the same Son of the Most High, according to the true faith is called the one from the virgin.

19. Do not be upset by what the prophet said, speaking of the Son alone, "This is our God, no other can be compared to him."[53] From what he said about no other being compared to him, no one should think that, as concerns the person, the Father is the same as the Son. The blessed Jeremiah, filled with the Holy Spirit, says, "This is our God. No other can be compared to him." Since he said first, "This is our God" that in this we might know not to compare another to him because there is no God apart from him. Thus by nature there is no other God apart from the Father, thus there is no other God apart from the Son, nor is there another God apart from the Holy Spirit, because the Father is not one God and the Son, a second God, and the Holy Spirit, a third God, and apart from this God of ours there is no other God. Accordingly, the Father is our God in such a way that there is no other in comparison to him; the Son as well

51. Mt 1.21. 52. Lk 1.31–32.
53. Bar 3.36.

is our God in such a way that there is no other in comparison to him; no less the Holy Spirit as well is our God in such a way that there is no other in comparison to it because apart from this one God, there is no other God. Concerning him, David says, "For who is God except the Lord? And who is a rock besides our God?"[54] And he says of himself: "See now that I, even I, am he; there is no God besides me."[55] Concerning this the blessed James as well says, "You believe that God is one. You do well. Even the demons believe that and tremble."[56]

20. Therefore, by nature no other God will be compared to the Son because no other God will be compared to the Father nor will any other God be compared to the Holy Spirit. In their persons, however, the Father is one, the Son another and the Holy Spirit, a third; nor is the Father himself the one who is the Son nor the Holy Spirit himself the one who is the Father or the Son; but one and the same God the Father and the Son and the Holy Spirit. For the Son himself shows that the Father is different in person and the Holy Spirit is different also, saying, "But there is another who testifies on my behalf and I know that the testimony he gives on my behalf is true."[57] And lest anyone think that this was said about John, a bit later he says, "But I have testimony greater than John's. The works that the Father gave me to accomplish, these works that I perform testify on my behalf that the Father has sent me. Moreover, the Father who sent me has testified on my behalf."[58] He also says that the Holy Spirit is a different person when he says, "If you love me, you will keep my commandments. And I will ask the Father and he will give you another Advocate to be with you always, the Spirit of Truth."[59] Concerning whom he also says in another text, "When the Advocate comes whom I will send you from the Father, the Spirit of Truth that proceeds from the Father, he will testify to me."[60] But the majesty of the Father

54. Ps 17. 32 LXX; Ps 18.31.
55. Dt 32.39.
56. Jas 2.19.
57. Jn 5.32.
58. Jn 5.36–37.
59. Jn 14.15–17.
60. Jn 15.26.

and of the Son and of the Holy Spirit is one which does not move from one place to another. The highest and true divinity cannot move from one place to another, because it is always totally present everywhere. The same one majesty of the Trinity is by nature one infinite divinity. But, as I said above, the Trinity is one nature in such a way that it is not one person. Accordingly, the Son, with the infinity of his majesty, which he has in common with the Father and the Holy Spirit, remaining, has alone taken up human nature into the unity of his person. Wherefore, for him, there is no communion of the flesh taken up with the Father and the Holy Spirit because the person is not common to the Father and the Son and the Holy Spirit.

21. The Trinity as a whole made that form of a servant which the Son alone took up into his person. For he alone is the Word and the evangelist says truly, "The Word became flesh."[61] And to that Word the Father gave the command to become flesh, not to some other word. For the Father has one Word through which he made and makes all things, through which he said and says all things. This Word was sent by the Father when the Word became flesh; but in order that he be sent, the Father did not speak to him with some transitory words. The eternal Word, born of the Father, this is the eternal command of the Father because the eternal generation of the Son is itself the eternal speaking of the Father. This Word then is heard by each one, when the truth of his divinity and Incarnation is recognized. For just as each person has a word in his heart when he thinks and this word is not expressed externally unless clothed in a physical sound, so that when the sound is received, it can come to the attention of others, although that word is manifested by the sound of the speaker, it is never separated from the interior of the heart. And so in a marvelous way, it happens that it all comes to others by means of a physical sound and yet in a spiritual way it all remains in the heart of the speaker. So also the Word of God the Father born from the

---

61. Jn 1.14.

Father, remained in the Father; it would never have been recognized by us if it had not been clothed with the substance of the flesh as with a physical sound. Therefore, while the whole Word came to us when it became flesh, as a spirit, it remained totally with the Father; equal to the Father from whom he was born from eternity and, in order that he could be received by us, lessened, thanks to the flesh accepted. And through this, the Lord born from the Lord, the Lord remained in the form of God, and, that he might come to his servants, from a handmaid he received the true form of a servant.

22. But certain people, with less understanding of the mystery of the acceptance of this form of a servant, when they hear from us that one essence of the Holy Trinity is proclaimed, they either deny or doubt that it could have happened that the Son who is proclaimed by God inseparable from the Father and the Holy Spirit according to the deity both alone accepted for us the true form of a servant and also remained notwithstanding inseparable with the Father and the Holy Spirit. But without a doubt this seems impossible to those who do not catch sight of the invisible things of God through those things which have been made because they do not understand them. If they were to pay attention to the common use of human nature, they would find the right lines of understanding also in that great mystery of piety. Therefore, since one is the true divinity which in itself has three altogether inseparable persons because of which the Trinity itself is one God, and in creatures there is no nature inseparable in three persons, let us turn our attention to what is done in each human person in whom we do not find three persons in one nature, but two natures in one person. In a marvelous work of his power, God, from two natures, i.e., from the rational soul and the flesh, has composed the one nature of a human being and has commanded the one person of a human being to remain in the soul and the flesh. Behold in a human being are two natures in one person, as we say that the Trinity is three persons in one nature.

23. Here let us note that from these two natures remaining in one person, certain things are done in common which are neither accepted nor possessed in common. Namely, we find in ourselves that something comes about in one operation of flesh and soul which we still attribute either to the flesh only or to the soul only. For most certainly, as the flesh alone is fed with bodily foods, so the soul is nourished spiritually by the word of God. And still in order that the flesh which is made from the earth, be fed with earthly foods, with the soul cooperating, inasmuch as life comes from the soul, usefully having one function in itself of working and another of the soul cooperating with it. In this there are present at the same time both from life that it may eat and from foods that it may live. When food is consumed, it is a work common to the flesh and the soul; although the food belongs properly to the flesh only. In receiving the word of God, by which spiritual food the soul alone is fed, in order that it may attain to the same food, it makes use of the function either of the eyes or of the ears. An interior feeding is not achieved without the working of the flesh. Therefore, just as in this case is found the working of each nature, when it is a question of receiving one thing, so we believe that the human nature of the only-begotten God was made at the same time by the Father and the Son and the Holy Spirit, but, mercifully for our salvation, was taken up by the Son alone.

24. You add that one of you at the banquet said afterwards that God did not make flies, fleas, scorpions, and bedbugs, but after the fall of the angel, the unworthy Devil, all these things were made by the Devil himself. And while you were saying that God made all things and these were very good, you said that you ought to consult me about this, so that I might satisfy him about this, whether before the transgression, when God made all things, then these things were made or whether it was after the transgression of Adam. These were the words with which you letter ends. There are two parts to this question. You inquire whether God made all these things and when he made them.

25. First, therefore, I see that there must be a discussion as to whether God made these things. Here the blessed John the evangelist shows us what we ought to believe when he says, "In the beginning was the Word and the Word was with God and the Word was God. He was in the beginning with God. All things came to be through him and without him, nothing came to be."[62] See that the holy evangelist, filled with the Holy Spirit, in a few words has taught us in a salutary way not only about the Creator but also about the creature. For what he says, "In the beginning was the Word," the orthodox faith understands in two ways, i.e., either that the Son was in the Father because by nature the Father and the Son are one principle, or that not only the Father, but also the Son, is without beginning. Most certainly this is called a true beginning because it is preceded by no point of origin. But whatever began to be in the beginning was made by the work of God creating nor can it have one nature with the Creator; for this is subject to a beginning, because God created it from nothing.

Accordingly, that is rightly said to be in the beginning, to which it is natural to exist always apart from any beginning of existence; this eternity without a beginning is true divinity. This is found by nature in the one Son, who was born from the Father, and in the one Holy Spirit who proceeds from the Father and the Son. This, therefore, is what the evangelist is saying, "In the beginning was the Word," just as if he were to say, "The Word always was." Whatever a person wished to think of as a beginning, he does not find that that Word began at some time to whom it is natural not to have begun at some time at the beginning but always to exist in the beginning. Then saying, "And the Word was with God," he shows the nature of the Word is neither temporal nor spatial. For the Word which was in the beginning has nothing from the beginning of time, it has nothing from a spatial location, which was with God before every creature subject to time and space. Then saying, "And the Word was God," he

---

62. Jn 1.1–3.

shows the one nature of the Father and the Son, while he said that the Word which was with God was nothing other than God by nature. The evangelist, speaking first of the Word, uttered the name of a truly existing person which, however, is not common to the Father and the Son. For the Son alone is called the Word.

26. The natural significance demanded that just as the name of a person, so also the name of the nature be shown forth in the Word. Therefore, the blessed evangelist subsequently added: "And the Word was God," and thus fulfilled the duty of holy preaching by introducing not only the person but also the nature of the only-begotten Son of God; so that also calling the Word by the name of the person, he might show forth the Son of the Father; and naming God by the common name, he demonstrated that he was of a single nature with the Father. Then, in order that from the unity of the work, the unity of nature might be urged the more, the blessed evangelist added, "All things were made through him and without him nothing was made." Who said this? Namely, the one who, reclining on the breast of Wisdom itself and of the Truth, received the true knowledge of the incomprehensible majesty; who, just as he knew that the Father and the Son are one God, so also knew that all things were made by the Father through the Son. Whence, St. John so universally understood all these things which were made through the Word that he said, "All things were made through him and without him, nothing was made." Therefore, whoever strives to deny that flies, fleas, scorpions, bedbugs, or whatever else by which mortal sensitivity is offended were made by God so that he may say that they were altogether not made, or if he says they were made but not by the Father through the Son, what else remains except that he say that John the evangelist lied in his preaching? For he said "all things were made through him and without him, nothing was made."

27. Therefore, there is nothing which the Father, who made all things, did not make; nor is there anything which the Father did not make through the Son, without whom

nothing was made. Accordingly, whatever something is by nature, it is necessary that it be assigned among the works of him through whom all things were made and without whom nothing was made. Full of the Truth, the evangelist bears witness that in the teaching of the Holy Spirit, Paul as well, the vessel of election and teacher of the nations in the faith and the truth, did not cease to teach us, saying what we have already cited above: "For us there is one God, the Father, from whom all things are and for whom we exist, and one Lord Jesus Christ, through whom all things are and through whom we exist."[63] He took care to explain all these same things even more clearly in another text: "For in him were created all things in heaven and on earth, the visible and the invisible, whether thrones or dominions or principalities or powers; all things were created through him and for him. He is before all things and in him all things hold together."[64] Lest anyone, hearing that all things in heaven and on earth were created through Christ and in Christ, because the sea is not named here, and he think that those things which are in the waters are alien to the work of the divine creation, first of all, let him pay attention to the beginning of Genesis itself. There, with God commanding, the waters produce swarms of living creatures and the birds which fly over the earth and let him recognize that the creation of the fish and birds in the waters is the same as the Creator on land of the trees and grass, likewise in heaven the Creator of the lights and stars. Just as he knows that God first made the heavens in which he made the lights and stars, earlier made the earth which, at his command, produced grass and trees, so he made the waters from which, as he says, the fish and the birds equally took their origin. Nor would he create something from the waters by the Word, if he had not before made the same waters by the Word. Hence it is that David was not silent about everything—heaven, earth, sea—with all that are in them, having been made by God, when he says,

63. 1 Cor 8.6.
64. Col 1.16–17.

"Happy are those whose help is the God of Jacob, whose hope is in the Lord their God, who made heaven and earth, the sea and all that is in them."[65] Since, therefore, the authority of the prophet bears witness that the heaven, the earth, the sea, and all that is in them, have been made by God, Paul the Apostle also asserts that all things in the heavens and on the earth, visible and invisible, whether thrones or dominions, principalities and powers, were created in the heavens, by what reason or by what truth does someone not wish to believe that flies and scorpions, fleas and bed-bugs have not been created on earth, by the same one whom he cannot deny the thrones, dominions, principalities, and powers were created in Christ? Therefore, must that God who, creating above the heavens, constituted legions of angels, be denied on earth to make scorpions, on the same earth where he made human beings, beasts and cattle, birds and fish?

28. What, I ask you, is so displeasing about scorpions that anyone should think that they are not made by God? For there is nothing in the body of a scorpion which does not suggest the praise of the Creator. First of all, that bodily structure of members, put together and arranged harmoniously, the symmetry and equality of the parts, then the soul giving life and feeling to the body; who would dispute that these are all good things? Without question, that power of poison, which is found to be harmful to human beings, is regarded as something to be dreaded in the body of the scorpion. Would that from it human beings might learn to pay attention to the punishment for transgression and cease lyingly assigning the good works of God to the Devil. For they little notice how strong among the works of God is the fittingness of nature, how profitable his way in individual matters, or how harmful immoderate excess. In cases where God does not permit a great deal of it, who does not also praise the works of God in the very chastisements, when he sees the sinner being punished by divine affliction? For, as it

---

65. Ps 145.5–6 LXX; Ps 146.5–6.

is written, God made the human being straight, whom he thus set as lord over all the things which he had created on land and sea, so that he might subject everything to his power. He demanded the obedience of due servanthood from the one to whom he had given free choice of will. He who served his Lord with fitting devotion, also received the power of unshaken domination over those things to which he himself was superior. He did not lose anything of those things he had received so long as he himself paid what he owed. But, offending the Lord by the transgression of a command, that recalcitrance which he, as a despiser, showed to God, he immediately found in his own body, when he, after he began to be evil, lost control over his own genital organs. How could he remain the master of all those things which he had received from God, who, scorning God, had first lost the rights of mastery over his own body? Hence he came to have a body subject to infirmities and death. From then on, with just retribution following, it came about that he who did not fear the death of the soul in sin, feared the death of the body in pains. Having lost the peace which the blessed one attained, he, very miserable, was pestered by the tiniest animals.

29. And so it was that after the sin of the first human being, because of which human nature is universally subject to the reign of sin and death, the human being is still master of camels, horses, cattle, elephants, and other large quadrupeds but is upset by the bite of a bed-bug and flea. Although all these animals which are greater in body and have greater strength, tamely serve the human race, these tiniest animals which with the greatest of ease can be crushed, held between only two fingers, can never be reduced to harmlessness. It is clear that this has been done by divine judgment, so that from those animals over which the human race is master, it might know how great a dignity it had before the transgression; but from those animals by which it is upset and harmed, it might know how low it had fallen because of the transgression. Into our power God has delivered the greater ones, withdrawn the lesser, at the same time showing

what the goodness of the Creator has brought to human beings and what their own wickedness has inflicted on sinners. Therefore, through the transgression of the first human beings, as the penalty for such a great crime, a severe weakness of nature has come upon the human race. Not that human beings might give in to certain evil natures, but that human weakness might know the punishments and dangers resulting from the dysfunction of good natures. That a flea bother a person and a scorpion kill, this is the result, not of the creation of evil beings, but of the dysfunction of good natures, which followed from the justice of the judge, following upon the wickedness of a recalcitrant person. God, whose true works and right paths the holy Azariah very rightly confesses in his prayer, because he is supremely good, all things whatever that he makes, he makes well.

30. So it is that by a marvelous work he fittingly makes use of even the very dysfunction of natures, by which human sins are punished. Immutable justice which gives to each one his due, does this so that he causes the dysfunction of one to another of whatever nature, to fit in with his works in every case. Any nature while it fits in less with another nature for salvation should not from that be thought evil because it is harmful. For every nature-qua-nature is good. But often when problems are brought upon one nature because of another nature, it gives in to the contradiction and weakness submits. For often even things themselves, i.e., the natures themselves, only those in which there is usually undoubted harm, if they are tempered by fitting moderation from the others, they are changed from being a mortal danger to remedies for health, something we find first of all in the poisonous animals themselves. For certain people say that when a sharp, fiery feeling arises in the body, it is rapidly extinguished by scorpions ground to a powder and applied. But since some may think that this is perhaps uncertain or false, certainly no one is permitted to deny this, that something remarkable is found in snakes. No one is unaware that vipers are poisonous by nature. By a poisonous bite, they kill much more rapidly than scorpions kill with a poisonous sting; and

still, in order that it be shown that not evilness of natures but dysfunction harms, we know that from the flesh of vipers, tempered by some other fitting things, medicines are made against the bite of vipers. They are usefully applied, not only for those who are stung by scorpions but also for those who will be bitten by vipers. Who would not admire the wisdom of God in this? Who would not glorify his goodness and praise his providence? He does not shut up[66] his compassion in anger for from the source from which he made dangers arise for sinners, from the same source he made assistance available for those exposed to danger, so that from the source from which we believe there came misfortunes because of our iniquity, we know that there are gifts from his goodness as well. Who may make known the praise of the Creator with adequate words when he so created one and the same viper that at the same time it bears in itself both destruction and healing? While living, it brings death but when dead, it restores health. Who, I ask, does these things, except the one to whom the Church sings of mercy and judgment?

31. Who is unaware of how bad the species called scammony[67] is for the healthy, if taken by itself, and how useful it is for the sick if correctly mixed with other types? And in order that I speak of these things which are always sought by all and by whose daily use not only illness but even the very health of human life is found to be in need of, let us speak of bread and wine, of which neither one is right for the person with a fever. For we observe that the drinking of wine and sometimes even bread are forbidden by doctors to the sick. This happens, not because bread and wine are bad, but because they are not right for the sick person. For later on when they begin to be appropriate, food contributes to the strengthening and preservation of health; but their immoderate consumption takes away strength from the strong

---

66. In the Latin text of CCL XCI, 338, lines 846–47, I believe that 'continet' is to be preferred to 'contineris'.

67. Scammony or convolvulus, some types of which produce a milky juice which is used as a purgative.

while it makes the healthy ill. See how important are God's way and the coherence of things, for his creatures for whom lack of moderation and dysfunction are contraindicated. When nature is damaged, there is not the malice of nature but resulting illness for them as anyone will easily find, in the case of almost all creatures, whoever thus considers that they have been created good by the highest Good in such a way that he recognizes in them the inexpressible and indescribable goodness of the Creator. Because of this, he must be loved before all else, he who is bound to be both merciful and just even in those things we realize are punishments for our wickedness. He raises up the weak from the same place he crushes the recalcitrant. Because when pride goes before, misery has immediately overtaken the person, the merciful and just God, from the source from which he puts pressure on pride, from the same source he brings to bear comfort for wretchedness.

32. So, that son of the Church, who, as you say, proposed these things, asserting that flies, scorpions, fleas, and bedbugs were made not by God but by the Devil, should be careful lest he be deceived and seduced by the death-dealing cleverness of the Manichees who, stuck in darkness as they are, strive to bring in a god of light and a god of darkness and to proclaim two principles by nature, contrary to each other. Because they say that the nature of light is good and the nature of darkness bad, they are led by their own error to this, that they do not hesitate to assert that in all the things that are in the world, some are good but some are bad natures. They say that those are bad by which their senses are offended and those good by which they are soothed by enjoyment, "without understanding" as the Apostle says, "what they are saying or what they assert."[68] To say something about light and darkness, whose natures, in principle, they think are contrary: Is not, first of all, their assertion about these things false because darkness, which they say is contrary to light by nature, in fact has no nature? Light and

---

68. 1 Tm 1.7. On Manichaeism, see EEC I.519–20.

darkness are not two natures. Where there is no light, there the very absence of light is called darkness by name; just as the absence of sound is called silence, just as the absence of clothes is called nudity; just as a vessel into which no substance either of liquid or anything else is poured is called empty; just as in ourselves, it is called hunger where there is no food; it is called thirst where there is nothing to drink.

33. Therefore, all these things which I have recalled and things similar to them, about which up to now I have remained silent in order to keep a certain moderation in this discussion, are indeed without a doubt, contraries, not, however, through their own natures but through presence and absence, i.e., that contrariety by which either something is possessed or something is not possessed. Accordingly, although they are contraries, their effects are not always contrary; for that physical light which the Manichaeans think is the principal good, because it is good, since it has been created by the highest good, insofar as it is good, that the substance of life must naturally be given precedence over it. Although it is good, sometimes it does not become salutary but punishing for those who use it in an unfitting way. It strengthens healthy eyes but causes pain to sick eyes; it refreshes those who are all right and assails those who suffer. On the contrary, suffering eyes gain some rest from darkness and when the doors and windows are closed they feel some relief from that pain which they suffer because of the light and are strengthened to see the light by a certain fittingness of the darkness. See how the light is less fitting, the more it damages; and the darkness is the more fitting, the more it is helpful and just as the brightness of the light helps healthy eyes, so the obscurity of the darkness has usually helped those in pain. Because of this, when something is done in the right way, the one effect of light and darkness is to help the eyes. For just as the healthy are aided by the light, so the ill are refreshed by the darkness. For when the weary are lost in sleep, in some way they are aided by the darkness so that, seeing again, by means of light, they are restored, vigorous, and strong. As for sick and tired eyes, being removed from

the good light restores health and strength, so it is for the whole body, if when it is sick, it is kept from consuming its usual nourishment. But these are not contrary to the sick and harmful to them because they are evil by nature but because they are not right for their illness; for sickness does not endure all the things which health takes. So often the infirmities of the body are made worse by those same things by which a healthy body is refreshed. So that sometimes a healthy body is helped by the use of these things which, taken in excess, are harmful, and when some thing is taken for reasons of preserving health in an unfitting way, illness results. The very use of clothing as well, if used in an unfitting way, will be able to harm, not help. Whether because of some lack or by illness of body, who does not do harm to himself by using either winter clothes when he feels hot or summer clothes when it is cold.

34. It is tedious to point out indications of fittingness by many examples when they cannot be missed by those who are observant. Accordingly, all natures which exist, which live, which are conscious, which understand, since they have been made by God, i.e., by the supreme Good, are good. If they were not made by the highest Good, they would not be good; and if they were not good, they would not have anything good in themselves. And first, because life is something good and such a good that it is loved by all living beings, if there were any nature that was not made by the supreme Good, it could never exist. I say this concerning animals, i.e., concerning a substance which lives and feels; but as for those natures which neither live nor feel, this itself—that they exist—they have from the creation of him who is good in the supreme degree, because not only to live but also to exist is good, and what exists in the supreme degree is the Supreme Good.

35. Therefore, there is no evil nature, whether living or not living; and because of this, all natures, because they are natures, are good. But certain of them, although they are good from the creation of God, have become punishments for human beings for the punishment of sin, not because of

their own nature, but because of human guilt. Whence it has been shown to the person made in the image of God how much evil he has brought on himself who has been brought to this, so that the ruin of death is inflicted on him by small animals. So, in all animals, in all plants, and in all creatures generally, whatever a human being discerns is deadly for himself, let him not say that there is an evil nature in them, but let him recognize in them vengeance for his own wickedness. For we have been brought low by fleas and bed-bugs, after we were recalcitrant to God; and the sting of the scorpion has become mortal for a human being, after, of his own accord, he preferred to be wounded by the sting of death. For "the sting of death is sin."[69] By that sting, the human race first wounded itself unto death in such a way that he made it also pass to and through his offspring. This happened in such a way that even in those in whom the grace of God overcomes the reign of sin, frequent and multiple dangers from the punishment for sin would not be lacking. So it is that in this mortal life, even just people and those living holy lives are not free from troubles and dangers of this kind because as long as they live in this life, they are not free from sin. So the blessed John says, "If we say we are without sin, we deceive ourselves and the truth is not in us."[70] The holy Apostle James also bears witness that "we all fall short in many respects."[71]

36. But the sins of the saints are not like those of the wicked. For the sins of the saints are light; the sins of the wicked are serious. Among the sins of the wicked, either human perversity thinks wrongly about God or human lust brings a person to the desires of the flesh or human cruelty harms the neighbor. Concerning those who sin against God, Wisdom says, "But those who miss me injure themselves; all who hate me love death."[72] Concerning those who live in a depraved way, the Apostle says, "If anyone destroys God's Temple, God will destroy that person; for the Temple of

---

69. 1 Cor 15.56.
71. Jas 3.2.
70. 1 Jn 1.8.
72. Prov 8.36.

God, which you are, is holy. Let no one deceive himself."[73] Speaking about hatred for one's brother, the blessed John says, "Whoever says he is in the light, yet hates his brother, is still in the darkness. Whoever loves his brother remains in the light, and there is nothing in him to cause a fall. Whoever hates his brother is in darkness; he walks in darkness and does not know where he is going because the darkness has blinded his eyes."[74]

37. The sins of the wicked come about in three ways. Either they are bound up with sacrileges or vices or crimes. For they commit sacrilege when they do not believe rightly concerning God and depart from the true faith either because of fear of temporal misfortunes or desire for temporal advantages or by blindness or perversity of heart alone. They sin by vice when unrestrained or obscene in themselves; they live in a shameful fashion. Then they sin by crimes when they cruelly harm others, either by damages or by some kind of oppression. The blessed Apostle calls both of them reprobate whether sinning capitally in faith or in works, saying about those who contradict the true faith, "Just as Jamnes and Jambres opposed Moses, so they also oppose the truth, people of depraved mind, unqualified in the faith."[75] In a similar way, rebuking those who under the profession of the true faith live in evil deeds and crimes, he says, "To the clean, all things are clean, but to those who are defiled and unbelieving, nothing is clean; in fact, both their minds and their consciences are tainted. They claim to know God but by their deeds they deny him. They are vile and disobedient and unqualified for any good deed."[76] But when the saints sin, they fall in some sin by human weakness or human pleasure in such a way that they neither contradict the true faith in a pertinacious way nor do they pollute themselves with vices nor do they harm their neighbors by crimes. The blessed Apostle shows this when he says, "For the grace of God has appeared, saving all and training us to reject god-

---

73. 1 Cor 3.17–18.
74. 1 Jn 2.9–11.
75. 2 Tm 3.8.
76. Ti 1.15–16.

less ways and worldly desires and to live temperately, justly, and devoutly in this age."[77] In another text, the same blessed Apostle warns us "not to think more highly of ourselves than one ought to think, but to think soberly."[78] And so in this tripartite division in which he says that we live soberly and justly and devoutly, it seems to me that he lives soberly who does not follow the pleasures of depravity; he lives justly who never harms his neighbor and is beneficent toward him insofar as he is able; he lives devoutly who for no reason will depart the community of the unity of the Church and within the Church without hesitation holds those things he knows most certainly belong to the knowledge of the true faith. But those things of which he is unaware, concerning which he has doubts, he inquires into with humility and patience until, if there is something about which he thinks otherwise, he will come to know it with God revealing it to him.

38. But this sobriety, justice, and devotion which should be in all the faithful are so linked among themselves that if one of them is absent, the others which seem to be present are useless. That sobriety by which anyone abstains from vices does not save unless it be devout and just, i.e., that it both believe rightly in God and freely expends on the neighbor what charity demands. Justice, by which each one expends on his neighbor that which he delights to expend on himself, is not fruitful if it is not sober and devout. Devotion, by which there is right belief in God, is dead if either sobriety of morals or charity toward the neighbor is not held. Therefore, true salvation for the soul is acquired if both devotion in faith and justice in charity and sobriety in chastity and frugality are held.

39. According to the divine words, it is one thing for the saints to sin and another for the wicked. Hagar,[79] the maidservant of Sarah, would not have been driven out unless she had been proud, and Sarah herself would not have been guilty unless she laughed. The former became proud, seeing

77. Ti 2.11–12.
78. Rm 12.3.
79. See Gen 21.10f.

that she had conceived; the latter laughed, doubting that she would conceive. Each sinned but the sins are not equal. In one of them human weakness doubted; in the other, human boldness exalted itself rebelliously. Therefore, Hagar deserved to be driven out by command of the divine severity, but Sarah deserved to be blamed by the calm leniency of the divine voice. And because the sin in that doubting was light, confirmed by the word of the divine promise, she put aside the doubt and received most certain faith, through which she also received the power to conceive, as the authority of the Apostle bears witness, saying, "By faith, Sarah herself, received the power to conceive, even though she was past the normal age, for she thought that the one who had made the promise was trustworthy."[80]

40. In another text, we have found that the sins of the saints and of the wicked are not equal. The sins of the former are light and need to be purged by correction in time; but the sins of the latter are serious and deserve to be punished by the endless burning of eternal fire. For at the waters of contradiction, the sons of Israel sinned in one way, rebels against God in every way; Moses, in another way, who contradicted God, not through boldness but through weakness, presumed too little about God's workings; he became like the blessed Peter who heard from the Lord: "O you of little faith, why did you doubt?"[81] So the rebelliousness of the Israelites deserved to be condemned with eternal punishment; but in Moses's case, the punishment of his sin amounted to this, that only entrance into the promised land was denied him. Moses himself has borne witness that the Lord was angry with him, not on account of his own sin, but on account of them, saying in Deuteronomy, "Even with me the Lord was angry, on your account, saying, 'You also shall not enter there.'"[82] Holy David as well shows that Moses was afflicted because of the sin of the people. "They angered the Lord at the waters of Meribah, and it went ill with Moses on their account."[83] The people angered the Lord; Moses

80. Heb 11.11.
82. Dt 1.37.
81. Mt 14.31.
83. Ps 105.32 LXX; Ps 106.32.

doubted about a work of the Lord; and because the sins of anger and doubt were not equal, the holy Moses, although he was afflicted on their behalf, still he was not condemned with them to eternal punishment.

41. And in order that we may briefly take a look at something found in human day-to-day living, from which we may the more easily take an example, let us have a look at the souls of baptized men, as well as the women joined to them in marriage. For the Apostle points out the great mystery of marriage itself in Christ and in the Church. So a soul faithfully cleaving to Christ is just like a wife living faithfully with her husband. In the very chastity of her marriage, she often saddens the spirit of her husband but preserves the faith of the marriage bed with pure chastity. She dispenses her husband's property prudently and temperately. In this, she both sins against her husband and still lives chastely and faithfully with her husband. As human weakness sometimes causes her to sin in the eyes of her husband, conjugal chastity makes her happy to remain attached to her husband. But that woman who, whether leaving her husband's house or, in the very dwelling of her husband, becomes involved in adultery, or wastes her husband's property, is not judged worthy of forgiveness, but is held liable to mortal guilt. So the soul which, giving in to the Devil, is either brought down by infidelity or caught up in crimes.

42. Concerning these people, the Apostle says that "neither fornicators nor idolaters, nor adulterers, nor boy prostitutes, nor practicing homosexuals, nor thieves nor the greedy, nor drunkards, nor slanderers, nor robbers will inherit the kingdom of God."[84] But concerning those who sin lightly, it is said: "for though they fall seven times, they will rise again."[85] This one is said to sin and still is called truly a just person. For he does not fall in such a way so as to cease being a just person because it is written: "Though we stumble, we shall not fall headlong, for the Lord holds us by the hand."[86] Therefore, the Lord is still present to the just per-

---

84. 1 Cor 6.9–10.　　　　　　85. Prov 24.16.
86. Ps 36.24 LXX; Ps 37.24.

son who falls because he does not sin in such a way that the Lord departs from him. For the weakness of the flesh, he has concupiscence, but he does not give in to the concupiscence, having been strengthened by the power of the grace of the Spirit. Concupiscence itself is the law of sin, found even in the members of the saints, from which, however, the grace of God through Jesus Christ our Lord frees the just who are his own. Christ who "bore our sins in his body on the cross, so that, free from sin, we might live for righteousness."[87] When the just person falls, he contracts debts; but the debts of the just person are such as can be forgiven in daily prayer, when he truthfully says, "Forgive us our debts as we forgive our debtors."[88]

43. Therefore, the sins of the saints are from necessity of weakness; the sins of the wicked are from the intention of the worst will. In the former, the birth of sin is such that the effect does not follow. Because although it is born through weakness, it is overcome by the grace of God. The bad will drives those deprived of the help of grace wherever depraved lust leads. Therefore, the faults of the saints are called sins, not crimes, for which they are corrected by a father in such a way that they are not condemned by a judge. This correction belongs to judgment but a fatherly one by which God mercifully both judges and beats his children, so that he snatches them away from the punishment of eternal damnation. The blessed Apostle, showing this, says, "If we discerned ourselves, we would not be under judgment; but since we are judged by the Lord, we are being disciplined so that we may not be condemned along with the world."[89] The blessed Peter also affirms this, saying, "For it is time for the judgment to begin with the household of God; if it begins with us, how will it end for those who fail to obey the Gospel of God? And if the righteous one is barely saved, where will the godless and the sinner appear?"[90]

44. No faithful and wise person calls the faith of the saints weak, if he sees the distress of any adversity happen to them

---

87. 1 Pt 2.24.
89. 1 Cor 11.31–32.

88. Mt 6.12.
90. 1 Pt 4.17–18.

in the time of this life. For bodily health and weakness are found to be common to the faithful and the unfaithful, to good and evil; and so the adversity of bodily illness touches both in common, because sometimes health also is given in time to both in common. The just are distinguished from the wicked not by the state of their body but by faith and life. Therefore, at the same time, they bear in the body the troubles and dangers of the present life which they put up with in fact with a different intention. They do not groan equally in the evils of this life because they do not equally love the good things of this life. The wicked want this: to have a peaceful life now, without problems, so that they do not lack transitory and temporal goods. The just hate the dangers and troubles of the present life so that they may enjoy God whom they love, seeking true rest in him, in whom they hope to have eternal blessedness. Accordingly, they do not love temporal goods, which they know will quickly disappear. When they use them, they do not seek the fulfillment of greed but the means whereby charity may be restored and weakness kept from collapse; they do not seek from them joy as from personal pleasure but some modest consolation like provisions for the road when they are available.

45. And since we are currently discussing the view of that person who does not believe that flies and scorpions, fleas and bed-bugs could have been made by God, this also one must be wary of, lest someone come up with this idea, altogether foreign to the Catholic faith, not from the errors of the Manichaeans, but from a reading of the divine Scriptures: ". . . the law is good, provided that one uses it as law."[91] He does not use the law legitimately who, concerning the words of the law, does not understand that which should be understood. I say this because we read in Exodus that the rod of Moses which Aaron carried was turned into a serpent by God's work; there it is also said that Pharaoh's magicians, whom the Apostle calls Jamnes and Mambres, did as much

91. 1 Tm 1.8.

so that by magical incantations, their rods were turned into serpents. Then, when Aaron struck the waters of the river and they were turned into blood, Holy Scripture recalls that they did the like by their incantations. Afterwards, when the waters were struck, and Aaron brought forth frogs which covered the land of Egypt at once, those sorcerers are said to have done similar things, relying on their accursed arts. But afterwards, it came about, that, when the earth was struck, gnats were produced, the evil of the magical art was not able to do anything like it. Where first the one who asserts that flies were made by the Devil, knows that he is a liar, seeing that the Devil and his angels, even when they were permitted to do other things, failed when it came to flies. So, who does not see that whether it be serpents from rods or frogs produced from the waters, that the renegade angels made them because God permitted it; but gnats, i.e., flies, they were not able to make because God did not permit it?

46. Sometimes by the hidden and incomprehensible judgment of God, the bad angels are permitted to make certain things to test the good and seduce the evil. But they themselves do not create what they make but they are permitted to bring forth something which we can see from the hidden breast of the Creator God, which we cannot see. As the Devil was not able to create serpents or frogs, although with God's permission he brought them forth, just as he was not the creator of the fire when, to test Job he, with fire falling from heaven, consumed his sheep together with the shepherds. Nor was he the creator of the wind, when a wicked wind blowing out of the desert, struck the four corners of the house and crushed all the children of holy Job in one simultaneous ruin. The omnipotent God alone created the various natures, i.e., the elements of this world. In secret and hidden places, he sets certain seeds of things, hidden to us, but visible to the angels, from which, as the opportuneness of the work and time require, by the hidden counsel of his wisdom, God either commands that certain things be brought forth by the good angels or permits them to be shown through the bad angels. By permitting these latter

things, God shows how much power he has given to the holy angels when he has given the ability to do certain things in the material creation even to the wicked angels. And so it is that our Savior did not stop forewarning his faithful, saying, "False Messiahs and false prophets will arise and they will perform signs and wonders so great as to deceive, if that were possible, even the elect."[92] And the blessed Apostle, speaking of the Antichrist, says, "And thus the lawless one will be revealed when the Lord Jesus will kill with the breath of his mouth and render powerless by the manifestation of his coming, the one whose coming springs from the power of Satan in every mighty deed and in signs and wonders that lie, and in every wicked deceit for those who are perishing because they have not accepted the love of truth so that they may be saved. Therefore, God is sending them a deceiving power so that they may believe the lie, that all who have not believed the truth but have approved wrongdoing may be condemned."[93]

47. By these testimonies and others of a similar nature, we shall know that all natures have been created by God's work. Whenever we are harmed it is not nature that ought to be declared evil but found unpleasant to us because of our weakness. Hence the fitting admonition is applied to us so that with a humble heart, we fear the justice of divine power. No wise person either believes or says that not only the bad but even the good angels are creators of natures. For God, as we said above, made all things in wisdom, which wisdom "reaches mightily from one end of the earth to the other, and orders all things well."[94] Therefore, he orders all things because in it the Father made all things. Therefore, just as God in wisdom created the angels in heaven, so in it he created maggots on earth; and he who placed thrones, dominions, principalities, and powers on high, on earth made scorpions, fleas, and bed-bugs. He who created the hen, created the fly as well; but he gave the latter by which the proud one

92. Mt 24.24.
94. Wis 8.1.

93. 2 Thes 2.8–12.

is put to confusion; the former by which strength is restored to the weak. Hence, it is that willingly one gets food from the former, unwillingly one suffers a feeling of disgust from the latter; so that at least this one receives not only comfort from God from the former; but also is forced to recognize what his sin deserves in the latter.

48. Accordingly, let that person see to it that he is not seduced by that name by which Beelzebub, the prince of demons is called in the Gospel, which is interpreted as 'Prince of the flies'. This has not been said because the Devil could create flies; it is one thing to be a prince, another to be a creator. For the angel, speaking to Daniel the prophet, says "So, Michael, one of the chief princes, came to help me."[95] And a little later: "There is no one with me, who contends against these princes except Michael, your prince."[96] We find that not only angels but human beings as well are given the title 'prince'. For it is written: "The princes of the peoples gather as the people of the God of Abraham."[97] And it is said to the Church: "In place of your ancestors, you, O king, shall have sons; you will make them princes in all the earth."[98] And in the books of Moses, we know they are called "princes according to the tribes."[99] Even though human beings or angels are called princes, they must not be called creators, not only of angels and human beings, but even of certain irrational animals or certain bodies. For even Beelzebub himself, whose name is interpreted as prince of the flies, is called prince of the demons; he rules over them as the first author and instigator of wickedness, not as creator and founder of their nature. For the evil angels have God as the maker of their nature; but they have the Devil as the source of their wickedness. The whole multitude of rebel angels was made good by God, by whose free kindness they arose in order to exist; by their own will, they adhered to the Devil, that they might fall. Accordingly, he is called their prince not because he created them but because he drew them with

95. Dn 10.13.
96. Dn 10.21.
97. Ps 46.10 LXX; Ps 47.9.
98. Ps 44.17 LXX; Ps 45.16.
99. Cf. Gen 25.16.

him into the fall for their destruction. Therefore, what is called the prince of flies is shown to be prince of the wicked; another text of Scripture refers to him by saying, "Dead flies destroy the perfumer's sweet ointment."[100] Who destroy except those who grieve the Holy Spirit either by the crime of infidelity or by the filthy obscenity of unclean deeds, while befouling themselves either with a false faith or an evil way of life? With great concern, the Apostle forbids this, saying, "And do not grieve the Holy Spirit of God with which you were sealed for the day of redemption."[101]

49. They destroy in themselves the oil of sweetness, they who do not make use of the mystery of spiritual grace with the right order of life. The oil cannot be destroyed by those who destroy just as the Holy Spirit is unable to feel any sadness when the same ones cause grief in accord with their bad will. For, concerning the Son of God himself, it is said to the Hebrews: "Do you not think that a much worse punishment is due the one who has contempt for the Son of God?"[102] Christ is the Son of God, the power of God, and the wisdom of God, which is never trampled upon, because he is never stained. Concerning it, it is said in the book of Wisdom: ". . . because of her pureness, she pervades and penetrates all things; . . . therefore nothing defiled gains entrance into her. For she is a reflection of eternal light, a spotless mirror of the working of God, and an image of his goodness."[103] Therefore, the evil grieve the Holy Spirit but the Holy Spirit cannot be grieved; the evil trample on the Son of God but the Son of God is never trampled upon.

50. While the evil are said to grieve the Holy Spirit and trample on the Son of God, the Son of God and the Holy Spirit each remains ungrievable and untrampleable, just as the Savior says in the Gospel, "Every one who looks at a woman with lust has already committed adultery with her in his heart."[104] If while he is committing adultery, she remains chaste, how much more does the divine substance of the

100. Eccl 10.1.
101. Eph 4.30.
102. Heb 10.29.
103. Wis 7.24–26.
104. Mt 5.28.

Son of God and of the Holy Spirit remain without sadness and in bliss even though the evil try to cause grief and to trample!

51. Let none of the faithful say that any nature could have been created by the Devil at the beginning; lest, while he affirms that certain animals arose with the Devil as creator, they consequently also ascribe those things from which they take their origin to the workings of the Devil. For certain types of flies originate either from the excrement of bodies or from rotten plants or flesh. Often we see some flies born even from vegetables. The corn weevil is accustomed to exist in corn. Whoever asserts that animals of this sort were created not by God, but by the Devil, why does he not also assert that wood, grains, vegetables, plants, and flesh from which they are born, have been made by the Devil? Consequently, when he sees worms taking their origin, not only from human cadavers, but also from living bodies, since sometimes the meaning of carnal human mortality is shown by worms, he will claim without a doubt that the Devil is also the author of human bodies. But when everyone who believes rightly and understands rightly, does not dare to assign the origins of any creature to the good angels, how does he assign the power or ability to create any kind of animal to that angel cast down and excluded from his divinity by the vice of his own corruption? This is what no one would dare to assign to him even if he had remained in the angelic dignity without any vice.

52. Not without purpose at the very beginning of Genesis, does Scripture, speaking of all things which have been made, confirm that God made all things, saying of each thing, "And God made it and God saw that it was good."[105] And he finished all these things on the sixth day in which nothing could be missing which he made afterwards. Because God, foreknowing what is to come, just as he knew that human beings would sin, so, of all the things which he made, he salutarily prepared not only consolations but also

---

105. Gen 1.

scourges for him. For it is the same hand of the good father which gave to his son both food and punishment; the first that he may live, the second that he may live well; the first lest he faint from weakness, the other that he, lacking discipline, not scorn his father's commandments, "for whom the Lord loves, he disciplines . . . ; he scourges every son he acknowledges."[106] The abundance of temporal goods is of no avail, if someone, by an evil life, lacks eternal goods. If he lacks them, it is necessary that he be given over to eternal evils which he is unable to be without.

53. Therefore, let each one restrain the boldness of his thought. Just as there are things in which he delights, so also let him not doubt that these things by which he is offended were also naturally made by God. His wisdom which reaches mightily from one end of the earth to the other and orders all things sweetly,[107] shows the beauty of his creation even in those things which corruption destroys; also, in the tiniest animals, showing the splendor of each one of its kind. He made the tiniest flies, however much smaller they are than the great elephants, they are so much more agile. Although there is in each such a difference in the size of the members, there is no difference in the praise for the divine work. For who is a sound thinker and seeing the invisible things of God, understood through those things which have been created, does not praise God the Creator in the maggot as he praises him in the elephant? Or would not praise the same in the flea whom he praises in the cow? For as much as the spirit is accustomed to praise those markings which the diligent activity of craftsmen accomplished in jewels, with how much more wonder will the sight look upon even smaller things?

54. It must be confessed, therefore, that God created all things. But these things by which human transgression is afflicted by the divine will, when it is sought whether they were created by God before Adam sinned or after he sinned, the

106. Heb 12.6.
107. Cf. Wis 8.1.

appropriate answer is that these things, born either from the waters or from the earth, were established when God created them at the very beginning, by the Creator who not only knew the nature of the human being which he made but also marvelously foreknew that the same human beings would sin. Nor did he make those things in such a way that before sin, the human being would either recognize them as harmful or fear them. So no touch of an earthly creature could harm him since, by divine gift, he had been set up as lord of all things. The transgression of the human being himself, not the work of the Creator, made these things harmful and ruinous for a human being. The kindness of the one who created did not do this but the justice of the one who judges.

55. Those things which we see arise from the rotting of flesh or of fruits, we say that they did not arise when in those six days, God made everything very good; but those things were made in such a way that in time those other things might later be born from them. Even human flesh has become subject to that corruption when it is written: "Mortals cannot abide in their pomp; they are like the animals that perish,"[108] so that the necessity of corruption and death always dominate the body of the sinner. From those two evils, the bodies of the just must be freed through the grace of God; but not in this time in which, just as God "makes his sun rise on the good and the bad, and causes rain to fall on the just and the unjust . . . ,"[109] so also he caused not only Herod the unbeliever to be consumed by worms, but also he permitted his servant Job to break out with sores and worms. But in the future, the bodies of the just will feel no troubles of corruption and mortality, when that in them which is corruptible will put on incorruptibility and that which is mortal will put on immortality. In that life of the good and that misery of the evil, whatever will be, whether for the good or for the evil, will be full and eternal. There consolations will not

---

108. Ps 48.13 LXX; Ps 49.12.
109. Mt 5.45.

be mixed with sufferings nor will sufferings be added to the consolations. There the eternity of joys and tortures will remain without end. The evil will not hope for joys nor the good fear sadness. An eternal rejoicing of minds will always continue in the good, and wailing and gnashing of teeth will persist in the evil. The company of demons will hold the wicked for eternity, but equality to the holy angels will take up the blessed just forever.

56. Accordingly, singing to God of mercy and judgment, let us not scorn the time of mercy, so that we may come to the judgment without dread. Let us hope for a judge whom we know as the Redeemer. Let our works be those for which eternal rewards are given. Just as we fear and avoid the troubles of the present time, so we must give thought to how much we must flee eternal punishments. Let us keep away from evils and do good things; in the time of divine retribution, everyone will find that which he desires from his works here, as the Apostle says, "A person will reap only what he sows because the one who sows for his flesh will reap corruption from the flesh, but the one who sows for the spirit will reap eternal life from the spirit."[110] So the same Apostle warns us, saying, "For if you live according to the flesh, you will die, but if by the spirit, you put to death the deeds of the body, you will live."[111] Therefore, let us here put to death in spirit the deeds of the flesh and, dead to sin, let us live for God. Let not the prosperity of the world corrupt us nor its adversity break us. In heart, let us migrate from living in this world, from which we are rapidly going to migrate in the body; that that heavenly dwelling may receive us, concerning which the Apostle says that we have an eternal dwelling from God, a house not made by hands, in the heavens. Concerning this dwelling it has been written: "Happy are those who live in your house, ever singing your praise."[112] There, just as there is an eternal dwelling, so there is eternal praise. Those who live there always praise God because they are always ex-

---

110. Gal 6.7–8.
112. Ps 83.5 LXX; Ps 84.4.

111. Rm 8.13.

ulting about God and in God; and just as for those who give praise, there is the sweet eternity of a holy dwelling, so the eternal sweetness of giving praise remains for those who dwell there.

LETTERS 11 AND 12.
BETWEEN FERRANDUS AND FULGENTIUS

It is generally agreed that the two exchanges of letters between Fulgentius and Ferrandus date to the final period of the former's life, the time after his return to Africa from the second period of exile in Sardinia. Langlois suggests that chronologically the second exchange (letters 13 and 14) precedes the first (letters 11 and 12).

The main burden of Ferrandus's question in letter 11 revolves around the issue of a young man who was proceeding satisfactorily through the stages of the catechumenate but who became seriously ill and moribund before the actual conferral of the sacrament. Was his baptism valid and efficacious? Could even the baptized be saved without receiving the Eucharist?

LETTER 11. THE LETTER OF FERRANDUS
TO FULGENTIUS

ERRANDUS THE DEACON sends greetings in the Lord to the most blessed and holy Father, Bishop Fulgentius, to be received with all veneration.

1. Those who are lacking in earthly goods and who are not fed by the continual labor of daily work or the industry of honest artisanship, or perhaps by profitable business, are accustomed, after hunger has eliminated shame, to seek their sustenance before the gates of rich people, breathing prayers, and to assault the kindly ears of noblemen with at times relentless begging. For beggars know that silence will get them nowhere. But I, who labor under shortage of the poor person's inventiveness and with few cares barking, am permitted to work for the food of wisdom by daily meditation on the divine text. In addition, being less able with my

11. FERRANDUS TO FULGENTIUS

own strength, i.e., with my discussions or thoughts, to investigate doubtful things, to explain obscure things, to distinguish and define contrary things, I pound on the door of the heavenly Father with repeated groans. But when again I, to whom it is opened as quickly as I wish, convict myself of being unworthy, then with suppliant voice I beseech those who have received from the inner chambers of the king the money of my Lord to dispense, that they may deign to relieve our hunger with at least modest resources.

Because you desire to multiply the profits of one of those talents entrusted to you and you share without consuming envy the most precious pearl of the heavenly scribe which, after having expended all you had, as a most faithful merchant, you procured to be generally acquired, possessed, and enjoyed, bring forth from your treasure, I beg you, out standing dispenser, at the same time new things and old, with which you may enrich the needy, feed the hungry, teach the unlearned, show to the hesitant what road to follow.

2. The slave of a certain religious man, an adolescent in age, an Ethiopian in color, from, I believe, the furthest parts of a barbarous province, where the dry parts of human beings are blackened by the heat of the fiery sun, was brought forward. He had not yet been cleansed by the sprinkling of the saving bath or whitened by the glittering grace of Christ. Therefore, because of the zeal of his Christian owner, he was handed over to the Church to be initiated into the ecclesiastical sacraments, becoming, according to custom, a catechumen. After a very brief period, as the paschal solemnity was approaching, he was presented, enrolled, and instructed among the *competentes*.[1] Knowing and grasping all the venerable mysteries of the Catholic religion, when the scrutiny had been solemnly celebrated, he was reclaimed from the Devil by the exorcism. He renounced him without hesitation and, as custom here required, was brought forward to hear the Creed. Further, with clear voice, in the sight of the faithful

---

1. *'Competentes'*: Within the catechumenate, those chosen for baptism on the next Easter vigil.

people, pronouncing the words of the holy Creed from memory, he received the pious rule of the Lord's prayer. Now understanding at the same time both what to believe and what to say in prayer, he was being prepared for the coming baptism, when suddenly he was overtaken by violent fevers and was in agony as the deadly illness grew. The shortness of time persuaded us that he should be put off to be washed at the fountain with the others or, rather, held back. Why go on with more details? The hour wished for by all arrived, in which the acquired people, buried with their Redeemer through baptism, laid aside the old life and, renewed, took up the new faith of the Resurrection. Then he, at his last breath, without a word, without a movement, without senses, unable to answer the priest posing the questions, was brought forward by presenting hands. Totally absent in mind, he received baptism, while we answered for him as for an infant. Dying a little while later, as far as I can see, he never realized that he had received it in this present life.

3. Now I ask whether the fact that his voice had been taken away did him any harm as regards the gaining of eternal happiness. For I greatly fear lest the Lord, to whom all things are possible, denied him the ability to speak because he judged him unworthy of the blessing of a second birth. For I do not see how that age, capable of reason, could be purified by someone else's confession. Do we not believe rightly that only children, who we know are damned only because of original sin, are saved by the faith of those who bring them? With the divine justice doing this in marvelous ways so that in some way where one's own, i.e., actual, sin is found not at all and one's own will is not required; but through the abundance of grace, through the faith of others, salvation is given to those to whom guilt has been attributed. But this man lived by his own free will; beyond that which he took from his roots, without a doubt he, overcome by his own concupiscence, contracted many things. Bound by the chains of many sins, he will not be saved except by his own freely-willed faith which in that place of redemption, he neither willed nor was able to confess. Knowing nothing, he

was altogether unable to will anything. Or perhaps the past confession when he was conscious merited the forgiveness of sins when he was unconscious? But I hesitate to say this lest someone say to me in truth: Therefore, he would have been saved, even if he had not made it to the very washing of the body; since, as you assert, he had deserved the merit of purification through the mysteries already accomplished.

4. Finally, why do we not also baptize the dead whom sudden death often carried away from sacred baptism, though their will and faithful devotion were known to all? If I am tempted to agree with someone giving such an answer, from it the great absurdity follows that people will think that, if those mysteries alone suffice for conferring the fullness of salvation, one goes to the water of the eternal font not to be reborn but already reborn. I see that in this question the view of the canons can be brought forward. They command that the sick, "if they are unable to answer for themselves, but of their own will have spoken their own testimony in their own danger, are to be baptized."[2] With this definition, I think it a question more of a command of what the Church ought to do rather than an indication of what he may receive. That is, that the minister of the word should be free of the guilt of negligence, not that he be shown to be partner and participant of justice. Most of all, because although I see that many are moved by this matter, often still I am more agitated, hesitating as to what kind of view should be held concerning those who, even if they are legitimately baptized with sound mind, with death very speedily intervening, are not allowed to eat the flesh of the Lord and to drink his blood. Note especially the words of the Savior to the faithful, saying, "Unless you eat the flesh of the Son of Man and drink his blood, you shall not have life in you."[3] So we ask that you instruct us with a swift response, whether it is detrimental, how much it is detrimental, or whether it is detrimental at all, if someone baptized in the name of the Holy

---

2. *Breviarium Hipponense* 32. CCL 149.42.
3. Jn 6.53.

Trinity is deprived of the sacred food and drink. Please reply at the same time to both questions which, by presumption of charity, we believe must be asked and which, we suggest, will be very useful for many. May our God deign to preserve your Paternity for our edification, Sir, always a father to me.

LETTER 12. THE LETTER OF FULGENTIUS TO FERRANDUS

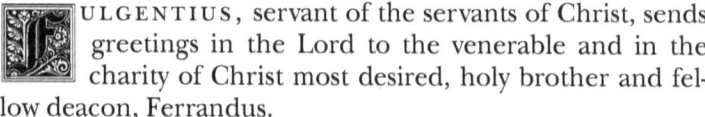ULGENTIUS, servant of the servants of Christ, sends greetings in the Lord to the venerable and in the charity of Christ most desired, holy brother and fellow deacon, Ferrandus.

1. (I.) Holy brother, I rejoice that the flame of charity in your heart which is spread through the Holy Spirit is nourished by constantly growing grace; because of it I recognize something clear in the letter among those many things which seem doubtful; lest, while there is uncertainty in the very sacrament of human salvation, it be thought that the grace of the Savior is given to believers in vain.

2. Therefore, you say that the slave of a certain religious man, an adolescent in age, an Ethiopian in color, by the zeal of his Christian masters was handed over to the Church to be initiated into the ecclesiastical sacraments, and, according to the custom, was made a catechumen. Notwithstanding, after a very brief period, as the paschal solemnity was approaching, he was presented, registered, instructed among the *competentes*, knowing and grasping all the venerable mysteries of the Catholic religion. When the scrutiny had been solemnly celebrated, he was reclaimed from the Devil by the exorcism, whom he renounced without hesitation, just as the custom of the Church of Carthage, where, God willing you still serve as a deacon, demanded, he was to hear the Creed he will profess. Further, with clear voice, in the sight of the faithful people, pronouncing the words of the holy Creed from memory, he received the pious rule of

12. FULGENTIUS TO FERRANDUS

the Lord's Prayer. Now understanding at the same time, both what to believe and what to say in prayer, he was being prepared for the baptism to come. You say that he was overtaken by violent fevers and was in agony as the deadly illness grew. You add that the shortness of time persuaded you that he should be put off to be washed at the fountain with the others or, rather, held back. You also say that when the hour wished for by all arrived in which the acquired people, buried with their Redeemer through baptism, laid aside the old life and, renewed, took up the new faith of the resurrection., then at his last breath, without a word, without movement, without senses, unable to answer the priest posing the question, he was brought forward by presenting hands. Totally absent in mind, he received baptism, with you answering for him as for an infant. Dying a little while later, as far as you can see, he never knew that he had received it in this life.

3. (II.) Therefore, when this story was completed, then you ask whether the fact that his voice had been taken away did him any harm as regards the gaining of eternal happiness. Indeed, you testify that you are afraid lest the Lord, for whom all things are possible, denied him the possibility of speaking because he judged him unworthy of the blessing of a second birth. You also say that you do not see how that age, capable of reason, could be purified by someone else's confession, since we rightly believe that only small children, whom we know are damned only because of original sin, are saved by the faith of those who bring them. With the divine justice doing this in marvelous ways so that somehow where one's own, i.e., actual, sin is found not at all nor is one's own will required; but through the abundance of grace, through the faith of others, salvation is given to those to whom guilt has been ascribed because of the sins of others. But this man, as you assert, lived by his own free will, without a doubt he, overcome by his own concupiscence, contracted many things beyond that which he took from his own roots. Bound by the chains of many sins, will he be saved except by his own freely-willed faith which in that place of redemption, he

neither willed nor was able to confess? Knowing nothing, he was altogether unable to will anything.

4. With these words of yours, from fear of being asked questions, you bring up other things again, saying that perhaps the past confession when he was conscious merited the forgiveness of sins when he was unconscious. But you say that you hesitate to say this lest someone say to you in truth: Therefore, he would have been saved even if he had not made it to the very washing of the body since, as you assert, he had deserved the merit of purification through the mysteries already accomplished. Finally, why do we not also baptize the dead whom sudden death often carried away from sacred baptism, but their will and faithful devotion were known to all? Then you add that if you are tempted to assent to someone proposing such answers, from it the great absurdity follows, that people think that if those mysteries alone suffice to confer the fullness of salvation, then one came to the waters of the eternal font, not to be reborn, but already reborn.

5. Finally, lest anyone think that your most vigilant understanding and most devout concern were not posing enough questions, you add that the view of the canons can be brought forward, the canon which commands that the sick, if they are unable to answer for themselves but have given testimony to their will by speaking, in case of danger to themselves, are to be baptized. But by this definition, you say that you think that it is a question more of what the Church must do rather than an indication of what he may receive. That is, that the minister of the word be free of the guilt of negligence, not that he be shown to be a partner or a participant in justice. Most of all, because although you see that many are moved by this matter, as you say, often still you are more agitated, hesitating as to what kind of view should be held concerning those who, even if they are with sound mind legitimately baptized, but with death very speedily intervening, are not allowed to eat the flesh of the Lord and drink his blood. Because of the words of the Savior which are known to the faithful: "Unless you eat the flesh of the

Son of Man and drink his blood, you do not have life in you."[1] Then you ask that, with a swift response, I instruct you whether it is detrimental, how detrimental it is, or whether it is detrimental at all, if someone baptized in the name of the Trinity is deprived of the sacred food and drink. Therefore, since at the same time, charity commands us to reply to both, it is worthy that charity freely obeys the charity that gives the command. But we hope that, for paying the debt, the grace of charity of him by whom charity itself is inspired will deign to be present.

6. (III.) First of all, it is necessary for us to recall that declaration which the free benevolence of the Savior has promulgated for all for the salvation of the human race; that declaration which the Lord himself, the more tenaciously he wanted it to inhere in our minds, the more he deigned to promulgate it at a later time in all his commandments. After the resurrection, as he was about to ascend to heaven in his body but would remain on earth with his own in his divinity, he said these things to his disciples: "Go into the whole world and proclaim the gospel to every creature. Whoever believes and is baptized will be saved; whoever does not believe, will be condemned."[2] Well here did the Lord say that he who believed and was baptized is saved, but he showed that the one who does not believe must be condemned without hesitation. But in the case of the nonbeliever, no mention was made of baptism. For the one who does not believe, whether he is baptized or is not baptized, without a doubt, will be condemned.

7. This statement by which the Lord decided and defined that every nonbeliever must be condemned with an everlasting punishment, not only those whom the end of this life finds foreign to the sacrament of baptism, but also there is no doubt that all heretics must be condemned by divine decision. For if faith, which the blessed Paul, filled with the divine Spirit, asserts is one, it is faith which is true, not

---

1. Jn 6.53.
2. Mk 16.15–16.

feigned, because "the aim of this instruction is love from a pure heart, a good conscience, and a faith that is not feigned."[3] How is one said to believe if he does not hold the truth of the faith? Whatever the spirit of a believer contains which is known to be foreign to the truth of the faith, of necessity is a lie. The Lord hates all who do iniquity and will destroy those who tell lies. Wherefore, Wisdom as well says in Proverbs, "For my mouth will utter truth; wickedness is an abomination to my lips."[4] Therefore, they who do not hold the truth of the faith in heart and mouth do not receive salvation in baptism. Because of this, although they have the appearance of piety which consists in the sacrament of baptism, by refusing the power of piety, they receive neither life nor salvation. But what remains for such people except eternal damnation which, not true, but feigned faith will bring forth for them? In such people, there is no charity from a pure heart, because, according to the statement of the blessed Peter, the Lord purifies the hearts of his own by faith; nor can there be purity of heart where there is no faith because that must not be called faith where it is not true. Since charity from a pure heart is there where faith is not feigned but true (the heart is purified not by the feigning of faith but by the truth), it is clear that with the heretics in whom there is not the truth but the counterfeit of faith, charity from a pure heart is never found. For how can they have a good conscience in whom that prince of evil dwells through unbelief? Therefore, they, unless they are converted and saved by the truth of faith, will be condemned for the crime of unbelief because they have not loved him in whom they did not believe according to the truth of the faith. There cannot be a good conscience in them where it is clear a deadly lack of faith has held out against the true faith until the end of their life.

8. Let no one be moved because the blessed Apostle called something faith, albeit feigned, because in another

---

3. 1 Tm 1.5.
4. Prov 8.7.

place, just as he preached one God, so also he preached one faith. For the blessed Apostle called it that, not according to the truth of the matter, but according to the opinion of the nonbelievers. For that which was being preached by the pseudo-Apostles, the same he also called 'Gospel', and the blessed Paul confirms that it is not the Gospel. In his letter which was written to the Galatians, this is contained in these words: "I am amazed that you are so quickly forsaking the one who called you by the grace of Christ for a different Gospel (not that there is another)."[5] For how is there another Gospel, if not a different one, except that it is different according to the error of the unfaithful but not "another" according to the truth of the faith? So also faith is feigned by those who lack faith according to their own opinion, by whom the true faith which the Holy Spirit gives, is not possessed. Also the same blessed Apostle points out knowledge by a false name, saying, "O Timothy, guard what has been entrusted to you. Avoid profane babbling and the absurdities of so-called knowledge."[6] Just as that which is called falsely by the name of knowledge is not knowledge, so too faith which the divine spirit has not poured in, but a human spirit fashions for itself, is truly not faith; and because of this, that which is called faith according to their own opinion still is not faith. For we have found even some being called gods in the sacred words, whom even the divine words themselves indeed testify are not gods. For it is said in the psalms: "For all the gods of the peoples are idols."[7] Jeremiah also says, "The gods who did not make the heavens and the earth shall perish from the earth and from under the heavens."[8] In another text, those whom he calls gods, he shows are not gods. For he says, "Cross to the coasts of Cyprus and look, send to Kedar and examine with care; see if there has ever been such a thing. Has a nation changed its gods, even though they are no gods?"[9]

5. Gal 1.6–7.
6. 1 Tm 6.20.
7. Ps 95.5 LXX; Ps 96.5.
8. Jer 10.11.
9. Jer 2.10–11.

9. We find the name of God in the Holy Scriptures, as many as now come to mind, spoken of in four ways. For God is spoken of according to the truth of nature, that the Holy Trinity is one, true, and unchangeable God, who says, "See now that I, even I, am he; there is no God besides me."[10] And concerning whom David says, "For who is God except the Lord? And who is a rock besides our God?"[11] This is the one and only God who alone is God by nature. From this one true God, certain ones, in order that they might be gods, did not have it by nature but received it by the gift of grace. Concerning such gods, it was Moses to whom that one true God said, "See, I have made you, like God to Pharaoh."[12] Of such people are also those to whom it is said: "I said, 'You are gods, children of the most High, all of you.'"[13] Therefore, these gods received that grace to be gods which they received to become the children of God. The evangelist says that "to those who did accept him, he gave power to become the children of God, to those who believe in his name, who were born, not by natural generation, nor by human choice, nor by a man's decision, but of God."[14] Likewise, to them it is said: "I said, 'You are gods, children of the most High, all of you.'"

10. Therefore, two of those ways of naming are praiseworthy; one by which he is called the true God by nature; the other which, through grace, God has granted to whom he willed. Still they are distinguished from each other by a great difference. That way, by which in the name of God the truth of nature is shown, shows one God by the truth of the name of the nature in such a way that it never permits them to be called gods in themselves. Hence it is that, just as the Father alone or the Son alone or the Holy Spirit alone is truly called God, so at the same time, the Father and the Son and the Holy Spirit are truly named not three gods but one God. That Trinity, one God, has this, that they are three persons

---

10. Dt 32.39.
12. Ex 7.1.
14. Jn 1.12–13.

11. Ps 17.32 LXX; Ps 18.31.
13. Ps 81.6 LXX; Ps 82.6.

but are not three gods, because that Trinity is one true God. Therefore, the Son of God, not only according to his true divinity which he has from the nature of the Father, but also according to the true flesh which he has by nature from the body of his mother, is both believed and proclaimed as true God by us. Since the eternal divinity of the Son with his full humanity and the same full humanity of the Son with his eternal divinity is one person in the Trinity; and he completely in his divinity and in his humanity, the only-begotten Son together with the Father and the Holy Spirit is one God. But the other way, which is not that of nature but of grace, without any error in faith, accepts the name of gods in itself; because it contains only the multitude of the adopted, to whom, the Highest Trinity, the one true God, has given the power to become the children of God. (IV.) Therefore, in the former way, the clarity of nature is recognized; in the latter, there is the gift of grace.

11. The two remaining ways by which either some thing or some person is called god are more worthy of condemnation than praise. There is obvious blame in each case because in neither of them can either nature or grace be present. For one is according to a disposition for evil concupiscence; the other, according to erroneous opinion. For the spirit, given over to carnal concupiscence makes that which it loves above all else its god. Hence it is that the blessed Apostle speaks without hesitation of certain ones who are wise in the things of this world but whose belly is their god, saying, "Their end is destruction. Their god is their stomach. Their glory is their shame. Their minds are occupied with earthly things."[15] Here I think that the Apostle has read "occupied with earthly things," instead of "love earthly things." Such a meaning I think is contained as well in that text where the above-mentioned Apostle says, "If then you were raised with Christ, seek what is above, where Christ is seated at the right hand of God. Think of what is above, not of what is on earth."[16] Showing how they must not think of

15. Phil 3.19.   16. Col 3.1–2.

these earthly things, a little later, he added, "Put to death, then, the parts of you that are earthly; immorality, impurity, passion, evil desire, and the greed that is idolatry."[17] When he commanded that our members, which are on the earth be put to death, he commands that the lust for earthly things in us be put to death. For this reason he says in another place, "Now those who belong to Christ have crucified their flesh with its passions and desires."[18] He also wants us to consider ourselves dead, saying, "Consequently, you too must think of yourselves as dead to sin and living for God in Christ Jesus."[19] Each one lives for that thing which he loves and shows himself dead to that the affection for which he has put to death in himself. They who love earthly things are preoccupied with earthly things; and they make their belly their god who surrender the service of their heart to the seductive pleasures of gluttony.

12. The opinion indeed of human error lyingly fashions for itself the name of god to its own destruction in two ways. This twin opinion of error punishes heretics no less than pagans; while it subjects both the former and the latter to itself by it, so that, at the same time, it binds all with different bonds of varied falsity. The true God being left behind, pagans serve the superstition of false gods; heretics, thinking false things about the true God, resist the truth of the true religion. It is clear, therefore, that heretics are bound by the chain of deadly error and those whom the Church endures as stubborn enemies must not be called 'the faithful', seeing that he is guilty of infidelity, either by believing and not giving up false things about the true God, or by adoring a false god under the name of the true God.

13. (V.) Therefore, since we have opened up the start of the discussion concerning that statement of the Lord in which he decreed that "Whoever believes and is baptized will be saved,"[20] we believe that that boy has been saved. In him, we find there was nothing lacking of those things which pertain to the work and effect of baptism. The work of the

17. Col 3.5.
18. Gal 5.24.
19. Rm 6.11.
20. Mk 16.16.

12. FULGENTIUS TO FERRANDUS 485

second birth consists in faith and confession, the effect in regeneration. "But to those who did accept him, he gave power to become children of God; to those who believe in his name."[21] Therefore, they believe in order to become children of God since, for this purpose, they receive the grace of faith, that, believing, they may receive the grace of the sacrament. For it is worthy that while "one believes with the heart and so is justified and one confesses with the mouth and so is saved,"[22] it is clear, however, that, just as the work of faith and confession pertain to the catechumen, so the effect of baptism pertains to the minister; and while the confession of the true faith is proclaimed by the former, it follows that the grace of the saving mystery is completed when the latter baptizes.

14. In the Acts of the Apostles, we see this rule observed in the action of St. Philip. He was admonished by the Holy Spirit to proclaim the Lord Jesus Christ to the eunuch and when, at that point, they came to some water, the eunuch asked, saying, "Look, there is water. What is to prevent my being baptized?"[23] First, he drew forth from him the act of confessing, and then he rightly ministered the effect of holy baptism to him. So he answered the eunuch, "If you believe with all your heart, you may."[24] And because the eunuch's confession came before, subsequently, through the ministry of Philip, there was fulfilled in him the effect of holy regeneration. By what justice will he who has accomplished the work of faith and confessing not gain the effect of holy regeneration? For if the order of work and reward is attended to, the work is in the faith and confessing, the reward is in baptism. When anyone is judged worthy of baptism because the merit of faith and confession has preceded, to him the sacrament of holy baptism must be given as a reward. "For the laborer deserves his payment."[25] He who has accomplished the works of believing and confessing, divinely given by devotion of heart and mouth, should not be deprived of

21. Jn 1.12.
23. Acts 8.36.
25. Lk 10.7.
22. Rm 10.10.
24. Acts 8.37.

the reward of baptism. For he was to be questioned at the hour of baptism about that which he had previously confessed in the recital of the Creed. Therefore, the fact that his voice was taken away did him no harm in the matter of gaining eternal happiness since that voice, as long as it was able, remained steadfast in the confession of faith. It was taken away, not changed; nor was what it had said abolished when it could no longer speak because as long as he was able to know, he did not change his statement.

15. But you say, "I greatly fear lest the Lord, to whom all things are possible, denied him the ability to speak because he judged him unworthy of the blessing of a second birth." Here rather let us recognize that our God was not forgetful of his mercy. If he took away the man's voice, still he did not take away his life so that what he sought, believing and confessing, he received while still living.

16. But it is doubted "how that age, capable of reason, could be purified by the confession of another." On the contrary, it is purified by his own confession, for whom then the subsequent confession by others could not have been of avail, if his own confession had not preceded. Therefore, the confession of others was without a doubt of avail for him because it did not come before him unwilling but subsequently came to his aid as he weakened. What in him the illuminated will began by believing and confessing, this fraternal charity completed on his behalf. (VI.) For we read that the Lord said, "Everyone who acknowledges me before others, I will acknowledge before my heavenly Father."[26] As long as he had the ability to speak, that confession was not lacking. Therefore, who will dare to say that that confession is unworthy of salvation, which he saw not rejected by perversity of will but silenced by necessity of infirmity? The tongue was weakened but the conscience was not perverted. The Apostle says, "Since then we have the same spirit of faith, according to what is written, 'I believed, therefore I spoke,' we too believe and therefore speak."[27] So he who believed when the

26. Mt 10.32.
27. 2 Cor 4.13.

spirit of faith was accepted, and spoke, since the same Spirit whom he had accepted in order to believe, could have been lacking, if he denied. Since he did not deny, assuredly he did not lack it. As a believer, he spoke by the very Spirit who redeemed him, though silent, since the second birth is accomplished by the same Spirit by which the second belief is given. Accordingly, because the will to believe and confess was not lacking to him when he was healthy, the necessity of remaining silent did not tell against him when he was ill.

17. (VII.) But it is true that "we believe rightly that only children whom we know are damned only because of original sin are saved by the faith of those who bring them. With the divine justice doing this in marvelous ways so that, in some ways, where one's own actual sin is found not at all and one's own will is not required; but through the abundance of grace, through the faith of others, salvation is given to those to whom guilt has been ascribed because of the sins of others." You add that "he lived by his own free will; beyond that which he took from his roots, without a doubt he, overcome by his own concupiscence, contracted many things. Bound by the chains of many sins, he will not be saved except by his own freely-willed faith which in that place of redemption, he neither willed nor was able to confess. Knowing nothing, he was altogether unable to will anything." These, dearest brother, are your words which are contained in that letter which you sent.

18. Accordingly, first of all the nature of original sin must be attended to, something which, committed by some, has been spread to others by a defect in generation. In its cleansing, if, when it is a question of that age in which there can be no confession of one's own, through the faith and confession of others, salvation is given to children to whom guilt has been ascribed because of the sins of others. But when there is question of ages with the use of reason, one's own confession is sought. By that reason, since they are alive and understand, having derived from life original sin and from their understanding a sin stemming from their own activity, we say rightly and without hesitation that he has been saved,

because he, when he understood, believed, and what he believed he confirmed with his own confession. And then, although no longer understanding but still living, he received the sacrament of holy regeneration. For through the sacrament of holy baptism, that life is freed from the bonds of original sin, which had been bound by the chains of the same sin. And because the power of holy baptism is so great that when it found life in which it loosed that chain of original sin, it washed away as well by the blessing of the second birth all those things which it found which had been added later. The Apostle says, "For after one sin, there was the judgment that brought condemnation; but the gift after many transgressions brought acquittal."[28] Rightly then do we believe that he has been saved. Before baptism, belief and confession from understanding were not lacking in him and at the hour of baptism, life remained, although in a weak and feverish man. The life which contracted original sin, because when it was able, it gave testimony of its conscience and understanding, even when it was not able to confess, it received the forgiveness of original sin by the merit of that confession. Above all, with the assistance of the fellowship of ecclesiastical unity, by which it came about that the confession given in time past, since he was not able to give it at the hour of baptism because of the weakness of the body, he would give it with the help of fraternal charity with the result that he was assisted by the word of the members of that company to which he was to be assigned. When that original sin had been forgiven, none of the faithful doubts that all the sins which he had contracted by his own will were forgiven. We have no hesitation in saying that the confession of the past when he was conscious merited the forgiveness of sins even when he was unconscious.

19. (VIII.) The fear that someone might say that he "would be saved, even if he never got to the baptism of the body," need not turn our spirit from this view, since we are not saying that he could have been saved solely by his confes-

---

28. Rm 5.16.

sion without the sacrament of baptism. For "whoever believes and is baptized will be saved."[29] So we affirm that that adolescent, because we know that he believed and confessed, was saved through the sacrament of baptism. If he were not baptized, not only unconsciously but also consciously, never would he be saved. The way to salvation lay in confession, salvation in baptism. For at that age, not only would confession without baptism have availed him nothing, but not even baptism would have been of any use for salvation to him if he did not believe and confess. Therefore, God willed that his confession avail him because he preserved him in this life all the way to holy regeneration. Just as he, because he wished it, sought the gift of holy regeneration, so God, because he willed it, gave it.

20. (IX.) We do not, however, baptize the dead because none of their sins, whether original or actual, because it is at the same time common to the soul and flesh, is forgiven them if the soul is separated from its flesh. "For we must all appear before the judgment seat of Christ, so that each one may receive recompense, according to what he did in the body whether good or evil."[30] Therefore, the soul which sinned in the body and did not believe when it was in the body is never saved without the flesh. And for this reason, it will receive the evil which it did in the body, not the good, which it did not do, when it was in the body. The flesh without a soul cannot be baptized because it will not receive the forgiveness of sins. For a thing which is not living, just as it cannot sin, so it cannot have penance for sins. How can the sacrament of forgiveness be given where there is no life? Or how is the flesh baptized for the forgiveness of sins where there is no soul with which it was at the same time a partner in sin? Even if there was a person with the will and faithful devotion when alive, who still dies without the sacrament of baptism, that person could not be baptized dead, because the soul, whose will and devotion were faithful, had gone forth from that body. And so, this man whose case we are

29. Mt 16.16.
30. 2 Cor 5.10.

now discussing was worthily baptized since his soul, whose faithful will and devotion were known to all, remained in his flesh up to the hour of holy baptism. Those mysteries which are performed in the Church before baptism cause a person to be conceived spiritually, not reborn. Hence it is that he will come to salvation if the second birth will bring him to the light. For that light, a person is prepared by these mysteries but is brought forth by the sacrament of baptism. This is what I spoke about above that in those mysteries is the work of salvation, but the effect of salvation in baptism, which, not the onset of illness but only a change of will, can negate for him.

21. (X.) Accordingly, that statement of the canons of the fathers must be most firmly held which commands that the sick, "if they are not able to answer for themselves but have expressed testimony of this will, in case of danger to themselves, be baptized." For the holy fathers saw that the will is not guilty which is known to be impeded but not changed, and they must not refuse the sacrament of baptism where the firmness of the will is known. Making this decision, the holy fathers declared both what the Church must do and what he receives. Nor would the Church have done this if he had received no benefit from this action. For since the Apostle bears witness that the Church of the living God is the "pillar and foundation of Truth,"[31] if it has some part among the mysteries of faith, where it is not the firm truth, it is not the "pillar and foundation of truth" in all the mysteries. Whatever firmness is taken away from its sacraments, of necessity it is taken away from the Church itself. For the Church is not truly called the "pillar and foundation of truth," if it is found unsound in the most basic mystery of human salvation. But because it is truly called the "pillar and foundation of truth" by the Apostle, whatever according to the canons of the Church itself is given and received within it, among the holy mysteries of human redemption and reconciliation, is given with firm truth, is received with firm truth.

31. 1 Tm 3.15.

22. It is so commanded in Proverbs: "Hear, my child, your father's instruction and do not reject your mother's teaching,"[32] so that we may never reject the general canons of holy Mother the Church, i.e., those which the most harmonious assent of all the bishops confirms. Therefore, who would think that useless which he hears from God must never be rejected? Therefore, if one who is baptized is not saved, there is no culpability if this is neglected; nor will the minister of the word, if he has not done this, be held guilty of negligence if the one in whose case this happened, cannot be a sharer in justification. For someone is accused of the guilt of negligence where the effect of the action is not despaired of. And just as one who does not do what is useful is justly accused of negligence, so rightly the labor of the one who devotes his work to superfluous matters is rejected as null and useless. But if also in this matter, invalid labor is expended, without a doubt, null as well will be the statement of the Apostle Paul in which he said that "each one will receive his wages in proportion to his labor."[33] Without a doubt he was speaking of the ministers of Christ and the dispensers of the mysteries of God just as the text of the same letter indicates. For he had said before, "I planted, Apollos watered, but God caused the growth."[34] What did it mean for Paul to plant or Apollos to water except that Paul planted by preaching the word of salvation, Apollos watered by administering the sacrament of baptism? Therefore, when the Apostle said, "Therefore, neither the one who plants nor the one who waters is anything, but only God who causes the growth,"[35] that he might show that the reward for that planting and watering remains firm, he immediately added, "each will receive wages in proportion to his labor." Showing that the labor of the divine work cannot be empty, in another text of the same letter, he speaks as follows: "Therefore, my beloved brothers, be firm, steadfast, always fully devoted to the work of the Lord, knowing that in the Lord, your labor is not in vain."[36]

32. Prov 1.8.
33. 1 Cor 3.8.
34. 1 Cor 3.6.
35. 1 Cor 3.7.
36. 1 Cor 15.58.

23. But that is the work of God which is so expended on each living person that it can profit either the soul or the body of the one who has received it. And those things which are of use to the soul, it is necessary that they also be of use to the body; but not all the things which are of advantage to the body pertain to the advantage of souls, such as food, drink, clothing, or shelter which are of avail to the soul, not of the received, but of the giver. The sacrament of baptism is given to a person for this, that the soul be saved with the flesh. Assuredly what the minister gives is useless if he does not give it for this purpose, viz., that he who is baptized may receive the gift of eternal salvation. To no purpose is the sacrament of redemption given if the one to whom it is given is not redeemed. But if we single out one word of your letter for attention, no doubt will remain in this matter. For you said that this was ordered in the canons of the fathers "that the minister of the word be free of the guilt of negligence." But how does the minister incur guilt in this negligence if there is no advantage in zeal? For to no purpose does one contract guilt for negligence, unless he did not do what he should have done; but he ought to have done it, because if he had done it, it could have been of some use. Therefore he contracted the guilt of negligence because he did harm by not doing something which, without a doubt, would have been of use, if he had done it. So, therefore, according to the canons of the fathers, that sick person, whose will does not lack the attestation of his neighbors, must without a doubt be baptized so that both the minister of the word is free of the guilt of negligence, and he becomes a partner of and sharer in justification.

24. (XI.) But none of the faithful ought to be surprised in these things "who even if they are legitimately baptized with sound mind, with death coming on more quickly, they are not allowed to eat the flesh of the Lord or drink his blood," because of that statement of the Savior in which he said, "Unless you eat the flesh of the Son of Man and drink his blood, you do not have life in you."[37] Anyone can consider

---

37. Jn 6.53.

this not only according to the mystery of the truth but also according to the truth of the mystery, and, doing so, he will see that this comes about in the very washing of holy regeneration. For what is going on in the sacrament of holy baptism, except that believers become the members of the Lord Jesus Christ and belong to the structure of the body in the unity of the Church? For the blessed Apostle says to them, "Now you are Christ's body and individually parts of it."[38] He shows not only that they are sharers in the very sacrifice but that they are the holy sacrifice itself, while he commands them to show themselves humbly to be a living victim for God, saying, "I urge you, therefore, brothers, by the mercies of God to offer your bodies as a living sacrifice, holy and pleasing to God."[39] In a similar teaching, the holy Peter also says, ". . . like living stones, let yourselves be built into a spiritual house to be a holy priesthood to offer spiritual sacrifices acceptable to God through Jesus Christ."[40] Whence blessed Paul in a certain place had said, "The cup of blessing that we bless, is it not a participation in the blood of Christ? The bread that we break, is it not a participation in the body of Christ?"[41] In order to show that we are the true bread itself and the true body, he immediately added, "Because the loaf of bread is one, we, though many, are one body, for we all partake of the one loaf."[42] Whence he says in another text, "One body and one Spirit, as you were also called to the one hope of your call."[43] And again: "Rather living the truth in love, we should grow in every way into him who is the head, Christ, from whom the whole body, joined and held together by every supporting ligament, with the proper functioning of each part, brings about the body's growth and builds itself up in love."[44] For, confirming again that we are the flesh of the Lord, he says, "For no one hates his own flesh but rather nourishes and cherishes it, even as Christ does the Church, because we are members of his body."[45] So,

---

38. 1 Cor 12.27.
39. Rm 12.1.
40. 1 Pt 2.5.
41. 1 Cor 10.16.
42. 1 Cor 10.17.
43. Eph 4.4.
44. Eph 4.15–16.
45. Eph 5.29–30.

since "we though many are one bread and one body,"[46] then each one begins to be a participant of that one bread when he begins to be a member of that one body, because in the individual members when in baptism he is joined to Christ the head, then already as a living victim, he is immolated for God. As he becomes a sacrifice by that gift of birth, so also he becomes a temple. As the blessed Apostle teaches, saying, "Do you not know that you are the Temple of God and that the Spirit of God dwells in you?"[47] The one who becomes a member of the body of Christ, how has he not received what he himself is becoming? When he becomes a true member of that body of him, whose body is the sacrament in the sacrifice. Therefore, by the regeneration of holy baptism, he becomes that which he is to receive from the sacrifice of the altar. We know that the holy fathers without a doubt believed and taught this. The blessed Augustine preached a sermon on this matter, altogether splendid and apt for the edification and instruction of the faithful. I have chosen to add the whole of this sermon to this letter because it is not long and in its very brevity is full of great instruction and sweetness.

25. A Sermon of the blessed Augustine, bishop[48] (s.272):

What you behold now on the altar of God, you saw there last night as well. But you have not yet heard what it is, what it means, and of how great a reality it is the sacrament. What you see then is bread and a cup. This is what your eyes report to you. But your faith has need to be taught that the bread is the body of Christ, the cup, the blood of Christ. Perhaps this rather brief statement might be sufficient for belief, but belief requires instruction, for the prophet says, 'Unless you believe, you will not understand.'[49] So now you can say to me, 'You have taught us to believe. Explain, so we may understand.'

For the following thought may arise in someone's mind:

46. 1 Cor 10.17.
47. 1 Cor 3.16.
48. Augustine *Sermo* 272. PL 38.1246–48. Trans. Daniel Sheerin, *The Eucharist*, Message of the Fathers of the Church, vol.7, 94–96.
49. Is 7.9.

'We know whence our Lord Jesus Christ took flesh, from the Virgin Mary. As an infant he was nursed. He was brought up. He grew. He attained manhood. He suffered persecution from the Jews. He was hanged on the wood; he was killed on the wood; he was taken down from the wood. He was buried. He rose on the third day. When he willed, he ascended into heaven; to there he lifted up his body. Thence will he come to judge the living and the dead. Now he is there, enthroned at the right hand of the Father. How is the bread his body? And the cup, or what is in the cup, how is that his blood?

These things, my brothers, are called sacraments for the reason that in them one thing is seen but another is understood. That which is seen has physical appearance, that which is understood has spiritual fruit. If, then, you wish to understand the body of Christ, listen to the Apostle as he says to the faithful, "You are the body of Christ, and his members."[50] If, therefore, you are the body of Christ and his members, your mystery has been placed on the Lord's table, you receive your mystery. You reply 'Amen' to that which you are and by replying, you consent. For you hear 'the Body of Christ' and you reply 'Amen'. Be a member of the body of Christ so that your 'Amen' may be true.

But why in bread? I provide nothing of my own at this point; rather let us listen together to the Apostle who said, when he was speaking about this sacrament, 'We, though many, are one bread, one body.'[51] Understand and rejoice. Unity! Verity! Piety! Charity! 'One bread.' What is this one bread? 'Many . . . one body.' Remember that bread is not made from one grain but from many. When you were exorcised you were, after a fashion, milled. When you were baptized, you were moistened. When you received the fire of the Holy Spirit, you were baked. Be what you see, and receive what you are.

That is what the Apostle said about the bread, and he has already indicated quite well what we are to understand of

50. 1 Cor 12.27.
51. 1 Cor 10.17.

the cup, even though he did not say it. For just as in the preparation of the bread which you see, many grains were moistened into a unity, as if there were taking place what Holy Scripture says about the faithful, "They had one mind, one heart towards God,"[52] so also in the case of the wine. Brothers, recall whence wine comes. Many grapes hang in the cluster, but the liquid of the grapes is mixed in unity. So also did Christ the Lord portray us. He willed that we belong to him. He consecrated the mystery of peace and unity upon his table. He who receives the mystery of unity and does not hold fast to the bond of peace receives not a mystery for himself, but testimony against himself.[53]

26. I think, holy brother, that our discussion has been confirmed by the sermon of the outstanding doctor, Augustine. Up to a point, there should be no doubt for anyone then that each one of the faithful becomes a sharer in the body and blood of the Lord, when he is made a member of the Body of Christ in baptism and is not alienated from the fellowship of that bread and cup, even if, before he eats that bread and drinks that cup, he leaves this world in the unity of the Body of Christ. He is not deprived of the participation in and benefit of that sacrament when he is that which the sacrament signifies. Pray for us, always vigorous and strong in Christ, holy and venerable brother.

LETTER 13. THE LETTER OF FERRANDUS TO FULGENTIUS

Here Ferrandus poses a variety of questions for Fulgentius: Are the persons of the Trinity separable or not? Is it necessary to affirm that the divinity of Christ was born, was crucified, and died? Did the soul of Christ have full knowledge of the Deity? If the three persons of the Trinity reign together, why does the liturgical ending of prayers speak of only the Father and the Son reigning? Finally, what is the significance of the two cups in the Lukan account of the Last Supper? Ful-

---

52. Acts 4.32.
53. Augustine, *The Eucharist*.

13. FERRANDUS TO FULGENTIUS

gentius's response to these questions makes letter 14 the longest of the letters translated in this volume.

ERRANDUS THE DEACON sends greetings in the Lord to the most blessed and holy Father, Bishop Fulgentius, to be received with all veneration.

1. I have often wanted to ask about many things out of a desire to learn but the difficulty of finding someone to carry the letters because of the length of the journey forbade calling upon an absent teacher with frequent letters. So now, taking advantage of the present occasion, I have gathered up everything I could into one and, so that your answer may be prolonged the more, I pose my questions briefly; asking and begging you through Christ from whom you hear within what you teach externally so that you may truthfully tell me:

2. Whether the Trinity, inseparable because of one and the same nature, work and will, must be said to have separable persons or, rather, must be proclaimed to be altogether inseparable in the persons. Or, whether God, the Son of God, just as he is said to have been born, suffered, died, crucified; so it is necessary that we affirm that his divinity was born, suffered, died, crucified; although whether God or divinity is named, only the flesh is understood to be mutable and able to suffer, according to which God or divinity was able to suffer what he could not in his own nature. Thirdly, I ask whether the soul of Christ has altogether full knowledge of the deity which assumes it and how the Father and the Son and the Holy Spirit know each other; so does the same Son know by the fact that he is human, in the same way know himself as God, from each and in each substance wholly comprehending the Father. Or perhaps, just as with bodily eyes he does not see God as spirit, lest the dignity be attached not to the human being, but the nature is believed to be changed within, so the entire essence of the divinity is not seen or comprehended by the rational soul, even with devout understanding and perfectly clean heart, lest any creature capture the Creator.

Allow me, I beg you, to ask another question. For I want to propose several things at once since there is no opportunity for asking about individual matters one by one. We believe and confess that there is one reign of the Father and of the Son and of the Holy Spirit, knowing that they rule over all creatures together. Therefore, why in priestly prayers does the Catholic Church throughout almost all the regions of Africa traditionally say, "Through Jesus Christ, your Son, our Lord, who lives and reigns with you in the unity of the Holy Spirit"? As if the Son alone possessed the Kingdom with the Father, to be sure "in the unity of the Holy Spirit," so that, while uniting those who reign, the Holy Spirit is not indicated as reigning at the same time. Answer these things, I beg you, quickly, and with the pleasant honey of heavenly words, feed the one who with rude words consults you about matters unknown. Also with diligent exposition explain why it is that as Luke the Evangelist is going to tell about the Lord's Supper, first he says that he took the cup and immediately gave it to the disciples to be shared among themselves and then, when he took the bread, said, "This is my body." And then, after he had eaten, he likewise took the cup again, saying, "This cup is the new covenant in my blood which will be shed for you."[1] Was the one cup given a second time or one first and then another after? And whichever it is, to what mystery does it belong concerning which the others who wrote the Gospels have remained completely silent? I beg of you, do not put off a reply nor by a long wait keep in suspense a spirit that is ready. We ought to deserve at least a part of your working time.

3. I ask as well that you have sent to us the book concerning the rule of the true faith[2] so that it can be reread, and the letter to John, bishop of Thapsus,[3] in which I recall there was a full discussion concerning not yielding to a certain wicked judge. I have taken two codices and given back to young Hermias[4] his own. Have as well a copy of the letter concerning prayer sent here again, the letter which you were

---

1. Lk 22.17–20.
2. Presumably the treatise *De fide ad Petrum* translated in this volume.
3. John of Thapsus or Tharsis. See "Johannes 4," PCBE, 608.
4. Hermias. See PCBE, 553.

gracious enough to send me here. For while many wish to read it because of its brilliance, given my forgetfulness, we are unaware of who has it now. As a suppliant, I greet the holy priests, deacons, and their blessed congregation. May our God graciously preserve your Paternity unharmed for our edification, Father.

LETTER 14. THE LETTER OF FULGENTIUS TO FERRANDUS

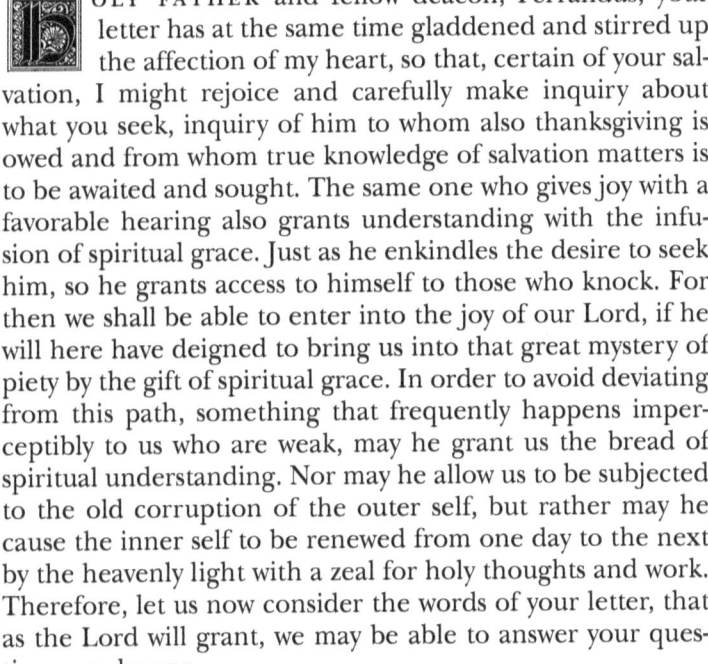OLY FATHER and fellow deacon, Ferrandus, your letter has at the same time gladdened and stirred up the affection of my heart, so that, certain of your salvation, I might rejoice and carefully make inquiry about what you seek, inquiry of him to whom also thanksgiving is owed and from whom true knowledge of salvation matters is to be awaited and sought. The same one who gives joy with a favorable hearing also grants understanding with the infusion of spiritual grace. Just as he enkindles the desire to seek him, so he grants access to himself to those who knock. For then we shall be able to enter into the joy of our Lord, if he will here have deigned to bring us into that great mystery of piety by the gift of spiritual grace. In order to avoid deviating from this path, something that frequently happens imperceptibly to us who are weak, may he grant us the bread of spiritual understanding. Nor may he allow us to be subjected to the old corruption of the outer self, but rather may he cause the inner self to be renewed from one day to the next by the heavenly light with a zeal for holy thoughts and work. Therefore, let us now consider the words of your letter, that as the Lord will grant, we may be able to answer your questions one by one.

2. For you demand that I tell you truthfully "whether the Trinity, inseparable because of one and the same nature, working and will, must be said to have separable persons or whether in the persons as well, it must be proclaimed as alto-

gether inseparable." Doubtless you recognize these as the words of your first question.

3. Where are we to start in our consideration that the Trinity must not be called inseparable if those three persons can be separated in some measure? For that is truly said to be inseparable which can in no way be separated. For what is not separated but can be separated is not inseparable. But if anyone thinks that the persons in the Trinity can be separated, then the Trinity must not be said to be an inseparable Trinity but a unity. For the Trinity is found in the persons, the unity in the nature. But I do not know whether our assertion can be supported by the truth when we say that the nature is inseparable in such a way that we assert that persons of the same nature are separable; since one nature, which cannot be divided in the persons by its very inseparability, does not show that the persons can be separated. For, not to go on longer, we find the separation of nature apart from the separation of person in human beings themselves. For no one doubts that human flesh pertains to human nature; but there can be a separation in it, if any member is cut off from the body. Still this amputation cannot in itself bring about a separation of the person. For when a hand or a foot is cut off from the body, the person of the human being is not also separated together with the same member, although there may come about some separation in the nature a part of which is cut off in the member. But that human being, if he is still alive after he loses the member, will not be lacking in the fullness of the definition of nature by which a human being is called a mortal, rational animal. Having the true definition, it is necessary that he also have his own person with the nature, although he has a part of the nature, i.e., a part of his flesh, separated from himself. But when human beings are separated from their persons, they are also, without a doubt, separated from their nature. A person is not separated when a hand or a foot is separated from the body; but a nature is separated in the separation of persons, when human being is separated from human being. Therefore, the inseparable unity of nature cannot have separable persons.

4. Accordingly, we must consider that one and the same nature of the Trinity fills the whole in such a way that there is not something where it is not. So it is that it is everywhere complete and in no way contained in a place; it is complete in individual spirits and bodies and complete at the same time in all creatures. Now we are not speaking about grace by which God with a free gift of his mercy offers himself to human beings for their salvation, but about nature by which God both fills and contains all the things which he made; according to this, he says, "Do I not fill heaven and earth?"[1] And according to this, the blessed David says to God himself, "Where can I go from your spirit? Or where can I flee from your presence? If I ascend to heaven, you are there. If I make my bed in Sheol, you are there."[2] And concerning Christ who is the Wisdom of God, it is said, "She reaches mightily from one end of the earth to the other, and she orders all things well."[3] Concerning the Holy Spirit, too, divinely-inspired Scripture puts it this way: "Because the Spirit of the Lord has filled the world and that which holds all things together knows what is said."[4] In this text, it is the voice of the heart, not of the body, that is meant, namely the voice, not of bodily speaking, but of interior thought. That voice, which God alone hears calling when in secret he alone sees it thinking. Therefore, he says the following, "Therefore, those who utter unrighteous things will not escape notice and justice, when it punishes, will not pass them by."[5] Showing where this unrighteous speaking is, in order that it may be recognized as pertaining more to the conscience than to the tongue, this Holy Scripture subsequently revealed, saying, "For inquiry will be made into the counsels of the ungodly."[6] I have said this because it is said of the Holy Spirit that "that which holds all things together knows what is said."[7] Holding all things together, the Holy Spirit is not less than the Father or the Son; and, having a knowledge of

1. Jer 23.24.
2. Ps 138.7–8 LXX; Ps 139.7–8.
3. Wis 8.1.
4. Wis 1.7.
5. Wis 1.8.
6. Wis 1.9.
7. Wis 1.7.

inner thought, the true God is recognized as the one who knows hidden things. The knowledge which grasps hidden things without a doubt also grasps things to come, something which the true faith assigns to the true God with the holy Susanna calling upon the true God in this fashion: "O eternal God, you know what is secret and are aware of all things before they come to be."[8] Therefore, the Trinity, i.e., our God, true and good, eternal, immutable and infinite, is totally everywhere according to the infinity and omnipotence of his nature, although he does not live in all according to the largesse of his grace.

5. Hence it is that when God says through Jeremiah, "Am I a God nearby . . . and not a God far off?"[9], the aforementioned prophet says to the same God concerning certain ones, "You are near in their mouths, yet far from their hearts."[10] Therefore, God is close to the good both by nature and by grace; by nature by which he creates; by grace, by which he saves; by nature, he makes them human; by grace, by which he justifies sinners; by nature, by which he causes them to be born from human beings; by grace, by which he gives them the power to become children of God; by nature, by which he brings it about that they live; by grace, by which he brings it about that they live soberly, justly, and piously; by nature, by which he brings them to live for a short time in this world; by grace, by which he brings them to reign in heaven without end. In the evil, God is present only by his natural infinity and omnipotence; by which he brings them to existence, to live and to feel, to be rational, to have free choice of the will; but free, not freed. For free will remains even now in human beings by nature which those in whom God willed it, he graciously frees by grace. For from this free will, the first human being became a slave of sin. Thus human freedom began to be evil because the goodness of the will was taken away by free decision itself and so by the very same human decision, freedom began to be evil. Be-

8. Dn 13.42. 9. Jer 23.23.
10. Jer 12.2.

cause of this, for him and for all who would be born through sexual intercourse, it would mean captivity by the enemy. Therefore, God, as we said before, through the infinity of his nature, both fills and contains his whole creation; and in this way, the Father fills all, the Son fills all, the Holy Spirit fills all because the Father and the Son and the Holy Spirit are by nature one God. But the one nature of the Father and the Son and the Holy Spirit, i.e., of these three persons, is not like the human nature of three human beings. In the case of the latter, there is one nature in such a way that both their souls and their bodies are separated and although there is a unity of nature in the three human beings, still in no one of them is there a flesh and soul common with the other two. Hence it is that any creatures, i.e., of the same nature, can be separated from one another because each one individually cannot be everywhere in its entirety; for when, through the grace of faith it happens that they have "one heart and soul of the multitude of believers,"[11] still in their persons they can be separated by being in different places even though they are not separated by the affection of the heart; and some of the faithful can become unbelievers and be severed from the fellowship of that one soul. But the nature of the Trinity, which alone is everywhere in its entirety, just as it holds itself everywhere one and entire, so it cannot undergo a separating of the persons.

6. At times those persons are given individual names, but the Trinity willed to show itself inseparable in the persons in such a way that there is no name thereby which any one person is called that is not either fitting to the three by a unity of nature or shows that one is referred to the other, even with its individual name. For concerning those words by which the Father and the Son and the Holy Spirit are properly spoken of in relation to themselves, in which, indeed, not the individuality of each person but the communion of one essence is shown, there is no name which can befit the Father in such a way that it cannot befit either the Son or

---

11. Acts 4.32.

the Holy Spirit. For by nature the Father is called God; but by nature the Son is also God, by nature the Holy Spirit is also God; still there are not three gods but by nature the one God is the Father and the Son and the Holy Spirit. The Father is omnipotent but the Son is omnipotent; the Holy Spirit is omnipotent but still there are not three omnipotent gods but the one omnipotent God is the Father and the Son and the Holy Spirit. The Father is eternal, without beginning; the Son is eternal, without beginning; the Holy Spirit is eternal, without beginning; but still there are not three eternal gods, but the one eternal God is the Father and the Son and the Holy Spirit. The Father is infinite but the Son is also infinite; the Holy Spirit is also infinite; but still there are not three infinite gods but the one infinite God is the Father and the Son and the Holy Spirit.[12] Therefore, wherever any one name is such that, at the same time, it can fit both the three and the individual persons without making any difference and is singular in the nature in such a way that it cannot be plural in the persons, how do we say that the persons are separable when we do not see a plural number being accepted in the name? For whatever is said in the singular only according to nature, it is necessary that it be communicated as well in the persons inseparably and the truth itself shows that the persons cannot be divided when whatever name, by which still each person is spoken of in relation to itself, not to another, just as it is spoken of in one in the singular, so also it is named in the singular in the three. For in one person, one angel is spoken of, one human being is spoken of; but if there were three persons of angels or human beings, neither one angel nor one human being could be named; because in these three persons, which are found in either angelic or human nature, there is not one angel or one human being, but, without a doubt, it is necessary that three angels or three human beings be named; otherwise, that plurality of either angelic or human persons cannot be spo-

---

12. The wording is reminiscent of the Athanasian Creed. See J. N. D. Kelly, *The Athanasian Creed* (London: 1964), esp. 33–34.

ken of as either one angel or one human being; because these three persons, either angels or human beings, can be separated; therefore, the three persons themselves do not receive at the same time the one singular denomination of nature; but doubtless, they are called either three angels or three human beings.

7. We are not unaware that through the grace of God it can come about that many human beings can be called by some name in the singular such as that which we spoke of above: "There was one heart and one soul of the multitude of believers,"[13] still it is called one soul in such a way that souls are spoken of, i.e., of the faithful, not of the impious. For the Lord spoke to his faithful disciples to whom he said, "By your perseverance, you will secure your lives."[14] The blessed Peter also says to the faithful, ". . . believing in him, you rejoice with an indescribable and glorious joy as you attain the goal of your faith, the salvation of your souls."[15] Also it is said in the book of Wisdom: "The souls of the righteous are in the hand of God."[16] We know as well that the blessed Apostle said to the Thessalonians whose election he knew of from God, "May the God of peace himself make you perfectly holy and may you entirely, spirit, soul, and body, be preserved blameless for the coming of our Lord Jesus Christ."[17] But also in the hymn of the three boys, one also reads, "Bless the Lord, spirits and souls of the righteous."[18] We know through the grace of God that the holy Church is called a virgin, as the Apostle says, ". . . I betrothed you to one husband to present you as a chaste virgin to Christ,"[19] but in that one virgin herself, virgins in the plural are also named. For we read, "Virgins will be brought to the King after her."[20] Nor is there any doubt that there is one Church which is spread throughout the whole world which is called by the Apostle, "the Church of the living God, the pillar and foundation of

13. Acts 4.32.
14. Lk 21.19.
15. 1 Pt 1.8.
16. Wis 3.1.
17. 1 Th 5.23.
18. Dn 3.86 LXX; Dn 3.64.
19. 2 Cor 11.2.
20. Ps 44.15 LXX; Ps 45.14.

truth."[21] Still this is one Church in such a way that in it many are called churches. For the blessed Apostle himself says, "And I was unknown personally to the churches of Judea that are in Christ."[22] But also he says that he sent a brother to the Corinthians "who is praised in all the churches."[23] He revealed in the beginning of the same letter that he had also written to the churches of Galatia. Showing that his faithful are a light, our Lord says to his disciples, "You are the light of the world,"[24] and yet the blessed James does not hesitate to call the children of God lights, saying, ". . . All good giving and every perfect gift is from above, coming down from the Father of lights. . . ."[25] Therefore, in all of these we find the word both in the singular and in the plural; the plural because the very quality of the nature shows that all creatures are separable; but singular because in order that there be one soul, one spirit, one virgin, one Church, one light, this that one Trinity has brought about by its grace; this in nature as well as in the persons is inseparable in such a way that whatever there is said about the one as well as about the three persons in the singular is not said in the plural. Therefore, the persons of the Father and the Son and the Holy Spirit cannot be separated, for whom one name by nature is so fitting that there cannot be a plural in the three persons; with the exception of this by which they are called persons, there can be no other name in the Father and the Son and the Holy Spirit which is not given in the singular only. But scarcely could the inadequacy of human speech find this one so that at least it would say that there are three persons; so that if even this were not said, that there is a Trinity would not be believed and from that complete silence, a danger to faith would be born.

8. Wherefore, according to the truth of the Christian faith, we say that the Father and the Son and the Holy Spirit are by nature one God. It is necessary, however, that just as we say that the Trinity is one God, we thus speak of one om-

21. 1 Tm 3.15.
22. Gal 1.22.
23. 2 Cor 8.18.
24. Mt 5.14.
25. Jas 1.17.

nipotent, one eternal, one infinite, one great, one most high; and whatever God, insofar as he has given to human beings, not only in the individual persons, but also at the same time in three is named in the singular in relation to itself. Lest, from the fact that Father is the name of one person, the Son also is said to be only one person in the Trinity, likewise, also, when the Holy Spirit is spoken of in its own right, the individuality of one person is emphasized, anyone might wish to assert and establish three separable persons, in that one name from these three befitted each person in such a way that there could be no common name for the three persons. Whoever attempts to assert this as an objection, if his belief conforms to what he is saying and holds in his conscience what he expresses with his tongue, he is not paying enough attention to the fact that these names are, without a doubt, relative. In any such relative name, it is certain that one person is meant in itself in such a way that henceforward it is referred to another [person] and not only in those things which are the same, just as brother is spoken of in relation to brother, friend to friend, neighbor to neighbor, but also in those things which are different, just as father is spoken of in relation to son, son to father, begetter to begotten or begotten to begetter; with any of these names, two persons are normally to be understood. For in these names, one person is not spoken of in the singular in such a way that by its very name, it is not referred to another; for by a relative name, any person is spoken of in itself in such a way that it is not spoken of in relation to itself only. Therefore, to declare the evidence of inseparability, that one and true divinity willed to be named in an incommunicable fashion in the individual persons in such a way that one person could not be understood without the other. For when the Father is referred to the Son or the Son to the Father, even though the individual names can fit only individual persons and what is proper to the persons altogether refuses the communion of those two names, still the Father is not recognized without the Son nor is the Son without the Father. For that relation of a personal name forbids that the persons be separated which, even when it does not name them at the same time, it makes them known at the same time. No one can hear any one of these names without being forced to understand the other as well. The blessed John tells us this, saying, "No one who denies the Son has the Father but whoever confesses the Son has the Father as well."[26] Consequently, as he said, the Father is referred inseparably to the Son and the Son is referred inseparably to the Father. Therefore, the person of the Father is not separated from the person of the Son, however many times either the Father alone is named or the Son, seeing that the Father is not spoken of, unless he is referred to the Son; nor is the Son spoken of unless he is referred to the Father. For in the name of the Father, the begotten is recognized in such a way that from it, he also who has been begotten is made known, and the naming of the one begotten reminds us that the person of the begetter is to be recognized. Hence it is that just as the Father is possessed by the one who confesses the Son, so he is not possessed by the one who has denied the Son.

9. Therefore, whoever says that the person of the Father and the Son are separable, let him show that in either of them, there is some personal name that is of one person in such a way that it cannot be referred to the other. But because this is not at all the case, without a doubt, this pertains to the true faith that just as we do not confuse those three persons of one and inseparable nature, so we do not dare separate them in any way. Inasmuch as the Trinity itself has deigned to show us this clearly in such a way that even in these names, by which he willed persons to be recognized one by one, he does not allow one to be understood without the other. For, except that the Father and the Son are spoken of in relation to each other, where it is necessary that one be referred to the other inseparably, since these are indeed the names of persons, no less is every contradiction lacking in that personal name of the Holy Spirit; it is not

26. 1 Jn 2.23.

called any thing other than a person when the Holy Spirit is spoken of than that which both the Father and the Son are called by nature. For the Father too is a spirit by nature and the Son is a spirit by nature; and the Father is holy by nature and the Son is holy by nature. Therefore, how can the person of the Holy Spirit be separated in any way from the person of the Father or of the Son since the Holy Spirit has this in its very name as a person which it is known to have in common with the Father and the Son by unity of nature? For by this name, it is not referred to the Father only like the Son; nor to the Son only like the Father; but at the same time, it is referred to both the Father and the Son when it is called the Spirit of both the Father and the Son. And since the Holy Spirit itself is called a gift, it is referred inseparably to the giver. The blessed David, knowing of this inseparability of persons, said to God, "Where can I go from your spirit? Or where can I flee from your presence? If I ascend to heaven, you are there; if I make my bed in Sheol, you are there."[27] Certainly, he would not have said this, if he knew that the person of the Holy Spirit was separable from the person of the Father. So he said that he could not go away from the Spirit of God nor flee from God himself in any way because he knew that God is in his Spirit and the Spirit of God is in God inseparably. This is not just as a creature is in God but just as his Spirit who is not of another nature than is God himself in whom he is. The holy Apostle shows this in that place where he said, ". . . This God has revealed to us through the Spirit. For the Spirit scrutinizes everything, even the depths of God."[28] He immediately brought in the example of the human spirit, saying, "Among human beings, who knows what pertains to a person except the spirit of the person that is within? Similarly, no one knows what pertains to God except the Spirit of God."[29] Therefore, just as the human spirit which is in him knows what is in a person, because it is of the same nature as the human being in whom it

---

27. Ps 138.7–8 LXX; Ps 139.7–8.   28. 1 Cor 2.10.
29. 1 Cor 2.11.

is (where I think that rather the inner person should be understood), thus also no one knew the things of God except the Spirit of God, because through unity of nature, he is in God in such a way that there is nothing in God which the Spirit cannot know because of its unity of nature.

10. Only unity of nature possesses this fullness of knowledge; through it his Spirit is in God in such a way that by nature he is one God with him. Still he is in God and is one God with him in such a way that he does not have one person with him, as the spirit who is in a human being has with him. But that example of knowledge for unity of nature which allows there to be no difference in knowledge in the Father and the Son and the Holy Spirit, it is most certain that this is what the blessed Apostle meant; because that one inseparable nature, all of it is in itself by nature, not different but one, and it is clear that it is entirely in the three persons just as in the individual persons. To indicate the proper person of the Holy Spirit, in its teaching on the same Spirit, apostolic authority was careful to state, "We have not received the spirit of the world but the Spirit that is from God."[30] This can in no way be said of the spirit of a human being which is said to be in a human being in such a way that it is not said to be from a human being. But the Holy Spirit that is in God by unity of nature is also from God by the property of the person. Therefore, through that unity of nature, through which no one knows the things of God except the Spirit of God, this too is understood as the Son says, "No one knows the Son except the Father and no one knows the Father except the Son and anyone to whom the Son wishes to reveal him."[31] Through the same unity of inseparable nature, the Son bears witness that he is in the Father and that the Father is in him. For with the disciples he said, "If you know me, then you will also know my Father."[32] When Philip asked that the Father be shown to him, the Lord himself replied in this way, "Have I been with you for so long a time

30. 1 Cor 2.12. 31. Mt 11.27.
32. Jn 14.7.

and you still do not know me, Philip? Whoever has seen me, has seen the Father. How can you say, 'Show us the Father'? Do you not believe that I am in the Father and the Father is in me? The words that I speak to you I do not speak on my own. The Father who dwells in me is doing his works. Believe me that I am in the Father and the Father is in me, or else, believe because of the works themselves."[33] Therefore, from the fact that the Father and the Son and the Holy Spirit are inseparable, it follows that they work inseparably. But if that Trinity could have separable persons, there also would be some separated works of the Trinity. For if we would pay attention to what Holy Scripture says of Wisdom: "For she is a reflection of eternal light,"[34] just as we see the reflection inheres inseparably to the light, so must the Son be recognized as impossible to separate from the Father. Apostolic authority proclaims that he is "the refulgence of his glory, the very imprint of his being,"[35] following which the blessed Ambrose in his hymn for morning prayer proclaims that the Son is the reflection of the Father's glory.

11. With that example, it is fitting that we believe that the persons of the Father and the Son and the Holy Spirit are inseparable by which the only-begotten God himself has joined and united the divine and human nature in the unity of his person in such a way that they cannot in any way be separated from him. For in the one person of the only-begotten God, who "like a bridegroom comes out from his wedding canopy,"[36] the union of each nature remains inseparable. Nor, therefore, must anyone think that either nature could have been broken apart from the other, because through the taking up of death, both the lifeless flesh lay in the tomb and the soul, with the flesh dying, descended into Hell; seeing that, even when with death intervening, the soul departed from the flesh, each nature remained insepa-

---

33. Jn 14.9–11.
34. Wis 7.26. Wisdom was long a figure of the Logos; since it is feminine, the new RSV translates it as 'she'.
35. Heb 1.3.
36. Ps 18.6 LXX; Ps 19.6.

rable in Christ because the infinite divinity deserted neither his soul in Hell nor his flesh in the tomb. To such an extent is each nature inseparable in Christ that because of this, Eutyches fell into error and, seeing one person in Christ, impiously proclaimed one nature as well in him, wishing to confuse what he says could not be separated. So, as this man rushed into the crime of impiety in the matter of the two natures which he knew were inseparable in the one person, just so did Sabellius because of the blindness of deadly infidelity go astray in the case of the three persons on account of the unity of nature, not understanding that the persons of the Father and the Son and the Holy Spirit exist without confusion which he heard remain inseparable in fact by the unity of nature. But the inseparable Trinity conquered both; the unconfused unity trampled on both; each one, alienated from the womb of Mother Church, went away; each one wandered from the womb of the most pious mother and buried himself and his accomplices in the pit of impiety. For in God, the true Trinity, there is not only a unity of nature but also the property of the persons remains unconfused and inseparable and notwithstanding, just the same, in the one person of Christ, the full truth of the two natures remains unconfused and inseparable.

12. But if in Christ, on account of the unity of the person, there is an inseparable union of the divine and human nature (since neither eternity without a beginning, nor simplicity without mutability, nor infinity without a boundary is found to be common to both natures by nature; because, in one and the same Christ, there is both the true divine nature by which he is God born from the Father by nature without a beginning and a true human nature by which, in the fullness of time, God was created a human being by nature from the virgin; in the former, co-eternal with the Father, in the latter, later than his mother; according to the divine nature, always everywhere in his entirety, nor ever or anywhere confined to a place; according to the human nature, on a certain day, he will come from heaven to judge the living and the dead), how much inseparability must we be-

lieve there to be in those three persons, in whom is by nature both unity and eternity and simplicity and infinity? The blessed Ambrose truthfully proclaims and confirms this in his first book on the Holy Spirit, writing as follows: "Who then shall dare to say that the Holy Spirit is separated from God the Father and Christ, when through him we merit to be according to the image and likeness of God?"[37] And, in another place he says, "For who can separate the Holy Spirit from the Father and the Son when, indeed, we cannot name the Father and the Son without the Spirit? For no man can say 'the Lord Jesus' but by the Holy Spirit.' So if we cannot name the Lord Jesus without the Holy Spirit, surely we cannot proclaim him without the Spirit."[38] This inseparability of the three persons is asserted without hesitation also by the blessed Augustine. In the first book *On the Trinity* when he said that the Son alone was born of the virgin Mary, and that the Holy Spirit alone in the form of a dove [came] down on Jesus who was being baptized, and on the day of Pentecost came on the disciples in divided tongues as fire, and that the Father alone was the voice which said, "You are my Son,"[39] when the Son was baptized by John, and when the voice sounded, saying, "I have glorified it and will glorify it again,"[40] showing once again that the Father and the Son and the Holy Spirit are inseparable, brought forward this statement, saying, "Although the Father, the Son, and the Holy Spirit, as they are inseparable, so they work inseparably."[41] You perceive how the blessed Augustine leaves no suspicion of separable persons here, when he asserts that the Father and the Son and the Holy Spirit, just as they are inseparable, so they work inseparably. Confirming this statement with such a conclusion, he says, "This is also my faith, since it is the Catholic faith."[42]

---

37. Ambrose, *De spiritu sancto* I.VI.80; CSEL 79.48; FOTC 44.63–64.
38. Ibid., I.XI.124; CSEL 79.68; FOTC 44.80.
39. Mk 1.11, Lk 3.22.
40. Jn 12.28.
41. Augustine, *De Trinitate* I.IV.7; CCL 50.36; FOTC 45.11.
42. Ibid.

13. In another part of the same book, he says, "Finally, on account of their very inseparability, it suffices at times to name the Father alone, or the Son alone, as the one whose countenance will fill us with joy. Nor is the Spirit of both of them, i.e., the Spirit of the Father and the Son excluded from this unity, and this Holy Spirit is properly called, 'the Spirit of Truth whom this world cannot receive.'[43] For this is the fullness of our joy than which there is nothing greater: to enjoy God the Trinity in whose image we have been made. On this account, the Holy Spirit is sometimes spoken of in such a way as if he himself alone were sufficient for our blessedness, and he alone does suffice, for this reason, because he cannot be separated from the Father and the Son, just as the Father alone suffices for us because he cannot be separated from the Son and the Holy Spirit, and accordingly the Son alone suffices because he cannot be separated from the Father and the Holy Spirit."[44] This is the view of the blessed Augustine according to the truth of the Catholic faith concerning the inseparability of the Father and the Son and the Holy Spirit. In case someone should accept this only in relation to the nature and not also according to the persons, a little later in the same book he took care to show this even more clearly and obviously, saying, "But in order to intimate the Trinity, the names of the persons are also given and while certain things are predicated of each one separately, this is not to be understood as excluding the others, on account of the unity of this same Trinity and the one substance and Godhead of the Father, the Son, and the Holy Spirit."[45] In another text of the aforementioned book, he drives this home even more fully, when he said concerning the Son, "For inasmuch as he is less than the Father, he prays, but inasmuch as he is equal to him, he listens with the Father." Showing the inseparability of the persons, he says, "Therefore, he certainly does not exclude himself from that

---

43. Jn 14.17.
44. Augustine, *De Trinitate* I.VIII.17–18; CCL 50.52; FOTC 45.25–26.
45. Ibid., I.IX.19; CCL 50.55–56.; FOTC 45.29.

which he said, 'For the Father himself loves you,'[46] but wants it understood in the same sense as those statements that we have mentioned above, and for which we have given a satisfactory explanation: that as a general rule, each person in the Trinity is mentioned by name in such a way that the others are also understood to be there. Therefore, 'the Father himself loves you' is so said as to be logically understood also of the Son and the Holy Spirit."[47] Likewise, further on, the same Saint Augustine speaks as follows: "From the many modes of expression in the divine books, we have already shown that what is said about each one in this Trinity is likewise said about all of them, on account of the inseparable activity of the one and the same substance."[48] In the fifteenth book of *On the Trinity* when, concerning this image that is within us, he wished to put forward some lines for the understanding of the Trinity, among other things he says, "On the contrary, the inseparability in that highest Trinity, which incomparably surpasses all things, is so great that although a trinity of men cannot be called one man, yet that Trinity is called and is one God, nor is that Trinity in one God but it is the one God. Nor again, as this image, which the man is who has these three, is one person, so is that Trinity . . . but there are three persons, the Father of the Son, the Son of the Father, and the Spirit of both the Father and the Son."[49] In the same fashion, after a bit, he says, "Yet we do not find that, as in this image of the Trinity, these three are not the one man but belong to the one man, so in the highest Trinity itself, whose image this is, are those three of one God, but they are the one God, and there are three persons, not one."[50] Saying these things and understanding the inseparability of the same three persons in the revelation of the Trinity itself, he follows up by saying with admiration, "And what is indeed wonderfully ineffable, or ineffably wonderful, is that, al-

---

46. Jn 16.27.
47. Augustine, *De Trinitate* I.X.21; CCL 50.59; FOTC 45.32.
48. Ibid., I.XII.25; CCL 50.64.; FOTC 45.37.
49. Ibid., XV.XXIII.43; CCL 50A.520–21; FOTC 45.509.
50. Ibid., FOTC 45.510.

though this image of the Trinity is one person, while there are three persons in the highest Trinity itself, yet this Trinity of three persons is more inseparable than that trinity of one person."[51]

14. I have no doubt that these words of the blessed Augustine which we have cited from the first and last book of *On the Trinity* are completely sufficient; especially with your intelligence and interest with which you very frequently and with understanding read his words, so that you are able to find in them many similar things which show the inseparability of the Holy Trinity, not only in nature but also in the persons. Therefore, these three persons are spoken of one by one that they may be known, not that they may be separated, in whom there is no separation, just as there can be no confusion in them. Nor must those three persons because they cannot be confused on that account be considered as separable since they are altogether inseparable both in what they are and in what they do. And let no one dare to assert that those three persons are separable since he is able to find none either existing or acting before another, none after another, none without another. Where just as by nature there can be no separability of action, there by nature remains an incomparable unity of will. Let us turn our attention to what way either a human being or an angel is separated from God that we may be able to understand without hesitation the inseparable Trinity. For Holy Scripture says that "perverse thoughts separate from God" and that "wisdom will not enter a deceitful soul or dwell in a body enslaved to sin" and that "a holy and disciplined spirit will flee from deceit and will leave foolish thoughts behind."[52] Isaiah too affirms that iniquities come between God and human beings. The Holy Trinity is itself the faithful God in whom there is no wickedness. "The Son of God came to take away sins and in him there is no sin, for sin is lawlessness."[53] Taking away sins, he brought charity. Therefore, he removed that by which we

---

51. Ibid.
52. Wis 1.3–5.
53. 1 Jn 3.5,4.

were separated from God and gave that by which we are inseparably joined to the Holy Trinity. Therefore, the Apostle cries out with confidence, "For I am convinced that neither death nor life nor angels nor principalities nor present things nor future things nor powers nor height nor depth nor any other creature will be able to separate us from the love of God in Jesus Christ our Lord."[54] Therefore, if the Trinity with charity being infused causes our souls to adhere to itself inseparably, because "whoever is joined to the Lord becomes one spirit with him,"[55] how can the Trinity itself have separable persons when the Trinity itself is one God and, through this, is one charity because "God is love"?[56] Charity never permits division, [charity] which from many hearts and many souls makes one heart and one soul in itself.

15. Then comes this your second question, following in due course: "Whether God, the Son of God, just as he is said to have been born, to have suffered, died, been crucified; so it is necessary that we affirm that his divinity was born, suffered, died, was crucified; although whether God or divinity is named, only the flesh is understood to be mutable and able to suffer, according to which God or divinity was able to suffer what he could not suffer in his own nature."

16. To these words of yours, I respond briefly. Whatever is said, there will be nothing prejudicial to the faith by which the Catholic Church truthfully believes and proclaims that by nature the divinity of the Son of God remains impassible and immutable. For the blessed Apostle says, "We proclaim Christ crucified, a stumbling block to Jews and foolishness to Gentiles, but to those who are called, Jews and Greeks alike, Christ the power of God and the wisdom of God."[57] See what the Apostle says of the crucified Christ, that he is the power of God and the wisdom of God. In another text, joining together power and divinity, he speaks of "his eternal power and divinity."[58] If, therefore, the power of Christ is not un-

54. Rm 8.38–39.
55. 1 Cor 6.17.
56. 1 Jn 4.8.
57. 1 Cor 1.23–24.
58. Rm 1.20.

worthily spoken of as crucified according to the flesh, why cannot divinity be spoken of in the same way, as crucified according to the flesh? When "according to the flesh" is added, it was shown that it was not his divinity but his flesh that was subjected to the passion. We also see this pointed out by apostolic authority. For when the blessed Paul the apostle said, "Christ crucified, the power of God and the wisdom of God," lest the power itself and the wisdom be thought of as capable of suffering by nature, he took care in another text to open up salutarily the mystery of crucified power and wisdom, saying of Christ, "For indeed he was crucified out of weakness but he lives by the power of God."[59] We know that Christ the Son of God is truthfully called by the words of the prophet 'mighty God' when Isaiah says, "For a child has been born for us, a son given to us; authority rests upon his shoulders; and he is named Wonderful Counselor, Mighty God, Everlasting Father, Prince of Peace."[60] Does not the Apostle in one text point out the eternal power and divinity of this mighty God? Nor does the true faith proclaim the eternal power and divinity of the Father in such a way that it does not believe in the eternal power and divinity of the Son or the Holy Spirit; since by nature the eternal power and divinity of the Father and the Son and the Holy Spirit are one. Therefore, Christ, the mighty God, is also truly God, just as divinity is truly mighty because it is power. Therefore, it is the true faith which truly believes and proclaims that Christ is the mighty God and knows that Christ crucified is the power of God and the wisdom of God as preached by the Apostle; just as, in faith, he knows and says that, according to the flesh, the power is crucified, so he does not hesitate to confess that, according to the flesh, the divinity is crucified; for Christ the mighty God is God in such a way that he is his divinity; while he is mighty is such a way that he is his power.

You know that what I am speaking about has been dis-

59. 2 Cor 13.4.
60. Is 9.6.

cussed most fully in the book *On the Trinity* by the blessed Augustine; here he shows that each person in the Trinity, at least in these names which are applied to it, not metaphorically, but properly, that it is in itself that which it is proclaimed as having by nature. For we say that either the Father or the Son or the Holy Spirit is the living God, great, wise, mighty, good. In all of these things, each of which is applied to each person in the Trinity, that God is God by divinity; great is great by greatness; wise is wise by wisdom; mighty is mighty by power; good is good by goodness; indeed, he is God in such a way that he is his divinity; he is great in such a way that he is his greatness; he is wise in such a way that he is his wisdom; he is mighty in such a way that he is his power; he is good in such a way that he is his goodness. The same holy Augustine frequently intimates this in the books mentioned above so that I have taken care to insert a certain text from his fifth book in this little work. For when he speaks about God and about his greatness, among other things, he says the following: "He is great by that greatness which is identical with himself. Hence, as we do not speak of these essences, so we do not speak of these greatnesses, for in God to be is the same as to be great. For the same reason we do not speak of three greats, but of only one great, because God is not great by a participation in greatness. He is great by himself being great, for he himself is his own greatness. Let the same also be said of the goodness, the eternity, the omnipotence of God, in fact of all those attributes which can be predicated of God when he is referred to as he is in himself and not in a metaphorical sense or by a comparison, if indeed the human mouth can say anything about him as he properly is."[61] In the eighth book, putting forth the same view from that natural simplicity of the Trinity, among other things, he says, "Thus the Father is God, the Son is God, the Holy Spirit is God; the Father is good, the Son is good, the Holy Spirit is good; and the Father is omnipotent, the Son is omnipotent, and the Holy Spirit is omnipotent; but yet there

---

61. Augustine, *De Trinitate* V.X.11; CCL 50.218; FOTC 45.188–89.

are not three gods, nor three goods, nor three omnipotents, but one God, one good, and one omnipotent, the Trinity itself. And the same applies to anything else that may be said of them, not in relation of one to another, but individually in respect to themselves. These things are said according to essence, for in them to be is the same as to be great, to be good, to be wise, and whatever else is predicated of each person therein with respect to themselves or of the Trinity itself."[62]

17. From these words of the blessed Augustine, it is clear that this is of Catholic truth, that when in God we name divinity, greatness, goodness, power and whatever else in these things which is properly said in respect to itself, we know most certainly that in these different names there are not different things (just as in a human being who is subject to quality), but that one thing which is the essence or nature. Hence it is that the blessed Augustine himself says in the fifth book of *On the Trinity* that God must be understood "as good without quality, as great without quantity,"[63] because the immutability of a simple and omnipotent essence can be subject to no accidents, where the divinity is the same as the eternity and majesty, the greatness is the same as the power and the goodness. Therefore, from this rule of the truth we know that whatever is being said truthfully concerning the majesty, the eternity, the power of God according to the flesh, we do not deny that it is said truthfully about his divinity as well. The blessed Augustine himself in the first book of *On the Trinity*, showing that God the Son according to the divinity has what he is and is that which he has, speaks as follows: "For it is not, as with the creature, so with the Son of God before the Incarnation and the created nature which he assumed, the only-begotten through whom all things have been made, that what he is, is one thing and what he has, is another thing, but it is rather this: that which he is, is at the same time that which he has. This is expressed more

---

62. Ibid., VIII.Intro.; CCL 50.268; FOTC 45.243.
63. Ibid., V.I.2; CCL 50.207; FOTC 45.176.

clearly in that place if there is anyone capable of grasping it, where it is said: 'As the Father has life in himself, so he has given to the Son to have life in himself.'[64] For he has not given to one already existing and not having life in order that he may have life in himself, since by the very fact that he is, he is life. Therefore, the sentence, 'He has given to the Son to have life in himself,' means that he has begotten the Son as unchangeable life, which is eternal life.[65]

The same blessed Augustine, in his exposition of the Gospel of John, when he treats of the very words of the Lord, speaks as follows: "But the Son of God was not as if at first without life and [then] he received life. For, if he so received it, he would not have it in himself. For what does 'in himself' mean? That he himself is life itself."[66] And a little later in the same work, he confirms this, saying, "For the Apostle said, 'You were once darkness, but now you are light in the Lord.'[67] When he said, '. . . but now you are light,' he added 'in the Lord.' Therefore, there is darkness in you, 'light in the Lord.' Why light? Because by participation in that light you are light. But if you withdraw from the light by which you are enlightened, you return to your darkness. Not so Christ, not so the Word of God. But how? 'As the Father has life in himself, so he has given to the Son also to have life in himself,' so that he does not live by participation, but he lives without change and in every respect he himself is life."[68] And a little after this, the outstanding teacher, the holy Augustine says, "Therefore, what is said 'He has given to the Son' is such as if it were said 'He begot a Son'; for he gave by begetting. As [the Father] gave that he might be, as he gave that he might be life, and so he gave that he might be life in himself. What does it mean, he might be life in himself? He would not need life from another source, but he would be

64. Jn 5.26.
65. Augustine, *De Trinitate* I.XII.26; CCL 50.66.; FOTC 45.39–40.
66. Augustine, *Tractatus in Johannem* XXII.9; CCL 36.228; FOTC 79.206.
67. Eph 5.8.
68. Augustine, *Tractatus in Johannem* XXII.10; CCL 36.229; FOTC 79.206–7.

the fullness of life by which others, believing, might live while they live."[69]

18. Therefore, from these words of the well-known bishop Augustine, with all the obscurities removed, we are taught that saving the immutability, eternity, and impassibility of the divinity of the Son of God, whatever is said of his majesty, eternity, and power according to the taking up of the flesh, is not incompatible if it is said of his divinity in the same way according to the flesh. Therefore, what has been taken up by the Son of God is proved to have been taken up by his divinity, by his majesty, by his power, by his eternity. In order that the truthful assertions of the holy Fathers may show this, we first bring forward the letters of the most blessed Pope Leo, glorious pontiff of the Apostolic See, writing to Flavian, bishop of the city of Constantinople. In this letter, because he marvelously expressed the true faith concerning the Incarnation of the Lord, he destroyed every error of heretical depravity. For in this letter, the same glorious bishop, no less endowed with the truth of the apostolic faith than outstanding because of the dignity of the Apostolic See, said this: "In the preservation, then, of the real quality of both natures, both being united in one person, lowliness was taken on by majesty, weakness by strength, mortality by the immortal. And in order to pay the debt of our fallen state, inviolable nature was united to one capable of suffering so that (and this is the sort of reparation we needed) one and the same mediator between God and men, the man Jesus Christ, could die in the one nature and not die in the other."[70] The above-mentioned bishop of the Apostolic See follows up and says, "In the whole and perfect nature of the true man, then, the true God was born, complete in his own nature, complete in ours. But by 'our' we mean that which the Creator formed in us at the beginning and which he took upon himself to redeem it."[71] You perceive how that apostolic teacher

---

69. Ibid., FOTC 79.207.
70. Leo *Epistola* 28; N.Tanner, *Decrees* I.78b; FOTC 34.95–96.
71. Ibid., FOTC 34.96.

says by this faith that God took upon himself to redeem the things which he created in us in the beginning, by that same faith he says that humility was taken up by majesty, weakness by strength, mortality by eternity. When the maj-esty, power, and eternity of the Son of God are spoken of, nothing other than his divinity is being referred to. Therefore, let us not doubt that the divinity of Christ took up whatever the majesty of Christ, the power and eternity of Christ took up. Hence it is that in the same letter a not-dissimilar statement is contained a second time; since the same very blessed leader of the Roman church affirms with a most clear declaration the divinity and the humanity just as God and man. For in the same letter he says, "From the mother the Lord took his nature, but no fault, and the Lord Jesus Christ, born from a virgin's womb, does not have a nature different from ours just because his birth was an unusual one. He who is true God is also true man; there is no falsity in this union, wherein the lowliness of man and the greatness of the divinity are mutually united. Just as God is not changed by his show of mercy, so the man is not changed by being swallowed up in majesty."[72] In another text, the same very blessed Pope Leo professes that the divinity is covered by a veil of the flesh, saying, "Already when he came to be baptized by John, the precursor, lest it be unknown that divinity was being covered by a veil of flesh, the voice of the Father, thundering from heaven said, 'This is my beloved Son in whom I am well-pleased.'"[73] Here immediately he confidently names that divinity, God, and that flesh he unhesitatingly calls a human being, saying, "And so, he whom the cleverness of the Devil tempts, as if he were a man, is accompanied by the ministration of angels, as to God."[74] Again, in another text of the same letter, he says, "Although in the Lord Jesus Christ, there is one person of God and man, it is only from one of these sources that contempt comes to both in common and

---

72. Ibid., Tanner, 79ab; FOTC 34.97.
73. Ibid., Mt 3.17. FOTC 34.98.
74. Ibid., Tanner, 79b, FOTC 34.99.

from the other source that glory comes to both in common. From us he has a humanity less than the Father; from the Father, a divinity equal to the Father's."[75] The firmness of this declaration is made known to and impressed upon the minds of all the faithful in such a way that he affirms that in this faith the life and progress of the Catholic Church stands, saying that the Catholic Church lives and progresses by this faith so that it is believed that there is not a humanity without a true divinity nor a divinity without a true humanity.

19. Here as well, Pope Gelasius of blessed memory, assuring the continuity of teaching, treads the path of the true faith and the apostolic confession with altogether similar steps. For in that book, which the aforementioned venerable bishop wrote against those who refuse to believe in the undivided truth of the two natures in the Lord Jesus Christ but confuse them by the profession of one nature, preserving the continuity of the apostolic proclamation, he affirms that the two natures in Christ are unconfused and inseparable, saying, "It is necessary that these same be spoken of as existing undivided and inseparable in one and the same person because of that union in such a way that they may remain what they are."[76] And a little later: "When God alone is spoken of, is the human being denied? When humanity is spoken of, is the deity removed from there? When the Son of Man is spoken of, is not the Son of God also adverted to as a result? When the Word of God is spoken of, is not the flesh which it became also understood at the same time? When his flesh and body are brought up, is not the divinity without a doubt also shown?"[77] Likewise, in another text of the same book, concerning those who try to assert that there is one nature in Christ, he speaks as follows: "For also when they say that there was one incarnate nature, wishing in this way to present as it were a single [nature], in no way do they es-

75. Ibid., Tanner, 80a, FOTC 34.99.
76. Gelasius, *De Duabus Naturis in Christo*, ed. E. Schwartz (Munich: Publizistische Sammlungen zum Acacianischen Schisma, 1934), 91.
77. Ibid.

cape the reality of two. For while it is said that one nature of the divinity was incarnated, with the ambiguities removed, there will be one that was incarnated and the other is shown as incarnate; since the nature of the deity which was incarnated will not be the same as the nature of the flesh by which the incarnated is established; nor is the very nature of the deity incarnated but the nature of the flesh is recognized as incarnate; just as the very nature of the flesh did not cause itself to come forth, elevated because of the deity, because the divinity did not come forth from any other source than that which came forth incarnate from the womb of the virgin mother; and the flesh has not been united to the deity except in that same womb, with the Holy Spirit coming from above and the power of the Most High overshadowing."[78] Likewise, a little later, he says, "So, let them try to escape from that pit of their own madness by which they are imprisoned; and let them openly confess either that they are among the number of those who impugn the true body of Christ; or let them not dare to deny it, not unless it is true for this reason without which it cannot be true. Just as when we speak of the one God and we proclaim that we are speaking or acting according to God, otherwise it cannot be true, unless we confess that there is the true divinity and that there is the nature of the deity remaining in the property of his substance."[79]

20. St. Ambrose, too, in the first book of *On the Faith* in one and the same place, just as he professes that Christ is God and a human being, so there he professes the divinity and the flesh, saying, "The prophets proclaim, the Apostles hear the voice of one God. In one God did the Magi believe, and they brought in adoration gold, frankincense, and myrrh to Christ's cradle, confessing by the gift of gold his royalty and with the incense worshipping him as God. For gold is the sign of kingdom, incense of God, myrrh of burial. What then was the meaning of the mystic offerings in the

78. Ibid., 92.
79. Ibid., 93.

lowly cattle stalls, save that we should discern in Christ the difference between the Godhead and the flesh? He is seen as man; he is adored as Lord. He lies in swaddling-clothes but shines amid the stars; the cradle shows his birth, the stars his dominion; it is the flesh that is wrapped in clothes, the Godhead that receives the ministry of angels. Thus the dignity of his natural majesty is not lost, and his true assumption of the flesh is proved."[80] All these things which were written above the blessed Ambrose confirmed by this conclusion, saying, "This is our faith. Thus did God will that he should be known by all. . . ."[81] The blessed Ambrose brings the previous discussion to a close with this statement in such a way that he says that this is our faith, teaching very clearly that as we speak of God and a human being, so we should never hesitate to speak of divinity and flesh. Also in the second book of the same work, he says this: "A truce then to vain wranglings over words for the kingdom of God, as it is written, does not consist in persuasive words but in power plainly shown forth."[82] The same Saint Ambrose follows up by saying, "Let us take heed to the distinction of the Godhead from the flesh. In each there speaks one and the same Son of God for each nature is present in him."[83] And further on: "This is he who came down from heaven, this he whom the Father has sanctified and sent into this world. Even the letter itself teaches us that not the Godhead but the flesh needed sanctification."[84] The blessed Augustine also, in his book on faith, hope, and charity which you know is called the *Enchiridion* by many, speaks as follows: "Who could expound in words apt to their subject the single statement, 'The Word was made flesh and dwelt among us' so that we might believe in the only Son of God, the Father Almighty, born of the Holy Spirit and the Virgin Mary? 'The Word was made flesh'; flesh was assumed by the divinity; divinity was

---

80. Ambrose, *De Fide* I.IV.31–32; CSEL 78.15–16; NPNF 10.205–06.
81. Ibid., I.IV.33; CSEL 78.16; NPNF 10.206.
82. Ibid., II.IX.77; CSEL 78.84; NPNF 10.233.
83. Ibid.
84. Ibid., II.IX.78; CSEL 78.85; NPNF, 10.234.

not changed into flesh."[85] See that the blessed Augustine shows the divinity capable of the taking up of flesh which he bears witness is no less capable of the taking up of death as well. For in the book on the presence of God, he speaks as follows: "Through our head we are reconciled to God, because in him the divinity of the only-begotten Son shared in our mortality, that we might be made sharers in his immortality."[86] Then, immediately pointing out the greatness of this mystery, he added these words: "This mystery is far removed from the hearts of the prideful wise; consequently, not from the truly wise."[87]

21. All these statements of the holy Fathers show that what is said of the only-begotten God, is not unfittingly also proclaimed of his divinity. We know in their defense of Catholic truth, that there are either heretics given over to perversity or Catholics less instructed in the mystery of correct belief; when they hear what is being said of the Son of God, being said as well of his divinity, still they know that the one divinity of the Father and the Son and the Holy Spirit is no less proclaimed by us; in some measure, they must be persuaded that the communion of divinity brings about a communion in the taking up of the human nature; and just as from the communion of the flesh, let it be thought that there is a communion of the human birth, suffering and death in the Father and the Son and the Holy Spirit. Therefore, in order that neither the former wickedly lay snares nor the latter be deceived possibly from lack of care, both ought to think that the one substance of the Trinity is proclaimed by us in such a way that we do not say that there is one person of the same Trinity. So the whole, which is the nature itself, is common to the three persons but in such a way that there is still something by which each person is properly recognized, something still that is neither separable nor can be common. For we say that it is proper to the Father that he

---

85. Augustine, *Enchiridion* X.34; CCL 46.68; FOTC 2.399.
86. Augustine, *Epistolae* 187.20; CSEL 57.99; FOTC 30.237.
87. Ibid., l87.21; CSEL 57.99; FOTC 30.237.

beget; we say that it is proper to the Son that he alone was born from the Father alone; proper to the Holy Spirit that it proceeds from the Father and the Son. In these properties, there is no separation of nature but a certain recognition of the person. Although begetting is proper to the Father alone, the Son is not separated by it, because with the Father begetting, the Son is born. And although birth is proper to the Son, he is not thereby separable from the Father who begets, because the birth of the Son would not be true by nature unless he had been begotten by the Father. Therefore, although with the Son being born, the Father has begotten, and with the Father begetting, the Son has been born, still neither has the Son begotten with the Father nor has the Father been born with the Son. The Son has been born from the nature of the Father, and the Father has begotten the nature of the Son from himself. That property of the persons is inseparable in such a way that neither begetting nor birth can be common to the two persons. Although, unless there were by nature two persons of the Father and the Son, neither could one beget or the other be begotten. But if heretics seek to reject this in the case of God the Father and God the Son, let them either be instructed or confounded by the clear example of human generation. For a human father precedes a human son in time because he himself also began in time. The Son would not be born in time from him unless the nature of the father was subject to a beginning in time. From this, it appears very clearly that God the Son was born from God the Father without a beginning because that Father begot the Son from himself who did not begin to exist just as he does not cease to exist; and still when a human father is recognized as having preceded the birth of his son by nature, in that same begetting of the son, the son is not separated from the father nor the father from the son, because with the father begetting, the son is begotten. And since that begetting is the cause of the birth and the birth cannot be separated from the begetting, that begetting is not separated from the birth in such a way that in one and the same nature, one begets and the other is born.

22. Therefore, that begetting and birth are inseparable by nature in such a way that communion neither of begetting nor of being born can be present at the same time in both persons. Because the property of the persons has this so that neither does the Son beget himself with the Father from whom he is begotten nor is the Father born with the Son being born from him. Therefore, in the unity of nature there remains the unconfused truth of the persons, in which there is something which is found to be not common but proper. Therefore, the unbegotten God who, together with the Father and the Holy Spirit, has one and the same nature in such a way that he has a person, not common altogether, but proper, therefore, he did not have the receiving of the form of a servant in common with the Father and the Holy Spirit, because he received the truth and the fullness of the form of a servant, not in the unity of nature but only in the unity of his own person. For he who truly and fully is God, the same became truly and fully human, when a rational soul and flesh without sin was accepted by the only-begotten God into the unity of his person. Therefore, human nature was accepted by the only-begotten God in such a way that there was only one person of the divinity and humanity, not one nature. Accordingly, the Son, when he took up the full nature of our humanity, was not separated from the Father and the Holy Spirit. But he did not take up the same nature at the same time with the Father and the Holy Spirit because there did not come about in him one nature of divinity and flesh so that from this one might believe that there was an incarnation of the entire Trinity, but there is one person in Christ, which the only-begotten God has inseparable from the Father and the Holy Spirit but still one that he does not have with the Father and the Holy Spirit. So Christ has his own proper humanity with which his divinity does not have one nature but has one person. Because this person of the only-begotten God is not the person of the Father and of the Holy Spirit, the form of a servant is rightly believed to have been accepted by the Son alone, since there is one person of his divinity and flesh, not one nature. For in Christ, there is

not one person of the divinity and another of the humanity, but there is one person for both natures, nevertheless, of this one and the same person, there is a divine nature and a human nature. Wherefore, because the working of the Trinity is inseparable, the entire Trinity made the form of a servant which the only-begotten God received; it is certain that this was made by the entire Trinity but pertains only to the person of the Son of God. Just as there is in it one working of the entire Trinity, there is not a common taking up by the Trinity in it. The fact is that what is proper to the person (because the Father himself is not as the Son nor is the Holy Spirit himself as Father or the Son) shows that there is something made by the Father and the Son and the Holy Spirit which still was received only by the Son.

23. No example of this sort of thing can be found in creatures, because, with the exception of the Trinity which is by nature the one true God, there is no nature which can have three inseparable persons in it. Because in each human being we find the flesh is not that which the soul is nor are both of one nature, although from the two is formed and constituted one human nature; still in each human being, there is one person. Accordingly, in those two natures which we know have one person, let us look for something similar, so that we may find here something coming about by the common working of the soul and the flesh which still pertains to the substance of the soul alone or to the substance of the flesh alone. So let us try to figure it out and let us understand, to the extent that the Trinity grants, how something could be done at the same time by the same three persons by one working, something which the entire Trinity does inseparably but in such a way that what has been done pertains to one person of the Trinity. So, when we eat, we provide for the flesh, not the soul; and yet in the very taking of food by which the flesh alone is fed, the soul is at work equally with the flesh because the flesh without the soul, just as it does not live, so it does not eat. So, in order that the flesh alone take food, at the same time, there is one work for both the flesh and the soul, and what the flesh alone re-

ceives by a natural property, through the unity of the person, the soul is also at work together with the flesh. Therefore, the work is common but the receiving is not common; nor does the soul in the event desert the flesh when it eats. It still combines the function of its working with the flesh in such a way that, through the same communion of effort, the flesh alone receives the life-giving support. There is something like this in the same unity of the person, the very soul of the human being affirming for itself if, when it assigns to the function of divine reading the disposition of the heart, by which, without a doubt, not the exterior but the interior person is nourished; and most of the time the soul is well fed rather than the fasting flesh. Is it not so that the soul may take nourishment from the reading and it participates in a function of the corporeal members? Reading is impossible without the eyes of the body; what it reads with the eyes of the body, it understands with the eyes of the heart; and in this way, the soul works together with the flesh, from which it alone is nourished and alone receives in itself what it does not do alone. So on account of one person, two natures work together inseparably and on account of their properties, one often receives what it alone does not do, indeed what it in no way does without the other. And although this altogether suffices for the complete line of knowledge, in order that we may rise above what we see here in two natures and one person to, insofar as the very Trinity deigns to grant, the understanding of three persons in one nature; even in the very person of our Redeemer, a clear and undoubted knowledge of this matter is demonstrated for us. For he has joined and united each nature in the unity of his person in such a way that in the one person of the only-begotten God, neither can the divinity be separated from his humanity nor the humanity from his divinity. For the indissoluble union of the Word and flesh came about when the Word became flesh; in him, the unity of person has remained in such a way that the property of each nature can neither be divided nor confused. Accordingly, the functions of each nature in the one Christ are common in such a way that, although Christ is not divided in strengths and weaknesses, still there is something that in the working of each nature is not common to both natures.

24. For, in order that I may now keep silent about that ineffable conception and birth, by which the eternal God was conceived and born in time in such a way that still in the very communion of the virginal conception and birth, it was the property by nature solely of the flesh initially to exist from the flesh of the mother, to be formed into members and to be brought to the maturity of birth in the passing of time and activity, then to grow with the going and coming of the stages of life and to arrive at the perfect measure of youth in his time. What shall we say concerning those works and sufferings after that since there was in him by nature an inseparable true flesh, a true rational soul, and a true divinity? Nevertheless, those things which the truth of nature had either deigned to suffer or to do in such a way that the whole Christ remained inseparable in suffering or in working and what the union in the person showed as common to the divinity and the humanity, still this the same Christ demonstrated as proper to each nature in himself by the truth of the nature. So, assuming the hunger of our weakness, the whole Christ brought about that hunger of his, and, in order that he take food, the whole Christ likewise brought it about; still, by nature, just as the flesh alone bore the hunger, so the flesh alone, by the working of the whole Christ eating, received the food. Wearied by the journey, Jesus sat by the well; divinity could not feel that weariness, but neither, according to the soul, must Christ be said to have felt that weariness in any way. That he sat pertained by nature only to the restoring of the wearied flesh; still in that restoration, the work was common to the deity and to the soul. Thus in that time of the suffering and death, who does not see that in one and the same Christ the properties of the natures remain inseparably in the very communion of the works? His soul was saddened unto death. But immutable divinity cannot be a receiver of sadness nor can flesh ever feel sadness. Therefore, sadness belongs solely to the rational

soul which cannot be present by nature either in the divinity or in the flesh. In his person, the whole Christ deigned to bring sadness upon himself. He brought about his own sufferings, he who had nothing which could suffer unless he willed it. Therefore, the whole Christ brought it about that he be saddened; but by nature, only the rational soul received that sadness in itself. So when Christ, at one and the same time, both lay in the tomb and descended to Hell, who does not see the inseparable work of each nature? And who does not clearly recognize in that one and inseparable work things proper to the flesh and the soul and the divinity? The whole Christ brought it about that he could lie in the tomb according to the flesh; but by nature the flesh alone was capable of burial. That Christ according to the soul descended to Hell was the single work of both natures, that is, the divine and the human; but that descent was natural to the soul alone. Just as at that time, the whole Christ did not cease to work in heaven and on earth, but it belonged to divinity alone not to be contained in a place and those things which pertained to the governing of the universe, to work naturally and equally with the Father. Hence it is that in all those works of suffering and death, apostolic authority assigns to one person working what the whole Christ worked in himself in such a way that it shows without a doubt what belongs to which nature. For the blessed Paul says of one and the same Christ: "For indeed he was crucified out of weakness, but he lives by the power of God."[88] And the blessed Peter uttered prophetic words from the Psalms in such a way that he said that the soul of Christ, which he knew had descended into Hell, was not abandoned in Hell. The same Peter the apostle says of the blessed David: "But since he was a prophet and knew that God had sworn an oath to him that he would set one of his descendants upon his throne, he foresaw and spoke of the resurrection of the Messiah, that neither was he abandoned to the netherworld nor did his flesh see corruption."[89] Therefore, all these things the one

88. 2 Cor 13.4.
89. Acts 2.30–31.

Christ has done according to the single person and the one work of both natures is recognized in such a way that what must be assigned to which nature is not denied. Therefore, let each one be instructed by these examples, so that what he here knows in the consideration of the natures, he may understand there in the persons, and let him not doubt that the human nature of Christ has been made by the working of the whole Trinity but that it belongs only to the person of the only-begotten God.

25. Your third questions is: "Does the soul of Christ have altogether full knowledge of the deity which assumes it, and how do the Father and the Son and the Holy Spirit know each other; so does the same Son know by the fact that he is human, in the same way know himself as God; from each and in each substance wholly comprehending the Father. Or perhaps, just as with bodily eyes, he does not see God as spirit, lest the dignity be attached not to the human being, but the nature is believed to be changed within; so the entire essence of the divinity is not seen or comprehended by the rational soul, even with devout understanding and perfectly clean heart, lest any creature capture the Creator."

26. Dear brother, when I read these words in your letter, I confess that I was more pressed by the discussion because we are being compelled to speak of something that we are not able to think of sufficiently and worthily. For the distinction being considered between Creator and creature demonstrates the incomprehensible and inexplicable greatness of the Creator to the created intellect. For the peace of God excels every intellect and the one who ascends above the Cherubim flies on the wings of the winds.[90] You know that the 'Cherubim' are interpreted as the fullness of knowledge. What, therefore, is "to ascend above the Cherubim" except to go beyond every fullness of knowledge with incomprehensible height? But confidently and without a doubt, we say these things concerning the holy angels and holy people, anyone of whom is called 'god' by the free gift of divine

---

90. Cf. Phil 4.7; Ps 17.11 LXX; Ps 18.10.

adoption but in such fashion that the God of the angels or the God of human beings is not being spoken of. But when we speak of the soul of Christ, we are speaking about that rational spirit to whom not only God came by grace but whom the divinity itself took up in the unity of the person. For by that soul, Christ is one with the Word; by that soul, the only-begotten God is one with the Word. And because the only-begotten God is equal to the Father and he who does not know the whole Father cannot know the whole Son, let us be careful lest, since the soul of Christ is not believed to know the whole Father, knowledge of not only the Father but also of himself and of the Holy Spirit as well, be denied in some part to the one Christ himself. It is extremely hard and thoroughly foreign to a healthy faith to say that the soul of Christ, with which it is believed that he has by nature one person, does not have full knowledge of his own deity.

27. If we believe this, it is necessary that that proclamation of the blessed John the Baptist, in which he attributed to Christ a singular gift of the Spirit and one without measure, be rendered meaningless. I refer to the statement: "[God] does not ration his gift of the Spirit."[91] Since our ancestors too in us receive a measure of this gift, they profess that in Christ there abides the fullness of the Holy Spirit. For the blessed Ambrose, in the first book on the Holy Spirit, among other things, says, "I will pour out of my Spirit."[92] He did not say, 'my Spirit,' but 'of my Spirit,' for we cannot take the fullness of the Holy Spirit, but we receive so much as our Master divides of his own according to his will.[93] Therefore, Saint Ambrose, showing that we receive not the fullness, but of the fullness of the Spirit, that he may show that Christ has received the entire fullness of the Spirit, a little while after this, says, ". . . so too, the Father says that he pours out of the Holy Spirit upon all flesh; for he did not pour him forth entirely but what he poured forth abounded for all. Therefore,

91. Jn 3.34.
92. Joel 2.28.
93. Ambrose, *De Spiritu Sancto* I.VIII.92; CSEL 79.54–55; FOTC 44.69.

it was poured upon us of the Spirit, but in truth, the Spirit abode over the Lord Jesus, when he was in the form of man, as it is written: 'He upon whom you shall see the Spirit descending and remaining on him, he it is that baptizes with the Holy Spirit.'[94] Around us from abundant provision is the liberality of him who bestows; in him abides forever the fullness of the Spirit."[95] Of course, the blessed Ambrose clearly and without a doubt shows that within the soul of Christ is the full knowledge of his complete divinity, when he says that around us is the liberality of the giver in abundant provision, in him abides forever the fullness of the whole Spirit. That he may say this, he calls attention to these words of the blessed John, where he says, speaking of the Son himself, "[God] does not ration his gift of the Spirit."[96] Also the blessed Augustine, by the same illumination of the Holy Spirit, perceiving and understanding this, affirms that it must be accepted only in the case of the person of Christ. For when he expounded the same text of the Gospel and the very words of John the Baptist came up where he says, "[God] does not ration his gift of the Spirit," the same blessed Augustine added this: "What does this mean: 'For [God] does not ration his gift of the Spirit'? We find that God does give the Spirit by measure. Hear the Apostle saying, '... according to the measure of the giving of Christ.'[97] He gives to men by measure; he does not give to the only Son by measure."[98] Likewise, he says in the same homily, "... So too there are various gifts of the faithful, distributed [to them] as to members according to the measure proper to each. But Christ, who gives, does not receive according to measure. For hear further what follows, because he had said about the Son, 'For not according to measure does God give the Spirit. The Father loves the Son and has handed over all things to him.'"[99] Of course, the blessed Augustine shows by

---

94. Jn 1.33.
95. Ambrose, *De Spiritu Sancto* I.VIII.92–3; CSEL 79.55; FOTC 44.69.
96. Jn 3.34.   97. Eph 4.7.
98. Augustine, *Tractatus in Johannem* XIV.X.2; CCL 36.148; FOTC 79.74.
99. Jn 3.34–35; Augustine, *Tractatus in Johannem* XIV.X–XI; CCL 36.148–49; FOTC 79.75.

the testimony from the Gospel what we must think about the soul of Christ when Christ himself, who gives the Spirit, has not received according to measure. For he it is who gives, he who receives; and because he is powerful enough to give according to measure, therefore, he could not receive according to measure. Remaining in the form of God, he gives the Spirit; receiving the form of a servant, he has received the Spirit. But because he gives according to measure, therefore, he himself has not received according to measure; what he gives according to measure, he has received the totality of; for according to measure, he gives to many sons, but the only Son has not received according to measure; because he is truly human in such a way that he is true God.

28. In the two books which he wrote *On the Lord's Sermon on the Mount*,[100] the blessed Augustine had once explained this text of the Gospel in a different way. Yet in his *Retractations*, he corrected this interpretation, approving and confirming what he later understood in a better way, in that exposition of the Gospel, he confirmed what ought to be accepted concerning Christ alone. Showing this in the first book of his *Retractations*, he says, among other things, "In another place, though I cited this text as a proof: 'For not by measure does God give the Spirit,' I did not yet understand that this is, more truly, to be understood in a proper sense about Christ. For if the Spirit were not given to other men by measure, Elisha would not have asked for twice as much [Spirit] as was in Elijah."[101] Therefore, in these words of the blessed Augustine, let us note above all what he says: viz., that it is given to other human beings according to measure. So he said this, to show that he believed this not about the divinity but about the humanity of Christ to which God did not give the Spirit according to measure, since the Apostle bears witness that grace is given to each one "according to the measure of Christ's gift." So, therefore, the blessed Augustine did not say "to human beings" but "to other human

---

100. Augustine, *De Sermone Domini in Monte* I.VI.17, CCL 35.17.

101. Augustine, *Retractationes* I.XVIII-3; CCL 57.56; FOTC 60.80; Eph 4.7; 2 Kgs 2.9.

beings" except to show that it was given to that man in singular way, not according to measure, but that the whole fullness of the Spirit was in him. He was true man by nature in such a way that the same was also true God by nature, receiving the whole in the truth of the flesh, which by the gift of the deity he grants according to measure. Therefore, to the one who gives grace according to the measure of his gift, God has not given the Spirit according to measure. In Christ, according to the truth of the Catholic faith, we confess that in the unity of the person, there are at the same time both divinity and a rational soul and the flesh, in whom still the divinity could not receive the Spirit because, according to divinity, the Father and the Son and the Holy Spirit are one God. As great as the Father alone is, he is just as great with the Son and the Holy Spirit; and as great as the Son alone is, just as great is he with the Father and the Holy Spirit; and as great as the Holy Spirit alone is, just is great is he with the Father and the Son. There no one of the three persons has anything less than the two where in each person the divinity is full in such a way that it is both one in the three persons and full in each of them. Therefore, the divinity of the Son could not receive the Holy Spirit since the Holy Spirit itself proceeds from the Son just as it proceeds from the Father and is given by the Son just as it is given by the Father; nor could that nature whence the Spirit itself takes its origin either expect or receive its gift. That Spirit is completely of the Father; it is completely of the Son because by nature it is the one Spirit of the Father and the Son. Accordingly, as a whole, it has proceeded from the Father and the Son, it remains completely in the Father and the Son; because it remains in such a way that it proceeds, it proceeds in such a way that it remains. Whence by nature it has this fullness of unity with the Father and the Son and the unity of fullness so that it has the whole Father and the whole Son, and it, as a whole, is possessed by the Father; as a whole, it is possessed by the Son. Therefore, the divinity of the Son did not receive the Holy Spirit with which the Holy Spirit is of one nature and from which it has whatever it has, indeed, from which it is that which it is; because what it has by nature, that it is. Therefore, it remains that the soul of Christ receives the Spirit which still it has not received according to measure and so has received as a whole. For when a measure is not spoken of, there is the fullness of perfection and the perfection of fullness.

29. But who this Spirit is, whom Christ did not receive according to measure, the prophet Isaiah shows us, who, speaking about Christ, says, "A shoot shall come out from the stump of Jesse and a branch shall grow out of his roots. The Spirit of the Lord shall rest on him, the spirit of wisdom and understanding, the spirit of counsel and might, the spirit of knowledge and the fear of the Lord."[102] Therefore, Christ received the Spirit, but he did not receive it according to measure. But if God did not give the Spirit to the soul of Christ according to measure, it is necessary that he have no lessening of wisdom or knowledge. For that Spirit is the Spirit of wisdom and understanding, of counsel and might, of knowledge and piety. And for this reason, this privilege of perfection pertains not only to the divinity of Christ but also to his soul which the blessed Apostle attributes to Christ himself, saying, ". . . in whom are hidden all the treasures of wisdom and knowledge."[103] For if he has received the Spirit of wisdom and knowledge not according to measure, it is necessary that he have all the treasures of wisdom and knowledge. But if something of this fullness be taken away from him, it follows that he be proclaimed to have received the Spirit according to measure. And who is it to whom God has given the Spirit not according to measure if Christ has received it according to measure? To the extent that the Spirit is given, to that extent is knowledge of divinity received. But where the Spirit is not according to measure, it is necessary that there be full knowledge of the infinite divinity. Complete fullness is given where the Spirit is not given according to measure. But not fullness but "from his fullness we have all received, grace in place of grace."[104] Where it is

102. Is 11.1–2.　　　　　　　　103. Col 2.3.
104. Jn 1.16.

shown that even in that grace of vision, which will be given in place of the grace of faith, it is not the fullness itself but from his fullness that we will receive grace in place of grace. We will be filled with this itself, which we will receive from his fullness insofar as through his grace we will have the capacity. The prophet shows us this when he says, "In your presence there is fullness of joy."[105] And again: "Satisfy us in the morning with your steadfast love."[106] And again: "We shall be satisfied with the goodness of your home. . . ."[107] But, in order that we be filled, from his fullness, we shall receive. Concerning Christ, Paul, the teacher of the nations, says, "For in him all the fullness was pleased to dwell."[108] Concerning him, the same one says, "For in him dwells the whole fullness of the deity bodily."[109] Therefore, I do not think that full knowledge of divinity is lacking in anything to that soul, who is one in person with the Word; Wisdom took him up in such a way that the same person is Wisdom itself; it has become master of all things to such an extent that with its divinity itself it is one person in the Trinity, i.e., Christ crucified, whom the Apostle Paul proclaims as the power of God and the wisdom of God.

30. But if the soul of Christ has a lesser knowledge of his godhead in anything, he does not have in himself the whole of wisdom and the whole of power. He has a participation in Christ, he is not himself Christ, if he has a part of the knowledge of his divinity. The Apostle asserts that we are participants in Christ, saying, "We have become partners of Christ. . . ."[110] Whence it is said to Christ himself: "Therefore, God, your God, has anointed you with the oil of gladness beyond your companions."[111] The oil of gladness with which Christ was anointed is without a doubt the Holy Spirit, as blessed Peter says, "How God anointed Jesus of Nazareth with the Holy Spirit and power."[112] Him, therefore, "God anointed beyond his companions" to whom "He gave the Spirit, not ac-

105. Ps 15.11 LXX; Ps 16.11.
107. Ps 64.5 LXX; Ps 65.4.
109. Col 2.9.
111. Ps 44.8 LXX; Ps.45.7.
106. Ps 89.14 LXX; Ps 90.14.
108. Col 1.19.
110. Heb 3.14.
112. Acts 10.38.

cording to measure," in whom "dwells the whole fullness of the deity bodily," "in whom are hidden all the treasures of wisdom and knowledge." The blessed Apostle marvels at the depth of his wisdom and knowledge, saying, "Oh, the depths of the riches and wisdom and knowledge of God!"[113] The true faith confesses Christ as most high completely, not only according to the divinity but also according to the humanity. For Mother Zion says, "This one and that one were born in it for the Most High himself will establish it."[114] And in fact who would dare to deny him as Most High whom God not only begot from himself who is the Most High but also "exalted" the one born from the virgin "and bestowed on him the name that is above every name that, at the name of Jesus, every knee should bend of those in heaven and on earth and under the earth and every tongue confess that Jesus Christ is Lord to the glory of God the Father?"[115] But if the soul of Christ does not have full knowledge of his divinity, he will not attain to the full depth of the wisdom and knowledge of God. Let Christ be proclaimed as most high, not in full but in part, if his soul is proclaimed by the faithful to be below the depth of the riches of the wisdom and knowledge of God. For in whom does God exalt us if not in the one who raises our souls to himself? To the extent that he lifts our souls to himself, to that extent does he make known to us the truth of his knowledge and love. For who would say that the soul of Christ either perceives less of the truth or has less charity? For Christ is himself Truth. Therefore, how is that soul said to have less knowledge of truth in itself which is in a unique way the soul of Truth itself? Thus, one must not discuss the soul of Christ as one might discuss some angelic or human spirit which can participate in the true God but is not the true God as Christ is. He, receiving perfect flesh and a perfect rational soul, i.e., a full human nature, into that eternal person of his divinity, just as by nature he is completely a true human being, so he is completely true God because just as in his divinity, he has the com-

113. Rm 11.33.
114. Ps 86.5 LXX; Ps 87.5.
115. Phil 2.9–11.

plete nature of his humanity, so in his humanity, he has the complete substance of his divinity, all the majesty, all the immutability, all the power, all the wisdom, all the omnipotence. For the only-begotten God deigned to take up human nature in such a way that it is God himself who is a human being and it is the same human being who is God. Accordingly, the fullness of divinity is in the human being Christ just as there is the fullness of humanity in God. Therefore, just as Christ the human being has it in a unique way that he is true God, so in a unique way he knows his full divinity.

31. We can say clearly that the soul of Christ has complete knowledge of his godhead; still I do not know whether we ought to say that the soul of Christ knew his deity in the way that the very deity knows itself, or rather, that this should be said that he knew as much as it knew but not in the way it knows. For the deity knew itself in such a way that by nature it found itself to be what it knew; but that soul knew its complete deity in such a way that still the soul itself is not the deity. Therefore, that deity itself is by nature its knowledge; but that soul has received from the deity itself what it fully knows that it may know; therefore, the deity of Christ by nature is that which it knows; but that soul, in that it knows its deity, does not find that it is what it knows. Not, therefore, as the Father and the Son and the Holy Spirit know themselves, has Christ become known to his own soul according to his divinity, since while it is true that that soul has a full knowledge of the Trinity, still it does not have one nature with the Trinity. For it is one thing for something to know what it is by nature, another thing to know what it is not by nature. God the Spirit does not see with bodily eyes. So, when the blessed Augustine in the letter which he wrote to Italica,[116] albeit with few words, still with a sufficient response, has convinced certain ones who wanted to believe this about Christ, that he saw God the Father with his bodily eyes. For the eyes of the body have this, that they see not only bodies but they cannot see if, between themselves and

---

116. Augustine, *Epistolae* 92.5, CSEL 34.441, FOTC 18.52–53.

those things which they see, there are not distances consisting of some space in between. Hence it is that, although they see many other things, they cannot see themselves nor do they see in themselves when they see outside themselves; for the vision itself is obscured if anything to be seen is brought into contact with the eyes themselves. Therefore, whoever thinks that God can be discerned with the eyes of the body, it is our first duty to say that God is separated from the very eyes by a corporeal space; whoever wishes to know by what kind of eyes God is seen, let him think of the fact that God himself is wisdom, he is truth, he is charity. Wherefore, with whatever kind of eyes are wisdom, truth, and charity seen, with the same kind of eyes is that wise, true, and loving divinity seen. God does not promise the vision of himself to the eyes of the body but to the eyes of the human soul to which he gives a capacity for wisdom, truth, and love. Therefore, the rational spirit has received from God that it see God; it has received it through grace whom still it can see, not outside itself, but in itself. For God is not contained in a place but is perceived by love, and, therefore, is not seen by the one in whom he does not live. God lives in the soul in a much more inward fashion than the soul lives in the body, since the former spirit is the Creator, the latter a created spirit. Therefore, to the extent that any soul of a holy human being has knowledge of that most high God, to that extent has it received the grace of inward vision. So I do not know how we receive the only-begotten of the Father, full of grace and of truth, if either we say that something of the fullness of grace is missing from that fullness of truth or we think that the whole fullness of truth is not in that fullness of grace; since, indeed, in him most certainly the only-begotten of the Father is recognized as full of grace and of truth, if not only in the one himself the full grace of humanity and the full truth of divinity are recognized, but also the fullness of truth has in itself the fullness of grace, by which the full humanity is in his divinity; and the fullness of grace has in itself the fullness of truth by which the full divinity is in his humanity; in such a way that fullness of truth has in itself the fullness of grace and the fullness of grace has in itself the fullness of truth.

33. The whole fullness of truth is not possessed when something is not known of the truth itself. May it be far from us that we think about Christ in that way. For the whole fullness of grace is in that fullness of truth in such a way that that full deity fills his whole humanity; and the fullness of truth is in that fullness of grace in such a way that that full humanity, just as it has a full and unique incorruption and immortality of the flesh, so according to the soul, it has uniquely a full knowledge of the deity. Therefore, Christ is full of grace and truth in such a way that, just as in the divinity there is a full reception of his humanity, so in his humanity there is a full knowledge of the divinity. Let us not be afraid to assert that the soul of Christ knows his complete deity, lest from this it be said that he is of one nature with the deity itself; since, indeed, if true reasoning requires this that in the fullness of knowledge necessarily there is a unity of nature; to begin with, God himself, because he knows fully all the things which he has made, it will be said that he is of that nature of which are those things which he made and knows. The one who believes or asserts this is not provided with Catholic truth but is possessed by Manichaean impiety. Then that is likewise to be considered, that the very soul of Christ, from whatever part it is said to have knowledge of its deity, immediately it is said that from that part it has one nature with its deity. This is so much madness. For we too, we hope that we, by the grace of God, will see God but to the extent that we will see, to that extent, we will know without a doubt; since the apostolic authority points out both to us; for the blessed Paul says, "At present, I know partially; then I shall know fully, as I am fully known."[117] and John, beloved by Christ, asserts without hesitation that ". . . when it is revealed, we shall be like him, for we shall see him as he is."[118] But that vision is not only of the flesh, according to which alone, only the Son will be seen by the impious for

---

117. 1 Cor 13.12.
118. 1 Jn 3.2.

their eternal condemnation; but there will be a vision of the deity, according to which the Trinity itself will offer itself to be seen by the just in such a way that that unending vision of the deity is itself the inexhaustible fullness of blessedness. Hence, blessed are the clean of heart for they will see God."[119] Therefore, to the extent that we shall see the divinity of the holy Trinity, to that extent we shall receive the gift of the grace to be able to see. But still not to the extent that we shall see, to that extent shall we be consubstantial with the divinity itself. For we also see many things with the body which are not of one and the same nature with our flesh. Our eyes see light although they are of one nature and light is of another. Indeed, the blessed John said, "... when he is revealed, we shall be like him, for we shall see him as he is."[120] But he said 'like', by imitation of justice, for example, not by unity of nature. According to this imitation, the blessed Paul says, "Be imitators of me, as I am of Christ,"[121] and the blessed John says, "Whoever claims to abide in him, ought to live just as he lived."[122] Indeed the creature comprehends the Creator to the extent that the Creator allows himself to be comprehended.

34. Hence it is that the blessed Augustine does not refuse these words but takes them up without hesitation. For in the same homily in which he had expounded this text: "God does not ration his gift of the Spirit,"[123] then in a certain place he speaks of the Son himself: "For as God, remaining with the Father, among men he became a man so that, through him who became a man for you, you might become such as grasps God. For man could not grasp God; man could see the man but could not grasp God. Why could he not grasp God? Because he did not have the eye of the heart by which he could grasp. Therefore, there was a thing within, wounded, and a thing without, healthy; he had healthy eyes of the body, he had wounded eyes of the heart. He became man for the body's eye so that, believing in him who

119. Mt 5.8.
121. 1 Cor 11.1.
123. Jn 3.34.
120. 1 Jn 3.2.
122. 1 Jn 2.6.

could be seen bodily, you would be cured to see him himself whom you could not see spiritually."[124] With these words, the blessed Augustine shows that in spiritual things, to comprehend is to see, nor is to see anything other than to understand, nor is to understand anything other than to know. Hence it is that in the book on the presence of the Lord, when he gives to the Son alone the full capacity for divinity, he shows that the full knowledge of divinity is in him alone. In the book mentioned above, he uses these words: "Thus God, who is everywhere present and everywhere wholly present, does not dwell everywhere but only in his Temple, to which, by his grace, he is kind and gracious, but in his indwelling he is received more fully by some, less by others. Speaking of him as our head, the Apostle says, 'For in him dwells the whole fullness of the deity, bodily.'"[125] Pay attention, I ask, in these words of the blessed Augustine to the most certain distinction between the head and the members. By those to whom God gives the Spirit according to measure, in his indwelling he is received more fully by some, less by others. What is "being received" except being understood and known? When the same blessed Augustine wishes to speak of Christ, see what he says, "Speaking of him as our head, the Apostle says, 'For in him dwells the whole fullness of the deity, bodily.'"[126] The blessed Augustine himself says that God, indwelling, is received; wherefore, the fullness of divinity is received by him without a doubt in whom dwells the very fullness of divinity. But it is received in him in whom it is known. Therefore, in him in whom dwells all fullness of divinity, the full knowledge of that fullness cannot not be present. Hence it is that the blessed Augustine a little further on in the same book, says the following: "What then? Are we to think there is this difference between the head and the other members that divinity may dwell in any given member however outstanding, as some great prophet or

---

124. Augustine, *Tractatus in Johannem* XIV.XII.2–3; CCL 36.149–50; FOTC 79.76.
125. Augustine, *Epistolae* 187.38–39; CSEL 57.116; Col 2.9; FOTC 30.252.
126. Col 2.9.

apostle, yet not 'all the fullness of the Godhead' as in the head which is Christ? In our body there also is sensation innate in the individual members but not so much as in the head, where it is clear that all the five senses are centered; for there are located sight and hearing and smell and taste and touch, but in the other members there is only touch. But, perhaps, besides the fact that 'all the fullness of the Godhead' is found in that body as in a temple, there is another difference between that head and the perfection of any of the members. There is, indeed, in the fact that by a certain unique assumption of humanity, he became one person with the Word. Of none of the saints has it been, is it, or will it be possible to say, 'The Word was made flesh';[127] none of the saints by any supreme gift of grace received the name of only-begotten Son, so as to be called by the name which is that of the very Word of God himself before all ages, together with the humanity which he assumed. Therefore, that act of becoming man cannot be shared with any holy men, however eminent in wisdom and sanctity."[128] Therefore, it is certain that the view of the holy Fathers fits with the heavenly Scriptures which they most clearly bear witness to and proclaim to us as divinely inspired, i.e., to all the adopted that this is a partial knowing and receiving of divinity infused by grace, insofar as the will of the giver gives it; in Christ, however, i.e., in his soul, there is present a full knowledge of the complete divinity.

35. The following section of your letter contains a fourth question: "We believe and confess that there is one reign of the Father and of the Son and of the Holy Spirit, knowing that they rule over all creatures together. Therefore, why in priestly prayers does the Catholic Church throughout almost all the regions of Africa traditionally say, 'Through Jesus Christ, your Son, our Lord, who lives and reigns with you in the unity of the Holy Spirit'? As if the Son alone possessed the Kingdom with the Father, to be sure 'in the unity

127. Jn 1.14.
128. Augustine, *Epistolae* 187.40; CSEL 57.116–17; FOTC 30.253–54.

of the Holy Spirit,' so that, while uniting those who reign, the Holy Spirit is not indicated as reigning together."

36. I shall say candidly what I know about these words. As often as I have subsequently thought about them, I know that there was nothing there other than our ancestors' building up a defense of the truth of the faith against many heresies. First you should pay close attention to what we say in the conclusion of the prayer: "through Jesus Christ, your Son, our Lord." We do not speak through the Holy Spirit. This the Catholic Church does not celebrate together to no purpose, on account of that mystery by which the mediator between God and human beings, Christ Jesus, became a human being, a priest forever according to the order of Melchisedech, who entered once for all into the sanctuary with his own blood, not through figures of the truth made by hands but into heaven itself where he is at the right hand of God and intercedes for us. The Apostle, seeing in him the function of a high priest, says, "Through him then let us continually offer God a sacrifice of praise, i.e., the fruit of lips that confess his name."[129] Therefore, through him we offer the sacrifice of praise and prayer, because through his death we have been reconciled when we were enemies. Through him, who deigned to become a sacrifice for us, our sacrifice can be acceptable in the sight of God. Wherefore the blessed Peter admonishes us, saying, ". . . and, like living stones, let yourselves be built into a spiritual house to be a holy priesthood to offer spiritual sacrifices acceptable to God through Jesus Christ."[130] For this reason, therefore, we say to God the Father, "Through Jesus Christ, your Son, our Lord." For you know well that it is sometimes said: "Through the eternal priest, your Son, our Lord Jesus Christ." Therefore, when there is mention of a priest, what is being shown other than the mystery of the Lord's incarnation, in which the Son of God, "though he was in the form of God, emptied himself, taking the form of a servant,"[131] according to

---

129. Heb 13.15.   130. 1 Pt 2.5.
131. Phil 2.6–7.

which "he humbled himself, becoming obedient to death,"[132] "for a little while was made 'lower than the angels',"[133] and possessing the equality of unity with the Father? Even though the Son, remaining equal to the Father, was made less because he deigned to come in the likeness of human beings. He made himself less, when he emptied himself, taking the form of a servant. The lessening of Christ is the very self-emptying; nor is this self-emptying anything other than the taking of the form of a servant.

37. Christ, remaining in the form of God, the only-begotten God, to whom with the Father we offer sacrifices, taking the form of a servant, has become a priest through whom we are able to offer a living, holy sacrifice pleasing to God. Nor could we have offered a sacrifice if Christ had not become a sacrifice for us, in whom, the very nature of our race is a true, saving sacrifice. In order that the only-begotten himself who by nature is true God also become a true priest, he deigned to receive in the person of his divinity, not the person of our humanity but the nature. For if, in the mystery of the Incarnation, he had received the nature of a human being together with the person, there would not be one Christ in two natures, God and human being, but in two persons there would be one God and the other, a human being. But Christ is one, true Son of God and human, because that only-begotten Lord who always had his own person, received into that person of his the truth of the nature of a servant. Accordingly, Christ remains inseparable because, although one of the natures in him is of the divinity and the other, the nature of a servant, still in one and the same Christ, that person of eternal divinity is also the person of the assumed humanity. Therefore, Christ is one and the same whom the receiving of the form of a servant shows to be a little less than the angels and the unity of nature proves to be equal to the Father. The Arians stumble against this mystery in such a way that, paying attention to the office of high priest in him,

132. Phil 2.8.
133. Heb 2.9.

they are unwilling to take up the question of deity. Hence it is that they also say, "Glory to the Father through the Son," so that they are unwilling to say, "Glory to the Father and to the Son." Therefore, since they are heretics who do not believe that the Son is of one divinity with the Father, likewise, there are others who are not afraid to deny the truth of the flesh in the Son of God; the most holy Fathers have treated of this problem fittingly and usefully. For when we show that we offer our prayers through the eternal Priest, the Lord Christ, we confess that the true flesh of our race is in him; according to what the Apostle says, "Every high priest is taken from among men and made their representative before God to offer gifts and sacrifices for sin."[134] So when we say, "your Son," and we add "who lives and reigns in the unity of the Holy Spirit," we recall that unity which the Father and the Son and the Holy Spirit have by nature, where the same Christ himself is shown as having exercised a priestly office for us, to whom there is a unity of nature with the Father and the Holy Spirit. See, I ask, how many heretics are convicted by this text. First of all, our faith is distinguished from the error of the Manichees, when we offer our prayers through that priest who consequently is a true priest because he has offered himself as a true sacrifice for us. Unhesitatingly, the Apostle affirms this, saying, "So be imitators of God, as beloved children, and live in love, as Christ loved us and handed himself over for us as a sacrificial offering to God for a fragrant aroma."[135] He would not offer a true sacrifice if the truth of the flesh were not in him. After he rose from the dead, the high priest himself showed the truth of this sacrifice to his disciples and offered to be touched, saying, "Touch me and see, because a ghost does not have true flesh and bones as you can see I have."[136]

38. Hence our faith is also distinguished from the error of Eutyches; although he did not dare deny the incarnate Word, still when he does not confess that the very flesh of

---

134. Heb 5.1.
135. Eph 5.1–2.
136. Lk 24.39.

the Word was taken from the flesh of the virgin, he in fact empties the mystery of the high priest. In that statement which I cited above, the Apostle contradicts him, saying, "Every high priest is taken from among men and made their representative before God."[137] And in another text: "Surely he did not help angels but rather the descendants of Abraham; therefore, he had to become like his brothers in every way, that he might be a merciful and faithful high priest before God to expiate the sins of the people."[138] Therefore, by these words in which we show that we offer our prayers through Jesus Christ, the true faith repulses every error, which does not confess the truth of the human body in Christ. But because Christ is not only a true human being, but also by nature is true God and one God with the Father and the Holy Spirit, justifiably we say to God the Father, "who lives and reigns with you," in that unity of nature which he shows saying, "The Father and I are one."[139]

When similarly our faith is distinguished not only from the error of Arius and Sabellius but also from that of Nestorius, in the very word 'unity', just as the substance of the Father and the Son is known not to be different, so when we say, "who lives and reigns with you," it is shown that there is not one person of the Father and the Son. It also is apparent that the eternal priest is himself the true Son who reigns with God the Father in the unity of nature. So when we say, "in the unity of the Holy Spirit," we show the one nature of the Holy Spirit with the Father and the Son. Unity of nature, what else does this show but the Trinity, one God, and from this, that there is one reign? For difference in nature can show difference of power in the kingdom. But where there is unity of nature in the kingdom, there also remains one power of reigning; but in that reign, they can have difference of power, they to whom the power itself is granted by grace, not available from nature. There is not difference but unity of power in the Trinity which grants the power itself to

137. Heb 5.1. 138. Heb 2.16–17.
139. Jn 10.30.

anyone according to its will because it has ineffably a unity of nature. See what the blessed Augustine thinks about the Holy Spirit in the sixth book *On the Trinity* where he says, "Therefore, the Son is equal to the Father in everything and is of one and the same substance."[140] Immediately he added, "Wherefore the Holy Spirit also subsists in this same unity and equality of substance. For whether he is the unity between both of them, or their holiness, or their love, or whether the unity, therefore, because he is the love, and the love, therefore, because he is the holiness, it is obvious that he is not one of the two. Through him, both are joined together; through him, the begotten is loved by the begetter and in turn loves him who begot him; in him, they preserve the unity of Spirit through the bond of peace, not by a participation but by their own essence, not by the gift of anyone superior to themselves but by their own gift."[141] And a little later: "The Holy Spirit is, therefore, something common, whatever it is, between the Father and the Son. But this communion itself is consubstantial and co-eternal, and if this communion itself can be appropriately designated as friendship, let it be so called, but it is more aptly called love. And this again is a substance, because God is a substance and 'God is love' as it is written."[142] Likewise, in another text of the same book, he says, "And therefore, the Holy Spirit is also equal, and, if he is equal, he is equal in everything on account of the highest simplicity which is in that substance. And, consequently, there are not more than three: the one loving him who is of him, the one loving him of whom he is, and the love itself. If love is nothing, how can it be said, 'God is love'? If it is not a substance, how is God a substance?"[143] Therefore, with these words the blessed Augustine did not hesitate to say that the Holy Spirit, like the love and holiness, so also is the unity of the Father and the Son; to proclaim in faithful trust not only that he is something common

---

140. Augustine, *De Trinitate* VI.IV.6; CCL 50.235; FOTC 45.206.
141. Ibid., VI.V.7; CCL 50.235; FOTC 45.206.
142. Ibid., FOTC 45.207.
143. Ibid., VI.V.7; CCL 50.236; FOTC 45.207.

between them but also that the communion is consubstantial and co-eternal. Therefore, this is said by Catholics that from the very name of unity, there is one essence and from this one reign and in the same one reign, one power of the Trinity and one majesty is recognized by the faithful; lest either the Son or the Holy Spirit thus be thought to reign with the Father according to divine nature in the manner in which an inferior reigns with the more powerful; but that unity of the Holy Spirit, which is the communion of the Father and the Son, while it proves the unity of divinity in that reign, teaches that there is one eternity of reigning, one power, one majesty, and one rule of the highest Trinity.

39. The letter contains a fifth and last question in these words: "Why is it that as Luke the evangelist is going to tell about the Lord's Supper, first he says that he took the cup and immediately gave it to the disciples to be shared among themselves and then, when he took the bread, said, 'This is my Body,' and then, after he had eaten, he in the same manner took the cup again, then said, 'This cup is the new covenant in my blood which will be shed for you.'"[144] You then follow with the question proposed with this, and you say, "Was the one cup given a second time or one first and then another after? And whatever it is" you say, "to what mystery does it belong, concerning which the others who wrote the gospels, have remained completely silent?"

40. Certain ones have wanted to understand this passage in the Gospel in such a way that they assert that two cups were not given by the Lord but rather they affirm that this was said by anticipation; otherwise, there is one cup which is remembered as given to the disciples, as passed around before and drunk afterwards. Certain ones affirm that a cup was given a second time. But whether one thinks it is the former or the latter, each interpretation is such that it is in no way foreign to the true faith. For those who think that a cup was given a second time said that this was done symbolically. Others, asserting that in the first cup, the Lord prefigured

---

144. Lk 22.17–20.

his own suffering; in the second, the suffering of the faithful. Others said that in each cup that is shown which was commanded in the Old Testament, that he who did not celebrate the Pasch of the first month by eating the lamb, carries it out in the second month by eating the goat. It seems to me that here too there is some other mystery befitting the Christian faith so that in each cup each covenant ought to be understood. Especially since truth itself has shown this to us in such a way that no difficulty remains for inquiries, for the Lord himself deigned to call the cup which he gave to be drunk the new covenant, as the content of the words of the Gospel shows. This is attested to unhesitatingly by the three evangelists, Matthew, Mark, and Luke. These are the words of Matthew: "While they were eating, Jesus took bread, said the blessing, broke it, and giving it to his disciples said, 'Take and eat. This is my body.' Then he took a cup, gave thanks, and gave it to them, saying, 'Drink from it, all of you, for this is my blood of the covenant, which will be shed on behalf of many for the forgiveness of sins.'"[145] Mark, to explain the mystery of the Lord's bread and cup, says this: "While they were eating, he took bread, said the blessing, broke it, and gave it to them and said, 'Take it; this is my body.' Then he took a cup, gave thanks, gave it to them, and they all drank from it. He said to them, 'This is my blood of the covenant which will be shed for many.'"[146] The account of Luke who, it is certain, spoke of the cup a second time, is put in order and unfolded in these words: "Then he took a cup, gave thanks, and said, 'Take this and share it among yourselves; for I tell you that from this time on, I shall not drink of the fruit of the vine until the Kingdom of God comes.' Then he took the bread, said the blessing, broke it, and gave it to them, saying, 'This is my body which will be given for you; do this in memory of me.' And likewise the cup after they had eaten, saying, 'This cup is the new covenant in my blood, which will be shed for you.'"[147] Hence it is that the

---

145. Mt 26.26–28.
146. Mk 14.22–24.
147. Lk 22.17–20.

blessed Paul too, recalling the most sacred mystery of that supper, makes known no other cup than the one called the New Covenant by the Lord. For among other things, he says, "For I received from the Lord what I also handed on to you, that the Lord Jesus, on the night he was handed over, took bread, and, after he had given thanks, broke it and said, 'This is my body that is for you. Do this in remembrance of me.' In the same way also the cup, after supper, saying, 'This cup is the new covenant in my blood. Do this, as often as you drink it, in remembrance of me.'"[148]

41. Therefore, by the attestation of the words of the Gospels and the apostolic writings on the word 'cup', at least on that text, it is not permitted to understand the covenant as anything other than divine. Nor is there any doubt that in other texts the grace of suffering was intended by the Lord when the word 'cup' is used. For what did he wish to be understood when he said to the sons of Zebedee, "Can you drink the cup that I am going to drink?"[149] And in the very hour in which he willed to be taken captive by the hands of wicked men, by these words, warning the blessed Peter to put his sword back in its sheath, showed that the cup he would drink was the cup of his suffering, saying, "Put your sword into its scabbard. Shall I not drink the cup that the Father gave me?"[150] In that situation he also showed that in that cup suffering is to be understood, when, torn away a stone's throw from his disciples, to die for the sins of human beings, he truly showed in himself feelings of human weakness; and, in order that he might deign to take away despair from the weaker members, power itself which willed to be our head, did not refuse to express by divine love what his members would afterwards express with human fear. Hence it is that Luke the evangelist recalls that he said, "Father, if you are willing, take this cup away from me."[151] Matthew also testifies that these were his words: "My Father, if it is possible, let this cup pass from me."[152] But Mark, to show what we ought to

148. 1 Cor 11.23–25.
149. Mt 20.22.
150. Jn 18.11.
151. Lk 22.42.
152. Mt 26.39.

understand by that cup, says, "He advanced a little and fell to the ground and prayed that if it were possible the hour might pass by him."[153] What do we think might be meant here by the holy evangelist by the term 'hour' except that concerning what the Lord says, "My hour has not yet come,"[154] and about which the evangelist John says, ". . . no one laid a hand upon him, because his hour had not yet come."[155] The hour, not of a coerced death but of a voluntary suffering; that hour without a doubt in which he took up a triumphal death and loosing the pains of Hell, he himself became mercifully and marvelously the death of death, as he had already said through the prophet, "O Death, where are your plagues? O Sheol, where is your destruction?"[156] This is the hour the blessed evangelist subsequently showed was called by the Lord in prayer by the name of 'cup' with the prayer of the same Lord added, in which he said, "Abba, Father, all things are possible to you. Take this cup away from me."[157] So it is clear that to pray that this hour pass from him was the same as saying that the cup be taken from him. Where, as I said, our head proved that the weakness of his members was taken up in him, to whom he knew he would give the power to suffer in order to teach that not for this reason would the merit of suffering be lost, if to a person who is going to suffer for the faith and love of Christ, a trepidation of the will comes on from the weakness of the flesh and strives to shake the willingness of the spirit, but rather the human will must subject itself to the divine will and perfect strength by weakness with the gift of the grace of the Spirit prevailing; retaining the ability given to itself by it, there would be no uncertainty as to whose will should be given priority over its own will, and thus the human being would patiently overcome that which it wished for because of human weakness and would happily attain to that which the divine will helpfully called it.

42. Therefore, the will of Christ could not be different

153. Mk 14.35.
154. Jn 2.4.
155. Jn 7.30.
156. Hos 13.14.
157. Mk 14.36.

from that of the Father since in the Father and the Son, the unity of nature always preserves one will. But he who, taking up human nature, came to save the nature which he made, uttered as well the words of the same nature, not with a deceitful but with a completely authentic taking up. With a most merciful goodness, he also took up its feelings, feelings indeed which the flesh had from fear of dying, not from a lust for sinning; for he who did not know sin, without sin, took up the feelings, not of wickedness, but of our weakness. For concerning him, the blessed Peter says, "He committed no sin and no deceit was found in his mouth."[158] Accordingly, because he did no sin, he did not have a will different from the will of the Father; and because there was no deceit found in his mouth, so there was no hesitation in uttering authentic words from feelings of human weakness. Therefore, although in those words of our Savior in which he spoke of a 'cup', suffering is to be understood, his own as well as that of his saints (in which meaning the blessed David also spoke of a 'cup', namely in that text where he says, "What shall I return to the Lord for all his bounty to me? I will lift up the cup of salvation and call on the name of the Lord."[159] Showing that that cup is nothing other than the death of the saints, he immediately added, "Precious in the sight of the Lord is the death of his faithful ones."[160]) By the word 'cup' is also to be understood the perfect grace of charity by which the strength for undergoing suffering for the name of Christ is infused. This is given in such a way that even if the opportunity by which anyone may undergo suffering for Christ is lacking, there is still such great strength in the heart by a divine gift that nothing is lacking for putting up with punishment, scorning life, and undergoing death for the name of Christ. This is well understood in that text in the Psalm where it is said: "My cup overflows," and he had just said before: "You anoint my head with oil."[161] What

---

158. 1 Pt 2.22.
159. Ps 115.12–13 LXX; Ps 116.12–13.
160. Ps 115.15 LXX; Ps 116.15.
161. Ps 22.5 LXX: Ps 23.5.

must be understood by "head anointed with oil" except a mind strengthened by the gift of the Holy Spirit? The shining quality of this oil is the unconquerable fortitude of spiritual grace by which the holy drunkenness is poured into the inner depths of the heart so that every affection of the heart, overcome, is consigned to oblivion. Filled with this drunkenness, the spirit learns to rejoice always in the Lord and to consign to contempt whatever he loved in the world. We drink this drunkenness when, having received the Holy Spirit, we possess the grace of perfect charity which drives out fear. Hence it is that the blessed Ambrose in his hymn for morning prayer taught us to ask for the grace of this drunkenness when we say, "In joy, let us drink the sober drunkenness of the Spirit."[162]

43. So, in other texts, the word 'cup' may be understood in some other way according to the rule of the true faith, but in this text of the Gospel, which we are now discussing, we are not permitted to understand it other than what we are taught by the words of the Lord himself, our teacher, who says, "This cup is the new covenant in my blood."[163] From this rule by which this cup is called the new covenant, in that cup which he gave earlier is understood the old covenant, not without reason. Therefore, the Lord himself, who granted both covenants to his faithful, gave each cup. So also in that same supper, he ate the Jewish Passover which had to be taken away, and he gave the mystery of his body and blood which had to be instituted for the salvation of the faithful. He ate the Passover of the Jews in which Christ was promised in order to come to our Pasch in which Christ is immolated. Next, note what Luke the evangelist recalls that he said to his disciples. For he spoke as follows: "When the hour came, he took his place at table with the Apostles. He said to them, 'I have eagerly desired to eat this Passover with you before I suffer....'"[164] Before he voluntarily suffered for

162. Ambrose, Hymn 2.23-24, "Splendor paternae gloriae." See Ambrose, *Hymni*, ed. J. Fontaine (Paris, 1992), 186-87.
163. Lk 22.20.
164. Lk 22.14-15.

them, he ate the Pasch by which it was signified that he was to suffer. There is also something in the words of the Lord which should be studied more attentively by the faithful in which the distinction between the two covenants can be seen. For the blessed Luke says concerning the cup which he mentioned first, "Then he took a cup, gave thanks, and said, 'Take this and share it among yourselves.'"[165] Concerning the bread and the cup given after, he says, "Then he took the bread, said the blessing, broke it, and gave it to them, saying, 'This is my body, which will be given for you; do this in memory of me.' And likewise the cup after they had eaten, saying, 'This cup is the new covenant in my blood which will be shed for you.'"[166] It does not seem to me to be without purpose that here a certain distinction of wording has been made by the very wisdom of God; seeing that he gave the first cup to be received in such a way that he commanded that it be shared, saying, "Take it and share it among yourselves."[167] He did not say this at all in the case of that cup which he gave with the bread. There he points out his body and blood and asserts that the same cup is the new covenant in his blood, saying, "This cup is the new covenant in my blood, which will be shed for you."[168] There is no mention of sharing the cup, as there is likewise in the other two evangelists, viz., Matthew and Mark, just as their words, which we cited above, clearly show. Therefore, the Lord commanded that this cup, in which we have said that the Old Testament is indicated, be taken and shared in order that the Apostles, instructed by the gift of heavenly wisdom, would receive the Scriptures of the old covenant with reverence but in such a way that they, having received the spirit of discernment, might know what was to be observed and what omitted among those commandments. For this is to divide rightly so that each one knows what he must omit and what he must maintain according to the fittingness of the time.

44. Hence it is that the Church of the living God, which is

165. Lk 22.17.
167. Lk 22.17.
166. Lk 22.19–20.
168. Lk 22.20.

the pillar and foundation of truth, distinguishes with a most careful division the times of Christ to come and of Christ coming. Omitting the sacrifice by which it was promised that Christ would suffer, it offers this sacrifice in which Christ is shown as already having suffered. For it divides the time for celebrating circumcision from the time for receiving baptism. Holy Church retains the most salutary way of this dividing as well in the matter of the commandment of the feast of the new moon, seeing that it does not pointlessly sound off with the trumpets of the Jews, but it does not cease to proclaim that each one is renewed in the spirit of his mind and puts on the new self. All these things it salutarily divides which it now hears with veneration in the reading but no longer celebrates in practice, turning the ear of the heart to the words of the Apostle, with which the blessed Paul instructs all the faithful, saying, "Let no one, then, pass judgment on you in matters of food and drink or with regard to a festival or new moon or sabbath. These are shadows of things to come...."[169] For, expounding the mystery of circumcision, he says, "See to it that no one captivates you with an empty seductive philosophy according to human tradition, according to the elemental powers of the world and not according to Christ. For in him dwells the whole fullness of the deity bodily, and you share in the fullness in him who is the head of every principality and power. In him you were also circumcised with a circumcision not administered by hand, but, stripping off the carnal body, with the circumcision of Christ. You were buried with him in baptism...."[170] These and things like them, the Church has both received wisely and divides; by receiving, it believes in the truth promised; by dividing, it knows from God himself about the truth already fulfilled; it does not await in figures for the truth to be fulfilled but holds that it is fulfilled in the truth. For the holy Church knows that God is faithful in his words and holy in all his deeds. Whence, just as in the Old Testament, it understood as faithful the words of God who

169. Col 2.16–17.
170. Col 2.8–12.

promised, so in the New Testament, it recognizes the holy works of God who fulfills what he had promised. For certain words of the God who promises were mysteries of the Old Testament by which Christ was promised to us. These words have passed but from it there came the fulfillment of those things which were promised. Therefore, we begin with a giving of thanks in the very sacrifice of the body of Christ in order to show the truth that Christ is not going to be given but that he has been given for us in truth; and by the fact that we give thanks to God in the offering of the body and blood of Christ, let us recognize that Christ is not still to be killed for our iniquities but that he has been killed; that we are not going to be redeemed by that blood but that we have been redeemed. For the proclamation of the blessed Peter is true, when he says, ". . . you were ransomed from your futile conduct handed on by your ancestors, not with perishable things like silver and gold but with the precious blood of Christ as of a spotless, unblemished lamb."[171]

45. Therefore, the holy Church separates figures from the truth, shadows from the body, as the holy Apostles taught, who salutarily received from the Lord the cup to be shared among themselves. So the Lord gave to the disciples the dividing up of this cup because from their teaching, the holy Church has received the knowledge of this division. He says that they may divide among themselves, i.e., that in the unity of the Spirit and the bond of peace, they may distinguish the mysteries of the New Testament from the cessation of the old mysteries; something that he did not command be done by the Apostles in the case of the cup of the new covenant. For in the New Testament there is no division of the mysteries but of the gifts which are not within the ability of human beings but in the power of the Holy Spirit. "There are different kinds of spiritual gifts but the same Spirit; there are different forms of service but the same Lord; there are different workings but the same God who produces all of them in everyone."[172] Hence it is that when "to one is given through

---

171. 1 Pt 1.18–19.   172. 1 Cor 12.4–6.

the Spirit the expression of wisdom; to another, the expression of knowledge according to the same Spirit; to another, faith by the same Spirit; to another, gifts of healing by the one Spirit,"[173] and the other things which the words of the Apostle have woven together are not given to human beings for dividing up, but "One and the same Spirit produces all of these, distributing them individually to each person as he wishes."[174] This dividing which he did not give to human beings but which the Trinity has reserved to itself alone, in another text, the blessed Apostle admonishes "not to think of oneself more highly than one ought to think, but to think soberly, each one according to the measure of faith that God has appointed."[175] And because the division of the Father and the Son and the Holy Spirit is one, therefore, the Christ, who is the wisdom of God, says in Proverbs, "I walk in the way of righteousness, along the paths of justice, endowing with wealth those who love me and filling their treasuries."[176]

46. Therefore, each cup is given to the Apostles by the Lord but it is not commanded that each be divided; a dividing was necessary in that case in which a distinction had to be attended to. Hence it is that we know of and we receive with veneration that in the Old Testament certain mysteries were properly celebrated as figures in that time; but we do not celebrate them in the same way as they used to be celebrated because dividing the time of promise from the time of the truth fulfilled, we now retain those mysteries handed down to us by Christ, by which we recognize and hold that Christ is not going to suffer but that he has suffered for us; we show, not by our presumption, but by the tradition of the fathers that by the word 'cup', the old covenant also ought to be understood. For the holy Augustine in his exposition of the seventy-fourth psalm, when he came to this text where it is said: "For in the hand of the Lord, there is a cup with foaming wine, well mixed; he will pour a draught from it and all the wicked of the earth will drain it, down to the

---

173. 1 Cor 12.8–9.
175. Rm 12.3.

174. 1 Cor 12.11.
176. Prov 8.20–21.

dregs."[177] Among other things he says, "The cup of pure wine full of the mixed seems to me to be the Law which was given to the Jews and all that Scripture of the Old Testament as it is called; there are the weights of all manner of sentences. For therein the New Testament lies concealed, as though in the dreg of corporal sacraments."[178] And although the same blessed Augustine distinguishes those mysteries of time past from the commandments to be carried out in life, as it were, dividing the cup, he afterwards recalled what was said: "You shall not kill; you shall not commit adultery."[179] And a certain number of things which are found in the text of the decalogue, these the holy Augustine himself appended, saying, "All these things belong to the wine. But those things carnal have as it were sunk down in order that they might remain with them, and there might be poured forth from thence all the spiritual understanding. But 'the cup in the hand of the Lord,' that is, in the power of the Lord: 'of pure wine,' that is, of the mere Law: 'is full of mixed,' that is, is together with the dreg of corporal sacraments. And because he humbles the one, the proud Jew, and the other he exalts, the pagan who confesses, 'He has inclined from this to this,' i.e., from the Jewish people to the people of the Gentiles. Inclined what? The Law. A spiritual meaning has been distilled from it. Nevertheless, the dregs have not been emptied out for all the carnal mysteries have remained with the Jews."[180] From these words of the blessed Augustine I think that the understanding of that 'cup' lies open by which the dividing of the dregs and the wine can be known in the truth of the spiritual mystery; but not in such a way that anyone would wish to cast away the Old Testament because he sees that its mysteries have ceased. The New Testament must be held with ven-

---

177. Ps 74.9 LXX; Ps 75.8.
178. Augustine, *Enarrationes in Psalmos, Ps 74.12*; CCL 39.1033.; NPNF, ser. 1, 8-354.
179. Dt 5.17-18.
180. Augustine, *Enarrationes in Psalmos, Ps 74.12*; CCL 39.1034.; NPNF, ser. 1, 8-354.

eration in such a way that the Old Testament is not abandoned in any way. This seems to me to be indicated under the words 'old' and 'new friend' in the book of Ecclesiasticus when it is said: "Do not abandon old friends, for new ones cannot equal them."[181] The divine word announcing in advance this unlikeness which is in the mysteries of each covenant says through the holy Jeremiah: "The days are surely coming, says the Lord, when I will make a new covenant with the house of Israel and the house of Judah. It will not be like the covenant that I made with their ancestors."[182] In this way there comes the New Testament, not like the Old Testament, brought to an end by the Lord, that one in which the Lord gave the fulfillment of the commandments and, with the old mysteries taken away, instituted the different mysteries of revealed truth; and so what he promised in the Old, he perfected in the New. Accordingly, since the knowledge of the mysteries of the New Testament can be truly salvific and sweet, if the promise which went before in the mysteries of the Old Testament is recognized as true, as is said with Scripture: "Do not abandon old friends, for new ones cannot equal them," he immediately added, "A new friend is like new wine; when it has aged, you can drink it with pleasure."[183] What is 'aged' except that the type of the New Testament appears in the Old Testament? Thus this new wine is drunk with pleasure, if its meaning and promise are recognized in the Old Testament.

47. The Lord made this new wine age in the heart of the disciples, when, approaching these two who were going to the village of Emmaus, he accompanied them; and when they told him of the things which had been done in his suffering, as if he were unaware, then he said to them, "O how foolish you are! How slow of heart to believe all that the prophets spoke!"[184] See, I ask you, how the new wine ages that it may be drunk with pleasure. Therefore, the Lord added, "Was it not necessary that the Messiah should suffer

181. Sir 9.10.
183. Sir 9.10.
182. Jer 31.31–32.
184. Lk 24.25.

these things and enter into his glory?"[185] The holy evangelist, as he aged the new wine to be drunk by them with pleasure, says, "Then, beginning with Moses and all the prophets, he interpreted to them what referred to him in all the Scriptures."[186] Then, they themselves showed the fire of newness and sweetness conceived from the aging wine, saying, "Were not our hearts burning [within us] while he spoke to us on the way and opened the Scriptures to us?"[187] He did it again, saying, "These are my words that I spoke to you while I was still with you, that everything written about me in the Law of Moses and in the prophets and psalms must be fulfilled. Then he opened their minds to understand the Scriptures."[188] Thus did he make the new wine age sweetly when without hesitating he showed that the promises of the New Testament appear in the reading of the Old Testament; nor should a new friend be prized in such a way that the old is abandoned, because the new remains like in faith, although it seems to be unlike in the celebration of the mysteries. But the faith of the New and the Old Testaments is one. Among the ancient fathers, faith believed in the promises which it believes have now been fulfilled in us. The faith was promised in our fathers; in us the faith itself of the truth shown forth has been fulfilled; so, because that old friend and the new one are joined indissolubly and one is not held salutarily without the other, the new wine must age so that it will be drunk with pleasure by the faithful.

185. Lk 24.26.
186. Lk 24.27.
187. Lk 24.32.
188. Lk 24.44–45.

INDICES

GENERAL INDEX

Abragil, 42
Acacian schism, 23 n.27
Adam, and Eve, 99, 315
adoption, of man, 216, 372, 377, 391, 482–83, 502, 534–35
adultery, 283–84, 319
Ambrose, St., 513, 525–26, 535, 558
angels, 75, 78–80, 95, 98–99; fall of, 80–81, 210, 466–67; evil 464
apollinarianism, 403
Arianism, 17, 30, 38–40, 42, 139, 234, 259–75, 359, 366–67, 379 n.52, 387–92, 395, 401–2, 429, 403, 411, 417, 549–51
Augustine, St., 10, 59, 190, 191, 192–94, 228–29, 253, 254–55, 256–58, 494, 513–16, 519–21, 526, 536–37, 545–46, 552, 562; *City of God*, 256–57, *Confessions*, 345, *De Trinitate*, 384, *Enarratio*, 10, *Enarrationes in Psalmos CXVIII*, 346 n.11, *On the Perfection of Justice*, 191, *On the Predestination of the Saints*, 230–32
Aurelius, bishop of Carthage, 36

baptism: adult, 474–80, 484–92; body of Christ and, 493–96; church and, 88–89, 103–104, 134–35, 140; circumcision and, 560; Eucharist and, 475–76, 478, 492; faith and, 485; formula for, 61, 240, 368, 377, 399; grace and, 249–50; need of, 88, 101–102, 104, 134; of children, 282–83, 474, 487; of dead, 489; rebaptism of heretics, 40, 138, 253–54; salvation and, 479, 484, 491–92; subsequent sins, 356; lifegiving, 391
beautific vision, 545
Beelzebub, 466
birth, 528

body, temple of God, 151, 244, 377
Boethius, 291
Boniface, bishop of Carthage, 49, 52
Breviarium Hipponense, 475 n.2

Cassian, John, 21–22
Chalcedon, Council of, 23 n.27, 59 n.1, 381 n.57
charity, 132, 188, 341–47; good will and, 344; love and, 342–43
Chifflet, Pierre-François, 3
children: raising of, 290; baptism and, 282–83, 474, 487
Christ: baptism of, 93, 513; birth of, 525–26, 532; coming of, 432, 434–35; church and, 246–50, 315; creation and, 243, 448–49; divinity of, 65–66, 68, 71–74, 91–96, 260–65, 270, 272, 274–75, 303, 370–76, 379 n.52, 380–82, 392, 402–404, 409, 415–16, 420–21, 424, 429–48, 504, 510–13, 517–34; forgiveness and, 114–15, 138; Holy Spirit and, 535–47; humanity of, 65–66, 68–74, 95, 275, 375–76, 403–6, 410, 436–38, 441, 523, 529, 532–47, 557; humbling of, 71–74, 96; Judge, 81–82, 100, 106, 162; King, 87; knowledge of, 497, 534–47; lamb of God, 100, 162, 254; mediator, 66–67, 74, 97, 380–82, 522, 548; passion of, 555–57; priest, 548–52; savior, 162; one person, 66, 95–96, 408, 419–35, 511–12, 517–34, 538, 541, 549; relation to the Father, 375–76, 402, 433–34; servant, 73, 94, 312, 374, 409, 431, 444–45, 529, 548–49; spouse of virgins, 314, 328, 333; two births of, 66, 94, 428; two natures, 67, 71, 73, 95–96, 375, 402–4,

569

(Christ *continued*)
408–11, 419–20, 431, 511–12, 517–34, 538, 541, 549; Truth, 91, 271; Wisdom, 243, 270, 511 n.34; *see also* incarnation
Christian: name of, 370; dead to sin, 484; life of, 459
Church: Christ and, 133–34, 136, 246–51, 315–16, 505, 546–47; faith of, 517, 524; holy spirit and, 249; oneness of, 139, 251–52; nations of, 257; salvation and, 88–89, 100, 104, 133–34, 136, 138, 178, 254–55; virginity of, 315–17, 505; Noah's Ark and, 135, 257; threshing ground, 105, 133; humanity as body, 318; one, 139
circumcision, 560
Claudius (Fulgentius's father), 7
Claudius (Fulgentius's brother), 14
confession, 171–73
continence, vows of, 90, 105; *see also* virginity
contraries, medicinal purposes, 455–56
conversion, 117, 119–21, 123–25, 129, 131, 143, 145, 152, 174; gift of, 127; forgiveness and, 129–30, 356; God's desire for, 36; lack of, 177–78; time for, 160, 170, 173–181, 358
covenent, new and old, 553–65
creation, 74–77; Christ and, 68, 72; diversity of, 78–79; dysfunction of, 446–72; good of, 75–77, 98, 105, 210–11, 450, 452, 456, 465; governance of, 76, 87, 214, 219, 221–22, 450–51, 469; grace of, 79–80; image of God, 63; purpose of, 79; resurrection and, 166–67, 169; spiritual, 80
Cyprian, 135–36, 384

damnation, 100, 176, 293–94; *see also* hell
Datianus, primate of Byzacena, 56
death: eternal life and, 293; first and second, 166–69, 195–96, 225–27; grief over, 292–93; judgment and, 293–94; of flesh, 145; of spirit, 145; sin and, 293, 391
despair, 86, 116–17, 119, 120, 173–74, 182, 355
Donatists, 386

Ephesus, council of, 381 n.57
eternal life, 83, 200–201; *see also* reward
Eucharist, 233; and Arian controversy, 234–59; spiritual sacrifice, 250, and Abraham, 237–38; formula for, 234, 237–41, 247–48
Eugippius, Abbot of Lucullanum, 3, 341 n.1
Eulalius, Pope, 21–23
Euthymius, 111
Eutyches, 381–82, 512, 550–51
Eve, 71
evil: cause of, 167–68, 215, 221, 424–25, 464; nature and, 465; nature of, 454–56; persons, 457–62; privation and, 98, 130, 455–56; occurance of, 462–63, 470–71
exorcism, 473

Fabianus, 52
faith: catholic, 481–82; imperfect, 338–40; incarnation and, 87–88, 116, 138, 162, 205; knowledge of God and, 203; lack of, 82; law and, 209, 247; need for, 59–60, 100, 114, 165, 298, 425, 479–80, 485; object of, 137–38; works and, 84–85, 116, 130, 131, 147, 165, 177, 181, 297–98, 326
fall: from church, 134; into sin, 158–60, 217–18; of creation, 451–54, 457; of man, 210, 388, 451–52
Fastidiosus, 387–92, 401, 406, 421–22
Faustus, bishop of Praesidium Diolele, 11–13, 15, 28, 256–57
Faustus, bishop of Gaul, 47
fear, of God, 199–22, 123, 161
Felicianus, bishop of Ruspe, 4
Felix, abbot, 15–16, 17–21, 28, 34, 50
Felix, Arian priest, 3, 17–20

GENERAL INDEX 571

Felix, deacon of Ruspe, 30–32 n.38
Ferrandus, 3–4, 472–76
flesh, law of, 338
flood, 135–36
foreknowledge, 102–3, 147–48, 179, 193, 202, 210, 218, 220, 227–33; causation and, 210, 215
forgiveness, 84–86, 111–87; conversion and, 358–59; despair and, 86, 116–17, 119, 120, 173–74, 182; free will and, 356; penance and, 147–48, 357–58; repentance and, 357; time for, 117, 140–43, 148, 157–58, 163, 178–80, 298
fornication, 283–84, 297, 319
free will, 79–80, 127–28; cause of sin, 217, 223–24, 232, 272, 502; forgiveness and, 356; grace and, 502; servitude and, 451
Fulgentius, St., life of: childhood, 6–7; family, 6–8, 13–15; faith of, 21, 43; intelligence of, 5, 7, 22, 36, 39–40; miracles of, 3, 17, 43–44, 51; vocation of, 8–13; health, 13–14, 19, 31; mercy of, 20, 43, 45; sanctity of, 5, 12–14; teacher, 5, 17, 40, 46, 52; poverty of, 13–14, 23–25, 33, 36, 51; persecution of, 17–21, 29; esteem during life, 18–19, 22, 25–26, 28–29, 31–32, 40–41, 48–49, 52; virtues of, 5, 8, 13, 15–16, 24, 27–28, 31, 35–36, 43–44, 46, 50, 53–54, 341; Travels: 21–53; stay in Africa, 16–21; travels to Egypt, 21–24; stay in Medidi, 21; Siracusa, 23; stay in Rome, 24–25; travels to Junca, 27; taken to Ruspe, 30–32; return to Carthage, 48–49; travels to Cercina, 53; return to Ruspe, 53; ordination, 28; made abbot, 15, 28; made bishop, 31; Sardini: first exile, 35–37; second exile, 42–47, 111, 187, 279, 383, 472; monasteries of, 4, 6, 16, 21, 26–27, 34, 45; love of monasticism, 8, 21–23, 26, 33–34, 38; illness and death, 53–54; burial, 55; other works: *Against Pinta*, 41, *Admonition*, 42

Gabardilla, 17
Gaiseric, King, 6
Gelasius, Pope, 524
glorification, 202, 207–9
God: attributes of, 504, 519–20; charity, 345; eternity, 92, 148, 447; generosity of, 198, 218; goodness of, 98, 198, 211, 215; greatness of, 519, 538; immutability, 203–4, 270, 350, 401, 517–18; incorporeal, 399–402; infinite, 94, 243–44, 430; justice of, 196–97, 204, 212, 219, 222, 360; knowledge of, 497, 542–43; omnipotence, 76, 133, 148, 204; omnipresence, 396–400, 501–3; omniscience, 102, 144, 219, 326, 330, 501; truth, 372; allows evil, 167–68, 215, 221, 464; creator, 75–76, 92, 98, 393, 399, 447–50, 463–69, 534; judge, 152; physician, 334–35, 355–56; source of all good, 75, 309, 334–36; teacher, 194; name of, 236, 504–8, 520; nature of, 39, 42, 61–64, 91–93, 139, 241, 243–44, 251, 260, 264, 367–73, 377–78, 416–19, 426–27, 430–34, 442–45, 499–517; three persons, 39, 61–63, 92–93, 368, 416–17, 427, 443–45, 499–517; relations between persons, 64, 260–63, 427, 508, 525, 528; properties of persons, 427–28, 527–28; works of, 64, 393–94; inseparability of persons, 240–41, 393–401, 415–16, 497, 503–17, 519–20, 527; equality of persons, 39, 62, 72, 91, 138, 263, 367–83, 448
goods: eternal, 298; temporal, 137, 298–9; giving up, 300; life, 459; ordering of, 211–12
Gordianus (Fulgentius's grandfather), 6
grace, 330–36; beginning, 87–88, 113, 119–20, 148–49, 197–98, 200–202, 207, 209, 219, 314, 349; cause of, 102; debt and, 197–98, 200; dependence on, 120–22, 200–202; free will and, 502; gift of, 127, 200–202, 207–9, 215,

572 GENERAL INDEX

(grace *continued*)
  223–24, 228, 298, 501; nature and, 336, 430; need for, 351–52; prayer and, 334, 338; sin and, 172; time for, 298; understanding and, 499
guilt, vessel of, 223–24

heart, hardness of, 85–86, 119, 122–24, 126, 129, 140–43, 160, 171, 175, 178
hell, 82, 100–101, 106, 114, 145, 150, 156, 162, 167–69, 222, 225, 272, 294
heresy: anger of God, 264, 371–72; correction of, 260; idolatry, 372–73; piety and, 146, 234; salvation and, 106, 136; sin of, 104, 130–31, 137–38, 233–34, 421–22, 458; holy spirit and, 252–53
heretics, avoidance of, 240, 247; church and, 512; conversion of, 139–40, 142–43; separated from church, 252–53; sensuality of, 416–17
Hilderic, King, 47
holy spirit: advocate, 244, 368; annunciation and, 114; baptism and, 93, 253; Christ and, 535–47; church and, 249; coming of, 93, 435–36; creator, 376–77; divinity of, 42, 91–93, 241–45, 372–95, 498, 501, 509–11, 513–16, 518, 552–53; forgiveness and, 140–41; gifts of, 114, 141–42, 245–47, 317, 342–43, 394; good soul and, 268; grace and, 113; grief over sin and, 467; heresy and, 252–53; love and, 254, 342–46; measure of, 534–47; mission of, 241; omnipresence of, 94; procession of, 63, 64, 94, 538, 547–53; reign of, 551–53; sacrifice and, 241–42
homoousia, 42, 379 n.52, 386, 392
hope, 121, 208
humility, 330
Hunneric, King, 11 n.14

incarnation, 41, 64–70, 94, 96–97, 380–83, 388, 429–41, 445, 511– 12, 517–34, 538, 541, 549; marriage and, 249; trinity and, 406–8, 416, 418–21, 424, 438–41, 527, 529–30
Illustris, bishop, 37
impiety, 126, 130–31, 146, 234
indwelling, 265–73, 502, 516–17, 521, 543
inheritance, eternal reward, 142–43, 150, 158–59, 165, 177, 182, 200, 207, 209, 294, 340
insects, worms and, 464, 468, 450, 469–70
Isola, Antonio, 3, 45 n.55

Januarius, bishop, 37, 347 n.13
Jerome, St., 190, 314
Jerusalem, 148
John, bishop of Thapsus, 498
judgment, 141, 146, 149–50, 176, 213, 228, 293–94; of angels, 80; punishment and, 81–82, 84, 100, 127, 160–61, 164, 178–81, 213
Juliatheus, 42
Junca, Council of, 51
justification, gift of, 60, 83, 87, 100, 128, 148, 202–3, 206–7, 216

kingdom of God, 87, 106, 129, 182, 200
knowledge, sin and, 127–28

last supper, 498, 553–65
law: end of, 247; faith and, 209; new and old, 97; of flesh, 338–39, 462; sacrifices of, 74, 97, 100; salvation and, 121–24, 152–56, 171; sin and, 196
Lazarus, 170
Leo the Great, Pope, 280, 522–523
liberty, 311–12
life, good, 145–46, 295, 311, 459; evil, 295; living in God, 273–74, 502, 516–17, 521, 543
light, grace and, 127, 136–38; truth and, 194, 199
Logos, 379 n.52, 511 n.34
love: of God, 211–13, 152, 312–13, 346; of neighbor, 132, 146, 312–13, 346; of world, 152, 214;

obedience and, 346; debt of, 188–89, 312–13; of flesh, 326; rationality and, 211

magi, 525
macedonianism, 379–80
man: fickleness of, 78; image of God, 212, 264, 377, 411–13, 417; knowledge of God, 542–45; living in God, 273–74, 502, 516–17, 521, 543; nature and person, 500, 510, 515; pilgrims, 335; reconciled through Christ, 436–38; sinful nature of, 331; sons of God, 372, 377, 482–83; soul, 412; speech, 413–14; temple of holy spirit, 151, 244, 377; union of body and soul, 271, 418, 445–46, 500, 503, 530–31
manichaeanism, 130, 256, 380, 382, 403, 454–55, 463, 544, 550
Marcellus, of Ancyra, 380 n.56
Mariana (Fulgentius's mother), 7
marriage: anxiety and, 295–96, 301, 318; authority of spouse, 286; chastity and, 90, 281, 296, 461; children and, 290; death and, 295; debt, 90, 281–82, 288, 296–97; divorce and, 90, 105, 301; figure of church and Christ, 319; fruits of, 282; gift of, 297, 299–300; holiness of, 105, 318; incarnation and, 249; institution of, 89, 105, 282; modesty and, 288; of baptized persons, 461; remedy for weakness, 89–90, 281, 318; sin and, 90, 281–83; unity of, 249, 286; virginity and, 317–20; vows and, 91, 105, 279–81, 285–87
Martin of Tours, St., 3
martyrdom, 88, 101
Mary, 70–71, 95, 114, 130, 247–48, 315, 380–81; cp. to Eve, 71, 95, 130; symbol of church, 315; annunciation and, 114, 247–48, 442; cooperation of, 404
medicine, 455–56
mercy: gift of, 219, 223; justice and, 116–122, 146, 149, 153–55,

159–64, 197, 215, 220, 223, 359–60; vessel of, 223–24
merit, 84, 163, 298, 313; and penance, 170–80
modalism, 379 n.51
monasticism, 23
monophysitism, 23 n.27, 381 n.57
Moors, invasions, 16 n.17
Moses, 95, 236
mourning, for sin, 126, 133, 168, 337

nature, 465, 468; fall of, 451–54; grace and, 336, 430; singular and plural, 505–06
Nestorius, 381–82, 551
Nicea, Council of, 42 n. 51
Noah, 135–36, 236

Old Testament: foretelling of Christ, 97, 256, 405–6; faith of patriarchs, 208–9, 235–36, 238–39; fulfillment of, 560–62; prefiguring baptism, 135–36; prefiguring confession, 136–38; widows in, 303–4
Optatus of Milevis, St., 255, 258
order, 214
original sin, *see* sin

Patripassianism, *see* Sabellianism
Pelegianism, 47–48
penance, 89, 170–80, 357–58; delay and, 85, 115–16, 147, 153; forgiveness and, 125, 147–48; time for, 84–85, 101, 115–16, 147–48, 157
perseverance, 110, 112–13, 122, 134, 158–60, 309, 333–40
Photinianism, 190, 380, 382
Pinta, bishop, 41
poison, 450, 452–53
Pontianus, bishop of Thenae, 55
prayer, 334, 338
predestination, 87, 103, 112–14, 187–233; to death, 192, 195, 204; of good and evil, 193, 196, 212–15, 219–25, 229–32; to punishment, 194, 204, 219, 221–22; of works, 206, 225, 227–28, 230–31; foreknowledge and, 147–48, 179,

(predestination *continued*)
193, 202, 210, 218, 220, 227–33; causality and, 210; of evil, 194, 204, 210, 214–16, 229, 232; to glory, 204, 216, 221–22; justice and, 204, 212, 219, 222; limit of, 205, 212; of fall, 217–18; promise and, 220–21, 228; prediction and, 220–21; free will and, 204–6
pride, 210–12, 228–30, 325, 325–27
Primasius, bishop of Cagliari, 45
privation, 455–56
Prosper, 231–32
punishment, 144–45, 150–51, 156, 165, 169, 194, 196–97, 204, 219, 221–22

Quodvultdeus, bishop, 51–52

rational soul, salvation and, 86–87, 99
Redemptus, 21
repentance, 143, 145, 152; confession and, 171–73; forgiveness and, 357; time for, 177
resurrection: general, 164–65; of wicked, 83, 87, 101, 165, 168; of good, 164–65; first and second, 166–67; bodily, 82–83, 86–87, 101, 165; of animals, 86
riches, eternal, 362–64; worldly, 348–53, 362–64, 483–84
Romulus, 348
Rufinianus, bishop, 24
Rusticiana, 291

Sabellianism, 139, 378–79, 428–29, 381, 512
sacrament, 494–95
sacrilege, *see* heresy
saints: sins of, 457–62; perfection of, 222; sufferings of, 553, 557, 559
salvation, 150–51; God's desire for, 122–23, 149, 195, 199, 226; grace and, 334, 336, 349, 351–52; martyrdom and, 88, 101; faith and, 60, 87–88, 100, 114, 116, 138, 162, 165, 205, 298; of children, 127–28; outside church, 106, 136;

rational soul and, 86–87, 99; sacraments and, 130
sanctity: degrees of, 317; works and, 115, 120, 143, 145–46, 147, 158, 165, 169, 283, 298
Satan, 71, 80–81, 100, 104, 106, 114, 446; power to create, 468; tricks of 116–19, 131, 210, 222, 324–325, 337
Scripture, meaning of, 256–58, 553
second coming, Christ, 98, 106, 145, 162–63
self: hatred of, 156; love of, 211–13
sex, and sin, 128; and marriage, 90, 281–83, 296; illicit 283–84, 297, 319
sin: cause of, 217, 223–24, 232, 272, 502; death and, 161, 168, 200, 213, 227, 272, 325; effects of, 100, 128, 167, 334–35; forgiveness and, 461; grace and, 172; heresy and, 233–34, 416–17, 421–22, 458, 480, 484; law and, 196; order and, 214; original sin, 69–71, 81–82, 99–100, 114, 128, 217–18, 220, 457, 487–88; personal, 114, 224, 227, 232; pride and, 210–12, 228–30, 325, 325–27; punishment, 80–81, 98, 129, 131, 144, 195, 210; regret and, 337; responsibility and, 161, 167, 334; separation from God, 397, 516–17
Sinai, Mount, 95
Son of God, 93, 372, 376, 429–39, 444, 518, 520–23, 526, 537, 548
Son of Man, 376, 441
soul, human, 265–67, 271; interior life of, 267–68; thought and, 264–65, 273–74; *see also* man
spiritual adornment, 301–302, 307–308
spouse, Christ as, 302, 306, 314, 328, 333
Sufes, Council of, 51–52

tears, 337–38, 340
Theoderic, King, 24–25
Theodore, Senator, 347
theology, method, 256–58, 261
thought, 264–65, 273–74

GENERAL INDEX

Thrasamund, King, 38–41, 47
Tome of Leo, 23 n.27
Trinity, *see* God, Christ, Holy Spirit

understanding, sight and, 544–46

vengence, *see* wrath
Victor, primate of Byzacena, 31 n.36
vir, 315
virago, 315
virginity, 310–33; gift of, 314–17, church and, 315–16; anxiety and, 318; spouse of, 306, 314, 328, 333; fasts and, 322–23; fruits of, 321; good of, 255, 257–58, 283, 289, 296, 306; highest call, 317–20; humility and, 328–29, 332; reward for, 317; spiritual and bodily, 316, 321, 324; spiritual combat and, 332–33; temptations and, 321–25; virtue and, 314, 319; vows and, 285–86, 288; weakness and, 288–89
viriliter, 315
virtue, 214, 311–12
Vitalis, prior, 34
vows, 90–91, 284–88

warfare, spiritual, 338–39
wicked, actions of, 457–62
widowhood, 257–58, 291–310; marriage and, 297; purpose of, 306; fasts and, 304–306; charity of, 307–8
wife, behavior of, 301
will, function of, 204; love and 343–45; predestination and, 206
within, existence, 265–73
word: breath and, 262; of God, 68, 72, 74, 92, 94–96, 260–65, 270, 272, 303, 374, 382, 394, 415–16, 418, 421, 424, 439, 441, 444–45, 447–48, 547, thought and, 264–65, 273–74
works: good, 84, 88–89; as prayer, 302–303; lack of, 169–70; merit and, 298; salvation and, 115, 120, 143, 145–46, 147, 158, 165, 169, 283, 298; tears and, 337–38, 340
world, desire for, 483–84
wrath: of God, 85, 118–19, 121, 125, 144, 153, 161, 163, 205, 215, 219, 222–23, 264; vessel of, 223–25

INDEX OF HOLY SCRIPTURE

Old Testament

Genesis
1: 468
1.26: 63, 411
1.27: 63
1.31: 211
2.21–23: 315
8.20: 236
12.7–8: 235
12.18: 204
13.2–4: 236
21.10: 459
25.16: 466
26.23–25: 238
35.1: 238
35.6–7: 238

Exodus
3.14: 92
3.15: 235
7.1: 482
20.2–3: 371
20.5–6: 118
34.6–7: 118

Leviticus
4.21 [LXX]: 100

Deuteronomy
1.37: 460
5.17–18: 563
6.4: 61, 91, 369, 371
6.13: 61, 91, 369, 370
20.5: 371
23.21–23: 285
32: 371
32.4: 213, 217, 268, 269
32.7: 424
32.39: 91, 369, 378, 443, 482
43: 371

Joshua
2: 136

Ruth
3.15: 367

2 Samuel
12.13: 172

1 Kings
8.27: 431

2 Kings
2.9: 537
2.9–10: 245
4.34: 385

Judith
8.4–5: 304
8.7–8: 304

Job
7.1: 339
14.4: 70
14.16–17 [LXX]: 144
31.3: 144
33.4: 376
36.10–12: 143

Psalms
1.6: 226
4.2: 363
4.4: 265, 412
4.5: 266

5.8: 391
7.9: 171
7.12–13: 122
8.4–5: 375
10.16: 268, 269
11.5: 154, 156, 196
11.6–7: 154
11.7: 117, 217
14.2: 193
14.3: 192
16.11: 540
17.8–9: 331
18.10: 534
18.28: 194
18.30: 339
18.31: 369, 443, 482
18.44: 31
19.5: 383, 406
19.6: 240, 248, 511
19.10: 218
22.1: 390
22.10: 374
22.16–18: 405
23.1: 21
23.5: 557
23.6: 201
25.7: 126
25.10: 117, 231
25.15:337
27.3:202
27.14: 309
30.6: 330
30.7: 330
30.8: 330
31.24: 315
32.1: 128
32.9: 99
33.6: 376, 394
33.11: 401

INDEX OF HOLY SCRIPTURE   577

34.9: 218
34.16: 227
34.18: 364
36: 10
36.9: 270
37.3: 309
37.5: 330
37.23: 198
37.24: 461
37.28: 206
37.39–40: 150
38.5: 335
38.6–7: 329, 337
38.8: 329
38.9: 330
39.13: 180
45.7: 540
45.11–13: 302
45.14: 505
45.16: 466
47.9: 466
49.6: 351
49.12: 470
50.17: 152
51.1–2: 125
51.3: 125
51.5: 70
51.8: 113
51.17: 364
55.19: 167
55.20: 167
55.22: 309
59.10: 201
60.12: 198, 396
62.3: 281
62.10: 363
63.8: 249
65.4: 540
65.14: 284
66.13–14: 284
68.28: 198
72.11: 371
73.1: 218
73.18: 212
73.19: 213
73.27: 212, 249, 399
73.28: 302
74.12: 92, 563
75.8: 563

76.11: 91
77.10: 165, 349
80.2: 433
81.11–12: 168
82.6: 482
84.2: 117
84.4: 471
84.7: 301
84.12: 214
85.8: 113
86.13: 272
86.15: 72, 117
87.5: 67, 541
90.14: 540
94.7–8: 85
96.5: 481
100.3: 434
101.1: 117, 197
102.25–27: 92
103.1–5: 355
103.5: 293
103.8–13: 215
103.10: 216
103.10–12: 164
103.13: 216
104.24: 72, 393
104.30: 376
104.32: 349
106.32: 460
109.20: 275
110.3: 96
112.4: 206
115.3: 204, 314
115.5: 214, 220
116.2: 201
116.5: 117
116.8: 272
116.12–13: 557
116.15: 557
116.16: 374
119.11: 137
119.19: 345
119.73: 331
119.103: 218
119.133: 339
119.175: 229
124.7: 337
126.5–6: 364
126.6: 203, 338

127.1: 330, 335
127.4: 335
135.6: 148
139.7: 377
139.7–8: 94, 397, 501, 508, 509
139.7–10: 243
140.5: 32
142.3: 324
143.2: 220
145.13: 309
145.18: 60, 143
146.5–6: 92, 450

Proverbs
1.8: 491
2.6: 192
2.11–12: 362
2.17–18: 271
3.7–8: 143
4.27: 226
5.22–23: 144
8.7: 480
8.20–21: 562
8.21A [LXX]: 405
8.22: 405
8.22–23: 389
8.23: 95
8.25: 95, 405
8.30: 270
8.35: 198, 199
8.36: 234, 457
9.1: 405
9.12: 391
11.31: 126
18.3: 355
20.9: 331
24.16: 461

Ecclesiastes
5.4–5: 285
10.1: 467

Song of Songs
2.4: 155, 214

Wisdom
1.1: 433
1.3–5: 397, 516

578 INDEX OF HOLY SCRIPTURE

(Wisdom *continued*)
1.4: 344
1.5: 287, 433
1.6–7: 397
1.7: 94, 243, 377, 501
1.8: 501
1.9: 501
1.12–13: 195
1.13: 217, 388
2.1: 264, 265, 271, 413
2.24: 101, 195
3.1: 505
3.11: 151
3.17–18: 293
4.1: 267
4.8–10: 294
4.11–14: 295
5.1–5: 149
5.4: 150
5.5: 150
7.20: 402
7.24–26: 467
7.26: 511
7.27: 267
7.30: 355
8.1: 94, 243, 394, 398, 430, 465, 469, 501
8.17: 271
9.15: 208
9.17: 417
10.15–16: 267
12.18: 204
15.2: 274

Sirach
1.4: 394
1.5 [LXX]: 394
1.8–9: 394
2.10: 309
2.12: 287
2.14: 434
2.15: 434
3.17–18: 310
3.18: 328
3.19: 44
3.26: 143
5.5–6: 144

5.7: 85, 153, 175, 364
6.5: 187
7.1–3: 144
7.16: 145
7.30: 556
9.10: 564
10.12: 212
10.13: 210, 315
12.7: 145
18.20: 146
21.1: 85, 358
21.1–2: 144
21.9–10: 145
29.12: 303
30.24: 154
34.30–31: 124
35.21: 337

Isaiah
1.16–20: 123
3.12: 271
6.3: 64
7.9: 494
7.14: 406
9.6: 406, 518
11.1–2: 539
11.4: 94
30.15: 84, 123, 124, 125, 360, 365
45.11: 203, 215, 230, 406
45.21–22: 118
48.16: 242
49.8: 154, 156
52.13: 95
53.7: 406
54.22: 360
55.1–7: 356
55.6–7: 179
55.7: 357
55.8–9: 400
56.4–5: 317
59.1–2: 397
62.2: 316
62.4: 316
62.4–5: 315
62.5: 316
65.13–14: 221
66.2: 113

Jeremiah
2.10–11: 481
2.19: 218
2.21: 217
8.4–5: 360
10.11: 481
10.23–24: 229
12.2: 502
23.23: 502
23.23–24: 399
23.24: 77, 94, 501
31.31–32: 564

Baruch
3.25: 242
3.35: 424, 426
3.36: 442
3.36–38: 441
3.37: 424, 426

Ezekiel
18.4: 196, 391
18.20: 272
18.21–23: 122
18.21–24: 359
18.24: 122
18.26: 160
18.26–28: 359
18.30–32: 195
18.32: 226
33.11: 85
36.26–27: 198
36.27: 207

Daniel
3.26–31: 365
3.41–42: 365
3.64: 505
10.13: 466
10.21: 466
13.42: 102, 502

Hosea
1.7: 370
13.14: 556

Joel
2.12–13: 361
2.13: 338
2.28: 535

INDEX OF HOLY SCRIPTURE 579

Habbakkuk
2.4: 272, 425
3.11: 137

Zephaniah
3.8–10: 239

Malachi
2.17: 213
4.2: 137

New Testament

Matthew
1.18: 114, 248
1.20: 248
1.20–21: 114
1.21: 442
3.7: 205
3.12: 106
3.17: 65, 93
4.4: 418
5.3: 350
5.4: 354
5.7: 155
5.8: 545
5.14: 506
5.16: 207, 308
5.25–26: 152
5.28: 467
5.44–45: 132
5.45: 470
6.1: 308
6.12: 89, 462
6.19–20: 307
6.24: 434
7.7: 289
7.7–8: 356
7.12: 132
7.13–14: 152
7.17: 354
7.21: 143
8.22: 226
9.2–3: 266
9.3–4: 413
9.6: 179
10.28: 196
10.32: 486
10.32–33: 116, 138
11.19: 212
11.27: 510
11.28: 163
11.29: 95, 326, 350
12.28: 394
12.33: 354

12.35: 187, 266
13.43: 209
14.31: 460
15.8: 399
15.19: 266
15.19–20: 217
16.13: 440
16.15: 440
16.16: 489, 440
16.17: 348, 440
16.18–19: 134
16.19: 85, 141
16.27: 162
17.21–22: 441
19.6: 249
19.12 : 89, 300
19.17: 156
19.26: 272
19.29: 300
20.1–16: 177
20.22: 555
23.3: 247
23.12: 350
23.37: 148
24.24: 465
25.34: 163, 200,
 222, 294
25.41: 104, 163,
 222, 294
25.46: 106, 206, 221
26.26–28: 554
26.39: 555
26.41: 120
26.27–28: 115
27.3–5: 357
28.19: 368, 377

Mark
1.11: 513
10.18: 218
14.22–24: 554
14.35: 556

14.36: 556
16.15–16: 479
16.16: 484
16.19: 420

Luke
1.35: 248
1.78–79: 137
2.21: 96
2.37: 305
2.51: 8
3.7–9: 161
3.17: 161, 162
3.22: 513
3.36–37: 305
4.18: 242
4.21: 242
5.20: 413
5.22: 266
5.31: 355
5.31–32: 121
6.21: 364
6.25: 364
6.37–38: 289
6.46: 171, 326
7.29: 265
9.26: 116
10.7: 485
10.35: 189
11.19: 191
12.20: 307
12.47–48: 127
14.11: 211
15.7: 362
16.15: 326
16.19: 299
16.25: 363
16.25–26: 170
17.5: 245
18.9–14: 327
19.10: 162, 359
21.19: 505

580 INDEX OF HOLY SCRIPTURE

(Luke *continued*)
22.14–15: 558
22.17: 559
22.17–20: 498, 553, 554
22.19–20: 559
22.20: 558, 559
22.42: 555
23.46: 390
24.5: 303
24.25: 564
24.26: 565
24.27: 565
24.32: 565
24.39: 95, 380, 550
24.44–45: 565

John
1.1: 72, 260, 262, 270, 374, 381, 415
1.1–2: 92, 441
1.1–3: 68, 447
1.3: 263, 374, 393
1.9: 147, 354
1.12: 216, 485
1.12–13: 482, 391
1.14: 68, 374, 390, 415, 441, 444, 547
1.15: 389, 404
1.16: 200, 381, 539
1.29: 100, 359
1.33: 536
2.4: 556
3.5: 88
3.14–15: 439
3.16: 93, 439
3.16–17: 65, 162
3.16–18: 429, 440
3.18: 93
3.19: 293
3.20–21: 199
3.21: 395, 396
3.27: 208, 330
3.34: 535, 536, 545
3.34–35: 536
3.36: 205
5.1: 65
5.14: 121

5.17: 65
5.18: 368
5.19: 368, 395
5.21: 368
5.25: 163
5.26: 521
5.28–29: 87, 163, 293
5.30: 162
5.32: 443
5.36–37: 443
5.44: 209
6.33: 191
6.38: 27
6.53: 475, 479, 492
7.30: 556
8.16: 368
8.26: 162
8.34: 129
9.35–38: 439
10.17: 95
10.18: 420
10.30: 66, 96, 376, 551
10.34–36: 439
12.28: 513
12.48: 162
13.10: 103
13.34: 345
14.6: 91, 291, 354
14.7: 510
14.9: 96, 415
14.9–11: 511
14.10: 96, 272
14.15: 165
14.15–17: 244, 268, 443
14.16–17: 368
14.17: 514
14.23: 242, 267, 432
14.26: 242
14.28: 96, 376
15.5: 330
15.22: 432
15.26: 94, 242, 443
16.27: 514
17.1: 440
18.11: 555
20.17: 440
20.22: 94

20.22–23: 142
20.28: 370
23.24: 243

Acts
1.11: 98
2.30–31: 95, 533
2.36: 389, 404
4.32: 252, 398, 496, 503, 505
5.3–4: 288
8.36: 485
8.37: 485
10.38: 540
17.28: 262, 274
20.28: 97
20.34–35: 255
24.22: 362

Romans
1.8: 207
1.9–10: 313
1.17: 366
1.18: 125, 372
1.20: 92, 517
1.24: 168
1.25: 372
1.26: 168
1.28: 168, 230
1.36: 263
2.1–6: 361
2.4: 141
2.4–6: 141
3.5–6: 205, 223
3.8: 129, 151, 357
3.26: 197
4.4: 224
4.20–21: 204
4.21: 208
5.2: 150
5.5: 140, 142, 189, 245, 249, 251, 312, 342, 398, 435, 436
5.6: 97, 356
5.10: 97, 437
5.16: 488
5.20: 172
6.11: 484
6.20: 311

INDEX OF HOLY SCRIPTURE 581

6.21: 311
6.22: 311, 432
6.23: 161, 200
7.2: 295
7.22: 339
7.23: 339
7.25: 339
7.24–25: 337
8.3: 410
8.7: 326
8.9: 93
8.12–13: 145
8.13: 471
8.15: 244
8.18: 201
8.23: 391
8.29: 103, 148
8.29–30: 202
8.30: 197, 203
8.32: 65, 438
8.35: 393
8.38–39: 393, 517
9.1–4A: 126
9.5: 96, 376, 382
9.14: 268, 269
9.16: 352
9.19: 148
9.22–23: 223
9.28: 60
10.3: 327
10.10: 139, 485
11.22–23: 121
11.33: 541
11.36: 92, 199, 396
12.1: 493
12.3: 459, 562
12.5: 399
12.6–8: 317
12.9–10: 345
12.12: 365
13.1: 282
13.8: 188
14.23C: 177
15.13: 142
15.30: 313

1 Corinthians
1.23–24: 517
2.5: 107
2.10: 417, 509

2.11: 271, 509
2.12: 207, 417, 510
2.13: 244, 256
2.14: 252, 416
2.15: 107
2.16: 209
3.6: 491
3.7: 102, 491
3.8: 160, 491
3.16: 151, 244, 494
3.16–17: 377
3.17–18A: 151
3.17–18: 458
4.7: 188, 208, 330
6.9–10: 82, 129, 284, 461
6.15: 318
6.17: 517
6.19: 244, 377
6.19–20: 92, 318
6.20: 377
7.1: 281
7.1–2: 318
7.2: 297
7.2–3: 281
7.3: 90
7.4: 282, 286
7.7: 296, 319
7.9: 89
7.25: 189, 254
7.28: 285, 296
7.32–34: 318
7.34: 292, 295
7.37: 90, 285
7.40: 297
8.6: 262, 441, 449
9.9: 87
9.26–27: 160
9.27: 322
10.6: 315
10.12: 120
10.16: 493
10.16–17: 257
10.17: 493, 494, 495
11.1: 545
11.23–25: 555
11.31–32: 462
11.32: 365
12.4–6: 394, 561
12.8–9: 245, 562

12.8–11: 343
12.11: 394, 395, 562
12.12: 249
12.13: 249, 399
12.27: 493, 495
13.1: 246
13.2: 104
13.2–3: 246
13.4–6: 344
13.12: 544
13.13: 251
14.40: 214
15.3: 419
15.40: 155
15.41: 76
15.41–42: 317
15.42–44: 101, 166
15.51: 83, 101, 164
15.52: 83, 101, 165
15.53: 83, 101, 165
15.54: 83
15.56: 457
15.58: 491

2 Corinthians
3.4: 331
3.5: 313, 336
4.13: 269, 486
4.17: 201
4.17–18: 300
4.18: 137
5.3: 178
5.4: 67
5.7: 202
5.10: 87, 154, 489
6.1: 195
6.2: 154, 156, 157
6.2B: 154
7.10: 292
8.9: 330, 409
8.18: 506
9.10: 227
10.3: 339
10.12: 329
11.2: 315, 505
11.27: 322
12.21: 126, 284, 361
13.4: 67, 383, 410, 518, 533
13.13: 142

INDEX OF HOLY SCRIPTURE

Galatians
1.3–5: 439
1.22: 506
1.22–24: 308
1.6–7: 481
2.20: 438
3.14: 235
3.16: 235
3.19: 246
3.27–28: 348
4.4: 95, 374, 404, 436
4.4–5: 68
4.5: 436
5.6: 141, 176, 298, 324, 423, 436
5.13: 312
5.17: 338
5.19–20: 82
5.19–21: 129
5.21: 284
5.22: 342
5.24: 484
6.1: 120
6.7: 157
6.7–8: 471
6.7–10: 157
6.8: 158, 227, 323
6.9: 158
6.10: 160

Ephesians
1.3–4: 247
1.3–5: 215
1.4–5: 103
1.5: 103
1.9–10: 203
1.13–14: 142
1.14: 247
2.1–5: 226
2.3: 100
2.7: 201, 218
2.8–10: 199
2.14–18: 248
2.19–22: 250
3.17: 267
4.1–3: 142, 252
4.4: 398, 493
4.6: 441
4.7: 536, 537

4.13: 315
4.13–16: 250
4.15: 245
4.15–16: 493
4.17–18: 367
4.30: 467
5.1–2: 550
5.2: 74, 254
5.8: 521
5.23: 248
5.25: 318
5.28–30: 319
5.29–30: 493
5.30–31: 249
5.32: 249
6.4: 290
6.18: 244

Philippians
1.10–11: 308
1.23: 208
1.29: 200
2.1: 251
2.6: 72, 374, 375
2.6–7: 414, 548
2.7: 73, 374
2.7–8: 71
2.8: 436, 549
2.9–11: 436, 541
2.12: 352
2.12–13: 120
2.13: 199, 206, 336, 352
3.9: 209
3.12: 202, 208
3.15: 107, 208
3.19: 233, 483
3.20: 272
4.7: 534

Colossians
1.16: 393
1.16–17: 243, 449
1.18: 249
1.19: 540
2.3: 539
2.5: 214, 398
2.8–9: 261
2.8–12: 560
2.9: 540, 546

2.12: 391
2.16–17: 560
3.1–2: 483
3.3–4: 350
3.5: 484

1 Thessalonians
1.9–10: 91, 205, 372
2.5–6: 308
2.9: 255
4.13–14: 292
5.3: 205, 225
5.23: 505

2 Thessalonians
2.8: 94, 465

1 Timothy
1.5: 135, 247, 425, 436, 480
1.7: 454
1.8: 463
1.12–13: 127
1.13: 224
2.4: 148
3.15: 490, 506
3.16: 388
4.4–5: 89
5.5: 302
5.6: 226, 303, 305, 322
5.11–12: 285
6.20: 314, 481

2 Timothy
2.19: 156
2.20: 133
2.25–26: 102, 149
3.8: 131, 458
4.1: 82
4.4: 111

Titus
1.15–16: 458
1.16: 326
2.11–12: 459
2.11–13: 145
2.12: 146
3.7: 67

Hebrews
  1.3: 96, 402, 511
  2.8: 339
  2.9: 375, 549
  2.11–12: 438
  2.16–17: 551
  2.16–18: 437
  3.1–2: 437
  3.12–13: 85
  3.12–14: 160
  3.14: 540
  4.12: 303
  5.1: 437, 550, 551
  10.29: 467
  11.6: 23, 60, 177
  11.11: 460
  11.39–40: 208
  12.6: 469
  13.4: 89, 281, 284, 319
  13.15: 548
  13.20–21: 199
  13.21: 199, 207

James
  1.14: 195, 196
  1.15: 286
  1.17: 208, 270, 311, 313, 336, 506
  1.18: 274
  1.25: 334
  2.13: 154, 155
  2.14: 326
  2.17: 177
  2.19: 326, 369, 443
  2.20: 177
  3.2: 331, 339, 457

  3.15: 326
  4.4: 152
  4.6: 212, 331
  4.8–10: 364
  5.1–5: 363

1 Peter
  1.8: 505
  1.18–19: 561
  2.5: 250, 493, 548
  2.11–12: 151
  2.22: 557
  2.24: 462
  3.1–4: 301
  3.5: 301
  3.5–6: 319
  3.15: 367
  3.20–21: 135
  4.8: 140, 143, 355
  4.17–18: 462
  4.18: 126
  5.5: 212

2 Peter
  2.4: 82
  3.9: 147, 149, 360

1 John
  1.2: 270
  1.8: 331, 457
  2.1–2: 356
  2.6: 545
  2.9–11: 458
  2.11: 293
  2.15–16: 214
  2.16: 340
  2.18: 176

  2.23: 508
  3.2: 274, 544, 545
  3.4: 196, 516
  3.4–6: 213
  3.5: 196, 516
  3.7: 198
  3.15: 156
  4.7–8: 398
  4.8: 517
  4.16: 354
  4.18: 188
  5.1: 441
  5.4: 207
  5.6: 92
  5.20: 91, 372

Jude
  19: 252, 253, 416

Revelation
  1.7: 98
  1.16: 94
  2.11: 167
  3.19: 362
  3.20: 267
  6.10: 153
  6.11: 153
  6.16–17: 294
  14.4: 317
  20.6: 167
  20.10: 225
  20.11: 167
  20.14–15: 225
  21.8: 226
  22.11–15: 174
  22.12: 176

www.ingramcontent.com/pod-product-compliance
Lightning Source LLC
Chambersburg PA
CBHW030527010526
44110CB00048B/615